RIGHT AND
REASON

AUSTIN FAGOTHEY, S.J.   Professor of Philosophy
University of Santa Clara
Santa Clara, California

RIGHT AND REASON

Ethics in theory and practice

Third edition

THE C. V. MOSBY COMPANY
Saint Louis   1963

Imprimi potest: JOHN F. CONNOLLY, S.J., Provincial
Nihil obstat: BENEDICT M. BLANK, O.P., Censor Librorum
Imprimatur: ✠ JOSEPH T. McGUCKEN, S.T.D., Archbishop of San Francisco
August 14, 1962

Third edition
Copyright © 1963 by
THE C. V. MOSBY COMPANY

Third printing
(All rights reserved)
Previous editions copyrighted 1953, 1959
Printed in the United States of America
Library of Congress Catalog Card Number 63-14251
Distributed in Great Britain by Henry Kimpton, London

PREFACE

I am grateful to my readers for making a third edition of this book possible. Although much of the old is retained, it is in a sense a new work. The general point of view and the conclusions derived remain those of the Aristotelian-Thomistic synthesis but are approached from a new starting point, that of modern value theory. This approach to ethics is common enough today, but its union with the ancient and medieval tradition is a radical venture and an original contribution, appearing here in an English text for the first time. I wish to express my debt to Father Joseph de Finance, S.J., of the Gregorian University, Rome. His Latin work, *Ethica Generalis,* is the first to unite value theory with Aristotelian-Thomistic ethics. His personal assistance and review of the manuscript have made the third edition of this textbook possible. The latter's shortcomings are due, of course, entirely to its author.

The problem method has been maintained: introducing one of the major questions of ethics, explaining how it arose and why it is a problem, giving the main schools of thought on the subject with sufficient historical background, stating the arguments for and against each proposed solution, weighing the arguments against one another, and finally resolving the problem, if it can be resolved, in the light of the evidence and reasoning involved. The use of ordinary and current language rather than technical and latinized vocabulary, quotations from classical and modern philosophers, short summaries at the end of each chapter, and reading lists encouraging the student to go to the sources—these remain features of this edition as well as of previous editions. They have been thoroughly revised and brought up to date.

Some teachers used to the two former editions will find the present work a disconcerting innovation, while others will think that the changes have not been radical enough. Since it is impossible to please everybody, this middle stand may be best for most. Those who prefer the old approach can take the chapters in the order to which they are accustomed and omit any material they dislike. Those with more radical views may find the book a point of departure for launching out on their own and exhibiting to the class what the author should have said, always an excellent use for a textbook.

The main changes are as follows: The presuppositions of ethics are posed less dogmatically. The human act rather than the end of man is taken as the starting point. Subjective morality and conscience are discussed before rather than after objective morality. The good is viewed first as value, then as ought, and lastly as end, and an attempt is made to synthesize these three aspects. Greater stress is placed on the intrinsic nature of the good, independent of its rewarding character. Happiness and the end of man are postponed as the crowning point of ethics rather than its start and source. The legalistic attitude and the casuistic use of conscience have been de-emphasized. Some obvious and uninteresting material on the titles to property has been compressed. There is a more realistic assessment of socialism. The chapter on war has been rewritten to include the provocative question of modern nuclear warfare. In general, technical and academic topics have been bypassed in favor of matters in which the modern student is vitally interested.

The list of persons to whom I owe gratitude is becoming too large for expression. Besides Father de Finance, I wish to single out especially Father Robert H. Taylor, S.J., and Father Vitaliano Gorospe, S.J., both of whom prodded me to undertake the present revision along the lines it has assumed. Finally, I wish to thank my superiors, my teaching colleagues, and my students for their criticism, advice, and encouragement.

Austin Fagothey, S.J.

ACKNOWLEDGMENTS

Grateful acknowledgment is hereby made to the various authors and publishers who kindly granted permission to quote from the following works:

To the Oxford University Press and the Clarendon Press for permission to quote from *The Dialogues of Plato,* translated by B. Jowett; from *The Works of Aristotle Translated Into English,* edited by W. D. Ross; from Epicurus' *Letter to Menoecius,* translated by Cyril Bailey; from T. H. Green, *Prolegomena to Ethics;* from J. B. Scott, *Classics of International Law: Selections From Three Works of Francisco Suarez.*

To Random House for permission to quote from *Basic Writings of St. Thomas Aquinas,* edited by Anton C. Pegis (quotations from *The Summa Theologica,* I-II, qq. 6-114, are from this source); and from E. A. Burtt, *The English Philosophers From Bacon to Mill.*

To Benziger Brothers for permission to quote from *The Summa Theologica of St. Thomas Aquinas,* translated by Fathers of the English Dominican Province (quotations from *The Summa Theologica,* I-II, qq. 1-5, 21, II-II, and III suppl. are from this source).

To Professor Lewis W. Beck and the University of Chicago Press for permission to quote from L. W. Beck, *Kant: Critique of Practical Reason.*

To Houghton Mifflin Company for permission to quote from Benjamin Rand, *The Classical Moralists.*

To Charles Scribner's Sons for permission to quote from *Descartes Selections,* edited by Ralph M. Eaton; and from *The Range of Reason* by Jacques Maritain.

To T. & T. Clark, Edinburgh, for permission to quote from St. Augustine's *The City of God,* translated by Marcus Dods; and from Kant's *Philosophy of Law,* translated by W. Hastie.

To E. P. Dutton & Company for permission to quote from St. Augustine's *The City of God,* translated by J. Healey, Everyman's Library.

To George Allen & Unwin, London, for permission to quote from Bertrand Russell, *Mysticism and Logic*.

To the Harvard University Press for permission to quote from Cicero, *De Natura Deorum*, translated by H. Rackham, Loeb Classical Library.

To the Hafner Publishing Company for permission to quote from H. W. Schneider, *Smith's Moral and Political Philosophy*.

To Routledge and Kegan Paul, London, for permission to quote from Carl von Clausewitz, *On War*, translated by J. J. Graham.

To Charles H. Kerr & Company for permission to quote from their edition of Karl Marx' *Capital*.

To the Fordham University Press for permission to quote from St. Robert Bellarmine, *De Laicis, or the Treatise on Civil Government*, translated by K. Murphy; and from Le Buffe and Hayes, *Jurisprudence*.

To Victor Gollancz, Ltd., and Dover Publications, Inc. (publishers of American edition) for permission to quote from *Language, Truth and Logic* by A. J. Ayer.

To the Journal Press for permission to quote from "Anthropology and the Abnormal" by Ruth Benedict, *Journal of General Psychology*, vol. 10, pp. 59-82, 1934.

CONTENTS

10   *Contents*

ETHICS AS

A STUDY

THE GOOD LIFE

The good life and how to live it must always have been the subject of human speculation. From the wooden plow to the tractor, from the rude hut to the skyscraper, from the bow and arrow to the latest form of nuclear weapon, man has been devising tools for the accomplishment of purposes, means for the attainment of ends. He knows what these things are for, because he has made them with a definite end in view. No great intellectual leap is required for man to turn his question from his products to himself and ask: What am I for, what goal am I destined to achieve, what is the purpose of human life?

Man does not feel that the giving of meaning to his life, the achievement of his destiny, is something optional for him. He has a strong sense of the inner dynamism of his being, of the driving forces within him urging him to act, of the gathering together of these acts into the spending of a life, of the identification of that life with himself. Not just any way of living will carry this drive of his nature to its goal. He must prevent others from acting in certain ways against himself, and sees that he too must refrain from such acts against others. There is a right way and a wrong way of living, and the right way ought to be followed. What is the law of good living and what demands that this law be kept?

Man is both realist and idealist. When he cannot change the existing situation, he adapts himself to it, as he must if he is to survive. But he is constantly casting around for a way of bettering the situation. Adaptation to environment is necessary up to a point, after which it becomes stagnation. This discontent with things as they are, this creative aspiration to embody in reality what has been envisioned in thought, this

13

idealistic yearning of the imperfect for the perfect, is applied by man not only to his surroundings but to himself. He cannot essentially re-fashion himself in body or mind, but he can redirect what remains of his life. If there are better ways of living than he has lived, must there not be some best way? If so, what is this best way, what is the pattern, the model, the ideal of the good life?

We have no record of any such primitive speculations, but in the dawn of history we find that man had already asked these questions and given some sort of answer to them. In fact, we find rather complex codes of conduct already existing and embedded in the customs of the tribe. This was prescientific knowledge, subject to all the errors and whimsies of non-scientific thinking, but out of material suggested by these primitive codes of conduct an awakened intelligence could fashion a science of the good life.

ORIGIN OF ETHICS

The transition from nonscientific to scientific knowledge began, in our Western culture, with the Greeks. By the sixth century before Christ they had reduced primitive speculations to some sort of order or system, and in-tegrated them into the general body of wisdom called *philosophy*. After a brilliant period of speculation on the structure of the universe, they began in the days of the Sophists and of Socrates to turn their insatiable curiosity on themselves, on human life and society. Nothing was too sacred for their penetrating scrutiny. As seafarers and colonizers they had come into close contact with various surrounding peoples and were struck by the variety of customs, laws, and institutions that prevailed. They began to ask themselves whether their own were really so superior, and, if so, why. In time their study led to an examination of all human conduct, and this part of philosophy they called *ethics*.

Ethics comes from *ēthos*, the lengthened form of *ĕthos*. Both words mean *custom*, but *ēthos* denotes a more fixed type of custom and is often used to mean a man's character. The Latin word for custom is *mos;* its plural, *mores,* is the equivalent of the Greek *ēthos*. From *mores* we derive the words *moral* and *morality*. Ethics is also called moral philosophy.

By derivation of the word, then, ethics is the study of human customs. Some are mere conventions, such as table manners, modes of dress, forms of speech, and etiquette. These are fads and fashions, varying in different parts of the world and at different times, and we feel that we can change them as we please. They are *manners,* not morals. But there are other cus-toms which seem more fundamental, seem to rest on something inherent in human nature, such as telling the truth, paying our debts, honoring our parents, respecting the lives and property of others. We judge that such conduct is not only customary but *right,* that to deviate from it would be *wrong,* that it results not from arbitrary whim but from some abiding prin-ciple in human nature. These are *morals,* and it is with these alone that ethics deals. Hence ethics is the study of *right and wrong* in human conduct.

WHAT ETHICS STUDIES

We are partly on our way toward framing a definition of ethics. Ethics has for its purpose to interpret this fact of human life: the acknowledgment of right and wrong in human conduct. We find in the human race taken generally a tendency to judge that there are three kinds of acts:

(1) Those that a man ought to do
(2) Those that he ought not to do
(3) Those that he may either do or not do

At this point in our study we do not yet determine whether this judgment is correct or mistaken; we simply note that it is a fact of experience that men do judge in this way. So important are these judgments considered that men will regulate their whole lives in accordance with them and will even sacrifice life itself rather than diverge from them. We apply these judgments not only to our own conduct but to the conduct of others; we punish people and even put them to death for doing what we think they ought not to do, or for not doing what we think they ought to do. The man who does whatever he wants, with no regard for what he *ought,* is outlawed from society and hunted down like a wild beast.

Philosophy, as an interpretation of human life, cannot afford to overlook a fact of such significance, but must investigate it and determine all that it entails. If men are correct in distinguishing right from wrong, we need to know why and on what grounds this judgment is justified. If men are mistaken in distinguishing right from wrong, we also want to know why, and how such wholesale error can be accounted for. Without prejudging the case in either way, ethics is a necessary study with a large and legitimate field of inquiry.

Every distinct branch of learning must have a subject matter *(material object)* which it studies from a certain definite aspect or point of view *(formal object)*. The subject matter of ethics is human conduct, those actions which a man performs consciously and willfully, and for which he is held accountable. The aspect or point of view from which ethics studies human conduct is that of its rightness or wrongness, its *oughtness,* if we may manufacture a noun corresponding to the ethical verb *ought,* which is the real verb in every ethical judgment. Ethics is not interested in what at man *does,* except to compare it with what he *ought* to do. We call those actions right which a man ought to do, and those actions wrong which a man ought not to do. The investigation of the *ought* is the distinctive feature of ethics and separates it from every other study.

RELATION TO OTHER STUDIES

Besides its relation to the other branches of philosophy, of which it forms a part, ethics is also related to the other human and social sciences. These all have the same broad subject matter, but ethics differs from them by its distinctive point of view.

Anthropology and ethics both deal with human customs on various levels of culture and civilization. Anthropology studies the origin and development of human customs, without passing any judgment on their moral rightness or wrongness, but it is this rightness or wrongness alone that interests ethics. Anthropology testifies to the existence of moral notions, however queer, among primitive tribes; ethics borrows such data from anthropology, but goes on to criticize the moral value of these concepts and customs.

Psychology and ethics both deal with human behavior, with the abilities and acts of man. But psychology studies how man actually does behave, ethics how he ought to behave. Sanity and sanctity, a well-adjusted personality and a morally good character, despite an incidental relationship between them, are essentially different things; so too are their opposites, madness and sin, psychic eccentricity and moral depravity. What motivates a man to a deed, good or bad, is different from the goodness or badness of the deed he does. Ethics is dependent on psychology for much information on how the human mind works, but always passes on from how man does act to how he ought to act.

Sociology, economics, and *political science* study man's social life, and so also does ethics. But the same difference of viewpoint remains. These three sciences deal with man's actual social, economic, and political institutions, what they are and how they function; ethics determines what they ought to be in terms of human rights and duties. A hard and fast line between these three sciences, and between them and ethics, would render all four studies impractical. The endeavor to remedy the social, economic, and political ills of mankind involves an application of ethics to these three fields. Such a combination is sometimes called *social, economic,* or *political philosophy.* But ethics, precisely as ethics, always preserves its distinctive point of view, the *ought.*

The *study of law* is perhaps more closely related to ethics than is any other study. Although both deal with law, and therefore in some way with the *ought,* the civil law and the moral law do not always perfectly correspond. The study of civil law deals only with external acts and positive legality, ethics with internal acts of the will and the tribunal of conscience. There is a difference between crime and sin, legal immunity and moral worth, outward respectability and true virtue of soul. A mingling of ethics and the civil law on a wider field gives us the *philosophy of law,* the study of how laws *ought* to be framed and interpreted, a study some writers call jurisprudence.

Another distinction remains, but resting on quite different grounds. *Moral theology* and ethics both study the rightness and wrongness of human conduct; they differ in the source from which they derive their knowledge and in the method of pursuing their conclusions. Moral theology proceeds from the standpoint of divine revelation and ecclesiastical law, ethics from the standpoint of natural human reason alone. They differ somewhat in content and purpose also, since moral theology teaches the effective supernatural Christian life with the view of attaining a supernatural end.

As strictly a part of philosophy, ethics is not allowed to appeal to revealed sources for its facts or arguments nor should it discuss ecclesiastical legislation. Philosophy and religion are often concerned with the same problems, but their approach to them is quite different and should never be confused. Ethics is philosophy and not religion.

ETHICS AS SCIENCE AND ART

The view has been expressed that ethics may be an interesting study but can never be a science. The scientific world is still largely under the spell of that nineteenth century mode of thinking originated by Auguste Comte and known as *positivism,* which eliminates all metaphysics from philosophy and restricts scientific knowledge to facts and relations between facts. They say that the scientific method is one of exact mathematical measurement, but virtue and vice can never be measured in this way; that science proceeds by prediction based on hypothesis and followed by experimental verification, but human conduct, especially if regarded as free, is too unpredictable; that science deals with facts and the laws governing them, but ethics only with opinions on what ought to be and never wholly is; that science engages in the hardheaded pursuit of wresting from nature her secrets, but ethics is lost in a nebulous quest for ever-beckoning yet ever-escaping ideals and aspirations.

The answer to such complaints is to give a definition of science. If science is so defined as to apply to the physical or experimental sciences only, then ethics will not be a science. But this is too narrow a definition. The word *science* in the sense of any body of systematized knowledge is still in current use, and ethics is surely this. The definition of science as the *certain knowledge of things in their causes* is traditional among philosophers; ethics preeminently fulfills this definition, for it studies the purpose or final cause of human life, the principles and laws governing the use of means to this end, and establishes its conclusions with demonstrative thoroughness. Like every other science, including the physical, ethics will have its disputed points, but these will be shown to revolve around a solid core of established truth. Nor is it right for one group of scientists to rule out of court the legitimate subject matter of another science; there is need of a science of the *ought,* for the *ought* itself is a fact demanding explanation quite as insistently as the physical universe.

But is not ethics an *art,* the art of good living, rather than a science? It is both. As a science it discovers, explains, and demonstrates the rules of right conduct. As an art, in a very broad sense of this term, it applies these rules to the conduct of an individual man and results in the good life actually lived. A good life is indeed a work of art. But it is obvious that the art of ethics must be practiced by each person for himself, as the shaper of his destiny and the sculptor of his soul; ethics as a subject taught and studied can only give him the principles, and so comes under the heading of science.

Sciences are either theoretical or practical: theoretical, if their purpose is the mere contemplation of truth; practical, if they are also directed to action. Since ethics is directed to enable a man to act and live rightly, it is a *practical* science, standing somewhere between a purely theoretical science and its corresponding art. A science which gives rules or norms for acting is called normative, especially if these norms have to do with man's inner perfection rather than with the making of external objects. Since ethics sets down the norms for right living, it is a *normative* science.

PRESUPPOSITIONS OF ETHICS

Every science has to begin somewhere, and therefore starts by laying down certain presuppositions. These are truths or propositions not proved by the science in question but presupposed by it. They are not to be thought of as unwarranted assumptions, but rather as statements borrowed from another discipline whose province it is to investigate and establish them. There would result either an endless series or a circular process, were it not for the science of metaphysics. This alone rests on no deeper foundations; as the science of first principles, it takes on itself the task of testing and proving the fundamental postulates and general presuppositions of all other sciences, and thus assumes a unique position in the hierarchy of knowledge.

We shall try to begin our study as independently as possible, starting with commonly experienced data and observed facts, but we shall find that interpretation of these facts and pursuit of their underlying principles will make us draw more and more on other branches of philosophy. The earliest part of our study should be acceptable to all men of good will, be they materialists, atheists, agnostics, naturalists, humanists, pragmatists, relativists, or philosophers of any other persuasion. But it will be increasingly difficult, as we proceed to deeper levels, to find any ultimate foundation for moral values and obligations on such terms. The basic continuity of metaphysics and ethics then becomes more evident.

If one is willing to grant its presuppositions provisionally, while awaiting their demonstration in some future course, ethics may be studied anywhere in the philosophy curriculum. Because of the advantage of having already mastered these matters, it is customary to make ethics the last branch of philosophy to be studied.

Ethics, like most studies, presupposes that man can know truth, that his mind can reason logically, that the world exists and can be known, that actions take place, that people can communicate, and dozens of similar propositions. Since the days of Immanuel Kant, three philosophical truths have been singled out as of particular importance to ethics:

1. *The freedom of the will.* Does moral responsibility result from the bare fact that a man does the act he does without external compulsion, even if he was so internally conditioned that he could not have chosen otherwise in the situation? Or does it result only from a free choice of good or evil, free in the sense that he could have chosen otherwise?

2. *The immortality of the soul.* Should a man limit himself to what is achievable in this life, and in that case what goal is there worthy of his effort? Or will the human spirit outlive the present life, so that he must consider the effect of his acts on himself not only here but for an ever-lasting hereafter?

3. *The existence of God*. Is man, as individual or as socially united, his own highest good, so that he imposes moral obligation on himself and is its ultimate source? Or is the law of right living imposed on man from above, because he comes from the Creator's hand and is destined to return to Him?

It is evident that acceptance or rejection of all or any of these three propositions will profoundly affect one's whole ethical outlook. Ethical systems have been built without as well as with them, but the conclusions are vastly different. These three problems are not answered by ethics, but the student must come to ethics with his mind made up about them.

METHOD OF ETHICS

Sciences have at their disposal two main avenues of approach to their subject matter. Which shall be used depends on the nature of the subject matter itself and of the viewpoint adopted, since means are chosen with a view to the end.

1. The *deductive, a priori*, or *rational method* starts with accepted axioms, principles, definitions, and postulates, and proceeds to their application. The mathematical sciences are the outstanding examples of this method.

2. The *inductive, a posteriori*, or *empirical method* starts with the given complex world of experience and proceeds by observation, experiment, and classification to the framing of general laws. This method is characteristic of the physical sciences.

The method of ethics is mixed. It is no mere spinning of a string of conclusions from ideas found embedded in our minds with no reference to experience. On the other hand, it cannot be built up on a basis of experience alone, which is limited to the *is* and cannot touch the *ought*. Ethics begins with a definite view of the universe and of man drawn from experience and refined by metaphysics, from which certain moral principles follow as logically demanded. Ethics develops the implications of these principles and points out their application to the various spheres of human conduct. As a practical science, it deals, not with some imaginary utopia, but with human life as it is actually lived.

Aristotle, in his *Nicomachean Ethics*, follows some such combined method. Starting with commonly accepted notions on the good and the end, and identifying these with happiness, he goes on to a study of the virtues that are the essential means to happiness. He returns at the close of his work to take a second look at happiness, which now stands out in a clearer light as the proper goal of all human effort.

St. Thomas, in the second part of his *Summa Theologica* and in the third part of his *Summa Contra Gentiles,* follows a more deductive approach. Starting with God as creator of the world and its provident ruler, as the last end of man and the source of his happiness, St. Thomas deduces from the eternal law in God the natural law in man, from the infinite light of divine reason the borrowed light of human reason shining to guide man's steps, from God the exemplar of all holiness the delineation of the virtues that man must cultivate within himself. It is a grand vision and the proper approach for one who writes as a theologian.

Today many followers of St. Thomas, while adhering to both his principles and conclusions, recognize that St. Thomas never wrote a philosophical ethics of his own and speculate on how he would do so. They think that he would not follow the deductive method that works so well in theology, but rather an inductive method starting with man, with man's acts, his values and ideals, his inescapable sense of the *ought,* the inner urgency of his drive toward the fulfillment of his nature, the utter necessity of following his reason which is his only natural guide; and then proceeding to seek justification for these observed facts, finding it ultimately in God, on whom man and the whole moral order are squarely based.

The study of morals may proceed in either way and the conclusions, if validly derived, should be the same. We shall try to follow the second method as more appropriate to a philosophical study such as ethics is meant to be. But any method is only a tool. It will be diversified to meet the various problems as they arise.

DEFINITION AND DIVISION OF ETHICS

Having explored the study of ethics and mapped out its territory, organization, and function, we can now summarize our discoveries in a definition. *Ethics is the practical normative study of the rightness and wrongness of human conduct as known by natural reason.*

First we shall take up basic ethics, then applied ethics. *Basic* ethics lays down the broad principles that must govern all human conduct, and must logically come first. *Applied* ethics gives these basic principles specific application to man's chief forms or patterns of conduct. Since man's actions are infinitely variable, we can study only the main types or classes of actions, much as physicians classify diseases and lawyers classify crimes, though each individual case is somewhat different. Applied ethics is subdivided into *individual* and *social,* according as it considers man without or within the framework of social organization.*

SUMMARY

Ethics originated in speculation on the good life, and was systematized into a part of philosophy by the Greeks, who called it ethics from their

---

*Basic ethics was formerly called *general* ethics and applied ethics was called *special* ethics. But *general ethics* is now often understood to mean the whole of ethics for man in general, as opposed to medical ethics, legal ethics, business ethics, etc.

word for custom. But it deals only with customs involving the idea of right and wrong, with *morals*.

Its purpose is to study this fact of experience, that men distinguish right from wrong and have a feeling for the *ought*. The *subject matter* of ethics is human conduct; its *point of view* is that of rightness and wrongness, of *oughtness*.

Ethics is related to all the human and social sciences, but is always distinguished from them by its unique point of view, the *ought*. Ethics is distinguished from moral theology by restricting itself to natural reason as opposed to revealed religion.

If ethics is called a *science*, it is not in the sense of the experimental sciences, but in the sense of the philosophical sciences. Ethics is a *practical* and *normative* science. It is also an art, but only the science can be taught.

It borrows the normal epistemological *presuppositions* of any body of learning, and expects the student to have made up his mind on the freedom of the will, the immortality of the soul, and the existence of God.

Its *method* is a mixture of induction and deduction, rising from the experience of human behavior to a knowledge of human nature, and then applying its general laws to particular cases.

Ethics is defined as: *the practical normative study of the rightness and wrongness of human conduct as known by natural reason.*

Ethics is divided into basic and applied; applied ethics is further divided into individual and social.

READINGS

1. Read Aristotle's preface to his *Nicomachean Ethics*, bk. I, ch. 1-3. This can be found in McKeon's *Basic Works of Aristotle*, as well as in numerous other editions. Note that by "political science" Aristotle means ethics, and that he does not think it a fit study for young men.
2. St. Thomas' *Commentary on Aristotle's Ethics* would be very helpful if it were put into English.
3. Cronin's *Science of Ethics*, vol. I, ch. I, gives much useful material.
4. Maritain, *Essay on Christian Philosophy*, pp. 38-43, 61-100; *Science and Wisdom*, pp. 107-127, discusses the relation between ethics and moral theology; he argues for a Christian ethics distinct from, yet subalternated to, moral theology.
5. D'Arcy, "Religion and Ethics," in Anshen (ed.), *Moral Principles of Action*, ch. 24.
6. St. Thomas' proofs for the presuppositions of ethics are found in his *Summa Theologica:* for God's existence in I, q. 2, a. 3; for free will in I, q. 83, a. 1; for immortality in I, q. 75, a. 6. Some of the surrounding material should be read to make the argument clear. Pegis' *Basic Writings of St. Thomas Aquinas* is a convenient edition.
7. Leibell's *Readings in Ethics* devotes the first 152 pages to matter touched on in this chapter. It has a wide selection of material on the presuppositions of ethics.

*   *   *

The introduction and first chapter of the ordinary textbooks give their presentation of the matter we have here. In the reading lists following each chapter we shall rarely refer to textbooks of ethics, since their organization is such that the student can easily find the corresponding matter for himself. It will be our policy to suggest readings that the student might otherwise overlook.

CHAPTER 2

HUMAN CONDUCT

PROBLEM

There are no good or bad babies, but there are good and bad men. How does the change come about? Obviously by the lives, the conduct, the actions of the persons in question. Man has no moral character to begin with, but builds up one for himself by the way he lives. Before we can determine what moral goodness or badness is, and how it gets into the acts one performs and from them into the man himself, we should look at the thing in which moral goodness or badness can dwell. What sort of acts can a man do? Are all sorts of acts capable of becoming morally good or bad, or only some of them? If only some, what are these acts and what differentiates them from the rest? We can portion out our inquiry as follows:

(1) What is human conduct?
(2) How is human conduct under our control?
(3) How can the will command the acts of other faculties?
(4) What qualities of the human act have ethical import?
(5) How is responsibility entailed in the human act?

HUMAN ACTS

Man's actions taken collectively are called behavior or conduct. *Behavior* is more of a psychological word and is applied even to animals, whereas *conduct* has a strictly ethical meaning and is exclusively human. Conduct consists of acts, but not of all or any acts a man can perform. It is customary to call the kind of acts constituting conduct *human acts*, making this expression a technical term with an exact and restricted meaning. St. Thomas puts it as follows:

> Of actions done by man those alone are properly called human which are proper to man as man. Now man differs from irrational animals in this that he is master of his actions. Wherefore those actions alone are

properly called human of which man is master. Now man is master of his actions through his reason and will, whence too the free will is defined as the faculty of will and reason. Therefore those actions are properly called human which proceed from a deliberate will. And if any other actions are found in man, they can be called actions of a man, but not properly human actions, since they are not proper to man as man.*

Hence there are two kinds of acts:

1. A *human act (actus humanus)* is one of which man is master, one that is consciously controlled and deliberately willed, so that the agent is held responsible for it. These human acts constitute human conduct and form the subject matter of ethics.

2. An *act of a man (actus hominis)* is one which a man happens to perform, but he is not master of it, for he has not consciously controlled it, has not deliberately willed it, and for it he is not held responsible. Such are acts done in infancy, sleep, delirium, insanity, or fits of abstraction; they have no ethical significance and do not constitute human conduct.

Note carefully that the distinction here is not between acts of the rational order and those of the sentient or vegetative order. It is true that rational acts, such as thinking and willing, are proper to man in the sense that he alone can do them, whereas sentient and vegetative acts, such as eating, sleeping, walking, growing, are actions that man has in common with other beings. This is how psychology classifies them to understand human nature; but ethics tries to explain human *conduct,* and its whole question is whether man is master of his acts or not, be they of the rational, sentient, or vegetative order.

Man is the only creature in this world who can think, but if his thoughts simply run along by association without his conscious direction and control, such thoughts are only *acts of a man,* not *human acts,* even though they are of the rational order. On the other hand, eating and sleeping are by their nature merely animal acts that man does in common with brutes, but they become *human acts* if the man does them knowingly and willingly. To put food in the mouth while in a distracted state of mind is an *act of a man,* but to determine deliberately to eat this food is a *human act.* To be overcome by drowsiness and fall asleep is an *act of a man,* but to go to bed intentionally for the purpose of sleeping is a *human act.* Hence, though it is impossible to have a *human act* unless it is guided by intellect and will, the act itself so guided can be of any sort. In other words, a human act can be either physical or mental in nature provided it is deliberately willed.

PSYCHOLOGICAL BACKGROUND

Human conduct is the result of a complex psychological process. There is an interplay of man's two specific faculties, intellect and will. A warning should be issued not to take the accompanying description too mechani-

---

*St. Thomas, *Summa Theologica,* I-II, q. 1, a. 1.

cally. Intellect and will are but abilities or faculties by which the whole man acts. It is the person who acts by means of his abilities. The abilities are not independent agents, little persons inside the larger human person, nor are they geared like the wheels and levers of a machine. If we speak of the intellect or will as doing anything, we mean that the *man,* the *person,* does them with his intellect or will. We give the briefest summary of this process with a view to its ethical import.

For a man to act he must first be attracted by some good. When he perceives something as good, there arises in him a liking for it. If he sees that it is not only good in itself but also good for him, his liking becomes a desire or *wish.* A wish may remain ineffectual, but if he further understands the good as possible of attainment, this intellectual insight moves his will to an act of spontaneous *intention* or tendency toward the good, a stretching forth to gain the object without yet counting the cost in effort and loss of other goods. He now turns his intellect to the task of weighing the reasons for and against the carrying out of this intention and the various sets of means by which it might be accomplished. This act of the intellect is called counsel or *deliberation,* whose outcome is to arrive at one of two practical judgments: "This is to be done here and now," or "This is not to be done here and now." The matter has now been laid out for his decision. He now knows thoroughly what to do and the reasons why. The stage is set for his verdict, the supreme act of expression of his being as a self-directed person. He accepts one or the other of these alternative practical judgments of the intellect by a free act of decision of his will. Cutting off deliberation, he makes the alternative chosen the *last* practical judgment. The yielding to one rather than the other, after deliberation, is the deliberate act of the will. It has two moments: taken absolutely, as a yielding to the attraction of the object and an acquiescence in the judgment of the intellect, it is called *consent;* taken comparatively, as a preference of one alternative over the other, it is called *choice.* Then by the act of *command,* a guiding act of the intellect, he directs his will in the *use* of the means to carry his decision into execution. Finally, there come the perception that the end is attained and its *enjoyment.*

In all there are six acts of the will. Three are about the end: *wish, intention,* and *enjoyment.* Three are about the means: *choice, consent,* and

	Intellect	*Will*
End	Perception of the good Judgment of attainability	Wish Intention
Means	Deliberation Last practical judgment	Consent Choice
Execution	Command Perception of attainment	Use Enjoyment

use. Each act of the will is preceded by an act of the intellect, the most important of which is *deliberation.**

In the accompanying scheme the word *intention* is taken in a technical sense. The intention that precedes deliberation can mean only the spontaneous movement of the will toward embracing a perceived good. It is entirely outside our control whether we shall have such a reaction or not. Recognition of this attraction in us starts off the process of deliberation, a kind of debate with ourselves whether to yield to it or to resist it. If yielded to by consent after deliberation, the intention persists until the execution of the act. Then we say that the act was done with *deliberate intent,* and the act is a human act. But the initial intention before deliberation and consent is not a human act, but only a spontanenous tendency.

Deliberation itself is not a human act unless we reflect on it and initiate a secondary deliberation. We spontaneously begin to weigh motives for and against our contemplated course of action without recognizing that we are doing so. But if our attention is turned to the fact that we are deliberating, the question arises whether we should continue our deliberation or break it off. If we decide to continue, our act of deliberating becomes a human act, but the original point at issue is not yet a human act, because we have not yet consented to *it* but have consented only to deliberate about it. Such reflections on our own acts can become quite complex.

Deliberation consists of a series of practical judgments for and against the contemplated course of action. The last practical judgment is not distinct from the deliberation but is simply that one among all these judgments that the will consents to and accepts. It is the consent of the will that makes this judgment the last one, thus ending the deliberative process. Likewise *consent* and *choice* are not two distinct acts, but the consent to one alternative is the choice of it over its opposite, and vice versa. Only in a case where no two alternatives are offered could there be consent without choice.

It may seem surprising to see *command* listed as an act of the intellect rather than of the will. St. Thomas takes command as an act of ordering and directing, involving an understanding of the fitness of means to end; this is properly an act of the intellect, though no execution of the command is possible without an accompanying act of the will.

There is no need of considering each of the stages mentioned above as a distinct act; they blend together in the most confusing fashion and are much more complicated than can be described conveniently. We must, however, always distinguish the indeliberate from the deliberate acts of the will, that is, the act which preceded from the act which follows deliberation. The most important part of the process is *consent,* for it is this which makes the act ours in the sense that it is chargeable to us. Up to that point it was not a *human act;* afterwards it is.

---

*St. Thomas, *Summa Theologica,* I-II, qq. 8 and 13, preamble.

COMMANDED ACTS

The will can control not only its own acts but the acts of other faculties as well. By the will we make decisions but rely on other faculties to carry them out. By the will we decide to walk, but the will cannot do the walking; it must command the muscles of the legs to carry out the decision by performing the act. By the will we decide to think, but the will cannot do the thinking; it commands the intellect, the faculty of understanding, to turn its attenion to this thought rather than that. The will can command itself, as when it decides to reach a decision now or to put it off till later. St. Thomas speaks, as we have done, of acts commanded by the will, but *command* itself *(imperium)** he makes an act issued by the intellect, but moved thereto by a previous act of the will, the act of choice, and coming before the next act of the will, the act of use. When we speak of the will commanding, we are only using a short expression for the whole process.

The will can command, then, both external bodily acts and internal mental acts. I decide to study, and this decision is the act of the will itself. I take out my book, turn to the lesson, bend my eyes on the page; these are external bodily acts commanded by the will. I focus my mind on the matter, understand what I am reading, fix it in my memory; these are internal mental acts commanded by the will. Thus study is a mixed act involving the use of the eyes in reading and of the intellect in understanding, both under command of the will.

Which of these is the *human act?* It might seem that only the act of the will itself, the act which the will as a faculty performs or elicits, the so-called *elicited act* of the will, is the *human act.* In the strictest sense this is true, for it is in the will that choice and consent reside, and it is these that give an act its specifically human character. Hence if a man decides to do something with clear consent of his will, but is prevented by circumstances from carrying out his decision, he is responsible for this consent. Thus a man can be guilty of murder in intent although he never gets the chance to carry it out.

But commanded acts share in the consent of the will that commands them. Man's will is his controlling faculty and he is held responsible for all that he controls through his will, both for the internal acts of the will itself and for the acts of other faculties that the will commands. Both are human acts, but the former are so in a stricter sense.

ETHICAL CONSTITUTION OF THE HUMAN ACT

After this brief survey of the psychological background of the *human act,* we must now determine the properties which characterize it from the ethical standpoint. A *human act,* or *human conduct,* has three qualities:

(1) Knowledge
(2) Voluntariness
(3) Freedom

---

*Summa Theologica, I-II, q. 17, a. 1.

Of these voluntariness is the one which essentially constitutes the act a human act. Knowledge is an essential prerequisite without which the act cannot be voluntary. Freedom is connoted in nearly all our human acts and ordinarily follows from the fact that the act is voluntary.

Knowledge

Conduct springs from a motive and is directed to an end. The will is a blind faculty, a faculty of striving and not of knowing, and cannot act unless enlightened by the intellect. The intellect proposes the good and the will tends toward it. Also, the end cannot be attained without the use of suitable means, and the will, being blind, cannot see the suitability of these means. So the intellect is needed, not only to propose the end to be attained, but also to pass judgment on the fitness of the means to the end and to devise a course of conduct that will efficiently lead to the end. The intellect must think this all out before presenting it to the will for its decision.

The activity of the intellect is especially apparent in the process of deliberation, where the motives for and against cannot be weighed unless they are known. There must also be advertence to what one is about, a focussing of attention on the acts being done so that a man is conscious or aware of his acts. Advertence is impossible without a certain amount of reflection, by which the mind turns back and looks at itself acting. The person both knows that he knows and knows that he wills.

Advertence and reflection occur in varying degrees, thereby affecting the human character of the act. An act is a *human* act only insofar as it is known. Any part or circumstance of the act that the doer does not advert to is not attributable to him. This works both ways: a man who willfully kills another without knowing that the victim is his father commits murder but not parricide; a man who steals money not knowing that it is counterfeit is morally guilty of theft, though he gets no profit out of it.

Voluntariness

To have a human act, it is not sufficient that it be guided by knowledge; it must also be *willed*. An act which comes from both knowledge and will is called *voluntary*, an adjective formed from the Latin word for *will*. A voluntary act is a willed act, one that neither is forced on a person from without nor arises spontaneously from within. After much groping about, Aristotle suggests the following definition:

> Since that which is done under compulsion or by reason of ignorance is involuntary, the voluntary would seem to be that of which the moving principle is in the agent himself, he being aware of the particular circumstances of the action.*

Aristotle thus grants voluntariness to acts done by children and animals. He recognizes that sensation is knowledge and sense appetite is an inner

---

Nicomachean Ethics, bk. III, ch. 1, 1111a 22.

principle of action; besides, the Greek words for *voluntary* and for *will* are not etymologically connected like the Latin *voluntarium* and *voluntas*. While not wishing to contradict Aristotle, St. Thomas points out that animals' actions can be called voluntary only in an analogous and participated sense (like our modern use of the term *animal intelligence*), and that the voluntary agent must know not merely the circumstances of the act, but the end to which it leads. St. Thomas puts his definition in these terms:

> It is of the nature of a voluntary act that its principle be within the agent, together with some knowledge of the end.*

Throughout his whole discussion it is evident that the inner principle referred to is the will. Hence his definition may be amended thus: *A voluntary act is one which proceeds from the will with a knowledge of the end.*

Voluntariness is one of our simplest and most familiar notions. We should not take the impression that there is anything recondite or mysterious about it. A voluntary act is simply a *willed act,* one in which the agent knows what he is about to do and wills to do it. The difficulty is that some of the words we commonly use to indicate this kind of act have certain connotations we do not wish to stress. We say that a person acts willingly, willfully, intentionally, deliberately, or voluntarily; these all mean the same in the present context. To act willingly one does not have to act gladly and eagerly; to act willfully it is not necessary to be wayward or obstinate; to act intentionally does not require that one act vigorously or ostentatiously; to act deliberately there is no need of acting slowly and painstakingly; to act voluntarily it is not necessary to volunteer or freely offer oneself for some work. The English words often have these shades of meaning, but we use them simply in the sense that a person *knowingly wills* what he does.

Freedom

Freedom (in the sense of free will, as we take it here) is the ability, when all requisites for acting are present, of either acting or not acting, of doing this or doing that. Ordinarily all voluntary acts are free acts, but the concepts are not the same. A free act supposes two or more eligible alternatives, at least the alternatives of acting or not acting. If only one is possible, yet that is what the person would knowingly and willingly take were choice offered, his act would be voluntary without being free. Such an act would proceed from the will with a knowledge of the end (voluntary), yet one would be unable to refuse it (not free).

Does this ever happen? Only in one case: when man is confronted with the perfect good. This is so overwhelmingly good that there can be no motive for refusing it, and man cannot act without a motive. In this life the desire for happiness in general is of this type, as is the actual possession of God in the next life. But for all practical purposes voluntariness

---

*Summa Theologica, I-II, q. 6, a. 2; but his main discussion of this matter is in a. 1.

and freedom coincide, and in our study we can neglect the slight distinction between them.

Though every free act is voluntary, and every voluntary act except the one mentioned above is free, these two words have a different flavor. *Voluntary* emphasizes the strength with which the will knowingly adheres to the good proposed and pursues its aim. *Free* emphasizes the fact that the will is choosing this alternative at the very moment when it could be choosing the opposite. Hence strong emotion is said to increase voluntariness but diminish freedom; if the emotion becomes so strong that the man does not know what he is doing, he cannot will, and both voluntariness and freedom are destroyed.

We might put actions done by men on five levels. *Violent* acts are imposed from without and the subject is more properly said to be acted on than to act. *Automatic* acts come from within but are not guided by knowledge, as in reflexes and secretions. *Spontaneous* acts, if we distinguish them from automatic, come from within and are guided by knowledge, but not by knowledge of the end as end; such are acts of sensation, intellection, and the first uncontrolled movements of the appetites. *Voluntary* acts come from the will guided by knowledge of the end as end. *Free* acts are voluntary acts in which there is the factor of choice. Only the last two types of acts can be human acts.

CONSEQUENCES OF VOLUNTARINESS

A voluntary act, as the product of a man's own will guided by his own reason, is the actual exercise of his mastership over his conduct. Though the act is done and finished, it is still referable to its master as *his act.* The basic explanation of why it was done rather than not done is that *he willed it,* and thus it remains forever related to him. This relation we express by the words *responsibility* and *imputability.* They express the same relation between the agent and his act, but they look at the relation from different sides: we say that the agent is responsible, answerable, accountable for his act and that the act is imputable, chargeable, attributable to the agent. Responsibility for a bad act is called *guilt,* but we have no corresponding word for this in a good act. To determine the degree of a person's responsibility for an act is the same as to determine how far the act was voluntary on his part.

Besides the relation between the agent and his act, there may be a further relation of both to reward or punishment. An act is a transitory thing, lasting only so long as it is being done, but rewards and punishments are not always given immediately on the doing of the deed. A murderer kills his victim and is apprehended years later; we feel justified in punishing him now, though his evil act lasted only a moment. A soldier receives a medal for bravery long after the battle is over; we feel that, though his deed is only a memory, something of it remains in him and calls for a reward. Some kind of moral entity must be produced in the doer by his deed to connect him with the reward or punishment to come. This property or essential consequence of a human act is called *merit*. To merit something is to earn it, to deserve it, to be entitled to it as payment or to be liable to it as punishment. Further pursuit of this subject must be postponed, since it would carry us into the fields of law, right, sanction, and justice.

SUMMARY

What precisely is conduct? It consists of *human acts*. In contrast to mere *acts of a man, human acts* are those of which man is master by consciously controlling and deliberately willing them.

The *human act* is the result of a complex psychological process involving wish, intention, deliberation, choice, consent, use, and enjoyment. The decisive point is the *consent* of the will following the deliberation of the intellect. It is here that the person yields to the attractiveness of the object and commits himself to it.

Commanded acts, acts of faculties commanded by the will, share in the consent of the will and are also considered *human acts* in a borrowed sense.

A *human act* has three qualities: knowledge, voluntariness, and freedom.

Knowledge points out the end and the means to it, guides deliberation, and provides advertence and reflection, without which there can be no consent of the will.

Voluntariness means that the act is really willed, that it proceeds from the will with a knowledge of the end. It supposes that the agent knows what he is doing and wills to do it.

Freedom adds to voluntariness the possibility of choice. All free acts are voluntary. All voluntary acts are also free, except desire for and possession of the perfect good.

Some main consequences of voluntariness are *responsibility* in the agent, *imputability* in the act, and *merit* in both.

READINGS

1. Aristotle, *Nicomachean Ethics,* bk. III, ch. 1-5, treats of voluntariness. This chapter tries to reduce to a small space what St. Thomas says in the Summa Theologica, I-II, qq. 6, 8, 11-17 (*Basic Writings,* vol. II). In q. 9 he discusses what moves (motivates) the will, and in q. 10 he shows that the will is not moved of necessity (not necessitated). This follows up what he had said in Part I, qq. 82 and 83, on free will (*Basic Writings,* vol. I).
2. Gilson, *Moral Values and Moral Life,* ch. II. Also *The Christian Philosophy of St. Thomas Aquinas,* pp. 251-256.
3. Farrell, *A Companion to the Summa,* vol. II, ch. II, III.
4. Cronin, *The Science of Ethics,* vol. I, pp. 28-33.
5. Bourke, *Ethics,* ch. 3, contains an excellent summary of St. Thomas' treatment.
6. Klubertanz, *Philosophy of Human Nature,* ch. 10.

CHAPTER 3

RESPONSIBILITY

PROBLEM

From the acts man performs we have separated out those over which man has control. We have fixed the point of control in the consent of the will, prepared for by the deliberation of the intellect. If the consent can be thrown to either alternative, for or against, the person himself is the cause of his own decision, and is therefore responsible for the act chosen. There is no other reason why this act was done rather than not done except that the man himself, by the choice of his will under the guiding light of his intellect, made that act to *be*. The act is *his* insofar as *he* did it.

Is a man equally responsible for all his human acts? Not all knowledge is equally clear nor does the will consent always with equal decisiveness. What proceeds from the will may be closely or remotely connected with the will-act itself, and may share in its voluntariness in varying degrees. We must therefore see the factors that enhance or limit a man's responsibility by increasing or diminishing his control, making the act more or less *human*, more or less *his*. The following points come up for discussion:

(1) Can there be voluntariness in not acting?
(2) How much attention is needed for a voluntary act?
(3) Are unwanted but foreseen consequences voluntary?
(4) What destroys or weakens our responsibility?

POSITIVE AND NEGATIVE VOLUNTARINESS

There is a difference between *not willing* to do something and willing *not to do* something. In the first case there is no act of the will and therefore no voluntariness. In the second case there is an act of the will, an act of deliberate omission or refusal, and this is quite voluntary. Hence voluntariness can be positive or negative, according as we will to do something or to omit something, and both of these are different from a state of nonvoluntariness, which is an absence of willing.

The state of *not willing* is often psychologically impossible to maintain. We *do not will* so long as the doing of an act does not even cross our mind. But when we think of it, and especially after we have reflected on it and deliberated about it, we must do either of two things: take it or leave it, will to do it or will not to do it. One course is as voluntary as the other. Negative voluntariness is not the same as no voluntariness, just as a negative number is not the same as zero.

ATTENTION AND INTENTION

For my act to be voluntary I must knowingly will it. But must my mind be focussed on the act at the very moment I am doing it? Can I be responsible for an act done in a state of complete distraction? For any responsibility to remain, must a previous decision to act still influence my behavior or may it have entirely ceased its influence? Can I be responsible for something which I never did will but presumably would have willed if I ever thought of it?

To answer such questions, it is customary to distinguish four levels of intention with which an act is performed, representing a progressive diminution of voluntariness.

An *actual* intention is one that a person is conscious of at the moment he performs the intended action. The person pays attention not merely to what he is doing but also to the fact that he is here and now willing it.

A *virtual* intention is one that was once made and continues to influence the act now being done, but is not present to the person's consciousness at the moment of performing the act. Thus a man walks to a definite destination; his intention was actual on starting out, but soon becomes virtual as his mind drifts onto other subjects while he takes the right turns and arrives where he wanted to go. What he willed was the whole series of acts that would bring him there, but he need not be thinking of his destination every step of the way. After his first decision, the subsequent acts could be carried out while his mind is completely distracted from its original purpose.

A *habitual* intention is one that was once made and not retracted, but does not influence the performance of the intended act. Though called habitual, it does not imply any habit; it is an intention that was once *had,* and is still had only in the sense that it was never revoked, for no psychic remnant of it need remain in the mind. A man accepts an invitation to dinner and intends to go, but in the meantime becomes thoroughly drunk and happens to stagger into the dinner without the slightest idea of where he is or why he is there. A man fully resolves to kill his enemy but is prevented by circumstances from carrying out his intent, though he never revokes it; later, while hunting, he shoots at what he thinks is an animal, but finds that he has accidentally shot his enemy.

An *interpretative* intention is one that has not been made but presumably would have been made if the person were aware of the circumstances. If the literal application of a law would cause more harm than good, one might interpret the mind of the lawgiver and relax the law in this particular case. If a repentant thief cannot return stolen goods because he cannot discover the owner, he may give them to the poor on the presumption that this would be the will of the owner in the present circumstances.

For an act to be voluntary an actual intention is not necessary, but a virtual one suffices. The habitual and interpretative intentions indicate that the person's will (either once actually had or merely presumed) is objectively carried out, but not by the person's own voluntary act. An habitual intention, however, is sufficient for the fulfillment of certain kinds of obligations; for example, if I give you a gift, completely forgetting that I already owe you the money in payment of a debt, the debt is satisfied.

FORESEEN CONSEQUENCES

There is a difference between the way in which the act itself is voluntary and the way in which its consequences are voluntary. That is *voluntary in itself*, or *directly voluntary*, which is the thing willed, whether it be willed as an end or as means to an end. That is *voluntary in cause*, or *indirectly voluntary*, which is the unintended but foreseen consequence of something else that is voluntary in itself; the agent does not will it either as end or as means, but sees that he cannot get something else without getting it; he wills the cause of which this is a necessary effect. Thus one who throws a bomb at a king to assassinate him, knowing that he will kill the king's attendants also, directly wills the throwing of the bomb (as means), also directly wills the death of the king (as end), and indirectly wills the death of the attendants (as consequence) though their death gives him no profit. But a consequence which is neither intended nor foreseen is involuntary, such as the death of one who unexpectedly rushes up to the king after the bomb has left the thrower's hand.

The assassin just described, since his act is wrong from the start, is morally responsible for all the deaths he foresaw would result from his act, whether he wanted them or not; he had no right to will them or to permit them. But good or indifferent acts also may have bad effects, which can be foreseen. Is one always obliged to avoid them? This question of the *indirect voluntary*, as it is often called, of those effects that are merely voluntary in cause, poses a problem of the utmost importance in ethics. Since we have not yet seen the factors which can make a human act good or evil, it will be better to postpone our treatment of the *indirect voluntary* or the so-called *double effect principle* to the chapter on moral determinants.*

MODIFIERS OF RESPONSIBILITY

Voluntariness is *perfect* if the agent has full knowledge and full consent. It is *imperfect* if there is something wanting in the agent's knowledge or

---

*See pp. 101-113.

consent or both, provided he has both in some degree. If either the knowledge were wholly lacking or the consent were wholly lacking, there could be no voluntariness at all. The question now arises: What renders voluntariness imperfect, reducing the specifically human character of the act and making the agent less responsible? Since we are not interested here in the strength of the will-act, but in the agent's self-control, we shall call them *modifiers of responsibility*. There are five main ones:

(1) Ignorance, affecting the knowledge
(2) Passion, affecting the consent of the will
(3) Fear, opposing to the will a contrary wish
(4) Force, actual use of physical compulsion
(5) Habit, a tendency acquired by repetition

Ignorance

Lack of knowledge exists in varying degrees. The term *ignorant* is usually applied only to persons and not to things incapable of knowledge. One capable of knowledge but lacking it may or may not have an obligation to have such knowledge. Neither a sea captain nor a doctor needs to know music or archaeology; such merely negative ignorance has no ethical import. But the case would be different if the sea captain piloted a ship without knowing navigation, if the doctor tried to practice without knowing medicine; ignorance in these instances is a privation of knowledge that ought to be present. Ignorance may exist without error but is implied in all error; one who mistakes Smith for Jones does not know either man.

Ignorance either can or cannot be overcome. Ignorance that can be overcome by acquiring the requisite knowledge is called *vincible ignorance*. Ignorance that cannot be overcome because the requisite knowledge cannot be acquired is called *invincible ignorance*. A person can be invincibly ignorant for one of two reasons: either he does not realize his state of ignorance, and so it does not cross his mind that there is any knowledge to be acquired; or he does realize his ignorance, but his efforts to obtain the knowledge are of no avail. Ignorance should be taken relatively to the person: Can this man obtain the information with a reasonable amount of effort, such as normally prudent and good men would feel obliged to use in the circumstances and in time for the decision he must make?

The culpability of vincible ignorance depends on the amount of effort put forth to dispel it, and the amount of effort called for depends on the importance of the matter and the obligation of the agent to possess such knowledge. One who makes a little effort, but not enough, shows some good will but insufficient perseverance. One may know that the knowledge can be obtained, but is too lazy or careless to search for it. One may doubt whether the knowledge can be obtained, and after a little effort may hastily but wrongly judge that it cannot. One may make no effort at all, either with full knowledge that the ignorance is vincible, or not caring whether it is or not. One may deliberately avoid knowledge in order to plead ignorance as an excuse, such as refusing to read notices or dodging those who might inform him; this sort of pretense is called *affected* or studied ignorance.

1. *Invincible ignorance destroys responsibility.* Knowledge is requisite for voluntariness, and in the case of invincible ignorance this knowledge is not obtainable. Therefore what is done in invincible ignorance is not voluntary. A man who passes on counterfeit money, not suspecting that it is counterfeit, does no wrong. His act of *paying* is voluntary, but not his paying *in worthless money.*

2. *Vincible ignorance does not destroy responsibility.* The person knows that he is ignorant and that he can gain the knowledge. By deliberately failing to make sufficient effort he allows himself to remain in ignorance, and the effects that follow from this ignorance are voluntary in cause, for they are foreseen consequences. A surgeon, knowing that he has not sufficient knowledge for a difficult operation that can be postponed, performs it anyway and kills the patient; though he did not want the patient to die, he deliberately exposed him to serious and unnecessary danger, and is responsible for the death.

3. *Vincible ignorance lessens responsibility.* The less knowledge there is, the less voluntariness there can be. Though the ignorance itself is realized, the effect of the ignorance is only vaguely perceived. In the example above, the surgeon is not sure that he will kill the patient, but knows only that it is a probable effect. He is less guilty than one who would deliberately plan to kill a man in this way.

4. *Affected ignorance in a way lessens, in a way increases responsibility.* It lessens it, as does all lack of knowledge, since the person does not see clearly the full import of what he is doing. It increases it if the person intends to use the ignorance as an excuse; the removal of the risk of punishment is an added motive for the will; he is not only willing the act but willing the ignorance as a means of facilitating the act.

Passion

It is difficult to get a word that means precisely what we want here. The older writers call it *concupiscence,* but this term has become too ambiguous. Concupiscence originally meant simply desire, then any motion of the sensitive appetite, then that part of the sensitive appetite which is opposed to the irascible part, then the rebellion of the sensitive appetite against the dictates of reason (a theological term indicating a result of original sin), from which it comes to mean proneness to evil in general, and then proneness to evil especially in the matter of sex. The native English word is *lust,* and it has gone through a similar evolution. Because of possible misunderstanding, these two words are better avoided in the present context.

The idea we want here is that of any very strong motion of the sensitive appetite. The word *feeling* is too weak; *emotion* is stronger but not strong enough. The word *passion* seems to suit best, though it is not perfect, for it puts too much stress on two emotions, anger and love, and we mean them all.

We shall not enter into a psychological discussion of the passions—their nature, number, and varieties. We are interested only in the effect of the passions on a human act. We usually speak of the passions as affecting the *freedom* of a human act rather than its voluntariness, for passion may make us will a thing more strongly, but with less self-control. It is in this sense that passion is sometimes said to *increase voluntariness but lessen freedom.* Passion certainly increases the force of the will-act, but this is more of a psychological than an ethical consideration. The man who has less self-control has less responsibility, and his act is that much less a *human act.*

The passions may arise spontaneously before the will has acted. When an object is presented to the senses, the sensitive appetite is stirred up almost automatically and reacts by sudden feelings of joy, anger, hatred, grief, shame, pity, disgust, and the like. These emotions, if felt very strongly, are what we mean by the passions. They often occur in us without our will or against our will. Passion of this kind is called *antecedent,* because it comes before the will can act.

We can also intentionally stir up our passions by brooding on the objects that arouse them. We can actually make ourselves angry by vividly rehearsing insults in our imagination, or frightened by the hair-raising details of a horror story, or sad by an exaggerated indulgence in self-pity. Passion thus deliberately aroused is called *consequent,* because it comes after the free choice of our will. Antecedent passion is but an *act of a man,* but consequent passion is a *human act.* Antecedent passion becomes consequent when it is recognized for what it is, and then is deliberately retained or fostered.

1. *Antecedent passion may destroy responsibility.* If the passion is so sudden or violent as wholly to prevent the use of reason, it makes deliberation impossible and the act performed under its influence is neither free nor voluntary. Experience shows that complete loss of control sometimes happens, though rarely.

2. *Antecedent passion does not usually destroy responsibility.* In most cases a man even while upset by passion remains master of his acts. Enough knowledge and consent remain for his act to be both voluntary and free, and he is held responsible for it. That this case is the normal one is also evident from experience.

3. *Antecedent passion lessens responsibility.* It makes calm intellectual deliberation more difficult. The motives on each side cannot be weighed with perfect impartiality. The will is predisposed more strongly toward one side than the other, and its freedom of action is hampered. Hence an act done with passion, when free, is less free than one done with cool premeditation and no disturbing influences. The act may be more voluntary in the sense of a greater onrush of the will, but it is less so in the sense of self-control and moral responsibility dependent on calm judgment.

4. *Consequent passion does not lessen responsibility but may increase it.*

The state of passion is deliberately aroused or fostered, and is therefore voluntary in itself. The act resulting from the passion is voluntary either in itself or in its cause. A man intentionally broods over an insult in order to nerve himself for an act of revenge; he is using the passion as a means and the revenge as an end, and both are voluntary in themselves. A man who does not want to kill foresees that his continual brooding over his wrongs will get him into such a state of frenzy that he will kill; yet he deliberately continues to nurse his anger, and as a result becomes insane with rage and kills his enemy; his state of passion is voluntary in itself, but his act of killing is voluntary in cause.

Fear

Fear is the apprehension of impending evil. It can be an emotion, a disturbance of the sensitive appetite, when it appears as a sudden fright-producing reflex or as an impulsive act of avoidance. In this sense fear is one of the passions and follows the laws on the passions stated above. But there is also an intellectual fear, comprising an understanding of a threatened evil and a movement of the will to avoid this evil by rationally devised means. This kind of fear may have no emotional component. Thus a man may steal because he is afraid of poverty, may lie because he is afraid of disgrace, may murder because he is afraid of blackmail. This is the kind of fear we mean as a separate modifier of responsibility.

In estimating its effect on responsibility, fear must be taken relatively to the person and his circumstances. What would produce a slight fear in one person may produce grave fear in another; some are naturally cautious while others are bold, some have little aversion to a condition that others would find intolerable. A lesser evil that threatens us now may produce more fear than a greater evil still far off.

Fear is a modifier of responsibility only when it is a *motive* for acting and not a mere accompaniment of our act, when we act *from* fear and not merely *with* fear. A soldier deserting his post in battle through cowardice is motivated by fear; if he stays at his post despite the danger, he may have just as much fear but it does not influence his conduct.

1. *Fear does not destroy responsibility.* It is true that the emotional type of fear can throw a person into such a panic that he loses all self-control. But the intellectual type of fear we are dealing with does not produce such an effect. The person calmly looks about for an escape from the threatened evil and makes a deliberate choice. He could choose to face the evil but prefers to yield to his fear instead of resisting it, and therefore wills what he does.

2. *Fear lessens responsibility.* An act motivated by fear is one that we will, but would not will except for the fear we experience. This admixture of reluctance weakens the consent of the will, leaving us with a divided mind and a hankering for the other alternative, thus lessening our self-control.

If a person's decision is clear-cut and straightforward, so that he acts without any regret or reluctance, his act is voluntary and the alternative he did not choose is involuntary. But when he acts regretfully and reluctantly, when he chooses something he would rather not be obliged to do, there is a conflict between his *will* and his *wish*. His will is what he deliberately chooses; his wish is what he would like if circumstances permitted.

The time-honored example is that of the sea captain who throws his cargo overboard to save his ship in a storm. The act contains both a voluntary and an involuntary aspect: voluntary in the sense that he does it deliberately and intentionally with sufficient knowledge and consent, for he could refuse and try to weather out the storm or even let his ship sink; involuntary in the sense that he would rather not have to do this and, if there were no storm, certainly would not do it. So he *wills* to jettison his cargo, *wishing* that he did not need to.* Despite the contrary wish (technically called a *velleity*), the captain is held responsible for this act of jettisoning the cargo, but not as responsible as he would be were there no contrary wish present. The unwilled wish itself is involuntary, since it was not consented to, and does not constitute human conduct.

Acts done under *duress* and *intimidation* have fear as a motive. These are acts extorted under threat of evils to be inflicted by another human will. Unless the person becomes so emotionally upset as to become temporarily insane, a matter of passion rather than of intellectual fear, acts done under duress and intimidation are responsible acts, for the person could have refused and taken the consequences. As we shall see later, contracts unjustly extorted through fear can be invalidated by positive law; they are rendered invalid not because they are not willed, but because positive law uses its authority to nullify such contracts for the common good.

Force

Force, violence, or compulsion is external physical power making one do something against his will. In common language, one who yields to a threat of violence is said to be *forced,* yet this is not really force but *fear,* and the person's voluntariness is to be judged by the rules on fear. As a distinct modifier of responsibility, *force* must be understood in its strictest sense as no mere threat but the *actual use of physical might*. If I hand over my money to a thug because he thrusts a gun at me, that is fear; if he physically overpowers me while he rifles my pockets, that is force.

Force cannot reach the will directly, for it touches only external acts and not the internal act of the will itself, in which voluntariness resides. We can continue to will the opposite, no matter how violently we are forced to do the act. Hence the act we are forced to do is involuntary, so

---

*The medieval Latin terminology for such a state is *voluntarium simpliciter et involuntarium secundum quid* (voluntary simply and involuntary in a certain respect). Attempts to translate such language are more confusing than helpful to the English reader. The common words *will* and *wish* as we used them seem to convey the idea adequately enough, though they do not exactly correspond to the Latin terminology.

long as the force is resisted. Somebody else may have the physical strength to make us *do* something, but he cannot make us *will* it.

The act a violent aggressor is trying to make us do may or may not be evil in itself. If it is not, we may yield to it and comply with his demands; our rights are outraged and injustice is done against us, but we ourselves are not doing wrong, only saving ourselves further harm. One who is kidnapped need not struggle (and this is true of one acting from fear as well as force), for there is no moral wrong in merely going off to another place. But in a case such as rape, where consent would involve moral wrong, resistance is required.

How much resistance? At least internal resistance, which consists in withholding the consent of the will, and passive external resistance, which consists in noncooperation with the aggressor. Active external resistance, which consists in positively fighting the aggressor, is also necessary when without it the withholding of consent would be too difficult to maintain, but not when it would be useless and there is no danger of consent.

Force, consented to reluctantly but really, lessens responsibility because a contrary wish is present. If, however, the person actually wants to do what he is being forced to do and only pretends to resist, there is no genuine violence brought to bear and the person is fully accountable for what he does.

Habit

The nature and kinds of habit will be discussed when we come to the virtues; here we are interested only in the way habit may affect our responsibility for an act. For our present purpose we may define a habit as a constant way of acting obtained by repetition of the same act. When a habit has been acquired, the actions follow from it spontaneously and almost automatically, so that deliberate guidance becomes unnecessary.

1. We may set out *deliberately to acquire* a habit, as when we try to learn a sport or to play a musical instrument. Then the habit is voluntary in itself, and the acts resulting from it are either voluntary in themselves if performed with the intention of acquiring the habit, or at least voluntary in cause if they are the unintended but foreseen consequences of the habit.

2. We may not intend to acquire a habit for its own sake, but *voluntarily* perform acts which we know are *habit-forming*, as a person who takes up smoking. Here the acts done are voluntary in themselves and the forming of the habit is voluntary in cause, since we know that we cannot do habit-forming acts without getting the habit. After the habit has been acquired, acts unintentionally following from it are also voluntary in cause.

3. We may discover that we have *unintentionally* acquired a habit, either because we did not realize that we had done the same thing in the same way so often, or because it did not occur to us that such actions were habit-forming. In this case we are not responsible for the existence of the habit or for the acts that unintentionally follow from it, so long as we re-

main ignorant that we have the habit. Only a gross lack of reflectiveness could cause this condition to remain indefinitely, but it can happen.

In whatever way we may have acquired the habit, as soon as we fully recognize our condition we face the choice of either keeping the habit or trying to get rid of it. In either case a new act of the will is called for; the act of getting and the act of keeping are two separate acts, and each may be voluntary.

If we decide to *let the habit remain,* our possession of the habit now becomes voluntary in itself and the acts that unintentionally follow from the habit are voluntary in cause. The habit, however acquired, now falls into the first category mentioned above.

If we decide to *get rid of the habit,* as we are obliged to do if the habit is bad, we are now the victim of two opposite pulls, the voluntary decision of our will to suppress the habit and the involuntary persistence of the habit itself. Long-standing habits of a certain type are not overcome in a day, and when our vigilance is relaxed will inadvertently spring out into the corresponding act. Success in this struggle is bought only by constant watchfulness and effort. If we let down the guards, we shall soon find ourselves drifting back to the old familiar way. Our responsibility for such acts depends on the amount of advertence at the moment when the act is performed, and also on the amount of effort we put in to get rid of the habit. Here, just as in the dispelling of vincible ignorance, we are obliged to put in an amount of effort proportional to the importance of the matter. Depending on these factors and on the person's sincerity, the responsibility for acts done from habit may be perfect or imperfect or nonexistent.

*   *   *

To these five modifiers of responsibility it is possible to add others, such as sleepiness, sickness, pain, alcohol, drugs, and other conditions that reduce awareness and self-control. They do not seem to involve any new principles beyond those already discussed.

Abnormal mental states will, of course, seriously affect the capacity of a person to perform human acts. The lighter neuroses will probably only lessen voluntariness, while the deeper psychoses may destroy it entirely. The mentally ill may have complete self-control at times or along certain lines, and none or little at other times or in other forms of behavior. A kleptomaniac may be a very rational person except when under the spell of this particular compulsion; these acts are involuntary, but not the other acts the person performs. Each case is different and must be judged by itself.

The same principles seem applicable also to the refined methods of physical, mental, and social torture used by the Communists, beginning with "brainwashing" and aiming at total "thought control." It is said that in such a long, drawn-out process, everyone has his breaking point. If so, the victim has full responsibility at the start, suffers a gradual diminution of it as the inhuman routine continues, and after the breaking point, if there really is one, he ceases to be a responsible person. He need not be reduced to actual insanity. It is sufficient that he cannot control his moral judgments or the actions resulting from them. Whether he has any moral responsibility left only the victim himself really knows, though a psychologist could make a good inference. What we have said applies to the victim. The perpetrator of this horror stands guilty of his own barbarity and of all its foreseen consequences.

SUMMARY

Voluntariness is *positive,* if one wills to do something; *negative,* if one wills to omit something; *none,* if one does not will.

Intention is *actual,* if now present to consciousness; *virtual,* if unconsciously continuing to influence the act; *habitual,* if once made, never retracted, and not now influencing the act; *interpretative,* if it would have been made had the agent ever thought of it.

An act is voluntary *in itself,* also called *directly* voluntary, if willed either as end or as means; voluntary *in cause,* also called *indirectly* voluntary, if it is the unintended but foreseen consequence of something else that is voluntary in itself. Unforeseen consequences are involuntary. Note that what is only *indirectly* voluntary, voluntary *in cause,* is nevertheless voluntary.

Voluntariness is *perfect* if there is full knowledge and full consent; *imperfect,* if there is some flaw in one or both.

Ignorance is lack of knowledge in one capable of it. Invincible ignorance cannot be overcome and destroys responsibility. Vincible ignorance can be overcome and does not destroy, though it lessens, responsibility.

Passion is any strong emotion. *Antecedent* passion, arising spontaneously, lessens responsibility and may, though rarely, destroy it. *Consequent* passion, deliberately aroused or fostered, does not lessen responsibility but may even increase it.

Fear is the apprehension of impending evil. Fear affects voluntariness only when it is the motive for acting. It does not destroy responsibility, but lessens it because of the contrary wish mingled with our actual will.

Force is actual external physical power making us act against our will. The act is involuntary if we withhold consent.

Habit is a constant way of acting through repetition of the same act. The acquisition of a habit may be voluntary in itself, voluntary in cause, or involuntary. One who finds he has acquired a habit must choose either to keep it or get rid of it. Responsibility for habitual acts depends on the amount of advertence and on the effort to get rid of the habit.

READINGS

1. Plato, *Laws,* bk. IX, especially from §860 on.
2. Plato in the *Lesser Hippias,* a work of doubtful genuinity, discusses the question whether it is worse to do wrong voluntarily or involuntarily; the conclusion he hints at is hardly acceptable, but it stimulates thought.
3. Aristotle, *Nicomachean Ethics,* bk. III, ch. 1-5.
4. St. Thomas, *Summa Theologica,* I-II, q. 6, on voluntariness; q. 76, on ignorance;

q. 77, on passion; q. 78, on malice and habit. These are in the *Basic Writings*. In I-II, qq. 22-48 (omitted from the *Basic Writings*) St. Thomas gives a lengthy treatment of the passions. This is summarized in:

    a. Gilson, *Moral Values and Moral Life,* ch. IV; also, *The Christian Philosophy of St. Thomas Aquinas,* pp. 282-286.

    b. Farrell, *Companion to the Summa,* vol. II, ch. V, VI, VII; read also ch. II, on the human act and its modifiers.

5. The following have matter pertinent to this chapter:

    a. Cronin, *The Science of Ethics,* vol. I, pp. 33-45.

    b. Rickaby, *Moral Philosophy,* pp. 27-31, 41-64.

    c. James, *Principles of Psychology,* vol. I, ch. IV; *Psychology, Briefer Course,* ch. X; *Talks to Teachers,* ch. VIII. This is James' famous chapter on habit and well worth reading.

    d. Hunter, *Brainwashing,* gives a graphic journalistic account of Communist thought control in Red China.

CHAPTER 4

CONSCIENCE

PROBLEM

How far an individual man is responsible for his acts he alone knows. Others judge him, but they can see only the externals. A man knows when he has been misjudged by others, and can know it only by comparing their judgment with his own and passing a final judgment on both these judgments. This form of reflective knowledge, of awareness of his own responsibility, is sometimes confused with conscience but is more properly a form of *consciousness*.

A man judges, not only whether and how far he is responsible for his acts, but also whether these acts are good or bad. As was said in the beginning, ethics rests on a fact of experience: men's conviction that some acts are right and ought to be done, others are wrong and ought not to be done, still others are indifferent and may either be done or not. Whether such judgments are correct or not is another question, but the fact is that men do make them. The power to do so is called *conscience*.

Since we have been dealing so far with such subjective aspects of the human act as voluntariness and responsibility, and since morality first presents itself to our experience as a personal reflective judgment on our acts long before we have identified the principles on which such judgments should rest, it will be convenient to continue with the subjective aspects of morality before passing to the objective. All men, no matter what their system of morals might be, make judgments of conscience. The study of conscience is, or should be, outside the realm of controversy. It is when we try to find an objective basis for conscience and its judgments that ethical systems begin to diverge. But beyond all ethical systems and common to them all is the requirement that a man be true to himself and that he follow the good as he sees it. We have the following points to discuss:

(1) What is morality?
(2) What is conscience?

(3) How is the judgment of conscience formed?

(4) Must we always follow the dictate of conscience?

(5) May we act with a doubtful conscience?

(6) How can doubts of conscience be solved?

MEANING OF MORALITY

Morality is the quality in human acts by which we call them right or wrong, good or evil. It is a common term covering the goodness or badness of a human act without specifying which of the two is meant. The opposite of *moral* is properly *unmoral* or *nonmoral,* terms which indicate that the act has no moral significance at all, that it is simply unrelated to morals. The word *amoral* is also used in this sense but is more often applied to persons deficient in a sense of moral responsibility. Since the word *immoral* means morally bad, it indicates an act that has a definite moral quality (a bad one). When clearly opposed to *immoral,* the term *moral* means morally good. Thus *moral* and *unmoral* are contradictories, for everything either has or has not some reference to morals; *moral* and *immoral* are contraries, as marking the extremes of good and bad within the field of morals while excluding the morally neutral and irrelevant.

In judging the morality of a human act, we may take into consideration the subjective peculiarities of the agent and look at the act as conditioned by his knowledge and consent, background, training, prejudices, emotional stability, and other personal traits. We ask whether this individual person did right or wrong in this particular case, whether this particular act was good or bad *for him.* Morality so considered is *subjective* morality and is determined by whether the act agrees or disagrees with the agent's own conscience.

But we may also abstract from such subjective conditions, which, though always present in any individual act, can be known directly only by the personal conscience of the doer. We can simply look at the kind of act performed and at the outward circumstances apparent to any observer. We ask not whether this individual is excused from responsibility for the act because of his ignorance or passion or any other modifier of responsibility, but whether *any* normal person with full command of his faculties is allowed deliberately to will that kind of act. We are judging the objective nature of the act done, not the subjective state of the doer. Morality so considered is *objective* morality.

If we ask, "Is murder wrong?" "Is truthfulness right?" we are asking about objective morality. If we ask, "Did this man fully realize what he was doing when he killed that man?" "Did this man intend to tell the truth when he blurted out that remark?" we are asking about subjective morality.

Morality in its completeness includes both its subjective and its objective aspects. It is futile to ask which is more important. Unless acts have a rightness or wrongness of their own with which the judgment of conscience should be in agreement, anybody's judgment is as good as anybody else's and ethics becomes a mere listing of opinions. Ethics as a study stresses objective morality. But each one has his own life to live, must account for his deeds as he saw them, and is rated good or bad on his sincerity in following his conscience even if his moral judgments have been objectively incorrect. In this sense subjective morality is paramount.

MEANING OF CONSCIENCE

Conscience is sometimes called the voice of God, but this expression is to be understood metaphorically, not literally. It does not mean that we get a special revelation from God about each act we are going to do. God speaks to us through our ordinary human nature and through the ordinary faculties of that nature. Supernatural manifestations are outside the scope of ethics.

In the popular mind conscience is often thought of as an "inner voice," a "still small voice," telling us what to do or avoid. Doubtless, most people do experience a reaction of the subconscious based on their childhood environment and training, a tendency to approve or disapprove of things for which approval or disapproval was shown in childhood. Such latent prepossessions, whether predilections or prejudices, will often give correct moral estimates if one has been brought up well. A result of such early psychological experiences may be a vague unidentifiable feeling, a sense of unease and even of "guilt" in departing from the established pattern, even when the feeling is recognized as unreasonable. All this is not what is meant by conscience as we take it.

Conscience is not a special faculty distinct from the intellect. Otherwise our judgment about the rightness or wrongness of our individual acts would be nonintellectual, nonrational, the product of some blind instinct. Conduct of this kind would be unworthy of one whose chief characteristic is rationality. Conscience is but the intellect itself in a special function, the function of judging the rightness or wrongness of our own individual acts.

Conscience is a function of the practical intellect. It does not deal with theoretical questions of right and wrong in general, such as "Why is lying wrong?" "Why must justice be done?" but with the practical question: "What ought I to do here and now in this concrete situation?" "If I do this act I am thinking of, will I be lying, will I be unjust?" It is the same practical intellect by which I judge what to do or avoid in other affairs of life: how shall I run my business, invest my money, protect my health, design my house, plant my farm, raise my family? Like other human judgments, conscience can go wrong, can form false moral judgments. As a man can make mistakes in these other spheres of human activity, so he can make mistakes in personal conduct. But in making any such practical judgment, man has no guide other than his intellect.

Conscience may therefore be defined as the practical judgment of reason upon an individual act as good and to be performed, or as evil and to be avoided. The term *conscience* is applied to three things, and though the definition just given expresses the last of the three, it implies the other two. Conscience means:

(1) The intellect as the faculty of forming judgments about right and wrong individual acts
(2) The process of reasoning that the intellect goes through to reach such a judgment
(3) The judgment itself which is the conclusion of this reasoning process

Deriving the judgment of conscience

The reasoning process involved in arriving at a judgment of conscience is the same as in any logical deductive argument. Deductive reasoning supposes a major premise or general principle, a minor premise or application of the principle to a particular case, and a conclusion necessarily following from the two premises.

The major premise employed in forming the judgment of conscience is a general moral principle. Medieval writers use the word *synderesis* to mean the habit of general moral principles, the habit of possessing such principles formed in mind and ready for use as the basis of one's conduct. What the broad metaphysical principles of contradiction, sufficient reason, causality, and the like are to theoretical reasoning, the principles of synderesis such as "Do good and avoid evil," "Respect the rights of others," and "Do as you would be done by," are to practical moral reasoning. The major premise may be either a principle of synderesis or a conclusion derived from it but held by the individual as a general rule of conduct. The minor premise brings the particular act here and now to be done under the scope of the general principle enunciated in the major. The conclusion logically following is the judgment of conscience itself. Examples:

Lies are not allowed.
This explanation of my conduct is a lie.
This explanation of my conduct is not allowed.

Mistakes that may harm people must be corrected.
The mistake I just made is one that may harm people.
The mistake I just made must be corrected.

What belongs to no one may be kept.
This object I just picked up belongs to no one.
This object I just picked up may be kept.

We often draw the conclusions of conscience so quickly that we are not aware of their syllogistic form. But if we reflect on the process of reasoning we have gone through, we can readily see that it is syllogistic in nature. It usually takes the shortened form of an enthymeme: "Should I say this? No; that would be a lie"; "Must I correct this mistake? Yes; it may hurt someone"; "May I keep this? Of course; no one else owns it." Some of the principles involved (the major premises) may be so simple that we have never expressly formulated them, though we have been acting on them for years.

KINDS OF CONSCIENCE

Conscience may be a guide to future actions, prompting us to do them or avoid them, or a judge of our past actions, the source of our self-approval or remorse. The former is called *antecedent* conscience, the latter *consequent* conscience. For the purpose of ethics antecedent conscience is more important. Its acts are chiefly four: commanding or forbidding, when the act must either be done or avoided; persuading or permitting, when there is question of the better or worse course without a strict obligation.

Since the judgment of conscience is the judgment of the intellect and the intellect can err, either by adopting false premises or by drawing an illogical conclusion, conscience can be correct or erroneous. A *correct* conscience judges as good what is really good, or as evil what is really evil. Here subjective and objective morality correspond. An *erroneous* conscience judges as good what is really evil, or as evil what is really good. All error involves ignorance, because a person cannot make a false judgment in his mind unless he lacks knowledge of the truth. This ignorance involved in error is either vincible or invincible ignorance, and so we speak of error too as being vincible or invincible. Hence we have a *vincibly erroneous* conscience if the error can be overcome and the judgment corrected, or an *invincibly erroneous* conscience if the error cannot be overcome and the judgment cannot be corrected, at least by means any normally prudent man would be expected to use.

Conscience may also be certain or doubtful. A *certain* conscience judges without fearing that the opposite may be true. A *doubtful* conscience either hesitates to make any judgment at all, or does make a judgment but with misgivings that the opposite may be true. If it makes no judgment, the intellect remains in suspense because it either sees no motives or equal motives on both sides. If the intellect judges with fear of the opposite, it assents to one side but its judgment is only a probable opinion. There are varying degrees of probability, running all the way from slight suspicion to the fringes of certitude.

The fact that people differ in their sensitivity to moral values gives habitual characteristics to their judgments of conscience. We call consciences *strict* or *lax,* tender or tough, fine or blunt, delicate or gross, according as they are inclined to perceive or overlook moral values. A *perplexed* conscience belongs to one who cannot make up his mind and remains in a state of indecisive anguish, especially if he thinks that he will be doing wrong whichever alternative he chooses. A *scrupulous* conscience torments its owner by rehearsing over and over again doubts that were once settled, finding new sources of guilt in old deeds that were best forgotten, striving for a kind of certainty about one's state of soul that is beyond our power in this life. Scrupulosity can be a serious form of spiritual self-torture, mounting to neurotic anxiety, that is more of a psychological than an ethical condition. The person needs to learn, not the distinction between right and wrong, which he may know very well, but how to stop worrying over groundless fears, how to end his ceaseless self-examination and face life in a more confident spirit.

Having seen what conscience is and the main forms it takes, we must now discuss our responsibility in following what conscience approves or disapproves. There are two chief rules, each of which involves a problem:

(1) Always obey a certain conscience.
(2) Never act with a doubtful conscience.

ALWAYS OBEY A CERTAIN CONSCIENCE

Notice the difference in meaning between a certain and a correct conscience. The term *correct* describes the objective truth of the person's judgment, that his conscience represents the real state of things. The term *certain* describes the subjective state of the person judging, how firmly he holds to his assent, how thoroughly he has excluded fear of the opposite. The kind of certitude meant here is a subjective certitude, which can exist along with objective error. Hence there are two possibilities:

(1) A certain and correct conscience
(2) A certain but erroneous conscience

1. A *certain and correct conscience* offers no difficulty and our obligation is clear. The person judges what conduct is required of him here and now. His judgment is correct and he is certain of its correctness.

What degree of certitude is required? It is sufficient that the conscience be *prudentially certain.* Prudential certitude is not absolute but relative. It excludes all *prudent* fear that the opposite may be true, but it does not rule out imprudent fears based on bare possibilities. The reasons are strong enough to satisfy a normally prudent man in an important matter, so that he feels safe in practice though there is a theoretical chance of his being wrong. He has taken every reasonable precaution, but cannot guarantee against rare contingencies and freaks of nature.

In moral matters strict mathematical certitude (metaphysical certitude, the opposite of which is a contradiction) or even the certitude of physical events (physical certitude, the opposite of which would be a miracle) is not to be expected. When there is question of action, of something to be done here and now, but often involving future consequences some of which are dependent on the wills of other people, the absolute possibility of error cannot be wholly excluded; but it can be so reduced that no prudent man, no one free from neurotic whimsies, would be deterred from acting through fear of it. Thus a prudent man, having investigated the case, can say that he is *certain* that this business venture is safe, that this criminal is guilty, that this employee is honest. Prudential certitude, since it excludes all reasonable fear of error, is much more than high probability, which does not exclude such reasonable fear. One may, of course, define certitude so strictly as to make it mean absolute certitude only; but such a one is quarreling over mere words and must find another term to indicate what we have been describing in common language.

2. What happens when one has an *erroneous conscience?* Of course, if the error is *vincible,* it must be corrected. The person knows that he may be wrong, is able to correct the possible error, and is obliged to do so before acting. But a vincibly erroneous conscience cannot be a certain conscience. This is seen by asking how any conscience can become vincibly erroneous. A man may merely have a probable opinion which he neglects to verify, though able to do so. Or he may once have judged certainly yet erroneously, and now begins to doubt whether his judgment was correct or not. As long as he did not realize his error, his conscience was invincibly erroneous; the error has become vincible only because he is no longer subjectively certain and has begun to doubt. A vincibly erroneous conscience is therefore a name for a conscience that was either doubtful from the beginning or else was once subjectively certain but erroneous, and has now become a doubtful conscience. It will be handled under the discussion of doubtful conscience.

If the error is *invincible,* we seem to have a dilemma. On the one hand, it does not seem right that a person should be obliged to follow an erroneous judgment; on the other hand, he does not know that he is in error and has no means of correcting it. We solve the apparent dilemma by remembering that conscience is a subjective guide to conduct, that invincible error and ignorance are unavoidable, that any wrong which occurs is not done voluntarily and hence is not chargeable to the agent. A person acting with an invincibly erroneous conscience may do something that is objectively wrong, but since he does not recognize it as such, it is not subjectively wrong. The person is free of guilt by the invincible ignorance bound up in his error.

Hence a certain conscience must be obeyed, not only when it is correct, but even when it is invincibly erroneous. Conscience is the only guide a man has for the performance of concrete actions here and now. But an invincibly erroneous conscience cannot be distinguished from a correct conscience. Therefore if one were not obliged to follow a certain but invincibly erroneous conscience, we should be forced to the absurd conclusion that one would not be obliged to follow a certain and correct conscience.

The will depends on the intellect to present the good to it. The will-act is good if it tends to the good presented by the intellect, bad if it tends to what the intellect judges evil. Invincible error in the intellect does not change the goodness or badness of the will-act, in which morality essentially consists. If a man is firmly convinced that his action is right, he is choosing the good as far as he can; if he is firmly convinced that his action is wrong, he is choosing evil in intention, even though the act may not be objectively wrong.

NEVER ACT WITH A DOUBTFUL CONSCIENCE

The man who is acting with a certain but invincibly erroneous conscience is avoiding moral evil as far as he can. It is not his fault that his judgment is mistaken and he has no reason for believing that it is mistaken. But the same cannot be said of one who acts with a *doubtful* conscience. He has reason for believing that his intended act may be wrong, yet he is willing to go ahead and perform it anyway. True, he is not certain that he will do wrong, but he will not take the means to avoid this probable wrongdoing. The man has no care for right or wrong, and if his act turns out to be objectively right this is only accidental. Therefore it is never allowed to act with a doubtful conscience.

What, then, must a person with a doubtful conscience do? His first obligation is to try to solve the doubt. He must reason over the matter to see if he cannot arrive at a certain conclusion. He must inquire and seek advice, even of experts if the matter is important enough. He must investigate the facts in the problem and make certain of them, if possible. He must use all the means that normally prudent people are accustomed to use, in proportion to the importance of the problem. Before deciding on an important course of action, business and professional men take a great deal of trouble to investigate a case, to secure all the data, to seek expert advice, besides thinking over the matter carefully themselves. The same seriousness is demanded in moral affairs.

What if the doubt cannot be solved? It may happen that the required information cannot be obtained because the facts are not recorded or the records are lost or the law remains obscure or the opinions of the learned differ or the matter does not admit of delay for further research. If it is never allowed to act with a doubtful conscience, what can one in doubt do? It may seem that the answer is easy: do nothing. But often this will not help, for omissions can be voluntary and the doubt may concern precisely the question whether we are allowed to refrain from acting in this case.

The answer to the difficulty is that every doubtful conscience can in actual practice be turned into a certain conscience, that no one need ever remain in doubt about what he must do. If the *direct method* of inquiry and investigation described has been used and proved fruitless, we then have recourse to the *indirect method* of forming our conscience by the use of reflex principles. Note that we are not offered a choice between either the direct or the indirect method. We *must* use the direct method *first*. Only when the direct method yields no result may we go on to the indirect method.

FORMING ONE'S CONSCIENCE

Recall what we said previously on invincible ignorance. It occurs in two possible cases:

(1) Either a man does not know that he is in ignorance, or
(2) He knows it but cannot get the needed information.

The first case is one of invincible ignorance or error, but not one of doubt; the person's conscience is subjectively certain, and he must follow his certain conscience, whether correct or invincibly erroneous, as was previously proved. But the second case is one of doubt, for here the person realizes his ignorance and consequently doubts what he ought to do. The important thing to notice is that the doubt is really double:

(1) What is the actual truth on the matter in hand?
(2) What is one obliged to do in such a situation?

The first is the *theoretical* or *speculative* doubt, and this is the question that cannot be answered, because the direct method was used and failed to yield results. The second is the *practical* or *operative* doubt, and this alone we claim can be solved in every instance.

Though many doubts are invincible theoretically, every doubt is vincible practically. A person can become certain of what he is obliged to do, how he is expected to act, what conduct is required of him, while remaining in a state of unsolved theoretical doubt. Thus, though the rightness or wrongness of the action is not settled in the abstract, this man becomes certain of what he in these actual circumstances is obliged or allowed to do, and therefore he acts with a certain conscience. In other words, he finds out the kind of conduct that is *certainly* lawful for a *doubting* person. This process of solving a practical doubt without touching the theoretical doubt is called *forming one's conscience.*

REFLEX PRINCIPLES

The process of forming one's conscience is accomplished by the use of *reflex principles,* so called because the mind uses them while reflecting on the state of doubt and ignorance in which it now finds itself. Two such principles are of application here:

(1) Take the morally safer course.
(2) A doubtful law does not bind.

The morally safer course

By the *morally* safer course we mean the one which more surely preserves moral goodness, more certainly avoids wrongdoing. Often it is physically more dangerous. Sometimes neither alternative appears morally safer, but the obligation on each side seems equal; then we may do either.

It is always *allowed* to choose the morally safer course. If a man is certainly not obliged to act but doubts whether or not he is allowed to act, the morally safer course is to omit the act; thus if I doubt whether this money is justly mine, I can simply refuse it. If a man is certainly allowed to act but doubts whether or not he is obliged to act, the morally safer course is to do the act; thus if I doubt whether I have paid a bill, I can offer the money and risk paying it twice.

Sometimes we are *obliged* to follow the morally safer course. We must do so when there is an end certainly to be obtained to the best of our power, and our doubt merely concerns the effectiveness of the means to be used for this purpose. Here the undoubted obligation to attain the end implies the obligation to use certainly effective means. A doctor may not use a doubtful remedy on his patient when he has a sure one at hand. A lawyer may not choose to defend his client with weak arguments when he has strong ones to present. A hunter may not fire into the bushes if he doubts whether the moving object is a man or an animal. A merchant may not pay a certainly existing debt with probably counterfeit coin or advertise probably damaged articles as first class goods. In such cases the person's obligation is certain and he must use means that will certainly fulfill it.

But there are other cases in which the obligation itself is the thing in doubt. Here we have a very different question. The morally safer course, though always allowable, is often costly and inconvenient, sometimes heroic. Out of a desire to do the better thing we often follow it without question, but, if we were obliged to follow it in *all* cases of doubt, life would become intolerably difficult. To be safe morally, we should have to yield every doubtful claim to others who have no better right, and thus become victims of every sharper and swindler whose conscience is less delicate than ours. Such difficulties are avoided by the use of the second reflex principle: a doubtful law does not bind.

A doubtful law

The principle, *a doubtful law does not bind,* is applicable only when I doubt whether or not I am bound by an obligation, when my doubt of conscience concerns the *lawfulness or unlawfulness* of an act to be done. I may use this principle in both the following situations:

(1) I doubt whether such a law exists.
(2) I doubt whether the law applies to my case.

For example: I may doubt whether the game laws forbid me to shoot deer on my farm, whether the fruit on my neighbor's tree hanging over my fence belongs to him or to me, whether I am sick enough to be excused from going to work today, whether the damage I caused was purely accidental or due to my own carelessness. It is true that there are contained here questions of fact that cannot be settled, but they all bring up questions of lawfulness or permissibility of action: Am I allowed to shoot the deer, to pick the fruit, to stay home from work, to refuse to repair the damage? Does any law exist, applicable to my case, which certainly forbids me? If the direct method fails to prove any, then I am morally justified in doing these things on the principle that *a doubtful law does not bind.*

The reason behind this principle is that promulgation is of the essence of law, and a doubtful law is not sufficiently promulgated, for it is not sufficiently made known to the person about to act here and now. Law imposes obligation, which is usually burdensome, and he who would impose an obligation or restrict the liberty of another must prove his right to do so. A man is presumed free until it becomes certain that he is restrained, and therefore a doubtfully existing restraint or law loses its binding force.

Be careful to distinguish these cases from those which fall under the other principle. I may not roll boulders down a hill in the mere hope that they may not hit anyone on the road below, but I may cart off boulders from property that is only probably mine. I may not leave poisoned food about on the chance that no one will care to eat it, but I may manufacture clearly labeled poison if such manufacture is only probably forbidden by law. In the first instances there is no doubt about the law: I am not allowed unnecessarily to jeopardize human life. It may happen that no harm results, but the acts are certainly dangerous and *the morally safer course must be chosen.* In the second instances the law itself of not seizing others' property or of not manufacturing certain products is of doubtful application to my case, and I may take advantage of the doubt in my favor, for *a doubtful law does not bind.*

How doubtful does the law have to be to lose its binding force? Must the existence or application of the law be more doubtful that its nonexistence or nonapplication, or equally so, or will any doubt suffice to exempt one from the obligation? Such questions were hotly debated during the seventeenth and eighteenth centuries, more by moral theologians than by philosophical ethicians. The view that survived as the most tenable in theory and the only one workable in practice is called *probabilism*. It does not require a weighing of probabilities on either side of the case, but merely requires that it be *solidly probable* that a law does not exist or does not apply to my case for me to be free from its obligation. Solid probability means that the reasons against the law's existence or application are not frivolous or fictitious but valid and weighty, even though they may not be more so than the reasons in favor of the law. No proposition can be certain if there are valid and weighty reasons against it. If it is not certain, it is doubtful, and if it is doubtful it does not bind. To list all the reasons on both sides and weigh their relative merits is often a hopeless task, baffling the best experts. The average man has neither time nor knowledge nor ability for such a comparison. In practice decisions must be made promptly, and yet be made with a certain conscience. The theory of probabilism enables one to do so.

CONCLUSION

The whole matter of forming one's conscience may seem to involve a great deal of subtlety, as if we were whittling down moral obligation to its lowest terms. Is not this contrary to straightforward simplicity and sincerity? In answer, the first thing to note is that one can always follow the morally safer course. But in ethics we are studying not only what is the better, nobler, and more heroic thing to do, but also exactly what a man is strictly obliged to do. A generous man will not haggle over good works, but an enlightened man will want to know when he is doing a strict duty and when he is being generous.

Accurate moral discrimination is particularly necessary in judging the conduct of others. In our personal lives we may be willing to waive our strict rights and to go beyond the call of duty, but we have no business imposing on others an obligation to do so. The borderline between right and wrong is difficult to determine. It is foolish to skirt it too closely, but we are not allowed to accuse another man of wrongdoing if he has not done wrong. This is why we were obliged to detail these principles so carefully.

SUMMARY

Morality means the rightness or wrongness of human acts. It is *objective* or *subjective,* according as it overlooks the personal peculiarities of the doer of the act or takes them into consideration. The norm of subjective morality is conscience.

Conscience is not a special faculty, but a function of the practical intellect judging the concrete act of an individual person as morally good or evil. The reasoning used by the intellect is a deductive syllogism, the major premise being an accepted moral principle, the minor an application of the principle to the case at hand, the conclusion the judgment of conscience.

Antecedent conscience is a guide to future acts, *consequent* conscience a judge of past acts. A *correct* conscience judges good as good, evil as evil; an *erroneous* conscience judges good as evil or evil as good. A *certain* conscience judges without fear of the opposite; a *doubtful* conscience either makes no judgment or judges with fear of the opposite. Conscience is *strict* or *lax* according as it tends to perceive or overlook moral values.

Always obey a certain conscience. A *certain and correct* conscience is but the clear and proper perception of one's moral duty. Prudential certitude, the exclusion of any *prudent* fear of the opposite, is all that can be expected in moral matters. A *certain but erroneous* conscience must also be followed because the agent cannot distinguish it from a correct conscience and has no other guide; the act is subjectively right even if objectively wrong.

Never act with a doubtful conscience. To do so is to be willing to perform an act whether it is wrong or not, refusing to take the means to avoid evil.

A person in doubt must first use the *direct method* of inquiry and investigation to dispel the doubt. If this yields no results, the *indirect method* of forming one's conscience may be used, which consists in solving not the *theoretical doubt* (what is the actual truth?), but only the *practical doubt* (how should a doubting person act in this case?). The practical doubt can always be solved by using one of two reflex principles:

1. *Take the morally safer course.* This is always allowable, but is often costly. It *must* be used if the case concerns not the lawfulness or unlawfulness of an act, but the effectiveness of means used to an end that must certainly be attained.

2. *A doubtful law does not bind.* This principle may be used only when there is question of the lawfulness or unlawfulness of an act, when either the existence or application of a law is in doubt. A doubtful law is not sufficiently promulgated and hence has no binding force, for promulgation is essential to law.

Probabilism holds that to bind, a law must be certain, and no law can be certain if there are solidly probable reasons against it, no matter how strong the probability for it may be. It is practically impossible to weigh the degrees of probability on each side; probabilism makes it unnecessary.

READINGS

1. St. Thomas, *Summa Theologica,* I, q. 79, aa. 12, 13, on synderesis and conscience; I-II, q. 19, aa. 5, 6, on an erroneous conscience. Read also from St. Thomas' *De Veritate,* translated into English under the title Truth, vol. II, q. 16, on synderesis, and q. 17, on conscience. The matter of this chapter was not very thoroughly developed in St. Thomas' time, though what he says contains the germ of future speculations.
2. Cronin, *Science of Ethics,* vol. I, ch. XIV.
3. Rickaby, *Moral Philosophy,* pp. 133-143, 152-158.
4. Newman, *Grammar of Assent,* pp. 105-112.
5. Leibell, *Readings in Ethics,* pp. 341-364, repeats some of the above selections and adds more.
6. D'Arcy, *Christian Morality,* pp. 73-101.

CHAPTER 5

THE GOOD

AS VALUE

PROBLEM

The individual man relies on his own consciousness to determine the degree of his responsibility for his acts, and on his own conscience to judge the good or evil, the rightness or wrongness, of these acts as done in concrete circumstances by him. There is no more ultimate court of appeal in this world than the testimony of conscience. But subjective morality alone is insufficient. If this were all we had, there would be as many judges of morality as there are persons, and sincerity would be the same as truth in moral matters. Conscience can be erroneous as well as correct; error can be vincible as well as invincible. When objective truth is attainable, conscience cannot rest satisfied with a subjective opinion that it knows may be false. Our next endeavor, therefore, must be to find whether there is an objective morality with which the judgment of conscience should be in agreement, and, if so, what that morality is. Henceforth the whole of our study will be devoted to this pursuit. We begin by asking:

(1) What is meant by value?
(2) Do values really exist?
(3) Are value judgments valid as knowledge?
(4) What distinguishes moral values from other values?
(5) What is the importance of the moral ideal?
(6) How are moral values primitively known?

VALUE

The modern study dealing with value is called axiology, from the Greek *axios,* meaning *worthy.* The term *value* or *worth* seems to have its origin in economics, but long before the rise of axiology as a formal study, it was applied analogously to other aspects of life. Axiologists start out with initial disagreement on the definition of their main term. We all know what a value is, but cannot define it without committing ourselves to a school of thought as yet unexamined and untested. Let us begin with the subjective side, on which there seems to be more agreement.

One thing appeals to us in some way, whereas something else does not. What appeals may supply a need, satisfy a desire, arouse an interest, stimulate an emotion, provoke a response, motivate a deed, or merely draw an approval. The existence of subjective values—valuations or evaluations or value judgments, as some prefer to call them—is a matter of experience. We do make value judgments, whether these judgments are justified or not, whether they have any real content to them or not. Some of these judgments are noncomparative, in which we merely express our approval or disapproval; others are comparative, and by putting them in order we can construct a scale of values. A full scale would be too complex for anyone to complete, but we all have some constant preferences that represent known points on our scale.

Some general characteristics of value immediately appear. Values are bipolar, with a positive and a negative pole: pleasant, painful; easy, difficult; strong, weak; rich, poor; beautiful, ugly; true, false; good, bad. The positive pole is the one preferred; the negative pole is better not called a value at all but a disvalue. Values are not homogeneous but of many kinds, some quite unrelated, and this is why the construction of a complete scale of values is so difficult; there are too many crosscuts. Values transcend facts in the sense that nothing ever wholly comes up to our expectations; even if anything should, it only shows that our expectations were pitched too low and we want something further. Values, though not wholly realizable, clamor for realization. They should exist, they deserve to be, even if we have no way of bringing them into existence.

EXISTENCE OF VALUE

Do values really exist or do they belong wholly to the domain of thought? Do we call a thing valuable because it possesses some real property in itself or because we clothe it with a value by our attitude toward it? The subjectivist philosopher, to be consistent, must adopt the latter view. But even objectivist philosophers, who in their general epistemology admit the existence of real being that is there independently of our thinking, can be subjectivist on the question of value. Things exist, they say, but whatever value they have is conferred on them by us; there is objective being, but no objective value.

In this view values should be wholly arbitrary. Let us admit it of some values. The thing has no intrinsic worth, at least for us, but we give it a value because of our peculiar prejudices, our psychological conditioning, our unacountable tastes and fancies. In other cases the value is given by human convention, like the value of paper money, of credit, of reputation, of academic degrees, or of styles of architecture. But these conventions are not wholly subjective; if they have no backing in reality, we consider them fraudulent and their value vanishes.

That there are some objective values is evident from a partial list of them. In the biological realm life is a value, death a disvalue, as is seen in our tendency to survival. As a lesser mark of the same thing, health is a value, sickness a disvalue. The reason is not merely the fact that most people prefer one to the other, but its congruence or incongruence with the kind of beings we are. In the sensitive sphere pleasure is a value, pain a disvalue. A normal person will bear pain for the sake of a greater value, but not for itself. In economic life prosperity is a value, poverty a disvalue. Some economic values are merely subjective, as fads and fashions, some are artificially created by advertising and salesmanship, but the basic economic goods are needed for human living. From the esthetic standpoint beauty and taste are values, ugliness and tawdriness are disvalues. In the area of the mind knowledge, truth, and intelligence are values; ignorance, error, and stupidity are disvalues. In social life courtesy and companionability are values; boorishness and surliness are disvalues. As traits of character alertness, energy, and resourcefulness are values; dullness, laziness, and negligence are disvalues.

We are not arbitrary about which of these are values and which are disvalues, though we differ in our judgments on how much a particular person or thing embodies them. If it is claimed that these are but abstractions and therefore subjective because they exist only in the mind that conceives them, we say that, like all universal ideas, they are drawn from the data of experience and have their concrete fulfillment in existing persons, things, and actions. It is a fact that we evaluate goods to buy, persons to employ, students to reward, and friends to live with. We are not wholly arbitrary but see something in them that makes them deserving.

The foregoing is meant to be introductory to the question of moral values. Are there moral values distinct from other values such as those mentioned above, and are these moral values objective?

THE EMOTIVE THEORY

The most devastating answer to this question is given by the modern school of *logical positivism,* beginning with the Vienna Circle in the early 1920's but spreading rapidly to England and the United States, where empiricism and pragmatism had prepared for it a congenial home. The movement is now on the decline, being succeeded by the school of *analytic philosophy,* which continues the same attitude in a more conciliatory form. It will suit our purpose better to look at the older logical positivism, which represents this position in its uncompromising purity.

Beginning with an understandable revulsion from the abstract and apparently meaningless jargon of many metaphysicians, among whom Hegel was a chief offender, the logical positivists analyze the meaning of propositions. By their criteria they find only two kinds of meaningful statements: those that are statements of identity and those that can be verified by experience. The former are tautologies, true but impractical; their domain is that of pure logic and pure mathematics. Only the latter can contribute to the advancement of scientific knowledge. Metaphysical assertions belong to neither class and must be discarded as neither true nor false, but meaningless. What about value judgments? They also are neither tautologies nor statements of fact, but are normative, laying down rules, expressing the *ought*. Thus they are noncognitive but emotive. They are wishes, exhortations, or commands, but not genuine propositions. Only the grammatical form is indicative; they are veiled optatives and imperatives. A. J. Ayer expresses this view with particular clarity and bluntness:

> Fundamental ethical concepts are unanalyzable, inasmuch as there is no criterion by which we can test the validity of the judgments in which they occur. . . . The reason why they are unanalyzable is that they are mere pseudo-concepts. The presence of an ethical symbol in a proposition adds nothing to its factual content. Thus if I say to someone, "You acted wrongly in stealing that money," I am not stating anything more than if I had simply said, "You stole that money." In adding that this action is wrong I am not making any further statement about it. I am simply evincing my moral disapproval of it. It is as if I had said, "You stole that money," in peculiar tone of horror, or written it with the addition of some special exclamation marks. . . .
>
> If now I generalize my previous statement and say, "Stealing money is wrong," I produce a sentence which has no factual meaning—that is, expresses no proposition which can be either true or false. . . .
>
> In every case in which one would commonly be said to be making an ethical judgment, the function of the relevant ethical word is purely "emotive." It is used to express feelings about certain objects, but not to make any assertion about them.
>
> It is worth mentioning that ethical terms do not serve only to express feeling. They are calculated also to arouse feeling, and so to stimulate action.*

The last part of this view, that ethical judgments are used to influence action in others, is developed by C. L. Stevenson,† together with the notion that such judgments do have an assertable content: the fact that the speaker does have such an emotional attitude. But this is the assertion of a psychological fact, not an ethical one.

Logical positivism, criticism of which properly belongs to epistemology, concerns the moralist because it wipes out with one blow all meaning to ethics. The decisive argument against it is that the emotive theory itself is neither tautological nor verifiable by experience, and therefore falls by its own criterion. That emotion may accompany ethical judgments is no reason to deny that ethical judgments have a cognitive content. Most

---

*Ayer, *Language, Truth and Logic,* pp. 107-108.
†Stevenson, *Ethics and Language.*

people are convinced that their value judgments do have meaning, that they are in fact the most important of all judgments, and no amount of telling them otherwise alters this fact. More specifically:

1. If ethical judgments are not assertions that can be true or false, what are they? Reductions of them to commands, wishes, persuasions, exhortations, or propaganda does not work, for these are all judged for their ethical content. I can command you, knowing that I ought not to issue the command and you ought not to obey it, yet I want you to.

2. If ethical judgments are mere expressions of approval, how do we distinguish between actual approval and right approval? If it is a true statement of fact that I do approve, is it not also true that I can approve or disapprove of my approval, and thus make a true ethical judgment about my factual judgment?

3. To judge a thing to be right and to decide to do it are not the same. To seek approval for the second is to ask for encouragement and support; this is emotional. To seek approval for the first is to ask a question demanding a yes or no answer; this answer is either true or false, and these are genuine ethical judgments.

4. Empirical statements are not rejected because they are not mathematical, nor mathematical statements because they are not empirical. Neither, then, should ethical statements be rejected because they are neither of these, but have their distinctive subject matter and criteria.

5. To say that ethical judgments are justified but their justification lies in something else than their truth, is merely to invent a new language in which truth is given a restricted meaning contrary to common usage.*

MORAL VALUES

The answer to the logical positivists' denial of moral values, as the ones which concern us, assumes two phases:

(1) Explanation of the meaning of moral value
(2) Proof for the existence of moral value

The common estimate of mankind separates moral values from other values. We say that a man is a good scholar, athlete, businessman, politician, scientist, artist, soldier, worker, speaker, entertainer, companion, and yet that he is not a good man. We say that someone else is a failure at some or perhaps even all of these, and yet that he is a good man. On what do we base such judgments? Why do we separate out this last value? Because we recognize that it is distinct from the others and more fundamental, more valuable than the other values.

Moral values are understood to be those which make a man good purely and simply as a man. They are not external objects which, though they may help a man to become the kind of being he ought to be, are not the man himself. Nor are they qualities or attributes of the man himself but outside his control, such as having good health or long life

---

*These criticisms are condensed from Ewing, *Ethics.*

or family status or bodily beauty or mental acumen or artistic talent or a magnetic personality. These are all values but no one can command them. Moral values are personal, not only because a person has them, but because they are the expression of each one's unique personality in the innermost center of its being, as shown in the act of free choice. Moral values, therefore, reside both in the acts a man freely chooses to do and in the results of those acts on the character of the man. There are morally good or bad human acts and morally good or bad men.

A shark attacks one of two swimmers at the beach. The other comes to his rescue and, braving the danger, wards off the shark and brings the wounded companion to shore. We feel pity for the one who was bitten, but pass no moral judgment on him. He did not act but was acted on. Toward the rescuer our attitude is quite different. His swimming may have been awkward, his lifesaving technique faulty, his approach to the shark unscientific, his act unseen and unpublicized, and the whole venture useless because the victim died. Even one whose feelings are not aroused to admiration cannot help judging the act to be fine and noble and worthy of approval. It has no value but one, and that is its *moral* value. Suppose an opposite case. The shark attacks both swimmers. To save himself, one of them deliberately kicks his companion into the path of the shark's mouth, thus gaining time to scramble on shore while the shark is occupied with its morsel. As an act of self-saving it has value, for it was done quickly, efficiently, cleverly, and resourcefully. But we cannot approve. The only excuse for such an act would be instinct or panic. As a willful, deliberate act it merits condemnation.

Two husbands have wives afflicted with a lingering and incapacitating disease. Both families are alike: five children, moderate income, no hope of remedy. One husband does his best to be both father and mother to the children, works overtime to pay for his wife's care, and spends what time he can with her to brighten her days. The other man decides that he has had enough, deserts wife and children, gets work in a distant city under an assumed name, and is not heard of again. Our emotional attitude toward the wives and children is one of congratulation in one case and compassion in the other, but we cannot judge them morally as persons. Toward the husbands also our emotional reactions differ, but there is a remaining element beyond all emotion. By our intellectual judgment we have to approve of the first husband and disapprove of the second. It is not a question of consequences. Suppose that the deserted dependents are better taken care of by public charity than the husband could have done for them. Still we must condemn his action as morally wrong. The moral value and disvalue remain in these two cases as irreducible elements.

Examples of this type could be multiplied indefinitely. But these are sufficient for our purpose: to isolate the characteristics of moral value as distinct from any other value.

1. Moral value can exist only in a *free* being and his *free* acts. By willing moral good a man becomes good. It cannot happen accidentally. It makes no difference whether the act is succsessful or not. It is done intelligently in the sense that the agent knows what he is doing and wills to do it, but it need not be brilliantly planned and executed.

2. Moral value is *universal* in the sense that what holds for one holds for all in the same conditions. The reason is that it shows the worth of a man *as a man*. Even when no one else could duplicate one man's circumstances, all would approve of his action as the right thing to do in the case, whether they would have the strength to do it or not.

3. Moral value is *self-justifying*. So at least it appears on the surface, though we shall have to delve deeper into it later. We suspect that any further justification of moral value will be found to be part of the moral order itself and not some extrinsic reason. Even the truth must be pursued morally, though it be the truth about morals.

4. Moral value has a *preeminence* over every other value. A moral value can be compared only with another moral value. If a moral value conflicts with another type of value, this other must take a subordinate place. We think that a man simply must be true to himself as a man, no matter how much else he might lose in the effort.

5. Moral value implies *obligation*. We shall have much to say on this, but for the present it seems implied in the four points just given. Man may disregard all other values and we shall call him foolish, stupid, clumsy, improvident, and many other epithets, but we can still retain respect for him as a man. Not so if he loses his moral integrity.

THE MORAL IDEAL

The foregoing discussion brings out the fact that we do form for ourselves an ideal of human conduct and an ideal of manhood. These are not two ideals, for a man's conduct is his life. It is only good conduct that can make a good man, and a man is called good because his past acts show him to be the kind of man from whom good acts are expected.

We find it impossible not to form such an ideal, since it is implied in every moral judgment and we do make moral judgments. The word *ideal* should not be understood here as some romantic fancy, a knight in shining armor, some sort of superman with unearthly powers, the kind of being that could not happen in real life. What we use in moral judgment is not an imaginative ideal nor an esthetic ideal, but a *moral* ideal. It is true that no one ever perfectly lives up to it, but it must mean the ideal he *can* live up to because he *ought* to, and sometimes does. The ideal as an ideal does not exist in reality, but it is not subjective in the sense of being arbitrary. It is knowledge and has the same sort of being that knowledge has, a being in the mind with a reference to and basis in reality. The ideal is constructed by taking the various kinds of acts that experience shows us men perform, dropping from them all discordant notes, supplying all omissions, and heightening the whole to the limit of human ability. The man whose acts are all of this type is our ideal of the moral man.

As the artist has an ideal of the perfectly proportioned human body, as the scholar has an ideal of the perfectly intelligent human mind—and, being human, these are not beyond the possibility of realization—so we all have an ideal of the perfectly self-controlled and self-conducting human being. So far as a man approaches this ideal, he has moral value and is good. So far as he admits into his life what ruins this ideal, he has moral disvalue and is bad.

The notion of the good as expressed here is that of the intrinsic or perfect good as opposed to the instrumental or perfective good. The ideal is good, not as leading to something else, not as a means useful to something further, but in itself. It has value because it has what it ought to have to be itself in the fullest expression of itself. This is the good in the highest sense, for what is good for another ultimately supposes something for which others are good, and this last is good in itself.

This conception of the good admittedly derives from Plato. But the unacceptability of his interpretation of ideals should not prejudice us against what is true in his thought. We have no direct vision of the ideal and no former life from which to derive it, but must manufacture it from the data of experience. How do we do this? What is the origin of our moral ideas and ideals?

KNOWLEDGE BY CONNATURALITY

A person need not have studied ethics to know right from wrong. Ethics makes a formal and sophisticated investigation into the moral notions we already have, confirming or correcting our more primitive knowledge. How did we get this primitive knowledge and how accurate is it? A child of today will get it from his parents, teachers, and companions, from religious instruction, social custom, and civil law. But how did they get it? Furthermore, the child turned youth will begin to criticize what has been told him, thus showing some source of knowledge besides tradition.

This primitive way of knowing is called by St. Thomas* *knowledge by inclination* or *by connaturality*. It is a self-awareness that reveals our own natures to ourselves, a direct experience of the powers we possess, of their clamor for exercise, and of the appropriate objects on which they are to be exercised. We do not have to reason the matter out to know what our eyes and hands and legs are for, what our minds and wills are for. We use them without question, knowing without argument that it is right to use them. Men sought food before they studied the science of nutrition, reproduced without benefit of genetics, trained their children before child psychology, formed families and cities without sociology, spoke without linguistics, claimed their due without law courts, and lived moral lives without a formal study of ethics.

This knowledge is an act not of the intellect alone, but of the intellect

---

Summa Theologica, I-II, q. 94, a. 2; II-II, q. 45, a. 2.

plus the affections and appetites, the emotions and the will. It is non-conceptual, nonlogical, nondiscursive knowledge, rational in the sense that it is done by the reason or intellect, nonrational in the sense that it is not argumentative or demonstrative or scientific. In it the head consults the heart.*

> It is through connaturality that moral consciousness attains a kind of knowing—inexpressible in words and notions—of the deepest dispositions—longings, fears, hopes or despairs, primeval loves and options—involved in the night of the subjectivity. When a man makes a free decision, he takes into account, not only all that he possesses of moral science and factual information, and which is manifested to him in concepts and notions, but also all the secret elements of evaluation which depend on what he is, and which are known to him through inclination, through his own actual propensities and his own virtues, if he has any.†

We began our study of ethics with the recognition of a fact, that men do have a sense of right and wrong, that they do make moral judgments. Our study would be incomplete if we made no effort to isolate the kind of knowledge that accounts for this fact. We should not be disturbed at being unable to describe it more clearly, for it is the nature of prescientific knowledge to be obscure, unformulated, and unreflective. When we reflect on it, conceptualize it, define its terms, catalogue its contents, pose its problems, and prove its theorems, it ceases to be knowledge by connaturality and becomes moral philosophy or ethics. Knowledge by connaturality is not immune from error and needs the criticism, correction, and development ethics can give it. But in practical living the two continue side by side, for a reflective study does not eliminate the very thing it is studying.

Through this knowledge by connaturality man first recognizes moral value and forms his moral ideal. It has the further function of giving man his first sense of moral obligation and of putting him in touch with the natural law. But for the present we are concerned with it as the natural source of our sense of values and of the greatest among these, moral value.

SUMMARY

Value or *worth* is a term used for anything that appeals to us in any way. At least subjective values exist, for we do make value judgments and have preferences. Values are bipolar, heterogeneous, idealized, yet calling for realization.

Some values may be purely subjective but others are *objective*. We cannot be wholly arbitrary about them. As ideals they exist in the mind, but are formed by the mind's abstractive power from the data of experience.

---

*Simon, *Critique de la connaissance morale,* ch. 3.
†Maritain, *The Range of Reason,* ch. 3, p. 26.

The *emotive theory*, stemming from *logical positivism*, holds that value judgments, being normative, are noncognitive; they are but disguised wishes, not propositions. Such a conclusion is based on an inadequate theory of meaning.

Moral values are those which make a man good simply as a man. They can exist only in a *free* being and free acts, are *universal* since they pertain to man as man, are self-justifying and independent of other values, are *preeminent* over every other value, and imply *obligation*.

It is impossible not to form a scale of values in which there is some top value or highest good. In such a scale the moral value claims the highest place. The ideal human life ideally lived is the *moral ideal*. That we all have such an ideal, seen with more or less clearness, is evident from the fact that we do make moral value judgments.

The moral ideal guiding our moral judgments is first known through knowledge by *inclination* or *connaturality*. This is unformulated and un-reflective, nonconceptual, nonlogical, nondiscursive. Ethics is the endeavor to formulate, criticize, correct, develop, and prove these primitive moral judgments.

READINGS

1. Much of the matter for this chapter is based on Joseph de Finance, *Ethica Generalis*, published in Latin at the Gregorian University, Rome, but unfortunately not translated.
2. The classic work on value theory is R. B. Perry's *General Theory of Value*, supplemented by his later work, *Realms of Value*. See also Pepper, *The Sources of Value*.
3. Lepley (ed.), *Value, a Cooperative Inquiry* and *The Language of Value*, are symposia of contemporary American philosophers on value theory. These works treat value from a behavioral rather than from an ethical standpoint.
4. Modern theories of value are criticized from the Scholastic viewpoint in Ward, *Philosophy of Value*, and *Values and Reality*.
5. On the emotive theory the following two books are indispensable:
   a. Ayer, *Language, Truth and Logic*, especially ch. 6.
   b. Stevenson, *Ethics and Language*.
6. Ewing, *Ethics*, is well worth reading as a whole, but chiefly for its criticism of the emotive theory.
7. On knowledge by inclination or connaturality read:
   Maritain, *The Range of Reason*, ch. 3.

CHAPTER 6

THE GOOD

AS OUGHT

PROBLEM

One of the chief features of the moral good is its obligatory character. The good is a value, and the highest good is an intrinsic value, whose sole reason for being good is itself, its own inner worth in the scale of being. As we said, it clamors for being, it deserves to be, it ought to exist, it is an ideal that should be realized.

Of itself, however, the fact that a thing ought to be does not imply that I am the one who should make it be. In the esthetic sphere we say that a work of art ought to be in the sense that it is a noble conception worthy of production and it would be a shame not to bring it to light, yet no particular artist is strictly obliged to create it. We can say the same of every other value except one. Moral value not only ought to be because it is a worthy ideal, but also because I am strictly obliged to bring it into being in my life.

We have hinted at the reason for this difference, that other values affect man only in some particular and optional aspects of his life, whereas moral values affect the man as a man. Why is he *obliged* to make himself the kind of man he knows he ought to be? Who or what imposes this obligation on him? This investigation will take several chapters and we shall begin with the easiest and most superficial answers. The crudest opinion is that morality is a man-made thing, artificial, fictitious, and avoidable in itself, that morality is convention and the only thing that motivates its observance is fear of social disapproval with its sanctions. We shall discuss:

(1) The meaning of conventional and natural morality
(2) Whether all morality comes from the civil law

(3) Whether it comes from custom and social pressure
(4) Why obligation is intrinsic to the moral good

CONVENTIONAL AND NATURAL MORALITY

To set the question, we must define two other conceivable kinds of morality besides subjective and objective. An act that is neither good nor bad of its own very nature but becomes so only because it is commanded or forbidden by some law or custom is said to have *conventional* or *extrinsic* morality. An act that is good or bad of its own very nature independently of any command or prohibition is said to have *natural* or *intrinsic* morality.

That conventional morality exists is evident, for no one can deny the existence of laws, such as the laws of the state or the unwritten law of custom, which issue abundant commands and prohibitions, rendering good or bad many actions which would otherwise be morally indifferent. Hence the question is not one of choosing between conventional and natural morality but whether *besides* conventional morality there is *also* natural morality. To sum up the question:

(1) Are acts good only because they are commanded, bad only because they are forbidden? Is all morality merely *conventional?*
(2) Or are there any acts commanded because they are good, forbidden because they are bad in themselves? Is there a *natural* morality?

The theory which says that all morality is determined by convention, that it is the result of someone's arbitrary will commanding or forbidding certain kinds of acts, that it is not based on something intrinsic in the human act itself or in the nature of man, is known as *moral positivism* in the broadest sense of the term. It is so called because it holds that all morality rests on *positive law*, enacted or customary, as opposed to natural law. The theory takes two main forms, according as the convention or arbitrary decision to consider some acts right and others wrong is the result of:

(1) The laws of the state—*moral positivism strictly so called*
(2) The customs of men—*social pressure theories*

MORAL POSITIVISM

Some think that no act is wrong unless there is a law against it, and the only law they acknowledge is the civil law. Where the arm of the law cannot reach, anything goes. Morality is thus the product of civilized life, which necessarily entails political organization. Morality is made the same as legality. This popular misconception has had few philosophical defenders, but there are two of great influence.

Thomas Hobbes and probably Jean Jacques Rousseau maintain that before man organized himself into a political community there was no right and wrong. The state itself is not a natural society but the result of the social contract, a purely conventional agreement whereby men give up part of their natural rights (liberty to do anything they please) in order to preserve the rest. Once civil society is formed, it commands and forbids certain actions for the common good and this is the beginning of right and wrong. Therefore there are no acts right or wrong of their very nature but only because commanded or forbidden by the political state.

Hobbes and Rousseau differ greatly in their views on the state of nature, on the form of the social contract, on the mode of transferring rights, on the seat of sovereignty; but these belong rather to their theories on the state. Here we are interested only in the fact that they deny natural or intrinsic morality. One may wonder what value morals can have if they are but arbitrary conventions of man, but Hobbes and Rousseau both insist on the validity of morality once the state has been established.

A few key passages will show Hobbes' view:

> During the time men live without a common power to keep them all in awe, they are in that condition which is called war; and such a war as is of every man against every man. . . .
>
> To this war of every man against every man, this also is consequent: *that nothing can be unjust.* The notions of right and wrong, justice and injustice, have there no place. Where there is no common power, there is no law; where no law, no injustice. Force and fraud are in war the two cardinal virtues. . . . It is consequent also to the same condition, that there be no propriety,* no dominion, no *mine* and *thine* distinct; but only that to be every man's that he can get; and for so long as he can keep it. . . .†
>
> Where no covenant hath preceded, there hath no right been transferred, and every man has a right to everything; and consequently, no action can be unjust. . . . Before the names of just and unjust can have place, there must be some coercive power, to compel men equally to the performance of their covenants, by the terror of some punishment greater than the benefit they expect by the breach of their covenant . . . and such power there is none before the erection of a commonwealth.‡

It may be unfair to class Rousseau among the moral positivists. He seems rather to think that man in his primitive state of innocence naturally did what is right without the formulation of any moral rules. But, whatever his general theory, he lays himself open to the charge by the opening words of his *Social Contract:*

> Man is born free, and everywhere he is in chains. Many a one believes himself the master of others, and yet he is a greater slave than they. How has this change come about? I do not know. What can render it legitimate? I believe that I can settle this question. . . . The social order is a

---

Propriety here is but the old form of the word *property.*
†Hobbes, *Leviathan,* ch. XIII.
‡*Op. cit.,* ch. XV.

sacred right which serves as a foundation for all others. This right, however, does not come from nature. It is therefore based on conventions. The question is to know what these conventions are. . . .*

Since no man has any natural authority over his fellow-man, and since force is not the source of right, conventions remain as the basis of all lawful authority among men. . . .†

The passage from the state of nature to the civil state produces in man a very remarkable change, by substituting in his conduct justice for instinct, and by giving his actions the moral quality they previously lacked.‡

We readily admit that the state can pass laws on indifferent matters and make them binding in conscience. As guardian of public order and safety, the state decrees that we shall drive on the right side of the road, though either side might have been chosen. Thus the state gives extrinsic morality to an act intrinsically indifferent. But not all acts are of this kind. There are some acts the state cannot command and others the state cannot forbid. No state could survive that commanded murder, theft, perjury, and treason, or that forbade kindliness, honesty, truthfulness, and loyalty. Such actions were good or bad before there was any state. They are not good or bad because the laws of the state command or forbid them, but the state is obliged to command or forbid them because they are good or bad in themselves.

SOCIAL PRESSURE THEORIES

The theory that morality is mere custom has always been widespread since the days of the Sophists and Skeptics of ancient Greece. Some give legitimacy to the custom after it has been introduced, while others advocate its abolition. One who wishes to do away with morality must adopt some such theory to explain how men ever became deceived into thinking that right and wrong exist.

Some think that morality was imposed on men by clever and influential persons to keep the common people in subjection; by the force of public opinion and the weight of tradition the ordinary man accepts the moral code and wears the chains forged for him; only a few bold spirits assert and achieve freedom. This is the philosophy of the world's moral rebels. Bernard de Mandeville§ gives the idea expression but thinks it a providential arrangement.

The opinion of Friedrich Nietzsche‖ is not very different. In the beginning there were no good and bad, only the strong and the weak. The strong with their masculine virtues of power, cunning, and ruthlessness

---

*Rousseau, *Social Contract,* bk. I, ch. 1.
†*Op. cit.,* bk. I, ch. 4.
‡*Op. cit.,* bk. I, ch. 8.
§Mandeville, *Enquiry into the Origin of Moral Virtue.*
‖Nietzsche, *Genealogy of Morals,* and other works.

despised the weak with their feminine virtues of patience, obedience, and kindliness; and the weak feared the strong. Each class admired its own qualities and condemned the opposite; thus arose the distinction between master morality and slave morality. By weight of numbers, assisted by the influence of Christianity, slave morality triumphed. This outcome was a disaster. The common herd does not count, and it is the duty of society to produce an aristocracy of "Supermen," who will be the embodiment of the masculine virtues and will restore the master morality. The "Superman" will be beyond all good and evil, a law to himself.

Karl Marx and Friedrich Engels with their Communist followers hold the materialistic conception of history, according to which moral, political, artistic, social, and philosophical ideas are determined by the economic conditions of society. Each age, people, and class forms its ideas to suit its own peculiar economic situation. According to communistic belief, the economic changes to be brought about by the downfall of capitalism will require the formation of a new morality to supplant the present outmoded "bourgeois" morality.

Social evolutionists, of whom Herbert Spencer* is typical, trace the first beginning of moral ideas in animals. As man gradually evolved from a brutish condition, these moral ideas underwent a parallel evolution. Ways of acting that were found profitable developed into primitive tribal customs, which with the progress of civilization were gradually purified into our present system of morals. This will give way to a still higher system as the evolutionary process continues.

Positivism,† founded by Auguste Comte,‡ considers ethics a part of sociology, which Comte makes the supreme science. Moral customs grew out of social customs and fluctuate with the changes in society. Friedrich Paulsen,§ though hardly to be classed as a positivist in general, holds that there can be no universal morality in the concrete, that the moral code is different for each person, and that every moral philosophy is valid only for the sphere of civilization from which it springs. John Dewey‖ reduces morals to customs, folkways, established collective habits, but he admits

---

*Spencer, *Principles of Ethics,* of which the *Data of Ethics,* sometimes published separately, forms the first part.

†*Positivism,* as a general system of philosophy, is not to be confused with *moral positivism,* which is a specific answer to our present ethical problem. *Positivism,* as a general system of philosophy, holds that metaphysics is useless and that philosophy is limited to the facts and laws discovered by the *positive* or experimental sciences. *Moral positivism* is so called, not because it has anything to do with the positive sciences, but because it admits only *positive morality* based on positive law, as opposed to natural morality based on natural law. Most positivists will also happen to be moral positivists, but one can be a moral positivist without at all subscribing to the positivism of Comte and his followers.

‡Comte, *Cours de philosophie positive.* A convenient exposition of his philosophy in English is Harriet Martineau's *Positivist Philosophy of Auguste Comte.*

§Paulsen, *System of Ethics,* introduction, especially pp. 19-25.

‖Dewey, *Human Nature and Conduct,* pt. I, sec. V.

that they so form the texture of our lives that there is no escaping from them. More will be said of his ethical relativism later.

All such views received new cogency from a nonphilosophical source, the rise of cultural anthropology and Freudian psychology. These studies are not necessarily committed to a definite ethical view, but in the hands of some have been used to bolster the social pressure theory of moral obligation. They so concentrate on origins that they have difficulty getting man beyond his childhood, whether racial or individual.

Tribal tabus, however artificial and fictitious they may seem, often serve a purpose in the culture in which they flourish, though advanced peoples have grown out of them. Civilized mores are but a lingering remnant of the same thing in a more advanced style. Both have the same obligatory force: social pressure. It is easier to conform than to push against the demands of the crowd, and what is really only expediency becomes invested with an aura of duty.

> We recognize that morality differs in every society, and is a convenient term for socially approved habits. Mankind has always preferred to say, "It is morally good," rather than, "It is habitual," and the fact of this preference is matter enough for a critical science of ethics. But historically the two phrases are synonymous.*

While some thus reduce ethics to anthropology, others make it a form of psychology, so that the sense of moral obligation is identified with submerged psychic feelings of guilt. The person vaguely feels bound, but is unable to account for this inner sense of obligation until his early life is dredged up from the depths of the unconscious, and the feelings of guilt are seen as stemming from repressed infantile encounters with social, especially parental, disapproval. It would be foolish to deny anthropological and psychological facts with their bearing on ethics, but this reductionist type of reasoning is highly suspect.

All the foregoing opinions are but samples of this type of theory. They agree in reducing morality to social pressure and differ in their way of trying to account for the existence and influence of social pressure. They all deny that there is any intrinsic morality, that there is any basis in the nature of things for the distinction men commonly make between right and wrong. To assess this view we must see what is meant by custom.

What is custom?

Custom arises by repetition of the same kind of act in the same way. It is the external result of habit. Why do men repeat acts? Because the first time they did a certain act they found it pleasant or useful, and they want to obtain the same good again. In the beginning men do not repeat acts merely because they have done them once or twice before,

---

*Ruth Benedict, "The Concept of the Normal," taken from Mandelbaum, Gramlich, and Anderson, *Philosophical Problems,* p. 346.

but for the sake of some advantage. Until the custom has been formed, custom itself is not the source of action. Customs and traditions have their value as passing on to future generations in ready-made form the profitable experiences of our elders. As historical connections with the past, as the cement of cultural continuity, they are the mainstay of every civilization.

But custom can also act as a drawback. Over a long period of time circumstances may radically change, and acts which were formerly advantageous may now in the new conditions become useless or even harmful, yet men by force of habit continue to perform them without reflecting why they do so. Thus men continue to observe certain rites and ceremonies long after they have forgotten their meaning. Traditions can so pile up that a whole people will persist in doing a thing in a wasteful or illogical manner even after they recognize its absurdity, because they find it easier to conform to prejudice than to try to make men abandon familiar patterns of behavior. Our clumsy calendar, our irregular English spelling, our uncomfortable formal dress are instances.

As we noted in the very beginning of ethics, there are two kinds of customs: *manners,* which are mere customs, and *morals,* which are customs, it is true, but not mere customs. Mere customs, acts which are repeated solely because they have been done before, can be changed by lapse of time, by powerful authority, by continual propaganda, and popular re-education. This change may be difficult to accomplish, but history shows that even the most deeply lodged traditions, if they are mere traditions, can be broken. But this is not true of all customs, not of the kind called *morals,* for there are:

(1) Some customs that cannot be abolished, and
(2) Some kinds of acts that can never be made customary

Some customs never abolished

Eating and breathing are customs, but men cannot be reeducated to do without them. Conversation and exchange of ideas are customs, yet only a fool would try to prohibit them. Music and artistic expression are customs, but there is no prospect of ever eradicating them wholly from any people. The reason is that, though customary, they are not mere customs, but are founded on man's physical, mental, and emotional needs.

These instances are drawn from outside the field of morality, but the same conclusion holds true of man's moral life. It is customary for men to respect the lives and property of others in peacetime, to love their children, to pay their debts, to tell the truth, to be faithful to their friends, to fulfill their promises, to help others in distress. But these are not mere customs. If they were, they could be abolished and the opposite custom introduced. Not only would men refuse to accept the opposite custom, but there would be an end to human life and society. There would be no property, no children, no commerce, no talking, no friends, no promises, and no man would live to maturity much less produce a second generation. Here we are only using a few obvious examples and not trying to set up a full code of morality. We say only that some customs cannot be abolished, and the reader can take what examples he wishes.

We may call such acts customs in the broad sense of something done over and over again, but they are not mere customs in the sense that the only reason why they are done is that they have been done before. They represent the way man must live if he is to have a human life at all. Therefore such acts are good, not because they are customary, but because of their very nature. They are good in themselves, and were so before they became customary.

Some acts never customary

We cannot make it customary for man to walk down the street shooting people indiscriminately, for witnesses in a lawcourt to lie, for soldiers to desert in battle, for hosts to poison their guests, for every man to slander his neighbor's character and run off with his neighbor's wife. There must be some reason why such acts could not be established as customary. It is because such acts are evil in themselves and of their very nature. They are destructive of the fundamental capacities and requirements of man, and hence of human nature itself.

Of course there are men who do these things, but that is not the point. The point is that this kind of conduct is branded as wrong, and we are trying to find out why. Such conduct must ever be the exception, not the rule; the isolated instance, not the practice of the group; a blot on humanity, not the accepted ideal. If it becomes too widespread, it threatens the very existence of the society within which it grows. In our tolerance of human behavior, customary or otherwise, there is a limit beyond which, if we are to survive, we cannot go. There is a vast difference between antisocial conduct which people view with an amused or annoyed forbearance and the life of the outlaw whom society is forced for its own protection to hunt down like a beast. This latter kind of conduct can never become so prevalent as to be the accepted custom of the race, and even if it should nothing could make it moral. Morality, therefore, is based on something deeper than custom.

We do not deny that some evil customs may be adopted even by a whole people or nation, but history shows that no block of humanity can thus deteriorate without paying the price. Nations as well as individuals can be guilty of immoral conduct, and can become outlaws from the family of nations. We are experiencing in the world today the results of international immorality, and the lesson to be drawn from it is this: You can't live that way!

OBLIGATION AS INTRINSIC TO GOOD

The reduction of moral obligation to political or social pressure, to the commands or conventions of men, does not square with the facts. In the earliest stages of human development, both of the individual and of the race, probably little discrimination is made between physical and moral necessity. But as the child grows up and as primitive people arrive by self-examination at a more sophisticated attitude, the confusion disappears and the distinction is recognized. Compulsion from without is seen to be not the same as obligation from within. There is a difference between what I *must* do or suffer the penalty, and what I *ought* to do whether there is a penalty or not.

Thus a person emancipates himself from sole dependence on social and political pressure, from the laws and customs of the tribe or city or nation with their sanctions, and recognizes those rules that are proper to a man as a man. He is still a member of the group and strongly influenced by its approval, but he has grown critical of it and has found a norm for his criticism. Even those who attack all moral obligation do so in the name of sincerity, authenticity, and freedom, as liberating man from the weight of superstition, prejudice, and conformity. Thus they attack existing moral values and obligations for the sake of other moral values and obligations, rejecting the socially accepted code for one of their own making. Since we are not saying here what are the correct moral values but only that there are *some,* we could hardly find a better instance of the impossibility of reducing moral obligation to social approval than in those who criticize society itself in the name of morals.

Recall the case of the shark fighter or wife deserter in the last chapter. Or take the case of a man offered a huge fortune for one act of betraying his country's military secrets to the enemy. Minimize the dangers and enhance the advantages as much as possible. The act is foolproof and he is in clover for life. Yet it *ought not* to be done. Why not?

Eliminate the *legal* sanction. Suppose that the man is not only certain of not being caught, but finds some loophole by which he does not even break any existing civil law and could not be prosecuted for any crime. Yet he sees himself a traitor to his country and cannot approve his act.

Eliminate the *social* sanction. Since no one will know, there is no one's disapproval to be feared. Yet he deserves that disapproval even if he does not get it. How different when social sanctions are not deserved! We do not blame ourselves when we are innocent, but blame society for condemning us unjustly. If society can act immorally, social approval is not morality.

Eliminate the *psychological* sanction. The feelings of depression, disgust, and shame, the inability to eat or sleep with the twinge of remorse and guilt, may disturb him, but others can be immune to such feelings, and even in him they can come from other sources. The moral element remains. If by some drug the guilty *feelings* could be removed, if some merciful amnesia could blot out all memory of the sordid act, the *guilt* itself, the *ought not,* the *wrong* persists untouched though no longer perceived.

Eliminate the *religious* sanction. Were God not to punish it and were we certain that He would not, even in this absurd hypothesis the act ought not to be done. The doer might feel glad to escape, but would know that he did not deserve to escape. The act is of the kind that God ought to condemn and we would be disappointed in Him if He did not. We would begin to question God's justice, so that God Himself would no longer measure up to the ideal. This is perhaps the clearest indication of the absoluteness of the moral order.

What remains is the *moral* sanction. It is intrinsic to the very act itself, identical with the deliberate choice of the will, the relationship between the doer and his deed. Moral value, measured by the moral ideal, carries its necessity with it, a necessity unique and irreducible to any other. It is not a logical or metaphysical necessity based on the impossibility of thinking contradictions or of giving them existence. It is not a physical necessity, a *must* that compels us from without, destroying our freedom. Nor is it an internal impossibility of acting otherwise built into our nature, likewise destroying our freedom. It is a *moral* necessity, that of the *ought,* guiding us in what we recognize as the proper use of our freedom. It is a freedom that is a necessity and a necessity that is a freedom.

Moral necessity is *objective,* for, though it affects me, the acting subject, it comes from the object, the kind of act I the subject am performing. The act in its real being is something contingent that may or may not be, but in its ideal being as held up to my reason and will for deliberation and choice it assumes a practical necessity demanding decision. The demand is *absolute.* Bad use of artistic, economic, scientific, and other particular abilities is penalized by failure, not by fault, because I had no obligation to pursue these endeavors and hence no absolute obligation to succeed in them. But I cannot help being a man and absolutely have to succeed as a man. If I am a failure at it, it is my fault. I do not become bad in a certain line, but become a *bad man,* for the use of my freedom is *the* expression of my personality. In despising moral value I despise myself. According as I accept or reject a moral value, I rise or fall in my own worth as a man. Moral value is the scale by which I necessarily rate myself, unavoidably judge myself. This judgment is not merely a subjective opinion, but an objective estimate of my true worth in the scheme of things. This rise or fall is not something optional; I am not allowed to fall. It is not a question of whether I am interested in my own betterment; I am not allowed not to be. It is not a disjunctive necessity: Do this or take the consequences. It is simply: Do this. I am not allowed to expose myself to the consequences of not doing it. In fact, whatever consequences there are must themselves be judged by this moral criterion, and ultimate consequences must contain their own moral worth.

The ethical theory we have been defending here is that good ought to be done for its own sake, purely and simply because it is good, independently of what it may lead to. But good acts do have consequences, are done for a purpose, and it is to this aspect of the moral good that we now turn after summing up our conclusions.

CONCLUSIONS

We readily admit that there are some actions which are right or wrong merely because someone in authority has commanded or forbidden them. These actions are determined by positive law. The state has the right to forbid some actions not otherwise wrong for the sake of good order, and human customs may sometimes have the force of law.

But there are other actions so good of their very nature that no human law or custom could make them bad; and there are other actions so bad of their very nature that no human law or custom could make them good. Besides, no human law or custom can make acts that are good or bad in themselves become indifferent acts. But they can, by command or prohibition, make acts that are indifferent in themselves become extrinsically good or bad.

It must be insisted on that diversity of opinion on morals does not affect the arguments given. However much opinions may differ, there is a common denominator of moral action among men, and the arguments are drawn from this alone. Men may dispute whether this particular act is murder, theft, lying, or adultery; but there is no dispute that all sane men condemn murder, theft, lying, and adultery in general, and recognize that such acts cannot be made the standard of good conduct by any law or custom. If not, there must be some reason why not, and this can be found only in the very nature of such acts.

We may tie all these strands of argumentation together as follows: If all morality were conventional, all actions would be right or wrong because commanded or forbidden, approved or disapproved, either by the state or by society, by law or by custom. But some actions are such that the command or prohibition, the approval or disapproval of the state and its laws, of society and its customs, could not be otherwise, for any other mode of behavior would be destructive of the state, society, and of humanity itself. Therefore not all morality is conventional, but there is also a natural morality.

SUMMARY

Is all morality conventional, or is some morality natural?

Many hold the theory that all morality is conventional, resulting from the command or prohibition of the state and its laws or from the approval or disapproval of society and its customs, but that there are no acts good or bad of their very nature. The theory takes two forms:

1. *Moral positivism.* Hobbes and Rousseau say that there was no morality before the formation of the state, and morality now consists in obedience or disobedience to the civil laws. The argument against this is that the state can give conventional morality to indifferent acts, but no state can be completely arbitrary in its laws; there are acts every state must command and other acts every state must forbid, because human life itself demands it; these acts were moral or immoral before there was any state.

2. *Social pressure theories.* These are held by philosophers as widely separated as Spencer and Nietzsche, Comte and Marx. Custom can attain the force of law and give conventional morality to indifferent acts. But not all morality can be based on custom, for some customs cannot be abolished and some kinds of acts can never be made customary. The only reason for this is that these acts are good or bad independently of any custom, and custom is not the source of all morality.

Such theories fail to distinguish the *must* from the *ought*, compulsion from without and obligation from within. Why obey the law or custom? Force and fear are physical, not moral necessity. Eliminate legal, social, psychological, even religious sanctions, yet the person is *morally obliged* to do some actions and avoid others. He sees their objective relation to his nature and to his intrinsic worth *as a man.*

Conclusion. Some acts have only a conventional morality; of themselves indifferent, they become good or bad only because someone in authority has commanded or forbidden them. But there are other acts which have natural morality; they are good or bad of their very nature, and no human law or custom, no form of social approval or disapproval can make them otherwise.

READINGS

1. Plato's *Gorgias,* §481 to the end, and *Republic,* bk. I, §338, to bk. II, §368, are pertinent to the subject.
2. Cicero, *De Legibus* (On Laws), bk. I, xiv-xvi.
3. St. Thomas, *Summa Theologica,* I-II, q. 18, a. 1. Also *Summa Contra Gentiles,* bk. III, ch. 129. Natural morality was taken for granted in St. Thomas' day and is not given extended treatment.
4. Farrell, *Companion to the Summa,* vol. II, ch. IV.
5. Cronin, *Science of Ethics,* vol. I, pp. 104-123; 160-174.
6. Rickaby, *Moral Philosophy,* pp. 109-115.
7. D'Arcy, *Christian Morals,* ch. I.
8. Deploige, *Conflict Between Ethics and Sociology,* a criticism of Comte's positivism as developed by Émile Durkheim and Lucien Lévy-Bruhl. The first and last chapters give a good idea of it.

* * *

Some writers prefer to combine their treatment of this matter with that of the Norm of Morality or the Natural Law.

CHAPTER 7

THE GOOD

AS END

PROBLEM

The good is our constant quest. We are not born possessing it but are born seekers of it. Our existence is a passage from potentiality to actuality, from capacity to fulfillment, from perfectibility to perfection. Our emptiness clamors to be filled, and whatever satisfies our hunger is called a good.

Where does the moral good fit into this quest? If it is a general characteristic of the good to be sought after, this should show itself most intensely in the highest and best of goods. If the moral good is primitively known by connaturality or natural inclination, that inclination is *toward* something. If the moral good is not only a value to be contemplated but an obligation to be carried out, then it presents itself to us as an end to be attained, an aim to be followed, a goal to be reached, a purpose to be accomplished. A thing is not good because it is sought; rather, it is sought because it is good. That a thing is perfect in itself is prior to its being perfective of something else, and that is why we began with the good as value. Yet it is a fact that the good is sought, and this aspect of the good we must now explore. We ask:

(1) Does everything act for an end?
(2) Does human life have a purpose?
(3) Is man limited to short-range, relative ends?
(4) Has he some absolutely last end or purpose?
(5) Is it one and the same for all men?
(6) How are value, ought, and end related in the good?

THE PRINCIPLE OF FINALITY

Aristotle begins his *Ethics* with what looks like a definition of the good: "The good is that at which all things aim."* It is a popular question among modern ethicians whether the good can be defined, especially since G. E. Moore's essay on the topic.† His reasoning is that the good is a simple experience unanalyzable into anything simpler; since all definition is analysis of a concept into its components, the concept of the good is undefinable. The good, as the simplest of ethical ideas, could be analyzed only into something nonethical. This is not to define it but to lose it. Reduction of moral values to physical qualities involves what he calls the *naturalistic fallacy.* That we cannot define the good does not mean that we cannot know what it is; we know it by experiencing it. Whatever our view of Moore's general ethical position, we can agree with his rejection of reductionism. Aristotle's is a true statement, but it is not a strict definition and not meant to be.

Aristotle defines an *end* as "That for the sake of which a thing is done,"‡ and locates it among his four causes. For him all change is a process whereby some given underlying substrate (the matter) acquires a new specification or determination (the form) through the action of an efficient operator (the agent) moved to act by the attraction of some good (the end). Such a view of the universe with its constant changes supposes teleology or purposiveness, a directed world in which all things have an aim, as opposed to the *mechanistic* theory that all changes come about by chance. A directed world needs a principle of direction, and the name for it is *nature.* Each being is so structured that it acts only along certain definite lines. The nature is not some outside driver, not something distinct from the being which acts, but its very self. It is the *essence* of each being considered as the principle or source of its activity. Direction supposes not only a nature, an inner moving principle to make a thing go, but also a target toward which to move. So nature and end are correlative terms. Natural activity is teleological activity.

This briefest sketch of the Aristotelian metaphysical background, which is the one adopted here, was necessary to explain the inner dynamism of the human being, how it is *natural* for man to seek the good as his *end.* That the nature of a being structures it to act along definite lines is not a bar to freedom. Some beings have a free nature, are built to act freely, and it is natural to them to guide themselves to their end by free choice. Others lack freedom and automatically run along the tracks that their nature has laid. In either case they tend to ends.

Every end is a good and every good is an end. An end would not be sought unless it were somehow good for the seeker, and the good by being

---

Nicomachean Ethics, bk. I, ch. 1, 1094a 3.
†G. E. Moore, *Principia Ethica,* ch. 1, also reprinted separately as "The Indefinability of the Good."
‡*Physics,* bk. II, ch. 3, 194b 33; Metaphysics, bk. V, ch. 2, 1013a 33.

sought is the end or purpose of the seeker's striving. No activity is possible except for the attainment of some end, for the sake of some good. This is the *principle of finality* or *teleology,* which St. Thomas explains as follows:

> Every agent of necessity acts for an end. For if in a number of causes ordained to one another the first be removed, the others must of necessity be removed also. Now the first of all causes is the final cause. The reason of which is that matter does not receive form save in so far as it is moved by an agent; for nothing reduces itself from potentiality to act. But an agent does not move except out of intention for an end. For if the agent were not determinate to some particular effect, it would not do one thing rather than another: consequently in order that it produce a determinate effect, it must of necessity be determined to some certain one, which has the nature of an end.*

In other words, before it acts, a being with potentiality for acting is in an indeterminate condition, and can either act or not act, act in this way or in that way. No action will ever take place unless something removes this indetermination, stirs the being to act, and points its action in a certain direction. Hence the principle of finality, "every agent acts for an end," is implicit in the concepts of potency and act, and in the whole notion of causality. If every agent acts for an end, the human agent certainly does so.

Whatever one may think of teleology in the world at large, no sane man can deny that human beings act for ends. Even one who tried to prove that they do not would have this as his end in view. Failure to adapt one's conduct to rational ends is the accepted sign of mental derangement. The very admission, therefore, that there are such things as rational human acts is an admission that human beings do act for ends, at least for short-range ends in view. That they must act for a last end or ultimate goal remains to be seen.

THE END AND MORAL GOOD

The question arises: If all things, including man, inevitably seek an end which is also the good, how can any act fail to be good, how can human conduct go wrong? The good as end, as perfective, as good *for,* has various meanings among which we must sort out the moral good.

The thesis of the metaphysician, that "every being is good," refers only to *ontological* or *metaphysical* goodness. It means only that every being, by the very fact that it is a being, has some goodness about it and is good for something, contributing in some way to the harmony and perfection of the universe. Every being also has a certain amount of *physical* goodness, which consists in a completeness of parts and competence of activity. Though some things are physically defective, they are good insofar as they have being, defective insofar as they lack being. But from the fact that

---

*St. Thomas, *Summa Theologica,* I-II, q. 1, a. 2; see also *Summa Contra Gentiles,* bk. III, ch. 2, 3, 16.

every being is good for *something,* it does not follow that every being is good for *everything.* What is good for one thing may not be good for another, and what is good for a thing under these circumstances or from this aspect may not be good for the same thing under different conditions or from another standpoint. Metaphysics considers the good in its broadest scope and so can find good in everything in some way; ethics considers the good in the limited line of voluntary and responsible human conduct and often finds this line strangely warped. The murderer levels his gun and fells his victim. It is a good shot but an evil deed. As a piece of marksmanship it is admirable, but as an act of human conduct it is damnable. There is some good in all things, but it need not be the ethical or *moral* good.

Because not everything is good for everything, it is up to man's judgment to determine what things are good *for him.* Human judgments are open to error, and therefore he may mistake the *apparent* good for the *true* good. Unless a thing at least appears to be good we could not seek it at all, for it could make no appeal to our appetites, but we can easily confuse what is good for something else with what is good for us, or what would be good for us in other circumstances with what is good for us here and now. If some lesser good makes impossible the attainment of the highest good, then this lesser good is not the true good for us. The moral good must always be the true good.

So there are degrees in goodness. We may seek a good not for its own sake but as a means to some further good; it is desirable only because it leads to something more desirable. This is the *useful* good, and it is good only in a qualified and analogous sense; such are all tools and instruments. We may seek a good for the satisfaction or enjoyment it gives without considering whether it will be beneficial to our whole being; it delights us now and may be harmless, but offers us no guarantee that it may not hurt us in the long run and unfit us for the greater good. This is the *pleasant* good, and it attracts us most vividly. Or, lastly, we may seek a good because it contributes toward the perfection of our being as a whole, because it fits a man as such. This is the *befitting* good, the upright and honorable, the noble and righteous, and it is good in the fullest sense. The moral good, while it may also be useful and pleasant, is always and necessarily the befitting good.

We should add here a classification popular with modern writers, that has some parallel with the one just given though they do not perfectly correspond. It is a classification into instrumental good, inherent good, and intrinsic good. *Instrumental* good is about the same as the useful, that which is good merely because of what it leads to. *Intrinsic* good is that which is a value in itself independently of any effect it may have on anything else; it corresponds to the perfect good. The befitting good is an intrinsic good, which is also man's highest good; hence the befitting good is the intrinsic good plus another aspect of goodness: it is both perfect and perfective. *Inherent* good is somewhere in between. It differs from instrumental inasmuch as it does not lead to something else that is good for me; *it* itself is good for me. It differs from intrinsic good inasmuch as it is not conceived as having value in itself but only for me. Pleasure obviously comes under this heading, though it need not be the only thing that comes under it.

Our analysis of the kinds of good shows that human conduct must always be directed toward the good in some sense, but that this is not always the moral good. To make it the moral good is life's purpose and our responsibility.

THE LAST END AND HIGHEST GOOD

Must we link up the various intermediate and subordinate ends man may have into some ultimate and all-inclusive end? Single acts are directed to an end, but is it also necessary that the sum total of one's acts, one's whole life, be directed to some last end and highest good?

No infinite series of ends

A thing is intended either for its own sake or for the sake of something else. The former is an *end,* the latter a *means.* A means always supposes an end; it is called a means precisely because it lies in a mean or middle position between the agent and the end, and its use brings the agent to the end. The same thing may be both means and end in different respects, for it may be sought both for its own sake and for the sake of something further. This is called an *intermediate* end, and there may be a long series of such intermediate ends, as when we want A in order to get B, B in order to get C, C in order to get D, etc.

That which is sought for its own sake and not for the sake of anything further is a *last end* or *ultimate end.* It closes the series of means and ends. It may be a last end only in a relative sense, meaning that it closes a particular series but the whole series is directed to some further end; thus the reception of an academic degree terminates one's education but education itself has the further purpose of fitting one for life. In the full sense of the word, and as we take it here, the last end means the *absolutely last end,* which is directed to no further end at all, but to it everything else is directed. Since the end and the good are identified, a being's absolutely last end must also be its highest good.

In a series of means and ends we must distinguish the order of *intention* from the order of *execution.* The first thing that comes to mind (the order of intention) is the end, and the means are chosen with a view to accomplishing the end; but in the actual carrying out of the work (the order of execution) the means must be used first, and the last thing that is obtained is the end. This is an important step in our argument, for, whatever may be thought of the possibility of an infinite series in other matters, an infinite series of means and ends is quite impossible, and so there must be an *absolutely last end* to which the whole of human life is directed. Here is St. Thomas' proof:

That which is first in the order of intention is the principle as it were moving the appetite; consequently if you remove this principle there will be nothing to move the appetite. On the other hand, the principle in execution is that wherein operation has its beginning; and if this principle be taken away no one will begin to work. Now the principle in the intention is the last end; while the principle in execution is the first of the things which are ordained to the end. Consequently on neither side is it possible to go on to infinity; since, if there were no last end, nothing would be desired nor would any action have its term nor would the intention of the agent be at rest; while, if there is no first thing among those that are ordained to the end, none would begin to work at anything and counsel would have no term but would continue indefinitely.*

When a man uses A to get B, B to get C, C to get D, he must (unless he is acting at random and irrationally) first desire D, and then find out that to get D he needs C, to get C he needs B, to get B he needs A. Thus his planning (intention) is in inverse order to his acting (execution). That which is first in intention is last in execution, and vice versa. Thus the steps are as follows:

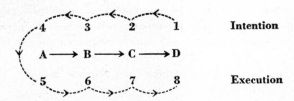

They are first planned out in the mind and then transferred to execution. If the planning went on forever, nothing would ever be done, for in rational action the execution cannot begin until the planning is complete. There must then be a point A (the proximate means) at which planning ends and execution begins. This closes the series on one side. But to arrive at point A in the planning, it was also necessary to begin somewhere. Neither A nor B nor C is wanted for itself. Unless there is some point D which is wanted for itself, neither A nor B nor C would be thought of and no plan would be formed. Hence there must be some point D (the last end) which starts the whole process going. This closes the series on the other side. Hence in any intelligent procedure apart from fitful and random behavior, one must already have the last end in mind before beginning the first act. Man therefore not only acts for an end, but for a last end.

But does not this argument prove too much and therefore nothing? The child, before it could perform its first act, would need to understand its last end and formulate a whole plan of life. We answer that the above was a description of *rational* activity, the use of means to end as directed by intellect in adult human behavior. At first the child's life lies on an

---

*Summa Theologica, I-II, q. 1, a. 4.

animal plane with no rationally understood goals. As its reason unfolds, the child begins to see some short-term objectives and plans for them with a rudimentary use of means and ends. But to every normal person the time must come when the problem of life's meaning becomes acutely insistent, the irrationality of haphazard living grows glaringly evident, and the former excuse of ignorance and immaturity vanishes before the clear light of developed reason. From then on a rational organization of life is imperative.

While this development is going on, the child is not left to drift aimlessly. So long as it cannot steer itself, it is steered by others. It is born into a family and meant by nature to accept parental direction, to be guided by the rules of the society it cannot yet criticize, and to rely on the knowledge by inclination and connaturality that spontaneously springs up within it. But it will have to go through some such process as we have described for a reasoned and reflective acceptance of a plan of life with consciously formed aims.

Opportunism

Not all agree with this analysis. To be content to live on a day-to-day or a year-to-year basis, confining oneself to immediate goals and neglecting remote ones, seeking proximate ends without bothering about a last end or supreme purpose, is a widely practiced philosophy of life called *opportunism*. Not so much a reasoned conviction as an attitude of intellectual and moral sloth, it merits the Socratic rebuff, "The unexamined life is not worth living."*

Opportunism is the unconsciously adopted philosophy of the child, rationalized and protracted into maturity. One may indeed consciously choose to float with the tide rather than set a course, to shun any fixed program so as to be free to reshape life as opportunity offers, above all to avoid encumbrance by embarrassing principles and responsibilities. This is the life of the moral tramp or ethical hobo, a form of life that can be chosen quite deliberately. But he who takes to it does not avoid having a last end; he mistakenly takes wandering itself for his last end by the very fact that he seeks nothing beyond. One may aim at aimlessness, rationally choose to live irrationally, but such conduct must be branded as unworthy of a man. As the vagrant is an economic anomaly and a social liability, so is the opportunist an ethical misfit and a human failure.

Relativism and pragmatism

Ethical relativism, passing far beyond any such crude attitude, examines life thoroughly, even scientifically, but arrives at a rather similar pragmatic conclusion. For the opportunist, there is too much trouble in finding out life's meaning if it has one. For the relativist, life can be somewhat meaningful in retrospect and in immediate prospect, but its total

---

*Plato, *Apology*, §38.

and ultimate meaning is undiscoverable by us now and unnecessary for relatively successful living.

For the relativist everything is relative; there are no absolutes. A last end would be an absolute, so there can be no such thing. Such an assertion, if it seem too absolute, can be softened into the observation that no supreme purpose for man has yet been identified with certainty. But the answer is not merely to drift with the tide, like the opportunist, not caring where. The relativist, especially of the pragmatist type, cares deeply and exhorts us to get the most out of life, to improve our condition as far as we can, to work earnestly for universal betterment. But he is acutely sensitive to our limitations and to the folly of being ambitious beyond our known possibilities. We may have no ultimate goal, but there are short-range goals that experience puts before us and by which we can guide ourselves. Like a sailor in a fog, we should steer in what seems the most likely direction at the moment, with a memory for the course we have traveled and with our eyes open for any clearing ahead. Life is subject to continual readjustment. We work chiefly by the trial-and-error method, experimenting with the data at hand. Morals seem to change from person to person, from age to age, from one form of society to another, as man progressively adapts himself to a constantly changing environment.

To many ethical relativists, the very idea of a last end appears too rigid and stifling. What would we do when we reached a last end? Would there be no further growth or progress? Without novelty and development the adventure of existence would lose all its zest. There is more joy in the excitement of the chase than in bagging the quarry.

Relativism is as old as Protagoras the Sophist with his motto, "Man is the measure of all things," and as new as John Dewey with his slogan, "We learn by doing." It is undoubtedly true that we learn *how* to do many things by getting in and doing them, but is this the way we learn *what* to do? We learn how to explode nuclear bombs by experimenting with them, but does this solve the question whether we should explode them at all? By his principles Dewey should put even the latter question on an experimental basis. His theory of the *continuity of means–ends*** says that, as there is no means that is not a means to an end, so there is no end that is not a means to a further end. The chain, therefore, of means and ends is necessarily indefinite in length, and the notion of a *last* end is essentially incoherent. Only felt wants demand satisfaction, and this situation automatically creates a new want. When we have finished one stage we experimentally cast about for the next stage in the on-going process. Anything like an ultimate fixed goal is both impossible as breaking off the continuity of means–ends, and undesirable as curtailing the flexibility and freedom of human progress. All this appeals especially to our day with its conviction that evolution is a fact but we do not know toward what we are evolving.

---

*Dewey, *Theory of Valuation.*

Ethical relativism does not succeed in eliminating a last end. That end is ultimate which has nothing beyond, and any provisional end now chosen becomes ultimate for the time being unless directed to something further. Thus proximate ends are lifted to the status of ultimate ends without deserving the honor. The motive behind relativism is often said to be intellectual humility, an acceptance of the limitations of the human mind, but genuine humility would show itself in the acceptance of truth when truth becomes evident more than in refusal to submit oneself to evidence. The real motive seems rather to be intellectual fear of being deceived or disillusioned, and if there is no further reason why the relativist adopts his relativism, he makes this his last end, whether he cares to call it so or not. Life does require continual adjustments, not of ends, however, but of means. We must be ready to alter our course only if there is some port for which we are making and if it is important to avoid being wrecked on the way. The excitement of the chase may be more exhilarating than the bagging of the quarry only if we know there is a quarry and some reason for engaging in the chase. And why must a last end be something static that would freeze all further growth instead of a condition of perpetually assured growth? If death is the end of all, as many relativists are willing to accept provisionally, it is the most static and rigid of all last ends, nothingness.

On his own grounds the relativist is unassailable, since he accords a relative truth to any argument that opposes him: "That may be true for you; the opposite is true for me." The nonrelativist puts forth his argument not in the hope of convincing the relativist, with whom he can find no common ground, but for the purpose of clarifying and establishing his own convictions.

ONE AND THE SAME LAST END

For the sake of method, we must next establish two propositions: first, that each individual man has but one last end and not several simultaneous and coordinate ones; second, that all men are alike in having the same last end to pursue and not different ones for different persons, classes, or races.

That each individual man has but *one* last end is proved by St. Thomas in three arguments, of which the first is the simplest:

> A man desires for his ultimate end that which he desires as his perfect and crowning good . . . It is therefore necessary for the last end so to fill man's appetite that nothing is left beside it for man to desire. Which is not possible if something else be required for his perfection. Consequently it is not possible for the appetite so to tend to two things as though each were its perfect good.*

In other words, if a man had several last ends, no one of them could satisfy him, for having attained any one of them he could still desire the

---

*Summa Theologica, I-II, q. 1. a. 5.

others; but a last end, because it is the highest good, must satisfy completely. This argument does not deny that the last end might be complex, consisting of a number of parts or a group of objects taken together, but it does deny that there can be many different objects each of which taken separately might be a last end in itself, and especially that there can be many alternative last ends between which we might choose. We have but one last end offered to us; we may take it or leave it, but we cannot find a substitute.

That all men have the *same* last end is evident from that fact that all men have the same human nature and therefore the same needs, tendencies, appetites, desires, or abilities craving satisfaction. Men can and do differ subjectively in their judgments on what constitutes their last end, but of these many conflicting judgments only one can be objectively true. What this true judgment is will form a large part of our inquiry; here we merely say that whatever it is, it must be valid for *all* men.

VALUE, OUGHT, AND END

In the last three chapters we have looked at the good under three aspects: as value, as ought, and as end. A more learned way of saying it is that we have seen axiological, deontological, and teleological ethics. The good as *value* stresses the intrinsic good, the perfect good, that which is good in itself irrespective of any goodness it may have for anything else. This must be the most fundamental aspect of the good. The good as *ought* stresses the fact that each thing ought to be as perfect as it can be, that the ideal is not merely something to be contemplated but to be put into act, and that this demand is laid on a free being in the form of moral obligation. The good as *end* emphasizes the obligation of any being, if it is not yet perfect, to strive toward perfection as its end, and to seek other goods as means to this end. These are not three kinds of good, but three ways of looking at the same good. The absolute good is the ultimate *end* that *ought* to be sought because of its supreme *value*.

SUMMARY

The *good* is that at which all things aim. As a primary notion it is not strictly definable. The good is *ontological*, the good of mere being; *physical*, the good of completeness; *moral*, the good of right living, of rightly directing free conduct to its due end. The *true* good really *is* good; the *apparent* good only seems so. The *useful* leads to something else that is good; the *pleasant* satisfies a particular appetite; the *befitting* perfects the whole man as such.

Though every being is ontologically good and has some physical goodness, it is not always morally good. The moral good is always the true good and the befitting good.

An *end* is that for the sake of which a thing is done. Every good is an end and every end is a good. A *means* is that which leads to an end. An end can be *proximate, intermediate,* or *ultimate* and any of them either absolutely or relatively so. An absolutely ultimate end or *last end* is not a means to anything further.

All human conduct is for an end and a good. This is a particular case of the principle of finality, "Every agent acts for an end." Since no agent can produce an undetermined effect, something must determine the agent to act rather than not, to produce this effect rather than that; what removes this indetermination is the end.

All human conduct is for a last end and a highest good. There cannot be an infinite series of means and ends, since intention and execution are in inverse order. The last end is the first thing desired; if there is no last end, nothing is desired and no activity can be started. Opportunists live haphazardly without bothering about a last end, but such conduct is irrational. Ethical relativists admit proximate ends without any last end, but to deny a last end in order to be free from commitment to it is to make such freedom itself one's last end.

There is but one last end for each man and it is the same for all men. Many alternative ends would leave a man wanting the others, and dissatisfied. Different ends for different men would contradict the specific unity of the human race.

The moral good has the three aspects of *value, ought,* and *end* inasmuch as it is an intrinsic worth in itself, a moral necessity demanding compliance, and a goal of our appetites seeking fulfillment.

READINGS

1. Read Aristotle's *Nicomachean Ethics,* bk. I, ch. 1-6.
2. The present chapter is an adaptation of St. Thomas' *Summa Theologica,* I-II, q. 1, not printed in the *Basic Writings of St. Thomas Aquinas,* but found in the Dominican Translation, vol. VI.
3. Read from St. Thomas' *Summa Contra Gentiles,* bk. III, ch. 1, 2, 3, 16, 22, and 24, found in the *Basic Writings,* vol. II. This is a different presentation of the same matter. Remember that some of St. Thomas' illustrations are drawn from antiquated physics and astronomy; they are not essential to his argument. Such cautious selectivity is always necessary in reading ancient and medieval writers.
4. St. Thomas' metaphysical development of the good is found in the *Summa Theologica,* I, q. 5, printed in the *Basic Writings,* vol. I.
5. The following modern writers have matter pertinent to this chapter:
   a. Cronin, *Science of Ethics,* vol. I, pp. 46-53, 89-97.
   b. Gilson, *Moral Values and Moral Life,* pp. 15-26.
   c. Adler, *Dialectic of Morals,* pp. 74-97.
   d. O'Connor, *The Eternal Quest,* ch. V, VI.
   e. Ward, *Values and Reality,* ch. I-IV.
6. A study of good from a different philosophical background is found in the following:
   a. Ewing, *The Definition of Good.*
   b. Ross, *The Right and the Good.*
   c. G. E. Moore's essay on "The Indefinability of the Good," *Principia Ethica,* ch. 1, is the source of much modern philosophizing on the ethical good. This, together with many modern articles, is reprinted in Sellars and Hospers, *Readings in Ethical Theory.*
   d. Dewey, *Theory of Valuation,* continues the views expressed in *Human Nature and Conduct.*
   e. Lewis, C. I., *Analysis of Knowledge and Valuation.* On the kinds of good.

CHAPTER 8

THE NORM
OF MORALITY

PROBLEM

The moral good, as it emerges from our study thus far, shows itself to be a value supreme among all values, imposing itself on us as an absolute obligation, so that to obtain it is the end and purpose of our existence. The moral order is not merely the creation of the individual conscience, though subjective morality has its importance; nor is it the creation of the collective conscience of society, though civil law and human custom can give a conventional morality to otherwise indifferent acts; nor is it a mere stage in man's evolutionary progress which he blindly pursues with no ultimate goal in sight, though man develops in moral knowledge as in all knowledge. Besides the subjective, conventional, and relative aspects of morality, there is a solid core of moral goodness that is objective, natural, and absolute. How can we find it?

Our task is to set up some norm by which we can distinguish which acts are good, which are bad, and which are indifferent in themselves. The following points come up for discussion:

(1) What is meant by a norm of morality?
(2) What faculty must we use to measure morality?
(3) How do we set up a norm of morality?
(4) How do we prove that this is the true norm?
(5) Is this norm really practical and proximate?

MEANING OF A NORM

A norm is a rule, standard, or measure; it is something fixed with which we can compare something else whose nature, size, or qualities we doubt. So a norm of morality will be a rule, standard, or measure by which we can gauge the goodness or badness of an act. It will be something with which an act must positively agree to be morally good, with which it must positively disagree to be morally bad, and toward which it must be neutral to be morally indifferent.

A norm may be proximate or ultimate. To find out whether a space is a yard long, we apply a yardstick to it. But how do the makers of yardsticks determine what a true yard is? They measure their yardsticks by some officially recognized yard beyond which there is no appeal, such as the metal yard bar kept in London or a definite mathematical fraction of the metal meter bar kept in Paris. In general, a *proximate* or *derived* norm is one directly applicable to the thing to be measured, and is here at hand ready for use; an *ultimate* or *original* norm is the last reason why the proximate norm is what it is. Theoretically, the same thing can fulfill the functions of both ultimate and proximate norms. It is possible to carry a thing to London or Paris and measure it by the metal bar there, but in practice this is inconvenient and it is usual to have two concrete embodiments of the same abstract measure, one for practical use and one for ultimate reference.

That there must be some norm of morality is evident. We have shown that there are some acts of their very nature good and others of their very nature bad; there must be something by which to distinguish one class from the other. There must be a proximate norm, for otherwise the measure would be useless, inapplicable to individual concrete acts, which are the only kind that can actually exist. There must be an ultimate norm, for otherwise there would be nothing to guarantee the validity of the proximate norm.

THE MORAL SENSE THEORY

Have we a special faculty for discovering and measuring morality? In the late seventeenth and throughout the eighteenth century a group of British moralists thought that the perception of moral good and evil is the work of some faculty distinct from the intellect or reason; this special faculty they called the *moral instinct* or *moral intuition* or *moral sense*.

Shaftesbury,* who was much taken up with speculations on the beautiful, recognized that besides its other forms there is also moral beauty, that a moral life is really a beautiful life. The sense of beauty he considered a special faculty of the mind, and when applied to moral beauty it becomes the moral sense. Moral beauty consists in a proper balancing of public and private affections, of selfish and social impulses, resulting in a well-rounded and harmonious life. This theory is called *moral aestheticism*.

Francis Hutcheson† developed Shaftesbury's views by separating the moral sense from the aesthetic sense, giving to the former the specific func-

---

*Shaftesbury (Anthony Ashley Cooper, third Earl of Shaftesbury), *Characteristics of Men, Manners, Opinions, and Times,* bk. I, pt. II, §3; bk. II, pt. I, §1.
†Hutcheson, *Inquiry into the Original of Our Ideas of Beauty and Virtue,* Treatise II, section I.

tion of distinguishing right from wrong. Joseph Butler* took the rather obvious step of identifying the moral sense with conscience, which he seems to consider a faculty distinct from the intellect. Thomas Reid, representative of the Scottish School of Common Sense philosophy, sums up the *moral sense theory* as follows:

> The abstract notion of moral good and ill would be of no use to direct our life, if we had not the power of applying it to particular actions, and determining what is morally good, and what is morally ill.
>
> Some philosophers, with whom I agree, ascribe this to an original power or faculty in man, which they call the *Moral Sense,* the *Moral Faculty, Conscience.* . . .
>
> In its dignity it is, without doubt, far superior to every other power of the mind; but there is this analogy between it and the external senses, That, as by them we have not only the original conceptions of the various qualities of bodies, but the original judgment that this body has such a quality, that such another; so by our moral faculty, we have both the original conceptions of right and wrong in conduct, of merit and demerit, and the original judgments that this conduct is right, that is wrong; that this character has worth, that demerit.†

Adam Smith, the economist, approaches ethics from the standpoint of psychological analysis. The moral faculty or conscience is an instinctive sentiment of sympathy, which he explains in a novel way:

> We either approve or disapprove of our own conduct, according as we feel that, when we place ourselves in the situation of another man, and view it, as it were, with his eyes, and from his station, we either can or cannot enter into and sympathize with the sentiments and motives which influence it. . . .
>
> When I endeavor to examine my own conduct, when I endeavor to pass sentence upon it, and either to approve or condemn it, it is evident that, in all such cases, I divide myself, as it were, into two persons; and that I, the examiner and judge, represent a different character from that other I, the person whose conduct is examined into and judged of.‡

These theories all demand some faculty distinct from the intellect to judge of right and wrong, either making this its sole function, or identifying it with the aesthetic sense or with conscience or with the sentiment of sympathy. David Hume,§ though not interested in any special faculty, agrees with Smith in reducing morality to feeling, especially to the sentiment of humanity, benevolence, or sympathy. The moral intuitionism of Ralph

---

*Butler, *Fifteen Sermons upon Human Nature,* Sermons II and III.
†Reid, *Essays on the Active Powers of Man.* Essay III, pt. III, ch. 6.
‡Smith, *Theory of Moral Sentiments,* pt. III, ch. 1.
§Hume, *Treatise on Human Nature,* bk. III; also *Inquiry Concerning the Principles of Morals.*

Cudworth* and Samuel Clarke† belongs in the same class of opinions, for, though they make the intellect the faculty of judging right from wrong, they have it do so, not by any process of reasoning, but by an immediate intellectual intuition of the eternal fitness of things, which is an expression of the Divine Ideas.

Criticism

There is no need for a special moral faculty distinct from the intellect. Moral judgments are not of an essentially different nature from other judgments. To understand is the function of the intellect. Any faculty other than the intellect would not understand why certain actions are good or bad. To make any such other faculty the norm would lower man's moral life to the instinctive and brutish. It is absurd to expect man to use his reason in the fields of science, business, law, and politics, but not in the realm of morals and in the goal of life itself.

To identify the moral sense with the aesthetic sense solves no problem, for we need no special faculty for the perception of the beautiful. It is true that there is moral beauty, that virtue is beautiful and vice is ugly, but this truth is more apparent in the abstract than in the concrete. Beauty must somehow be striking and attractive, but morality can pass unnoticed; beauty must give pleasure, but morality is often hard and costs sacrifice. Intellectual reflection is necessary to perceive the beauty of a moral life.

Conscience is the norm of subjective, not of objective morality. It is not a special faculty but only the name for the intellect judging the morality of a particular concrete act here and now. The judgment of conscience is the conclusion of a syllogism arrived at by a process of intellectual reasoning.

Sentiments, even the noblest such as sympathy, cannot be a reliable guide to right and wrong. They are constantly varying, depending on our physical condition and emotional mood. The same act would be good or bad according as one feels. Even if acts be classified by the feelings they commonly evoke, some objective reason must be assigned why they commonly evoke such feelings, and this objective reason will be the norm.

Though, according to many, we have an intuition of the first moral principles, for no process of reasoning can be carried back forever, such moral principles are very few, perhaps only one. Certainly we have no direct intuition of the moral goodness or badness of concrete acts here and now to be performed. If morality were intuitive and need not be established by rational argument, how could there be so many different opinions on morality?

RIGHT REASON

The faculty to be used in discriminating right from wrong can be no other than the human *intellect* or *reason*. Such a view is implicit in Aristotle,

---

*Cudworth, *Treatise Concerning Eternal and Immutable Morality,* bk. IV, ch. 6.
†Clarke, *Discourse Concerning the Unchangeable Obligations of Natural Religion,* I.

who devotes the whole of the sixth book of his *Nicomachean Ethics* to a search for the right rule which dictates the midpoint of virtue between excess and defect, finding it in the intellectual virtue of prudence or practical wisdom,* but this has to do more with applying the norm than setting up the norm itself. Prudence deals only with a single particular action, and cannot be a rule or norm, which must always have some universality.

St. Thomas, though not treating expressly of the norm of morality but merging it with his discussion of the eternal and natural law, has this to say:

> In human actions, good and evil are predicated in relation to the reason, because, as Dionysius says, the good of man is to be in accordance with reason, *and evil is to be against reason.*† For that is good for a thing which suits it according to its form; and evil, that which is against the order of its form. It is therefore evident that the difference of good and evil, considered in reference to the object, is an essential difference in relation to reason, *i.e.,* according as the object is suitable or unsuitable to reason. Now certain actions are called human or moral inasmuch as they proceed from the reason.‡
>
> In those things that are done by the will, the proximate rule is the human reason, while the supreme rule is the eternal law. When, therefore a human act tends to the end according to the order of reason and of the eternal law, then that act is right; but when it turns away from that rectitude, then it is said to be a sin. Now it is evident, from what has been said,§ that every voluntary act that turns aside from the order of reason and of the eternal law is evil, and that every good act is in accord with reason and the eternal law.‖

In saying that *right reason* is the norm of morality, we certainly do not mean that our reason has an intuitive vision of the rightness or wrongness of human acts in detail or that at birth our reason is equipped with ready-made moral principles that we can later apply to concrete cases by a simple use of formal logic. This would be but a variety of the moral sense theory. How then are we to know when reason is right? Logic teaches us how to draw the correct conclusion from the premises given, but it does not give us the premises. Where shall we search for these and how shall we know them when we have found them?

Reason has to be its own critic. To determine when reason is right and when it is wrong, there is nothing else to appeal to but reason itself. Knowledge can be known only by knowledge reflecting on itself. By reason we discover truth and by the same reason we are capable of error, just as by the will we seek the good and by the same will we can do evil by seeking the merely apparent good. The will seeks anything that reason proposes to it as good; it needs a norm but cannot be one. Reason needs a norm and

---

*See especially bk. VI, ch. 1, 1038b 17-35.
†Dionysius the Areopagite, *The Divine Names,* IV, 32.
‡*Summa Theologica,* I-II, q. 18, a. 5.
§*op. cit.,* I-II, q. 19, aa. 3-4.
‖*op. cit.,* I-II, q. 21, a. 1.

must also be one; it can find none but itself. How can this paradox be resolved?

We distinguish two uses of reason: reason rationally exercised, consistent with itself, faithful to its own law and function; and reason irrationally exercised, contradicting itself, enthralled by a law foreign to it and functioning to its own destruction. Reason used to plot a crime, for instance, is reason used irrationally, for only the means are rational and not the end; reason thwarts itself by its own cleverness in rationally arranging parts into an irrational whole. When reason is enslaved to serve irrational ends and when it is free to be fully itself, reason alone can know.

What guides has human reason for determining when it is right and when it is not? Reason looking at itself discovers several aspects under which it may be regarded as right reason:

1. *The dictate of right reason.* In our whole discussion here reason is taken as *practical* reason, reason not in its function of contemplating the true but of directing action. This it does by framing the practical judgments that constitute deliberation, presenting the good to the will for its acceptance, the arguments in its favor, the obligatory character of the moral good, and the *reasonableness* of choosing this course. Here reason is acting as a guide, a norm in the sense of a directing principle. This particular act is good if it conforms to the dictate of practical reason issued in this case. The question still remains, however, how we know that the dictate of practical reason was right and good.

2. *The habit of rational principles.* Practical reason not only issues a dictate concerning the moral goodness and obligatory character of a particular act, but relies on its habitual possession of rationally derived principles. This habit is also called right reason, supposing that these principles are rightly derived. This habit lies between *synderesis,* or the habit of first principles known by connatural knowledge, and the habit or virtue of *prudence* which applies the principles to individual acts. But again the question remains whether such habitually possessed principles are correct and whence they are derived.

3. *Rational human nature.* Right reason is also taken to mean human nature itself, since rationality is the essential and specifying element of human nature. Reason, reflecting on the human nature of which it is a part, sees the congruity of some actions and the incongruity of other actions with that nature, pronouncing the former good and the latter evil. Here indeed is an objective standard, but conformity of action with nature is the rule all over the universe, conferring physical goodness but not necessarily moral goodness. Why should it confer *moral* goodness in the case of *man* alone? Here human nature is to be taken, not as one nature among other natures, one thing among other things, but as something distinctive. It is human nature not merely as nature but as human, and what distinguishes it as human is rationality. It is rational human nature precisely *as rational.*

4. *Direction to a rational end.* It is characteristic of reason to direct to an end. Conduct not so directed is called *irrational.* An act is morally good that leads man to his last end, evil that hinders him from his last end. But is the act good because it leads to the end, or does it lead to the end because it is good? Reason can perceive the inner dynamism of the human being, his abilities and capacities craving fulfillment, and the suitability of certain acts and objects to contribute to the human being's fulfillment of his being. But the good as perfective, as completing natural tendencies, appeals only to the nature *as nature* and does not specify the moral good as such. The end itself must be a good if it is good to strive for it.

5. *The ideal of right reason.* Right reason can be identified with the objective order of reason, with the hierarchy of perfections and values that reason must necessarily acknowledge. Some values are seen to be nobler in intrinsic worth, more inclusive in scope, more compatible with other values, more productive of order and harmony in man himself and in his relations with the universe. Then moral value will consist in agreement with this objective order. Whatever is inconsistent with the ideal or would prevent its realization must be rejected as not a true good. Whatever harmonizes with the ideal and promotes its realization is the good. Since we have no direct intuition of eternal essences in some Platonic heaven, the moral ideal must be found by a process of abstraction and sublimation from the human beings and human acts we concretely experience. What does the abstracting and sublimating is human reason, and in forming the ideal it looks to human nature. But again it must be human nature precisely as *human*, as *rational*.

The norm of morality is found in right reason taken in its full scope. No one of the five aspects mentioned above is to be taken in isolation, but they must all be fitted together. Then we can know that reason is right. In the deliberation preceding an act we perceive the *dictate* of practical reason pointing out the right path, we check it against our *habitually* possessed code of rationally derived moral principles, we examine the principles and recognize that they express the logical consequence of the kind of *nature* we have, because the act we are contemplating will bring us to the attainment of the *end* to which our inner dynamism is driving us, and the end itself is seen by reason as not merely a good for us but as verifying in itself the *ideal* of the moral good.

If we limit ourselves to the proximate norm, this is perhaps as far as we can go. To see the ultimate guarantee of the goodness of human nature, of human reason, and of human ideals, we must pass from the proximate to the *ultimate* norm. We make this transition in the chapter on the eternal law. First we must make a more thorough investigation of human nature as seen by right reason.

HUMAN NATURE TAKEN COMPLETELY

We determine the useful or the pleasant good by noting its suitability to some partial aspect or particular craving of man. It may suit him in one way and harm him in another. But we are dealing here with the moral good, the befitting good, that must be good simply and without qualification.

Hence right reason must look to the whole man, to human nature taken adequately or completely.

1. *Human nature must be taken with all its parts.* These are man's essential parts, both metaphysical (animality and rationality) and physical (body and soul), as well as all the integral parts (members and faculties) that happen to be present in any individual man. Man is obliged to manage his complex nature and keep these parts working in harmony.

Man by nature is an animal and must live like an animal. He must take care of his body and minister to its needs. He must not ambition to live like an angel or disembodied spirit. Man's nature is such that he could not live in this way, and to try to do so would not befit him. Man's bodily needs are so vivid and insistent that there is little temptation in this direction, but it remains true that conduct suitable only to angelic nature is not suitable to human nature.

Man by nature is no mere animal, but a rational animal, and he must also live as a rational being. The life of a brute is not suitable to a man, who is expected to govern his conduct by intellect or reason. In man reason is the ruling faculty, exerting conscious control over the rest. The two parts of man, the lower and the higher, sense and reason, are to be kept in harmony, the lower faculties serving the higher; otherwise there is rebellion in the very nature of man. When a conflict arises, as happens often enough, between the lower and the higher, the higher faculties must be made to prevail. The lower faculties must receive what they need but be kept in their place. If reason is dethroned, the life of a mere animal takes the place of that of a rational animal, and the man remains a man in nature but becomes a beast in conduct.

2. *Human nature must be taken with all its relations.* There must be not only inner harmony between the parts and faculties that make up man himself, but also outer harmony between man and his surroundings. Man is not a solitary being but a part of the universe; he must fit himself into the total scheme of creation and occupy the place destined for him by the kind of nature he has. There are three essential relations and a number of accidental relations that may arise from circumstances or the fulfillment of certain conditions, such as marriage, parenthood, profession, employment, and the like. We need consider here the essential relations only, which make man:

(1) A created being, regarding God
(2) A social being, regarding his fellow man
(3) A possessive being, regarding the goods of the earth

Toward what is above man, human nature is *created* or contingent. It is dependent on God, the Necessary Being, the source of man's being. To arrogate absolute independence to himself is to refuse to accept his position as a creature, and thus to go against his nature, which is a created nature.

Toward beings on the same level, human nature is *social* or cooperative. Man is born into the society of the family and is made for companionship with his fellow man, on whom he is dependent to supply his needs and develop his abilities. Hence what promotes a well-functioning social life among men is good for man; what tends to disrupt human society and to sour this mutual helpfulness and cooperation is bad for man.

Toward things beneath man, human nature is *possessive* or proprietary. By his very nature man needs the use of material things: food, water, air, sunlight for the maintenance of life itself, and so many other less necessary goods for the development of his abilities and the living of a decent and cultured life, to which his rationality entitles him.

To sum up: That conduct is morally good which right reason shows to be befitting a rational animal, composed of soul and body, created by God, living with his fellow man, and supporting himself on the products of this earth. That conduct is morally evil which right reason shows to be unbefitting such a being. In any conflict between the rational and the animal appetites, the rational must prevail. In any conflict between the three essential relations, the relation to God comes first, to fellow man second, to the goods of this world third. This hierarchy is arranged according to the intrinsic worth and excellence of these two main parts of man and of these three orders of beings.

PROOF FOR THE NORM OF MORALITY

The foregoing was an exploratory investigation into the process of searching for and finding the norm of morality. We must now cast the results of our lengthy investigation into an argument, which may be stated as follows:

That by which we can discover what is morally good for man is, by definition, the norm of morality. But by the use of right reason examining human nature taken completely in all its parts and relations, we can discover the kind of activity which man ought to perform, which is therefore morally good. For a being cannot have a nature as the internal directing principle of its activity without being intended to act in accord with that nature and to maintain due order in all its parts and relations. And it cannot have a rational and free nature without being intended to direct the use of its freedom by the right use of its reason. Therefore right reason as applied to human nature taken completely in all its parts and relations is the norm of morality.

This argument shows us that man is no exception to the general rule, that every being must act according to its nature. But if man is no exception to the rule and we do not set up a norm of goodness for other beings, why do we do so for man? Because man is rational and free, whereas other beings in this world are not. Nonfree beings must act as their nature prescribes for them, and thus they necessarily fulfill their purpose in the universe. Man alone, being free, can act either according to his nature or against his nature. In all things the nature of the being is the norm of its activity. Since nonfree beings must necessarily act naturally, in them the norm is automatically applied and need not be definitely expressed. Since man ought to act naturally but can act unnaturally by abuse of his freedom, he needs rational formulation and conscious application of the norm of morality in his conduct.

PRACTICALITY OF THE NORM

How practical is such a norm? The foregoing argument proved that it is the true and correct norm of morality, but is it also a *proximate* norm capable of direct application to definite human acts? The following argument, since it does not show how rational human nature measures moral goodness, is not a substitute for the previous argument, is not a proof that human nature as judged by right reason is the norm of morality. But, presupposing the previous argument, it goes on to show the universal practical applicability of this norm.

A norm of morality, to be a truly practical and proximate one, must have the following characteristics:

1. *The norm must be such that from it the same rules of morality can be derived for all men.* By its nature a standard must be applicable to all the objects of a class. To say that each person has his own standard of conduct is the same as saying that there is no standard at all. Human nature has this first characteristic, for human nature is common to all men, and the rules derived from it by the exercise of right reason will be applicable to all human beings.

2. *The norm must be such that from it all the rules of morality can be derived.* Otherwise it would not be the complete norm, but it plus something else would be the norm. Therefore we take human nature completely with all its parts and relations, for this brings in everything that can concern a human act. Man, the doer of the act, is taken with all his parts, so that the act must be befitting to him as a whole, and the relations connect him with every possible object on which or toward which he can act, or that can in any way circumstance or condition the act. Human reason with its reflective power can embrace the totality of man's parts and relations.

3. *The norm must be immutable yet flexible enough to admit of varying applications according to circumstances.* If the norm is not immutable it is really no standard; yet it will be useless if it is not applicable to every possible circumstance of human conduct, for this is what it is supposed to measure. Hence the norm must be flexible but not elastic, like a tape measure which is fixed in length but can conform to any surface. Human nature has this characteristic, for it is immutable in essentials but accidentally variable, specifically the same but individually diversified, and human reason with its abstractive power can separate the essential from the accidental.

4. *The norm must be constantly present and manifest to all men.* Human acts entail responsibility and, if man could perform them without being able to find the norm of morality, he would be responsible for conduct whose morality he could not determine. He must therefore, whenever he is confronted with a rational choice, always be able to compare his conduct with the norm. But the only thing always present to a man in every conceivable circumstance is his own rational human nature. Wrecked on a desert island, he still has the norm of morality with him.

No other conceivable standard has these qualifications. If it were some external object distinct from man, it could be lost or left behind and might not be available when need for acting is present. If it were something internal to man but only accidental to him, it would not be present in all men, and those who lacked it would have no way of determining morality. If the norm were something essential to man but only a part of his essence, it would afford no guarantee that such conduct is suitable to the other parts of man's essence, and so would not measure human conduct as such. Therefore it must be the whole of man's essence or nature.

But the norm of morality is not only a standard or measure, but also a director and guide. Under the latter aspect it is especially designated as *right reason,* which is man's intellect capable of understanding human nature, of understanding it correctly, and of forming practical judgments that are objectively true concerning conduct befitting that nature. In this last function the concept of norm leads into that of law.

SUMMARY

A *norm of morality* is a standard to which we compare human acts to determine their goodness or badness. A *proximate* norm is immediately applicable to the acts; an *ultimate* norm guarantees the validity of the proximate norm.

The *moral sense theory* appeals to a faculty distinct from the intellect for judging right from wrong. There is no need for any such faculty; it would make moral conduct nonrational and thus unworthy of a rational human being.

Man distinguishes moral good and evil by his intellect or reason. Since reason can fall into error, it must be *right reason.* How do we know when reason is right? Reason itself must be the judge. Reason is right when it is rationally exercised, consistent with itself, faithful to its own law. Right reason is a dictate of practical reason, a habit of moral principles, rational human nature, direction to rational ends, a rationally developed moral ideal. As a norm right reason is all these together.

Right reason is concerned with human nature taken completely in all its parts and relations.

Parts	Metaphysical: animality and rationality
	Physical: body and soul
	Integral: members and faculties

Relations	Created: toward God
	Social: toward fellow man
	Possessive: toward the goods of the earth

Everything is intended to act according to its nature, since a nature is but the essence of a thing as the inner directing principle of its activity.

Reason is part of a rational nature and is the directing principle of free beings. Reason can criticize itself and know when it is right. Hence *right reason examining human nature taken completely in all its parts and relations* is the norm of morality.

This is a proximate and practical norm, for nothing else could fulfill these functions essential to a norm:

(1) It gives the same rules of morality to all men
(2) It gives all the rules of morality to each man
(3) It is immutable yet applicable to all cases
(4) It is always present and manifest to all men

READINGS

1. The problem of this chapter was not expressly formulated by ancient and medieval writers, but by reading between the lines we can see what norm of morality they actually took. The view expressed here is but a development of the concepts of *reason* and *nature* as they run throughout the whole Aristotelian-Thomistic philosophy. Hints are found in the *Summa Theologica*, I-II, q. 19, aa. 3-4; q. 21, a. 1; q. 59, a. 5; q. 71, aa. 1 and 2. Also in the *Summa Contra Gentiles*, bk. III, ch. 129 (this latter passage is not found in the *Basic Writings*). Thomists tend to emphasize *right reason*, Suarezians *human nature*, but neither view is wholly exclusive of the other.

2. Cronin, *Science of Ethics*, vol. I, ch. V. At first reading this author may seem to contradict the view we have expressed, but more careful reading should show substantial agreement. His secondary criteria of morality are not important for our purpose.

3. Leibell, *Readings in Ethics*, pp. 155-162, a selection translated from Victor Cathrein's *Philosophia Moralis*.

4. Ward, *Values and Reality*, ch. XI; also, *Christian Ethics*, ch. 6-8.

5. Selections from the school of British Moralists can be found in convenient form in Rand's *Classical Moralists*, Clark and Smith's *Readings in Ethics*, Melden's *Ethical Theories*. Criticism of these views is found in Cronin's *Science of Ethics*, vol. I, ch. XIV and XV.

CHAPTER 9

MORAL

DETERMINANTS

PROBLEM

By applying the proximate norm of morality we can tell whether a certain kind of human act is morally good, bad, or indifferent. If right reason shows that it agrees with human nature taken completely in all its parts and relations, the act is good; if right reason shows that it disagrees, the act is bad; if according to right reason it neither agrees nor positively disagrees but is neutral, this kind of act, abstractly considered, is morally indifferent.

But how are we to apply this norm to concrete cases? Just in what way and how far does the act agree or disagree with the norm? What must we look for in the act to see whether it is in agreement or disagreement? To answer, we must break down the human act into its elements in a way differing from our previous analysis. We now seek those elements which can be the sources of harmony or conflict between the act and the norm.

We may consider the act itself in its own very nature as an act, or we may consider the circumstances in which the act is performed. Among the circumstances we may single out one, the motive or intention of the agent, as of such importance as to be put in a class by itself. Two men may do the same thing but from different motives, or different things from the same motive, or the same thing from the same motive but in different circumstances. In each case the act can have a different morality because of a different combination of these three elements.

The accepted terminology since St. Thomas' time is to call these three sources, founts, or determinants of morality the *object,* the *end,* and the *circumstances.** But the terms *object* and *end* are here given such a precise technical meaning as to be too misleading in modern speech. By *object*

Summa Theologica, I-II, q. 18, aa. 2-7.

101

is meant the object of the will-act, that act which the will chooses to perform, and this is nothing else but the act itself which is deliberately willed. By *end* is meant the purpose for which the act is willed, and this may mean either the purpose the act is naturally fitted to achieve *(finis operis)* or the purpose the agent personally wishes to accomplish by willing that act *(finis operantis);* here the emphasis is almost entirely on the latter meaning. By *circumstances* are meant the various accidental surroundings of the act, and on these there is no ambiguity. In the interest of clarity we shall call these three sources of morality:

(1) The act itself, or what a man does
(2) The motive, or why he does it
(3) The circumstances, or how, where, when, etc., he does it

THE ACT ITSELF

Morality resides in the will, in the will's consent to what is presented to it as morally good or evil. But we cannot just *will;* we must will *something,* to do or omit some *act,* which is therefore (in St. Thomas' language) the *object* of the will's consent. Since we have proved that there are acts good or bad of their own very nature independently of any command or prohibition, it is evident that the consent of the will derives its morality first and foremost from the kind of act the will consents to. This is *what* the will wills; if the act willed is bad of its very nature, the willing of it must be bad; if the act willed is good of its very nature, and if there is nothing else about it to render it evil, the willing of it must be good. This point is so obvious that it hardly needs expression.

We must call attention to the fact that ethics studies acts not in the physical but in the *moral* order. The existence of verbs in any language shows that acts can be classified. No two performances of the act are exactly alike, but they are sufficiently so to afford a basis for a universal concept. We can make a classification in the physical order, regarding only the muscles used and the material objects displaced, as when we speak of sitting, standing, walking, talking, grasping, hitting, throwing. Such acts are morally indifferent in their nature; whatever morality they have must come from the motive and circumstances. We can also make a classification in the moral order by putting certain moral characteristics in our definition. When we speak of hating, envying, murdering, stealing, lying, or slandering, moral evil enters into the very definition of the concepts indicated by the words and thus belongs to the essence of the acts described. Verbs indicative of good acts, such as praying, loving, honoring, helping, protecting, or benefiting, do not always have such a clear moral connotation, but in some contexts it is quite evident. Acts which thus have morality included in their definition are good or bad of their very nature.

What may seem to be mere circumstances in the physical order can belong to the very essence of the act in the moral order. We distinguish seizure and theft, killing and murder, speaking and lying. The first of each pair indicates only the physical act, which may be right or wrong; the second means an act which is morally wrong in its nature. Theft is not mere seizure, but the seizure of another's property against his reasonable will; murder is not mere killing, but the direct killing of an innocent person; lying is not mere speaking but the saying of what one knows to be untrue. At first sight these added qualifications may seem to be mere circumstances, whether what I take is mine or another's property, whether the man I kill has lost his right to life or not, whether the words I utter express my thought or contradict it. But in the moral order these points are essential. The moral order is the order of *willing*, and some features cannot be detached from the act willed. You cannot will merely to kill but must will to kill some definite person; you cannot will merely to take but must will to take some definite thing; you cannot will merely to say but must will to say some definite words. So from the moral standpoint the innocence of the victim killed, the ownership of the goods taken, the truth of the words said are not accidental or circumstantial but essential. They do not merely add to a morality already present, but give the act its first moral quality and go to make up the very essence of the act in the moral order.

Look more closely at the case of theft. For an act to be theft (we are not proving this here but only taking it as an example), four elements are required and sufficient:

(1) That the act be an act of taking
(2) That the thing taken be another's property
(3) That the owner be unwilling to let me have it
(4) That his unwillingness be reasonable

Omit any of these four components and the act is not theft, for it is not theft to covet another's goods without taking them, or to take my own goods, or to borrow another's with his leave, or to deprive a madman of his own weapons. Add any further element and the act is more than theft: if we add that it is done by personal violence or fear, the act becomes robbery, and if it is also committed on the high seas, piracy; if we add that it is done by forceful entry into a dwelling, the act becomes housebreaking, and if this occurs at night, burglary. Such additions may or may not change the moral species of the act, as will be seen in our discussion on circumstances, but they are not necessary that theft be theft.

THE MOTIVE

A human act gets its first morality from the nature of the act the agent wills to do. Sometimes a man has no further reason for acting than the act itself, as in an act of loving God or of blasphemy. In this case the act done and the motive for doing it coincide. But more often a man uses his act as a means to something further, to some desired end or purpose not identical with the act itself, but either its natural outcome (walking for exercise, eating for nourishment, reading for entertainment) or some added personal aim of his own (walking to work, eating for sociability, reading to become a lawyer). In these cases, especially in the latter group, the act and the motive are different.

The *motive* is that which the agent has in mind when he acts, that which he consciously sets before himself to achieve by his act. It is called by many names: end, purpose, intent, intention, aim, goal, objective, even object (one reason why we avoided this term previously), but perhaps the least ambiguous in the present context is *motive*, which stresses the influence it has on the will in moving the agent to act.

In a murder the police look for the motive of the crime, knowing that one hardly ever kills for killing's sake, but to get revenge, to remove a rival, to seize the victim's money, to be rid of a blackmailer. The proverb, "no one is a liar for nothing," recognizes the need of a motive in lying, to get out of a difficulty or obtain an advantage. The influence this motive can have on the morality of the act prompted by it should be apparent.

When a man directs his act to some consciously intended purpose, he deliberately wills this purpose together with the act, and both are voluntary. The act itself is used as the means to accomplish this end. When a person deliberately uses a means to an end, in the one same act he wills both the use of the means and the attainment of the end. As the act itself can be morally good, bad, or indifferent, so can the end to which it is directed by the will of the agent. Therefore, in addition to the morality which the act has by its own nature, the act also derives morality from the motive with which it is performed.

The motive may give an indifferent act its first moral quality, either good or bad; thus one who borrows money with the firm intention of never returning it is not a borrower but a thief; one who refuses to testify in court because he wants his innocent enemy to be convicted turns his negative act of silence into one of hatred and injustice. The motive may strengthen or weaken in degree the same species of morality the act already has; thus one who falsifies his age to get out of military duty does not lie merely about his age but about his availability to serve his country; a clerk who pilfers a little money each day in order to build up to a predetermined sum cannot excuse himself by the smallness of each single theft. The motive may give to an already specified moral act quite a new species of morality; thus one who gives money to the poor for the sole purpose of being praised as a philanthropist turns his act of kindness into one of vanity, one who steals money to have the means of seducing his neighbor's wife is, as Aristotle* observed, more of an adulterer than a thief.

THE CIRCUMSTANCES

The circumstances are the various surroundings of the act, including everything affecting the act without belonging to its essence, except the

---

Nicomachean Ethics, bk. V., ch. 2, 1130a 24; as quoted by St. Thomas, *Summa Theologica,* I-II, q. 18, a. 6.

motive just discussed. The motive, as we said, is really a circumstance but was separated out for special treatment; we mean here all the other circumstances. A convenient way of listing the circumstances is to ask the familiar questions: *who? where? when? how? to whom? by what means? how often?* and the like. But not *what?* or *why?* since these ask for the act itself and its motive.

Some circumstances have nothing to do with morality: whether one poisons with strychnine or cyanide, slanders in English or French, steals with his right or left hand. But other circumstances do affect morality: whether one robs a rich or a poor man, murders a stranger or a friend or a parent, commits sin with a married or unmarried person, damages another's character in private or in public, charges exorbitant prices for food in normal times or when people are starving. These latter circumstances are the only kind we consider.

Some circumstances so affect the act as to make it a different *kind* of act from the moral standpoint, to put it into a different moral *species*. Dishonor to one's parents adds to insult a breach of filial piety. Intimate relations between persons married but not to each other are sins of injustice as well as of unchastity. Perjury in a law court is not merely lying but also a violation of religion and justice. Circumstances which thus change the species of the act are called *specifying* circumstances.

Other circumstances only change the *degree* of goodness or badness in the act while leaving it in the same moral species. Such circumstances exist in good acts but have no particular name, while in bad acts they are called *aggravating* or *extenuating* according as they increase or lessen the guilt of the wrongdoer. It is still theft whether one steals a large or a small sum of money, it is still drunkenness whether one has had five or fifteen too many, it is still slander whether one has partly or wholly ruined another's reputation. Such differences, though only in degree and not in kind, can be of the utmost importance.

It is evident that a human act can have its morality colored by the circumstances in which it is done. No act can be done in the abstract; every act actually performed is surrounded by a number of concrete circumstances involving persons, quantity, quality, place, time, manner, means, frequency, and relations of all sorts. These circumstances can be foreseen and willed in the willing of the act. In this event, they contribute to the morality of the act, either giving it a new moral species or a new degree within the species.

The fact that these are called circumstances should not lead us to think that they are negligible or unimportant. Sometimes they are made more of than the essence of the act and to them the will is chiefly directed. There are men who will lie but not to their mother, men who will steal but not from their friends, men who will kill but not a baby. Many otherwise indifferent acts receive their whole morality from circumstances, because they are done at the right or wrong time, in the right or wrong place, by the right or wrong means, in the right or wrong manner.

PRACTICAL APPLICATION

To be morally good a human act must agree with the norm of morality on all three counts: in its nature, its motive, and its circumstances. Disconformity in any one of them makes the act morally wrong. Just as to be physically healthy one must have all one's organs functioning rightly, and if only one organ is deranged the person is unwell, so to be morally healthy no element of immorality must be present in any of one's acts.

An act that is *bad in itself* cannot become good or indifferent by a good motive or good circumstances, and much less by indifferent ones. Nothing can change its intrinsically evil nature. No person is ever allowed voluntarily to will that kind of act in any circumstances or for any motive. That is why we must reject the false principle, "the end justifies the means." Though a good end renders good the use of indifferent means, a good end cannot justify the use of evil means. We are never allowed to do evil that good may come of it. A good motive and good circumstances may somewhat lessen the badness of the act, but it remains bad and forbidden. Each bad motive or circumstance added to an intrinsically bad act makes it worse.

An act that is *good in itself* becomes better by each good motive and good circumstance added to it. But any gravely bad motive or circumstance is sufficient to render the act wholly and gravely bad, no matter how good it may otherwise seem. If there is only one motive and it is slightly bad, it will make the whole act slightly bad, for the whole act is directed to this one end only. But when there are several motives or circumstances, a slightly bad motive or circumstance of minor importance will not render the act wholly bad, but only less good, for the act retains its natural goodness in a somewhat tarnished form. Thus a man may give alms out of benevolence touched with vanity, may obey legitimate superiors but discourteously, may work at his job but lazily or negligently, may tell the truth but with a little exaggeration. Such defects, commonly called *imperfections,* even though intended, cannot wholly ruin an otherwise good act. Nor can such defects so pile up as to render an intrinsically good act morally indifferent, for they either do or do not destroy the act's natural goodness; if they do, the act becomes bad; if they do not, it remains good.

An act that is *indifferent in itself,* since it has no moral quality of its own, must derive all its moral goodness or badness from the motive and circumstances. These must all be good or at least indifferent if the act is to be morally acceptable. Simply speaking, any bad motive or circumstance will make an indifferent act morally wrong. But this matter can get quite complicated. How shall we judge cases in which an indifferent act is surrounded by a mixture of good and bad motives or good and bad circumstances? When the act itself is indifferent, and each motive or circumstance can be separately willed, it is easier to consider such acts as virtually multiple, that is, as compounded of a good and a bad act. Here we really have two moral acts and can judge each on its own merits. A lawyer in defending an innocent man may win his case by bribing the jury; the act of vindicating justice for his client is good, but the act of violating justice by bribery is evil. The two parts of the total act do not necessarily imply each other and can be separately willed, for the case might be won without bribery, and bribery can be used for other purposes. However, if this be considered one whole act, it must be judged evil.

PRINCIPLE OF DOUBLE EFFECT

Often the mixture of good and evil occurs not so much in the act and its immediate surroundings as in the consequences that follow from it. In our discussion on voluntariness we saw that unintended but foreseen consequences are voluntary, though only indirectly so (voluntary in cause). How responsible are we for them? Are we obliged to make sure that every single consequence of each of our acts will be morally good, or at least not bad? If so, the scope of human activity becomes so limited as to make life unlivable. One who accepts a job when jobs are scarce cuts someone else out of a livelihood, a doctor who tends the sick during a plague exposes himself to catching the disease, a lawyer who must present this bit of evidence to win his case may put an innocent person under suspicion, a teacher who gives a competent examination knows that some will probably fail. We seem to be caught on the horns of a dilemma: either human life cannot be lived as it actually is, or we are compelled to do evil and to do it voluntarily.

We find the solution to the dilemma in the principle of the *indirect voluntary,* commonly known as the principle of *double effect,* one of the most useful ethical principles and one that must be thoroughly mastered. It is based on the fact that evil must never be *voluntary in itself,* must never be willed either as end or as means, for then it is the direct object of the will-act and necessarily renders the act evil. Nor may evil ever be *voluntary in cause,* as a foreseen but unwanted consequence, unless it can somehow be reduced to an incidental and unavoidable by-product in the achievement of some good the person is rightfully seeking.

Though I am never allowed to will evil, I am not always bound to prevent the existence of evil. Just as I may tolerate the existence of evils in the world at large, since I could not cure them without bringing other evils on myself or my neighbor, so I may sometimes tolerate evil consequences from my own actions, if to abstain from such actions would bring a proportionate evil on myself or others. Sometimes I cannot will a good without at the same time permitting the existence of an evil which in the very nature of things is inseparably bound up with the good I will. But I must not do so indiscriminately. Sometimes I am bound to prevent evil, and in these cases it would be wrong for me to permit it. How can we determine these cases?

The *principle of double effect* says that it is morally allowable to perform an act that has a bad effect under the following conditions:

1. *The act to be done must be good in itself or at least indifferent.* This is evident, for if the act is evil of its very *nature,* nothing can make it good or indifferent. Evil would be chosen directly, either as an end or as a means to an end, and there could be no question of merely permitting or tolerating it.

2. *The good intended must not be obtained by means of the evil effect.* The evil must be only an incidental by-product and not an actual factor in the accomplishment of the good. If the act has two effects, one good and the other bad, the good effect must not be accomplished by means of the bad, for then the evil would be directly voluntary as a means. Since the willing of the end implies the willing of the means, evil means pertain to the very *nature* of the act. We may never do evil in order that good may come of it. A good end does not justify the use of bad means. Hence the good effect must follow as immediately and directly from the original act as the evil effect. It is sometimes said that the evil must not come before the good, but this may be misunderstood; it is not a question of time but of causality; the good must not come *through* or *by means of* the evil.

3. *The evil effect must not be intended for itself but only permitted.* The bad effect may be of its own nature merely a by-product of the act performed, but if the agent wants this bad effect he makes it directly voluntary by willing it. The act then becomes evil in its *motive*. An evil intention it not to be presumed without evidence.

4. *There must be a proportionately grave reason for permitting the evil effect.* Though we are not always obliged to prevent evil, we are obliged to prevent a serious evil by a small sacrifice of our own good. Hence some proportion between the good and evil is required, and if it is lacking the act becomes evil by reason of its *circumstances*. What that proportion should be is often difficult to determine in practice, and properly belongs to applied ethics. For the present we can say that the good and the evil should be at least nearly equivalent. If the good is slight and the evil great, the evil can hardly be called incidental. Also, if there is any other way of getting the good effect without the bad effect, this other way must be taken; otherwise there is no good reason for permitting the evil.

Note that the act is not morally allowable unless all four conditions are fulfilled. If any one of them is not satisfied, even though the other three are, the act is morally wrong. Note also that the bad effect spoken of here is a physical evil of some kind. The double effect principle expresses the conditions under which it is not morally evil to permit a physical evil to happen.

An example will help to illustrate the application of the principle. A passer-by dashes into a burning building to save a child trapped there, though he may be severely burned and even lose his life. We recognize this as a heroic deed, but its justification is found in the principle of double effect:

1. The act itself apart from its consequences is merely an act of entering a building. This is surely an indifferent act and quite allowable.

2. It has two effects: one good (saving the child) and the other bad (burning or even death to the rescuer). But he does not save the child by means of dying or getting burned, but by means of reaching the child and carrying it or throwing it to safety. If he can do this without harm to himself, so much the better. The good effect is accomplished rather in spite of than by means of the bad effect, which is thus made only an incidental accompaniment in the rescue of the child.

3. If the rescuer were using this chance as an excuse for suicide, he would spoil the act by this bad intention, but there is no need for presuming any such intention.

4. There is a sufficient proportion: a life for a life. To enter a burning building to rescue some trifling possession could not be morally justified.

A few more cases will show how one or another of these four conditions can be violated:

1. An employee embezzles money to aid his sick child, hoping to pay it back later. Here the act itself of embezzlement (taking money belonging to another and falsifying the accounts) is not good or indifferent but wrong of its very nature, and cannot be justified by any good intentions or good effects which might follow. He must try to raise the money in some other way. The first condition is violated, and the evil is *voluntary in itself*.

2. A man living with an alcoholic rich uncle stocks the house with liquor, knowing that he will inherit a fortune when the uncle has drunk himself to death. The act of stocking the house with liquor is indifferent in itself. It has two effects, bad for the uncle by occasioning his death, good for the heir by bringing him his inheritance sooner. But the money cannot be inherited except through the uncle's death. The good effect (obtaining the money sooner) is accomplished by means of the bad effect (the uncle's death), and thus the second condition is violated.

3. A political boss distributes money to the poor to get them to vote for an unworthy candidate. Here the giving of money to the poor is a good act. The good effect (relieving poverty) is not accomplished by means of the bad effect (electing an unworthy candidate), but rather the other way round, the bad effect through the good. But the third condition is violated, because the evil is directly intended as an end. The main intention is to elect the unworthy candidate; it does not even need to be the main intention so long as it is really intended.

4. The owner of a private plane gets his pilot to fly him through exceedingly dangerous weather to complete a business deal that will net him a small profit. To fly a plane is an indifferent act; the danger has to do with the possible effect rather than with the act itself. The good effect (completing the business deal) is not obtained by means of the bad effect (possible loss of life). The bad effect is not intended for its own sake, for neither wants to die. But the fourth condition can easily be violated here, for there does not seem to be a sufficient proportion between the risk to their lives and the rather slight financial advantage to be gained. There is always a risk in flying and financial advantage can be great enough to justify it, but the present case supposes an excessive risk.

Though the above examples show how the principle of double effect can be violated, many of the ordinary actions of life find their justification in a correct application of the principle. Thus people may take dangerous occupations to earn a livelihood, firemen and policemen can risk their lives to save others, a surgeon can operate even though he may cause pain, a man can vindicate his honor even though other people's reputations suffer from his disclosures, a just war is allowable despite the great suffering imposed on people of both sides. If a man were obliged to avoid every deed to which evil could be incidental, he could do so little he might as well stop living.

EXISTENCE OF MORALLY INDIFFERENT ACTS

Most writers who discuss this problem agree with St. Thomas that, though a human act considered in the abstract can be morally indifferent, it cannot be so when considered individually in the concrete, and so every human act actually performed by a definite individual is either morally good or morally bad. St. Thomas' argument is clearest in his own words:

> It sometimes happens that an act is indifferent in its species, which is yet good or evil, considered in the individual. . . . And every individual act must needs have some circumstance that makes it good or evil, at least in respect of the intention of the end. For since it belongs to the reason to direct, if an act that proceeds from deliberate reason be not directed to the due end, it is, by that fact alone, repugnant to reason, and has the character of evil. But if it be directed to a due end, it is in accord with the order of reason, and hence it has the character of good. Now it must needs be either directed or not directed to a due end. Consequently, every human act that proceeds from deliberate reason, if it be considered in the individual, must be good or evil.
>
> If, however, it does not proceed from deliberate reason, but from some act of the imagination, as when a man strokes his beard, or moves his hand or foot, such an act, properly speaking, is not moral or human, since an act has the character of being moral or human from the reason. Hence it will be indifferent, as standing outside the genus of moral acts.*

This opinion is opposed by Duns Scotus and his followers. The controversy stems from the difference between the intellectualist and the voluntarist attitude. Voluntarists like Scotus hold that the will's freedom is so unrestricted as not to be determined even by the good as such; hence an indifferent act does not become good unless it is explicitly referred by an act of our will to our last end. God has put on us no obligation of referring every single act to our last end; therefore, if it is not so referred and yet is not evil from any other source, it will remain indifferent. Thus individual acts can be morally indifferent. Intellectualists like St. Thomas, on the other hand, hold that the will is free in regard to particular goods but is necessitated by the good as such. By the very nature of the human will,

---

*Summa Theologica, I-II, q. 18, a. 9.

which must necessarily seek the good as such, all man's acts are implicitly directed to his last end, unless they are incompatible with it or deliberately directed elsewhere. This implicit direction to the last end is sufficient to render these acts morally good.* So individual acts cannot be morally indifferent; those that are not deliberately evil are good. This latter view accords with the position we have consistently taken.

INTERNAL AND EXTERNAL ACT

Would it be correct to say with Abelard† that morality is found wholly in the intention, or with Kant‡ that morality consists solely in a good will, so that the external physical act is quite outside the scope of morals? Such statements can be true only in the sense that without intention and will no act can be moral or immoral, for a voluntary act requires knowledge and consent. But, as we have seen, there are some acts that one is never allowed to intend or will, and there are circumstances in which we are not allowed to intend or will an otherwise good act. Hence morality is not entirely dependent on our good intentions or good will.

Nor is it true that the external act is quite outside the scope of morals. Morality does reside primarily in the internal act of the will. The external act commanded by the will becomes morally good or bad only by sharing in the morality of the internal act. Though the internal and external acts are physically distinct, being done by different faculties and even at different times, they form *one moral whole*. Thus the external act acquires the same moral character as the internal act.

Does the external act add any goodness or badness to the internal act? Not essentially, for the external act, as we said, derives all its goodness or badness from the internal act. But it may do so accidentally, by being an occasion for the continuation, intensification, or repetition of the internal act. An internal resolve tends to grow pale unless its external execution is at least begun. When a man has started acting, he feels that he has committed himself, burnt his bridges behind him, and must go through with it. An act externally completed invites repetition and may be the start of a habit, which would never grow into being if the first act had remained a mere internal resolve.

Lack of opportunity to carry out a fully made resolve does not affect its moral character. One who has made up his mind to murder or steal, but cannot bring off the crime successfully, may escape civil punishment, but not moral guilt. One who risks his life to rescue a drowning man, only to bring ashore a corpse, will receive the full merit of his heroic deed, even though it was fruitless. Morality is not a matter of accident but of deliberate will.

Summa Theologica, I-II, q. 1, a. 6.
†Peter Abelard, *Ethica seu Scito Te Ipsum* (Ethics or Know Thyself). So at least he seems to say in ch. 7 and 11; but he modifies his statements in ch. 12 and 13.
‡Kant, *Foundations of the Metaphysics of Morals*, section II. Kant's views are discussed more thoroughly later.

CONCLUSION

The various strands of this seemingly scattered but very practical chapter tie together to form the ethical position opposed both to *moral subjectivism,* the theory that it matters little what you do so long as you mean well, and to *moral externalism,* the theory that what you do alone counts and your intentions go for nought. There are some things you cannot do and mean well. Let us give to subjective morality its due and recognize that a man is responsible for his action as it seemed to him at the moment when he willed it. On this he has the judgment of his own conscience. But when he knows that the action is of an evil kind by its own nature or that it will be rendered evil by objective circumstances, he cannot by the simple use of a good motive purify that act of its evil and render it innocent. Anything could be justified on such terms. Since he cannot change the act, what he has to do is to restrain his will and refuse to do the known evil. On the other hand, he is not to be held responsible for every consequence that follows from his act, even when it is foreseen, so long as it is merely an unavoidable by-product in the accomplishment of a good he is allowed to will.

SUMMARY

To apply the norm of morality to concrete cases, we must find out what there is in the act that can bring it into agreement or disagreement with the norm. We find three such sources or determinants of morality: the act itself, the motive, and the circumstances.

The *act itself* is simply what the agent wills, considering it not in the physical but in the moral order. We have proved that there are acts of their very nature good or evil, and the willing of them will accordingly be good or evil.

The *motive* or intention is what the agent personally wishes to achieve by the act over and above what the act naturally tends to. The motive, being consciously willed, contributes to the morality of the act, sometimes giving it a new kind of morality.

The *circumstances* are the accidental surroundings of the act. Some have no effect on morality; others have an effect, changing the act either in kind or in degree. Circumstances can be foreseen, and if so are willed in the willing of the act, thus contributing to its morality.

An act *bad in itself* cannot be made good or indifferent by motives or circumstances, though the degree of badness may be somewhat modified. An act *good in itself* is ruined by any gravely bad motive or circumstance; slightly bad ones weaken the act's goodness but do not destroy it. An act *indifferent in itself* gets all its morality from motives and circumstances; if any one of them is bad, the rest being indifferent, the act becomes bad; if some are good and others bad, it may be possible to resolve the physical act into two moral acts.

To try to avoid every act that has any bad effect would make life impossible. We are never allowed to will evil but are not always bound to prevent the existence of evil.

The *principle of double effect* has four conditions:

(1) The act must be good or indifferent in itself
(2) The good must not be obtained by means of the evil
(3) The evil must not be intended in itself
(4) There must be a sufficient proportion

All four conditions must be fulfilled. Violation of any one makes the evil directly willed, not merely permitted as an incidental by-product.

St. Thomas holds that there can be no indifferent act in the concrete, for it either is or is not directed, at least implicitly, to one's last end; if it is not bad, it is good. The Scotists disagree with this opinion.

Morality resides in the internal act of the will, which need not be carried out into external action; but, if it is, the internal act communicates its morality to the external act, for both form one moral whole. The internal act can be only accidentally affected by the external act.

READINGS

1. St. Thomas, *Summa Theologica*, I-II, q. 18 is the source for the material of the present chapter. Read also q. 19, aa. 1, 2, 7, 8, and q. 20. We have already called attention to the difference between St. Thomas' terminology and that used here. One of the first express uses of the double effect principle is found in St. Thomas, II-II, q. 64, a. 7, where he deals with self-defense.
2. Cronin, *Science of Ethics,* vol. I, pp. 97-104. This is reprinted in Leibell's *Readings in Ethics,* pp. 165-171.
3. Farrell, *Companion to the Summa,* vol. II, ch. IV.
4. Rickaby, *Moral Philosophy,* pp. 31-41. Rickaby speaks of the end in view, the means taken, and the circumstances; by "end in view" he refers to the motive, by "means taken" to the act itself. This is his way of clearing up the ambiguity in the terms *object, end,* and *circumstances.*
5. Leibell, *Readings in Ethics,* pp. 193-207, on whether the end justifies the means.

LAW

PROBLEM

The norm of morality affords us a standard to which our acts must conform to be moral. But the mere fact that a norm exists does not impose any obligation to use it. The norm enables me to find out whether my conduct is moral or not, but it does not of itself oblige me to make my conduct moral; just as a yardstick will enable me to find out whether the ditch I dug is three feet wide, but did not oblige me to dig it three feet wide.

Is there anything which *obliges* us to conform our conduct to the norm of morality? This is the problem of the existence of law, for *law* is the name given to that which imposes such an obligation. Law accounts for *oughtness*. Without law we have but an acknowledged relationship of means to end, what Kant called a *hypothetical imperative:* If you wish to be moral, the norm of morality shows you how to attain this wish. Should one say, "I am not interested in being moral," the norm of morality as a mere standard has nothing further to say; even as a guide it merely directs. But here *law* comes in to impose an absolute obligation, a *categorical imperative:* You have to be moral, whether you like it or not, and therefore you have to make your acts conform to the norm of morality.

In this chapter we do not prove the right of law to exist and to command us, but merely examine the meaning and implications of the term:

(1) What is a law?
(2) What is a moral law?
(3) How can one be under a law and remain free?
(4) Is the universe irrational or governed by law?
(5) What are the main kinds of law?

MEANING OF LAW

We do not deal here with laws in an improper or figurative sense. These are mere formulas expressing some sort of observed uniformity, such as the periodic law in chemistry, the law of diminishing returns in economics, or Grimm's law in philology; or they may express mere social customs, such as the laws of etiquette, parliamentary law, the laws of diplomatic protocol, which are the accepted procedures among modern civilized peoples, but might not prevail in other times and cultures.

Law in the proper sense is a rule and measure of acts directing them to their proper ends. It imposes some kind of necessity on the beings it directs. It may be of two kinds:

(1) Physical law, imposing physical necessity, or
(2) Moral law, imposing moral necessity

Physical law directs *nonfree* beings to uniform action toward their ends by an inner necessity of their nature. Though laws of physics, chemistry, biology, and allied sciences may be considered as mere formulas expressing how bodies are observed to act, we recognize that this observed uniformity does not happen accidentally. It is the very nature of the bodies and the structure of the universe that necessitates them to act as they do. This necessitation identified with the very nature of things and determining for them their mode of activity is what we call physical law. It is obvious that nonfree beings cannot rebel against their own very nature or essence, and that disobedience to physical law is impossible. Not so with moral law.

Moral law directs *free* beings to act toward their ends by imposing obligation on the free will. This obligation or duty or oughtness is called moral necessity. Since it is imposed on free beings, it cannot be physically compelling, but it is no less peremptory or demanding than physical law, since free beings must reach their ends just as thoroughly as nonfree beings. Hence moral laws *can* be broken by the beings bound by them, but they *ought not* to be broken, and moral necessity means precisely this: that they *ought not* to be broken. All other acts are regulated by physical law, but *human acts* are governed by moral law.

DEFINITION OF LAW

Law in its strictest sense means moral law. St. Thomas gives us the classical definition of it:

> "Law is nothing else than an ordinance of reason for the common good, promulgated by him who has the care of the community."*

An ordinance. This distinguishes a law from a mere counsel, a piece of advice, a suggestion put forth to make things easier, but without any real binding force. An ordinance is an order, a command, a mandate, imposing obligation or moral necessity. It is the imposition of the superior's will on the will of the inferior, and must be expressed in a mandatory or imperative form.

Summa Theologica, I-II, q. 90, a. 4.

Of reason. Law, though imposed by the superior's will, is formulated by his intellect as the planning and directing faculty. As directing beings to their ends, law must be no arbitrary whim but a dictate of right reason; it must be reasonable. To be reasonable a law should be *consistent,* both with itself and with other laws, for no one can keep contradictory obligations; *just,* respecting existing rights guaranteed by higher laws and distributing burdens equitably; *observable,* for no one can do the impossible or be reasonably expected to do what is too harsh and difficult; *enforceable,* otherwise only the good will keep the law and the wicked, who need restraint, will go free; *useful,* for a law is a means to an end and needless restriction of liberty serves no purpose.

For the common good. Thus a law differs from a command, order, precept, or injunction laid on an individual person. The latter may bind a person quite as strongly as a law, for a son must obey his father no less than a citizen must obey the state, but the two have different functions. A law looks always to the common good, the benefit of the community as a whole, not to private or personal good. A law is usually territorial, binding all in a certain region and only when they are in it, whereas personal orders follow the person everywhere. A law is at least relatively permanent, for it is a rule of action and rules are not made for single acts. A law is always from public authority, lasts until repealed, and may bind succeeding generations, but personal orders cease with the death or removal from office of the one who gave them.

Promulgated. Promulgation is making the law known to those whom it binds. Certainly a law is useless if those expected to obey it do not know of its existence. Proper promulgation does not require the superior to make sure that each and every subject knows the law, but it must be published in such a way that they can know it without too much difficulty. The manner of promulgation will depend on the nature of the law, the customs of the people, and on circumstances generally. Once promulgated, a law binds objectively though individuals be unaware of it; they can be excused subjectively through invincible ignorance. The civil law will not usually accept the excuse of ignorance, for there is no way of telling whether the person is lying.

By him who has the care of the community. A law must be authoritative. It must come from a lawgiver or legislator having jurisdiction. The lawgiver may be a physical person, which is a single individual, or a moral person, which is a body or board passing laws by joint action. Jurisdiction is the right to impose or administer a law; in a secondary sense it sometimes means the territory or sphere within which a superior may legitimately act. Jurisdiction pertains to the authority of a legitimate superior. It is evident that not anyone who pleases can pass a law, but something must set the lawgiver off from the rest and give him the right to command; this is his authority.

Thus we see that a law must be mandatory, reasonable, for the common good, promulgated, and authoritative. If any of these characteristics be lacking, an alleged law is not a genuine law and cannot impose moral obligation.

LAW AND FREEDOM

Freedom in its broadest sense means absence of bonds, ties, or restraints. Law is said to *bind* those subject to it, and whoever is bound finds his freedom curtailed to some extent. But not all freedom is necessarily good; in its broadest meaning the word covers a vicious license as well as true liberty. The purpose of law is to eliminate the first and promote the second. How does it produce this effect? One can be bound by various kinds of bonds and those imposed by law are of a special nature. There are three kinds of freedom corresponding to three kinds of bonds:

1. When we think of bonds there immediately come to mind such things as chains, ropes, bars, prison walls. The one bound is subjected to force, violence, coercion, applied from outside him. Such bonds impose *external physical necessity,* which compels or restrains bodily actions only and cannot touch the inner act of the will. Freedom from such external compulsion is called freedom of *spontaneity*. In this sense a man turned out of prison is set *free,* an uncaged animal roams about *freely.*

2. Less obvious but more rigorous bonds are imposed by the inner determination of a being's own nature. A being lacking free will is utterly subject to its own natural tendencies and instincts, and must act in the way its nature prescribes for it. The nature of a being imposes on it *internal physical necessity;* this is the domain of the physical laws, which are not the kind of laws we are dealing with in ethics. Freedom from such inner determination of one's nature is called freedom of *choice* or *free will,* which is the prerogative of a rational being. It is in this sense that we speak of a human act as being done voluntarily and *freely.*

3. In contrast to the two kinds of physical bonds, outer and inner, mentioned above, there are also moral bonds, which are ways of restraining the free will of rational beings by the authority of a commanding will. Moral bonds are *laws* in the strictest sense, moral laws as opposed to physical laws, and the necessity they impose is called *moral necessity,* which is the same as oughtness, obligation, or duty. Freedom from law, from dictation by a commanding will, is called freedom of *independence.* In this sense Americans by the War of Independence became *free* from the laws of England, a man whose wife has died is *free* to marry again, a man discharged from the army is *free* at least for a time from further military service.

Because the bonds are different, one kind of freedom may exist without the other. Hence a man can retain his free will and yet be bound by a law. He may be physically free to do an act, because he is able to do it, but he may not be morally free, because he ought not to do it.

Here we see the difference between the last type of freedom, freedom of independence, and the other two types. It is a perfection to be free from the compulsion of external force and from the determinism of a rigidly necessitating principle of action in one's nature, but it is no perfection in a creature to be free from *all* law. Freedom of independence has meaning only with regard to human laws, which are not passed universally for all mankind but for certain political divisions or classes of people. A man is free from the laws of other jurisdictions to which he does not belong, but he should be a citizen of some country and subject to its laws. Man cannot have complete freedom of independence from all human law, and he can have no independence at all from the natural moral law.

The freedom we have been considering is *freedom from*. More important is *freedom for*. The only reason why it is good for a person to be free *from* various restrictions and hindrances is that he may be free *for* the kind of life he is meant to live, for the attainment of his end. Freedom *from* is merely negative; freedom *for* is its positive complement. Law curtails freedom *from,* because it imposes obligations a man would otherwise be free from, but it enhances freedom *for,* because it enables a man to live the kind of life he has been created for.

The purpose of law, then, is not to impose undue hardship or needless restriction on people, as the anarchists would have it, but to protect and promote true liberty. Law tends to make men good, directing them to their last end and pointing out to them the means necessary to this end. Even in the lesser sphere of man's temporal welfare, human law fulfills the same function, that of pointing out means to end and the obligatory character of both. Law makes man free to attain his goal by directing him right, at the same time leaving him physically free to take or refuse this direction, since it does not destroy his free will. Thus law frees man from bondage to ignorance and error without lessening man's responsibility and self-control.

A man lost in a forest is not free to reach his destination because he does not know in what direction to go or what means to take. A signpost and a pathway do not destroy his freedom, but rather free him from the necessity of staying in the forest. He is still free to follow the sign and path or not, but if he refuses the penalty is that he remains lost. In like manner laws point out how we must act to attain our goal; we retain our free will to obey or disobey them, but the penalty for disobedience is that we cannot reach our end. True liberty, therefore, is not license to do anything at all however evil it might be, the freedom of outlaws, but the ability to direct ourselves with the help of laws to the good. In this sense it is correct to say that true freedom is the right to do what we *ought,* and law shows us where the *ought* lies.

EXISTENTIALISM

We have mentioned the *anarchists* as opponents of law. But theirs is a superficial opposition, a disliking for government and civil law. They think that human nature is good in itself and needs only to be let alone, that human reason without the interference of authority can be trusted to direct man's life reasonably. The real opponents of law are the existentialists. Though they make no attack on governments and civil laws, they remove all basis on which any law could rest. They deny that man has a human nature that could be either good or bad, and in their almost morbid abhorrence of rationalism put no trust at all in human reason.

The existentialist mood or attitude (they refuse to be called a school and have but scorn for philosophical systems) stresses *freedom* as its undefined primary presupposition. Freedom is not proved but is the basic datum. We find ourselves in this world, confronted with the bare fact of existence. We did not ask for it, but the fact is that we are here, *trapped into existence.* The world that we live in is a wasteland that makes no sense. We look around and see that most people live an animal life that is listless and unhappy, some almost a vegetable life that is barren and empty. The few who reflect on this meaningless existence become uneasy, then restless, and finally desperate. Life fills them with a sense of futility and despair, of anguish and nausea. What should we do? What should we believe? These are the agonizing questions, but there seems to be no answer. It is not only that human reason is too weak to work out a solution, but absurdity seems to be inherent in the universe itself. Even if we should find an answer, we should find it to be absurd.

Søren Kierkegaard and the theistic wing of existentialists solve the problem by faith. We cannot prove the existence of God or the claims of any religious group. Only God could enlighten us, but we do not know whether He exists or whether revelation is possible. All we can do is to make a *leap into absurdity,* choosing to believe as a pure act of our freedom, governed by no law, led by no motives. Before deciding to believe, we have no way of knowing whether it is the right decision, whether it is better to leap or not. The act of faith is not a rational act, but one of pure free will. For our choice we bear the full responsibility. We prepare for it by anguish and dread, mounting even to the horror of despair, that seizes us on the brink of decision. Having chosen faith in Jesus Christ as God Incarnate, "because it is absurd," Kierkegaard testified to his own personal enlightenment. But one can neither learn the truth nor teach it. One can only believe by faith and each man's faith is his own.

Jean-Paul Sartre and the atheistic wing of existentialists can find no comfort in faith, for they have decided already that there is no God and no future life. The world is not only meaningless, it is absurd. It is utterly arbitrary with no sense to it at all. There is no reason why the world should be as it is, why we should be in it, why we should live one way rather than another, why we should accept one set of beliefs and values rather than another. But there is the brute fact that we are here. We cannot avoid the necessity of choice. The absurd world must be confronted and accepted for what it is—absurd. By our decision, taken in absolute freedom, we become *authentic* individuals, not meaningless stereotypes or lifeless props on the fantastic stage of life, but meaningful characters in that drama of our own composition which is our life. By each decision we create ourselves and determine what we shall become. We are *condemned to be free.* Man begins with existence but no essence. His essence, *what* he shall be, he makes for himself by every free choice. Each choice is a dreadful responsibility, inevitably molding him into the kind of being he has chosen to be and interpreting the universe into the kind of thing he has chosen it to be. Each man is responsible for all mankind, for they too, their attitude to him and his attitude to them, are conditioned by his commitments. Hence man must engage in the work of society, for his is not only a being-for-himself but a being-in-the-world. All a man's commitments come to a head in death. No sooner has he made himself, created his essence, achieved his authenticity by the full use of his freedom, than the whole structure is swept away in death, the ultimate and tragic absurdity, the final irrationality in all this meaningless existence. Only by accepting this situation and freely committing himself to it can a man rise above the nausea of despair, shake off his paralysis, and acquire the courage to be, to be himself.

We cannot ask the existentialists to offer rational proof or listen to rational disproof. Perhaps the best philosophy to bring to an admittedly absurd world is an absurd philosophy, unless this be thought too rational a consistency. The existentialists seem to be paying the price for being intellectuals who disdain intellect. If the common herd who live unauthentic lives are being suffocated in the drab ooze of their own mediocrity, at least they may find solace in their animal faith. The intellectual is tortured by having the ability to understand, yet finding the world opaque to being understood. Hence all the distress, anguish, dread, and nausea. But is the world incapable of being understood? No man can have an omniscient understanding of it, but is that necessary? If, besides freedom in the human being, there is also law in the universe, law seen sufficiently in its broad outlines to function as a guide for man, then the whole existentialist case falls. The existentialist himself is unconcerned, since he is not out to convince anyone but himself and is prepared to expect his absurd world to contain absurd arguments. But the fact of law's existence should be sufficient refutation to satisfy all who have the humility to accept their reason as a limited one, whose knowledge is a slow and painful growth, but valid within its sphere.

Situation ethics is a practical conclusion from hazily existentialist premises. It holds that there are no rules of moral conduct universally valid, but every act must be judged from the concrete situation in which it occurs. The premises would have to be that there is no human essence or nature that can be known, that human reason is incapable of certain knowledge at least about man, that right reason reasoning about human nature cannot be a norm of morality, and that there is no such thing as a natural law.

We have admitted and emphasized that for its total morality, objective and subjective together, an act must be taken in its concrete situation. It is thus that the act is judged by conscience. Besides the act itself and its motive, there are also the circumstances that will color each act differently. Every act is done by a person who is unique. But it does not follow that there is no objective component in moral behavior, that human nature cannot be isolated by human reason like any other universal idea, that no general norms can be discovered by human conduct, or that there can be no natural law. These same grounds, if taken consistently, would also prove that there can be no civil law, in fact, no law at all. It may be that subjective morality has not received from moralists all the attention it deserves, but any such possible neglect would not be remedied by denying objective morality.

Much can be learned from existentialism with its insistence on freedom, subjectivity, personality, authenticity, and commitment, despite its pessimistic irrationalism. At least it faces important questions that might be more profitably explored by surer methods. But it is now time to return from the denial of law to its affirmation.

KINDS OF LAW

There are innumerable ways in which laws can be classified, and we shall take up now only such divisions as are pertinent to our immediate purpose.

According to their *duration* laws may be eternal or temporal. The law by which God governs the whole universe is the decree of His intellect and will identified with His essence, and since God's essence is eternal this is called the *eternal* law. Laws made in time are *temporal* laws, and these include all laws except the eternal law in God.

According to their mode of *promulgation* laws may be natural or positive. The law promulgated through the very nature of the beings it governs is called the *natural* law. It includes the physical laws as well as the natural moral law. It is customary to call the physical laws the *laws of nature* and to reserve the term *natural law* for the natural moral law, but this usage is not always kept. Laws promulgated by some external sign of enactment are known as *positive* laws, so called because they are *posited* or laid down. They are usually contained in definitely worded statutes or decrees, but this kind of formulation is not strictly necessary. Any legitimate sign of enactment, written, oral, or gestured, that signifies to the subjects that this is the law, is sufficient.

According to their *origin* laws may be divine or human. *Divine* laws are those in which God is the lawgiver. *Human* laws are those made by men. The eternal law and the natural law (both physical and moral) are divine laws. Human laws can be only temporal and positive. However, there can also be divine positive laws,* laws imposed on men by God's direct intervention and revelation, such as the Ten Commandments. It is true that the Commandments are in great part merely statements of the natural

---

*Divine positive law is what St. Thomas calls simply *divine law*. See *Summa Theologica*, I-II, q. 91, a. 4.

law, but the difference between natural law and positive law is not in the content but in the mode of promulgation; since they were promulgated by external signs, they are divine positive law. Human law is either ecclesiastical or civil, according as the society which passes the law is the Church or the state.

Having set down these commonly accepted definitions necessary for any intelligent discussion of the subject, we shall now take up the types of law that pertain to ethics.

SUMMARY

That which obliges us to make our conduct conform to the norm of morality is called *law*. Law, in the proper sense as opposed to the figurative, is *a rule and measure of acts directing them to their proper ends*. Law directing nonfree beings to their ends by the necessitation of their nature is *physical* law. Law directing free beings toward their ends by imposing obligation on their free will is *moral* law. Ethics treats of moral law only.

St. Thomas' definition of law (moral law) is: *An ordinance of reason for the common good promulgated by him who has the care of the community*. Hence it must be mandatory in form, reasonable in content, community-serving in purpose, knowable in manifestation, and authoritative in source.

The function of law is not to impose needless restraint, but to direct men to their last end without destroying their free will. As there are various types of bonds, there are various types of freedom: of *spontaneity*, opposed to external physical necessity; of *choice*, opposed to internal physical necessity; of *independence*, opposed to moral necessity. Law is a bond, a moral bond, opposed only to the abuse of freedom, not to true liberty.

Existentialism stresses the irrationality of life, the primacy of freedom, the unavoidableness of commitment, the dreadful responsibility of each decision, the confrontation of death, the purifying value of anguish and despair, issuing in a free act either of blind faith in God (theistic) or of accepting the ultimate absurdity of nothingness (atheistic). *Situation ethics* drops all moral rules and judges each act in its situation. Philosophies which eliminate the universality of human nature and the power of human reason have no room for law.

Kinds of law: The *eternal* law is the plan of God's wisdom directing all creatures to the end for which He created them; *temporal* laws are those made in time. The *natural* law is promulgated by being embedded in the very nature of creatures; *positive* laws are promulgated by some external sign. *Divine* laws are made by God; *human* laws by man.

READINGS

1. St. Thomas' treatise on law is one of the most famous and often quoted parts of his works. It is found in the *Summa Theologica*, I-II, qq. 90-108, all of it printed in the *Basic Writings*. Read qq. 90-92.
2. After St. Thomas the classical writer on law is Francis Suarez. Selections from his *De Legibus* (On Laws) are given in J. B. Scott, *The Classics of International*

Law: Selections from Three Works of Francisco Suarez. Read bk. I, ch. 3-7, 9, 12.

3. Blackstone, *Commentaries on the Laws of England,* Introduction, section II. This famous work begins by putting law on a solid ethical basis.

4. Rommen, *The Natural Law.* This excellent book deserves to be read as a whole. Chapters VIII-XII pertain to our material here.

5. Farrell, *Companion to the Summa,* vol. II, ch. XVIII.

6. Cronin, *Science of Ethics,* vol. I, ch. XIX.

7. Leibell, *Readings in Ethics,* pp. 301-313.

8. Gilson, *Moral Values and Moral Life,* ch. VI.

9. Gilson, *Spirit of Mediaeval Philosophy,* ch. XVI.

10. Gilson, *The Christian Philosophy of St. Thomas Aquinas,* pp. 264-270.

11. Le Buffe and Hayes, *The American Philosophy of Law,* ch. II.

12. Doolan, *Order and Law,* ch. 1-3.

13. On existentialism:

    a. Kierkegaard, *Fear and Trembling,* and *Sickness unto Death.*

    b. Camus, *The Myth of Sisyphus.*

    c. Marcel, *The Philosophy of Existence.*

    d. Reinhardt, *The Existentialist Revolt.*

    e. Collins, *The Existentialists.*

CHAPTER 11

NATURAL LAW

PROBLEM

The first kind of law we have to discuss is natural law. There is probably no more controversial topic in the field of morals than the meaning and existence of natural law. We shall limit ourselves in this chapter to these two points and take up later the question of the obligatory force and ultimate ground of the natural law. We have for consideration:

(1) What meanings has natural law had in history?
(2) Is there a natural law?
(3) How do we come to know the natural law?
(4) What prescriptions does the natural law contain?
(5) Is the natural law variable?

HISTORY OF NATURAL LAW

The term *natural law* has had its ups and downs in history, and has not been understood in the same sense in every age. It is important to see some of these swings in meaning, for an argument or a criticism that is valid in one period will not apply to the term as understood in a different historical context.

The early Greeks contrasted *physis* (nature) and *nomos* (law), the latter being understood in the sense of human convention and contrivance, so that a union of the two words in a phrase like *natural law* seemed contradictory. Yet they had a feeling for what is right and just beyond the laws of men. Plato is unintelligible without the Ideas of law and justice in which all human law and justice participate. Aristotle is more explicit:

> Particular law is that which each community lays down and applies to its own members: this is partly written and partly unwritten. Universal law is the law of nature. For there really is, as every one to some extent divines, a natural justice and injustice that is binding on all men, even on those who have no association or covenant with each other. It is this that Sophocles' Antigone clearly means when she says that the burial of

Polyneices was a just act in spite of the prohibition: she means that it was just by nature.

> Not of today or yesterday it is,
> But lives eternal: none can date its birth.*

The Stoics were the first to make wide use of the term *natural law*. For them it is the absolutely necessary course that nature fatalistically follows, with no distinction made between physical and moral law. Reason urges us to obey it willingly rather than have it forced upon us, because thus we intelligently comply with the inevitable law of our being. Cicero's remarkable passages are probably to be understood in a Stoic sense:

> There is a law, judges, not written but inborn, not learned or passed on by tradition but sucked from nature's breast. . . .†
> There is truly a law, which is right reason, fitted to our nature, pro-claimed to all men, constant, everlasting. It calls to duty by commanding and deters from wrong by forbidding, neither commanding nor forbidding the good man in vain even when it fails to move the wicked. It can neither be evaded nor amended nor wholly abolished. No decree of Senate or people can free us from it. No explainer or interpreter of it need be sought but itself. There will not be found one law at Rome and another at Athens, one now and another later, but one law, everlasting and un-changeable, extending to all nations and all times, with one common teacher and ruler of all, God, this law's founder, promulgator, and en-forcer. The man who does not obey Him flees from himself and, even if he escapes other punishments normally incurred, pays the supreme penalty by the very fact that he despises the nature of man in himself.‡

On the whole, the natural law as conceived by the Greeks is a rising beyond the particular and contingent to a universal and necessary ideal of conduct, describing how one must behave to be a real man, giving him a rule of life he transgresses at the peril of unhappiness in the frustration of his powers and the stultification of his being. It is not a law imposed by a legislator and enforced by his authority. With the Romans came the distinction between *jus* or right and *lex* or law, between what is just *(jus)* and the command to do it *(lex)*. For the natural law the only legislator could be God, as Cicero says, but He is not yet clearly portrayed as a per-sonal God.

Christianity introduced a new turn into this speculation by regarding nature as the product of God's creative act. God acting as lawgiver sets the law for His creation by His wisdom and enforces it by His will. His providence constitutes Him Governor of the universe, which He directs to its appointed end. Here we have the concept of the *eternal law* developed by St. Augustine, which is the old natural law of the Greeks but seen from

---

*Aristotle, *Rhetoric*, bk. I, ch. 13, 1373b 4. The quotation from Antigone is lines 456-457. Also, see Aristotle, *Nicomachean Ethics*, bk. V, ch. 7, 1134b 18.
†*Pro Milone*, iv, 10.
‡*De Re Publica*, III, xxii, 33. Quoted by Lactantius, *De Institutionibus Divinis*, VI, 8, 6-9.

the side of God the Creator and Lawgiver. The codification of Roman law brought the civil law into contact with the natural law; the law of nations *(jus gentium)* lies in the area where the two meet and partly overlap. By the thirteenth century studies in Roman and Canon Law, in ethics and politics, had laid the ground for an adequate philosophy of law, which first appeared in St. Thomas' *Summa Theologica* as the Treatise on Law,* with his fourfold distinction of eternal law, natural law, human law, and divine (revealed) law. But some unsolved difficulties remained. The medieval Church asserted her position as guardian of faith and morals. Are natural morals included too? Can there be an authoritative interpreter of natural law? If so, how does the law remain *natural?* These questions clouded an understanding of the natural law for some centuries and are not yet wholly dispelled.

Early Protestantism continued the medieval tradition, looking on nature as God's creation and on God as Supreme Lawgiver. But further difficulties arise. Any claims of the Church to be an interpreter of the natural law are rejected in favor of private individual conscience. But how shall it decide? The theory of total depravity, emphasized by Luther and still more by Calvin, seems incompatible with a natural law. Human nature, if totally depraved, offers no sure guidance for man's moral life. Nothing is left but the political state. An established religion, national rather than international, modeled on the union of nation and religion in the Old Testament, seemed to them man's best refuge. A theocracy like that of Geneva or Massachusetts, minutely regulating man's private life, was the logical outcome. In such a view the moral law is stressed, but its *natural* character seems to have disappeared.

It should be expected that the Enlightenment of the Age of Reason would carry us back to pre-Christian concepts. Natural law returns, but in a new guise. God as Lawgiver drops out. If He is acknowledged at all, He is conceived in deist fashion, unconcerned with the world and not governing it by His providence. Again we have natural law without an eternal law, without a lawgiver, without any really binding obligation. Again it is *jus* rather than *lex,* natural right or justice rather than a natural law in the strict sense. But the *natural* aspect of it, far from being abandoned, is reinforced and reinterpreted. In that rationalistic age human nature is regarded as eminently knowable by human reason. The method that reason pursues, however, is not a search for what is essential to man but for what is primitive in him, or if it seeks the essential it endeavors to find it in the primitive. The distinction between the essential and the accidental is confused with the distinction between the natural and the artificial. The way to find human nature, it was thought, is by stripping from man the artificial accretions of civilization so that he may be seen in his native state, in the so-called *state of nature.* The natural is understood to be the native or original or primeval, and natural man is man before or without the social

---

Summa Theologica, I-II, qq. 90-108.

contract that established him in society. Human nature is not so much the abstract essence of man as the unspoiled savage. Thus the Age of Enlightenment passes into the Age of Romanticism.

In the nineteenth century trust in rationalist procedures waned. Kant's separation of morality and legality put rights in the sphere of legality and made them a function of the civil law; for him there are no natural rights. He affirmed the moral law, but had it known intuitively and not by reasoning from human nature; thus understood, it is a moral law, but is it a natural law? The rise of the historical school of jurisprudence and the influence of evolutionary theories in Hegel and Darwin brought in the view of human nature as something constantly developing and progressing. Laws and morals, rights and duties change with changing man; they are products of human custom, relics of traditional folkways, variable for each focus of culture and for each stage of social evolution. Legal positivism and legal pragmatism appear on the scene after their philosophical counterparts, and relegate natural law and natural rights to the museum of discarded superstitions. The names may be kept because of the aura of veneration surrounding them, but all their substance is interpreted away. The legal profession especially is suspicious of any appeal to a higher law beyond the written law. And with good reason, if we remember the interpretations read into the "due process" clause of the Fourteenth Amendment canonizing the status quo and protecting vested interests. What guarantee have we of our rights with a judge who goes beyond the written law to decide a case by some private intuition he may have of a higher law?

The twentieth century, despite the persistence of legal positivism and pragmatism, is witnessing a tentative revival of natural law. There may have been abuses of the higher law theory, but what else do we have? The old question returns. Without natural law, what guide have our lawmakers but utility and expediency, trial and error? How can they determine what ideally ought to be the laws of states and the conduct of men? The dilemma is a serious one. Either there is no law beyond the civil law, and hence no natural rights, no court of appeal, no recourse from tyranny, and a man is subject to the arbitrary will of anyone who can control him by force; or there is beyond the civil law a higher law, but then each man is his own judge and, though it is evident to him that this higher law objectively embodies natural right and justice, his associates have no assurance that his judgment is correct. The first horn of the dilemma causes the appeal to a higher law, to which the founders of our country turned against the arbitrary decrees of Parliament. The second horn causes the qualm of the legal positivists, who see each citizen setting aside a civil law because it disagrees with his personal interpretation of a higher law. We are back again at Antigone's problem. It is not solved by putting the matter to vote and accepting majority rule, for that would mean no rights for minorities. The tyranny of the monarch would be exchanged for the tyranny of the mob.

The problem is insoluble for any society so based on skepticism and relativism as to maintain that human nature is unknowable, that rights and duties cannot be determined, that justice is an empty abstraction, that in morals there is nothing but opinion, and anybody's opinion is as good as anybody else's. Society can flourish only in some commonly breathed atmosphere of thought and principle, and must rest on some public philosophy. That the natural law seems to be the only possible one is the reason for its revival in our time.

EXISTENCE OF THE NATURAL LAW

That there is a natural law, at least in the sense in which the Greeks took it, follows from all we have said in our study this far. We have noted the existence of values and their objective basis, the preeminence and self-justification of moral value, its irreducibility to any other value and its absolutely imperative but noncompulsory necessity, the inner drive of each being toward the attainment of its end which is the fulfillment of its function in the universe, the ability of man by the use of his reason reflecting on his nature to distinguish moral good from moral evil in the living of his life. What remains is to point out that all this material put together adds up to a *law,* and, since it is rooted in man's nature, to a *natural* law.

That there are laws governing the activity of beings in the universe is evident from the very existence of scientific knowledge. An utterly haphazard world could not be studied. Formulas expressing the observed regularities of natural phenomena are rules of action that these beings carry out with remarkable constancy. Living beings, especially, direct their activity toward their self-preservation, growth, and reproduction, following the definite pattern of living prescribed for them by the kind of beings they are, by their structure and function, which is what we mean by their nature. Departure from nature's pattern does not happen spontaneously. A mild deviation imposed from the outside usually results in maladjustment and debility, an extreme one in death. To fulfill their function they *must* live naturally, that is, according to nature's prescription, and this is the *law* of their life.

The same law of nature which applies to inanimate, vegetable, and animal nature applies likewise to human nature. As it applies to each of the other three levels with a difference, so also it applies to human nature with a difference. Man is unique in being rational and free. Though subject to physical forces like any other chemically composed body having mass and energy, to the biological drives and urges that control the world of living organisms, to the sensitive reactions and appetites characteristic of brain- and nerve-equipped animals, yet beyond all these he can intellectually *know* what is good for him and can wilfully *choose* to follow it. By examining the kind of being he is, his nature, he can find the kind of conduct suitable to him and can see how this alone can lead him to what is good for him. He sees that modes of conduct that are inhuman or antisocial, abusive of himself or of his fellows, while conferring a temporary advantage, must be destructive of himself and of his race in the long run. He also sees that he cannot renounce his rational nature and the responsibility bound up with it. Come what may, he must maintain his human dignity or become intolerable to himself. He must demand that others treat him as a man, even when they refuse to, and he must deserve his own and their respect by behaving as a man.

Natural law tests itself in the laboratory of history. Superficial observation may seem to show such differences of detail in various cultures as to eliminate any universal pattern of human living, but more careful scrutiny detects a highest common factor in all moral codes. Even the most degraded savages are recognizable as human beings, not merely by the shape of their bodies, but chiefly by the way they live and act. Too great a departure from the normal mode of human behavior leads only to frustration and extinction. Individuals here and there, tribes and nations here and there may flourish though they have adopted an unnautral form of life, but they are rather the exceptions that prove the rule. History itself catches up with them and eventually punishes the folly of unnatural living. Living can be called unnatural only because it violates the rule set by nature, and this is what we mean by the natural law.

We might sum up the argument as follows:

Man must be directed to his proper good, to the fulfillment of his function in the universe and to the attainment of his end, by means that are both effective and suitable. They must be effective, powerful enough to produce the effect; otherwise, they are not really means at all. They must also be suitable to man's rational and free nature; otherwise, man alone of all creatures would be obliged by his own nature to go contrary to his nature. But the only means both effective and suitable is the natural moral law.

1. It must be a *law*. A mere wish, counsel, hint, or suggestion would not be effective, for it would lack binding force and could be disregarded without fault or penalty. It would be an insufficient motive in the face of difficulties. It would work when it is not needed, when the path is clear and the going pleasant; but it would not work when it is needed, when we must be goaded forward over the dark and rough spots of life. Nothing less than a law will do.

2. It must be a *moral* law. Physical laws are suitable only to nonrational beings. An internal determination or necessity of one's nature such as is found in nonrational beings would destroy man's free will and make him a living contradiction, a being made free but not able to exercise his freedom. External compulsion would mean that man must accomplish his end despite his will, and thus would do violence to human nature.

3. It must be a *natural* law. Every creature tends to its end by its activity guided by its nature, for a being's nature means nothing else but its essence considered as the principle of its activity. Man is no exception; he too has a nature and in him it fulfills the same function. Therefore man also can find that his nature is the means that will guide him to his end, and this is what we understand by the *natural law*. Besides, if it is necessary for man to know by the norm of morality which conduct is right and which is wrong, it is no less necessary for him to recognize his obligation of conforming his conduct to that norm. Both the norm and the law are found in rational human nature itself, and are properly called *natural*.

KNOWLEDGE OF THE NATURAL LAW

We tend to think of a law as a written decree or spoken command. But nothing of this sort is found in the natural law. We must insist that the natural law of itself is not formulated. Failure to understand this fact has led believers in innate ideas, partisans of the moral sense theory, and various schools of intuitionists to imagine that man has moral concepts and judgments ready made in his mind at birth or that he easily forms them by the use of some infallible special faculty. Critics of such views have hastily jumped to the conclusion that, if the natural law can be known only in this way, and since there is no such knowledge, there can be no such thing as a natural law. The fallacy is in the first premise: the natural law is not known in this way.

How then is it known? It begins with what we have called knowledge by connaturality or natural inclination. Without study or reflection, man in a pre-scientific and pre-philosophical condition simply follows the bent of his nature in using his powers for the purposes for which they obviously seem constructed. He is following the natural law but he knows it only as the blind man knows the hand that leads him. The individual in his growth to maturity and the race in its development toward civilization cannot remain always in this primitive condition.

Knowledge of the natural law is a slow growth. Man's nature is a rational nature, and he finds the natural law by the use of his reason in drawing conclusions about his own nature. He has no moral judgments formed at birth and ready for use, but must form them for himself. But he is equipped by his nature with ability for forming such judgments, has a natural tendency to use this ability, and his own nature is the object from which he draws his moral ideas and concerning which he frames his moral judgments.

Man has a natural interest in and facility for forming rules of conduct. He can reflect on himself and, finding himself interesting, is stimulated to self-observation. He can evaluate and criticize his own actions and the actions of others like him. He can understand the needs of his own nature and the suitability of his deeds to his needs. He can compare his conduct with his nature and understand the conformity or nonconformity between them. He can therefore draw up rules of conduct which will preserve and enhance this conformity. If he becomes a legislator in human society, he formulates such rules and promulgates them to his subordinates by some external sign; the law now becomes positive law. But such rules before formulation and external promulgation were already natural law.

All law is promulgated through reason because it is reason alone that can understand a law. This statement is true both of the natural law and of positive law. But positive law is manifested to reason by the help of some external decree or announcement intimating the mind of the lawgiver. The natural law is manifested to reason not by any external sign, but simply by a rationally conducted examination of human nature with all its parts and relations.

We may sum up our answer to the problem as follows: The natural law can be looked at formally or virtually. The natural law considered *formally* consists of the actual judgments of practical reason on what ought to be done or not done. The natural law itself is nothing else but the sum of these judgments, just as the civil law is a list of judgments telling citizens what they ought to do or not do. We have a thing *virtually* if we have the power *(virtus)* to produce it, even though we have not yet the thing itself. The natural law considered virtually is practical reason insofar as it has a natural tendency for making moral judgments. The natural law exists virtually in every rational being even before his reason is sufficiently developed to form the actual judgments. As the person advances in the use of reason and *forms* his moral principles, either with the help of moral training or by his own efforts, in him the natural moral law passes from the *virtual* to the *formal* state. A similar advance occurs in the passage of the race from a primitive to a cultured society. To aid people in this process of moral growth is the aim of ethics as a practical science.

CONTENT OF THE NATURAL LAW

How do we come to know the content of the natural law, what it actually prescribes?

Though man by the use of his reason is able to develop the natural law into a formal and explicit code of moral conduct, how many men actually succeed in doing so? Unless most men do so, the natural law, however excellent in theory, would prove itself an unfit instrument in practice. Anyone invincibly ignorant of the prescriptions of the natural law is excused from keeping them, but if most men were in this condition the natural law would not serve its purpose. How could it be called a *natural* law, if most of those possessing human *nature* were excused from its obligations?

So we find ourselves in a dilemma. On the one hand, we know a priori, from the demands of the natural law itself, that it must be sufficiently known to the generality of mankind. On the other hand, we know *a posteriori,* from experience, that there is much controversy and disagreement of opinion on matters of morality, betokening a widespread ignorance. Many of these disagreements can be discounted as dealing not with the principles of morality but with their application; the law itself is clear, and the argument is only about cases. But other controversies are not so readily disposed of and concern the very principles of morality. If these can be unknown, how is the natural law sufficiently promulgated?

The only way out of this dilemma is to recognize that the natural law consists of precepts of varying degrees of importance for the welfare of humanity, that the more fundamental principles of the natural law cannot be invincibly unknown by normal mature persons, whereas reasoned conclusions derived from them can be. St. Thomas says:

> There belong to the natural law, first, certain most common precepts that are known to all; and secondly, certain secondary and more particular precepts, which are, as it were, conclusions following closely from first principles. As to the common principles, the natural law, in its universal meaning, cannot in any way be blotted out from men's hearts. But it is blotted out in the case of a particular action, in so far as reason is hindered from applying the common principle to the particular action because of concupiscence or some other passion. . . . But as to the other, the secondary precepts, the natural law can be blotted out from the human heart, either by evil persuasions, just as in speculative matters errors occur in respect of necessary conclusions; or by vicious customs and corrupt habits, as, among some men, theft, and even unnatural vices . . . were not esteemed sinful.*

Levels in the knowledge of natural law

A more precise discrimination of these principles is called for. The more general the principles are the more impossible it is for them to be unknown, whereas the more particular and determinate they become the more possibility there is for ignorance and deception. We may distinguish:

(1) The first moral principle
(2) Common general principles or moral axioms
(3) Reasoned conclusions
(4) Particular applications

1. *There is one first principle of the natural law,* which in the practical field corresponds to the principle of contradiction in the speculative field. St. Thomas says:

> The precepts of the natural law are to the practical reason what the first principles of demonstrations are to the speculative reason, because both are self-evident principles. . . .
> That which first falls under apprehension is *being,* the understanding of which is included in all things whatsoever a man apprehends. Therefore the first indemonstrable principle is that *the same thing cannot be affirmed and denied at the same time,* which is based on the notion of *being* and *not-being:* and on this principle all others are based, as is stated in *Metaphysics* iv.† Now as *being* is the first thing that falls under the apprehension absolutely, so *good* is the first thing that falls under the apprehension of the practical reason, which is directed to action (since every agent acts for an end, which has the nature of good). Consequently, the first principle in the practical reason is one founded on the nature of good, namely, that *good is that which all things seek after.* Hence this is

---

Summa Theologica, I-II, q. 94, a. 6.
†Aristotle, *Metaphysics,* bk. IV, ch. 3, 1005b 29.

the first precept of law, that *good is to be done and promoted, and evil is to be avoided.* All other precepts of the natural law are based upon this; so that all the things which the practical reason naturally apprehends as man's good belong to the precepts of the natural law under the form of things to be done or avoided.*

This first principle can be stated in various ways: "Do good and avoid evil," "Lead a life in accord with reason," "Seek your last end." This primary truth which, as St. Thomas says, is self-evident, cannot be invincibly unknown to anyone who has the use of reason at all.

2. *There are other common or general principles based on the first principle,* following from it with immediate inference, or with mediate inference so simple and easy that no normal mature person can fail to make it. These principles can be regarded as moral axioms. They express the natural inclinations man has in common with all substances, such as "Preserve your own being," or in common with other animals, such as "care for your offspring," or the inclinations clearly and obviously springing from man's rationality, such as "Adore God," "Do not murder," "Treat others with fairness," "Be faithful to your friends." One could hardly know the first principle, "Do good and avoid evil," and fail to see what is good and what is evil in such obvious cases.

These common principles cannot be invincibly unknown to persons whose reason is developed, that is, to persons of normal intelligence, who have arrived at mental maturity, and have received an adequate moral education. If knowledge of the natural law is not innate but must be discovered by reason, it is to be expected that the feeble-minded through incapacity and children through immaturity will be deficient in it. The need for an adequate *moral* education may not be so commonly recognized, but it is a very important factor. Moral education need not run parallel with mental education. One may have no book learning at all, yet have received an excellent moral training; on the other hand, highly educated people of brilliant talents may be victims of defective or perverted moral training. These latter cannot be considered morally normal, for their moral reason is undeveloped. One brought up in an atmosphere of cynical misanthropy, one trained from youth in crime and degeneracy, one encouraged to rebellion against all authority, has had the moral side of his nature artificially blinded and starved. This cannot be called man's normal condition.

3. *There are remote conclusions derived by a complicated process of reasoning.* This does not mean that there is anything doubtful about these conclusions; the conclusion is certain and the logic perfect, but the reasoning is long and involved as in a difficult theorem in geometry. Untrained minds cannot follow it and even trained minds can become sidetracked through confusion or prejudice. Such moral questions as suicide, mercy-killing, duelling, divorce, polygamy, and contraception are examples in point. Some modern writers call these the *tertiary precepts* of the natural

*St. Thomas, *Summa Theologica,* I-II, q. 94, a. 2.

law; others, more in accord with St. Thomas' language, call them *secondary;* to avoid confusion we shall simply call them *remote conclusions.*

These precepts of the natural law can be invincibly unknown even by intelligent people living in a cultivated moral atmosphere. Error on these remote conclusions is due to the same sources as error in general. Moral education is obtained by the same faculties as other kinds of education. Since even educated people can be mistaken in other fields, in science, history, and politics, they can likewise be mistaken in moral matters when the argumentation becomes difficult and contradictory conclusions seem equally plausible. This possibility is what makes a scientific study of ethics so important for a fully educated man.

4. *There are applications of the principles of the natural law to particular cases.* Normal mature men may err in their application of any of these principles to a concrete case. The resulting misjudgment does not mean that they do not know the principles themselves, or that they are ignorant of the natural law, but only that they are inexpert in applying principles to practice, like one who knows mathematics but gets bogged down in working problems.

Thus we distinguish four levels in man's knowledge of the natural law. By the more common and general principles we mean the first two headings given above: the first principle and the simplest inferences from it. One may ask why the argument is restricted to these. Should not the remote conclusions, the so-called tertiary precepts, as part of the natural law, be equally well promulgated? Ignorance of the general principles, since they ramify into all fields of conduct and are the mainstay of all law and order on earth, would make moral life and human society utterly unlivable. Ignorance of the remote conclusions, though these are important enough, is not nearly so devastating; moral life and human society can still go on, however lamely. For example, promiscuity and polygamy, though both wrong, are not equal in their effects. Polygamous societies have functioned and flourished, though not as well as monogamous ones, but no human society has ever been totally promiscuous or could be.

Invincible ignorance of any precept of morality excuses from its observance, thus taking care of the individual's conscience. However, this is not the problem we are discussing. Widespread ignorance of the general principles of morality would be disastrous to the human race, and the natural law ensures that such widespread ignorance does not occur. But the remote conclusions are such that invincible ignorance of them can be tolerated without wrecking mankind, and we are left to draw these conclusions for ourselves.

Just as raw materials and necessities of life are scattered throughout nature and do not fail, but we are left to our own ingenuity in developing science, culture, and civilization, so we cannot fail to know the general principles of morality, but must use our own reason in working up the details of a complete moral system. And just as people depend on experts in other fields of knowledge, so those who have less ability or opportunity to study difficult matters in ethics can be guided by the teaching and example of persons whose intelligence and character they respect. Even here mistakes will occur, as they do in all things human, but we are not responsible for them if we act in good faith.

The terms *normal* and *mature,* used in the above discussion, may seem too inexact but greater preciseness in this matter is not possible because of the gradual way in which human reason develops. It depends on ability, age, opportunity, effort, habit, and environment, all of which shape the moral character of the person. There will be many borderline cases, but from these no conclusion can be drawn.

Apparent exceptions

Many difficulties can be brought up from the customs of primitive tribes and even from some civilized practices. To cover these in detail would take us too far into anthropology and sociology, but we can lay down a few norms for handling them. About any alleged practice we should ask:

(1) Are the facts certain?
(2) Are the moral implications properly interpreted?
(3) Is this a general principle or a remote conclusion?
(4) Is this a moral precept itself or its application?
(5) Are these normal and mature people?
(6) Is their ignorance really invincible?

The first thing is to verify the facts. The accounts of early explorers are full of fanciful tales uncritically lumped with true observations, and even modern anthropologists can draw hasty conclusions. Reports of tribes with no moral notions whatever were later disproved; primitive peoples jealously guard their traditions from strangers and share them only with proved friends. The acts of savages must be interpreted, not by the conventional standards of civilization, but against their simple forest background. To enter a house and pick up anything they see may not be theft for them, for they have no privacy and no idea that a man's home is his castle. Their cruelty and revengefulness can be exaggerated manifestations of courage and justice. In general, they learn far more vices from contact with civilization and from mistreatment by colonists than they ever practiced in their native condition.

Some practices are the result of inability to resolve an apparent conflict of moral principles. Human sacrifices were made on the principle that the best thing should be offered to God, and a man's dearest possession is his child. Cannibalism was done as a religious rite, to acquire a warrior's courage by eating his heart, and not as an ordinary source of food. Suicide too is sometimes done as an act of religion, as was also the custom of burning a man's wives and slaves on his funeral pyre. Killing deformed children, incurable sufferers, and the aged was thought an act of mercy, as some consider euthanasia today. Prolonged social injustice may cause one to think it right to take from the rich to help the poor. Duelling was regarded as an obligation of honor and to refuse a challenge as a manifestation of cowardice. Feuding and lynching are mistaken forms of family or public justice where organized law is not in force. These practices are not defended here, but only cited to show how an apparent conflict of moral principles may result in a faulty application of them or in conclusions wrongly reasoned from them.

It is possible also for people to become victims of moral depravity introduced in previous generations. Those who introduced the immoral customs did so with conscious knowledge of their immorality, but succeeding generations now come to take them as a matter of course, having grown up not in a normal but in a perverted moral environment. Tribes reduced to brigandage for a living may cease to see anything wrong in theft, at least from strangers. Slaves threatened with death for bringing bad news may come to feel justified in lying. The constant tolerance of concubinage by public opinion may dull the consciences of unreflecting persons. Public apathy toward political graft and unfair patronage may cause some to view them as perquisites of office. Ignorance in all such matters is not usually invincible, but may be in extreme cases.

NATURAL LAW ABSOLUTE OR RELATIVE

There are some who look upon the natural law as a rigid and stifling box put around their lives and cramping them into an unrelieved round of prescribed duties. Others, especially after reading our previous description, may find the natural law to be so vague and fluid as to be practically useless. Both views are exaggerations. The natural law is as absolute and as relative as human nature. Listen again to St. Thomas:

> To the natural law belong those things to which a man is inclined naturally; and among these it is proper to man to be inclined to act according to reason. Now it belongs to the reason to proceed from what is common to what is proper. . . . The practical reason is concerned with contingent matters, which is the domain of human actions; and, consequently, although there is necessity in the common principles, the more we descend toward the particular, the more frequently we encounter defects. . . . In matters of action, truth or practical rectitude is not the same for all as to what is particular, but only as to the common principles; and where there is the same rectitude in relation to particulars, it is not equally known to all.*

Some modern legal writers speak of a "natural law with a variable content,"† looking toward a compromise that will give them both the needed higher law on which human law should be modeled, and an adjustibility of this law to fit human progress. But the whole content cannot

---

*Summa Theologica, I-II, q. 94, a. 4.
†Rudolf Stammler, mentioned in Rommen, *The Natural Law,* p. 229, and Haines, *Revival of Natural Law Concepts,* p. 249.

be variable, since human nature is variable only within limits. Man's essence is unchangeable, but some properties flowing from his essence are adjustable to circumstances and capable of growth in the course of history.

It is perhaps better to say that, while the core of the natural law has absolute moral necessity, there are peripheral areas that have a conditional moral necessity. Man has some natural law duties that are consequent on certain conditions of life, such as marriage, employment, wealth, leadership and the like. They flow from man's social nature and are therefore natural, provided society has taken this form and he has this position in it. Since society itself, though natural, develops its institutions gradually, some conclusions of the natural law will not have application until a certain degree of cultural sophistication has been reached. Thus the natural law may permit to savages some forms of seizure and violence that could be only brutality or revenge in a civilized man. The former has no institutions for securing justice; the latter must use those society has established. The moral law of justice remains the same; only the mode of acquiring it is different. It is otherwise with the evils of predatory warfare, of slavery, or race prejudice. These were always contrary to the nature of man, but only lately has he become conscious of his duty to eliminate them. That he has not yet fully done so is proof of his need of further moral education.

What is said here is by no means meant to be a concession to relativistic morals. The relativist has no anchor at all and drifts anywhere on the tide of fickle human desire, giving morals no more stability than fads and fashions. Human nature is like a fixed anchor with some slack in the line, permitting a circle of swing around the center. It is the business of the moralist to pull the line taut and fix the position close to the center, but he should not try to abolish entirely the leeway nature itself gives him. By striving for absolute strictness and mathematical certainty he would not be following the law of his own nature.

SUMMARY

The history of natural law shows six periods: Natural law as natural justice for the Greeks and Romans, as participation in the eternal law for medieval Christians, as moral law imposed on corrupt human nature in early Protestanism, as the native and primitive in the Age of Enlightenment, as almost nonexistent in the positivistic outlook of the nineteenth century, as staging a fairly vigorous revival at present.

The natural law *exists*. Man must be guided to his end by means that are effective and suited to man's nature. Such means must be a *law* with binding force, for advice would be insufficient; a *moral* law, for inner necessity and outer compulsion would destroy man's free will; a *natural* law, for man is no exception to the general rule that every being is directed to its end by its nature.

The natural law is *promulgated* to man through his *reason*. At birth it is in man only *virtually;* by examining his nature with the light of his reason man develops the natural law into a *formal* code of moral principles.

The *content* of the natural law is sufficiently *knowable*. Its *general principles* cannot be invincibly unknown by normal mature persons, though its *remote conclusions* can be. The first moral principle, *Do good and avoid evil,* is known to all. Simple and obvious deductions escape only the abnormal or the immature or those with defective moral training. Difficult conclusions and applications can be invincibly unknown even by the learned, just as error occurs in other fields of knowledge. Hence the diversity of opinion in morals.

The natural law is as variable and invariable as human nature. The essence of man is unchangeable, but his properties and abilities are capable of development. Some precepts of the natural law are absolutely necessary, others contingently so. The natural law is absolute in its core, but admits of relativity in its details and applications. Since it is man's nature to live in history, it is natural for him to undergo moral growth.

READINGS

1. As instances of the recognition of the natural law among the ancients, see Sophocles' *Antigone,* especially lines 450-460; Cicero's *Pro Milone* (For Milo), iv; *De Re Publica* (On the Republic), bk. III, xxii; *De Legibus* (On Laws), bk. I, v, to bk. II, vii. Cicero, as a Stoic, does not sufficiently distinguish between physical law and moral law; also his application of the natural law in *Pro Milone* is much too wide.
2. St. Thomas, *Summa Theologica,* I-II, q. 94; see also q. 91, a. 2.
3. Suarez, *De Legibus* (On Laws), bk. II, ch. 5-15.
4. Blackstone, *Commentaries on the Laws of England,* introduction, section II.
5. James Wilson's lecture *Of the Laws of Nature,* found in his *Works,* vol. I, and in Adams, *Selected Political Essays of James Wilson,* gives eloquent testimony to the natural law as seen by an advocate of the moral sense theory.
6. Modern philosophical treatments of the natural law:
   a. Rommen, *The Natural Law,* is excellent; see also *The State in Catholic Thought,* ch. 5-8.
   b. D'Entrèves, *Natural Law,* is a highly recommended little book, stressing the historical and legal side.
   c. Messner, *Social Ethics,* bk. I, pt. I.
   d. Maritain, *The Rights of Man and Natural Law.* Of particular value is his essay "Natural Law and Moral Law" in Anshen (ed.), *Moral Principles of Action,* ch. 4.
   e. Cronin, *Science of Ethics,* vol. I, pp. 506-514, and especially ch. 16, on how we come to a knowledge of the natural law; see also ch. 19.
   f. Wild, *Plato's Modern Enemies and the Theory of Natural Law.*
   g. Rickaby, *Moral Philosophy,* pp. 132-152, 371-373.
   h. Farrell, *Companion to the Summa,* vol. II, ch. 18.
   i. Doolan, *Order and Law,* ch. 4-18.
   j. Leibell, *Readings in Ethics,* pp. 317-326. The article by Walter McDonald summarizes the views of Gabriel Vasquez, a Scholastic who differed from St. Thomas and Suarez.
7. The legal profession has recently written much on the natural law:
   a. Haines, *Revival of Natural Law Concepts.*
   b. McKinnon, *The Higher Law.* This excellent pamphlet is followed by further articles by the author in the *American Bar Journal.*
   c. Harding, *Natural Law and Natural Rights.*

d. *Natural Law Institute Proceedings,* published over some years at Notre Dame, contains many fine articles.

e. Wright, *American Interpretations of the Natural Law,* summed up in his conclusion, ch. 11, gives a different interpretation from ours.

f. Kelsen, *What is Justice?,* presents the author's essays against the natural law position. See Gerhart, *American Liberty and "Natural Law,"* for a political and religious attack on natural law.

CHAPTER 12

ETERNAL LAW

PROBLEM

Thus far our whole discussion of morality has centered about man. We began with the fact of experience, that man does make moral judgments. In our attempt to account for them, we first concentrated on their subjective side and saw that they suppose free choice, entail responsibility, and are approved or disapproved by conscience. We found that these judgments are not merely subjective, emotive, opportunistic, or relative to the person, but are based on an objectively existing moral order, comprising a unique type of value that imposes itself on us as an ought and attracts us as an end. We found extrinsic authority, human convention, and social approval insufficient to account for the moral good, and had to place its foundation in human acts themselves and their relation to the nature of man. Rational human nature, we saw, is both the norm of moral goodness and the law prescribing conduct according to that norm.

The natural law is in a certain sense the crowning point of our study. It is the glory of the human person that he is responsible for making a man of himself, not lawlessly, as some existentialists would have it, but according to the law of his being. He is thus a man in two senses: the man he was born, a being endowed with human nature and all its potential; and the man he makes of himself, the fulfillment of his potential, the product of his intelligently self-directed activity.

A philosophy that rests here might be called *naturalism,* because of its emphasis on human *nature,* but the term today has the misleading connotation of an atheism gone mild. It might better be called *humanism,* in one of its many senses, because in stressing *human* nature it lets man be his own highest value, his own source of obligation, and his own self-realizing end. This philosophy is not only capable of having a system of

140

morals, but one that is quite high and noble in its way, for it appeals to what is best in man taken simply as man. Aristotle has given the classic expression of it. Unlike some modern humanists, he is not argumentative against a higher source and goal for man, but with admirable reticence stays within the limits of his evidence.

Is such a philosophy sufficient? That is our present question. Can man, who is at least the proximate basis of the moral order, be also its ultimate basis, or must we look for something beyond man? Is the natural law sufficient for itself or must the natural law be a derivative of a still higher law? Does anyone impose the natural law on man? We shall consider:

(1) What is the ultimate norm of morality?
(2) Is there an eternal law?
(3) How is the natural law derived from the eternal law?

ULTIMATE NORM OF MORALITY

If a human act derives its moral goodness from its conformity with human nature taken completely as judged by right reason, we may further ask where human nature gets its goodness, which it can then communicate to an act conforming with it. Is man himself the highest good and supreme value?

It is here that ethics shows its dependence on metaphysics. If God does not exist, man is the highest being that experience has so far discovered in the universe and he will be the ultimate standard of his own worth. But if God exists, then man is not something ultimate, and rational human nature is but a proximate norm of morality, requiring the backing of an ultimate norm that can be nothing less than God.

In ethics we do not discuss proofs for the existence of God. Though the very fact of the moral order has been used as an argument for the existence of God—and expertly stated it can be a most cogent one—we refer the question of God's existence to the science to which it properly belongs, metaphysics. It is the business of the science of *being* to investigate the Ultimate in Being. Also, since we wish to avoid even the appearance of a vicious circle, of deriving God from morals and morals from God, there is a logical advantage in placing the existence of God on an independent footing.

One may say: If good and evil are recognizable by right reason inspecting human nature, if the moral order is knowable without reference to God, if atheists and agnostics can manage to live good moral lives, why bring God in? Because we have to. Right reason is a reliable guide only when it is faithful to its own law, judging every object by measuring its approach to the ideal. Since the ideal cannot be found in the empirically observable universe, it must be one of two things: either it is a mere abstraction that can only be thought of but cannot exist in reality, or it really does exist and exists as God. The atheist or agnostic can have only the mental abstraction as his supreme value and highest ideal. Often it is inspiring enough to motivate a good life, even a heroic one, for there are always men willing to pursue even the most wraith-like ideal. He then has the problem of rationally justifying a moral life on these unsatisfactory terms. The theist, on the other hand, knows that the ideal exists. He cannot separate the ideal which he seeks from the God whom he acknowledges. The Supreme Being is also the Supreme Value and the Highest Good. Since He is perfect, infinitely perfect, and since there can be only one such, the Supreme Being is necessarily the Best of beings. God takes the first place in every line of being, and value is not outside the line of being, since nothing is. For the theist, therefore, the moral order like everything else requires God as its ultimate foundation.

How is God as the Highest Good related to human action? Since God is Creator of the universe and exemplary cause of all things, whatever else exists or can exist must be a far-off and finite reflection, imitation, or participation of the Infinite Being. Man is no exception, for there can be none, and his preeminence in this created universe is due to the fact that a rational being's resemblance to God is closer and clearer than that of other beings.

This resemblance between God and man should exist not only in nature but also in action. The nature of a thing is its essence considered as the source of its activity, and there must be no disharmony between the activtiy and the nature from which it flows. If man must exist as an image of God, he should also act as an image of God. His actions should be the kind of actions that God can do. God's acts are all good because they correspond with His nature, which is Goodness Itself.

Man resembles God, too, in the gift of free will, and it is man's noblest privilege that he can freely guide himself to his end and freely cooperate with God in achieving the purpose of creation. But man is only a finite image of the Infinite. God is the Necessary Being, man but a contingent being; in God nature and activity are identified, in man they are not. In a being in which nature and activity are identified, even the freest acts must be in accord with the nature, and disharmony is impossible. In a being in which nature and activity are not identified, the acts must be kept in line with the nature by the careful and judicious use of freedom, or else disharmony will creep in.

Freedom in God because it is perfect cannot fail, cannot fall off from the ideal, cannot be abused. Freedom in a contingent creature (unless it is overwhelmed by the actual possession of the perfect good) by the very fact that it is contingent can fail, can fall off from the ideal, can be abused. It is only by deliberately abusing his freedom that man can do moral evil. When acting thus he does the kind of act that God cannot do, willfully destroying as far as he can the resemblance between himself and God. Because he cannot efface his resemblance to God in essence or nature, he always remains *ontologically good* no matter what he does; but when he twists his activity away from the pattern set him by God, he ruins the resemblance that ought to exist between his activity and God's activity, his life and God's life, and thus man can become *morally evil*.

As God is the Source and Norm of all being, so He is the Source and Norm of all goodness. The ultimate reason why a human act is good is that it shares in the goodness of God. The ultimate reason why a human act is evil is that it goes counter to the activity and nature of God, the fountainhead of all goodness.

We may sum up this argument as follows: The ultimate norm of morality must be the last and absolute standard to which we can appeal in judging the goodness of human acts. But the last and absolute standard of all goodness, whether of human acts or anything else, is the divine nature. Therefore the ultimate norm of morality is the divine nature.

THE ETERNAL LAW

If we must go behind right reason and human nature as the proximate norm of morality to find the ultimate norm in the divine reason and nature, must we not also go behind the natural law inherent in man to find its ultimate counterpart in God? Law requires a lawgiver and subjects. What we call the *natural law* from the standpoint of man the subject, we call the *eternal law* from the standpoint of God the Lawgiver. In a sense it is the same law looked at from the two sides. We give it different names to emphasize its double aspect: as actively proceeding from God the Creator, and as passively received in man the creature.

The eternal law expresses the necessary relation of the Creator to His creation. It is defined by St. Augustine as: "That law by which it is just that all things be most perfectly in order"* and also as "The divine reason or the will of God commanding that the natural order of things be preserved and forbidding that it be disturbed."† St. Thomas, after giving the gist of St. Augustine's definition, defines the eternal law as: "The exemplar of divine wisdom, as directing all actions and movements."‡

The eternal law includes both the physical laws and the moral law. God directs all His creatures to their ends, nonfree beings by the physical laws inherent in their natures and free beings by the moral law to which they are expected freely to conform their conduct. Ethics emphasizes the eternal law insofar as it contains the moral law.

St. Thomas proves the existence of the eternal law as follows:

Law is nothing else but a dictate of practical reason emanating from the ruler who governs a perfect community. Now it is evident, granted that the world is ruled by divine providence, . . . that the whole community of the universe is governed by the divine reason. Therefore the very notion of the government of things in God, the ruler of the universe,

---

De Libero Arbitrio, bk. I, ch. 6.
†*Contra Faustum Manichaeum,* bk. XXII, ch. 27.
‡*Summa Theologica,* I-II, q. 93, a. 1.

has the nature of a law. And since the divine reason's conception of things is not subject to time, but is eternal . . . therefore it is that this kind of law must be called eternal.*

The argument contains these three steps:

(1) God rules the world
(2) He rules the world by law
(3) This law is an eternal law

1. God, being intelligent, had a plan in creating the world. According to this plan He directs all things to the ends He has given them. God cannot be indifferent whether this plan is carried out, otherwise He would both will it and not will it. He must will that creatures carry out His plan as He intends it. This plan of God's intellect carried out by the decree of His will is what we call the eternal law.

2. This plan of God is truly a *law,* for it has all the elements required by the definition of law. It is an *ordinance,* a command, a decree of the divine will, a rule of action to guide His creatures to their ends; this is no mere counsel or bit of advice. It is an ordinance of *reason,* because it is directed by God's intellect which conceives the plan of creation and understands the relation of means to end. It is *for the common good,* because it establishes order and harmony in creation, by which each being, accomplishing its own end, will enable the whole universe to achieve the end God has put before it. It is *promulgated,* because God has embedded it in the very nature or essence of the creatures governed by it and has thus enabled them to observe it. It is *from competent authority,* for God is the Supreme Ruler of the universe He has created.

3. This law is an *eternal* law, for God is eternal, and His intellect and will, which are identified with His essence, are likewise eternal and unchangeable. The law is the plan in God's intellect carried out by the decree of His will, and, since God cannot have accidents, whatever is in Him is identified with Him. God does not pass from not knowing to knowing a plan, from not willing to willing its execution. Therefore such a law, identified with God Himself, is properly called eternal.

A difficulty may be brought up about the promulgation. How can a law be made known to creatures incapable of knowledge? The answer is that promulgation must be adapted to the nature of the creature, and, since rational creatures alone are capable of understanding the law, to them alone can it be promulgated in the strict sense of making the law *known.*

How can a law be promulgated even to rational creatures from eternity, when the creatures do not yet exist? One widely accepted solution is to distinguish between active and passive promulgation. Active promulgation is God's decree to make the law known to creatures if and when they exist; this must be eternal, for the plan of the universe existed eternally

---

Summa Theologica, I-II, q. 91, a. 1.

in God's intellect and the decree to activate this plan existed eternally in God's will. Passive promulgation is the actual knowing of the law by the creatures; this is not eternal for, until creatures exist, they cannot know or keep a law. Since the eternal law by definition means the law in the lawgiver (God) rather than the law in the subject bound by it (the creature), it is obvious that active promulgation is the only kind such a law can have. This is quite sufficient for it to be a genuine law.

ETERNAL LAW AND NATURAL LAW

In the last chapter our approach to the natural law was from an inductive and empirical angle. The proper order of knowledge is from the better known to the less known, and the natural law in man is much more apparent to us than the eternal law in God. The natural law has been found and accepted by philosophers who made no acknowledgement of an eternal law, but no one could go directly to the eternal law without having a well-developed body of theistic metaphysics.

St. Thomas, having such a metaphysics, proceeds in deductive fashion from the eternal law to the natural law. The eternal law established, the natural law follows as a corollary. It is instructive to compare his method with the one we have followed. They are in no sense opposed, but complement each other, arriving at the same conclusion by different routes. Deductive derivation of the natural law from the eternal law is a much simpler process than our laborious induction of the natural law from the facts of human life and our inference of an eternal law as its ultimate justification, but the deductive method is narrowly restricted in the type of person to whom it may appeal. St. Thomas' proof rests squarely on God, creation, and providence:

> Law, being a rule and measure, can be in a person in two ways: in one way, as in him that rules and measures; in another way, as in that which is ruled and measured, since a thing is ruled and measured in so far as it partakes of the rule or measure. Therefore, since all things subject to divine providence are ruled and measured by the eternal law, . . . it is evident that all things partake in some way in the eternal law, in so far as, namely, from its being imprinted on them, they derive their respective inclinations to their proper acts and ends. Now among all others, the rational creature is subject to divine providence in a more excellent way, in so far as it itself partakes of a share of providence, by being provident both for itself and for others. Therefore it has a share of the eternal reason, whereby it has a natural inclination to its proper act and end; and this participation of the eternal law in the rational creature is called the natural law . . . The light of natural reason, whereby we discern what is good and what is evil, which is a function of the natural law, is nothing else than an imprint on us of the divine light. It is therefore evident that the natural law is nothing else than the rational creature's participation of the eternal law.*

---

*Summa Theologica, I-II, q. 91, a. 2.

In all things in nature there are constant and uniform inclinations to attain definite ends. It is natural for the sun to light and heat the earth, for flowers to grow and bloom, for fish to swim and birds to fly, for man to think his thoughts and share them with his fellows. They are simply obeying the law stamped on their natures by their Creator. Here we see the eternal law at work in creatures, the divine reason and will guiding them to their ends. Here we see the temporal effect of the eternal law.

This temporal effect of the eternal law as showing itself in creatures is what we mean by the natural law. We call it the *natural* law because it is grounded in nature itself, and manifests itself through the nature or essence or constitution of things. The part of the natural law governing nonrational creatures is the natural *physical* law, and the part of the natural law governing rational creatures is the natural *moral* law.

Man is both a physical and a moral being. On his physical side man is governed by physical law in the same way as the other objects that make up the visible creation. But on his moral side, by his knowledge of the moral law and his freedom in applying it to his human acts, man becomes partaker in his own governance. He is allowed to cooperate freely with God in achieving the plan of creation. Hence man's share or participation in the eternal law is much larger than nonrational creatures can have. The classical definition of the natural law, taken in this restricted sense as identified with the moral law, has been given by St. Thomas: "The natural law is nothing else than the rational creature's participation of the eternal law."*

CONCLUSION

Though there are moral philosophers who succeed in giving some grounding to morality without God, their work is necessarily incomplete. The moral good in all its aspects, as value, as ought, and as end, remains without ultimate justification. The ideal they set up as the supreme value must be a perpetual mirage, the ought which they feel within themselves becomes an unreasonable urge toward that mirage, and the end they are striving for slips through their clutch forever at death. All they can say is: Be a *man* in the fullest sense. But man without God is not even man. Natural law without an eternal law is not even natural law in a correct sense, because it is a misunderstanding of human nature. Man is essentially a creature of God. To make a god of himself is man's greatest possible crime against his nature. Only invincible ignorance can excuse it. But to be in invincible ignorance of the greatest of truths is to be, albeit unwittingly, that much less of a man.

SUMMARY

Can ethics be built on man alone? Can man be the ultimate foundation of the moral order? Naturalists and humanists say yes. Theists say no;

---

*Summa Theologica, I-II, q. 91, a. 2.

beyond right reason and human nature there is an ultimate norm, and beyond the natural law there is the eternal law.

The *ultimate norm* is the divine nature. As human nature resembles the divine nature, human activity must resemble the divine activity. Man does right when he does what God does, wrong when he abuses his freedom to do what God cannot do.

There must be an eternal law in God. God cannot without contradiction be indifferent whether His plan of creation is carried out. The plan of His intellect and decree of His will that creatures attain their ends is the eternal law. This is truly a *law,* for it fulfills the definition of a law, and it is an *eternal* law, for an act of God's intellect and will is as eternal as God's very essence. It was promulgated by God from eternity, but it could not be received in creatures until these creatures existed.

The natural law can be approached in two ways: *inductively,* by an examination of man's nature, as was done in the previous chapter, or *deductively,* as St. Thomas does, defining the natural law as *the rational creature's participation of the eternal law.*

READINGS

1. St. Augustine's notions on the eternal law are found in *De Libero Arbitrio* (On Free Choice), of which there are several English translations, and in *Contra Faustum Manichaeum* (Reply to Faustus the Manichaean), of which an English translation is found only in the complete edition of St. Augustine's works and in the *Selected Writings of the Nicene and Post-Nicene Fathers.*
2. St. Thomas, *Summa Theologica,* I-II, q. 93; see also q. 91, a. 1.
3. Suarez, *De Legibus* (On Laws), bk. II, ch. 1-4.
4. Rickaby, *Moral Philosophy,* pp. 126-132; reprinted in Leibell, *Readings in Ethics,* pp. 313-317.
5. Cronin, *Science of Ethics,* vol. I, pp. 639-643.

CHAPTER 13

OBLIGATION

AND SANCTION

PROBLEM

Since the moral law binds without the use of external physical force and without any inner determination of our nature, just how does it accomplish its effect? What is this *oughtness, obligation,* or *duty* that law imposes; where does it obtain and how does it exert its binding power?

There are those who admit the existence of the moral law and admit God as the ultimate ground of morality, even if they do not use the term *eternal law,* yet they do not place the source of obligation in God but in the moral law itself. God is the Supreme Ideal, the Highest Value, but not the source of duty, the imposer of obligation, the Eternal Lawgiver. The aim of this view is the laudable one of keeping morality pure, free from the taint of self-interest, from the lure of reward and the fear of punishment; of safeguarding man's freedom, autonomy, and personal dignity so that he is under orders from no one; of eliminating the caricature of God as capricious despot of the universe and man's hard taskmaster. The most famous theory of this type is that of Immanuel Kant. But, on the other hand, can there be a law without a lawgiver, and can there be an obligation to no one? We ask:

(1) Can man impose moral obligation on himself?
(2) What is the nature of moral obligation?
(3) What is the ultimate source of moral obligation?
(4) How does moral obligation arise from the moral good?
(5) Does all moral obligation come through the natural law?
(6) What sanction is attached to the natural law?

KANT'S AUTONOMOUS MORALITY

Kant never tired of saying that two things ever filled him with admiration, "the starry sky above and the moral law within." On the moral law he based the whole structure of his philosophy, for after he had devoted his *Critique of Pure Reason* to demolishing the ability of human reason to discover truth speculatively, he tried in his *Critique of Practical Reason* to build it all up again on a practical and moral foundation. His thought is easier to follow in his *Foundations of the Metaphysics of Morals*.

He begins by stating that the good taken purely and simply is found only in a *good will,* and a good will is one which acts, not from natural inclination, but from *duty.* Only acts done from duty have moral worth. Even acts done in the line of duty but not from the motive of duty have no moral value. They lack the *form* of morality, that which precisely gives them their moral quality, and this can be nothing else but *respect for the law,* which is what he means by duty. Thus an act is not good because of the end to which it leads, but solely because of the motive of duty from which it is performed.

> The moral worth of an action does not lie in the effect which is expected from it or in any principle of action which has to borrow its motive from this expected effect. For all these effects (agreeableness of condition, indeed even the promotion of the happiness of others) could be brought about through other causes and would not require the will of a rational being, while the highest and unconditional good can be found only in such a will. Therefore the pre-eminent good can consist only in the conception of the law in itself (which can be present only in a rational being) so far as this conception and not the hoped-for effect is the determining ground of the will. This pre-eminent good, which we call moral, is already present in the person who acts according to this conception and we do not have to expect it first in the result.*

What is this law, respect for which must be the motive of an act to make it moral? It must be the pure concept of law as such. If any act I do is to be moral, I must ask myself: Can I make the maxim or principle on which this act rests into a universal law binding all?

> The shortest but most infallible way to find the answer to the question as to whether a deceitful promise is consistent with duty is to ask myself: Would I be content that my maxim (of extricating myself from difficulty by a false promise) should hold as a universal law for myself as well as for others? And could I say to myself that everyone may make a false promise when he is in a difficulty from which he otherwise cannot escape? I immediately see that I could will the lie but not a universal law to lie. For with such a law there would be no promises at all inasmuch as it would be futile to make a pretense of my intention in regard to future actions to those who would not believe this pretense or—if they over-

---

*Kant, *Foundations of the Metaphysics of Morals,* section I.

hastily did so—who would pay me back in my own coin. Thus my maxim would necessarily destroy itself as soon as it was made a universal law.*

Kant goes on to say that, whereas everything in nature works according to laws, only rational beings can have an idea of law and consciously conform their conduct to principles. This capacity is *will,* which is the same as *practical reason.* An objective principle of law binding the will is a command, stated as an *imperative* expressing the *ought.* An imperative may be *hypothetical* (if you want this end, you must use these means), or *categorical* (you must do this absolutely).

> If the action is good only as a means to something else, the imperative is hypothetical; but if it is thought of as good in itself, and hence as necessary in a will which of itself conforms to reason as the principle of this will, the imperative is categorical. . . .
>
> It concerns not the material of the action and its intended result but the form and principle from which it results. What is essentially good in it consists in the intention, the result being what it may. This imperative may be called the imperative of morality. . . .
>
> There is . . . only one categorical imperative. It is: Act only according to that maxim by which you can at the same time will that it should become a universal law.†

This statement of the categorical imperative is repeated often by Kant, sometimes with a slightly different wording and emphasis, but the underlying meaning is always the same. What in Kant's view makes an act morally wrong? It is in making an exception for myself, and thus contradicting the law in my own favor.

> When we observe ourselves in any transgression of duty, we find that we do not actually will that our maxim should become a universal law. That is impossible for us; rather, the contrary of this maxim should remain as a law generally, and we only take the liberty of making an exception to it for ourselves or for the sake of our inclination, and for this one occasion.‡

The fundamental reason why such conduct is wrong is that it subjects other persons (as means) to myself (as end), perverting the whole *realm of ends,* according to which each rational being, each *person,* must be treated never merely as a means but always as an end in himself. The dignity of the rational being, the nobility of a person as such, is therefore the fundamental reason why I must be moral. But this principle involves a further and startling conclusion. If I must not subject other persons as means to myself as end, I myself am not subjected as means to another as end.

---

*Kant, *Foundations of the Metaphysics of Morals,* section I.
†*Op. cit.,* section II.
‡*Ibid.*

Who then imposes the moral law upon me? I impose it on myself. This is what he calls the *autonomy* of the will.

> Reason, therefore, relates every maxim of the will as giving universal laws to every other will and also to every action toward itself; it does not do so for the sake of any other practical motive or future advantage but rather from the idea of the dignity of a rational being, which obeys no law except that which he himself also gives. . . .
> He is thus fitted to be a member in a possible realm of ends to which his own nature already destined him. For, as an end in himself, he is destined to be legislative in the realm of ends, free from all laws of nature and obedient only to those which he himself gives. Accordingly, his maxims can belong to a universal legislation to which he is at the same time also subject. . . . Autonomy is thus the basis of the dignity of both human nature and every rational nature.*

Kant goes on to derive from the moral law the three truths which he thought could not be established by speculative reason: the freedom of the will, the immortality of the soul, and the existence of God. Unless we are free, we can neither legislate the moral law for ourselves nor observe it. We can never reach but only approximate a perfect fulfillment of the moral law, but since our function in existence is always to tend to realize it more perfectly, we must be immortal. The One who does realize it perfectly, who is the absolute fulfillment of holiness and the ideal of all goodness, is God.

> Granted that the pure moral law inexorably binds every man as a command (not as a rule of prudence), the righteous man may say: I will that there be a God, that my existence in this world be also an existence in a pure world of the understanding outside the system of natural connections,† and finally that my duration be endless. I stand by this and will not give up this belief.‡

So these truths are neither mere hypotheses nor rational convictions, but practical postulates demanded by our moral needs which we accept on *belief*, an attitude Kant calls *pure rational faith*.§

Criticism

Kant's vigorous assertion of the moral law, his stern preachment of the claims of duty, the paramount importance he attached to the ethical issue, and the high seriousness with which he approached the fundamental problems of philosophy, acted as a powerful antidote to the materialism

---

*Ibid.
†By "outside the system of natural connections," Kant means that which is *not causally predetermined, as physical nature seems to be, but possessing free will.*
‡Kant, *Critique of Practical Reason*, pt. I, bk. II, ch. II, viii.
§*Op. cit.,* bk. II, ch. II, v, viii.

and hedonism of a shallower age. All this was to the good, but it should not
blind us to the defects of his system. We shall limit our criticisms to three:

(1) The motive of duty
(2) The categorical imperative
(3) The autonomy of the will

1. To rest all morality on the motive of *duty* is unnatural and inhuman.
Kant nowhere says that an act not done from duty is immoral, only that
it is nonmoral; nor does he say that to be moral it must be done from
pure duty alone. All he says is that unless the motive of duty is present
it cannot be moral, and, if it is done from both duty and inclination, only
the motive of duty can give it its morality. But even this is overplaying the
role of duty. Is it only her sense of duty and not her love for her child
that gives morality to a mother's devotion? Is it only cold obligation
and not large-hearted generosity that makes relief of the poor a moral
act? Certainly a sense of duty will be present in such cases, but love and
generosity are always esteemed as higher motives than mere duty and
give the act a greater moral worth. We fall back on duty only when
other motives fail. Duty is rather the last bulwark against wrong acting
than the highest motive for right acting.

How could Kant explain heroic acts, such as giving one's life for
one's friend? These are always thought the noblest and best, precisely
because they go beyond the call of duty. Kant is then faced with this
dilemma: either he must deny that heroic acts are moral, and thus fly
in the face of all human evaluations, so as to make his ethics useless in
practice; or he must make heroic acts a strict duty, thus putting a burden
on human nature that it cannot bear and robbing these acts of the very
quality that makes them heroic.

2. That the moral law commands us with a *categorical imperative* is
undoubtedly true, and Kant emphasizes it well, but his formulation of it
is faulty. The moral imperative is properly, "Do good and avoid evil,"
plus the more definite principles derived from this, rather than Kant's
formula, "So act that the maxim from which you act can be made
a universal law," which is only a negative rule. Evil ways of acting could
never become universal laws, for they are self-destructive; but there are
also good ways of acting that can never become universal laws, such as
a life of celibacy. Hence the reason for the moral goodness of an act is
not the fact that it can be made a universal law. Kant might answer that
we can will celibacy to be a universal law for a definite type of person
in definite circumstances; but this answer is no help, for if we start making
exceptions of this sort, the term *universal law* loses all meaning. It finally
narrows down to just one single case. To use Kant's own example, I might
will that anyone in my peculiar predicament could get out of it by lying,
and still have the law universal for that class of people.

To determine the goodness of an act wholly from the maxim which
governs it and not from the end to which it naturally leads is to adopt

a purely subjective norm of morality. All three determinants, the nature of the act, its motive, and the circumstances, must be considered, and not the motive alone. It is difficult to square Kant's view here with the acceptance of intrinsic morality.

3. Kant's recognition of the dignity of the human person is one of the most admired parts of his philosophy. But he carries it so far as to make a *created* person impossible. We must never use each other merely as means, but God may do with us what He pleases, short of contradicting His own attributes. To make the human will *autonomous* does violence to the rights of God the Creator. Kant is forced to this position by his rejection of the traditional proofs for God's existence, thus paying the price for faulty metaphysics. In Kant's system our reason for accepting God's existence is ultimately that we will His existence, for we need Him to justify morality to ourselves. As Kant says, this is a practical faith rather than a reasoned conviction. But here is another dilemma. Really God either does or does not exist; if He does not exist, we cannot will Him into existence simply because we feel a need of Him; if He does exist, the human will cannot be wholly autonomous but is subject to the law God imposes on us.

Kant correctly argues that there can be no morality without free will. But in his discussion of freedom there is always a confusion between freedom of choice and freedom of independence, as if one could not retain free will and still be under the command of another's law. To save freedom he demands autonomy, but by demanding autonomy he destroys all real obligation and therefore all real law.

The obligation an autonomous will imposes on itself is an obligation only in name. A will that binds itself is no more bound than a man who locks himself in but still holds the key in his hand. Kant does not think that we may either make or not make the moral law for ourselves as we please, or that we frame its provisions arbitrarily. We cannot escape from the categorical imperative, and the maxims that we will into universal laws cannot be otherwise than they are. Why not? If this necessity is founded on the very nature of things (and Kant thinks that it is, for it is our one grasp of the *noumenon,* the thing-in-itself), then it is determined for us by some other will than ours and to this will we are subject. Either there is no obligation or it is imposed on us from without. The only other alternative is an identification of the human will with the divine, the pantheistic trend taken by Kant's followers.

NATURE OF OBLIGATION

Either we impose the *ought* on ourselves or it is imposed on us from the outside; if from the outside, it must come either from God or from our fellow man, for nothing beneath us can bind us; if from our fellow man, it must arise from fellow man politically organized into the state or from the broader general requirements of group living. The only other alternative is to deny the existence of any moral obligation.

Moral obligation does not come from *oneself*. We have just discussed Kant's version of this theory and found it unacceptable. One cannot have authority over oneself and be subject to oneself in the same respect, be one's own superior and inferior. A lawmaker can repeal his own laws. If man made the moral law for himself, he could never violate it, for he cannot will both its observance and its violation at once, and his act of violation would simply be an act of repeal. Such a law could impose no obligation.

Moral obligation cannot come from *fellow man*. We examined moral positivism but found that it eliminates rather than explains moral obligation. As persons all men are equal. No man or body of men has original jurisdiction over another so as to bind him under moral guilt, under pain of losing his intrinsic value as a man. What obligation have men to obey the state? Of itself the state can exert only physical compulsion, unless it can appeal to the authority it receives from a source beyond itself that enjoins obedience to the state as part of the moral law itself. Lesser groups have even less authority. Hence moral obligation cannot come from fellow man, whether taken individually or as organized into society.

Moral obligation, therefore, can come only from *God*. But a negative argument by elimination is insufficient in so important a matter. Positive answers fall into two classes. *Voluntarists* have immediate recourse to the will of God. Man is obliged to live a moral life because God wills it, and no further reason need be sought why God wills it than the freedom and supremacy of the divine will itself. *Intellectualists* agree that God does will that a man live a moral life, but they are also concerned to show that the divine will, though supremely free, is not arbitrary or capricious, but governed by divine wisdom.

Voluntaristic theories

Writers who give preeminence to the will over the intellect tend to hold that acts are good because God commands them, evil because He forbids them. John Duns Scotus* thinks that all obligation comes from God's absolutely free will, and that adultery and murder in themselves are bad for man as contrary to his nature, but would not be wrong if God did not forbid them; he believes in intrinsic goodness or badness, but not in intrinsic rightness or wrongness. William of Ockham,† denying that universal ideas have a basis in reality, frees even the divine will from dependence on the divine ideas, and makes the goodness or badness of acts depend solely on the divine will. In one passage he says that God could even command His creatures to hate Him, and this hatred would then become meritorious. All acts are indifferent in themselves and become good or bad only because commanded or forbidden by God. Samuel

---

*Scotus, *Commentaria Oxoniensia*, III, d. 37, n. 5-8; IV, d. 50, q. 2, n. 10.
†Ockham, *Super IV Libros Sententiarum*, I, d. 17, q. 3; II, q. 19; III, q. 13; IV, qq. 8-9.

Pufendorf,* the celebrated German jurist, also attributes all morality to God's free will, but what he seems to mean is that God may create any creature He wishes, but then requires that the creature conform its conduct to its nature; this requirement, however, does not come from the nature of things but solely from God's will. None of these writers says that God actually is arbitrary or capricious in His willing. René Descartes† goes to a further extreme when he declares that even mathematical truths depend on God's free choice. If so, moral truths likewise would be no more than divine whimsies.

It is true that morality is dependent on God and that God's will is free, but the above explanation will not hold. We must not imagine God looking over the catalogue of possible human acts and arbitrarily picking out some which He determined to designate as wrong, but might just as well have picked out others. It is true that God commands good acts and forbids evil ones, but this will of His is not arbitrary or capricious; His will depends on His intellect and both His intellect and will depend on His essence.

There can be no contradiction in God. He cannot command man to perform the kind of act His own holiness makes impossible for Him, and He cannot forbid man to perform the kind of act His own holiness requires of Him. God cannot be cruel, unjust, unfaithful, untruthful, wanton, or perverse. He not only does not want to but He cannot, for to act thus would destroy His very Being, and He is Being by essence. Therefore He cannot command His creatures to act thus. These acts are not wrong because God has forbidden them, but God has to forbid them because they are wrong of their very nature.

Intellectualistic theories

Intellectualists make God the ultimate source of moral obligation no less than the voluntarists, but try to show how God Himself is included within the moral order of which He is the Author, just as He from whom all being flows is also Being. They begin with an analysis of obligation itself. St. Thomas‡ notes that necessity arises from the causes of a thing. From the efficient cause arises the physical necessity of compulsion and restraint, for these are brought about by the action of an external agent. From the material and formal causes arises the physical necessity of internal determination, for matter and form constitute the nature of a being and specify for it its type of activity; only intellectual natures having free will escape this determinism, and only insofar as they are free. We are left with the final cause, and it is from this that *moral* necessity or obligation arises.

---

*Pufendorf, *Elements of Universal Jurisprudence,* bk. I, definition II; *De Jure Naturae et Gentium,* bk. I, ch. 2, §6; bk. II, ch. 3, §4.
†Descartes, *Objections and Replies,* 6th set of objections.
‡*Summa Theologica,* I, q. 82, a. 1.

Moral necessity, which binds a free will without destroying its freedom, must come from the final cause, for only an end or good known by the intellect can move the will, either to arouse or to restrain it. But one cannot will an end and at the same time refuse to will the means necessary to the end; otherwise he would have a mere ineffectual wish, not a decision of the will. Four possibilities occur:

(1) Neither the end nor the means are necessary
(2) The end is necessary but not the means
(3) The means are necessary but not the end
(4) Both the end and the means are necessary

1. Obviously there is no obligation when both end and means are optional.

2. If there are several alternative means to the same end, there is no necessity of willing these means rather than those. Even if the end is absolutely necessary, other means can be used and the end can still be reached.

3. If the end is not absolutely necessary, there is no necessity of using the means even when they are the only possible means. This is always the case when the end is not an absolutely last end, for every intermediate end is also a means to a further end and is not necessary unless this further end is necessary.

4. The end is one that absolutely must be obtained at all costs, and there is but one means to it with no substitute possible. The means are necessary *if* they are the only means and *if* the end is necessary. By fulfilling both conditions, we pass beyond hypothetical necessity to categorical necessity and arrive at the absolute *ought* of moral obligation. We may now define it as the moral necessity of acting in a certain way, laid on the free will by the intellect perceiving the necessary connection of these acts as necessary means to a necessary end.

Applying this analysis to man's moral life, we find both requirements fulfilled:

(1) A necessary end absolutely to be obtained
(2) One necessary means with no substitute possible

1. Man has an absolutely last end, attainment of which is absolutely necessary for man. The human will is not free to seek or not seek the ultimate good, but must of its very nature seek it. It is the sole purpose for which man exists, the only reason why he has any being at all. The intellect perceives this design impressed on man's very nature as the objective order inherent in creation itself and exacted by man's being the kind of being he is.

2. Man has only one means of fulfilling his nature and reaching his last end, morally good human acts, and only one means of perverting his nature and losing his last end, morally bad human acts. The nature of man as a free being, who must earn his own moral worth and incur his own moral guilt, makes any substitute means impossible.

Can, then, genuine moral obligation arise merely from the necessary connection of necessary means with a necessary end, independently of any commanding authority? In a sense, yes. Before any authority can command, there must preexist the moral obligation of obeying the command. Moral obligation is entailed in the very idea of moral value. By the very fact that an act has moral value it is the kind of act that *ought* to be done. Just as the evidence of the truth imposes itself on the theoretical reason and demands assent, so the moral ideal imposes itself on the practical reason and commands consent. As the principle of noncontradiction stands on its own feet in the theoretical order, so the principle "Do good and avoid evil" stands on its own feet in the practical order. It manifests the intrinsic connection between an act to be done, as the necessary means, and the love of the good, as the necessary end. One cannot love the good and refuse that act.

Only the good can be of obligation, yet not every good is of obligation. Does not this show that obligation adds to the good the notion of some authority imposing it? Not for this reason alone. Good acts are of two kinds: those which *may* be done and those which *must* be done. In the former case there is an option because the end can be obtained in another way and the necessity is not absolute. In the latter case the omission of the act would make the end impossible. The difficulty can be solved at least proximately on the means–end level, and does not of itself imply an extrinsic legislator. But proximate reasons are insufficient.

The explanation given so far shows how it is possible for a nontheist to recognize and accept moral obligation. It also points up its own inadequacy as an explanation. It only *asserts* that the good is an absolutely necessary end without being able to explain *why*. We need more than a bare assertion to see that the necessity is not merely hypothetical but truly categorical, and thus a *moral* obligation. We need to see just what there is about the good that constitutes its overwhelmingly necessitating power yet at the same time leaves us freedom of choice, so that the obligation is absolute yet a moral one. We can do so only by tracing the good to a really existing source of goodness, to the absolute Being who is both absolute Goodness and absolute Freedom, the cause of goodness and freedom in us. Moral obligation remains in a truncated condition until God is put in at the apex.

It is because the order of our knowing is not always the same as the order of objective being that some men have a sufficient notion of moral obligation and acknowledge its binding force without having a clear and certain knowledge of God. In our way of knowing, starting with connatural knowledge, we rise from the actual values we experience to the formation of an abstract ideal of value, and then learn to identify this ideal with God. Some stop short of this last step, and thus are left with a firm sense of moral obligation yet no really existing personal being to base it on. The last step is philosophically necessary to complete and justify our knowledge.

Moral obligation, therefore, though having an incomplete basis in the very notion of moral value, is as a matter of fact imposed by a commanding authority, by the one who has established the end and the means and their necessary connection. This objective order of things, commanded by God's intellect and carried out by His will, is what we have called the *eternal law,* whose created counterpart is the *natural law,* that can be imperfectly reflected and formulated in *human law.* Thus God is the ultimate source of all moral obligation.

MORAL GOODNESS AND MORAL OBLIGATION

There remain some points to be clarified, especially the logical sequence of our concepts. Should God as the ultimate source of moral obligation be conceived as the Supreme Lawgiver, or as man's Last End, or as the Ideal of moral goodness? Another way of saying it: Does moral obligation stem from the fact that God is powerful or that He is good, and, if the latter, that He is good to us or good in Himself?

God is the Supreme Lawgiver, but acknowledgment of Him as Lawgiver presupposes the obligation to obey His laws. Rewards and punishments, by which laws are enforced, do not constitute obligation but envisage an obligation already there. Why must God be a just rewarder or punisher except that justice is part of the ideal of goodness that God must exhibit in the highest form? God's right to be obeyed, from which His function of Lawgiver stems, exists in God necessarily and is not freely assumed by an act of His will. God conceived after the manner of the Deists, as Supreme Being and Architect of the universe but morally indifferent, could not impose *moral* obligation. He might force us to do His will, but there is nothing moral in cringing before superior power. God cannot be the source of moral obligation unless He is good. He does will to be good, but His will merely confirms the goodness He already has.

Is God conceived as Last End the source of moral obligation? If the end is thought of merely as something I cannot help wanting, something without which I shall feel empty and wretched, then missing it would be a physical evil resulting in pain and grief, not necessarily a moral evil. I ought to seek such an end if I want to avoid misery, but the obligation is hypothetical only; failure would be folly, not moral depravity. To be the ultimate ground of *moral* obligation, the end must be more than a mere source of personal gratification. It must have ontological as well as psychological necessity. It must be something I ought to seek because it is the only reason why I exist at all, something that constitutes my whole value as a being, something without which I become an existential absurdity, a living contradiction, a mockery of my Maker, a blot on creation, and a travesty of myself. I am not allowed thus to ruin my being. To do so would not be mere folly but moral depravity, an overturning of the moral order and an attack on goodness itself. Hence the obligation to seek the Last End is a *categorical* and a *moral* obligation.

If it is my own being, why may I not ruin it? Here the nontheist arrives at what must be bedrock for him. If he admits moral obligation at all, the value of his own person as a partially realized abstract ideal can be the only ultimate reason for it. The theist answers: I may not ruin my being because it is not wholly my own. My intrinsic goodness is a received and participated goodness, good ultimately not on its own account but as a finite reflection of the Infinite Goodness. God is the Lawgiver whose will ought to be obeyed and the Last End that ought absolutely to be sought, but the ultimate reason that makes Him both is His Supreme Goodness in Himself.

God as the fullness of Being is wholly for Himself by knowledge and love of Himself. He is thus the most personal of beings, and as personal is the foundation of the whole moral order. Moral value and personal dignity coincide. Man has moral value because he is a person, and God is the supreme source of all moral value because He is the supreme source of all personality.

ALL OBLIGATION THROUGH NATURAL LAW

Moral obligation, whatever its source, is conveyed to man through the natural law. All human positive laws, therefore, if they are to impose any moral obligation, must derive this binding force from the natural law. There are only three reasons why a person obeys a law:

(1) The law commands what is personally advantageous.
(2) Threat of punishment makes it expedient to obey.
(3) The subject feels a sense of duty or moral obligation.

The first two reasons cannot guarantee obedience to the law. It will be kept as long as it seems advantageous or the vigilance of the police cannot be eluded. Since the subjects feel no moral obligation to keep the law, they will break it as soon as it becomes more expedient to break it than to keep it. In these cases it is not the law itself that binds the human will, but the attractiveness of what the law prescribes or the fear of the punishment threatened. A law, as a law, can bind the human will only by imposing moral obligation.

Human positive laws can impose no moral obligation on their own account, but can do so only if the natural law commands that just laws enacted by legitimate human authority are to be obeyed. Therefore human positive laws derive what binding force they have from the natural law. Divine positive law is only an apparent exception, for, though it imposes moral obligation on its own account, it is confirmed by the natural law, which commands that God's commands shall be obeyed. Therefore all moral obligation comes from the natural law, or at least (in the case of divine positive law) is accompanied by a parallel obligation from the natural law.

SANCTION

We saw that obligation is moral necessity, a necessity resulting from the final cause. The final cause is a motive urging a person to act but not destroying his free will. The only way that a lawgiver can get his law obeyed is by proposing a motive sufficiently strong to attract the subjects to free acts of obedience. Such a motive, such a means a lawgiver uses to enforce his law, is called a *sanction*. Sanction means the promise of reward for keeping the law or the threat of punishment for breaking the law, or both; it also means the rewards or punishments themselves. Its function is *antecedent,* to induce people to keep the law and to dissuade them from breaking it, and *consequent,* to restore the objective order of justice after the law has been kept or broken.

A *natural* sanction follows from the very nature of the act performed, as sickness from intemperance or loss of business from dishonesty to customers. A *positive* sanction is decided by the will of the lawmaker and has no natural connection with the act, as a fine for speeding or imprisonment for tax evasion. A *perfect* sanction is one that is both *strong,* in that it provides a rational will with a sufficient motive for keeping the law, and *just,* in that it sets up equality between merit and reward, demerit and punishment. An *imperfect* sanction is in some measure either weak or unjust or both.

As moral philosophers we must discuss the kind of sanction attached to the natural law. The following questions call for an answer:

(1) Has the natural law any sanction in the present life?
(2) Has the natural law a perfect sanction anywhere?
(3) What is the perfect sanction for the natural law?

1. Observance of the natural law brings about the harmony between our acts and our nature that we described when discussing the norm of morality, harmony between our animal and rational tendencies, and between our creatural, social, and proprietary relations. Barring accidents, there should result peace of mind, friendship, honor, prosperity, health, and a long life, as the result of the natural virtues of prudence, justice, fortitude, and temperance. Frequent violation of the natural law should result in remorse of conscience, loss of friendship, dishonor, poverty, disease, and an early death, as the expected consequences of folly, dishonesty, cowardice, and debauchery.

But, as life is actually lived, this sanction is imperfect. Too often the good suffer and the wicked prosper all life long. Unforeseen calamities play a large part in life and they are not distributed according to one's moral worth. Few violate the whole natural law, and the punishments for breaking part of it are offset by the rewards for keeping the rest. Crimes are concealed and the punishments avoided. It may be true in general that "crime does not pay," but in many particular instances it pays well. One may find a bad conscience easy to live with for a million dollars dishonestly gained. One may be put to the supreme test, to choose between death and sin, and no possible temporal reward can be offered for loss of life.

2. This imperfect kind of sanction to the natural law cannot satisfy God, the Perfect Lawgiver. A wise lawgiver assigns a sanction strong enough to achieve the end of the law. Otherwise it will appeal only to the upright who do not need it, and will fail to influence those whom the law is especially designed to curb. It must counterbalance any advantage to be gained in breaking the law. A just lawgiver assigns a just sanction, distributing rewards and punishments in proportion to the degree in which the law has been kept or broken, to the good or evil done. Otherwise a small observance might compensate for a grave violation. Since God is a wise and just lawgiver, He must assign a perfect sanction to the natural law. Since the sanction in the present life is not perfect, the perfect sanction must be applied in the life to come.

3. What does this perfect sanction consist in? It must be the gain or loss of our last end and highest good. No other sanction would be sufficient to make men keep the natural law. Those who deliberately refuse to use the means should be deprived of the end and those who deliberately choose evil should be deprived of the good. If even this threat does not always prevent wrongdoing, and experience shows that it does not, surely nothing less would do so. God Himself is unable to provide a stronger sanction, without encroaching on man's free will, for He cannot offer a greater reward or threaten a greater punishment than the gain or loss of the Highest Good. What this consists in is our next consideration.

SUMMARY

How does moral necessity, which is the same as oughtness, obligation, or duty, accomplish its effect?

Immanuel Kant held that we impose obligation on ourselves. Nothing, he says, is simply good except a good will. A good will is one that acts from the motive of duty. Duty is the necessity of acting from respect for law. The moral law commands with a categorical imperative: So act that the maxim from which you act can by your will be made into a universal law. The basis for the categorical imperative is the human personality. A person is never to be used as a means, always to be regarded as an end. The human will is an end in itself, autonomously imposing the moral law on itself.

Kant is criticized for overstressing the idea of duty, incorrectly formulating the moral imperative, and making the human will usurp the place of God while emptying obligation of all meaning.

Moral obligation cannot come from *oneself,* for any lawmaker can repeal his own laws, nor from *fellow man,* for as persons all men are equal and no one has original jurisdiction over another. Moral obligation must come from *God,* who alone determines by the *eternal law* the necessary connection between the observance of the moral law and man's last end, and makes the attainment of the last end absolutely mandatory. This determination of His intellect and will He manifests to us through the *natural law,* which is the proximate source of all obligation; from it alone *positive laws* derive their binding force.

Moral obligation is inherent in the very idea of the moral good and should be conceived as logically prior to any commanding authority, which presupposes an obligation to obey the command. Yet without a lawgiver it is incomplete, for there is no one to whom one is obliged. Nontheists can and do admit moral obligation, but on an insecure basis.

Sanction is the promise of reward or threat of punishment added to a law to secure obedience. There is an *imperfect* sanction to the natural law in the present life. Some evil acts have natural punishments, but they are not equally applied and are often evaded. There must be a *perfect* sanction to the natural law in the life to come. God must provide a sufficiently strong motive for keeping the law, and must distribute rewards and punishments justly. This perfect sanction, the strongest possible without destroying human free will, consists in the gain or loss of man's last end and highest good.

READINGS

1. The following give background material rather than matter directly on the subject of this chapter.
   a. Aristotle, *Nicomachean Ethics,* bk. VII, ch. 2, 3.
   b. St. Thomas, *Summa Theologica,* I, q. 82, aa. 1, 2 (first volume of the *Basic Writings*); I-II, q. 10, aa. 1, 2; q. 13, aa. 3, 6; *Summa Contra Gentiles,* bk. III, ch. 10 (all these in the second volume of the *Basic Writings*).
   c. Suarez, *De Legibus* (On Laws), bk. II, ch. 9.
2. Kant's *Foundations of the Metaphysics of Morals* and his *Critique of Practical Reason* present his ethical views. There are numerous commentaries. Paton's *The Categorical Imperative* is worth consulting.
3. Cronin, *Science of Ethics,* vol. I, ch. VIII, IX.
4. Rickaby, *Moral Philosophy,* pp. 109-125, 159-168.
5. Brosnahan, *Prolegomena to Ethics,* appendix A, "The Kantian Ought" reprinted in Leibell's *Readings in Ethics,* pp. 383-400.
6. Le Buffe and Hayes, *The American Philosophy of Law,* ch. IX.
7. Davitt, *The Nature of Law.* Contrasts the intellectualist or Thomistic with the voluntarist or Scotistic interpretation of obligation.

CHAPTER 14

HAPPINESS

PROBLEM

The conflicting claims of happiness and duty run all through the history of ethics. The *deontologists*, champions of duty, have had their say through the mouth of Immanuel Kant. Few of them would deny the claim of happiness but want to keep it secondary, as an added bonus for faithfulness to duty rather than an aim consciously to be pursued. This view appeals to men of sterner stuff and to the puritanical-minded, who equate happiness with enjoyment and have never learned to enjoy themselves with a comfortable conscience. The *eudaemonists*, champions of happiness, have also been vocal but we have not yet given them a hearing. We could have begun ethics with happiness, as Aristotle does, but postponed it for the sake of a more disinterested approach, wishing to show that the good is worthy of pursuit just because it is good in itself apart from its benefit to us. We also did not wish to be identified with those who do disservice to happiness by interpreting it as pleasure.

It is time now to hear the case for happiness. We shall not, however, contrast it with duty. The dichotomy is a false one. To achieve happiness is our duty if happiness is our end, and the doing of such a duty automatically brings happiness. Both duty and happiness are united in the good, for the ought and the end are good only if they have intrinsic value.

That we must seek happiness in the abstract will be much a matter of definition. The more important question for us is whether happiness is attainable. Can our pursuit of it be successful or are we doomed to be ever chasing a will-o'-the-wisp that constantly lures us on but ever eludes our grasp? It is a choice between ethical *optimism* and *pessimism*, according

163

as we engage in the inevitable pursuit of happiness with hope or despair. The following points sum up our study:

(1) What is the meaning of happiness?
(2) Do all men seek happiness?
(3) Do all men think happiness attainable?
(4) Is merely natural happiness a possible end for man?
(5) Is happiness really attainable somewhere?

MEANING OF HAPPINESS

Happiness we define as *desire satisfied by the conscious possession of the good*. The root meaning of *happy* is that of a person favored by fortune, one to whom good things *happen*. The equivalent word in other languages usually has the same basic meaning. Hence one may wonder, as Aristotle* does, whether a man should be called happy until he is dead, since misfortune may befall him in his old age. But we carry the word *happiness* beyond its linguistic origin and the uses of common speech. The man who is fortunate, lucky, successful, satisfied, cheerful, glad, or joyous may be comparatively happy in the sense that he has come closer to happiness than most, or has done so in some particular line, but he is not necessarily happy in the way the philosopher speaks of happiness. Thus *happiness* is an analogous term, applying to various signs of, approaches to, and contributions toward happiness. The philosopher is not interested in these diminished manifestations but in the full concept of happiness as such.

Happiness is not a passing feeling or emotion, such as joy or gladness, but is a lasting state or condition. One may be generally happy though suffering a temporary grief, just as another's chronic unhappiness may be punctuated by moments of joy. Nor is happiness a permanent quality of a person's character, a sunny disposition, a cheerful outlook on life, however much this may help to happiness; for some people can maintain such a disposition in the face of disappointment, whereas happiness is satisfaction. The immature and feeble-minded can have a cheerful outlook, but it is due to lack of appreciation, not to fulfillment and possession.

Animals are incapable of happiness. They tend toward ends and have appetites that can be satisfied by things good for them. Having sense-knowledge, they can *feel* satiated and are capable of a kind of contentment. The animal that has eaten all it can is content for the moment, though it will soon get hungry again. Only intellectual beings are strictly capable of happiness. They alone can reflect on their state and *consciously* appreciate the satisfaction they enjoy. Happiness is a subjective condition entailing the existence of desire in oneself, the consciousness of the existence of the desire, the actual satisfaction of the desire, and the consciousness that this desire is being or has been satisfied. Such a state can exist only in a being capable of reflection and self-consciousness, an intellectual being.

Nicomachean Ethics, bk. I, ch. 10, 1100a 1 to 1100b 10.

Even in man contentment is not happiness. A man can be content if he limits his desires by a judicious compromise, being willing to forego some desires in order that he may attain others. In this life such an attitude is often necessary, but no one is ever *fully satisfied* with a compromise; it is the best we can get in the circumstances, but we wish the circumstances would allow us more. If the desires exist, they want to be satisfied, not sacrificed for the benefit of other desires.

Perfect happiness comes from the complete possession of the perfect good, from that which *fully* satisfies *all* our desires. Boethius defines it as "a state made perfect by the aggregate of all good things,"* and St. Thomas as "the perfect good which lulls the appetite altogether."† Imperfect happiness falls off from the perfect by leaving some of our desires wholly or partially unsatisfied. One who is imperfectly happy is happy insofar as his desires are fulfilled and unhappy insofar as they are not. Resignation to this state of affairs, to a partial happiness mingled with unhappiness, is what we have called contentment; thus it is evident that contentment is not happiness itself.

Perfect happiness, again, may be considered as absolute or relative. *Absolutely* perfect happiness is incapable of increase and is applicable to God alone. *Relatively* perfect happiness is completely satisfying to a creature according to that creature's finite capacity. In other words, perfect happiness supposes a perfect correspondence between potency and act, potency for happiness and actual possession of it. God, who is Pure Act, is necessarily happy by His own very Being and to an infinite degree. A creature, composed as it is of potency and act, is rendered happy when its limited potency for happiness is actualized as far as its limitations allow.

ALL MEN SEEK HAPPINESS

That all men seek happiness in general, in the abstract, without specifying the object supposed to produce it, is evident from the very definition of happiness. We cannot desire something without at the same time wanting our desire to be satisfied; otherwise, we both do and do not desire it. But happiness is only a name for our self-conscious realization that our desires have been or are being satisfied; therefore we cannot desire anything without desiring happiness. One who would not crave happiness must have no desires, and such a one could not be human. St. Thomas put this with his usual clearness:

> Happiness can be considered in two ways. First, according to the general notion of happiness; and thus of necessity every man desires happiness. For the general notion of happiness consists in the perfect good. But since good is the object of the will, the perfect good of a man is that which entirely satisfies his will. Consequently to desire happiness is nothing else than to desire that one's will be satisfied. And this everyone desires.

Consolation of Philosophy, bk. III, prose 2.
†*Summa Theologica,* I-II, q. 2, a. 8.

Secondly, we may speak of happiness according to its specific notion, as to that in which it consists. And thus all do not know happiness, because they know not in what thing the general notion of happiness is found. And consequently in this respect not all desire it.*

Hence the human will is not free with regard to happiness in general. Man is so made that he must seek it. But man is free in the choice of concrete objects by whose possession he hopes to obtain happiness. All want to be happy, but not all know how to find happiness.

It is a psychological impossibility to desire misery for its own sake. Those who seem to take a morbid delight in making themselves miserable manifest a perverted condition, an exception which proves the rule by showing how unnatural such behavior is; what they really seek, subconsciously perhaps, is some form of sadistic or masochistic gratification they get from it, as the crank probably does from his meanness. While yearning for happiness in the abstract, one may judge that happiness in the concrete has become impossible through lack of means to reach it; the man in the throes of despair wants happiness so badly that he cannot face the idea of its loss. One may feel that it is better to endure present misery than the worse misery of making an effort to escape from it; thus the lazy abide in a filth and squalor they do not enjoy, and the timid let opportunities for self-betterment pass them by. Introverted visionaries may find the dream of happiness too engrossing to be shattered by the prosaic reality of hard work; they want happiness now in the only way they can get it now. A man who deliberately chooses an evil does so because of the good he sees bound up in it. At least he thinks it the lesser of two evils; he wants to be less unhappy and this is choosing what appears to be a relative or comparative happiness; thus the suicide seeks relief from life's wretchedness. So all these are but seeming exceptions to the universal law that all men seek happiness.

Happiness is the basic motive in everything we do. Our every act is motivated by some desire, satisfaction of which is intended as at least a partial ingredient in the sum total of our happiness. We often have to sacrifice some goods for the sake of others, we may mistakenly choose the apparent good in place of the true good, we may foolishly prefer some temporary enjoyment here and now to lasting bliss in a better world, but we do all this for happiness. It goes to show, not that we do not want happiness, but rather that we want is so much that we cannot stand the delay in waiting for it, and impatiently snatch at its partial and imperfect forms that appeal so vividly to the senses.

We need not be *explicitly* thinking of happiness in all that we do. We do not pause before each action and say to ourselves, "I am doing this in order to become happier." Now and then, when we reflect on the meaning of life, we may explicitly form this intention and it remains in the back of our minds governing the rest of our deeds. But even one who never

---

*Summa Theologica, I-II, q. 5, a. 8.

reflects on the purpose of life is acting *implicitly* for happiness, and this is what we have been at pains to show here.

PESSIMISM AND OPTIMISM

Is happiness attainable? No one will deny the possibility of some sort of imperfect happiness, at least for the more fortunate of men. But by definition this state is not wholly satisfactory. We want to know whether *perfect* happiness is attainable, or at least how closely we can approach to it.

The answer will depend chiefly on one's convictions about the existence of God and the immortality of the human soul. Atheists and materialists must limit man's destiny to the temporary happiness possible in the present life. Most of them advise resignation and contentment as about the best we can do. Many insist that we must simply toughen ourselves to face the fact that the quest for real happiness is futile. The following passage from Bertrand Russell eloquently states this view:

> That Man is the product of causes which had no prevision of the end they were achieving; that his origin, his growth, his hopes and fears, his loves and his beliefs, are but the outcome of accidental collocations of atoms; that no fire, no heroism, no intensity of thought and feeling, can preserve an individual life beyond the grave; that all the labors of the ages, all the devotion, all the inspiration, all the noonday brightness of human genius, are destined to extinction in the vast death of the solar system, and that the whole temple of Man's achievement must inevitably be buried beneath the debris of a universe in ruins—all these things, if not quite beyond dispute, are yet so nearly certain, that no philosophy which rejects them can hope to stand. Only within the scaffolding of these truths, only on the firm foundation of unyielding despair, can the soul's habitation henceforth be safely built.*

Such stoicism on a foundation of modern science is a typically Western form of pessimism. The Orientals approach the problem in a different way. The Brahmanists† and Buddhists,‡ for example, say that personal existence itself is necessarily painful because it is always accompainied by unsatisfied desire. Since the desires cannot be fulfilled, the thing to do is not to strive to satisfy them but to extinguish them so that they are no longer felt. Suicide is useless, for desire itself will reincarnate us. For the Buddhists the soul is not a substance; the soul is only what it thinks. When by asceticism and contemplation it has succeeded in stifling all desire, especially for continued existence, it will escape the wheel of birth, the cycle of reincarnation, and sink into the blessed state of Nirvana. Happiness is the utter peace of nonbeing, whether this mean total extinction or an unconscious and selfless existence.

---

*"A Free Man's Worship," in *Mysticism and Logic,* ch. III; reprinted in *Selected Papers of Bertrand Russell.*
†The *Bhagavadgita* is a sublime poetic expression of Hindu thought.
‡Of the numerous Buddhist writings the *Dhammapada* may be found the most profitable reading.

Interest in Oriental thought was awakened in Europe by Arthur Schopenhauer,* the prince of pessimists. He thought that life is so full of miseries that it is better not to live. The whole universe is but the manifestation of a primeval force, the *will-to-live,* which is the source of all the struggle and misery in life. The worst thing we can do is to propagate the race, because it only brings into existence more sufferers. The chief virtue is sympathy or compassion, by which we substitute the *will-to-let-live* for the *will-to-live,* and thus obtain some relief from the constant struggle. This wan glimmer of happiness is all we can hope for. For the apostles of absurdity, the atheistic existentialists, happiness is not only unattainable; it may not even be desirable.

Optimism rather than pessimism has characterized the Western tradition. Plato recognized that happiness in the possession of the very Idea of the Good is the goal of human living. It is to be sought in the present life but cannot be experienced here. In a former existence we once had it, but we fell from that blessed state by the commission of some sin. Our purpose now is to strive through the practice of virtue in successive lives to escape from the body, from this sensible world of becoming and decay, and to return to the intelligible world of Ideas, the world of true and lasting being, in which we shall eternally contemplate the Ideas in their full perfection. To this we are led by fleeting glimpses of the Ideas awakened in our memory by their imperfect copies in this shadowy sense-world. Happiness, though the road to it be long and arduous, is ultimately attainable.

Aristotle in his masterly analysis of happiness, though never expressly denying a future life, restricts his consideration to the present world. Happiness, he says,† is the end of man. It is not inactivity, but action, else one could be happy while asleep. It must be the highest kind of action, not done for something else but desirable for its own sake. It is not amusement, which is only relaxation between work. It is not found in producing things, since such actions are for the sake of the product and happiness is for its own sake. It is not action of the body or senses, but of what is noblest and best in us, our reason. It is not activity of the practical reason, for this is full of care and trouble, but of the speculative or theoretical reason which acts in quiet and leisure, for we work to have leisure. Hence it is not the activity of the soldier and statesman, but of the sage and scholar.

Because it is the good life, it is the life of virtue, and of the highest virtue, not merely of courage and temperance which fit a man for practical life, but of the intellectual virtues which fit a man for contemplation, the contemplation of the highest truth and good. The contemplative life is the most pleasant, leisurely, continuous, enduring, and self-sufficing. This is the life of God and it is the best.

Such a life is too high for man on earth. We must interrupt our con-

---

*Schopenhauer's main work is *The World as Will and Idea.*
†*Nicomachean Ethics,* bk. I, ch. 4-13, 1095a 13 to 1102a 10; and bk. X, ch. 6-9, 1176a 30 to 1181b 25.

templation of the true and the good to take care of our bodily needs. But we should devote ourselves not to what is mortal but to what is most god-like in us, and cherish the periods of contemplation to which we can attain. Happiness of a sort is possible even in the practical life. For it we need a sufficiency of health, maturity, education, friends, worldly goods, and length of days. But all of these should be made subordinate aids to the truly happy life, a life most like that of God.

These two strains of thought, one from Plato and one from Aristotle, but especially the latter, elevated to the supernatural plane by the data of Christian revelation, find their full flowering in the teaching of St. Thomas.* But St. Thomas is primarily a theologian and only secondarily a philosopher. He nowhere makes a complete study of the end of man explicitly under-taken from the standpoint of pure reason alone. But he gives the ground-work for such a study. We can sift out the data of Christian revelation and, putting them aside as beyond the philosopher's scope, see what is left. There remains the hypothetical natural man. The whole question of man's natural destiny rests on the question of the immortality of the human soul. If immortality cannot be proved on rational or philosophical grounds, then man's natural destiny could only be to achieve such happiness as is pos-sible in this world. If immortality can be proved on rational or philosophical grounds, then man's destiny even in the natural order lies beyond the bounds of the present life. Only on the second hypothesis is the problem of man's ultimate happiness open for further philosophical investigation.

MAN'S NATURAL DESTINY

The question can be put on several different levels:

1. We may ask, *What is the end of man attainable within the limits of the present life?* This is Aristotle's problem in his *Nichomachean Ethics;* within the limits set he has solved it admirably. But if (whatever Aristotle himself may have thought) man has an immortal soul, an end restricted to the present life could not be an absolutely last end but at most a relatively last end. To secure the latter is important enough, but incomplete. The in-dividual can reach but a semblance of imperfect happiness, and not every individual but only the fortunate few. Society, however, is temporal in its aims: to improve the welfare of mankind and to provide for its members at least the opportunity of pursuing such happiness as is obtainable in this life. This is why Aristotle's *Politics* is the logical continuation of his *Ethics* and why the study of both on this lowly temporal plane is so necessary, for in any case man must live this earthly life and live it right. But it does not envision man's ultimate destiny even in the natural order.

2. We may ask, *What is the absolutely last end of man in the state in which man actually exists, using all the sources of knowledge we actually have?* This is St. Thomas' problem in the two *Summas.* According to Chris-tian revelation, man has been lifted to the supernatural plane. By a free

---

Summa Theologica, I-II, qq. 3 and 4.

gift of God to which man has no natural right, man has been raised above his natural capacity and given a destiny to which he could not aspire if left to himself. This destiny is the Beatific Vision, a direct sight of the divine essence face to face. He has also been given, or rather has had restored to him by redemption, the supernatural gift of grace, which is the means by which he can merit the Beatific Vision as his everlasting reward. Since the existence of the supernatural order, of grace and glory, could not be known without direct revelation from God, and even its possibility could hardly be suspected, the Beatific Vision belongs to Christian theology and has no place in a purely philosophical study such as ethics. We mention it here only to show what we do not mean.

3. We may ask, *What is the absolutely last end of man insofar as it can be discovered by pure reason?* This is our question, and it is different from that asked by Aristotle on the one hand and by St. Thomas on the other. It asks, What are the full demands and requirements of human nature taken precisely as a human nature, and what is human nature itself ultimately fitted for in the scheme of creation? If the human soul is naturally immortal, obviously even its natural demands and capacities cannot be satisfied by the transitory goods of this life. If the Beatific Vision, as supernatural, transcends the demands and capacities of man's nature, there must be some absolutely last end to which man would be destined were he left on the purely natural plane. This is the end of man and the kind of happiness that ethics must determine.

It is objected that such a study is purely hypothetical, that man is not and never was in such a state of pure nature. Granted, but that does not in any way make our study useless or impractical. The supernatural should not be thought of as opposing the natural, but rather as presupposing the natural and adding to it. The supernatural is not unnatural, against nature, but, as its name says, *super*natural, above nature. Hence whatever is said here in ethics about man in the natural order remains true, though incomplete, about man in the supernatural order. The fact, then, that man actually has been raised to the supernatural plane does not invalidate any of the conclusions we reach in a purely natural study such as ethics.

Nor are we hinting that man may make a choice between the natural and the supernatural orders, that he may politely decline the gift of the supernatural and settle for the lower plane of the natural. No, he actually has been raised to the supernatural plane, like it or not, and may not insult his Creator by spurning His gift. There is but one absolutely last end to which man is destined in the actual order of things, and that is supernatural. What we mean is that the supernatural supposes, enfolds, and includes the natural, not destroying any of man's natural endowments, capacities, demands, and requirements, but rather fulfilling them in a better and nobler way while extending their reach to a higher plane. Ethics therefore remains a legitimate and useful, if incomplete and partial, study of man's last end and the means to reach it.

Moreover, not everything about human life has been expressly revealed to man by God. Many matters of utmost importance God has seen fit to let us discover by the use of our purely natural powers, which are also His gifts. Hence, moral theology helps ethics, completing it by extending it from the natural order to the supernatural, and ethics helps moral theology, confirming many of its pronouncements by reason and filling in the gaps where revelation is silent.

HAPPINESS IS MAN'S ATTAINABLE GOAL

From the existence of God and the immortality of the human soul, taken as philosophically established positions, it follows that happiness is man's natural destiny and that it is possible for him to attain it. The argument is stated in the form of five logically connected assertions.

1. *Man seeks happiness to the fullness of his capacity.* We have already seen that man has a desire for some kind of happiness, and that this is man's basic desire penetrating all his other desires. But man is not satisfied with only some degree of happiness. The slightest suspicion that more can be obtained will start a craving for that more. His intellect reaches out to truth indefinitely, and cannot rest so long as there is anything more to know. His will reaches out to good indefinitely, and cannot rest so long as there is anything more to seek. In like manner all man's faculties demand complete satisfaction. So man wants happiness as such, and all the happiness he can hold.

2. *Man's seeking for happiness is a natural tendency, one that springs from human nature itself.* Though man has no innate ideas, he has certain native drives or urges which spring into action as soon as the requisite concepts have been gathered from experience. On the sense level both man and animal have the drives popularly called instincts. On the rational level man has similar drives peculiar to himself, and the basic one is this tendency for happiness. Among all man's tendencies the one for happiness is unique, inasmuch as it is:

Universal, for it is found in all men without exception, appearing even in morbid and abnormal persons though with some distortion. One man may refuse to seek happiness here, another there, but no one can refuse to seek it somewhere.

Inescapable, for it lasts throughout life and cannot be got rid of. No man can quench the desire for happiness in himself, and, no matter how hard he may try not to feed it, the hunger grows in spite of him.

Irresistible, for it insistently demands satisfaction. Man's ceaseless unrest shown in his constant activity is only an expression of this basic impulse in varying forms. He who is not happy wants to be happy, and he who is happy wants to be happier.

3. *Such a natural tendency must have been implanted in human nature by its Author, God.* There must be an adequate explanation for the existence of such a basic urge. Since it is not accidental to man or casually acquired, but rooted in the very constitution of the human being, the only possible reason is that God made human nature that way. Just as the only adequate explanation why man is rational is that God created him rational, so the only adequate explanation why man seeks happiness is that God made him for happiness. Therefore responsibility for the existence of this natural tendency in man must be asumed by God Himself.

4. *A tendency implanted in human nature by God must be intended not for frustration but for fulfillment.* Here we must suppose that God has the attributes without which He could not be God, especially that He is truthful, wise, and good.

Truthfulness will not let God mislead man into thinking that happiness is possible if it is not.

Wisdom will not permit God to place in man's very nature an inescapable urge that serves no purpose.

Goodness will not allow God to put into man's nature a basic craving whose sole function would be to tantalize and torment him.

Truthfulness, wisdom, and goodness are found in God; lying, folly, and cruelty are not. Therefore, once God has implanted in man a drive toward happiness, He must provide *some* attainable object by which this urge can be satisfied. We are not yet concerned with what that object is, but only that there must be *something*.

5. *The fulfillment of this tendency, or the attainment of happiness, is man's last end.* From the preceding analysis it follows that God has destined man for happiness and has made it possible for him to attain it. Happiness, therefore, forms at least part of man's last end. But the happiness man naturally seeks is all-inclusive, the full satisfaction of all the desires that spring from human nature itself. We have no natural capacity for anything above, beyond, or beside it. Therefore it is no mere part but the whole of man's last end, so far as human reason can discover it.

Questions on the argument

Atheists and materialists object against this argument by denying the metaphysical premises on which it rests. The only answer to this is to refer them to metaphysics where these premises are established. But there are other difficulties drawn from the structure of the argument itself, and these we must see.

1. *We naturally desire health, wealth, and other goods, but cannot always obtain them; how then can we be sure that the natural tendency for happiness cannot be designed for frustration?* The word *natural* may mean anything that is not unnatural, not opposed to nature, or it may mean something positively demanded by nature as its proper goal. The lesser tendencies are natural in the first sense, happiness in the second sense. Health, wealth, and the rest are good and perfect some part of our being, but they must be subordinated to and sometimes sacrificed for the all-inclusive tendency, which is for the highest good.

2. *Animals have natural wants that we often see frustrated, and there is no future life for them to look forward to; how can we be sure that God will take care to satisfy man's natural tendencies?* Animals do not crave

happiness, which they cannot even form an idea of, but only a series of momentary sense-gratifications. They often fail to reach even these, because, not being persons, they are subordinate to the utility of each other and of man. Nature is so arranged that animals feed on one another and on plants, and this is one of the purposes they are naturally destined to serve. Hence they always fulfill one of the alternative purposes for which they exist: either they grow to full maturity, or they are consumed in the process of assisting other creatures to do so. Man, being a person, is not of this type.

3. *Not all men attain happiness, for some live evil lives and are unworthy of it; does not this show that this tendency not only can be but actually is frustrated?* We did not say that all men *will* attain happiness, but only that all men *can* attain it. It must be possible for all; if man lose it, the loss must be man's own fault. God must offer it, but man is free to take or refuse the offer. Hence man is destined to happiness conditionally, and the condition is that man voluntarily do his part to earn it.

4. *If a man's destiny consists in seeking his own happiness, how does he avoid the charge of being essentially selfish, which is a most unethical trait?* Self-seeking is wrong only when one seeks self inordinately, in the wrong way or in the wrong measure. Happiness does not come in certain quantities, so that if I have more you must have less. Every man in existence can attain all the happiness he is capable of without depriving any one else of the least. That man should be happy is God's intention, and he who seeks his own happiness is at the same time doing God's will. The very same acts by which a man achieves happiness are the acts by which he gives glory to God.

SUMMARY

Happiness is desire satisfied by the conscious possession of the good. It is a lasting subjective state that can exist only in an intellectual being. It is neither mere contentment nor a passing emotion nor a sunny disposition.

All men seek happiness in general, since all want their desires satisfied, but they differ in what they judge will make them happy. Those who appear to desire misery or choose evils are only seeming exceptions. Happiness is the basic motive in all we do, though we may seek it only implicitly.

Perfect happiness fully satisfies all our desires; *imperfect* has flaws in it. Because of man's finite capacities, his happiness cannot be *absolutely* but at most *relatively* perfect. *Supernatural* happiness, the Beatific Vision, pertains to theology and is outside the scope of ethics. Ethics, though limited to *natural* happiness, is not thereby limited to the present life; it treats of the highest happiness man is *naturally* capable of aspiring to, whether he reach it in this world or the next.

Is such happiness attainable? Pessimism says no. Oriental pessimists seek relief from suffering in the extinction of individual consciousness. Atheists and materialists counsel contentment with this life and the acceptance of death as the end of all. The optimistic Western tradition holds that happiness is man's last end and is attainable. The proof, presupposing God's existence and the soul's immortality, includes these steps:

(1) Man seeks all the happiness he is capable of.
(2) This is a natural tendency springing from human nature.
(3) Such a tendency is implanted in human nature by God.
(4) God cannot intend a natural tendency for frustration.
(5) He intends it for fulfillment as man's last end.

In answering objections, we say:

1. That only the tendency to happiness is positively demanded by human nature and other desires must be subordinated to it.

2. That animals are not destined for happiness because they are not persons, can have no idea of happiness, cannot desire it, and are meant for man's service.

3. That God must make happiness possible of attainment, but we can refuse it and thus miss our last end.

4. That seeking our own happiness is not selfish because it is our due, hurts no one else, and is God's will for us.

READINGS

1. Plato's writings are full of discussions on the end of man and happiness. The *Phaedo, Phaedrus, Symposium,* and bk. X of the *Republic* give Plato's idea of man's destiny.
2. Aristotle's *Nicomachean Ethics,* bk. I, ch. 4-13, and bk. X, ch. 6-9 should certainly be read.
3. Boethius' *Consolation of Philosophy,* especially bk. III. One of the most popular books of the middle ages.
4. St. Thomas' *Summa Theologica,* I-II, q. 3; also q. 5, aa. 5 and 8. As a theologian primarily, St. Thomas treats of supernatural rather than natural happiness; this is why he says that man cannot attain ultimate happiness (the Beatific Vision, which is supernatural) by his natural powers. But what he says is useful for philosophy with the proper reservations. The same holds true of his treatment of happiness in the *Summa Contra Gentiles,* bk. III, ch. 25-63 (in the *Basic Writings*).
5. Cronin, *The Science of Ethics,* vol. I, pp. 79-88.
6. Rickaby, *Moral Philosophy,* pp. 3-21.
7. Miltner, *Elements of Ethics,* pp. 34-49 (also quoted in Leibell, *Readings in Ethics,* pp. 182-191).
8. Adler, *A Dialectic of Morals,* ch. IV.
9. O'Connor, *The Eternal Quest,* the four appendixes.

*   *   *

Some of these writers do not separate their treatment of happiness itself and the object which will make man happy, and so bring in matter proper to the next chapter.

CHAPTER 15

PURSUIT OF

HAPPINESS

PROBLEM

Since men are not born happy, with all their desires satisfied, they must acquire happiness by the possession of something they previously lacked, some *object* that will produce this state of happiness in them. Our previous argument showed that there must be some such object. Now our question is: *What is the object in which man can find happiness?*

To put it in more technical language, we have treated the problem of man's *subjective* or *intrinsic* last end, that state of the man himself which his actions tend to realize and which is brought about within the man himself; there remains the question of man's *objective* or *extrinsic* last end, the object whose possession will bring about this subjective state within man.

Numerous candidates have been suggested for this position. There are two possible procedures:

1. By a process of elimination to exclude all but one, which then automatically becomes the object we are searching for.

2. By positive argument to prove the claims of the one legitimate contestant.

We shall use both methods, for they supplement one another. The first will make sure that we have examined all claims, and the second will show how really worthy the true claimant is. But first it might be well to sketch several historical schools of thought which are fundamental enough to have been treated in the beginning of our course, but are put here because they hold that man tends to an end, that his end is happiness,

175

that happiness is in some measure attainable, and that it consists in some specific good that they propose. These views are:

(1) Hedonism, proposing pleasure
(2) Utilitarianism, proposing social welfare
(3) Stoicism, proposing virtue
(4) Evolutionism, proposing progress

HEDONISM

Hedonism is one of the oldest, simplest, and most earthly of ethical theories. It has persisted throughout all ages, and many people who have never consciously formulated for themselves any philosophy of life live according to its principles. It holds that pleasure is the end of life and the highest good. Modern hedonists prefer to use the word *happiness* for *pleasure,* and this practice must be noted in reading them, for in speaking of happiness they refer to the admittedly imperfect enjoyments of this life only. Hedonists differ from opportunists by making pleasure a deliberate and even serious pursuit.

We find hedonism first formulated by Aristippus, leader of the Cyrenaic school of thought. Misinterpreting the teaching of his master, Socrates, who said that happiness is the end of life, Aristippus identified happiness with pleasure. He held that pleasure results from gentle motion and pain from rough motion, that intellectual pleasures may be higher but sense pleasures are more intense and it is the pleasure of the moment that is valued. An act is good insofar as it produces pleasure. Virtue is useful as restraining us from excessive passion, which is rough motion and unpleasant.

Hedonism was refined by Epicurus, who joined it to the physical theories of Democritus. It is the ethics most consistent with mechanistic materialism. For Epicurus the end of life is not intense pleasure, but an abiding peace of mind, a state of cheerful tranquility. Above all we must avoid fear of the gods and fear of death. Intellectual pleasures are better because more lasting, but we cannot do without sense pleasures. The wise man so regulates his life as to get into it the greatest amount of pleasure and the least amount of pain. Moderation is counseled to enable one to enjoy future pleasures. We must learn to restrict our desires within the bounds in which we think we can satisfy them. That is good which will increase our pleasure or our general peace of mind, and anything which decreases it is bad.

> We call pleasure the beginning and end of the blessed life. For we recognize pleasure as the first good innate in us, and from pleasure we begin every act of choice and avoidance, and to pleasure we return again, using the feeling as the standard by which we judge every good. And since pleasure is the first good and natural to us, for this very reason we do not choose every pleasure, but sometimes we pass over many pleasures, when greater discomfort accrues to us as the result of them. . . . Every pleasure then because of its natural kinship to us is good, yet not every pleasure is

to be chosen: even as every pain also is an evil, yet not all are always of a nature to be avoided. Yet by a scale of comparison and by the consideration of advantages and disadvantages we must form our judgment on all these matters. . . . When, therefore, we maintain that pleasure is the end, we do not mean the pleasures of profligates and those that consist in sensuality . . . but freedom from pain in the body and from trouble in the mind.*

UTILITARIANISM

The extension of hedonism beyond mere selfish pleasure to the pleasure of the group is called *utilitarianism*. It makes little difference whether we take hedonism as the general term, dividing it into egoistic and altruistic and putting utilitarianism under the altruistic division, or whether we restrict the term *hedonism* to the egoistic variety and identify utilitarianism with altruism. However they are classified, utilitarianism historically grew out of hedonism.

Jeremy Bentham,† successful leader of political and legislative reform in England, is regarded as the founder of utilitarianism. Starting with the idea that pleasure and pain are the only motives governing mankind, he goes on to show that personal pleasure and pain are dependent on the general happiness and prosperity of the whole community. Therefore in framing a hedonistic calculus, the calculation of pleasures and pains inseparable from any hedonistic system, we must consider the extent of pleasure and pain, the number of people affected by our policy of conduct. The moral goodness of an act is to be judged by its *utility* in promoting the common welfare of all as well as the personal advantage of each. The aim of human life is expressed in the *Greatest Happiness Principle:* "The greatest happiness of the greatest number." But, since Bentham wishes to promote the interests of the community at large chiefly because it will redound to oneself as a member of that community, his system is still more egoistic than altruistic.

In John Stuart Mill utilitarianism reached its full development. He recognized its strong roots in hedonism:

> The creed which accepts as the foundation of morals, Utility, or the Greatest Happiness Principle, holds that actions are right in proportion as they tend to promote happiness, wrong as they tend to produce the reverse of happiness. By happiness is intended pleasure, and the absence of pain; by unhappiness, pain, and the privation of pleasure.‡

But, whereas Bentham thought that units of pleasure and pain can be calculated arithmetically and that ethics can be made into an exact

---

*Epicurus' "Letter to Menoecius" in Diogenes Laertius' *Lives and Opinions of Eminent Philosophers,* bk. X, 27. Whether the letter is genuine or not, it is a good summary of Epicurean thought.
†*Introduction to the Principles of Morals and Legislation,* ch. I-IV.
‡*Utilitarianism,* ch. II.

science, Mill recognized that pleasures differ in *quality* as well as in quantity, that there are higher and lower pleasures.

> It is better to be a human being dissatisfied than a pig satisfied; better to be Socrates dissatisfied than a fool satisfied.*

An existence as free from pain and as rich in enjoyments as possible, both in quantity and quality, to be secured to all mankind, is the end of human action and the standard of morality. His proof is often quoted in logic books as an example of a fallacy:

> The only proof capable of being given that an object is visible, is that people actually see it. The only proof that a sound is audible, is that people hear it: and so of the other sources of our experience. In like manner, I apprehend, the sole evidence it is possible to produce that anything is desirable, is that people do actually desire it. . . . No reason can be given why the general happiness is desirable except that each person, so far as he believes it to be attainable, desires his own happiness. This, however, being a fact, we have not only all the proof which the case admits of, but all which it is possible to require, that happiness is a good: that each person's happiness is a good to that person, and the general happiness, therefore, a good to the aggregate of all persons.†

He goes on to show that virtue, far from being opposed to happiness, is one of the elements that make up happiness: the feeling of self-satisfaction in contributing to the common welfare even at personal expense. Thus with Mill hedonism becomes altruism.

STOICISM

The ancient philosophy most directly opposed to the hedonism of the Epicureans was *Stoicism*. Just as the Epicureans were preceded by Aristippus and the Cyrenaics, so Stoicism was preceded by Antisthenes and the Cynics. Antisthenes, like Aristippus, was a follower of Socrates, but exaggerated his master's doctrine in the opposite way. Admiring Socrates' abstemiousness, self-sufficiency, and disregard of convention, Antisthenes taught that virtue is not only the chief means to happiness, but happiness itself. Virtue is the only good, vice the only evil, and everything else is indifferent. The greatest error is to suppose that pleasure is a good. "I had rather be mad than glad," Antisthenes is reported to have said. The essence of virtue is self-sufficiency, independence from everything and everybody. The Cynics despised riches, pleasure, comfort, family, society, culture, and sometimes even common decency.

Stoicism made this attitude respectable by joining it to pantheism. The world, they said, is composed of the world body, consisting of coarse matter apparent to our senses, and the world soul, fine matter that blows as a wind through the world, giving it motion and making it a huge ani-

---

Utilitarianism, ch. II.
†*Op. cit.,* ch. IV.

mal. Man's body and soul are but limited portions of the world body and world soul. The world itself is God or Nature, for these are the same. Nature develops itself according to inexorable law, so that the universe can be called not only Nature and God, but also Fate and Destiny, Reason and Law. Hence Stoicism is a form of *materialism, pantheism,* and *fatalism.*

> Our individual natures are all parts of universal nature; on which account the chief good is to live in a manner corresponding to nature, and that means corresponding to one's own nature and to universal nature.*

Nothing else, they say, could ever happen except what does happen. Everything that will befall me is decreed by Fate; I can accept these decrees graciously or rebelliously, but accept them I must. Rebellion is but an emotional reaction against Nature, a childish pouting which can change nothing and only makes me miserable. Nature stands serene though I rail against it. The reasonable thing to do is to develop *apathy,* a state of indifference to all things, of complete control over my emotions, the only thing I can control. Emotion is irrational and bad; action according to reason, which shows me the inexorable law of Nature, alone is good; and this is *virtue.* Virtue is the only good. It is not a means to an end, but the end itself. "Virtue is its own reward."

> Virtue is a disposition of the mind always consistent and always harmonious; one ought to seek it out for its own sake, without being influenced by fear or hope or any external influence.†

The virtuous man stands firm though the world crashes about him; realizing his identity with Nature, he is beyond good and evil. There are no degrees in virtue, and he who has one virtue has all, for either he lives according to Nature or he does not; the former is the wise man or philosopher, the latter a fool. One may wonder how happiness fits into this view. But the Stoics insist that living according to Nature *is* happiness and it is possible by practicing Stoic virtue.

The modern pantheist, Baruch Spinoza, gives us a moral system that is fundamentally Stoic in tone, though based on the physical and psychological doctrines of Descartes. His great work, though entitled *Ethics,* is more of a metaphysical treatise embodying a complete pantheistic philosophy, culminating in the way man can reach "blessed immortality" by deliverance from bondage to his passions and by realization of his identity with Nature, which is God.

EVOLUTIONISM

The theory of evolution is but the expression in biological terms of the most influential concept of the nineteenth century, that of unlimited progress and of the perfectibility of man. All subsequent writings are colored

---

*Diogenes Laertius' *Lives and Opinions of Eminent Philosophers,* bk. VII, 53.
†*Ibid.,* 53.

by it, and it is not surprising that it should be seized upon as the ultimate purpose of life. To progress, to evolve, to develop, that is the important thing; it matters not where we are going so long as we are on our way. The process itself is valuable even though the goal be unknown.

Those who write in this strain are so numerous that only a few can be mentioned. Herbert Spencer is the philosophical prophet of evolution, which he joins to a utilitarian ethics. Life, he says,* is adjustment of internal relations to external relations. Conduct is good or bad according as it is well or ill adjusted to its end. Adjustment produces pleasure, lack of it pain. Ancestral experiences of pleasure and pain are transmitted to posterity through brain modifications and accumulated through many generations. We thus inherit ethical habits, doing now through a sense of duty what our ancestors found pleasant or useful. Man is as yet imperfectly adjusted and feels a conflict of egoistic and altruistic impulses, but evolution is tending to a reconciliation of egoism and altruism into a higher synthesis.

Quite a different form of evolutionism occurs in the successors of Kant, especially in those who adopt the idealistic pantheism of the Hegelian school. Among these Thomas Hill Green and Francis Herbert Bradley propose *self-realization* as the ultimate good.

> The one divine mind gradually reproduces itself in the human soul. In virtue of this principle in him, man has definite capabilities, the realization of which, since in it alone he can satisfy himself, forms his true good. . . . The idea in man of a possible better state of himself, consisting in a further realization of his capabilities, has been the moralizing agent in human life; it has yielded our moral standards, loyalty to which—itself the product of the same idea—is the condition of the goodness of the individual:†
>
> The final end, with which morality is identified, or under which it can be included, can be expressed not otherwise than by self-realization.‡

Both hasten to point out that self-realization is impossible outside society, in which the individual realizes himself as a member of a greater whole, the whole of humanity, which is the highest manifestation so far of the ever-evolving Absolute.

John Dewey§ abandoned an idealism like Green's for the form of pragmatism he calls *instrumentalism*. It is ethical relativism with a strong evolutionary bent. Thinking, he says, is functional, instrumental to action, not done for the sake of finding truth but of making life more satisfactory. A value is whatever a man finds satisfaction in doing in this world of experience. An ethical question arises when a man must choose between values. The good is always the better; an evil is only a rejected good.

---

*Data of Ethics, see especially ch. III, XIII, XIV.
†Green, T. H., *Prolegomena to Ethics*, bk. III, ch. II, A.
‡Bradley, F. H., *Ethical Studies*, Essay II, end.
§*Human Nature and Conduct*, pt. IV, I; *Quest for Certainty*, ch. X.

Selection is made by considering one's capacities, satisfactions, and the demands of the social situation, and by taking that which embodies the most foreseen possibilities of future satisfaction. But it is a mistake to think that we need a goal in order to progress. Satisfaction of an old want creates a new one, which leads to a new experimental adventure. Evolution is continuity of change, readjustment, and redirection. There is no fixed goal, for it is better to travel than to arrive.

PROCESS OF ELIMINATION

Though some of these theories deny that genuine happiness is attainable, they suggest substitutes that must be eliminated, thus serving to show that the argument deals with seriously accepted views and widely practiced philosophies. We come now to the statement of the argument, which is unavoidably lengthy because of its comprehensive character.

The object that can make man happy must be either man himself or something that is not man, but either below man, equal to man, or above man. It cannot be a being which is not man but equal to man, for we know of no such being and cannot seek something we do not know. Three alternatives remain:

(1) Something below man
(2) Man himself
(3) Something above man

Goods of fortune

The first main point is that things below man cannot make man happy. Such are the good things of this world, as wealth, family, honor, fame, position, power, influence. Not only can they be possessed with unhappiness, but they can cause unhappiness by the care and burden they impose. We have desires they cannot satisfy, such as the craving for knowledge and love. Some chance on them without forethought or labor while others cannot secure them even with the greatest effort, and they often come to the most unworthy. When obtained they have an uncertain existence and they all must be left at death. History shows that so many who had all that the world can offer nevertheless declared themselves restless and unhappy. These things are means, not ends. They are for man, not man for them.

Man himself

The second main point is that man cannot make himself happy. He cannot find his last end either in the possession of himself or in the possession of certain qualities of himself. There are three possibilities:

(1) Goods of body
(2) Goods of soul
(3) Goods of both body and soul together

Goods of body

Health, strength, beauty, physical skills, and other bodily endowments are all subject to the imperfections of the goods of fortune mentioned above. Without gifts of fortune that afford them scope for their proper exercise, they are often useless. And they are not lasting; the art of growing old gracefully consists in intelligently adapting oneself to their loss.

Goods of soul

Happiness itself is a subjective state experienced within the soul, and is therefore a good of the soul. So it may seem at first sight that we have found what we are looking for. But, though happiness is a good of the soul, it must be produced in the soul by the acquisition of something else. By goods of soul producing happiness we mean such things as:

(1) Knowledge, the good of the intellect, and
(2) Virtue, the good of the will

These are both highly estimable and a life dedicated to their pursuit is truly noble. No one could be really happy without them. But knowledge as such and virtue as such can give but a partial happiness at most, because they are means to the last end and not the last end itself.

Knowledge. The man who devotes himself to the life of learning has chosen wisely among the good things of this world, and he will probably be happier than most men, but he is chasing a phantom if he expects from it a fully satisfying happiness. The knowledge we can get in the present life is acquired by hard and toilsome study; it is never perfectly clear; it cannot be completed even in the longest lifetime; so much of it remains undiscovered and inaccessible; and the things that it reveals are so often disappointing and unsatisfactory. The fact that learning can be devoted to the service of evil as well as good shows that it is but a means that can be abused, not an end that *must* be a good, and that of itself it cannot make man happy.

Virtue. The Stoics in claiming that "virtue is its own reward" mistook entirely the idea of virtue. By its very notion virtue is a means and not an end. Virtue consists of morally good habits, and these habits are called good precisely because they lead man more easily and readily to his last end. Virtue is a straight way, a right direction, a true aiming at the highest good. But no one takes a way to a way or directs himself to a direction or aims at aiming. Unless some goal, mark, or target is set up, these have no meaning. So unless the good habits called virtues lead to some other object, there is no reason why they should be distinguished from any other habits or called virtues. All the goodness they have they derive from the end to which they lead, and therefore they cannot be the end themselves.

Besides, the practice of virtue in this life is no easy thing. Though accompanied by peace of conscience and spiritual exaltation, the practice of virtue demands self-control and self-sacrifice, mounting at times even to heroism. However admirable this may be, nothing painful or difficult is compatible with complete happiness, since one would be happier who could attain the same good without the pain and difficulty. The Stoic might stand firm while the world topples about him, but he could hardly be happy about it. Virtue is an indispensable means to happiness, but it is not that happiness itself.

Goods of body and soul together

The goods of neither body nor soul taken separately can make man happy, for those of the body cannot satisfy the soul nor can those of the soul satisfy the body. Should not, then, happiness be sought in the satisfaction of the whole man, of *both body and soul taken together?* Here again two possibilities arise, according as one seeks this satisfaction in enjoying a good already attained or in the very process of striving to attain it. In other words, the two alternatives are:

(1) Pleasure, or enjoyment of a good attained
(2) Progress, or the process of attainment

Pleasure. The possession of the goods discussed so far results in pleasure of some kind, either sensuous or intellectual. When we speak of pleasure as the aim of life, we mean both sensuous and intellectual pleasure combined into one object, and ask whether happiness can be found in a wise blend of physical and mental delights. This is the Epicurean ideal.

It is admitted that pleasure of some kind must be an ingredient in happiness. It is actually desired and without it we could not be satisfied. But the pleasure referred to here is the pleasure of this life only, the pleasure that can be derived with our present faculties from the objects that surround us in this world. To examine the hedonist theory we must first understand just what pleasure is.

There is no sense in trying to define pleasure. We know what it is by experiencing it, and there is no doubt about the experience. Attempted definitions are merely verbal, substituting one term for another. Psychologists have written extensively on pleasure, but what they say has little ethical import, except for the *hedonistic paradox,* the fact that intense mental concentration on the pleasure one is now experiencing causes the pleasure to disappear. This confirms the following analysis.

We have no special faculty of pleasure. We cannot just simply *enjoy.* We enjoy *this* or *that,* which means that we enjoy doing something or experiencing something. The doing or experiencing must occur by the use of some ability we possess, the main purpose of which is something else besides mere enjoyment. The fact that we distinguish between sensuous and intellectual pleasure shows that pleasure is an accompaniment of the use of other powers, either of the sensuous or intellectual order.

Since no one of our abilities has as its purpose pleasure and nothing else, pleasure is but the accompaniment of the normal exercise of abilities which exist for the accomplishment of some other purpose. We eat primarily to keep ourselves alive, though eating is also pleasant. We have eyes to perceive what we need and to guide our movements, though many sights also give delight. Sex is intended for the reproduction of the race, though it also has its pleasure. Intellect enables us to live a civilized life, and there is also enjoyment in a problem successfully solved. The same can be said of our other abilities.

The purpose of pleasure is to allure a person to exercise a natural function which is otherwise beneficial to the individual or the race. We might not take the trouble to eat unless we felt hunger and food had a taste. We keep our eyes open because we really enjoy looking. People would not shoulder the responsibilities of matrimony were it not for the pleasures of married life. We would give up hard thinking if we did not find problems an attractive challenge.

In the intention of nature pleasure is a means rather than an end. Men may make it an end and seek it for its own sake, but, if they make it the only end or the last end, they thereby exclude the end for which pleasure is adapted by nature as a means. By acting thus they contradict their own nature, act unnaturally and, therefore, immorally. So pleasure itself is not man's last end, although the attainment of the last end will undoubtedly bring pleasure, even the greatest possible pleasure, as its natural accompaniment.

The pleasures of this life are not attainable by all men at all times. To have some pleasures we must forego others. Pleasure is not lasting, for no faculty can be continuously exercised. Too much indulgence makes pleasure cloying and often brings its own natural punishment with it. Old age diminishes the possibility of pleasure and death ends it. Hence, though there is nothing wrong in legitimate pleasure, it cannot give man the happiness he craves.

Altruistic pleasure, as proposed by the utilitarians, though on a higher plane than egoistic, is also unsatisfactory. The joy we feel in kindness, in giving gifts, in helping others, in relieving distress, in social uplift, in works of charity and benevolence, is among the purest and best we can experience. The many who devote their lives to these activities are worthy of all praise. But again they will not find here their last end. Some have neither the time nor the means for such works. The joy that comes from them is often marred by ingratitude and misunderstanding. Schemes for the betterment of mankind are seldom fully successful, and often result only in bitterness and disillusionment. The philanthropist is by all means to be encouraged, but he must not expect his efforts to bring him undiluted happiness.

Besides, there is something incoherent in the altruistic ideal. If bettering others is our last end, what is the end of the men who are bettered? If we exist for the sake of other men, then what are the other men for? If everybody exists for the sake of everybody else, then, when the process is brought round full circle, there is really no last end for the whole of humanity.

These systems make man's temporal welfare his last end. If there were no God and no future life, the conclusion would be reasonable enough that man ought to get as much pleasure and as little pain out of his brief span as possible. But if there is a God and a future life, no such conclusion follows; man may provide for his temporal welfare to the fullest, yet miss his last end and slide into eternal ruin. These philosophers were not all atheists or materialists, but this only shows the inconsistency of their ethics; the fact of God's existence and the soul's immortality, if admitted as true, cannot be left out of a system of morals.

Progress. We come to the second way of combining the goods of both body and soul. By progress is meant the actualization of all man's potentialities, either of the individual or of the race.

It is argued that, since nature provides these potentialities in man, it must be nature's intention that we develop them to the full. It is true that this is nature's intention and we are obliged to develop our abilities, but it will not make us completely happy. Self-development is *one* of the ends of human life, but not the last end.

The process of self-development results in the fully developed man, but *man cannot be satisfied with himself.* He is not satisfied with the mediocre abilities he has received to begin with, and much less with the imperfect development he can give them. His noblest powers, intellect and will, stretch out to something infinitely beyond himself. The self-development possible in this life would consist in a combination of goods of soul, body, and fortune. Few men can succeed in acquiring these in sufficient proportion, and no one can keep them forever. A well-stocked memory of a life rich in experience, though it may make old age contented, cannot make it really happy.

A favorite view of the evolutionists is that of social progress, the development of the whole race. The end of the individual is to contribute toward the future good of humanity, and man who is now capable of little happiness must evolve into a higher race capable of more. But this answer is no solution. The future happiness of the race cannot benefit the individual now living, and he wants to be happy himself as well as to make others happy. This happiness could only be a greater material prosperity and a higher level of culture, an increase in the goods of body, soul, and fortune, and we have seen that these things, however increased, can never be fully satisfying. If individual men are for the whole race, then what does the whole race aim at? Progress for the sake of progress is futile; there must be some known goal or else movement to it is unreasonable. To devote oneself to the advancement of civilization is a worthy and high-minded enterprise, but it is not the last and supreme end of human life.

The term *self-realization,* used by some writers, is ambiguous. Taken narrowly, it may mean the same as the progress described above, a sort of evolutionary humanism. Taken broadly to mean the full actualization of man's potentialities in the possession of the Supreme Good distinct from himself, self-realization may be an apt term for man's attainment of his true Last End. For man's Self is realized only by possession of the Supreme Other.

God

The third main point is that man's happiness must be sought in something above man. From our whole discussion so far it follows that neither things below man nor man himself can make man genuinely happy. None of these things taken separately can satisfy, as we have seen. Nor can the combination of them all taken together, because no one can secure all of these goods in one lifetime, some of them are mutually exclusive and any choice among them will leave other desires unsatisfied, they are all fleeting and insecure, and over the whole of them is flung the shadow of death. The fact of death alone would have been sufficient argument to show that none of these transitory things could be the purpose for which we live. We reviewed them in detail because so many make them the "be all and end all" of life.

Above man we have God and angels. Angels cannot be proved by pure reason, and so fall outside our scope. Besides, no one ever suggested that man's last end is to be found in angels or other creatures superior to man, that man exists for their sake to be used or consumed for their well-being in the same way as animals are for the sake of man; the fact that man is a person renders this idea impossible.

It follows by the process of elimination that the only object which can make man happy, and thus is man's objective last end, is GOD.

Synopsis

To take in this long argument in one glance, the following synopsis may be helpful. Man's supreme good and objective last end must be one of these parallel alternatives:

Something below man
　　Goods of fortune: wealth, honor, power, etc.
Man himself
　　Goods of body: health, strength, beauty, etc.
　　Goods of soul:
　　　　Knowledge, the good of the intellect
　　　　Virtue, the good of the will
　　Goods of body and soul together:
　　　　Pleasure, enjoyment of a thing attained:
　　　　　　egoistic, self-centered delight
　　　　　　altruistic, doing good to others
　　　　Progress, the process of attainment:
　　　　　　of the individual, full self-development
　　　　　　of the race, advancement of humanity
Something above man
　　Angels or other unknown superior creatures
　　GOD

The validity of a process of elimination depends on the completeness of the disjunction, that is, on the assurance that no possible alternative has been overlooked. Though ethical systems have an infinite possibility of variation in detail, and as the history of philosophy progresses future theories will be proposed to supplant their predecessors, we can safely say that no theory is conceivable that cannot be classified under some one of the headings given above. Any such system which does not make God man's last end must, if it is to be taken seriously, fall into the category of those which make *man* his own last end. As we saw, man is inherently incapable of being his own happiness.

POSITIVE ARGUMENT

The following argument is independent of the process of elimination just given, but the two arguments reinforce each other. We need to show that for our happiness God is required and sufficient. If He is required, we cannot be happy without Him. If He is sufficient, nothing else is necessary.

God is *required,* for no lesser being will do. Man is by nature a rational animal, and rationality shows itself in two main tendencies: the tendency of the intellect to know all truth, and the tendency of the will to possess all good. But God, as natural theology shows, is perfect Truth and Goodness. Therefore without God man's intellect and will cannot be satisfied.

God is *sufficient,* for one who possesses God, though he may also enjoy creatures, has no strict need of them. There can be no truth that it is not found in Truth Itself, no good that is not found in Goodness Itself. God is the Infinite Being, possessing in Himself in an infinitely higher degree all the perfections found in all possible creatures. Therefore any desire that any creature could satisfy God Himself can satisfy far more completely.

NATURAL AND SUPERNATURAL HAPPINESS

The process of elimination and the positive argument, together with material given previously, prove that even on the purely natural plane man must be destined to a last end which is also his highest good, that this last end subjectively is happiness, and objectively is the attainment of God in some way superior to our feeble groping toward Him in this life.

Do we mean a direct intuitive vision of the divine essence? As we said before, pure reason apart from revelation cannot go this far. All that pure reason can establish is a knowledge and love of God fully proportioned to man's natural powers and capacities, so that they are not left frustrated but given thorough satisfaction. All that man can naturally aspire to, all that he is naturally equipped for, is an *analogical* knowledge of God with its resultant love, that is, God known and loved through His creatures. This is the type of knowledge and love strictly proportioned to the intellect and will of man as natural faculties. We may say that in such a state not God alone but *God plus His creatures* would be the object conferring happiness on us, but in this combination God is the essential element and the place of creatures could be taken by some sort of direct action of God on the soul.*

But do we not have an analogical knowledge with a corresponding love of God in the present life? Yes, but it suffers from two fundamental defects that prevent it from making us happy. Our knowledge of God in this life is not only limited but subject to *error;* the limitation is part of our essential finiteness, but the error is remediable and must be removed before we can be truly happy. Our love of God in this life is unstable and can be lost through *sin;* even a purely natural happiness must contain the element of security, so that once possessed it could never be in danger of being lost. Occasional error in the intellect and possible sin in the will are compatible with a state of trial, of progress toward the goal, but are incompatible with the state of term, with the enjoyment of the goal itself.

May the happiness we have been speaking of be called *perfect* happiness? The answer depends on the terminology one prefers. The definition of perfect happiness given previously is commonly accepted, but the application of the definition meets with wide disagreement, since *relatively perfect* may be taken as relative to different things. Relative to God's happiness, all finite happiness is limited; relative to the supernatural vision of God, all natural happiness falls short; relative to another creature, one with smaller capacity may have as much happiness as it can hold, though other creatures with larger capacities are happier; relative to itself, what can satisfy the same creature at one stage would be insufficient for it should its capacity for happiness expand. Hence one can hardly use the term *relatively perfect happiness* without explaining how it is to be taken.

The natural order of things, far from excluding the possibility of elevation to a higher plane, is open to the supernatural in the sense of having an *obediential potency* toward it. An obediential potency, which is a potency only in an extended sense, is merely negative and does not call for fulfillment. It means only that God can do with His creatures whatever He wants that does not imply a contradiction. Thus, if God works a miracle on or with a creature, it must obey Him. It has no positive ability to act miraculously but cannot resist the divine omnipotence acting on it or through it. Likewise, God can lift the whole of human nature to a higher plane, giving it an end and supplying it with means it does not naturally possess; if He does so, human nature is in no condition to resist. Hence a *natural last end,* even if it be called an *absolutely* last end in the natural order, cannot have that utter finality and ultimacy proper to

---

*For example, by means of *infused species,* or representations put directly into the soul by God. Such infused species, if they would be *due* to the soul in its disembodied condition after death, would not be strictly supernatural.

a supernatural last end, which is not even in obediential potency to anything higher.

So a *natural* happiness, even if complete on the natural plane, cannot be so thoroughly satisfying as a supernatural happiness, which transcends the natural limitations of all possible creatures. An analogical knowledge and love of God is certainly inferior to an intuitive vision of the divine essence and therefore is absolutely less perfect. But it can be called *relatively perfect* in one of the senses given previously, inasmuch as it is not defective in its kind, not subject to error and sin, as is our analogical knowledge and love of God in the present life. It means a knowledge and love of God *perfectly* proportioned to the *natural* capacities of this individual being. It seems therefore quite correct to speak of *perfect natural happiness,* provided this term, avoided by many writers, is properly explained and understood.

Would such a happiness be a static condition incapable of growth or progress? In the absence of experience we can only speculate on what such a condition would be like. It would be *objectively* static in the sense that God does not change and there is nothing further beyond God to attain to. But need it be static *subjectively,* on the part of the finite possessor? There is no intrinsic impossibility in the supposition that an analogical knowledge and love of God through His creatures would be a continuously expanding knowledge and a continuously deepening love, at each moment perfectly corresponding to the proximate capacity of the soul at that particular stage, but with a remote capacity of indefinite growth because God is the inexhaustible Source of everlasting new manifestations of His infinite perfections.

This matter has been put here for those who wish to relate philosophical and theological data. Not all accept our view. Some* think that man's natural tendency is only for happiness in the abstract without calling for a definite object, and that man could not have a determinate concrete last end in the natural order. They must face the charge that either natural man would be a monstrosity made for a happiness he could never get, or that he has a natural demand for the supernatural so that the supernatural ceases to be a free gift and becomes only natural. But these are their troubles. Our main concern is to show that man is destined to possess God in some way and only thus can he be happy.

QUESTIONS AND REMARKS

Further questions are suggested dealing with the attainment of God in a future life, whether that attainment be on a natural or a supernatural plane.

1. *God is infinite and man is only finite; how can man hope to attain God?* We must consider not only the object that is possessed, but also the way in which it is possessed. The object possessed, God, is the Infinite

---

*Joseph Buckley, *Man's Last End*, especially ch. 7.

Being, but man cannot possess God in an infinite way, in the way in which God possesses Himself. Man will be completely happy, in a way that fully satisfies his created nature, not infinitely happy. Man will know and love God as much as man can know and love, not as much as God in Himself is knowable and lovable.

2. *Why cannot finite man be satisfied by a finite good?* We must distinguish a proximate and a remote capacity for happiness. Proximate capacity refers to any particular moment or stage in a being's existence; remote capacity to the full scope of a being's potentiality. The human intellect is finite in its nature and in its proximate capacity, but unlimited in the range of its operation by which it tends to being as such, in its most all-embracing aspect. At no moment can the human intellect actually know all truth, yet no point can be reached at which it is incapable of knowing more. Hence its remote capacity can never be filled, but its proximate capacity can be filled, and this is the only sort of happiness possible in a creature. Only the Infinite Being can satisfy such a faculty, completely filling its proximate capacity with an inexhaustible reserve for its remote capacity.

3. *Will not man know that a higher degree of happiness is possible and thus be dissatisfied with what he has?* Each soul possessing God to the fullness of its proximate capacity will be as happy as it can be; but, since these capacities differ according to the good and evil done during life, each soul will recognize that other souls with higher proximate capacities are enjoying greater degrees of happiness. We may think that they will be envious of others or chafe at their own actual limitations. But neither of these is possible in a happiness which consists in complete conformity of the created will with the divine will. This whole objection, if carried to its logical extreme, would mean that man cannot be happy without being God. But the ambition to be God is satanic pride, the very opposite pole to happiness.

4. *If happiness supposes the satisfaction of all our desires, how can a spiritual being like God satisfy man's bodily desires?* When sentient and vegetative functions are sloughed off at death, they cease to need any satisfaction, for they are no longer there. Even if they did remain or if they should be restored to us by a resurrection of the body (as Christian theology teaches), God both could and would devise suitable satisfactions for them.

5. *How can man's soul be happy when separated from the body, since it is an incomplete substance, essentially the form of the body, and designed for union with the body?* St. Thomas speaks of the disembodied soul as being in a violent or unnatural state, but his meaning should not be exaggerated. Man is composed of two parts, one material and destructible (the body), the other spiritual and indestructible (the soul). In the natural course of events one is made to outlast the other. The human soul, being spiritual, is unique among forms in that it can continue to exist and operate (by intellect and will) without its partner.

6. *Would not the disembodied soul feel a lack of the pleasures it formerly experienced, and so not be happy?* We must distinguish what is essential to happiness from what is only contributory to it. The satisfaction of intellect and will in the possession of God is all that is strictly required to give us all the happiness we demand, and for this a body is not necessary. The satisfaction of any other powers that might be present together with the enjoyment of the society of other creatures, though insufficient by itself, can enhance the essential happiness already present.

SUMMARY

Where can man find the happiness to which he is destined? What is man's objective last end?

Hedonism or Epicureanism picks egoistic pleasure as man's last end, asserting that man, with no hereafter to look forward to, acts wisely in seeking the greatest enjoyment here.

Utilitarianism prefers the altruistic pleasure of seeking the greatest happiness of the greatest number, and measures morality by its utility in promoting the common welfare.

Stoicism holds that virtue is man's last end, despises pleasure, controls emotion by apathy, and cultivates resignation to inexorable Fate in a pantheistic universe.

Evolutionism sees man's destiny as evolution toward an unknown but higher state, in which the human race will find solution to its conflicts by further development of its potentialities.

The contrary view is that man can find happiness only in *the possession of God in the next life.* The proof is twofold:

1. *Process of elimination.* Nothing below man can make man happy, nor can man make himself happy; therefore, only something above man can do so, and this is God. Goods of fortune and goods of body are given to few, held with anxiety, and lost in the end. Knowledge is toilsome, incomplete, and unsatisfying. Virtue, besides being hard to practice, is but a means to the end and not the end itself. Pleasure is but a means used by nature to allure us to use our faculties for other ends, and cannot be constantly enjoyed. Service of others supposes that these others have some last end. Personal progress results only in a fully developed man who cannot be satisfied with himself. Progress of the human race does no good to the individual now and leaves unanswered what the race is for.

2. *Positive argument.* God is *required* to satisfy all man's desires, because the intellect tends to all Truth and the will to all Good. God is *sufficient,* because all perfection is found in the Infinite and whatever a creature can do God can do better.

Philosophical reason, though it can neither affirm nor deny a supernatural Beatific Vision, can establish man's destiny as at least a relatively perfect natural happiness, consisting in an analogical knowledge of God with its resultant love. This would have to be a condition of secure possession; there is no reason why it would have to be static or exclusive of perpetual growth.

Difficulties can be answered as follows:

1. God is infinite, but man can attain Him only in a finite way that yields a finite enjoyment of the Infinite.

2. Man's proximate capacity for happiness can be filled, but his remote capacity extends indefinitely.

3. One will not be envious of others' greater happiness because conformity to God's will is part of his own happiness.

4. Man's bodily faculties either will not be present or, if they are, will have their satisfaction.

5. As a subsistent form, man's soul is fitted to survive the body and can operate without it.

6. Possession of God gives essential happiness, which other enjoyments can only enhance but not constitute.

READINGS

1. Plato's *Philebus* is the classical dialogue on pleasure.
2. In the *Gorgias*, §492-500, Plato argues that pleasure is not *the* good.
3. Aristotle's *Nicomachean Ethics* has two sections on pleasure: bk. VII, ch. 11-14; bk. X, ch. 1-5.
4. Oates' *Stoic and Epicurean Philosophers* gives the fragments of Epicurus together with Lucretius' didactic poem *De Rerum Natura* (On the Nature of Things) embodying the philosophy of Epicurus; also the *Discourses* of Epictetus and the *Meditations* of Marcus Aurelius, which are the two great Stoic classics. These are found in a number of other editions.
5. Cicero describes and discusses Stoicism and Epicureanism, especially the former, in his philosophical works: *Academica, Tusculan Disputations, De Finibus, De Officiis, De Fato, Paradoxa Stoicorum.*
6. Diogenes Laertius' *Lives and Opinions of Eminent Philosophers* is found in full in the Loeb Classical Library. His account of the Cyrenaics is in book II, of the Cynics in book VI, of the Stoics in book VII, of the Epicureans in book X.
7. St. Thomas' *Summa Theologica*, I-II, qq. 2, 4, 5, is not found in the *Basic Writings*.
8. St. Thomas' *Summa Contra Gentiles*, bk. III, in the *Basic Writings*, vol. II, devotes chapters 25-63 to this subject. Read some of these chapters, especially 25, 27-34, 37-39, 47-48, 52-63. Remember that St. Thomas is treating primarily of theology and the Beatific Vision.
9. The works of the modern classical philosophers mentioned are available in various editions. The following collections are particularly useful:
   a. Rand, *Classical Moralists.*
   b. Clark and Smith, *Readings in Ethics.*
   c. Burtt, *English Philosophers from Bacon to Mill.*
   d. Commins and Linscott, *The World's Great Thinkers.*
   e. Melden, *Ethical Theories, a Book of Readings.*
10. There are many commentaries on the classical philosophers and any history of philosophy will give a digest on their systems. Sidgwick's *Outlines of the History of Ethics for English Readers* is a short standard work.
11. On the thesis maintained in the chapter read:
    a. Cronin, *Science of Ethics,* vol. I, pp. 53-79. Chapters X-XIII contain a valuable exposition and criticism of various ethical theories.
    b. Gilson, *Moral Values and Moral Life,* pp. 26-51.

c. Gilson, *The Christian Philosophy of St. Thomas Aquinas,* pp. 351-356. A different translation in Leibell, *Readings in Ethics,* pp. 174-181.

d. Farrell, *Companion to the Summa,* vol. II, ch. 1.

e. Adler, *Dialectic of Morals,* ch. II-III (on pleasure).

f. Rickaby, *Moral Philosophy,* pp. 21-27.

g. Ward, *Values and Reality,* ch. V-VI.

h. O'Connor, The Eternal Quest, ch. VII-IX. This whole book is on the question whether man can have a *natural* desire for the Beatific Vision. It is also the subject of his Aquinas Lecture, *The Natural Desire for God.*

i. Buckley, *Man's Last End.* This author maintains that man could have no determinate concrete last end in the natural order and that there could be no perfect natural happiness.

CHAPTER 16

VIRTUE

PROBLEMS

We have criticized the Stoic concept of virtue as its own reward, and have found it a means to the end rather than the end itself. But the fact that it is a means does not make it unimportant. The only means to the end are morally good acts, and the only way of assuring ourselves that our acts will be morally good is by turning them into a habit. Virtue and vice are but names for morally good and morally bad habits. Virtue testifies to good acts done, for there is no other way of acquiring a virtue, but it is also and chiefly the spring of further and better moral acts in the future. Virtue stands midway between a single good deed and a whole good life.

This chapter is mainly descriptive, but it does contain some problems. One is the paradox that good acts produce virtue and virtue produces good acts. Another is the Socratic concept of virtue as knowledge, from which it might seem that virtue ought to be studied rather than practiced. A third is to determine which among the almost innumerable virtues exert the chief influence on our moral life. Our remarks come under the following headings:

(1) Habit
(2) Virtue
(3) The intellectual virtues
(4) The moral virtues
(5) The four cardinal virtues

HABIT

By derivation *habit* means a *having*, and on this score anything we have is a habit. But over the centuries the word has been getting narrower in its meaning. Aristotle, after putting habit under the category of quality and calling it a lasting disposition,* gives this definition, often quoted by St. Thomas:†

> Habit means a disposition according to which that which is disposed is either well or ill disposed, and either in itself or with reference to something else.‡

So vague a definition made it necessary to distinguish *entitative* habits, or habits of being, from *operative* habits, or habits of acting. The former would be such qualities as health or strength or beauty, which we hardly call habits today. Modern language recognizes only operative habits, the tendencies we *have* in us from repeated acts.

We are born with a nature endowed with certain powers of acting. We begin to exercise these powers, and each time we do a thing we find it easier to repeat the action in the same way. Habit is beginning to take shape. It is an actualization of our potencies, but has the peculiar position of being midway between bare potency and full act. Nothing, of course, can be both in potency and in act toward the same thing in the same way, but it can in different ways. Take the example of a carpenter. As a child he was but a potential carpenter, having an undeveloped natural ability. Now that he has learned the trade, got the habit, he is an actual carpenter, one actually expert in this kind of work. But he happens at the moment to be asleep. Though he actually has the habit, he is not exercising it and is in a state of potency toward that exercise. When he awakes and starts plying his trade, he not only is an actual carpenter but is actually carpentering. Thus the habit is a sort of midway stage between undeveloped ability and expert operation.

Habit does not give us the power to *do* something; this we must have from our nature. But habit enables us to do something *more easily and readily*. If the habit is good, it turns our originally fitful and clumsy efforts into quick, smooth, and masterful action. If the habit is bad, it makes us fall more easily and readily into the undesirable course. This is why habit has been called a "second nature,"§ for, just as nature is the principle of action itself, so habit is the source of facility in action. The habit comes from the acts and the acts come from the habit, but in different ways: by acting repeatedly we acquire the habit, and the habit now acquired tends to manifest itself in acts.

Habits are typically *human* things. God can have no habits because He has no potentiality and does all things with perfect ease. Animals cannot have habits in the proper sense because their potentialities are too narrow and their lines of action are laid out for them by their nature through their

---

*Aristotle, *Categories*, ch. 8, 8b 27.
†St. Thomas, *Summa Theologica*, I-II, q. 49, a. 1, ff.
‡Aristotle, *Metaphysics*, bk. V, ch. 20, 1022b 10.
§Aristotle, *Nicomachean Ethics*, bk. VII, ch. 10, 1152a 30.

instincts; man can train animals to quasi-habits, but these are imposed from without and not developed by the animal alone. But man has a nature plastic enough to be molded in various ways. By his free choice he can do the molding himself to some extent and his environment will do the rest. Man cannot spread his abilities over the whole field of action possible to him, but must channel them along definite lines. Habits are these channels, cut deeper with each repetition for better or for worse, until the person's native temperament is carved out into the thing we call character.

Though all habits are acquired in the sense that we are not born with any fully formed, they differ greatly in the amount of effort needed for their development. The intellectual habit of first principles, the understanding and use of such truths as the principle of noncontradiction in the speculative order and the principles of synderesis or the first moral truths in the practical order, is virtually in the mind from the start. Other habits grow only by painstaking and persistent practice, and need constant exercise to keep them at the peak of efficiency, such as the arts, skills, and sports. Bad habits may result from defective development of our abilities, so that instead of ease and smoothness we beget a wasteful and bungling style of operation. Other habits develop no ability in us but only create a tendency to repetition; the acts are not done better but only more often until we fall into them inadvertently, such as swearing. Still other habits come from building up in oneself an organic craving, whether wholly acquired or the ripening of a predisposition, as in the use of drugs and stimulants. Finally, there are those forms of routine more properly called customs than habits, which however often repeated normally require a voluntary act each time, such as going to church on Sundays.

Habits are destroyed either by disuse or by contrary acts. Disuse starves out the habit and contrary acts replace it with the opposite habit. In rooting out bad habits it is important never to allow a single slip back into the habits, for one fall can undo the work of a long and painful conquest. Habits are useful servants created in us by own own acts, but they have a tendency subtly to enslave their masters; they must be kept in their place.

VIRTUE

Some habits perfect us only physically or mentally or socially, but if they perfect our nature taken completely they are good habits of living or conduct and are called virtues. Originally the word *virtue,* from the Latin *vir,* meant manliness, and the Greek ἀρετή had a similar sense. From excellence in battle it came to mean any kind of excellence, and that is how ancient writers use it. Only in modern times has it become restricted to an ethical sense. *Vice* likewise meant any kind of flaw, but now means only an ethically bad habit.

Socrates taught that virtue is knowledge and vice is ignorance. This doctrine runs throughout the writings of Plato, appearing in two often recurring questions: "Is virtue one or many?" and "Can virtue be taught?"

Plato explains how knowledge is the common element in all virtues, the courageous man knowing what to do in danger, the temperate man knowing how to restrain his passions, the just man knowing what rightly belongs to himself and to others. Virtue is therefore one, and since it is knowledge it can be taught.* He says that the philosopher alone has true virtue because he alone has true wisdom, and insists on the importance of attaining that wisdom.† Because of this conviction Socrates and Plato took their teaching mission so seriously.

The sublimity of Plato's thought should not blind us to its defects. If virtue is knowledge and vice ignorance, no one does wrong voluntarily; at most he could be censured for neglecting to acquire the proper knowledge. Plato admits this:

> No man voluntarily pursues evil, or that which he thinks to be evil. To prefer evil to good is not in human nature; and when a man is compelled to choose one of two evils, no one will choose the greater when he may have the less.‡

In his discussion of voluntariness, Aristotle directly argues against Plato's opinion:

> The end being what we wish for, the means what we deliberate about and choose, actions concerning means must be according to choice and voluntary. Now the exercise of the virtues is concerned with means. Therefore virtue also is in our power, and so too vice. . . . Now if it is in our power to do noble or base acts, and likewise in our power not to do them, and this is what being good or bad meant, then it is in our power to be virtuous or vicious.§

If our knowledge were perfect and if our appetites were under the full control of reason, Plato's theory would be correct. But in this life our knowledge is not perfect. A vicious act requires some voluntary clouding of knowledge, a willful refusal at the moment of acting to use the knowledge we have. We seek evil not for itself, but for some good found with it or through it. We try to concentrate on the good and overlook the evil, yet we know the evil is there and choose it voluntarily. Also, our control over our appetites is not the same as our control over our muscles. When we command our hand or foot it obeys, but when we command our appetites they can and often do rebel.

> The soul rules the body with a despotical rule, whereas the intellect rules the appetites with a constitutional and royal rule.‖

Protagoras, §359-361; *Republic,* bk. IV, §441-445.
†*Phaedo,* §68-69, 107-108; *Phaedrus,* §246-256.
‡*Protagoras,* §358; see also *Laws,* bk. V, §731, bk. IX, §860.
§*Nicomachean Ethics,* bk. III, ch. 5, 1113b 3; see also bk. VII, ch. 2-3, 1145b-22-1147b 19, regarding continence.
‖Aristotle, *Politics,* bk. I, ch. 5, 1254b 3.

Hence the necessity of training the other parts of our being to be subject to reason. Such training results in good habits, and these are virtues. In a virtuous person the passions and appetites are habitually subject to reason like the free citizens of a well-governed state, but in the vicious man they are an unruly mob. In any single act he can keep them in line and it is his fault if he does not, but by and large he will find the effort too great, will relax his control, and act against the law of reason. So, though there is some knowledge in all virtue and some ignorance in all vice, knowledge alone will not suffice to make men good.

INTELLECTUAL VIRTUES

Good habits of the intellect, enabling it to be a more efficient instrument of knowledge, are virtues in the broad sense. Their effect on a man's moral life is quite remote, for they may make him a better student of ethics, but not a better living man. Failure to exercise them results rather in involuntary mistakes than in wrong conduct. But, though less important for ethics, they are very valuable in themselves.

Aristotle* distinguishes three virtues of the theoretical or speculative intellect concerned with the contemplation of the true:

(1) *Understanding:* the habit of first principles, the habitual knowledge of primary self-evident truths that lie at the root of all knowledge

(2) *Science:* the habit of conclusions drawn by demonstrations from first principles, the habitual knowledge of the particular sciences

(3) *Wisdom:* the habit of knowing things in their highest causes, an ordering of all principles and conclusions into one vast body of truth

Then there are two virtues of the practical intellect, concerned with the two forms of action, making and doing:

(4) *Art:* the habit of knowing how to make things, how to produce some external object; it includes the mechanical, the liberal, and the fine arts

(5) *Prudence:* the habit of knowing how to do things, how to direct activity that does not result in tangible products, how to live a good human life

---

*Aristotle, *Nicomachean Ethics,* bk. VI. St. Thomas, *Summa Theologica,* I-II, q. 57. Different translations of Aristotle use different names to indicate these virtues; the following list may help to avoid confusion:

νοῦς	= understanding	= intuitive reason
ἐπιστήμη	= science	= scientific knowledge
σοφία	= wisdom	= philosophic wisdom
τέχνη	= art	= craftsmanship
φρόνησις	= prudence	= practical wisdom

MORAL VIRTUES

Though even the intellectual virtues have some remote reference to moral life, those which are more directly concerned with good living are called *moral* virtues. They are good habits in the appetitive part of the soul, directing the activity of the will and governing the passions of the sense-appetite. They enable us not merely to know what to do and how to do it, but they actually assist us in the doing of it. Doing a thing well is opposed to overdoing and to underdoing it, and consists in hitting the mean between excess and defect. This is Aristotle's famous doctrine of the *mean,* which he expresses thus:

> Virtue is a state of character concerned with choice, lying in a mean, i.e. the mean relative to us, this being determined by a rational principle and by that principle by which the man of practical wisdom would determine it. Now it is a mean between two vices, that which depends on excess and that which depends on defect; and again it is a mean because the vices respectively fall short of or exceed what is right in both passions and actions, while virtue both finds and chooses that which is intermediate. Hence in respect of its substance and the definition which states its essence virtue is a mean; with regard to what is best and right, an extreme.*

In other words, virtue is a habit of choosing the mean between the extremes of excess and defect in action, and this mean is determined by reason guided by the intellectual virtue of prudence. As too much or too little food, sleep, or exercise hurts the body but just the right amount promotes its health, so excess or defect in the habits of the soul hurts its health and "virtue stands in the middle." Virtue aims us at our end, and must neither overshoot nor fall short of the mark. Courage is a mean between cowardice and rashness, temperance between overindulgence and insensibility, generosity between stinginess and prodigality, friendliness between surliness and flattery.

The mean is not absolute but "relative to us," for what is the right amount for one would be too much or too little for another. A brave deed for a soldier would be foolhardy for a woman, a temperate meal for a wrestler would be overindulgence for a dyspeptic, a generous gift from a poor man would be a stingy one from a rich man. So the intellectual virtue of prudence is the guide by which the mean of the moral virtues is to be decided. Aristotle carefully notes that, though the virtue itself is a mean between extremes, the virtue is not to be practiced moderately but fully. The judge must go all out for justice, but justice itself is a mean between lenience and severity; the witness must be exactly truthful, but truthfulness itself is a mean between exaggeration and understatement. In acts that are

---

*Nicomachean Ethics, bk. II, ch. 6, 1106b 36. The translation uses some unusual expressions: "state of character" is *habit,* "rational principle" is *reason,* "practical wisdom" is *prudence.* The English edition of St. Thomas shortens the definition thus: "Virtue is a habit of choosing the mean appointed by reason as a prudent man would appoint it" (*Summa Theologica,* I-II, q. 59, a. 1).

bad in themselves there is no virtuous mean. It is not good to be moderately murderous or adulterous; we must simply not be so at all.

CARDINAL VIRTUES

Four virtues have been traditionally picked out as the most important in the ethical order. They are called *cardinal* virtues, from the Latin *cardo,* a hinge, because they are the four hinges on which the other virtues swing. Plato, though he probably did not invent them, makes his whole theory of the human soul and of the state dependent on them. Aristotle centers his *Ethics* on them and they have been universally adopted by Christian writers. St. Thomas divides the cardinal virtues as follows:

> The formal principle of the virtue of which we speak now is the good as defined by reason. This good can be considered in two ways. First, as existing in the consideration itself of reason, and thus we have one principal virtue called *prudence.* Secondly, according as the reason puts its order into something else, and this either into operations, and then we have *justice,* or into passions, and then we need two virtues. For the need of putting the order of reason into the passions is due to their thwarting reason; and this occurs in two ways. First, when the passions incite to something against reason, and then they need a curb, which we thus call *temperance;* secondly, when the passions withdraw us from following the dictate of reason, e.g., through fear of danger or toil, and then man needs to be strengthened for that which reason dictates, lest he turn back, and to this end there is *fortitude.*
>
> In like manner we find the same number if we consider the subjects of virtue. For there are four subjects of the virtue of which we now speak, viz., the power which is rational in its essence, and this is perfected by *prudence;* and that which is rational by participation, and is threefold, the will, subject of *justice,* the concupiscible power, subject of *temperance,* and the irascible power, subject of *fortitude.**

Prudence

Prudence is an intellectual virtue by essence, but it enters into the field of the moral virtues by pointing out the mean and suggesting ways of securing it. Without prudence fortitude becomes boldness, temperance becomes moroseness, justice becomes harshness. Prudence chooses the right means toward worthy ends; the choice of good means toward bad ends is mere cleverness or shrewdness, but not true prudence. As it is impossible to have the moral virtues without prudence, so it is impossible to have prudence without the moral virtues, for the rebellion of passion and will clouds reason, and prevents the formation of a prudent judgment.

The importance of prudence in the ethical life cannot be overestimated. Whenever a general rule of conduct, such as ethics devises, must be applied to a concrete case, prudence is called for. Rules cannot be given for prudence itself, because all rules must have some universality and prudence

---

*Summa Theologica, I-II, q. 61, a. 2.

deals with the single instance. How to break bad news gently, when to ask one's employer for a raise, whether to punish a fault or to let it pass this time, whom to pick out as the right man for the right job, how to arrange the troops for battle in a particular terrain, what legislation will best promote the common good and conciliate all interests—all such matters, great and small, are governed by prudence. The widest possible observation and experience of human behavior are the only teachers of prudence. It has little correlation with book learning. Some pick it up readily, some otherwise intelligent persons are slow to catch on, some geniuses are deficient in it. Imprudent people may commit few sins, for one does not consciously will to be imprudent, but their lives are a series of blunders. The virtue of prudence does not consist in a single prudent decision but is the acquired habit of always or nearly always using the right means to good ends.

There are a number of lesser virtues implied in prudence, such as memory, foresight, care, docility, caution, circumspection. Negligence, precipitation, inconsideration, recklessness, headstrongness, and the like indicate a defect of prudence. Craftiness, deceit, timidity, pusillanimity may result from an excess of prudence not balanced by other virtues.

Temperance

Temperance regulates the appetite in the use of sensible pleasure. It moderates our two main drives, toward self-preservation and race-preservation, and thus acts as a curb on excessive indulgence in food and drink and in the use of sex. Its opposed vices are gluttony and lust. Temperance does not mean total abstinence. There are some persons who find that any indulgence leads to temptations they cannot overcome, and for these total abstinence is the only cure; others for higher motives and for their spiritual perfection voluntarily give up some otherwise legitimate pleasures. But no creature is bad in itself, and the natural law merely requires that creatures be used with moderation and insofar as they help to worthy ends. The habit of doing this is temperance. Since most persons are inclined to excess in pleasure, the mean is usually short of one's desire, and closer to the side of restraint. People differ greatly in the strength of their sensuous cravings, and so the mean varies with different persons.

Temperance contains the subordinate virtues of abstinence and sobriety, chastity and continence. By analogy temperance also regulates cravings that are less animal in nature: humility moderates self-esteem, meekness anger, and modesty outward deportment. Lack of temperance appears in gluttony, drunkenness, lust, pride, cruelty, vanity. Too much restraint may produce insensibility, stolidity, sullenness, moroseness, fanatical austerity.

Fortitude

Fortitude, courage, or bravery inclines one to face danger and toil without flinching. As temperance is a bridle, so courage is a spur. Most people are inclined to quail before danger and courage drives us into it. But not everything that looks like a brave act is a manifestation of the virtue of fortitude. It does not consist in one brave act, but is a habit of self-mastery. To rush into peril out of anger, ignorance, or stupidity is no sign of fortitude; the truly courageous man acts from a rational motive, whereby he appreciates the danger while counting it the lesser evil. To our instincts death is the most dreadful of all things, but reason tells us that there are some things better than life and others worse than death. Fortitude enables us to overcome our abhorrence for death, and still more of lesser evils, when it is reasonable to do so. It frees us from slavery to fear, though it need not take away fear itself. The brave man may act with fear, but in spite of it faces the danger.

Fortitude implies patience, perseverance, constancy. Aristotle adds two unusual virtues: magnificence, to dare wisely in the matter of expense, and magnanimity, to dare wisely in the matter of honor. His often quoted picture of the magnanimous man,* the high-minded or superior man, which seems to be his ideal, leaves much to be desired in a paragon. Lack of fortitude is shown in cowardice, weakness, timidity, impatience, irresoluteness. Boldness, presumption, stubbornness, quarrelsomeness, ruthlessness are faults of the overbrave.

Justice

Justice inclines us to give to each one his own. It supposes at least two persons between whom there can be some sort of equality, so that each person receives what really belongs to him. Temperance and fortitude regulate our control over the lower appetites, but justice regulates the will's government over itself where dealings with another person are involved.

Justice is divided by Aristotle into general and particular. *General* justice is so broad as to cover all virtue that has any social significance and is therefore not the specific cardinal virtue of justice. *Particular* justice he divides into *distributive* and *corrective*. The latter is now more commonly called *commutative*, a name derived from the commutation or exchange of goods. We shall take them in inverse order.

Commutative justice exists between equals, that is between man and man, or between groups of men acting as if they were private persons negotiating on equal terms. Commutative justice is the basis of contracts. In a contract, such as barter or hire, the two persons start equal; when one has fulfilled his part of the contract the equality is unbalanced; then justice demands the restoration of equality by the other's fulfillment of his part. The same holds outside the field of voluntary contracts in those situations where nature itself demands the balance of equality. One who has injured another by depriving him of something rightfully his is obliged in justice to restore it to him. Commutative justice, when violated, carries with it the obligation of restitution. Justice remains outraged until proper compensation has been made to reestablish the balance.

---

*Nicomachean Ethics, bk. IV, ch. 3, 1122a 33; the Oxford translation calls him "proud," a term which can easily be misinterpreted.

Distributive justice is a relation between the community and its members. As its name indicates, it requires a fair and proper distribution of public benefits and burdens among the members of the community. Though existing in some way in all organizations, distributive justice applies chiefly to the state. It is the particular obligation of public officials, and is violated by favoritism and partiality. It does not exist between equals, but between a superior and his subordinates; the equality, implied in all justice, here means that each subordinate should get his proportionate share, a share equal to his just deserts. Distributive justice has its converse, the obligation of the members to contribute to the common good. In this aspect it has been called contributive justice.

Social justice is a modern term that has been given various meanings by various writers. The tendency now is to identify it with St. Thomas' *legal* justice, which is the same as Aristotle's *general* justice. Social justice refers to the organization of society in such a way that the common good, to which all are expected to contribute in proportion to their ability and opportunity, is available to all the members for their ready use and enjoyment. It shows itself more in economic, industrial, racial, and political relations, but is by no means restricted to them. It involves everything connected with being a good citizen or a good member of society and reaping what ought to be the reward of upright and cooperative social conduct, one's proper share of the benefits of social living. Any arrangement of society that excludes or hinders certain classes or groups within it from their fair share of the common good is a violation of social justice. Nearly the whole of social ethics is a study of social justice.

CONCLUSION

Man is obliged to train his abilities to make them fit instruments for the attainment of his end. He has a general obligation to make good use of his talents, as gifts entrusted to his stewardship, though he has no particular duty to develop any one of them rather than another. But he should choose some sphere of action proportional to his gifts and educate himself in it to the point of expertness and competence. He cannot do so without a fair degree of the intellectual virtues.

Far more important in his development as a person are the moral virtues. A man simply must master his passions and learn self-control. Since he must avoid evil acts, he must keep himself clear of the evil habits or vices which are the sources of such acts, and acquire as much of the contrary virtues as will ensure his ability to cope with the ordinary temptations of life. No one can succeed without a good grounding in each of the four cardinal virtues.

No one is born with virtues and they do not come to one by chance, but only by long and arduous training. Parents are the ones charged with the responsibility of beginning the training of their children to give them a moral start in life. Human life is so arranged that each succeeding generation fits into the preceding one, so that the virtues of parents, by instruction but much more by example, are passed on to their children. Parents must have what they are to transmit. Moral discipline must begin long before the child is old enough to appreciate its value or even its meaning. The exercise of parental authority should gradually dwindle until it vanishes with the coming of adulthood, which is not the time for fashioning the weapons but for having them ready for use.

Our treatment of virtue may seem too cursory for so important a topic, but it is meant only as a summary and an introduction. Most of the following chapters will consist of a more detailed examination of the various virtues. Some will be treated at greater length because of the problems they raise, but the difficulty of a topic does not always indicate its importance.

SUMMARY

Habit is a quality difficult to change, disposing a being well or ill, either in itself or in its relations with others. Habit is a partial actualization of our natural potencies, adding to nature by giving it ease in performance, the acts intensifying the habit and the habit facilitating the acts. Habits of acting are acquired by constant repetition, lost by disuse or contrary acts.

Good moral habits are *virtues,* evil ones *vices.* The Socratic doctrine that virtue is knowledge and vice is ignorance is countered by the Aristotelian teaching that the control of reason over the passions is not despotic but political. The appetites can rebel against reason, but ought not, and must be trained not to.

Intellectual virtues make the intellect a better instrument of knowledge. They are understanding, science, and wisdom in the speculative intellect, art and prudence in the practical intellect.

Moral virtues govern the appetites, both rational *(will)* and sensitive *(concupiscible* and *irascible).* They consist in the habit of choosing the *mean* between extremes, directed thereto by the intellectual virtue of prudence.

The *cardinal* virtues are the hinges on which the other virtues swing. They are *prudence* in the intellect, choosing right means toward worthy ends; *temperance* in the concupiscible appetite, restraining it from overindulgence; *fortitude* in the irascible appetite, spurring it on to face necessary danger; and *justice* in the will, giving each one his own or his due.

Justice is particular or general. *Particular* justice is either *commutative,* from man to man, restoring the balance of equality, or *distributive,* between the community and its members. These two comprise the cardinal virtue. *General* or *legal* or *social* justice regulates the whole of social living, comprising both the acquisition and apportionment of the common good.

READINGS

1. Plato has written hardly anything that does not deal with virtue in some respect. The *Protagoras, Phaedo, Phaedrus,* and book IV of the *Republic* are recommended. The *Charmides* and *Laches* are on temperance and courage.
2. Aristotle's treatment of virtue in the *Nicomachean Ethics* runs from bk. I, ch. 13,

to bk. VII, ch. 10 (1102a 5 to 1152a 35). This is the orignal source of the ideas found in this chapter.

3. St. Thomas follows Aristotle, omitting some points, developing others more thoroughly, and adding the theological virtues. His discussion of habits and virtues is found in the *Summa Theologica,* I-II, qq. 49 to 61; qq. 63 and 64; q. 65, a. 1; q. 66, aa. 1-5; q. 71, aa. 1-4. The Second Part of the Second Part (II-II) takes up the cardinal virtues in detail, but is not printed in the *Basic Writings.*

4. Rickaby, *Moral Philosophy,* ch. V.

5. Farrell, *Companion to the Summa,* vol. II, ch. VIII-XI.

6. Cronin, *The Science of Ethics,* vol. I, ch. XVIII.

7. Gilson-Ward, *Moral Values and Moral Life,* ch. V. See also ch. VIII-XI, one on each cardinal virtue in detail.

8. Leibell, *Readings in Ethics,* pp. 213-221, 236-245.

9. Gilson, *The Christian Philosophy of St. Thomas Aquinas,* pp. 256-264, 271-332.

10. Le Buffe and Hayes, *The American Philosophy of Law,* ch. XIII, on justice.

11. Brennan, Sr. Rose Emmanuella, *The Intellectual Virtues According to the Philosophy of St. Thomas.*

12. Pieper has three little books, one entitled *Justice,* another *Prudence,* and a third *Fortitude and Temperance.*

CHAPTER 17

RIGHTS AND

DUTIES

PROBLEMS

The ideas of law and justice imply the existence of such things as rights and duties. Applied ethics, which begins with the next chapter, consists almost entirely in determining just what man's rights and duties are. We must therefore investigate these very important ethical concepts. We can distribute the matter under the following questions:

    (1) What are rights?
    (2) What are the components of a right?
    (3) Are there natural rights?
    (4) How is right related to might?
    (5) What are duties?
    (6) What if rights and duties conflict?
    (7) What excuses one from duty?

MEANING OF RIGHT

The English word *right* has two main meanings, as illustrated in the following sentence: "It is right (morally good) for us to demand our rights (things owed us)." The two meanings stem out of the same root idea, the ethical concept of *oughtness:* how I ought to act, and how others ought to act toward me. Hence we have:

    (1) Right as opposed to wrong
    (2) Right as correlative to duty

Right originally means something that is straight, not crooked, in opposition to *wrong,* which is wrung or twisted from the straight. Right is something which squares with a rule or norm, as a right line or a right angle. In ethics *right* means that which squares with the norm of morality, and so is morally good. In this sense it is equivalent to the Latin *rectus,* from which we derive such words as rectify, rectitude, erect, direct, and correct. Our whole previous discussion of morality dealt with this meaning of the word *right.*

Right is also used as the equivalent of the Latin *jus,* from which we derive such words as just, justice, justify, jurist, juridical, injure, and perjure. In this sense right means that which is just: a just law, just deed, just debt, just claim. This is *right* as correlative to *duty,* and it is this sense of *right* that we must now study.

We cannot be obliged to keep the moral law and at the same time be deprived of the means necessary to this end. This obligation requires that we have the *power* both to do the things necessary for keeping the moral law ourselves and to restrain others from interfering with our observance of the moral law. No one can be obliged to the impossible; hence, if it is a fact that we are obliged, we must be *empowered* to fulfill our obligation. Power is of two kinds:

(1) Physical power or might
(2) Moral power or right

Might or physical power is the bodily strength needed to secure an end. It comprises not only our own skeleton and muscles together with all the tools, weapons, and machinery we can use, but also the bodily strength of all other persons under our command and the force of all the instruments they can use to help us accomplish our end. Thus a whole army can be at the disposal of a single man's will, and is an enormous extension of his personal might. Though applied by a will or even by many wills cooperating, physical power accomplishes its purpose by mere force, which is indifferent to the claims of justice and can be used to help or hinder the observance of the moral law. Hence might in itself is neither good nor evil, and becomes either by the will that directs it.

Right or moral power, on the other hand, works by appeal to another's will through his intellect. It points out to him that I claim something as mine, and that respect for my claim is necessary for him if he is to attain his own last end. In urging a right I equivalently say, "This is mine, a means given me to help me fulfill my moral function as a human being; if you try to interfere, you can do so only by doing wrong, incurring moral guilt, violating the moral *ought,* thus destroying your own moral worth as a man." Thus a right puts a moral bond on the free will of another so that, even if he can infringe my right physically, he cannot do so without committing an evil deed and incurring moral guilt with its corresponding sanctions. Hence a right is said to be morally inviolable, even when it is physically violable.

1. Right is defined as moral power over what is one's own, or more expressly, *moral power to do, omit, hold, or exact something.* Right as thus defined exists in the person possessing the right and is right in the primary sense.

2. By a figure of speech we transfer the word *right* from the person who has the right and apply it to the thing over which he has the right. We say, "I will get my rights," meaning some object rightfully mine, and "This man is deprived of his rights," meaning some object rightfully his. If a man were deprived of his right in the sense of moral power, he would have no right to the thing at all and could not legitimately claim it; what we mean is that he is deprived of some object to which he retains a right.

3. Right is founded on law. Right puts an obligation on others to respect the right. Since all obligation comes from law, and ultimately from the natural and eternal law, all right comes from law. Because of this fact, *law* itself is sometimes called *right,* a usage common in other languages, but infrequent in English. Since all right comes from law, rights are natural or positive, divine or human, ecclesiastical or civil, according to the kind of law which confers the right.

These three meanings of right are illustrated in the following sentence: A man is unjustly deprived of his rights (an object due him); recourse is made to the code of civil rights (the law); the man is given a fair trial to which he has a right (moral power to do, omit, hold, or exact something; in this case, to exact).

COMPONENTS OF A RIGHT

A right involves a system of relations in which there are three terms and a basis or foundation on which the relations are grounded. In the example of a workman having a right to his wages, we may separate four elements or components: the workman who has earned the wages, the employer who is bound to pay the wages, the wages the workman has earned, and the work done whereby the workman has earned the wages. In general, in every right we distinguish the

(1) Subject: the one possessing a right
(2) Term: those bound to respect or fulfill a right
(3) Matter: that to which one has a right
(4) Title: the reason why this subject has this right

Subject of a right

It can be only a *person.* Rights exist because we are obliged to guard the moral value of our being and fulfill our function by voluntary observance of the moral law, and thus to reach our last end. To this kind of action rights are essential, because if we must guide ourselves by use of our free will we must be guaranteed immunity from hindrance in our choice of the necessary means. Since only persons have free choice and are obliged by the moral law, only persons can have rights. Other creatures, acting spontaneously and without freedom or responsibility, need no such guarantee. God's rights are founded on the eternal law, identified with Himself and containing the moral law preeminently.

Therefore animals, not being persons, have no rights. Is there, then, no wrong in cruelty to animals? Cruelty to animals is wrong, but not as a violation of the animals' rights. Rather, it is a perversion of the natural relation which should exist between man and animals, and violates the duty man owes to himself and to God. To himself, because man must use animals in a way befitting man's own rational nature, and to inflict needless pain is unreasonable conduct. To God, the animals' supreme master, because He in His bounty has provided man with these creatures to be used for any reasonable and good purpose they can serve, but not merely to pander to man's sadistic craving for cruelty.

Vivisection is not wrong in itself, because animals are for man and may be used to help in the curing of man's diseases just as they may be used for other human purposes. But vivisection can easily become wrong through circumstances, by being performed in an unnecessarily inhumane or cruel manner. On this subject much sentimental nonsense is written. Why draw a line between pets and pests? Even the staunchest defenders of so-called animal rights think it proper to get rid of vermin, and it is irrational to acknowledge rights only in those animals that happen to please us. If dogs have rights, so must fleas.

The subject of a right may be not only a *physical* or *natural* person, an individual rational being, but also a *moral* or *juridical* person (sometimes called a conventional, fictitious, or artificial person) such as a society, firm, corporation, or government. People may act singly or in groups, by themselves or through representatives, and group action is in accordance with man's social nature. Man attains his end by social as well as by individual activity; but a society would be useless unless it can command the means necessary to achieve its purpose; therefore societies as well as individuals can have rights.

Term of a right

It must also be a *person*. This proposition is evident from the definition. The term is the one or ones morally obliged to respect or fulfill the rights of another, and only a person can have moral obligations.

Matter of a right

It can *never* be a *person*. According to the classical definition of Boethius, a person is "an individual substance of a rational nature."* This definition is so explained as to mean that a person is self-owned, self-possessed, self-controlled, and therefore master of his own acts, in such a way as to be ordered directly to God and to no other. A person cannot be subordinated to the interests of another to be used and con-

---

*Boethius, *De Duabus Naturis, seu Contra Eutychen et Nestorium,* III, translated in the Loeb Classics; St. Thomas, *Summa Theologica,* I, q. 29, a. 1.

sumed as a mere means for another's benefit. Kant spoke correctly when he said:

> Beings whose existence does not depend on our will but on nature, if they are not rational beings, have only a relative worth as means and are therefore called "things"; on the other hand, rational beings are designated "persons," because their nature indicates that they are ends in themselves, i.e., things which may not be used merely as means.*

Since in the exercise of any right the subject always subordinates the matter to himself and uses it as a means to his own end, it follows that the matter of a right can never be a person.

This conclusion does not mean that one person can never do a service for another. Social life is a constant interchange of services, and men were made by nature to be helpful to one another. When we hire people to work for us, we buy their labor, not their persons, and labor can be the matter of a right.

Slavery is wrong because it comes so close to treating a person as a thing. It is impossible to own a person, if we understand the word *person* in a philosophical sense. To own a slave's person would be to own not merely his body but also his intellect and will. These, however, always remain under the slave's control, and he is responsible for his voluntary acts like any other human being. It is precisely because a person is an intellectual being capable of voluntary and free acts that he cannot be owned. Though the slaveholder does not deprive a man of his internal freedom in the sense of free will, he does deprive the slave of his external freedom, which is one of the most precious attributes of a person and one of his most fundamental rights.

Slavery might be imposed as punishment for crime. If the state can put criminals to death, it should be able to impose lesser punishments. Imprisonment for crime is used in all societies, and the distinction between it and slavery is rather nominal. Under desperate conditions a man might sell himself into slavery. If he can hire out his services for pay, why not for mere maintenance; if he can do it for a time, why not for life? For good order the state should forbid such a contract, but it does not seem intrinsically wrong. These two forms of servitude, the penal and the voluntary, are the only ones for which even a semblance of moral justification can be found.

Slavery as an historical institution looked on slaves as property, as animated tools, to be bought and sold. There can hardly be anything more degrading to human dignity or more destructive of human rights than this revolting practice. There can be no possible moral defense for slave-hunting, nor for letting children be born into slavery, and what begins unjustly and in bad faith cannot be righted by the mere passage of time. That the civilized world accepted this institution for so long illustrates

---

*Kant, *Foundations of the Metaphysics of Morals*, section II.

the slow growth of moral social consciousness and the difficulty of seeing remote conclusions of the natural law.

Title of a right

It is the reason why this particular concrete right exists. Its purpose is to establish a connection between the subject and the matter of a right. For example, a man has a right to own property in general, but this is an abstract right, not specifying any particular piece of property. Something is necessary to give this particular man rather than someone else the right to this particular piece of property, to change the abstract into a concrete right. The contract of sale does this, and this fact is his title.

According to title, rights are congenital or acquired. *Congenital* or *native* rights come with birth; the title to these rights is the bare fact of existence as a human being. *Acquired* rights have as their title some contingent historical fact, such as purchase or inheritance or arriving at the age of twenty-one. But in either case the title is always some fact connecting this subject with this matter, this person with this thing.

The terms *alienable* and *inalienable* rights cause so much confusion as to be practically unusable in ethics. To alienate is to give away or to take away. No right, if it is a genuine right, can be taken away except by the one who has granted it. Positive rights can be taken away by the grantor and given away, or at least given up, by the possessor. Natural rights, since they are granted by God through the natural law, cannot be taken away by man's authority, and are in this sense inalienable. Can they be given up, waived, or renounced by the possessor? Some of them can, for though granted by nature, they are not strictly necessary in all possible conditions of life. Thus a man may bind himself not to own property or not to marry. But other rights are so indispensable that their exercise is also a duty. These may not be arbitrarily taken away nor voluntarily renounced, and are in this sense inalienable, but they may be lost as punishment for misuse. Thus parents have the natural right to rear their children, but may lose it because of incompetence or cruelty. Even so basic a right as that to life may be lost for serious crime. Some try to explain this matter by distinguishing between the right itself and the right to its exercise, but this seems a meaningless subtlety. Moral power which *cannot* or *must not* be exercised is not moral power. The only rights that would be absolutely inalienable in all senses would be such highly abstract formulations as the right to lead a moral life or the right to be treated justly. In much of the literature the term *inalienable right* simply stands for *natural right*.

NATURAL RIGHTS

We need not prove that there are such things as rights, for no one denies it. To deny all rights one would have to deny all law, and even the most extreme anarchists would admit some form of customary law. All law supposes rights and all rights suppose law. The concepts are inseparable. There cannot be a right unless all others are bound to respect that right, and that which binds them is law. There cannot be a law unless someone is charged with moral power to exact obedience to the law, that is, with the right to enforce it. Hence the saying, "No law, no rights," and vice versa.

Unanimity ceases when we ask: Which law is the origin of rights? Since no one denies that there are positive laws, no one denies that there are positive rights. The problem, then, centers on the existence of the natural law. If there is a natural law, there should be natural rights; if not, there can be none. So the main cleavage of thought is as follows:

(1) Are there no rights but positive rights?
(2) Besides positive rights are there also natural rights?

Moral and *legal positivists* are logically compelled to adopt the first position. If there is no natural law, there can be no natural rights, because there would be nothing to oblige people to respect such rights. Some moral positivists use the term *natural rights,* but by it Hobbes* means only that in the state of nature a man had a right to do whatever he was able to do, and Spinoza,† consistently with his pantheistic determinism, cannot distinguish between natural moral law and natural physical law, so that a man's natural rights are on the same plane as that of a rose to bloom or of a cat to purr. Such uses of the word *right* make it but an empty name, as Rousseau‡ correctly observes. Moral positivists must either deny that the commonly accepted natural rights of man are really rights or reduce them somehow to positive rights.

There is also a group of compromisers who will not go so far as to deny a natural moral law, but think that civil law should be studied independently of it. They make a complete separation between the juridical order of rights founded on the civil law and the ethical order of morals founded on the natural law. Hence they are not strictly *moral* positivists (no natural morality) nor *legal* positivists (no natural law), but *juridical* positivists (no natural rights). All moral and legal positivists must also be juridical positivists, but not vice versa. Of course, if one defines the word *right* in such a way that it can apply to positive rights only, then there would be merely a dispute on words, but these writers do not admit natural rights under any other name, and so are denying not the word but the thing. Because of these differences and the importance of the matter, it is worth risking some repetition to outline these views briefly. The chief sources suggested by moral, legal, and juridical positivists for all the rights they admit are:

(1) The state, by its constitution and statutes
(2) A contract, expressed or implied
(3) The concept of freedom, universal for all men
(4) Custom, manifesting the spirit of the people

---

*Hobbes, *Leviathan,* ch. XIV.
†Spinoza, *Theologico-Political Treatise,* ch. XVI; *Political Treatise,* ch. II.
‡Rousseau, *Social Contract,* bk. I, ch. III, IV.

The state

The notion that no one has any rights except those given him by the state has always been widespread in practice, if not in philosophical theory, throughout all ages from the ancient oriental despotisms to their modern counterparts. Tyrants have acted as if their groveling subjects' right to live and breathe were their own graciously granted favor. Even today some otherwise enlightened states declare in their constitution that the citizens have no rights except those expressly granted them by the state. Hobbes* gave this doctrine, that all true rights come from the state, its first clear philosophical expression; in it he is followed by others, such as Spinoza,† whose total system is of quite a different cast. Among American jurists Justice Oliver Wendell Holmes‡ thought that a right is but a prophecy that the state will use its courts and its might to sustain a man's claim. We may sum up our criticism of this view in the following points:

1. The state cannot be the source of its own right to existence, for it would have already to exist before it could confer this right on itself. To admit that the state has a right to exist is to admit that there is some source of rights prior to the state, that there are natural rights founded on the natural law. If the state has no right to exist, it exists solely by force.

2. The state's right to establish positive rights is a natural right of the state, given it by the natural law which requires men to organize themselves into civil society. Apart from force and fear, the state can bind its citizens to respect the positive rights it confers only by appeal to its own natural right to exist and function as a state, for, as we previously proved, all obligation comes from the natural law.

3. If the state were the source of all rights, it could give itself and withhold from its subjects any right it wished, and so could do no wrong. Tyranny would be impossible, for individuals could have no rights against the state. But man's right to life and limbs, to food and air, to marry and raise a family, come from the one who has given these things to man; this is not the state, but God. Man keeps his right to these even when the state violates it.

4. If the state were the source of all rights, one state could have no rights against another state, for a state can rule only its own subjects. There would be an end to all international rights. There could not be an unjustified war or a legitimate defense, for between states there would exist no rights that could be attacked or defended.

Contract

Hobbes and Rousseau, holding that the state originated by the social contract, trace the origin of rights both to the state and to a contract. But they differ in emphasis, Hobbes stressing the state more than the contract

---

*Hobbes, *loc. cit.*
†Spinoza, *loc. cit.*
‡Holmes, *Collected Legal Papers,* "The Path of the Law," "Natural Law."

and Rousseau the contract more than the state. Our criticism of this theory is that, though many rights originate in contracts, not all rights can result from contracts and no right can be wholly grounded on contract alone.

1. Before making a contract the contracting parties must first have the right to enter into such a contract. This right might come from a previous contract, and the latter from another contract previous to it, and so on. But the series cannot be infinite. The first contracting parties could not get this right from contract, and if they did not have this right from some source all succeeding contracts were null and void.

2. Contracts get their binding force from a precept of the natural law, which says that just compacts must be observed. Therefore all contracts are ultimately based on the natural law and imply natural rights. What else can bind us to keep them? Not fear of the consequences, for that is only yielding to force or expediency, and acknowledges no binding power in the contract as such.

3. Some rights cannot become the matter of a contract, such as the right to life and other nonrenounceable rights. These rights cannot result from a contract freely entered into and voidable at will. If they result from an implicit contract we are morally obliged to ratify, what produces this obligation and who has the right to impose it?

4. One cannot by contract acquire a right to something intrinsically wrong, as another's murder, for the man to be murdered already has his right to life. If the only reason why no such contract is permissible is that it would conflict with the original social contract, then the original social contract either could have been different so as to include a right to murder, or it had to be what it was and therefore had to guarantee some already existing rights, which we call natural rights.

Concept of freedom

Kant, following the jurisprudence of Christian Thomasius, separates legality from morality, the juridical order from the ethical order. Right or legality has to do with external action and comes from the state; ethics or morality has to do with the inner motive of duty and comes from the moral law. Both are derived from the absolute freedom of man, which is twofold: freedom from inner compulsion, the basis of morals, and freedom from outer compulsion, the basis of rights. Kant defines right as:

> The conception of the conditions under which the wishes of one man can be reconciled with the wishes of every other man according to a general law of freedom.*

All men have equal shares in the external goods of the world and the right to use as much of them as is consonant with the equal right of every other

---

*Kant, *Metaphysic of Morals*, pt. I, *Metaphysical Elements of the Theory of Right*, introd., B. Part I of this work has been translated by Hastie under the title, *The Philosophy of Law*.

man. Right pertains only to this external use; the motive from which he acts, whether the moral motive of duty or any other, pertains to the private sphere of ethics. This system of equal shares of free external action is the system of rights. This view is untenable for the following reasons:

1. Rights are not limited to external acts only. A father has a right to his child's love and not merely to the outward show of it, a man has a right not to be rashly judged in thought as well as not to be slandered in words. Both the internal act and the external act, the inner motive and the outward deed, form one voluntary human act. If civil laws can deal only with the external act, that is accidental and due to the limited applicability of such laws.

2. The legal and juridical order is part of the moral order, and hence there can be no complete separation of legality from morality. Apart from morals the word *right* has no real meaning, for all rights suppose obligation somewhere, and obligation belongs to morality. Positive law gets its binding force from the natural law, which prompts men to live in society and set up the legal order of the state. Positive rights, to be genuine, must be ultimately based on natural rights.

3. Not all rights are deducible from the concept of freedom limited only by the equal freedom of all others. A child's right to support from its parents is due rather to its natural needs; this can be reduced to freedom only by very far-fetched argumentation. There are rights we are not allowed to surrender, even if we do so freely; but if all rights are based on freedom, we should have the right freely to give up any right.

4. To say that we have a *right* to do anything we wish, so long as it hurts no one else, puts a strange twist on language. We should then have a right to practice private vices or to commit suicide, provided we allow others to do likewise. Kant of course brands these as immoral, yet by his definition he must acknowledge them as rights. Since there is a moral duty not to do them, no amount of equally shared freedom among men can create a right to them, for no right can contravene a higher duty.

Custom

The historical school of jurisprudence, a reaction against Kant, grew out of the philosophy of Hegel and found its juristic expression in the writings of Friedrich Karl von Savigny. It holds that every people unconsciously develops its own speech, manners, art, and culture, much as an individual develops his mannerisms and personality. Rights are part of this development, and are grounded in immemorial customs, which are the outward expression and unconscious product of the spirit of a people. The state is not the origin of rights, but can and should assist in their development, since the people show their spirit in their political institutions as well as in every other feature of their national life. In criticism of this theory we say:

1. Some rights do originate in custom, for some laws originate in custom

and right comes from law, but this cannot be true of all rights nor can it be the basic source of any right. Laws originating in custom get their binding force, not from mere custom, but from the will of the lawgiver at least tacitly approving the custom.

2. Mere repeated acts, mere customs, of themselves do not generate laws. The bare fact that my ancestors did a thing constantly is no reason why I must continue to do it. Progress is possible only by doing something new; but in this theory how could I get a right to do it? There would be no rights until a custom has been sufficiently established; by what right, then, were the first acts performed?

3. Customs, even national customs, can be evil as well as good. By doing bad acts often enough a people could secure a right to do them. Rights customarily violated could not be vindicated, because it would then become the custom, and therefore a right, to violate them. According to the theory, this would be the way in which rights are extinguished, but what then becomes of a right's moral inviolability?

4. Man is superior to his acts and therefore to his customs. They are for him, not he for them. The theory we are criticizing makes man subjected to and the victim of his outward practices, so that the individual counts for nothing and is wholly absorbed in the tribe, race, or state to which he belongs, not as a responsible person, but as an unconsciously operating cell.

Proof for natural rights

The foregoing criticism of the various forms of juridical positivism is itself a negative argument for natural rights. Having seen something of the historical background of this controversy, we are now ready to present the positive argument for natural rights, showing how they are demanded by the natural law, whose existence we have already proved. The argument is very simple:

There exists a natural law, which imposes obligations on man: to tend to his last end and to conform his conduct to the norm of morality as the only means to this end. But man cannot have such obligations unless he has a right to fulfill them, and a consequent right to prevent others from interfering with his fulfillment of them. Therefore there are rights which stem from the natural law, and these by definition are natural rights.

Whereupon it follows as a corollary that God, the Author of the natural law, is also the Author of natural rights, for which reason we speak of such rights as God-given rights.

RIGHT AND MIGHT

The separation of the legal and juridical order from the ethical order, that is, the separation of rights from morals, is practically equivalent to identifying right with might, for if rights do not rest on moral obligation, they rest on physical force or the threat of it. We defined a right as moral power and might as physical power, but we now need to examine more thoroughly the relation between these two. We say:

(1) Right and might are not the same.
(2) Some rights, but not all, imply the right to use might.

An interesting discussion of the claims of right and might occurs in Plato's *Republic*,* where Thrasymachus defends the proposition that right is might or justice is the interest of the stronger, claiming that all laws and rights are framed by men in power for their own advantage and to keep the rest in subjection. In the *Gorgias*† Callicles maintains the contrary proposition, that justice is the interest of the weaker, who by sheer force of numbers are able to extort concessions from the few strong, and these concessions become the people's rights bulwarked by laws and conventions. But such is conventional justice only; by natural justice the stronger ought to prevail simply because they are stronger. Plato agrees with neither of these views on justice, but has Socrates define it as "the having and doing what is a man's own"‡ whether he be strong or weak.

Right and might are two different things because there can be right without might and might without right. The natural law gives to each one the means necessary for keeping the natural law, but does not grant to each one the physical force necessary for securing and defending these means. The child depends on its parents, the wife on her husband, the sick and the aged on those who care for them. In fact, no man, however strong he be physically, is wholly independent of others. Since all men are equal in their ultimate destiny and in the obligations the natural law imposes on them, but unequal in physical strength and also in wealth and authority by which they can command the physical strength of others, the natural law must provide a safeguard against the encroachments of physical force. This safeguard it provides by the conferring of rights. Positive rights are conferred by positive law in the same way and for the same purpose, as a supplement to the natural law. Therefore, since right and might do not always correspond, they cannot be the same thing.

Though right and might are not the same thing, there is evidently some connection between them, because violated rights can be redressed only by the use of force. What is this connection? Hegel holds that not all might is right, but all right is might or at least implies might. He says:

> Abstract right is a right to coerce, because the wrong which transgresses it is an exercise of force against the existence of my freedom in an external thing. The maintenance of this existent against the exercise of force therefore itself takes the form of an external act and an exercise of force annulling the force originally brought against it.§

---

*Book I, from §336 on.
†From §481 on.
‡*Republic*, bk. IV, §433.
§Hegel, *Philosophy of Right*, §94.

The first use of force against a free being is a crime, so not all might is right; right implies a second use of force repelling the first unjustified use of it.

Two objections can be brought against this view: it restricts rights to external physical objects and acts only, and it confuses the essence of a right with a property of some rights.

1. One could limit the word *right* to external matters, but both English usage and the concept of a right as *moral* power counsel otherwise. We speak of a husband's right to his wife's devotion, of a mother's right to her children's love, of a benefactor's right to gratitude, of a man's right to his friends' loyalty. The subject imposes by the natural law a duty on the term, even though there is no way of physically compelling fulfillment of the duty; violation of the duty produces moral guilt, which is the proper effect of the exercise of moral power. Here there seems to be everything needed to constitute a genuine right.

2. Other rights can be enforced by the use of might. Physical actions can be exerted or restrained, physical objects can be defended or recovered by the use of physical force. Rights to such matters would be useless unless the natural law enabled us to protect and secure them. But even here the ability to resort to force is not the essence of the right. The right must already be a right before it can be vindicated by might. There is really a double right: the original right, such as the right to life or property, and a secondary right annexed to it, the right to use might in defense of life or property.

Rights which may thus be upheld by recourse to might, force, or coercion are called *coercive* or *coactive* rights; they are also called *juridical* rights, because they can be sued for in a law court which enforces its verdict by appeal to the executive arm or might of the state. In contrast to rights founded on loyalty, gratitude, friendship, benevolence, and similar virtues, all coercive or juridical rights are founded on *justice*. Their enforcement should normally be entrusted to the civil government, since the maintenance of justice, the adjudication of disputes, and the protection of its citizens' rights is the chief function of the state.

DUTIES

Limitation is a property of rights. Limitation is that point beyond which a right cannot be exercised without violating the right of another. Moral laws make up one organic system much like the physical organism. The functions of one organ are limited by the other organs of the body, each being apportioned its share of nutriment and having its sphere of exercise, but not to the detriment of other organs. No one organ is the whole organism, which is the complexus of all organs working harmoniously. If any organ encroaches on another, it works harm to the whole body. So each man has an end to fulfill and is endowed by the natural law with rights for this purpose, but the whole of creation also has an end to fulfill and no man may seek his own end in such a way as to frustrate the end of the whole.

Right is limited by duty. I may exercise my right up to the point where my duty to others supersedes my right. A right ceases to be a right when it injures others' rights. I have a right to build a bonfire on my own property, but not when it endangers the property of my neighbors. Parents have a right to their children's obedience, but not in choosing a state of life.

Duty is defined as *the moral necessity to do or omit something*. As *moral necessity*, it obliges and demands independently of compulsion, though the latter may be used to enforce it. This is duty in the primary sense. In a transferred sense duty also means the thing which must be done or omitted. The difference is expressed in the two statements: "He has a duty," meaning that he is morally obliged, and "He does his duty," meaning that he does the thing he is obliged to do.

Rights and duties are correlative and complementary. That they are so follows from the moral inviolability of a right. If I have a right, everyone else has the duty to respect my right; thus the term of a right becomes the subject of a duty. If I have a duty, someone else has a right to the thing I must do or omit; if no other man appears to have such a right, then at least God has it, as in my duty to preserve my life. If I have a duty, I have also the right to fulfill that duty and do all the things necessary for its fulfillment; otherwise it could not be a genuine duty. But if I have a right, I have not necessarily a duty to exercise that right; in fact, no man can exercise all his rights but must choose among them, for some of them are simultaneously incompatible, as the right to stand and the right to sit. God is the only exception to the correlativity of rights and duties. He has all rights and no duties; creatures have duties to Him but no rights against Him; men have both rights and duties toward one another.*

All duties, like all rights, come from law. Duties are divided in the same way as the corresponding rights and so are natural or positive, divine or human, ecclesiastical or civil. Besides these there is another classification of importance here: into affirmative and negative duties.

Affirmative duties follow from affirmative laws (commands) and require the performance of an act. *Negative* duties follow from negative laws (prohibitions) and require the omission or avoidance of an act. Care should be taken not to call affirmative laws and duties *positive*, for the word *positive* is already used in another sense, as the opposite of *natural*. Affirmative duties may connote negative duties, as "Honor your parents" connotes "Do not dishonor your parents." The importance of the distinction between affirmative and negative duties is that they impose a different type of obligation. Negative laws and duties require constant fulfillment every moment; one must never be doing the thing forbidden. Affirmative laws and duties impose a lasting obligation, in the sense that one is never exempt from it, but the obligation does not require constant fulfillment every moment: a

---

*Not all agree that there is this exact correlativity and complementarity between rights and duties, but it does follow from the definitions adopted here.

property owner is *always obliged* to pay taxes, yet he is not obliged to be *always paying* taxes but only when they are due.

CONFLICT OF RIGHTS AND DUTIES

This is a very practical problem, for it sometimes happens that one person has moral power to do a thing and another has moral power to prevent his doing it, or two persons have moral power to do or hold or exact the same individual thing each for himself, or the same person has two incompatible duties to discharge for two different people at the same time, or the same individual has a duty to one person to do a thing and also a duty to another person to refrain from doing it. What is to be done when a right conflicts with a right, a duty with a duty, or a right with a duty?

This question is easy enough to answer in theory. There can be no real conflict of rights and duties, either with one another or among themselves. All rights and duties are derived from law, and all law is derived from the natural law based on the eternal law in God. The natural law cannot both command and forbid the same thing; ultimately this would suppose a contradiction in God's will. Therefore the conflict is only apparent. The stronger right or duty prevails; the weaker simply ceases to be a right or duty at all. In other circumstances it would be a real right or duty, but in these circumstances it vanishes in the face of a higher claim. The stronger right or duty does not conflict with lesser ones but extinguishes them.

But how can we determine which is the stronger right or duty? In practice this can become exceedingly intricate and beyond the competence of the ordinary person. One of the chief functions of positive law, drawn up by professional legislators and applied through the courts of justice, is to settle disputed claims. The natural law prescribes that we shall set up such means for determining just which right or duty prevails, and in most of the matters that come under their jurisdiction the decisions of the courts, unless manifestly unjust, are binding in conscience. But not all matters are subject to the civil law and its courts; often the decision must be made on the basis of natural ethics. We can lay down only a few general norms. Other things being equal, the stronger right or duty can be determined from the following scheme:

The subject:
    (1) *The nobler person:* God before man, parents before their children
    (2) *The closer relationship:* closer relatives before remote one, friends before strangers

The term:
    (3) *The more common good:* world peace before personal comfort, public safety before private gain
    (4) *The wider social order:* the country before the family, the family before the individual

The matter:
    (5) *The graver matter:* the soul before the body, life before property

(6) *The greater urgency:* fighting a fire before reading a book, saving the living before burying the dead

The title:

(7) *The higher law:* natural law before positive law, negative duties before affirmative

(8) *The clearer title:* the certain before the doubtful, paying a debt before giving a gift

What makes these norms hard to apply is that in concrete cases other things are not equal. One right or duty may appear stronger according to one of the headings listed above, and the opposite right or duty according to another heading. The main use of the scheme is to show us what to look for.

1. A doctor is about to attend divine worship on Sunday when an emergency call comes for an urgent case; God comes before man, but the case cannot be postponed and the man may die.

2. A young man wants to take a college education but has no funds; the mind comes before the body, but if he does not eat he cannot study.

3. A son has been disinherited in a civilly valid will but for dubiously just reasons; the natural law prevails over the positive, but the positive title is clear and the natural one doubtful.

4. In time of war a man is torn between duty to his country and to his family; the common good prevails over a private good, but his family is related to him more closely than the bulk of the citizens.

For a solution of these and similar apparent conflicts of rights and duties no hard and fast rules can be drawn up. Each case must be taken in its concrete setting and every circumstance carefully weighed. In these matters there is no substitute for common sense, which is another name for the cardinal virtue of prudence. Most cases are settled by working out some proportion or compromise between the various factors and claims, except that the negative duty of never doing anything intrinsically wrong prevails over everything else. In the cases above:

1. It would be wrong for a doctor to be so engrossed in his profession as to have no time at all for the worship of God, but in this instance God can be served later and the sick man cannot; the doctor should tend to the patient.

2. A man must live before he can live well; the student must first provide for himself the minimum requirements of life, and after this he does well to devote himself to the things of the mind rather than to the things of the body.

3. The disinherited son may contest the will, but if the will is upheld in the civil courts he has no choice but to accept this decision; the parent may have done a private wrong in disinheriting him, but the son would commit a public crime if he attempted to seize the property by force or fraud.

4. Our country shows its sense of natural justice by requiring its citizens to come to its defense, yet deferring or exempting those who can least easily be spared by their dependents; this policy balances the claims of private and public good, and brings in the element of urgency.

It may happen that after the most careful investigation two rights or two duties or a right and a duty seem equally valid and equally certain. In this case one may do either, or, if the matter is divisible, do part of both. The bankruptcy laws are an instance of the latter, where no creditor can be satisfied in full but as equitable a distribution is made as the matter allows.

EXCUSES FROM DUTY

Duty is imposed by law, which by definition is reasonable and for the common good. The purpose is not to crush man with unreasonable burdens out of proportion to the good aimed at. According to the principle of double effect, the physical evils (burdens, losses, restrictions, inconveniences, dangers) sometimes unavoidable in the fulfillment of duty are to be incidental to the accomplishment of good and not disproportionate to it. Hence there are causes which can excuse from duty, because in these cases the duty really invades our right.

No one can do the impossible, and all excuses from duty can be reduced to impossibility of fulfillment taken in a broad and relative sense; we shall call it *hardship*. Some norms can be established by putting together three elements:

(1) The kind of hardship, inherent or incidental
(2) The kind of duty, affirmative or negative
(3) The kind of law, natural or positive

1. Only incidental and excessive hardship excuses from a duty. *Incidental* hardship arises from the particular circumstances of the person concerned, such as being sick or disabled or captive or destitute. If hardship essential to or inherent in the duty itself could excuse, there would be no duties; thus workmen are not excused from their work because it makes them sweat nor soldiers from battle because it endangers their lives. Hardship may run from practical impossibility through extreme, grave, and moderate difficulty to slight inconvenience. To be an excuse it must be *excessive*, out of proportion to the importance of the duty. A duty can be so necessary as not to admit of excuse, even in the face of death.

2. A *negative* duty arising from the *natural* law admits of no excuse whatever. Such a duty concerns matters forbidden by the natural law as intrinsically wrong. Not even God can give anyone permission to do such things, and we are obliged under pain of losing our last end to choose death rather than commit them. There is question here of the worst possible evil, moral evil, to which no other evil can be proportioned. We are not now dealing with excuses arising from the modifiers of responsibility but with objective morality.

3. An *affirmative* duty arising from the *natural* law admits of excuse because of impossibility or excessive hardship. There must, however, be no violation of negative natural duty involved; for instance, the omission of an act of worship must not be construed as a denial of God, the keeping of silence by a superior must not imply permission to his inferiors to act against the common good. Since affirmative duties do not require constant fulfillment every moment, the acts can often be postponed for more favorable circumstances when the hardship will not be present, and then they must be done; if they cannot be postponed, the obligation ceases entirely.

4. A duty arising from *human positive* law, whether *affirmative* or *negative,* admits of excuse because of impossibility or excessive hardship. Here also no violation of negative natural duty must be involved. Merely human duties, even the negative ones, do not concern matter that is intrinsically wrong, and the human laws that impose them are meant to be a help rather than a hindrance to human living.

SUMMARY

We have seen *right* as opposed to *wrong;* now we take up *right* as correlative to *duty.* In the latter sense *right* is moral power, appealing to another's will through his intellect, as opposed to *might,* which is physical power or force. Right is defined as moral power to do, omit, hold, or exact something. Things to which we have a right are often called our *rights.*

A right has four components: *subject,* the one possessing the right; *term,* the one bound to respect the right; *matter,* that to which one has a right; and *title,* the reason why this person has this right. The subject and term must always be persons; hence animals have no rights. The matter can never be a person; even slavery, one of the world's most flagrant violations of human rights, supposed a right only to the slave's services, not to his person.

All rights come from law, *natural* rights from natural law, *positive* rights from positive law. All admit positive rights, but are there natural rights? Moral and legal positivists deny the natural law; they can have no natural rights. Juridical positivists deny natural rights, though they may admit a natural law. Both these groups derive all rights from one or several of the following sources:

1. *The state.* If so, the state itself has no right to exist, has no basis for the positive rights it grants, can withhold from its subjects any right it wishes, and can have no rights against another state.

2. *Contract.* If so, the first contract was made without any right to do so, contracts have no binding power but force, nonrenounceable rights are subjected to contract, and one can by contract get a right to anything however evil.

3. *Equal freedom for all.* If so, rights are limited to external acts, legality is separated from morality which alone gives it meaning, all rights can be freely surrendered, and we can have a right to immoral acts provided they hurt no one else.

4. *Custom.* If so, mere repetition of acts begets a right to them, there were no rights until the custom was established, evil customs can create rights, and man becomes the victim of the customs his race unconsciously develops.

We deduce natural rights from the natural law. The natural law imposes obligations on man, who must therefore have moral power to fulfill them and prevent others from interfering with this fulfillment; such rights coming from the natural law are natural rights. God, who imposes the natural law, is the ultimate source of natural rights.

Right and *might* are different because they can exist separately. All men are equal in their moral obligations but differ greatly in physical strength. Rights are the natural law's safeguard to us against the encroachment of superior might. Rights concerning external matters due in justice imply the right to use might in their defense or recovery. This right of coercion is not the essence of any right, but a property of some rights.

Right is limited by *duty,* which is the moral necessity to do or omit something. Every right supposes a duty, and vice versa. *Negative* duties require constant fulfillment, *affirmative* do not.

There can be no real conflict of rights and duties; the stronger extinguishes the weaker. In practice it can be very difficult to determine which is the stronger right. The subject, term, matter, and title must be considered together with the factor of urgency.

Impossibility and excessive hardship are excuses from duty. Hardship inherent in the duty never excuses from it. Disproportionate hardship, depending on the importance of the matter, excuses from *affirmative* duty under *natural* law, and from both *affirmative* and *negative* duty under *human positive* law. *Negative* duty under *natural* law admits of no excuse whatever.

READINGS

1. Be sure to read Plato's *Republic,* bk. I, §336, to bk. II, §368, on the relative merits of justice and injustice, right and might.
2. Aristotle's treatment of justice in the *Nicomachean Ethics,* bk V, is pertinent to a study of rights, though not directly on the subject.
3. Read Aristotle's defense of natural slavery in his *Politics,* bk. I, ch. 4-7, to see how disappointing a great man can sometimes be. St. Thomas in his *Commentary on the Politics* (no available translation) simply expounds Aristotle's doctrine with little comment.
4. Cicero's *De Officiis* (On Duties) is rather a treatise on morals in general and runs through man's chief duties as connected with the cardinal virtues and man's chief stations in life. Cicero's views, though always high-minded, need to be taken with caution.
5. Read St. Thomas, *Summa Theologica,* I, q. 29, aa. 1, 2 (*Basic Writings,* vol. I), on person. The little St. Thomas has to say on right is found in the *Summa Theologica,* II-II, q. 57 (not in the *Basic Writings*).
6. A discussion of the term *jus* (right) as related to *lex* (law) in the usage of

Roman law is found in Suarez, *De Legibus,* bk. I, ch. 2 (in J. B. Scott, *Classics of International Law: Suarez*).

7. Kant's *Metaphysic of Morals,* pt. I, can be read in Hastie's translation entitled *Kant's Philosophy of Law.* The introduction is printed in Abbott, *Kant's Theory of Ethics,* pp. 265-284, which unfortunately stops short just before Kant's definition of right.

8. Le Buffe and Hayes, *The American Philosophy of Law,* ch. XI, XVI. Chapter V describes modern attempts to codify fundamental human rights. The appendix by John C. Ford is an excellent criticism of Holmes' legal philosophy.

9. Cronin, *Science of Ethics,* vol. I, ch. XX.

10. McKinnon, *The Higher Law.*

11. Maritain, *The Rights of Man and Natural Law;* see also his introduction and article in *Human Rights,* a symposium edited by Unesco.

12. Rommen, *Natural Law,* ch. XII.

13. Brosnahan, *Prolegomena to Ethics,* ch. XVII; also pp. 277-280.

14. Rickaby, *Moral Philosophy,* pp. 244-251.

15. Leibell, *Readings in Ethics,* pp. 405-428; also pp. 507-513, on vivisection.

16. Haas, *Man and Society,* ch. 4.

17. Harding, *Natural Law and Natural Rights.*

18. Ritchie, *Natural Rights,* and Strauss, *Natural Rights and History,* present a different philosophical background from ours.

CHAPTER 18

WORSHIP

APPLIED ETHICS

As a science both normative and practical, ethics cannot be satisfied to give only the general norms of morally good conduct, but must try to apply these norms to the chief types of human conduct. Though human acts taken individually are indefinitely variable so that no two are ever exactly alike, they can be classified under certain headings and the general norms can be made more specific so as to bring out more clearly the goodness or badness of each class of acts. Older writers, such as St. Thomas, built their whole treatment of applied ethics around the classification of the virtues and opposed vices. Modern writers prefer to make a specific investigation of the rights conferred and the duties imposed by the natural law. Each method has its advantages. We shall follow the latter method as more convenient for the treatment of modern problems.

Rights and duties are found to concern God, man, or nonrational things. Toward *God* we have duties, but we can have no strict rights against God which would put God under duty to man. Toward *man,* fellow man, we have both rights and duties in the strictest sense. We also speak of rights and duties toward ourselves, but this must be taken as a shorthand expression meaning that we have rights against our fellow man concerning ourselves and duties to God concerning ourselves; thus we must interpret the right to life and the duty to preserve it. Toward *nonrational things* we have rights but no duties, though we have duties to God and to ourselves (in the sense used above) regarding our use of them.

Among man's many duties as an individual, those to God take the first place in dignity. Man's whole duty of living a moral life is a duty to God, the Author of the moral law, but we are considering here the duties which have God as their direct object. We cover them quickly, not as casting any reflection on their importance, but because they are treated more adequately in the study of religion and theology.

PROBLEM

That God should be worshipped seems to follow immediately as a practical consequence from the fact of God's existence. The prevalence of religious worship throughout the world shows that man naturally and easily derives this conclusion. But no truth has escaped the challenge of some philosopher.

Kant expressed the view that religion consists merely in living a good moral life, in doing one's duty for duty's sake, without any special obligation of worshipping God. This idea is found in his work, *Religion Within the Limits of Reason Alone,* from which the following quotation speaks for itself:

> I take the following statement as a principle needing no proof: besides the good conduct of his life, anything a man imagines he can do to make himself pleasing to God is superstition and false service of God. . . .
>
> The delusion that religious practices of worship have any effect towards justification before God is religious superstition, just as the delusion of wishing to effect the same by seeking a supposed union with God is religious fanaticism.*

Friedrich Schleiermacher in his *Discourses on Religion* and other works held that religion is a feeling of awe in the presence of something limitless and mysterious, and that worship is the expression of this feeling. Religion is thus put on a subjective rather than an objective basis. Worship is not something due to God but something that satisfies our feeling of religious exaltation.

Others argue that worship is an attempt to give gifts to God who cannot possibly benefit by them, that since worship is useless to God it is out of place and a kind of presumption on our part, and especially that God who sees into our hearts cannot have the slightest use for outward rites and ceremonies which most religions employ to some extent.

Of course atheists do not admit a God to whom worship need be given. But the above opinions are expressed by those who admit God and the moral law, yet deny that the moral law requires worship of God.

Together with some background material, we treat the following points:

(1) What place has religion in philosophy?
(2) What is the meaning of natural religion?
(3) Does the natural law oblige man to worship God?
(4) What kind of worship is required?
(5) How are natural and revealed religion related?

NATURAL RELIGION

Natural religion comprises only those duties to God which man can discover by his own reason, whereas supernatural religion is dependent on

---

*Kant, *Religion Within the Limits of Reason Alone,* bk. IV, pt. II, §2 (my translation).

some revelation by God. Such a supernatural revelation could not contradict natural religion but could only add to it and clarify it, for the same God who makes this revelation is also the Author of nature and of man's natural reasoning powers. Though supernatural religion is outside the scope of philosophy and therefore of ethics, natural religion belongs strictly to philosophy, for any philosophy which admits the existence of God must discuss the duties which man by the use of his reason knows that he has to God.

Religion is the word used to indicate man's duties to God. It comes from the Latin *religio,* but scholars differ as to its more remote derivation. Cicero takes it from *re-legere,* to gather back, to read over again:

> Those who carefully review and so to speak retrace all the lore of ritual were called "religious" from "relegere" [to retrace or re-read].*

Lactantius, an early Christian writer, derives religion from *re-ligare,* to bind back:

> We are tied to God and bound back to Him by the bond of piety, and it is from this, and not, as Cicero holds, from careful consideration [re-reading], that religion has received its name.†

St. Augustine derives religion from *re-eligere,* to choose again:

> Him we elect or rather re-elect, for by our neglect we lost Him. Him therefore we re-elect (whence religion is derived), and to Him do we hasten with the wings of love to attain rest in Him.‡

But St. Augustine later retracted this opinion in favor of that of Lactantius.§ St. Thomas refers to all three views without deciding:

> However, whether religion take its name from frequent reading, or from a repeated choice of what has been lost through negligence, or from being a bond, it denotes properly a relation to God.‖

The derivation signifying a "binding back to God" finds most favor with Christian thinkers and has certainly colored the modern meaning of the word, whatever be its real etymological origin. Man is physically bound to God in the sense of depending on Him, and man's recognition of this bond constitutes a second or moral bond binding man again to God.

Religion taken objectively consists of three theoretical truths and three practical truths, the latter following logically from the former. These truths are:

(1) God in Himself is a being of infinite excellence and worth. Man owes Him special reverence.

---

*Cicero, *De Natura Deorum,* bk. II, xxviii.
†Lactantius, *Divinarum Institutionum,* bk. IV, xxviii.
‡St. Augustine, *City of God,* bk. X, iii-iv (Healey's translation).
§St. Augustine, *Retractations,* bk I, xiii.
‖St. Thomas, *Summa Theologica,* II-II, q. 81, a. 1.

Excellence → Reverence
Creator → Service
Last End → Love

(2) God is man's First Cause giving him being and all that he has. Man owes Him special service.

(3) God is man's Last End and Highest Good in whom alone he can find happiness. Man owes Him special love.

By performing these three acts one acquires a habit, and a good habit is a virtue. Hence religion taken subjectively is a virtue allied to justice. Justice is the virtue that inclines us to give to each one what is his own, and religion inclines us to give God what belongs to Him.

The object of religion is God, its motive is man's absolute dependence on and indebtedness to God, and its act is divine worship. By divine worship man gives to God the reverence, service, and love that is God's due; thus divine worship is said to be the duty that man owes to God.

The word *worship* is a contraction of *worth-ship* and means *worthiness*. It is an acknowledgment of another's worth, dignity, excellence, or superior position. Formerly it was applied to anyone of eminence and survives in the old title "Your Worship," which means no more than "Your Honor" or "Your Excellency." But the modern convention is to reserve the term *worship* almost exclusively for divine worship or the worship of God, which can be defined as the acknowledgment of God's infinite excellence and absolute lordship. Divine worship comprises three chief acts:

1. *Adoration* is the most distinctive act of divine worship and of the virtue of religion. It is a conscious, explicit, and formal acknowledgment of God's infinite greatness and our utter dependence on Him. Originally *adoration* meant only a *bowing* in sign of respect to a superior person, but modern usage restricts it, like *worship,* to acts directed to God alone. Persons and things held sacred because of their relation to God, such as saints, relics, images, and shrines, are said to be *venerated,* but not *adored.*

2. *Prayer* is a raising of the mind and heart to God. In its narrowest sense prayer is asking something of God, *pray* being merely another word for *ask,* but the term is extended to cover any act by which a man fixes his mind on God and intentionally thinks of Him, whether he uses any definite formula of words or not. Prayer itself is an act of adoration and adoration is hardly possible without prayer.

3. *Sacrifice* is the offering of some precious thing to God and its immolation or destruction to signify that we give back to God, as far as we can, what is His. Sacrifice is an act of adoration and is usually accompanied by prayer. The word *sacrifice* is used metaphorically to mean giving up anything, whether in God's honor or not, but we are taking it only in its original and strictly religious sense.

There are two secondary acts of divine worship: a vow and an oath. A *vow* is a promise made to God to do something pleasing to Him. An *oath* is calling on God to witness the truth of what we say. Though primarily directed to another end, a vow being directed to the good act we promise to do and an oath to the true statement we make, these acts at least implicitly acknowledge God's excellence, and thus are acts of religion.

OBLIGATION TO WORSHIP

The natural law obliges man to worship God. It does not, of course, prescribe any particular form that this worship must take, except that it be consonant with God's dignity and man's dependence, and in the absence of any revelation from God man would be left to the devices of his own reason to work out the details. The argument may be put as follows:

The natural law obliges man to conform his conduct to right reason and to human nature taken completely in all its parts and relations. But human nature taken completely includes man's relation of creaturehood or dependence upon God, the Infinite Excellence, the Supreme Ruler of the universe, man's First Cause and Last End; and right reason shows that acknowledgment of God's excellence and man's dependence is due to God from man, for God has the right to it by the very fact that He is God, and to His right corresponds man's duty. Therefore the natural law obliges man to acknowledge God's excellence and man's dependence on Him, and this acknowledgment is called worship.

One may ask: Is not the mere fact of dependence on God sufficient without an express acknowledgment of it? No, not for man. Nonrational creatures pay their debt to God by the bare objective fact of their dependent existence, since they have no intellects to recognize this condition. Rational creatures, on the other hand, are dependent on God not only for their existence, but also for the intellects and wills that formally specify their nature, thus making them capable both of understanding the debt they owe to God and of willingness to pay the debt. Intellects and wills are meant to be used, and the primary use to which they can be put is the recognition and acknowledgment of the Supreme Source from which they come. Such acknowledgment is worship. Deliberately to refuse it is equivalent to a declaration of independence against God and a repudiation of one's status as a creature.

Interior and exterior worship

The acts of divine worship may be either interior or exterior. They are interior, if done within the mind as acts of intellect and will; exterior, if they are carried out by some outward sign or bodily action.

Man owes God *interior* worship. This is evident from the fact that man's specific faculties are intellect and will, and it is only by these that man acts as man. Mere exterior acts, if not accompanied and directed by interior acts, are not voluntary, not even *human acts* in the technical sense, and have no moral value.

This worship should also be *exterior.* Though exterior acts unaccompanied by interior acts of intellect and will are empty formalities and worthless dumbshow, interior acts alone leave something lacking. It might be difficult to prove from the natural law alone a strict and absolute moral obligation to express interior worship in external acts, but the appropriateness of these acts and their accord with the natural law is evident from the following:

1. The natural law obliges man to worship God because this is fitting to human nature taken completely as seen by right reason. Man by nature is not a disembodied spirit, but composed of body and soul. The body is the lesser but a real part of man's nature, and should cooperate with the soul in giving honor to its Creator.

2. The soul naturally works through the body and the thoughts of the mind tend to express themselves in outward behavior, as in gestures, facial expressions, and attitudes of deference. Though some people are less demonstrative than others, no one can suppress all of these manifestations without a positive act of inhibition. Never to give any outward sign of one's thoughts is abnormal behavior. Why should a man be obliged to act in this way toward God? If he really thinks of God at all, sometimes he will show it.

3. Man's thoughts tend to wander if they are denied their natural expression. Outward surroundings are helpful to mental concentration. We can adore God on a busy street corner, but we can do it better in the quiet of a church where everything leads us to God instead of distracting us from Him. Hence without exterior worship the interior worship will not be performed properly.

Whether man owes God *civic* worship, an act of the socially organized community as such, has become rather an academic question in these days of the secular state.

Answers to objections

What about the arguments of Kant, Schleiermacher, and others mentioned previously?

1. Kant is correct in implying that acts of worship without observance of the moral law would be vain and insincere. There is no substitute for a good moral life, and to protest allegiance to God while breaking His law is to live a lie. But mere observance of the moral law is not enough. To refuse a king or president or other ruler any mark of respect or any recognition of his dignity on the ground that we keep his laws and that is enough, would be a gross insult even in the strictest democracy. The honor is given, not to the man, but to his office. To refuse honor to God is to refuse to acknowledge His office as Supreme Ruler of the universe. Besides, the duty of worship is part of the moral law and he who refuses God worship does not keep the whole moral law.

2. Schleiermacher is correct in seeing that there is such a thing as religious feeling, that emotion is a powerful factor in religious experience. But feeling is rather an accompaniment of religion than its essence. In performing divine worship man should naturally have the feeling both of exaltation and abasement that the sublime produces, but the worship itself is not directed to this feeling and does not consist in this feeling alone; in fact, it can exist without the feeling, and unemotional persons need not be worried if they cannot attain it. Worship is directed to a personal being, who can be loved and feared, honored and offended, who rewards and punishes, who has rights and to whom there is duty. Religious feeling is an excellent thing, but it must be based on reason; otherwise, it is unworthy of man whose essence is rational. Religion is only secondarily a psychological need of man; primarily it is a strict duty to God.

3. Worship based on the idea that God really needs it from us, that He cannot get along without it, that He in any way depends on us for it, and especially that we are doing God a favor rather than fulfilling a duty, would be mistaken and presumptuous. God has no need of our gifts but condescends to accept them, not for their intrinsic worth, but because they are all that creatures can do and are a token of our submission to Him. We owe Him acknowledgment of our dependence even though He has no need of us. God does not need external rites and ceremonies, but *we* do. We must act according to our nature, which has a natural inclination to express itself in outward action. These outward acts should not be done mechanically but with a sense of their meaning.

Vices opposed to religion

The two chief vices opposed to the virtue of religion are irreligion and superstition, the one by defect and the other by excess, not excess toward the right object but by setting up false objects of worship. Infidelity and fanaticism are extremes of religious *belief* rather than of worship.

Irreligion is a refusal of divine worship when it should occur. Worship is an affirmative duty that obliges only now and then, and the natural law does not prescribe any set times, but never to do it or to refuse it when circumstances plainly call for it is wrong. Positive law, whether divine or ecclesiastical or even civil, determines the natural law in this respect. Irreligion is a negative vice, but may be accompanied by positive irreverence, as in blasphemy, sacrilege, and simony.

Superstition is a wrong or perverted form of worship. Though the natural law does not prescribe the form that worship should take, it does forbid any form that is unworthy of God's dignity or man's nature. Two main forms of superstition are idolatry and magic. Idolatry is giving divine worship to something which is not God. Magic is attributing divine powers to objects which cannot have them. Perverted worship is no less an insult to God than no worship.

NATURAL LAW AND REVELATION

Though ethics deals with natural religion only, it does not deny supernatural religion but merely considers it outside the scope of a philosophical study. However, it must face the possibility of a supernatural revelation and determine what adjustments it must make in its own sphere if this possibility is realized. Since ethics deals with the natural law, it must answer this question: Supposing a supernatural revelation to have taken place, what then would the natural law prescribe to man regarding it?

1. If a man is certainly convinced of the existence of a divine revelation, he is morally bound by the natural law to accept it. God is not obliged to speak to the human race, but if He does so He must not be despised. If God speaks to man, man must listen, believe, and obey. The natural law demands this of man because of his status as a creature.

2. If a man doubts about the existence of a divine revelation, he is morally bound by the natural law to inquire further into it. He is bound also to give it the full and serious attention which the importance of the question demands, and hardly any question can be imagined more important. Until he has made the effort, he cannot plead invincible ignorance. His inquiries will either lead to certitude or leave him in doubt; if the former, he must follow his certain conscience; if the latter he may form his conscience according to the reflex principle, a *doubtful law does not bind,* and may refuse to accept the revelation until he is certainly convinced of it, meanwhile keeping his mind open for additional information. This way of treating the matter is only an application of our ethical principles, and takes no account of supernatural influences or the workings of divine grace on the soul.

3. If a man is certainly convinced that an alleged divine revelation is not what it claims to be, he is morally bound by the natural law to reject it. This case may involve an erroneous conscience, but a man is obliged to follow a certain conscience even when erroneous. It may be well to note here that, in the Christian scheme of things, the supernatural virtue of faith cannot be lost except through one's own fault. We are simply considering philosophical possibilities.

SUMMARY

Foremost among man's specific duties come his duties to God.

Atheists can admit no duty of worship. But among those who accept God's existence, *Kant* thought that a man honors God sufficiently by a good moral life without any express worship, and *Schleiermacher* thought that religion is but a subjective feeling akin to awe and that worship is whatever produces this feeling.

Duties to God, so far as they can be known by human reason unaided by revelation, constitute natural religion. *Religion,* according to a probable derivation, means a *binding back* to God. Objectively, it consists of three truths: man owes to God special reverence as the Infinite Excellence, special service as man's First Cause, special love as man's Last End. Subjectively, religion is a habit of fulfilling these three duties, a virtue allied to justice.

These three duties are fulfilled by *worship,* the acknowledgment of God's infinite excellence and absolute lordship. Worship involves adoration, prayer, and sacrifice.

The natural law obliges man to worship God. It is a fact that God is the Supreme Excellence and man is dependent on Him; God has a right that this fact be acknowledged, and the acknowledgment is called worship.

This worship must be both interior and exterior. Interior, because the exercise of intellect and will are necessary for a human act. *Exterior,* because man is not a disembodied spirit, the mind naturally expresses itself through the body, and outward surroundings help mental concentration.

There is no substitute for a good moral life, but this alone is insufficient as worship. Religious feeling is important, but it must be based on reason and on the objective fact of God's excellence. God does not need our worship any more than He needs us, but, given the fact that we do exist, we must acknowledge our dependence on Him. Outward ceremonies are for *our* benefit and accord with *our* nature, which is corporeal as well as spiritual.

Irreligion or no worship and *superstition* or wrong worship are the two main vices against religion.

One certainly convinced of a divine revelation is morally bound to accept it. One doubting about a divine revelation is morally bound to inquire into it; if convinced, he must accept it; if still doubting, he may follow the principle that a doubtful law does not bind. One certainly convinced that an alleged revelation is not from God is morally bound to reject it, since he must follow a certain conscience even when invincibly erroneous.

READINGS

1. St Thomas treats of the virtue of religion and its opposed vices in the *Summa Theologica*, II-II, qq. 80-100. This is not found in the *Basic Writings*, but occupies the whole eleventh volume of the English Dominicans' edition.
2. Some of St. Thomas' views on magic are found in his *Summa Contra Gentiles*, bk. III, ch. 103-110, reprinted in the *Basic Writings*, vol. II. Some of his ideas are very foreign to our modern outlook, but his attitude is remarkably critical and restrained, if we consider the age in which he lived.
3. St. Augustine's *City of God*, bk. X, ch. 1-7, is not explicitly on our subject, but may be a good introduction to this great classic.
4. Cronin, *The Science of Ethics*, vol. II, ch. I.
5. Gilson, *The Christian Philosophy of St. Thomas Aquinas*, pp. 333-350.
6. O'Brien, *Truths Men Live By*, ch. XIV-XX.
7. Newman, *Grammar of Assent*, ch. X.
8. Rickaby, *Moral Philosophy*, pp. 191-202.
9. Hettinger, *Natural Religion*, ch. VIII, IX.
10. Leibell, *Readings in Ethics*, pp. 432-450.
11. Farrell, *Companion to the Summa*, vol. III, ch. X, XI.

CHAPTER 19

LIFE

PROBLEM

After man's duties to God come man's rights and duties regarding himself. First among them is the right and duty to maintain himself in life, for there can be no further rights or duties without a subject to have them. Sometimes even life itself must be sacrificed for a higher good, but apart from these cases man's right to life is fundamental.

That man has a right to life is evident. The only way he can fulfill his function as a man, achieve his highest good and reach his last end, is by performing morally good acts. To perform such acts he must live. The natural law, therefore, confers on him the right to life.

But is this right also a duty? Is it a nonrenounceable right so that not only may no one lawfully take it away from him, but the person himself may not even give it up? Is it always wrong to deprive another of his life, even incurable sufferers, even unborn babies? What about self-defense, when a man can save his own life only at the expense of another's? Here we deal only with deliberate destruction of human life, saving marginal questions for the next chapter. Our questions are:

(1) May one kill oneself?
(2) May one kill another man?
(3) May one kill the incurable?
(4) May one kill the unborn?
(5) May one kill in self-defense?

SUICIDE

Life is a gift from God, but it is also a gift to man. God has His rights over human life, but how much of these has He transferred to

235

man? Some gifts are given outright and the receiver can do what he wants with them, even destroy them, for they are fully his. Other gifts have strings attached and their use is limited by certain conditions. Is God's gift of life to man an outright gift or a restricted gift? According as we decide this question, suicide will be morally allowable or forbidden.

Suicide is here taken in the strict sense, not as any killing of oneself, but as *the direct killing of oneself on one's own authority.*

Direct killing is an act of killing that is directly voluntary, that is, death is intended either as an end or as a means to an end. Either the action is capable of only one effect and that effect is death, or the action is capable of several effects including death and among these death is the effect intended. To commit suicide a man must intend his death either as end or as means.

Indirect killing is an act of killing that is indirectly voluntary; death is not intended either as an end or as a means to an end, but is only permitted as an unavoidable consequence. The action must be capable of at least two effects, one of which is death, and the agent intends not death, but the other effect. To avoid misunderstanding, it is better not to speak of the indirect killing of oneself as killing at all, but as the deliberate exposure of one's life to serious danger. Such exposure is not what is meant by suicide.

The killing is not suicide unless it is done *on one's own authority.* Two others might be thought of as having authority in the matter: God and the state. God, having a supreme dominion over all things including human life, could order a man to kill himself. The act would not be suicide, for the man would only be acting as God's instrument and carrying out His will. But to know God's will in such a case a special revelation would be needed; there is certainly no provision for anything like this in the natural law. The state might appoint a man condemned to death to be his own executioner, as in the famous case of Socrates. Whether the state has the right to do so or not is a disputed question, and of little application today, since the practice has been abandoned by all civilized peoples. Whatever be its morality, it is not suicide according to the accepted definition.

Suicide can be committed positively or negatively: positively, by the performance of some death-dealing act against oneself; negatively, by omitting to use the ordinary means of preserving one's life. It is suicide to starve oneself to death, to refuse to step out of the way of an oncoming train, to neglect to use the ordinary remedies against an otherwise fatal disease.

Wrongness of suicide

Various arguments either of a utilitarian or sentimentalist nature can be brought forth for and against the permissibility of suicide: how, on the one hand, it is folly to go on living after life has become an intolerable burden; and how, on the other hand, suicide is an act of cowardice and a refusal to face life like a man. But we shall base our argument wholly on the natural law. From the natural law and from man's status as a creature it follows that the right to life is a right that is also a duty, that life is a gift with definite restrictions and responsibilities attached.

Though God by the natural law gives rights to man, there are some rights God cannot give, for by their very nature they are exclusively God's. One of these is the *direct dominion* (sovereignty, ownership, proprietorship) over the human person, the compound of body and soul, that the suicide seeks to dissolve. What God gives to man is an *indirect dominion* over himself, the use and stewardship of his person, but no direct dominion, no right to consume and destroy his person at his own discretion.

The reason why God must reserve to Himself direct dominion over human life is the peculiar nature of a rational being, such as man is, who must deserve his last end by his free acts. By the eternal law God decrees that all His creatures attain the end for which He created them. Man can attain his end only by doing morally good acts. These acts take time, and the length of each man's life is the opportunity alloted him for doing them. It is for God and not for man to say that a sufficient number of good acts has been performed and that they are of sufficient quality to deserve the end. The suicide equivalently tells God that He will have to take the deeds performed and virtues developed so far, and that He will simply get no more. The creature thus tries to dictate to God what God will have to be satisfied with, in contradiction to what God in creating him has a right to demand from him. God cannot give such authority to a creature without ceasing to be God.

Therefore man is obliged to live out his life to the end of its natural span. God owns both man and man's works, and has a right to both. The actual performance of these works God has put under man's stewardship to be guided by man's free will, but the final approval of these works both in quantity and quality rests with God alone. The suicide, by making further works of his own impossible, invades God's exclusive right.

To sum up the argument: Any act contrary to our nature as dependent creatures is forbidden by the natural law. But suicide is such an act. As an exercise of *direct dominion* over the human person, it is the seizure of a right that is so exclusively God's that even God cannot transfer it to another. God cannot grant to man *direct dominion* over himself, since to do so would be to allow man to dictate to God the conditions for the attainment of his last end, and thus to assume supreme lordship over himself. Therefore suicide is forbidden by the natural law.

Questions on the argument

The following are a few of the more common difficulties against the wrongness of suicide:

1. *The argument seems to rest on a false foundation, that man can defraud God of His right; is it not impossible for any creature to defraud God of anything?* This objection is invalid because it would prove that no

sin is possible. No sin can actually hurt God, but that does not make sin allowable. God cannot be outwitted and is too wise for all our malice. From all eternity He has adjusted His providence to His foreknowledge that a certain man will freely commit suicide (or any other sin), and derives either from that man's punishment or from other creatures the external glory He might have derived from the rest of that man's natural life (or from the good contrary to any other sin). Man can never actually defraud God, but he is not allowed to *try,* or to be willing to do what would defraud God were He not infinitely beyond all possible harm. In this the malice of all sin consists.

2. *God has given man direct dominion over the lives of animals and plants, which he can destroy for his own purposes; why could not God give man direct dominion over his own life?* The difference is that these lower beings are not persons. Lacking free choice and an immortal destiny, they are not obliged to make themselves worthy of an ultimate goal. They are made for man's use and consumption.

3. *Does not God give direct dominion over human life in the cases of capital punishment and self-defense?* No; the killing may be direct, a directly voluntary act, but it is not an exercise of direct dominion, which is full control over a thing to dispose of as one pleases and at one's discretion. The state has no such control over criminals. It can take a life only on the authority of God, by the right communicated to it by God through the natural law, to be exercised not in any way the state pleases but only for proved crime after a fair trial. The same is true of self-defense. The defender kills the attacker only on God's authority manifested by the natural law and implicit in the defender's own right to life. The right to destroy does not of itself give direct dominion; a man who hires a wrecking company to destroy his house does not give them direct ownership over the house.

4. *If it is not wrong to interfere with nature to prolong life, why should it be wrong to interfere with nature to shorten life? Both curing and killing are interferences with nature; if man may cure (which no one will deny), why may he not kill?* If man had direct dominion over his life, he could do either. But indirect dominion or stewardship means that life is only lent to man for his use. Not only must a man not destroy what is under his stewardship, but he must use ordinary means and reasonable care to preserve it. It is not contrary to nature to use intelligently the remedies nature provides, to develop them scientifically, and to apply them as means of preserving life, as good stewardship requires. But to use them to destroy life is not stewardship, but the unjust assumption of direct dominion and the violation of God's rights.

5. *Though people suffering from temporary despondency should be prevented from harming themselves, there are some for whom life is really and irremediably hopeless; they are useless burdens to society and to themselves; is it not better for all concerned if they retire from the scene?* If there is no God, or God's rights and interests are ruled out of court, man may do with his life what he pleases. But if God exists and there is a life beyond this, no human being can be called useless. Suffering in itself has no earthly value and might be called the worst of earthly disvalues, but its moral and spiritual value can be tremendous. A man who faces suffering with heroic courage and patience is an example to his fellows, a credit to himself, and an honor to God. No such one can be called useless.

6. *It is lawful to choose a lesser evil to avoid a greater; since there are worse evils than death, why cannot the lesser be chosen?* Prudence so dictates, if there is a choice between two unavoidable physical evils and no moral evil is involved. Moral evil may never be chosen to avoid a physical evil, and suicide is a moral evil. But suppose one must choose between suicide and the commission of some other moral evil? No such predicament ever occurs. One is never forced to choose between sins. In conflicts between rights and duties the lesser yields. A person who cannot determine which is the genuine right or duty can always form his conscience and avoid subjective wrongdoing.

MURDER

The civil law uses three words to express the killing of another man: homicide, manslaughter, and murder. *Homicide* is the general word covering the other two, which are distinguished by the civil law for the purpose of preferring different charges and imposing different penalties. *Murder* is the worse charge and supposes malice aforethought; *manslaughter* is the lesser charge and supposes either that malice was not present or, if it was, that there are other extenuating circumstances. In each several degrees are recognized.

In ethics we find the distinction between murder and manslaughter of little help. There are undoubtedly different degrees of wickedness involved in killing men, but morality, which resides chiefly in the inner act of the will preceded by knowledge, does not always correspond with the amount and kind of evidence presentable in court. So long as the act of killing another man is both directly voluntary and unjust we shall call it *murder*, following the usage of common language rather than the technical language of the civil law. The advantage for ethics is that our definition of murder will exactly correspond to the kind of act against our neighbor's life forbidden by the natural law.

Murder is defined as the direct killing of an *innocent* person. It is *direct* killing, directly voluntary, so that death is intended as end or as means. Indirect killing, or the exposure of life to serious danger, is discussed later; it does not come under the heading of murder.

An *innocent* person has not forfeited his right to life. Murder is *unjust* killing, done without legitimate authority. This excludes killing another on the authority of God or the state, as mentioned before under suicide. The soldier killing the enemy in war and the executioner putting criminals to death are acting on the state's authority. The state, however, can commit murder by acting outside the scope of its legitimate authority. Killing in self-defense is not murder because it is authorized by the natural law, as will be discussed later. The word *innocent* must be understood as objectively innocent, for it is not murder to kill a maniac in self-defense. In suicide the killed, being also the killer, is not innocent.

That the natural law forbids murder hardly needs a separate proof if the argument against suicide is already admitted, for if a man is not allowed to take even his own life, much less would he be allowed to take the life of another. The plausibility offered for suicide, that a man's life seems to be his own, however fallacious as an argument, is not present at all in the case of murder.

Murder is forbidden by natural law because it violates the right of God, who has exclusive direct dominion over human life, the right of indirect dominion which each man has over his own life, founded on the essential equality of all men, and the right of the state to the service of each of its citizens and to the preservation of public order.

Murder has always been recognized as one of the worst of crimes and as the most glaring example of a morally evil act. But some are not convinced of the injustice contained in certain types of direct killing, and these must be examined further.

EUTHANASIA

Euthanasia or *mercy killing* is the giving of an easy painless death to one suffering from an incurable or agonizing ailment. Its advocates argue that the person will die anyway, that the purpose is not to invade the person's right to his life but only to substitute a painless for a painful death, that the shortening of the person's life merely deprives him of a bit of existence that is not only useless but unbearable, that for all the good he can do to himself or others his life is finished anyway. Some would leave the decision to a qualified physician; most would require the subject's consent.

Little need be said on this topic. While we can sympathize with the sentiments of pity and mercy inspiring this proposal, we can find no moral justification for it. If administered by oneself, euthanasia is suicide. If administered by another without the victim's consent, it is murder. If administered by another with the victim's consent or cooperation, it is suicide and murder combined.

The arguments for euthanasia are the same as those for justifying suicide. Its advocates do not consider it murder because the victim is willing. But this disregards the fact that the right to life is not at the disposal of the sufferer. Euthanasia takes no account of God's rights or of man's last end or of the value of patience. It flouts God's providence and the fact that God cannot allow a person to be tried beyond his strength. It appeals to sentiment in disregard of reason, and is the most flagrant use of the false principle that *the end justifies the means*. Once admit this, and there is an end to all morality. Even if euthanasia should be made permissible by civil law, for which there is strong propaganda in some quarters, nothing can make it moral.

FETICIDE AND ABORTION

Infanticide, or the killing of an infant already born, is plain murder. Whether the infant is too weak to live long, whether it is deformed or crippled, whether the parents already have too many children—such reasons are beside the point. The infant is certainly a human being with a right to life as good as that of any other human being.

What of the killing of a child before birth? The direct killing of the child within the womb, by cutting, crushing, craniotomy, or any such means is called *feticide.* The expulsion of a nonviable fetus, that is, of one too young to live outside the womb, is called *abortion.* It will be convenient to discuss these together.

Hastened birth, or the premature delivery of a viable fetus, is not abortion. A viable fetus is one that can live outside the womb. The fetus normally becomes viable about the seventh month, and with artificial incubation one even a few weeks younger may survive. To deliver a viable fetus before its time is not wrong in itself, since the child can be kept alive, but presents such a serious risk to the child's life that grave reasons are required to make it permissible. Such an action can be justified by the principle of double effect, the proportionate reasons being the danger to the health of mother, child, or both, if the gestation be allowed to reach its natural term. But to deliver or expel a nonviable fetus is abortion.

Abortion is murder because it is a direct killing, and no mere exposure of the child to danger. It is direct killing if the child is expelled before it is viable, for by this act it is taken from the only place where it can live and put in a place where it cannot live; there is no more efficient way of killing a person than this. It is no argument to say that the child dies from natural causes after it has been born; it has not been allowed to be born properly. All killing consists in interfering with nature in such a way that a person dies of it. A man who has been kept without food dies from the natural effects of starvation, but this also is murder.

It may be said that the direct killing of what is surely a human being is murder, but how do we know when the fetus becomes a human being? Aristotle* had the opinion that the embryo does not become human until some time after conception, and this seems to be the reason why he saw no wrong in early abortion. St. Thomas† and most medieval writers accepted Aristotle's opinion as a probable physical theory, but drew no such ethical conclusions. We do not know the exact moment when the

---

De Generatione Animalium (On the Generation of Animals), bk. II, ch. 3, 736a 24-737a 17.

†*Summa Theologica,* I, q. 118, a. 2, reply to obj. 2; *Summa Contra Gentiles,* bk. II, ch. 89.

human soul is put into the body to make it a human being, and this is why for all practical purposes we must consider the moment of conception as the first instant of the new human life. We cannot use probabilism here, for there is no doubt about the law and its application; we must not directly kill what is probably a human being. Just as we may not bury a man if he is only probably dead, because he is also probably alive, so we may not kill a fetus if it is only probably nonhuman, because it is also probably human. In such matters *the morally safer course must be followed*. The only morally safe course is to treat the embryo as a living human being, with the same right to life as any other person.

Hardly any moralist would try to justify the procuring of an abortion for the purpose of destroying the evidence of immoral sexual behavior or of obtaining relief from the burden of rearing an illegitimate child. One who performs immoral deeds must stand the responsibility for them, which falls on man and woman alike. Nature is not equal to the two sexes here, and in reputation as in physical anguish it is the woman who pays. She must stand her shame, while the man can hide behind the mask of anonymity. But, despite the inequality of social stigma, the moral responsibility is equal. Murder is no solution to previous sin, and abortion directly induced is murder.

The so-called *therapeutic abortion* brings up a very different problem. Consider the case of a legitimate pregnancy that is developing into a serious threat to the life of the mother, child, or both. Medical indications may show that the pregnancy cannot come to term, and that both mother and child will die. What then is to be done? Is it not better to save one at the expense of the other than to let both die? The answer is that it is surely better to do so, if it can be accomplished by means that are not morally wrong. But a direct killing of the fetus is morally wrong like any other act of murder. Mother and child have an equal right to life, and neither may be murdered to save the other. It is not allowed to do evil that good may come of it, to use evil means to obtain a good end. To save the mother's life is a physical good; to kill the child is a moral wrong. The principle of double effect is of no avail here, for the first condition is not fulfilled, since the act is intrinsically wrong.

Hence direct therapeutic abortion is contrary to the natural law. It is not only morally wrong, but in many instances medically unwise. No doctor can be absolutely sure that a mother will survive abortion or die without it. Some have died of it who might have lived and borne a healthy child, as can be judged from the cases in which the doctor advised it and the mother refused it, yet both mother and child lived. However, even if it be medically certain that both will die, a direct killing of the child or the mother is no *ethical* solution to an unfortunate occurrence. If in this situation one could save one's life by murdering another, why not in any case? Moral principles cannot be abandoned merely because they are difficult and the cost is high.

It should be noted that cases of this kind are not nearly as frequent as is sometimes imagined. Advances in medicine, especially in pre-natal care, are reducing them still further. Some danger will probably always remain, but taking childbirth calmly is the kind of courage nature demands of a woman.

We are faced with an entirely different situation if the death of an unborn child is only indirect, so that it is merely permitted and not willed as a means or an end. This situation of *indirect abortion* arises when the mother has some serious illness (pregnancy itself is not an illness but a natural condition), and the only workable treatment, whether medicinal or surgical, will have two effects: the cure of the mother's disease and the death of the child. This is the type of case to which the principle of double effect readily applies. The child is not directly attacked and its death, even if certain to follow, is an incidental and unavoidable by-product in the performance of a legitimate act. The mother herself needs the treatment no matter what effect it may have on the child, and the death of the child is not the means by which she is cured. She has a right to take such treatment and is morally allowed to do so.

The doctor has the responsibility of deciding whether the mother's condition is truly pathological and whether the treatment contemplated is the only effective remedy. It seems to be a solidly probable opinion that tubal pregnancies cause a genuinely pathological condition of the tube, because the process of implantation amounts to incipient rupture and hemorrhage.

To sum up: Abortion can be *spontaneous,* a miscarriage that is no one's fault, or *induced,* voluntarily brought about. Induced abortion can be *indirect,* the foreseen but unwanted consequence of doing something else, or *direct,* the expulsion of the fetus intended as end or means. Direct abortion is called *therapeutic,* if the purpose is the saving of the mother's life or health, or *criminal,* if the purpose is anything else. The first two distinctions are important for the moralist as dividing the involuntary from the voluntary and the indirectly voluntary from the directly voluntary. The last distinction, recognized in civil law, is of no value to the moralist, since all direct killing of another person on one's own authority is murder and contrary to the natural law.

Opposing arguments

We cannot leave this subject without clearing up the objections of those who claim that direct therapeutic abortion is morally justifiable.

1. *Is not the mother's right to life prior to that of the fetus, so that by a collision of rights the mother's prevails?* All human beings are equal in their right to life, and age gives no one any priority in the matter. It might be argued just as well that the mother has had at least some enjoyment of life and should yield to the child, if one but not both can be saved. If there is question only of indirectly permitting the death of one or the other, that one should be chosen who has the better chance of survival; but a collision of rights cannot be settled by the doing of something intrinsically wrong, as direct killing is. In this case each one's right yields to each one's duty, and neither may be murdered.

2. *Is not the physician bound professionally to save human life by every means in his power? Is he not bound morally to choose the lesser of two evils, which is death of one rather than of both?* The physician must use all legitimate means, but must not use means that are morally evil. His profession does not make the physician exempt from the moral law or master of human life. He should indeed chose the lesser of two evils if both are of the same order and either one or the other must be chosen, but the avoidance of physical evil (death) is not a justifying cause for the commission of moral evil (murder).

3. *Since this is a matter of life and death, is it not possible to apply the principle, necessity knows no law?* Extreme or grave necessity exempts from duty when there is a conflict of rights or duties and the lesser yields to the greater. But here the right of each life is equal, and both rights yield to a negative duty of the natural law which admits of no excuse whatever. No necessity however extreme can excuse the doing of something intrinsically wrong.

4. *Cannot the fetus be regarded as an unjust aggressor on its mother's life, and so forfeit its right to life? Is not the mother merely acting in self-defense?* This objection leads us into our next topic. For the moment we can say that it is absurd to think of an unborn child as an aggressor against its parents, who by their own voluntary act caused its presence in the mother's womb. We might as well give a man money, then call him an aggressor against our property, and murder him to get it back. Aggression does not consist merely in being present but in *doing* something; there must be an actual attack. If the pregnancy is developing into a miscarriage, this is one of those accidents that is no one's fault, surely no more the child's than the parents'.

SELF-DEFENSE

Man has a right to life, and therefore a right to the means necessary to preserve his life. On the other hand, a man has no private right over another person's life and may not kill him as a means to an end. What then may he do when his life is attacked and the defense of his own life involves the killing of the assailant?

The right to life is a coercive or juridical right, a right the protection of which may require the use of physical force. Though the exercise of physical force in defense of a right should normally be entrusted to the civil government, it is often impossible, when one's life is attacked, to appeal to the civil government. After the attack is over, punishment of the offender belongs to the civil government alone, because the factor of urgency is not present, but at the moment of the attack the victim must often use *self*-defense or there will be no defense. On what principles is self-defense morally justified, and how far may one go in defending one's own right to life?

The act of violating or attempting to violate another's right is *aggression*. As we use the term, it always means an *unjust* attack. Aggression against another's person rather than his belongings is properly called *assault,* but the more general word is used in this sense also. Mere intention to attack without any external attempt is not aggression, but there may be aggression without deliberate intention, as in an assault by a maniac. The distinction between an intentional or voluntary and an unintentional or involuntary aggressor describes the guilt or innocence of the person attacking, but we are interested here in what the man who is attacked may do. He needs to repel the threat to his life, whether the assailant means it or not.

Conditions of a blameless self-defense

There are conditions setting the limits beyond which defense of one's life would not be allowed by the natural law. One may say that there is no sense in discussing conditions until we have established that man really has the right of self-defense, but the conditions will enter into the argument and therefore must be seen first. We cannot prove that man has an unlimited right of self-defense, but only under certain conditions. There are four of them:

1. *The motive must be self-defense alone.* A moral act can be spoiled by a defect in any one of its three determinants: its nature, its motive, or its circumstances. If self-defense is but a mask for hatred or revenge, the act becomes evil because of evil intent.

2. *Force may be used only at the time of the attack.* The danger to one's life must be actual, not merely prospective. The mere fact that a man sends me a threatening letter does not allow me to go out and kill him, for many threats are never followed up. There would be an end to public order if anyone could use force to repel merely imagined attacks.

3. *Force may be used only when there is no other way of repelling the attack.* Recourse must be made to the police and public authority when possible. One need not run away from every fight, it is true, but should prudently try to avoid meeting a probable assailant. Persuasion or other nonforceful methods should be used if there is any reasonable hope of success.

4. *No more injury may be inflicted than is necessary to avert actual danger.* If I can save my life by injury less than death, I must not proceed further. If the assailant is knocked unconscious, there is no need to kill him. Evil more than is necessary is not inflicted for the sole purpose of defense.

The second of these conditions is the most difficult of application. In concrete cases it is often hard to determine just when preparation for attack turns into actual aggression. Mere purchase of a gun by my enemy with declaration that he intends to shoot me is not aggression. But I do not have to wait until he has actually shot at me, for then no further defense may be possible. Defense may begin as soon as the aggressor lifts his gun or even approaches to the oncoming fray, depending very much on the circumstances. Here the common estimate of men must be taken into consideration. In a matter as crucial as this, when the action to be efficient must be swift, it is impossible to draw fine lines and delicate discriminations, and it is better to favor the defender of life than the attacker. Individual conscience will decide subjective guilt or innocence in concrete cases; we are trying to discover objective principles for any act of self-defense.

Why self-defense is lawful

Self-defense seems to be merely an application of the principle of double effect, and so St. Thomas considers it. He says:

> Nothing hinders one act from having two effects, only one of which is intended, while the other is beside the intention. Now moral acts take their species according to what is intended, and not according to what is beside the intention, since this is accidental. . . . Accordingly the act of self-defense may have two effects, one is the saving of one's own life, the other is the slaying of the aggressor. Therefore this act, since one's intention is to save one's own life, is not unlawful, seeing that it is natural to everything to keep itself in *being*, as far as possible. And yet, though proceeding from a good intention, an act may be rendered unlawful, if it be out of proportion to the end. Wherefore if a man, in self-defense, uses more than necessary violence, it will be unlawful: whereas if he repel force with moderation his defense will be lawful, because according to the jurists, *it is lawful to repel force by force, provided one does not exceed the limits of a blameless defense.* . . . It is not lawful for a man to intend killing a man in self-defense, except for such as have public authority, who while intending to kill a man in self-defense, refer this to the public good, as in the case of a soldier fighting against the foe, and in the minister of the judge struggling with robbers, although even these sin if they be moved by private animosity.*

It should be easy to recognize in this passage the source from which the principle of double effect was derived, by broadening it to suit other questions besides that of self-defense. However, in applying the principle of double effect to self-defense a crucial problem arises: Is not the killing of an assailant a *direct* killing, so that in defending my life I am using an evil as means to a good? This is a serious difficulty, for it would indicate a violation of the first two conditions of the principle of double effect. On this matter there are two opinions:

One opinion holds that legitimate self-defense is always only an *indirect* killing. Though more fully expressed by his commentator Cajetan,† this opinion seems to be that of St. Thomas, as appears from the last sentence in the quotation just given, where the key word is "intend." Only one in public authority may *intend* killing another, even in self-defense. Ac-

---

Summa Theologica, II-II, q. 64, a. 7.

†Cajetan, *Commentaria* (Commentaries on the Works of St. Thomas), on the above passage. This is found in the Leonine Edition of St. Thomas, vol. IX.

cording to this opinion, all that I as a private person may do in defending myself is to produce a state of quiet or nonactivity in the assailant so that he cannot continue his attack. If I can accomplish this purpose without death, I am not allowed to go on and kill the man, as all admit. If my attempts to produce this nonactivity, a thing that is morally indifferent, result in death, that is incidental and regrettable. But I must not *intend* anything more than the quieting of the adversary, not his death.

The other opinion holds that in self-defense the killing may be *direct*. John de Lugo puts it as follows:

> We may intend whatever is necessary for the defense of our life. Sometimes the striking of blows alone is insufficient for this purpose, but the death of the adversary is necessary. His stubbornness is such that he will not cease from attacking you, either by himself or others, unless he dies. Therefore you can intend his death, not merely as the striking of a blow [from which death may follow] but as death, because it is useful to your safety not otherwise than as death. . . . The death of the aggressor is not merely connected with another means that is intended, but it itself, and as death, is useful and judged necessary to your defense.*

This latter opinion really falls back on a *collision of rights.* By the very fact that the assailant's attack is unjust, his right to life yields to that of the person attacked. The right to life of the two parties is no longer equal, but the aggressor temporarily loses his right to life by his unjust act of aggression. Killing in itself is not wrong, but what makes it wrong is its *injustice,* the invasion of another man's right. If that right is extinguished, there is no injustice present to make the act of killing wrong. To preserve a life to which one has a right, at the expense of a life that has been forfeited, is not a morally evil act.

It does not seem necessary to settle this controversy, because, if one is satisfied that the killing is only indirect, then it is permissible by the principle of double effect; but if one feels that the argument for indirect killing sounds too much like verbal quibbling, then one may have recourse to the collision of rights to show that in the case of legitimate self-defense even a direct killing is morally justifiable.

Whichever of these explanations be preferred, there is no doubt about the existence of the right of self-defense. The use of force is not in itself intrinsically wrong. It is so only when one has no right to use it. In the case of self-defense the natural law must confer that right. For:

1. The natural law cannot provide that the assailant who breaks the natural law thereby acquires a better right to life than the innocent person who keeps the natural law, so that on being unjustly attacked a man finds that his right to life becomes a duty to die.

2. The natural law cannot impose on the virtuous members of the population the duty to permit the criminal element, by their indiscriminate

---

*De Lugo, *De Justitia et Jure,* (On Justice and Right), Disputation X, section VI, §149.

and unchecked use of force, to seize control of human society and thus destroy its primary purpose.

Therefore under proper conditions the natural law, since it cannot be intended by its Author to defeat itself, permits the use of force even to killing in self-defense.

The argument proves that man has a right to self-defense. Is it also a duty? No. As we shall see, man has the duty to use ordinary means to preserve his life, but the killing of a human being, even if he is an aggressor, is surely an extraordinary means. Therefore nothing prevents a man from choosing the heroic course of giving up his own life rather than taking another's. Only in unusual circumstances could self-defense become a duty, for example, in the case of a public personage indispensable to the community's welfare.

One may come to the assistance of another whose life is unjustly attacked. Such assistance becomes a duty for custodians of public order because of their office, and for husbands, fathers, and others who have a natural duty to protect their charges. The casual by-stander, however, has only a general duty in charity to come to another's assistance in distress; if this goes so far as to require the killing of an assailant, it usually entails serious risk to his own life, a risk he is allowed but not obliged to take.

Unintentional aggression

The argument given above is expressly directed at *intentional* aggression, but applies with proper reservations to *unintentional* aggression. A man who has lost the use of his reason, either permanently or temporarily, cannot perform a voluntary act and cannot incur moral guilt, but he can be just as serious a threat to other people's lives. The same is true of a man who has the use of reason but does not realize that the act he is doing at the moment will kill someone; for him the act is voluntary only as far as he sees it, and its unforeseen consequences, though involuntary, can be fatal to others, who have a right to protect themselves against them.

Such acts are unjust aggression from the standpoint of the person attacked, because his right is actually, though unintentionally, violated. He may protect himself even to the killing of the assailant under the four conditions of a blameless self-defense. The unintentional aggressor's right yields to the defender's, not because of the former's fault but because of his misfortune. Human lives cannot be placed at the mercy of madmen, however blameless they may be, nor are we obliged to give up our lives in deference to another man's ignorance. Most assailants are malicious, but it is not necessary that they be so in order that we may exercise our right of self-defense against them.

Goods equivalent to life

Man has a right not only to life itself, but to a human life, a normal and decent life fit for a rational being. Man's right to defend his life would be of small value if he could not also defend his right to live that life in a manner befitting a man. This right entails the possession of certain goods that make life worth living, goods that some writers call equivalent to life. Force may be used to defend such goods even to the killing of the unjust aggressor, under the same conditions as apply to the defense of life itself. Such goods considered equivalent to life are as follows:

(1) Limbs and faculties
(2) Sanity
(3) Liberty
(4) Chastity
(5) Material goods of great value

The first four should be evident because of their personal nature. Many would rather die than submit to such evils as rape, insanity, blindness, or enslavement, and, whether they would or not, why should anyone have to yield to a fiend who tries to inflict them? Material goods, even of great value, may at first seem disproportionate to the taking of human life, but the social as well as the personal aspect must be considered, and the good of society requires that people be secure in the possession of their property. Acts of violence, whether against one's person or against one's property, cannot be allowed to go unchecked in society, and in the last resort they can be checked only by opposed violence. The attacker can easily save his life simply by desisting from his aggression.

Honor and *reputation* have been deliberately omitted here. They are as important as any of the goods listed above, for their loss can mean utter ruin, but they are not the kind of thing that can be defended by force. Self-defense is the repelling of force by force. Lies and slander are words and cannot be beaten back by fists or swords or pistols. Before a man has spoken against me and injured my reputation, there is no certainty that he will do so even if he threatens to; after he has spoken, the damage is done and then it is too late for defense; whatever I do then is revenge, that only hurts him but does not protect me. The use of physical force against him would only prove me physically stronger, but would not restore my reputation; if I use strength to force from him a recantation, it would not be generally believed under the circumstances. However, force short of killing may be the only way of closing the mouth of a reviler or slanderer who refuses to stop. There must be some remedy against a perpetual tirade.

The former practice of *duelling* cannot be morally justified. Duelling with intent to kill on both sides is a combination of murder and suicide. The intent to kill the adversary makes it murder, and the exposure of one's own life to an unnecessary risk makes it suicide. The imputation of cowardice against one who refuses a challenge is unjust and at best the result of an erroneous conscience. The civilized world is well rid of this immoral custom.

SUMMARY

Man's right to life is based on the fact that he must achieve his last end by morally good acts, and to do these he must live.

Suicide is the direct killing of oneself on one's own authority. God gives man only *indirect* dominion over himself, the stewardship of his person, but no *direct* dominion, the right to destroy his person, for this is so exclusively God's that He cannot give it away. It is for God to decide that man has had sufficient opportunity for good works; by suicide man arrogates this privilege to himself and invades God's exclusive right. Hence suicide is against the natural law.

Man cannot actually defraud God, but is not allowed to *try.* Man can be given direct dominion over animals because they are not persons, but not over himself. Good stewardship allows interference with nature to prolong, but not to destroy, life. No person is useless, if he can profit spiritually by bearing suffering with patience. One can choose the lesser of two evils that is not intrinsically wrong, but suicide is intrinsically wrong.

Murder, the direct killing of an innocent person, is forbidden by the natural law, because it violates the right of God to all life, of an innocent man to his life, and of the state to public order.

Euthanasia or mercy killing is suicide if done by oneself, murder if done by another without the victim's consent, both together if done by another with the victim's consent.

Feticide, the direct killing of the fetus within the womb, and *abortion,* the deliberate expulsion of the fetus before it is viable, are also murder. Though we do not know just when the human soul enters the embryo, we cannot use probabilism here but must follow the morally safer course. When a pregnancy endangers the life of both mother and child, neither may be *directly* killed to save the other; *therapeutic abortion* cannot be justified by the double-effect principle, by priority of right in the mother, by the lesser of two evils, by claiming that necessity knows no law, or by calling the child an unjust aggressor. But if the mother has a serious illness, she may be given necessary treatment even though the death of the child *indirectly* results.

Self-defense, the repelling of force by force, should ordinarily be entrusted to the civil government, but sometimes must be done personally. There are four conditions of a blameless self-defense:

(1) The motive must be self-defense alone.
(2) Force must be used only at the time of attack.
(3) There must be no other way of repelling the attack.
(4) No more injury may be inflicted than necessary.

Some say that self-defense must aim only at the quiescence of the assailant and death must be indirect. Others think that even a direct killing is allowable because of a collision of rights.

The natural law in giving the right to life gives the right to protect that life by all means not intrinsically wrong. Otherwise the natural law gives a better right to life to criminals than to the innocent, and the criminal element get a free hand in the control of society.

Self-defense is a right, but normally not a duty. We may defend others who are attacked, but are not obliged to risk our lives for those not under our charge.

We may defend ourselves against *unintentional* aggressors, because they are actually though guiltlessly invading our right.

We may also defend goods equivalent to life: limbs and faculties, sanity, liberty, chastity, material goods of great value. But honor cannot be defended by force; hence duelling is wrong.

READINGS

1. Read Plato's *Phaedo*, §61-62, which shows that Socrates, whatever we may think of his action, certainly did not intend to commit suicide; the famous death scene is at the end of the *Phaedo*. Plato's *Laws*, bk. IX, §865 to the end, describes what he thinks are the best laws on homicide and assault, with remarks on the nature of these crimes.
2. St. Augustine, *City of God*, bk. I, ch. 17-27, on suicide.
3. St. Thomas, *Summa Theologica*, II-II, q. 64 (not in the *Basic Writings*). A commentary in Farrell, *Companion to the Summa*, vol. III, ch. 8.
4. There is unfortunately no English translation of the works of Cajetan or de Lugo, so that the student could pursue their views on the moral basis of self-defense.
5. Cronin, *The Science of Ethics*, vol. II, pp. 93-110, argues strongly in favor of Cajetan's position; see also pp. 687-700 for some medico-moral problems.
6. Leibell, *Readings in Ethics*, pp. 457-473, 487-496, 498-502.
7. Rickaby, *Moral Philosophy*, pp. 202-224; favors Cajetan.
8. Durkheim, *Suicide*.
9. Sullivan, *Morality of Mercy Killing*.
10. The ethics of various medical practices are discussed in the following works:
    a. Healy, *Medical Ethics*, ch. 6, 8.
    b. McFadden, *Medical Ethics*, ch. 7-10.
    c. O'Donnell, *Morals in Medicine*, ch. 5.
    d. Bouscaren, *Ethics of Ectopic Operations*.
    e. Kelly, *Medico-Moral Problems*.
    f. Kenny, *Principles of Medical Ethics*.
    g. Ficarra, *Newer Ethical Problems in Medicine and Surgery*.

CHAPTER 20

HEALTH AND
SAFETY

Problem
Risk to life
Care of health
Mutilation
Sterilization

PROBLEM

Life can be lost not only by deliberate killing, but also by lack of proper positive maintenance. Health and safety are means toward the preservation of life and thus pertain to man's stewardship over himself. To what extent must one go to preserve life and health? May a man expose himself to serious danger or even to certain death in a good cause? Must he keep himself whole as well as alive, and what if he cannot do both? We must discuss:

(1) When may a man risk his life?
(2) How much care must be given to health?
(3) How and when is mutilation justified?
(4) May a person submit to sterilization?

RISK TO LIFE

The natural law forbids suicide, or the direct killing of oneself on one's own authority, but does not always forbid the indirect killing of oneself, or the deliberate endangering of one's life, even when the danger may be so great that death is certain. When we say that life is a nonrenounceable right and its preservation a duty, we do not mean that a person may never sacrifice it under any conditions, but only that he may not give it up at pleasure. When a person may rightfully risk his life is determined by the four conditions of the principle of double effect:

1. *The act.* The act itself must not be direct killing but some allowable act from which death might follow as a consequence. Direct killing would be suicide and evil in its very *nature.*

2. *The effects.* Death must be an incidental by-product in the accomplishment of the good and not the means by which the good is attained. To use death as a means to an end would also be direct killing, suicide, and evil in its very *nature*.

3. *The intention.* If death, however obtained, were intended, the act would become evil in its *motive,* for death would be the end of the agent and directly willed by him. Death must be merely permitted as unavoidably connected with the seeking of a legitimate end.

4. *The proportion.* Death is too serious an evil to be risked for the sake of a slight gain and can become an incidental by-product only in the pursuit of some good that makes the risk worth taking. If this proportion is lacking, the act becomes evil by reason of its *circumstances*.

It would indeed be wrong to risk one's life unless all these conditions are fulfilled, yet it is easy to see that cases frequently arise in which all the conditions are actually fulfilled. In this event, provided any other evil circumstances arising from other possible sources are excluded, the deliberate exposure of oneself to the risk of death is not morally wrong, and is therefore not forbidden by the natural law. Moral evil in a human act must come either from the *nature* of the act itself or from the *motive* of the agent or from the *circumstances* in which the act is done, and the proper application of the double-effect principle shows that none of these sources of moral evil is present.

This discussion gives the philosophical basis of what we all know through ordinary experience in the hazards of life. If we could never risk our lives, no one could serve in the army or nurse the plague-stricken or undergo a serious operation or fly an airplane or undertake any dangerous occupation. Human life as we know it would come to a standstill.

The fourth condition, the proportion, requires some additional remarks. How is it to be estimated? Except in cases in which death is certain, we must not balance the good we seek against death itself but against the risk of death. Is the good proportioned to the danger?

The danger may be:

(1) *Ordinary* or *extraordinary*
(2) *Proximate* or *remote*
(3) *Certain* or *probable* or barely *possible*

The greater the risk, the greater must be the desired good that can justify such a risk. There is an ordinary, remote, and possible hazard in driving a car or flying a plane, yet one may do so for mere pleasure. To drive on sleety streets or fly in bad weather is much more dangerous and requires a better reason. Conditions can become so bad that no driving or flying are allowable, except perhaps to save a life, and then we must see how much that life is endangered.

To save another from certain death we may expose ourselves to certain death. Such an act is usually allowable, but becomes obligatory only under special conditions. Those who, either by nature or by contract, have charge over the lives of others may and sometimes must take greater risks to protect their charges. Husbands will sacrifice themselves for their wives and parents for their children, following nature's prompting that the strong should protect the weak. Soldiers, sailors, policemen, firemen, doctors, nurses, and others with like occupations are obliged by contract, express or implied, to their duties even in the most serious danger.

The greater benefit an action or occupation is to society, the more dangerous it may be without overbalancing the proportion. Explorers like Columbus could take chances not otherwise permitted because of the enormous boon to mankind a successful voyage would bring, and so may the space travelers of the future. Dangerous work with radiation is justified when truly directed to the advancement of science or to national defense, under proper precautions both for the investigators and the public. Acrobats and daredevils are morally allowed to ply their trade only because their skill renders the danger remote. A man may do right in facing the ordinary risks of a hazardous occupation such as coal mining or dynamite manufacturing, and at the same time do wrong by creating extraordinary dangers for himself and others in his way of working, especially by despising the usual safety precautions.

The infinite variety of possibilities in this matter rules out the framing of any hard and fast norms. Positive law and custom, crystalizing man's age-old experience with danger, are helpful guides, but not infallible. We must ultimately fall back on experience, criticized and evaluated by the intellectual virtue of prudence; this we call common sense, and for it there is no substitute.

CARE OF HEALTH

The natural law obliges man to take reasonable care of his health. Reasonable care does not mean becoming a health crank but using the ordinary means of keeping healthy. Not to do so would be needless exposure of one's life to danger, for life itself is dependent on health. By ordinary means we refer to proper food, clothing, and shelter, due moderation in work and exercise, the avoidance of foolish risks and dangers, taking the usual remedies in sickness, seeking and following medical advice when necessary; all this supposes rather normal conditions, and does not contradict what was said above about exposing one's life to danger.

One is certainly bound to avoid excesses ruinous to health. But the chief wrong in dissipation and debauchery comes not so much from the ruination of one's health as of one's character. The evil of drunkenness consists partly in the physical deterioration it gradually induces, but far more in the unseating of reason from its ruling position, making the man a temporary beast, and in the disastrous social consequences involved in becoming unfit for any responsible work such as holding a job and supporting a family. The evil of indiscriminate sex indulgence often meets a natural punishment in the form of venereal disease, which one is obliged to avoid, but the real malice of unchastity is quite independent of such accidental physical effects. Acts of overindulgence are wrong as violations of the virtue of temperance, but an added evil accrues to them from the effect they can have on one's health.

Man is not obliged to preserve life and health by extraordinary means, for no one is obliged to do what is practically impossible or disproportionately difficult. A man in moderate circumstances is not obliged to undergo a serious and costly operation, to break up his home and move to another climate, or to adopt some regimen that would prevent him from earning a living and make him a burden on others. Health must be preserved, but not at all costs. Whether a means is extraordinary or not must be judged, not absolutely, but relatively to the person. A man with a serious heart ailment is not obliged to spend the rest of his life in bed, though he must cut out heavy exertion. A form of life tolerable to one man would be quite unbearable to another. Hence a person's subjective attitude must be considered here as well as his social and financial condition.

Doctors must go to all *reasonable* lengths to keep a man alive, if there is hope. But they should remember that the distinction between ordinary and extraordinary means is measured *humanly* rather than scientifically. A treatment may be common medical practice or involve standard hospital equipment, yet for this particular person the cure may be worse than the disease. Unless the patient or his family want it, there is no point in prolonging life, regardless of trouble and expense, for a few more days of torment or coma. Doctors have legal and professional responsibilities to consider, but neither doctor nor patient has a *moral* obligation to go beyond ordinary care, especially in terminal cases. It is often better to let nature take its course so that the man can die in peace.

MUTILATION

Mutilation is an action by which some part of the body is injured, destroyed, or separated from the rest of the body. The body is mutilated not only by cutting away some organ or member, but also by rendering useless some function or ability. To paralyze a part of the body by cutting the nerves is mutilation, but not a mere wounding or incision that will heal and leave no disability.

The same argument which proves that suicide is wrong also proves that unnecessary mutilation is wrong, whether we inflict it on ourselves or allow others to do it to us. If we have but stewardship or use-ownership over our person, we are obliged to preserve and keep intact the property of the full owner, who in this case is God. We may therefore not part with our members or carve up our bodies on our own authority.

But we are also obliged to preserve life and health, and sometimes this is impossible without undergoing mutilation. Good stewardship requires us to stay both alive and whole, but if we cannot have both, which must we or may we choose? If the mutilation involved great pain or risk, or reduced one to a condition in which life would not be worth living, it would be an extraordinary means of preserving life and one would not be morally obliged to submit to it.

Is it allowable to prolong life or to restore health by sacrificing a part or a function of the body? The difficulty is that mutilation is not a mere permitting of an evil, such as can be justified by the principle of double effect, but a direct attack on the wholeness of the body, an action directly voluntary, and therefore the accomplishment of a good by means of an evil. It is true that it is only a physical evil, but it is morally wrong to inflict physical evil unless one has a right to do so. This last phrase gives us the answer: we do have this right.

The principle involved here is this: *The part is for the sake of the whole.* By the natural order of things a part of the human body is subordinated to the good of the whole, the various organs and members and functions existing not for their own sakes but for the purpose of maintaining life in the whole organism. The part is the means and the whole is the end. Hence it is a legitimate act of stewardship to sacrifice, when necessary, the part for the sake of the whole.

Well-founded hope of notable improvement in health is proportionate reason for lesser mutilations. Deformities, by the fact that they are such, supply sufficient reason for attempting correction, provided this does not prove too dangerous. Plastic surgery is likewise justified, because of the social and psychological effects disfigurement can have on a person and because of the importance of a pleasing appearance in the modern competitive world.

Organ transplantation is a highly technical matter, on which we can make but a few remarks. Blood transfusions, skin and bone grafts, transplants from animals (except their sex glands) and from human cadavers are quite legitimate. The moral difficulty about transplants from other *living* humans is the unavoidable disability left in the one from whom the organ is taken. If the disability is not disproportionate to the good accomplished, some allow the operation, not on the principle of the part for the sake of the whole, which does not apply, but on the grounds of love for the neighbor, of which it is a most noble and generous instance.

STERILIZATION

Sterilization is a form of mutilation, for, though it can be done simply by ligature without depriving the body of a physical part, it renders impossible one of the body's natural functions, the power of reproduction. Because this power is for the race rather than the individual, it involves a special problem.

There is no difficulty about *indirect* sterilization, when sterility is but the foreseen effect of something else that is done; such cases are handled by the double-effect principle. Direct sterilization is the production of sterility itself as an end or a means. It follows the principles set down for mutilation: it is allowable if required for the life or health of the whole body. Mere sterilization is not at present the remedy for any disease, but should it become so it may be done. This form might be called *therapeutic* sterilization.

Some people wish to undergo sterilization to avoid parenthood, and some doctors wish to produce this condition when they foresee that future pregnancy would be dangerous for the woman. It is being advocated as a means of controlling overpopulation in underdeveloped countries. In such cases sterilization becomes a form of birth control. This whole question will be taken up later under marriage. For the present we can remark that such *contraceptive* sterilization is wrong for the same reason that contraception is wrong, with the added evil of making it a permanent condition.

May the state impose sterilization as a punishment for crime, especially for sex crimes? The argument for it is that, if the state can put criminals to death, it can decree lesser punishments, and for sex offenders it is a punishment that fits the crime. This argument is valid as far as it goes, but overlooks the point that punishment must also be effective. Castration might be an effective, though barbaric, punishment. But mere sterilization is useless because it destroys neither the desire nor the possibility of sex satisfaction, but only renders it unfruitful, a situation sex criminals would not resent. Hence *punitive* sterilization, despite a theoretical justifiability, is practically unworkable.

Sterilization is proposed chiefly as a *eugenic* measure. The study of eugenics deals with the improvement of the race, the development of a better breed of human beings by methods commonly used in the breeding of animals. Eugenists are alarmed by the low birth rate among the better and more successful classes of society, by the high birth rate among the poorer and less gifted groups, especially the mentally deficient. They see the best families dying off, while the diseased, feeble-minded, shiftless, and criminal elements are multiplying apace, thus bringing about a gradual deterioration in the general level of human excellence. So they argue that defective strains must be eliminated from the race.

The biological side of this topic is outside our purview, except to remark how very inadequate is our knowledge of human heredity. No more than probability can be obtained that the recurrence of the same defect is due to nature rather than to nurture; the skimpier the family history the thinner become the grounds for prediction. There is no real evidence that the human race is deteriorating; theoretically it ought to be if defective stock is multiplying faster than perfect stock, but genius has a way of cropping out in the most unexpected places. The crowding of our insane asylums only shows that the state now cares for many who were formerly left to private resources or not taken care of at all. The maladjustments produced by the hectic pace of modern life cannot be ascribed to heredity.

Even if sterilization were an effective measure for improving the race, in itself a laudable aim, is it a means that is morally permissible? Though surgically only a minor operation, sterilization is a major mutilation because it deprives one of a very important natural function. No one is allowed to submit to a major mutilation unless it is necessary to save his life or health. Eugenic sterilization is not done for the sake of the individual's life or health but solely for some problematic effect it may possibly have on the future of the race. Therefore in eugenic sterilization the reasons that alone can justify mutilation are not present, and this act is morally wrong.

If *voluntary* sterilization is thus morally wrong, the state has no right to order *compulsory* sterilization. Eugenic sterilization is not inflicted in punishment of crime, since it deals with disabilities that are presumably only hereditary. The state has the obligation to protect the individual in his rights and not to maim him for something not his fault. The good of society may require the segregation of harmful defectives, which adequately prevents any damage they can cause. The main reason why the state favors sterilization is that it can then turn defectives loose on society without fear that they will burden the state with families they cannot care for. This financial argument has no moral value whatever.

It may be objected that, just as the members of the individual body exist for the sake of the whole and may be sacrificed for the good of the whole, so may the members of the social body; defectives may be called on to sacrifice the possibility of offspring for the benefit of society. Only in a totalitarian state could such an argument be admitted. The citizen is not wholly for the state and has natural rights the state must protect, among which is the right to bodily completeness. According to this argument the state could kill them just as readily. No matter how much it would help the public welfare, the state has no right to kill or mutilate its citizens except in punishment for proved crimes.

SUMMARY

Deliberate exposure of life to risk is allowable when the four conditions of the *principle of double effect* are satisfied. Then the act is not wrong from its nature, motive, or circumstances. To estimate the proportion note that danger may be ordinary or extraordinary, proximate or remote, certain or probable or barely possible. Even when we are allowed to risk our lives, we are not obliged to, except under special conditions.

Man must take reasonable care of his *health,* but is not obliged to use extraordinary means.

Mutilation is the destruction of some member or function of the body. Since we have only indirect dominion over ourselves, mutilation is not allowable at will. Mutilation, since it is a direct attack on the wholeness of the body, is justified on the principle that *the part is for the sake of the whole,* and is allowable only to save life or, in lesser mutilations, to obtain a proportionate improvement in health.

Sterilization is depriving a person of the reproductive function. Like other mutilations, it is lawful when necessary for life or health. As a contraceptive measure, it shares in the immorality of contraception. As a punishment for sex crimes, it would be lawful if it were effective, but it is not. As a eugenic measure, it cannot be justified; not if done voluntarily, because it is not required to save the life or health of the individual; not if done compulsorily by the state, because the victim is guilty of no crime by which he would forfeit his natural rights.

READINGS

1. St. Thomas, *Summa Theologica,* II-II, q. 65, a. 1.
2. Leibell, *Readings in Ethics,* pp. 474-487, 1077-1090.
3. Connell, *Morals in Poliitcs and Professions,* ch. 10-11, treated from the standpoint of moral theology.
4. Most of the problems dealt with in this chapter are discussed at length in books on medical ethics. See:
   a. Healy, *Medical Ethics,* pp. 59-90, 121-156, 170-188, 280-308.
   b. McFadden, *Medical Ethics,* ch. 12.
   c. O'Donnell, *Morals in Medicine,* ch. 4.
   d. Flood, *New Problems in Medical Ethics,* vol. II. Also *Medical Experimentation on Man* and *The Ethics of Brain Surgery.* These are symposia of French doctors, too technical to interest the general reader but valuable to the medical student. The ethical summaries are good.
   e. Cunningham, *Morality of Organic Transplantation.*
   f. Schmiedeler, *Sterilization in the United States;* Lehane, *Morality of American Civil Legislation Concerning Eugenic Sterilization,* deal with this medical-legal-moral problem.

CHAPTER 21

TRUTHFULNESS

PROBLEM

After considering man's right to life, including his duties to respect his own life and the lives of his fellow men, we have now to consider man's duty to respect his neighbor's intellect, a duty fulfilled by observing right order in the communications between his own mind and the minds of others. One who speaks is obliged to speak the truth.

The problem arises from the fact that a man may also have an obligation to conceal the truth. He may be entrusted with a secret that he simply must not divulge. There might be little trouble on this point if people did not have the habit of asking questions, but the privilege of inquiring goes with the gift of speech. What can a man do when he is questioned point blank on a matter he must keep secret? We need to explain:

(1) What is a lie?
(2) Are all deceptions lies?
(3) What is wrong about lying?
(4) Why must secrets be kept?
(5) How can secrets be kept without lying?

MEANING OF A LIE

What is a lie? The literal-minded person may define a lie as any statement not in strict literal accord with actual facts. But no one with the faintest spark of imagination or the most primitive inkling of courtesy could confine his speech within such narrow bounds. Speech not only exchanges information, but also contributes to the amenities of life. Candor has its place, but the outspoken telling of the unvarnished truth on every occasion would lose us all our friends and make us unfit for society. Speech need not always be used thus, and so this literal-minded definition would require a distinction between lies that are allowable and those that are not, between so-called white lies and black lies. A far better procedure is to reserve the word *lie* for the misuse of speech forbidden by the natural law and to define it accordingly. To distinguish it from the looser usages of everyday speech we may call it a *strict* or *formal* lie.

There is a temptation to go to the opposite extreme and to reserve the word *lie* for falsehoods told to one who has a right to know the truth. It would so simplify the question, for there is no doubt that this kind of lying is wrong. The very admission that one has a right to the truth makes lying a violation of this right, and therefore an evil act. But the right of a person to know the truth can be violated by silence as well as by lying and so is not distinctive of lying as such. Lying seems to have its own peculiar malice distinct from its effects, from the lack of justice or charity by which the other's right is violated. May we say anything we want, no matter how untrue, to those who have no right to be told the facts here and now? Our listeners would have to assure themselves that we recognize their right to the truth before they could believe us. Truthfulness would be limited to what could be said under oath.

The correct definition must stand somewhere between these extremes. Commenting on St. Augustine's* definition of a lie as "a false statement uttered with intent to deceive," St. Thomas† says that it contains three things:

(1) The falsity of the statement
(2) The will to tell the falsity
(3) The intention to deceive

Of these three, the first provides only the material for a lie, for it is not a lie to say what is actually false while thinking it true, though it is a lie to say what is actually true while thinking it false; and the third point, the intended deception, is rather a consequence of lying and its usual motive than the lie itself. The essence of a lie, therefore, consists in the second element, the willful disconformity between one's thought and one's speech. From this analysis by St. Thomas we derive the commonly accepted definition of a lie as *speech contrary to one's mind.*

Conventionality of speech

The problem comes down to the nature of speech as a medium of communication and its function in human society. It is natural for man to speak, but, apart from a few obvious gestures and imitative sounds, there is no natural language. Language is conventional, the symbols used being

---

*St. Augustine, *De Mendacio* (On Lying), ch. 4; *Contra Mendacium* (Against Lying), ch. 12.
†St. Thomas, *Summa Theologica,* II-II, q. 110, a. 1.

developed by human artifice and dictated by custom. Hardly any word has a single univocal meaning whenever used, like the symbols of mathematics. Language is a peculiar mixture of logic and tradition, in which the conventions are undergoing subtle but continual change. By convention we distinguish fact and fiction, literal and figurative expressions, jokes and serious statements, emotional outbursts and sober information, ironical allusions and scientific data, polite compliments and solemn testimony. Often nothing but circumstances indicates the difference.

1. Speech, as we take it, is not limited to words but is *any sign used to communicate thought.* Looks, gestures, nods, winks, shrugs, facial expressions, tones of voice, even the circumstances in which something is said, are all signs capable of telling another what we think and, if used for this purpose, are speech. Lying is possible by any of these means.

2. The sign must be *intended* by the speaker *to convey a meaning.* Involuntary looks and gestures are not speech. It is not lying to conceal our emotions under outward calm nor to appear cheerful when we are sad, for we are not then intentionally using our appearance to express our real feelings.

3. The sign must be made *to another person,* for speech is communication between minds. It is impossible to lie to oneself, nor would it be lying to confide untruths to one's dog. Talk in other people's presence, when it is clearly not directed to them, is not speech to them. Eavesdroppers listen at their own peril.

4. The sign must be such as to *express the speaker's own judgment,* what he believes to be true. To lie, therefore, the speaker must express as true something he thinks to be untrue, or as certain something he does not know for certain. If he mistakenly thinks that what he says is true, though as a fact it is not, he does not lie; his speech is untrue but not untruthful.

5. *Fiction* is not lying, for the story is used as an expression of one's creative imagination and entertaining ability, not of one's factual judgment. But fiction can be lying if it is given all the outward marks of true history. Jokes and exaggerations are not lies if there is any circumstance to indicate that they are not to be taken seriously. But a joke can be a lie if there is no possible way of discovering that it is a joke.

6. *Figures of speech* are not lies. When a word has several meanings, its sense in this particular statement must be judged by the context and the meaning of the whole statement by the total situation. Sometimes we speak literally, sometimes figuratively, and the figurative meaning can be just as genuine as the literal.

7. Many *polite expressions* and *stereotyped formulas* have lost old meanings and acquired new ones through convention. "Not guilty" in a law court is a legal plea by which the accused does not confess but demands that the case be proved against him. "Good morning," "goodbye," "how do you do," "see you later" once meant something but are now mere forms of greeting and parting. There are times when compliments must be paid: "very becoming hat," "most enjoyable evening," "such a beautiful baby." Only the most naive would accept these remarks at their face value; sometimes their omission is far more significant and expresses a pointed insult. How far one can go in the use of polite excuses depends on convention. "Not at home," "in conference," "occupied," "too busy," "previous engagement" are recognized as urbane ways of putting one off, depending on the circumstances. Once these probably were lies, but use has softened their import. A convention is not a private meaning arbitrarily created by the speaker for the occasion but a system of signs commonly accepted.

8. *Circumstances* can be such that, though words are used, there is no formal speech because no communication is intended nor should it be expected. A captured soldier, for instance, may regale his captors with tall stories about the disposition of his own troops. Even if they are foolish enough to believe him, he is not lying because circumstances show that he is entertaining and not communicating. The case is different if he is put on parole and seriously accepts the conditions.

Lying and deception

Deception is the usual motive for lying, but we must not confuse these two concepts. Feints, disguises, impersonations, fictitious names, and other such pretenses are deceptions but not lies. The difference is in the lack of communication, of speech in the sense just explained. Deception is not wrong in itself but can become wrong from motives and circumstances if intended or foreseen as a cause of harm. The wrong comes not from the act done, which is indifferent, but from the harm that follows.

Most games are built on harmless deception. Even harmful deception may be permitted in the protection or vindication of one's rights, according to the principle of double effect. Thus stratagems and military maneuvers in war may be designed deliberately to mislead the enemy. Such deceptions are not lies because nothing is *said*, no judgment is expressed, no statement is made by the usual symbols of communication. Actions are done, it is true, but if the enemy takes a meaning out of them he does so at his own peril. The intent to deceive may be justified on the grounds that one is defending one's own rights and merely permitting the enemy to harm himself. Some even classify the presentation of forged passports and other documents to elude an unjust government as deceptions but not lies, because circumstances show that they are not communications but only an external compliance with demands the officials have no right to make.

Hugo Grotius* correctly distinguishes between lies and stratagems, but his application is poor; he classes among stratagems some actions that really are lies: to tell a falsehood in order to do someone a service, to use

---

*Grotius, *Rights of War and Peace,* bk. III, ch. 1.

false intelligence to encourage troops, and his approbation of Plato's "noble lie"* told for the public welfare. These are not stratagems, actions capable of a deceptive interpretation, but speech contrary to one's mind; in a word, lies. A free hand cannot be given to the worst form of lying yet invented, modern nationalistic mass propaganda.

WRONGNESS OF LYING

We have shaved down a lie to the minimum because people use speech loosely and give it other social functions besides that of communicating thought. There remains an irreducible residue: speech meant and taken in all seriousness as communication from mind to mind. The hearer trusts the speaker and has a right to be told the truth if he is told anything. Hence lying in the sense defined and explained, which we have called a *strict* or *formal* lie, is intrinsically wrong and forbidden by the natural law. St. Thomas' argument is a model of succinctness:

> As words are naturally signs of intellectual acts, it is unnatural and undue for anyone to signify by words something that is not in his mind. Hence the Philosopher† says that lying is in itself evil and to be shunned, while truthfulness is good and worthy of praise. Therefore every lie is a sin, as also Augustine‡ declares.§

The first of the following arguments is an expansion of St. Thomas' and the second an addition to it.

1. *Argument from the frustration of a natural ability.* Speech is an ability given to man by nature, and hence by the Author of nature, to communicate thought. This is its essential and primary end, without which speech would not be speech. But to use speech to lie, to communicate as thought what is not thought, to say what one knows to be untrue, is to abuse the ability of speech by destroying its essential and primary end, to use it contrary to the evident intention of nature's Author in giving it to man, and thus is a violation of the natural law.

2. *Argument from the social nature of man.* Human society is built on mutual trust and faith among men. It requires constant communication between men, and all these means of communication are comprised in the term *speech* as explained before. But if lying were morally allowed, we could never tell when a person is lying and when he is not, whether his next statement will be a lie or the truth; we could not even accept his assurance that the statement he is now making is the truth. His speech would cease to have any meaning for us, and, if this practice became widespread, there would be an end to human communication and thus to human society.

---

*Plato, *Republic*, bk. III, §389-414.
†Aristotle, *Nicomachean Ethics*, bk. IV, ch. 7, 1127a 28.
‡St. Augustine, *Contra Mendacium* (Against Lying), ch. 1.
§St. Thomas, *Summa Theologica*, II-II, q. 110, a. 3.

Questions on the arguments

Note that in all the following questions the term *lie* means a strict formal lie, as previously described.

1. *We use other abilities for purposes not intended by nature without considering this an abuse, as when an acrobat walks on his hands.* Abilities may have many secondary purposes for which it is quite lawful to use them, provided their fitness for their essential and primary purpose is not thereby destroyed. Thus we use speech for entertainment and there is nothing wrong with fiction recognized as such. But lying is no mere use of speech for a secondary purpose leaving the primary purpose intact, but a destruction of its primary purpose; this is an abuse and a frustration of nature's gift of speech.

2. *Can it not sometimes happen that the good of society is promoted more by a lie than by the truth, for instance, to save an innocent man's life or to avert war?* The trouble with this argument is that it can be extended to include murder or any other crime if done for similar reasons. Not the size of the evil but the kind is what counts. Moral evil may not be done to avert even the greatest of physical evils. To imagine that God cannot overcome such evils without our lies argues too high an idea of our own importance and too low an idea of divine providence.

3. *Could not a man be allowed to lie only in extreme difficulty?* Then speech is of value only in matters of small moment and loses all force when it is really needed. If we know from other sources that the man is in extreme difficulty, we also know that we cannot trust his words. Yet we often put a person in such a situation; we hale him into court precisely to make him tell a truth to which we have a right. If we do not know whether he is in extreme difficulty or not, we could find out from his own declaration made at a time when by supposition his words are worthless. But if we cannot trust a man in important matters, why should we trust him in anything?

4. *If we may repel force by force, may we not repel a lie by a lie?* There is no parallel between these cases. Physical force is not wrong in itself, but is one of man's natural powers and has its legitimate use. Unjust aggression is the use of force without any right to do so, and in this lack of right its evil consists. The attacker unjustly resorted to force and is repelled by a legitimate use of force; to repel the attack by a wrong use of force, violating the conditions of a blameless self-defense, would also be wrong. As there is a right and wrong use of force, there is a right and wrong use of speech. A lie is a wrong use of speech and is properly repelled by the right use of speech, which is telling the truth. To repel a lie by telling another lie is simply returning evil for evil.

5. *If self-defense allows us to go so far as to kill an attacker, why may we not save ourselves at much less cost by a lie?* This objection is merely an appeal to utility and fails to consider that there are acts intrinsically wrong. One may summon all one's powers and abilities to aid in defense against an unjust attack, but one must use these powers legitimately, not abuse them. Lying does not cease to be an abuse of the faculty of speech merely because it occurs under circumstances of threatened violence. One might as well say that a person may save his life by committing adultery, the abuse of a different faculty. We are not allowed to accomplish a good end by the use of intrinsically evil means.

SECRETS

The natural law obliges us always to tell the *truth* but does not oblige us always to *tell* the truth. If we speak, what we say must be true; but there are times when we may and times when we must refuse to speak.

We must reveal the truth when the other party has a right to it or when it is necessary for the fulfillment of some other urgent duty. When a lawful superior or a judge in court questions us on matters within the limits of his jurisdiction, he has a right to the truth and we must tell it. One with whom we enter into a contract has a right to know all the conditions of the contract, and we are not allowed to keep back any secret clauses from him.

We must not reveal the truth when it is a strict secret. A secret is knowledge which the possessor has the right or the duty to conceal; the natural law either permits or commands him to conceal it. For want of a better term we shall call a truth that one has a *duty* to conceal a *strict* secret. A person may be obliged to keep a secret because:

(1) The knowledge of its very nature is private
(2) He has promised not to reveal it

The first is called a *natural* secret, because the matter it deals with is private in nature. What belongs to a person's private life, to the closed circle of the family, to the status of business firms and corporations, to military and diplomatic affairs of governments, cannot be aired in public without injury to the parties concerned. Those who share in such matters are bound to keep them secret. Others who happen to find out about them are also bound in charity to keep them secret, but not to the jeopardy of their own rightful interests.

The second comprises secrets of *promise* and secrets of *trust*. If one promises not to divulge some information he has, he is bound to keep his promise, and this is called a secret of promise. Often knowledge is confided to another under the condition, expressed or implied, that the matter is confidential and not to be revealed, and this is called a secret of trust or an entrusted secret. Every secret of trust is also a secret of promise in the sense that a promise of secrecy is involved, but not conversely, for one may have accidentally found out a truth not intended for him and then promised not to make it known; in this case it is only a secret of promise. Both secrets of promise and of trust may also be natural secrets or not, depending on the nature of the matter. Professional secrets are typical examples of secrets of trust, and are usually natural secrets also. A secret of trust is the strictest kind of secret and binds in justice, because it is based on a contract expressed or implied. To have a secret of trust the matter must not already be public knowledge, must not have been made known to a third party without obligation of concealment, and must be something whose revelation would cause harm.

Why we must keep secrets

That the natural law at times *permits* the concealment of the truth should be evident from the nature of man. Besides being a member of society, a man is also an individual. He has not only social and public relations, but also private and personal affairs of his own. The natural law gives man a right to his own personal dignity and independence, to freedom from meddling and prying into his private affairs. To preserve this right the concealment of the truth is often necessary.

But more than this, the natural law at times *commands* the concealment of the truth. One of the purposes of speech and of human society itself is that man can get help from his fellow man, that he can get advice from his friends and consult experts without danger of making private affairs public, that when he organizes with other men for the pursuit of a common goal they can exchange information with one another without fear of betrayal to a hostile group. One of the main purposes of speech would be lost unless we can also control how far the knowledge we communicate will spread. For this purpose the concealment of the truth is sometimes necessary.

Extent of this duty

How far does the duty of keeping a secret extend? This is a question of a conflict of rights, when the right of one party to have a certain matter kept secret conflicts with the difficulties the other party experiences in trying to keep it secret. In general, one is no longer bound to secrecy:

(1) If the matter has otherwise been divulged
(2) If the other party's consent can rightly be supposed

The first of these conditions is self-evident, but the second needs some explanation. One may be expressly released from the obligation of secrecy and then is no longer bound. Even if this release is not expressly given, conditions may be such that it can reasonably be presumed, for no one has the right to expect a man to keep a rather ordinary secret at the expense of his life. The laws on excuses from duty, as previously explained, apply to natural secrets and secrets of promise; one is no longer held to keep the secret when doing so would cause grave hardship. However, one who has expressly promised to keep the secret even under grave hardship must keep his promise, unless it were morally wrong for him to have made such a promise. Graver reasons are required to release one from a secret of trust. But even this, strict as it is, may cease to bind if the holding of the secret would cause serious damage, not merely hardship, to the community at large, or to the holder of the secret, or to the giver of the secret, or to an innocent third party threatened by the giver of the secret.

Sometimes, however, the revealing of a secret would cause such damage to the community that it must be guarded at the expense of one's life. Military secrets are often of this type. The secret of the confessional is perhaps the only absolute secret, for the priest binds himself never to divulge it for any reason whatever, no matter how dire the consequences for himself or others; the very use of confession is predicated on absolute protection against discovery.

MENTAL RESERVATION

What means can one use to keep a secret when directly questioned about it? One means is to refuse to answer, to keep silence. This is the best thing to do if feasible, but it is not always effective in guarding the secret, for silence is often interpreted as consent. Evasion that distracts the questioner without giving him the information he wants is another method, but it requires more ready wit than some people can command. Sometimes the only feasible method is mental reservation.

Mental reservation is limiting the obvious sense of words to some particular meaning intended by the speaker. It is important to distinguish between a *strict* and a *broad* mental reservation.

A *strict* mental reservation, one in which the reservation is kept *strictly* in the mind, gives no outward clue to the limited meaning intended by the speaker, or even to the fact that he is limiting the meaning. You ask a person, "Did you eat?" and he answers, "No," meaning "no *meat*," but he ate other things. You ask, "Did you take my book?" and he answers, "No," meaning "not yesterday," but he took it today and has it now. In these cases the reservation is purely mental and in no wise communicated to the listener. The questions by all the conventions of language mean, "Did you eat anything?" "Are you responsible for the loss of my book?" A strict mental reservation is the same as a lie.

A *broad* mental reservation, one in which the reservation is only *partly* mental or mental in a *broad* sense, gives some outward clue to the limited meaning intended by the speaker, even though it may not be noticed or taken up by the listener. The clue may be nothing else but the circumstances in which the words are said. A doctor is asked whether his patient has a certain disease and answers, "I don't know," meaning, "I don't know, secrets apart and in my nonprofessional capacity." He may even answer, "No," meaning, "No, not insofar as I can tell you." The very fact of his profession is sufficient clue to his meaning, and the questioner ought to know that the doctor cannot speak in his professional capacity.

Equivocation, or the use of double meaning expressions, is a form of mental reservation. If both meanings are legitimate, even though one meaning may be more obvious than the other, it comes under the heading of broad mental reservation. In this type of equivocation the speaker says what is true, though his words are also capable of another meaning which is false; if the incautious hearer takes the wrong meaning, he is deceiving himself. Thus a person may speak of his child without saying whether it is his child by birth or adoption; if the hearer unhesitatingly takes it for a child by birth, that is his fault for making a hasty judgment. If, however, the meaning intended by the speaker is so recondite that it could not possibly be found out by the hearer, the equivocation would be equivalent to a strict mental reservation and a lie.

A broad mental reservation is not a lie. There is no discord between one's thought and one's speech because sufficient clue is given to the restricted meaning of one's words. Speech does not consist in words alone, but also in the speaker's manner and in the circumstances. In a broad mental reservation these sufficiently indicate the speaker's thought. It is true that the listener may not notice the clue given him, but it is objectively present. There is no obligation to point it out clearly, especially when the listener has no right to know.

May then a person use a broad mental reservation at any time and for any reason? A broad mental reservation is not a lie and is not intrinsically wrong; in itself it is a legitimate use of speech. But an act can become wrong by its motive or its circumstances. An unrestricted use of broad mental reservation would have ruinous social effects and would break down mutual trust among men. It is not the normal mode of speech, and we cannot be constantly combing over every sentence uttered to us to find possible hidden meanings. We expect our neighbor to speak to us with candor and sincerity, and take his words in their obvious sense in the ordinary transactions of life. The broad mental reservation is to be used only as a refuge to guard a secret from prying questioners who have no right to the information they seek. With this motive and in these circumstances a broad mental reservation is morally allowable, not otherwise.

CONCLUSION

By nature man is a social being, and the gift of speech is perhaps the chief means by which man's social life is carried on. Like all other gifts, speech may be used or abused, may be directed by man to the end for which it evidently exists or may be diverted from that end and frustrated of its natural purpose. This is why truthfulness is good and lying is wrong.

But speech can be abused in two ways: by saying what one knows to be untrue, and by revealing truths one has no right to reveal. One is never allowed to do the former, since here the abuse of speech is direct and therefore intrinsically wrong. One would have no difficulty about the latter were it not for other people's prying minds and impertinent questions; against these a man has a right to protect himself, a right which often becomes a duty when other people are involved. One in such a difficult situation is allowed, sometimes obliged, to summon all his ingenuity to extricate himself from the difficulty and to guard the trust others have placed in him. This and no other reason is why a broad mental reservation is lawful. To use it too readily and apart from such situations is a breach of sincerity and a destruction of mutual trust among men.

SUMMARY

A lie is *speech contrary to one's mind*. This definition indicates the kind of speech forbidden by the natural law. Speech is any sign used to communicate thought, including language, gestures, tones of voice, even circumstances. To lie a speaker must intend to express to another person as his true judgment a judgment that he knows is untrue. Deception is the normal motive for lying, but not all deceptions are lies. Fiction, jokes, figures of speech, and expressions of politeness are not lies, since speech must be interpreted according to convention.

Lying is *forbidden by the natural law*, because it is an abuse of a natural ability, destroying its essential and primary end, and because it is contrary to man's social nature, which requires mutual trust among men.

Lying is not mere use of speech for a secondary end, leaving the primary end intact. It may promote a particular good, but by evil means and at the expense of a greater good, mutual trust. There is no way of restricting lying to make it allowable in extreme cases only. There is no parallel between killing in self-defense and lying in self-defense, for one is a right use of force, the other a wrong use of speech.

A *secret* is knowledge the possessor has a right or a duty to conceal. A *natural* secret deals with matter private in nature, a secret of *promise* with matter one has promised to conceal after finding it out, and a secret of *trust* with matter confided after exacting a promise of secrecy.

The natural law at times *permits*, at times *commands* concealment of the truth. Man has a right to personal dignity and freedom from meddlers. He must be able to seek advice and consult experts without making private affairs public or being betrayed to his enemies.

We are excused from secrecy if the matter has otherwise been divulged, or with the other party's expressed or presumed consent. Even a secret of trust ceases to bind if serious damage would result from keeping it.

Mental reservation is limiting the obvious sense of words to some particular meaning intended by the speaker. A *strict* mental reservation gives no outward clue and is a lie. A *broad* mental reservation gives an outward clue and is not a lie, because the true meaning is expressed though the hearer fail to take it. The speaker allows the hearer to deceive himself. Broad mental reservation may not be used indiscriminately, but for a proportionately good reason, the guarding of a secret.

READINGS

1. Despite the fact that he allowed the "noble lie" in the *Republic*, II, §382, III, §414, Plato really has not much use for lying. Read the *Republic*, II, §381-383; V, §484-490.

2. Aristotle, *Nicomachean Ethics,* bk. IV, ch. 7, 1127a 13.

3. St. Augustine, *De Mendacio* (On Lying) and *Contra Mendacium* (Against Lying); both are translated in *Fathers of the Church, St. Augustine, Treatises on Various Subjects,* edited by Roy Deferrari. St. Augustine is treating a special aspect of the subject and later expressed his dissatisfaction with his work.

4. St. Thomas, *Summa Theologica,* II-II, qq. 109, 110. In the following three questions he continues with a discussion of hypocrisy, boasting, and irony, subjects kindred to truthfulness and lying. None of this is in the *Basic Writings;* see also II-II, q. 69, aa. 1, 2.

5. Grotius, *The Rights of War and Peace,* bk. III, ch. I.

6. Cronin, *The Science of Ethics,* vol. II, pp. 69-79.

7. Rickaby, *Moral Philosophy,* pp. 224-237.

8. Newman, *Apologia pro Vita Sua,* Note G.

9. Leibell, *Readings in Ethics,* pp. 528-564.

10. Regan, *Professional Secrecy in the Light of Moral Principles.* A thorough treatment of the whole subject.

11. Connell, *Morals in Politics and Professions,* ch. VIII. This book, written from the standpoint of moral theology rather than of pure ethics, has much useful material.

CHAPTER 22

JUSTICE AND LOVE

PROBLEM

Communication between men is an evidence of man's social nature. Communication extends beyond an exchange of information and ideas, the proper sphere of truthfulness, to an exchange of goods and services, a mutual helpfulness in activity, which is the twofold province of justice and love of fellow man. When this mutual aid is organized into cooperative work for a common goal, we have *society,* a complex form of human behavior to be considered later. But even apart from organized society men are constantly crossing each other's paths and must deal one with another on a personal basis. Such dealings are social only in the very broad sense that they involve more than one individual, not in the strict sense that they seek some common good precisely as common. We shall discuss some of these dealings here, grouping them under the following questions:

(1) Why should there be justice?
(2) How do contracts secure justice?
(3) When is a contract binding and when void?
(4) Is justice enough or must we love our fellow men?
(5) How far must we aid those in distress?
(6) How can we avoid contributing to others' moral harm?

JUSTICE IN HUMAN ACTS

We have seen that justice is one of the chief virtues and that it regulates man's will, so that he wills for himself what belongs to himself and wills for others what belongs to them. Besides being a virtue, a habit of giving to each his due, justice is predicated of single acts. Our stress here is on the act, how it comes to be a just act.

Why should there be justice among men? The notion is so primitive that it hardly needs proof. It is not innate but arises very early in our experience. Children and savages can tell fair from foul play. Even if they cannot define or explain justice, they know when they have been cheated. But reflective knowledge must go beyond inarticulate feelings and attempt a philosophical justification of justice.

Justice is derived from *equality*. Though accidentally unequal, all men are essentially equal. We all have the same human nature, the same last end, the same kind of means to reach that end. We all live under the same norm of morality and the same moral law. For its proper implementation, the natural law confers on us natural rights, which are the same for all. Though we cannot deprive anyone of his last end nor of the means absolutely necessary to it, we can interfere with another's ready and easy use of these means—we can violate his rights. To live as befits a man, one needs not only life, but food, clothing, shelter, liberty, education, property, recreation, companionship, and all that goes to make life tolerable as well as possible. To interfere with a man's use of these in such a way as to make his life a hardship and a burden, especially when we refuse to take the same ourselves, is to destroy his fundamental equality with us, to invade his rights, to be unjust.

Natural law and natural rights are thus the source from which justice flows. To protect himself in these rights man has instituted positive law, the paramount expression of which is the civil law. The civil law either expressly declares what the natural law already implicitly contains or determines more definitely what the natural law leaves vague. The primary aim of the state and of civil law is to secure for its citizens the greatest benefits that can be derived from communal living and to distribute these benefits justly.

There are many transactions that are too personal in scope to be determined by the civil law. In these matters, where neither the natural nor the positive law determines anything, the parties concerned determine what they shall do by free agreement. Such mutual agreements which concern the transfer of a right are called *contracts*. In a typical contract two men agree to exchange goods, services, or whatever can be transferred. As far as this transaction is concerned, they start equal; then one carries out his side of the bargain and upsets the original equality, whereupon the other is now obliged to do his part and restore the equality. Until the second party does his part, he is said to *owe* it, and it is said to be *due* the first party. What obliges each to do his part in view of the other's doing his part is commutative justice.

Thus we see three main sources of human rights, the preservation of which is justice and the violation injustice. To violate a *natural right* is to take from another man something that God has given him, an act of injustice against both God and man. To violate a *civil right* is to take from another man something the state owes him in distributive justice, and our interference with the state's duty to him is a crime against social justice. To violate a *contractual right* (if we may use the term, for a contract does not originate rights but transfers them) is not only a breaking of one's plighted word but a violation of commutative justice. No one is obliged to make a contract, but if he makes it he is bound in commutative justice to keep it. Both natural and civil law protect the sanctity of contracts, each in its own sphere. The civil law can enforce only those contracts that fall within its jurisdiction, but the natural law is the guardian of all justice.

The wide scope of justice makes it impossible to gather all its ramifications under one heading. Respect for our fellow man's life and person is due him in justice. Nearly all we shall have to say on property involves justice. Society is instituted to protect and promote justice, and so justice enters into the family and is the main purpose of the state. Violations of law both natural and civil call for punitive justice. Wars are fought to obtain peace with justice. So justice pervades our whole study. Before entering the field of social ethics, we must take a general view of that instrument of justice in individual transactions, the *contract*.

NATURE OF A CONTRACT

Many moralists define a contract as a *mutual agreement concerning the transfer of a right.* The commonly accepted legal definition is that of Blackstone: "An agreement upon sufficient consideration to do or not to do a particular thing."* These definitions are not opposed but help to explain one another.

1. A contract is an *agreement,* for there must be consent of at least two wills to the same object; an offer which is made but not accepted cannot be a contract, for only one party consents.

2. It is a *mutual* agreement, for the consent on one side must be given in view of the consent on the other side; two people who accidentally happened to will the same thing without doing so in view of each other's consent would not form a contract.

3. The parties transfer a *right* and therefore bind themselves in *commutative justice;* pacts, promises, and engagements based on truthfulness, loyalty, or charity can impose serious obligations but are not strictly contracts. The transfer of a right produces a corresponding obligation of doing or omitting something.

4. By natural law a valuable *consideration* or recompense is not necessary in all contracts, and so there can be gratuitous contracts such as gift or promise. But even here some intangible consideration in the form of affection, gratitude, or good will is normally to be expected.

5. The obligation in justice may be on both sides or only on one side, and so contracts may be bilateral or unilateral, onerous or gratuitous, but the *consent* must always be on both sides.

That there is a moral obligation to keep contracts hardly needs proof. One who makes a contract transfers a right to another. Then by breaking

---

*Blackstone, *Commentaries,* bk. II, ch. XXX, p. 442.

the contract he violates the right of another, the very right he has just transferred, and so acts unjustly.

To be binding a contract must be valid, and to be morally allowable it should also be licit. Any alleged contract may be valid or licit, or both or neither. A *valid* contract is one that really is a contract, one that holds good and binds the parties to it. An *invalid* contract is null and void and therefore not a contract, though it may look like one. A *licit* contract is one that was rightfully entered into, one that the contracting parties were allowed to make. An *illicit* contract is one that is forbidden by natural or positive law. Thus buying an article from its owner with my own money is valid and licit; buying extravagant articles with hardship to my dependents is valid but morally illicit; buying stolen articles without knowing that they are stolen is invalid but licit; buying an article that I know to be stolen is invalid and illicit. In the example given the buyer of extravagant articles must pay for them if he cannot return them, and so the contract is valid, but he did wrong in making the contract, and so it is illicit. Because it is always illicit to attempt a contract one knows to be invalid, it is only through invincible ignorance that a contract can be invalid but licit.

VALIDITY OF CONTRACTS

In every contract we can distinguish the contracting parties, the matter of the contract, and the mutual consent. These contribute the three main conditions for a valid contract:

(1) The contracting parties must be competent persons.
(2) The matter must be suitable for a contract.
(3) The consent must be mutual, free, and in proper form.

Contracting parties

That the contracting parties must be competent persons means that they must be able to understand the terms of the contract so that they can give voluntary consent to them. Because the making of a contract is a human act, one incapable of a human act is incapable of making a contract. The parties must have sufficient use of reason at least when agreeing to the contract. By natural law infants and the insane are excluded; also intoxicated, drugged, and hypnotized persons while in that condition.

Positive law, its purpose being to promote the common good, has from the natural law the authority to regulate contracts within the sphere of its jurisdiction. This authority it often exercises by decreeing that certain classes of persons are incompetent subjects with regard to certain contracts, or by setting down conditions for their competence, thus invalidating contracts they may attempt to make to their own, their neighbor's, or the state's harm. In this way the civil law can restrict the contracting power of minors, wives, and aliens.

Matter of a contract

In a contract the matter is that which the contracting parties agree to do or not to do. A contract can concern goods, services, actions, or omissions. For a contract to be valid the matter must be something *possible* under the terms specified and not unduly difficult, something *definite* so that both parties know what they are agreeing to, something morally *permissible* and not contravening prior obligations; if the matter is a physical object, it must be *existing* either in fact or in prospect, and must *belong to* the contracting party so that he has the right to dispose of it. These conditions merely express the fact that a contract involves the transfer of a right and the assumption of an obligation. One must have a right in order to transfer it and must be capable of an obligation before assuming it.

A contract to do evil is invalid, that is, null and void, for a contract imposes obligation and an obligation to do evil is canceled by a prior obligation not to do it. One who has agreed to do evil is not allowed to carry out the supposed contract. He did wrong to begin with in entering into such an engagement and would do further wrong by attempting to fulfill it. If he has been paid in advance, he must return the price, which he cannot claim by any title. The whole is a bad bargain and both must withdraw from it.

What if the evil is already done? Opinion is divided on whether the other party is obliged to fulfill his part of the agreement. The first opinion says that, if the conditions for a valid contract are not met, the whole transaction is void; both agents ought to have known that neither is bound to anything. The second opinion makes a distinction, arguing that the promise to do evil was indeed invalid, but the act by which it was carried out was a real expenditure of physical effort or mental ingenuity worth a price; that here was a valid subsidiary contract attached to the main invalid contract. Each of the parties may follow the probable opinion that is to his advantage, the one demanding and the other refusing payment. The doer of the evil deed may certainly ask for and accept the price, for even if he has no right to it by contract he may always ask for and take a gift.

Bribery is the offering of money for evildoing, especially for the shirking of duty. If the money is offered or promised on condition that one do the evil act and this condition is accepted, there is an attempt to make a contract about illegitimate matter, and the principles stated above apply: the evil act must be avoided and the money returned; or, if the act has been done, the money either must be returned or may be kept, according as one adopts the first or the second opinion. But if the money is offered merely to persuade or allure someone to do wrong, there is no contract because there is no promise in return. Though it is understood why the money is given, the absence of mutual agreement makes it no more than a gift; if we regard only the purely contractual aspect of commutative justice, one could take the money and still refuse to do the evil act. But morality is not limited to strict justice. No self-respecting person will soil his hands with a bribe, and public officials particularly must not jeopardize their freedom to act impartially for the common good.

Mutual consent

That which gives the contract its essence is the mutual consent of the parties. Consent implies offer and acceptance. The offer may be on one side and the acceptance on the other, or there may be both offer and acceptance on each side.

The *offer* remains open as long as the offerer wishes. It may cease by withdrawal on the part of the offerer, by refusal on the part of the one to whom it was offered, or by lapse of time. *Acceptance* may not be revoked, for it seals the contract. Conditions may be attached to the offer or to the acceptance, but these conditions must be made known to and accepted by both parties. Regulation of contracts is a typical matter for positive law and custom. In the absence of an agreement to the contrary the prevailing conventions should be followed.

Mutual consent must be an external manifestation of a free internal act of the will. It must be externally manifested, because a contract is between two persons and supposes communication between them. It must be internally given by a free act, because a contract is a *human act,* requiring an act of the will consequent on knowledge. Freedom of consent may be nullified by error or by fear.

Error voids a contract only insofar as it excludes consent. Any *substantial* error, whether involving deceit or not, invalidates the contract, for then the person consents to something quite different from the actual matter proposed, as when a person buys what he thinks is a live horse and gets a hobby-horse. Errors about slight and unimportant qualities do not affect the contract, as when a person finds that the horse he bought is of a slightly different color from what he thought it was. However, if such qualities were expressly stipulated so that the contract would not have been made except for them, the contract is invalid if the stipulations are not adhered to. Hence what is substantial to a contract may be determined not only by the nature of the contract itself and of the matter concerned, but also by the will of the contracting parties when they make a certain condition essential to the contract.

Fear voids a contract only if it destroys the use of reason, making voluntary consent impossible. This would be the strongly emotional, not the intellectual type of fear. Since even grave fear does not normally destroy voluntariness, the general rule is that contracts made from the motive of fear are valid, as far as the natural law goes. Fear may be artificially aroused in a person by the use of threats to extort his consent. Such unjust intimidation, though it leaves the contract valid, makes it voidable, that is, capable of being canceled without the intimidator's consent. It is valid because it is a human act but voidable because it is the result of injury which the intimidator is bound to repair. Also positive law, for the sake of the common good, can go beyond the natural law and render invalid from the beginning contracts extorted under intimidation and duress. Whether it does so and under what conditions the positive law itself would have to declare.

This completes our discussion of contracts in general. Various forms of contract, such as marriage contracts, employment contracts, commercial and property contracts, international treaties, and the so-called social contract, will be discussed each in its place. They differ greatly because of the different kind of matter they are concerned with. But all contracts have this in common—that they all deal with the transfer of rights and the consequent assumption of duties, to the observance of which each party binds himself in justice. Implicit understandings may be sufficient among friends, but the public solemnity of the formal contract acts as a guarantee to each party concerned that the other party will respect the right transferred, fulfill the duty assumed, and thus maintain justice.

LOVE AND HATE

Justice prescribes only the minimum obligations men have toward each other. But human relations should not be limited to bare fundamentals, to giving our neighbor no more than he can demand in strict justice as his right. The virtue that goes beyond justice and looks at the neighbor as a person to be respected, helped, and loved is traditionally known as *charity*. The word has suffered by the attrition of language. It is still the theological term for man's love of God and man's love of his fellow man for the love of God, the highest of the supernatural virtues. But outside theological usage and on the natural plane the word *charity* has fallen almost as low as *philanthropy* and means little more than relief of the needy. This is indeed a noble work and included in our present concept, but too narrow and slight in its emphasis.

We are looking for the counterpart of supernatural charity on the natural plane. It is hard to agree on a word for it. Some modern writers use *benevolence* and its native English translation, *good will,* which are rather weak; others prefer *love* or *friendship,* which are too emotional and selective. The idea we want includes these plus kindness, fellowship, brotherhood, neighborliness, humaneness, sympathy, helpfulness, thoughtfulness, unselfishness, but has a more universal range than any of them. We shall use whatever word seems best to fit the context, but especially the expression *love of the neighbor* or *love of fellow man.* It is truly love in its highest form, not indeed of that intensely personal and emotional sort that binds lovers into one heart, but of the wide, all-embracing type that takes in the whole of humanity as our brothers.

Justice and love of the neighbor are often contrasted, yet they spring from the same root. Justice is love limited to the absolute requirements of basic human equality; love is justice expanded to the fullest scope of the human person's dignity. Justice is minimizing and negative in emphasis:

do not take or keep from another what is rightfully his. Love is maximizing and positive: go as far as you can in giving to another what will help him. Love of the neighbor imposes duties that can be quite as serious and important as those in justice, though of a different nature. Since rights and duties are correlative, each one has a claim to his neighbor's good will, but it is a right of the noncoercive or nonjuridical type. Violations of it are moral wrongs or sins but not civil wrongs or crimes. They do not entail injury in the technical sense and do not demand restitution or punishment in this life.

We are obliged to love our neighbor as ourselves. The phrase "as ourselves" refers not so much to the degree as to the kind of love we owe our neighbor. The reason why we must love our fellow man is that he is a *fellow* man, created and loved by the same God who created and loves us, destined to enjoy in common with us the possession of the same Highest Good. Our fellow man's right to all this is equal to ours. As we wish ourselves all good and no evil, we must wish the same to him.

The vice directly opposed to love of the neighbor is *hatred*. It is not a passing fit of anger, however strong, nor is it mere dislike for a person. Some people naturally grate on us and we cannot help feeling repelled by them; this feeling is involuntary and we are not responsible for it. There is nothing wrong in avoiding such persons so long as we do not make them feel they are being despised. Hatred means that with deliberate malice we injure others or wish them harm or rejoice in an evil that befalls them. No proof is needed to show how wrong hatred is, for it goes directly counter to our social nature.

How for does the love of our neighbor go? Is hatred so evil that we must not hate even our enemies? The natural law does not rise to the heroic height of bidding us to love our enemies in the sense of doing them positive acts of kindness, but it does forbid us to hate them. The mere fact that another has done us evil does not give us license to do or wish evil to him, for then we should become as evil as he. Hence the perpetual refusal of forgiveness is wrong. The emotional difficulties to be overcome in the process of forgiveness may seem insuperable, but there is not a question here of emotion but of will. Hatred is one of the passions, but its ethical aspect consists in the doing or wishing of evil to others. As a human act it requires the voluntary consent of the will, and, whether we can master the emotion or not, hatred is the kind of thing we are not allowed to will.

If one who has injured us has committed a civil crime, we have the right in social justice to turn him over to the public authorities for punishment, and we may even have the duty to do so if otherwise he would continue his career of crime against the common good. The securing of justice is quite a different thing from personal hatred and the wreaking of private vengeance. We also have the right, but not the duty, to demand satisfaction to ourselves, for this is due us in justice, but we have not the right forever to refuse forgiveness, which is due him in simple humanity.

When actual enmity has occurred, reconciliation is in order. The one who has done the injury is bound to make the first steps toward reconcilation, and the offended party is obliged to accept such offers if they seem genuine and sincere. If, as so often happens, each accuses the other and excuses himself, neither may reject in advance the good offices of a mediator. Former friends who have been reconciled after a serious quarrel are not obliged to resume their previous intimacy, which might only renew the quarrel, but are required to show each other at least the common courtesies of life.

AID IN DISTRESS

We are morally obliged to come to the aid of a fellow man in distress. How strong this duty is depends on three factors:

(1) How great is his need
(2) How much trouble it will cost us
(3) How useful our help will be

Since we must love our neighbor as ourselves but not more than ourselves, we are never obliged, though we are allowed, in incur a hardship equivalent to the one from which we are trying to free him. To sacrifice ourselves for others is heroic and most admirable, but it can hardly be imposed as a duty, since we ourselves have rights and the other person also has a duty to us. And it would be unreasonable to be obliged to make futile gestures to those who are beyond our aid.

To refuse help to a man in extreme need even at serious hardship to ourselves is inhuman and inexcusable. If he is not in extreme but in really grave need, the obligation diminishes in proportion but is still serious. The less the need the less the obligation, but it does not disappear if we can help without undue difficulty. But to relieve the common hardships of humanity in general, since they are a part of life and too numerous for the resources of any one man, cannot be an obligation for private persons in ordinary circumstances. Those in charge of the public good must devise measures for relieving them; this is a duty in justice, but it should go beyond the demands of bare justice.

The rich have a duty to assist the poor. This obligation rests on the wealthy as a class rather than on any individual rich man, unless he be the only one in the community who could meet the situation. The relief of the poor can be done in various ways. If the government handles all of it efficiently and sufficiently, something that has probably never occurred in history, the rich would be doing their duty by paying their taxes. If the government does none of it, as was mostly the case in former ages, the wealthy are morally obliged to do it on their own initiative, and neither indifference nor laziness nor cupidity can excuse them. If it is done by private agencies with civic backing but relying chiefly on voluntary contributions, the rich man is obliged to contribute in proportion to his affluence. There may be a combination of all these means, but, whatever they are, the relief of the needy is no mere recommendation, but a strict obligation of the natural law. These remarks concern the duties of individuals. Later we shall discuss the duty of society to remedy unjust economic conditions.

The assistance we can give our neighbor is of various kinds, running all the way from saying an encouraging word to saving his life, but the greatest favor we can do him is to help him fulfill his moral function and reach his last end. He may express more gratitude for temporal gifts, but nothing can be of more genuine benefit to him than assistance in attaining the Highest Good. There are many ways in which we can give him active spiritual help, but one always at our command, no matter what our resources or station in life may be, is the example of our own good moral lives.

Directly opposed to helping our neighbor to a moral life is the doing of those actions that positively contribute to his moral downfall. These may be gathered under the headings of occasion for and cooperation with evil.

OCCASION OF EVIL

In modern usage the word *scandal* has lost most of its force. Originally it meant a stumbling block; applied to morals, it meant something we may stumble on and fall over on our way to our last end. Someone may kick it in our way with deliberate purpose of tripping us, or with the excuse that it is in his way and he cannot get by without knocking it into our path. In any case it meant some word or deed tending to lead another person into evil, an occasion for or allurement to wrongdoing. Probably because bad example fulfills this function so well, scandal has come to mean a shocked emotional reaction to someone's unseemly conduct and the spread of this feeling through malicious gossip. The word is then applied to the conduct and the gossip that are found to be shocking. To avoid being misunderstood, we shall substitute for the old word *scandal* the expression *occasion of evil*. Such an occasion may be only *given,* or only *taken,* or both *given and taken*. Hence the moral fault may be on either side or on both.

We *give* occasion of evil to another *directly,* if we intend his evil act as an end or as a means. To intend it as an end would signify a truly diabolical hatred. The usual motive for inducing others to evil is to use it as a means to one's own profit, as do those who make their living by providing lewd entertainment.

We *give* occasion of evil to another *indirectly,* if we do not intend the other person's evil act either as end or as means, but foresee it as a consequence of something else we do. Care for our neighbor's moral welfare obliges us to avoid even this as far as possible. But life would be intolerably difficult if we have to avoid all actions in which others might find temptation. Here the principle of double effect applies: the act we do must not be wrong in itself though we foresee it will be a temptation to another, the good effect we intend must not be accomplished by means of the other's evil act, we must not want but only permit the other's temptation, and there must be a proportionate reason for permitting it.

Occasion of evil is *taken but not given* when someone with peculiar subjective dispositions is led to evil by another person's innocent words or deeds. It may be due to the taker's *malice,* and then is wholly his fault. Or it may be due to the taker's *weakness,* to his ignorance, youth, inexperience, prejudices, untamed passions, or unconquered habits. Love of the neighbor requires us to avoid words and actions, otherwise harmless, which might be a source of moral danger to the innocent or the weak. People should be more circumspect in their behavior before children, should not tantalize beyond endurance those who have trouble controlling their tempers, should not offer liquor to inveterate or reformed drunkards, should not discuss publicly conditions of vice that must be discussed privately by those in charge of remedying the abuse. But sometimes such situations cannot be avoided, and it is here that the principle of double effect comes into play. There is no obligation, at serious inconvenience to oneself or to the public, to abolish everything that might entice the weak or innocent, though all reasonable precautions should be taken. It would be absurd to close all theaters, taverns, and amusements that are conducted in a generally respectable fashion simply because some people with abnormal weaknesses find them seductive. When the young, innocent, or prejudiced are unavoidably exposed to temptation, precautionary instruction is usually the best remedy.

COOPERATION IN EVIL

Cooperation in another's evil deed may occur by joining him in the actual performance of the act, or by supplying him with the means for performing it. If two men plan a robbery, one may hold the gun while the other relieves the victim of his valuables, or one may lend the other a gun to enable him to carry out the robbery alone.

There is *formal* cooperation when one not only helps another to do evil but also joins in his evil intention, as in the cases just mentioned. Formal cooperation is always morally wrong and cannot be justified under any circumstances.

There is *material* cooperation when, without approving another's wrongdoing, one helps him perform his evil act by an action of one's own that is not of its nature evil. Thus an employee is forced by robbers to open up the safe, the driver of a car is compelled by gangsters to drive them to the scene of intended murder, an orderly is commanded by his already tipsy officer to bring him more drink.

By definition material cooperation is not something wrong in its nature or in its intention, and becomes wrong only by reason of a circumstance, the circumstance that my otherwise innocent act aids others in their wrongdoing. They use my act as a means to their evil end, but I do not use their evil act as a means to anything. Consequently, if there is a proportionately grave reason for permitting this evil circumstance, material cooperation can be justified by the principle of double effect. Since the act I do is not wrong in itself, and I do not use the other's evil deed as a means to any end, and I have no wrong intention, the only remaining difficulty is that of the proportion. This proportion must be estimated by:

(1) The amount of evil my cooperation helps others to do
(2) The amount of evil that will happen to me if I refuse to cooperate
(3) The closeness of my cooperative act to the other's evil act

The first two points need no further explanation here, since they are determined by the principles on a conflict of rights. Love of the neighbor does not oblige me to suffer an injury greater than or equal to that which I am trying to ward off from him, but it does oblige me to suffer a small loss to prevent a great loss from happening to another, and it may even oblige me to sacrifice my life to prevent a huge public calamity. Here we are supposing that the cooperation is proximate, and this brings us to the third point which needs some further explanation.

Cooperation may be *proximate* or *remote,* depending on how close it comes to the actual evil deed of the principal agent. For example, a man who writes an immoral book does an act evil in itself; publishers who accept and edit such a book are formal cooperators; typesetters, proofreaders, and others who prepare the actual text are proximate material cooperators; those who merely run the presses, bind the books, and prepare them for delivery are remote material cooperators. The heads of bookselling firms that stock such books are formal cooperators, hired clerks who sell them are proximate material cooperators, secretaries who handle the business correspondence concerning them are remote material cooperators. The more proximate the cooperation, the greater the proportionate reason required to make material cooperation allowable.

Two other factors should be noted here. If my cooperation is *indispensable,* so that no one else could be substituted to help in the evil act, I have a greater responsibility because I can actually prevent the act from happening. If my cooperation is not indispensable, the evil will be done anyway and I may suffer serious harm by my refusal. Greater reason is required for indispensable cooperation. Also, greater reason is required to justify cooperation in persons who, because of contract or similar reasons, have an *explicit duty* to prevent that particular kind of evil from happening. This would occur in a soldier forced to cooperate with the enemy, a policeman with criminals, a watchman with burglars, a customs officer with smugglers.

The forms which cooperation can take are too numerous to mention, for it is possible to cooperate with almost any external act, at least by encouragement and support. Hired workers, because they engage their services to a company whose policy they do not determine, are particularly open to the danger of material cooperation. One may not keep a job with a company that continually and habitually does a morally objectionable business. If it does so only occasionally, employees need not be disturbed so long as their material cooperation is kept remote; but if they find that proximate material cooperation is demanded of them fairly frequently, they must have a grave reason for continuing in their job and must meanwhile make an earnest effort to get other work.

SUMMARY

Justice is derived from the fundamental *equality* of all men, based on their common origin, nature, and destiny. To maintain this equality man is endowed by his Creator with natural rights, defines for himself civil rights, and transfers alienable rights by contract. Justice demands respect for all three kinds of rights; interference with any is injustice. Commutative justice guarantees the sanctity of contracts and obliges to their observance.

A *contract* is a mutual agreement by which two or more persons bind themselves to do or omit something. A *valid* contract holds good and really binds, a *licit* contract is one lawfully entered into; a contract can be valid without being licit, and vice versa.

The *contracting parties* must be competent persons, with sufficient use of reason for a human act. Positive law may add further conditions.

The *matter* must be possible, existing, definite, transferable, and lawful. A contract to do evil is invalid and one is forbidden to fulfill it; one who has done so may ask and accept the price, though the other probably need not pay it.

The *mutual consent* means that each freely consents in view of the other's consent. Substantial error voids a contract, but not accidental error, unless it is about something expressly stipulated. Fear that destroys consent voids a contract; positive law may void naturally valid contracts made under duress.

Passing beyond the strict claims of justice, we are required to love our neighbor as ourselves, because he shares our human nature with us. Love is directly opposed to *hatred,* which is doing or wishing harm to another or rejoicing in his misfortune.

The natural law forbids us to hate even our enemies, and requires *forgiveness.* This is not opposed to turning criminals over to the state for punishment, nor to demanding compensation for our injuries. Enemies are bound to seek reconciliation, but need not resume a former intimacy.

We are obliged to *aid others in distress,* depending on the urgency of their need, the trouble to us, and the efficacy of our help. We are not obliged, though allowed, to help another at equal hazard to ourselves. To refuse to help one in extreme or grave need, when we can do it without undue difficulty, is wrong; but we are not obliged to go about relieving every common hardship we see.

An *occasion of evil* is a word or deed leading another to wrongdoing. Occasion is *given* directly if another's evil act is intended as means or as end; indirectly, if it is but a foreseen consequence of something one does. Indirect occasioning of evil is permitted when the principle of double effect is satisfied. Occasion for evil can be *taken* through malice of the taker, and this should be despised, or through his weakness or innocence, and this should be avoided if possible; if not possible, it can be regretfully permitted.

Cooperation is helping another to do wrong by joining him in the act or supplying him with the means. It is *formal* if we intend the evil we help to accomplish; it is only *material* if without intending the evil we help another perform his evil act by an act of our own not of its nature evil. Formal cooperation is always wrong. Material cooperation is allowable when the principle of double effect is satisfied. The proportion is worked out by balancing the evil we cooperate with against the evil we are threatened with if we refuse, and by estimating how close our cooperation comes to the evil. A very strong reason is needed to justify *proximate material* cooperation; lesser reasons suffice for *remote material* cooperation.

READINGS

1. Plato's treatise on justice takes up bk. I and the first part of bk. II of the *Republic*.
2. Aristotle's *Nicomachean Ethics*, bk. V, is all on justice. His much admired treatise on Friendship in books VIII and IX of the *Nicomachean Ethics* is somewhat related to our subject and well worth reading for its keen insight into human nature. St. Thomas's commentary on these two books has been translated and entitled, *St. Thomas Aquinas on Aristotle's Love and Friendship*.
3. Cicero's *De Amicitia* (On Friendship).
4. St. Thomas on justice: *Summa Theologica*, II-II, qq. 58-59, 61-62. He writes of the supernatural virtue of charity, including both the love of God and of the neighbor, in his *Summa Theologica*, II-II, qq. 23-44, not found in the *Basic Writings*. Among these q. 26 is on the order of charity, q. 31 on beneficence, q. 34 on hatred, q. 43 on scandal.
5. Farrell's *Companion to the Summa*, vol. III, ch. III, IV, V, gives his excellent commentary on this part of St. Thomas.
6. Pieper's little book, *Justice*, is well worth reading.
7. Gilson, *Moral Values and Moral Life*, ch. 9. Also *The Christian Philosophy of St. Thomas Aquinas*, pp. 306-332.
8. Messner, *Social Ethics*, pp. 213-220, 231-235.
9. Rommen, *The State in Catholic Thought*, pp. 184-192, 319-326.
10. Doolan, *Order and Law*, ch. 22-31.
11. Haas, *Man and Society*, ch. 3, 5.
12. Le Buffe and Hayes, *American Philosophy of Law*, ch. 13.
13. Cahill, *Framework of the Christian State*, ch. 24-26, has a chapter on each of the three kinds of justice. Goes into particulars not pertaining to this chapter.
14. Cronin, *Science of Ethics*, vol. II, ch. 9.
15. Leibell, *Readings in Ethics*, pp. 221-269, 427-431, 450-457.
16. Connell, *Morals in Politics and Professions*, throughout.
17. Johnston, *Business Ethics*, ch. 5.

CHAPTER 23

SOCIETY

PROBLEM

We start with the easily observed fact that a man is not alone in the world but lives in company with others like himself. Many living beings thrive in groups, clusters, colonies, or herds, in which there may be some degree of cooperation and even a primitive form of leadership. But society is considered to be uniquely human and therefore must consist in something more than mere togetherness, be it of place or of activity. Given the fact that man does live in society, we ask why he does so and what there is about human society that makes it different from other ways of living together. We may formulate our questions as follows:

(1) Why do men live in society?
(2) Is man naturally social?
(3) What is society?
(4) What is the common good?
(5) What are the main kinds of society?
(6) Must there be authority in society?
(7) What is the source of authority?

WHY MEN LIVE IN SOCIETY

At the risk of oversimplification, we can reduce the answers to this question to three main headings:

(1) Man is naturally social and is prompted to form society by the demands and impulses of his rational nature working through his free will.

(2) Man is not naturally social but by free compact formed society

for certain advantages and continues to live in it through habit and training.

(3) Man has evolved from lower animals, and his social nature is but a higher development of the gregarious instincts of his brute ancestors.

1. The first opinion is the traditional one. Throughout ancient and medieval times, except for a flurry of dissent among the Greek Sophists, it was taken for granted that man is a social being by nature. This view is implicit in Plato and expressly formulated by Aristotle in the beginning of his *Politics,* where he declares: "Man is by nature a political animal."*

2. In the seventeenth and eighteenth centuries this view was challenged by Hobbes and Rousseau, who laid the foundations of *moral positivism.* Both envision a primitive condition called the *state of nature,* of man without society. Hobbes, who makes man antisocial, pictures the state of nature as one of constant predatory warfare. Rousseau, who thinks man only extrasocial, describes it as an era of blithe and carefree innocence. According to both, man's gift of intellect enabled him to see the advantages of cooperative action, to frame the social contract, and thus to pass from the state of nature to that of society. Having given up his liberties by the social contract he need never have made, man is now the slave of the monster he has created. Society is not natural to man but only conventional; its undoubted advantages are counterbalanced by its unnatural restrictions. Now it is impossible to return to the state of nature, and man must make the best of the situation. Hobbes counsels complete submission; Rousseau, a fight for a recovery of at least some of our lost liberties. The "back to nature" movement with its hatred for the artificialities and conventionalities of civilization found its inspiration in Rousseau, the great Romanticist.

3. The nineteenth century saw the rise of the evolutionary theory, giving a new turn to the philosophy of *evolutionism.* All atheistic and materialistic philosophies demand some form of evolution, since they cannot otherwise explain how man came to be. The stumbling block had always been the leap from matter to mind, from body to spirit. Darwin's achievement consisted in proposing a scientifically plausible method by which an evolutionary process could be explained wholly within naturalistic terms. If man is continuous with the lower animals, if his mind is but a more highly evolved form of organic life, brought into being by the accidental formation of a protoplasmic blob in the slime of the ancient seas, then no great leap from matter to mind is needed. Why not extend the principle beyond the biological sphere and make it a general philosophical interpretation of the universe? The typical representative of this movement for his age was Herbert Spencer. For him, man's ethical, religious, economic, political, and cultural development is but the most

---

*Aristotle, *Politics,* bk. I, ch. 2, 1253a 2.

recent part of man's evolutionary progress. Such too is the origin of human society. Man is naturally social because he evolved from animal ancestors of the herding type, whose gregariousness adapted them for survival in their environment. This is modern naturalism, which is miles away from anything resembling the natural moral law. Because of its materialistic hypothesis, we hand over this third theory to other branches of philosophy for criticism and concentrate on the other two views.

To summarize: The first answer takes a middle stand between the two others. It agrees with the second in making society somehow dependent on human reason and free will, but disagrees with its theory that society is merely the result of an arbitrary contract. It agrees with the third opinion in making society natural to man but disagrees completely with its view of human nature, that man's highest mental operations are continuous with and differ only in degree from his lowest biological urges. Synthesizing the two opinions, it says that society is natural to man because it springs out of man's rational and free nature.

SOCIETY NATURAL TO MAN

That man is naturally social is brought out by the following characteristics of human nature:

1. Man abhors solitude and craves companionship. Some solitude is good for man, but excessive solitude can go so far as to unhinge reason. Men spontaneously seek others and enjoy their company, whereas loneliness sets up a veritable hunger in the soul.

2. Man cannot take care of himself alone. The child must be reared by its parents for many years. Even in adult life a solitary man cannot supply himself with the bare means of subsistence, not to speak of the goods required for living a decent life befitting a human being.

3. The gift of language fits man to communicate with his fellows, to discuss projects of common interest, to agree on means and ends for cooperative effort. Unless man were to live a social life, the faculty of speech would be given to him for no purpose.

4. Intellectual and moral development require constant communication of ideas among men, an exchange possible only in society. If small isolated communities stagnate because they are out of touch with new ideas, how much more would this condition be true of single individuals?

From these facts we draw our conclusion. Human nature has properties which fit and impel man to live in company with his fellow men and to cooperate with them for common ends. This cooperation is more accurately obtained if men bind themselves thereto, each guaranteeing his help to the rest so that all can depend on it. When men bind themselves together in this fashion, they have formed society. Since they so act by the prompting of nature, society is natural to man.

This argument proves only that society is essential to man in general. It does not prove that every individual must live in society or that a hermit's life is intrinsically wrong. Society can get along without the few who count themselves out, and renounce both its burdens and benefits, so long as they do nothing to impede its functioning. There is something unnatural in a solitary life undertaken out of misanthropy or hatred for the human race. But there is no reason why one may not be a solitary for higher motives, to avoid the temptations of the world, to devote oneself to contemplation, to concentrate on personal spiritual perfection. But this cannot be the life of men in general. Aristotle is right in saying that the life of solitude is fit only for a beast or a god.*

DEFINITION OF SOCIETY

What sort of thing is society as it emerges from the proof just given? We notice that several elements are necessary:

1. There can be no actually existing society without *members*. The number of persons is not specified, but there must be at least two; otherwise there can be no togetherness or commonness of interests and activity.

2. The members must be united in a *stable* or *enduring* way. A single act of working together may be only a haphazard occurrence. The union need not last forever or for life but must last for some considerable time.

3. The members must *cooperate* or work together for the attainment of some *end*. This end will be some *common good* that all the members will share in and that no member could accomplish singly.

4. Society is held together by bonds, *moral bonds* of means and end. Either the members bind themselves by contract, pledge, or agreement, or else the bonds are imposed upon them by some law, natural or positive.

5. To guide the cooperative effort to the common good, society must be equipped with that moral power called *authority*. Authority is the right to determine the means and direct the members in their use.

Hence we may define society as an *enduring union of a number of persons morally bound under authority to cooperate for a common good.*

An examination of the four causes of society will help to bring out the idea more clearly:

1. The *material* cause is the members, the human beings capable of entering into society. Since society is a moral union supposing agreement of wills, only rational beings can form society. Herds of animals are not societies.

2. The *formal* cause is the moral bond uniting the members. Form is that which determines matter, and it is the moral bond which distinguishes these human beings from others, constitutes a society out of them, and makes them members of it. Some writers identify this moral bond with authority and say that authority is the form of a society; others consider that authority is rather a property flowing from the essence of society. Without entering into this theoretical dispute, we can say that authority is at least an essential property of society.

3. The *efficient* cause is the one who brings about the moral union

---

*Aristotle, *Politics*, bk. I, ch. 2, 1253a 29.

among the members, the one who puts the form on the matter. This is the founder of the society, and in a lesser way those who keep it going. The efficient cause may be the members themselves or someone outside the society. In a remote sense, we may think of man's social nature itself as the efficient cause of society.

4. The *final* cause is the good sought by the members, that which they hope to gain by their cooperative effort. This will differ for each different kind of society. Since society itself is a means to an end, the nature of the society will be determined more by its end than by any other factor.

It is easily seen that society is not a physical thing. The only thing physical about it is the members and their actions. But it would be a mistake to say that society is not real. Of course it is not a substance, for it has no existence of its own separate from the individuals who compose it; it is not a kind of superperson built out of people, as the living body is made up of cells. Metaphysically, society falls under the category of *relation*. A society is not a single relation but a number of relations unified and systematized into an *order*. The relations are accidents inhering in men and linking them together in a definite way. Relations can be real, but we must not expect of them any reality except that of a relation. An order is not a substantial entity distinct from the things that are ordered, but this does not mean that the order is not real. The order is real if there are real beings really ordered in that way.

If society is not a physical being, what kind of being is it? It has more than ideal or intentional being, for that would only make it an idea or knowledge in the mind of some knower. Perhaps it is best called a *moral being*. Not every relation, but only a unified system of relations is an order. Not every order, but only an order resulting from a human act, a decision of the will relating means to end, is a moral being. Not every moral being, but only a moral being resulting from the simultaneous decisions of many human wills to cooperate toward a common end and achieve a common good is a society.

THE COMMON GOOD

The common good is the end for which society exists. It is not the absolutely last end of society, for all things human exist for man and man exists for God. The common good is therefore an intermediate end, an end that is also a means toward man's happiness and God's glory. When we say that the common good is *the* end of society, we mean that it is the end that is distinctive of society as such.

Society is a temporal thing, and it exists for a good realizable in this world.* The common good is the temporal welfare of the community,

---

*Here we are not considering the Church, which could not tend toward its supratemporal end unless it were equipped by God its Founder with supernatural means. Societies studied in ethics do not have this advantage.

taken both collectively and distributively. The collectivist stresses the first element only, making the common good an entity over and above the individual good, the former absorbing the latter. The individualist sees only the second element, making the common good a mere sum of individual goods. An adequate view of society and the common good must find a place between these extremes. The common good is realized only in the individuals who make up society, but it is a good that they could achieve only by the interaction of many cooperators.

To have a common good which can be the end of society, it is not enough that it concern several persons. That might give us two inter-dependent private goods, such as we find in contracts of exchange. If an employer is interested only in profits from business and an employee only in wages from his labor, each benefits the other, but they have not a common good in the strict sense. To have a really common good as the end of their joint effort, the employer must be genuinely interested in the welfare of his employee and the employee must have at heart the success of the business he works for, and these two interests must be merged in one common enterprise. They must help each other not only accidentally, because their private goods are entangled, but essentially, because they share in the one same good. For lack of this the employer-employee relation normally found today is not a society.

Negatively, the common good consists in the establishment and maintenance of *order*. Each knows his place, his relations to others, his rights and duties as compared with others' rights and duties toward him. Each can rely on the other not to interfere; each is guaranteed a wide enough scope for private action and the development of his own personality. There result peace, harmony, security, opportunity, and freedom. Cooperation for the maintenance of order must be done by all for the benefit of all and is thus a truly common good.

Positively, the common good consists in giving to others and receiving from them powers and resources that as individuals none would possess. It is both active and passive, both supplementation and participation; a single word for it is *union,* or even better, *communion.* Scattered rain-drops over a wide enough area may, if added together, equal the force of a waterfall, but they cannot do the work of a waterfall harnessed to a turbine. The common good is not an arithmetical sum of each individual's contribution but something new resulting from the channeling of human energy and the mobilization of nature's resources. The economic products of an advanced civilization depend on the genius and labor of thousands of men who invented the machines, developed the processes, and continue to work them. The literature and art of a culture must be built up over the centuries and stored in books, monuments, libraries, and museums that we may now delight in them and absorb the great minds of the past into our own. A family depends on the two sexes and the love between them; mutual protection and support exemplify the negative common good of order, but the primary end, the begetting and rearing of children, is the best illustration of the positive common good of communion.

The means society uses to develop and share the common good are often called *institutions*. These are such things as schools, libraries, laboratories, hospitals, police, military forces, public utilities, corporations, banks, stock exchanges, law courts, and countless others. Some of them are also societies in their own right, but as institutions they are regarded as instrumental causes used by society for storing and distributing the means to the common good.

The common good is to be shared in by all. The negative aspect of the common good should be shared in *equally*, for it consists in the absence of interference and the affording of opportunity. Even if nature does not give equal opportunity to all, there should be no artificial human restrictions on such opportunities as nature does offer. The positive aspect of the common good should be shared in not equally but *proportionately*. The proportion is a blend of equal and unequal elements. There should be equality between one's contribution to society and one's share in the distribution of society's benefits, but, as not all contribute equally, neither should all receive equally. This establishment of social justice, the foremost task of society, is so difficult that in this imperfect world we can hope for no more than an approximation.

But here the dynamic character of the common good becomes apparent. It is the end of society, but, since it is never perfectly attained, society is never static. Temporal welfare is a thing that can be constantly bettered. Even if a society should once achieve a condition of perfect social justice, new conditions would arise with new difficulties to be met, and the problem of adjustment would have to be faced anew. The common good is thus the driving force in social progress.

If the common good is constantly changing, how can men agree upon it so as to will it together? The common good taken formally or abstractly (the general welfare as such, without specifying anything definite) always remains the same and must be willed by all the members of society. Thus society always has an end and the same end. But the common good taken materially or concretely (the specific good to be achieved here and now and the means to it) varies with circumstances and need not be willed or even known by each and every member; it is sufficient that each accomplishes his part. Each soldier wills victory in the abstract, but only the high command plans the precise steps by which the battle is won. How the parts the members play fit together is determined and willed by the leaders of society in their exercise of authority.

KINDS OF SOCIETY

When we say that man lives in society and that it is natural for him to do so, we do not refer to any specific grouping. Society in this sense is the abstract concept of men living together in interdependence and interaction for the sake of some unspecified common good that can be vaguely referred to as their general welfare. This is *society* but not *a society*. In concrete fact men break up into numerous overlapping groups, each of which is a society.

Some of these groups are informal and unorganized. They are often spoken of as *communities* rather than societies: ethnic, linguistic, geographical, neighborhood, class, cultural groups. They are united by the fact of their common interest rather than by any deliberate act of the will. Opposed to these are *associations,* which are deliberately organized for specified ends under a definite authority. These are societies in the strict sense of the word.

Societies in the strict sense are either natural or conventional. A *natural* society is one that is required by nature and has its end set by nature. Its necessity and purpose are manifested to man by the natural law. We have already proved that it is natural to man to live in society, but it does not follow therefrom that nature specifies any definite societies to which man must belong. Are there, then, any natural societies? In the following chapters we shall show that there are two: the family and the state. *Conventional* societies are artificial products of human convention, founded by the free agreement of men who set the end and choose the means. Clubs, fraternities, athletic leagues, business firms, labor unions—all such organizations are conventional. They may be established or abolished without affecting human nature as such. If some of them are necessary, their necessity is not absolute but dependent on historical contingencies that are not universal.

We can classify societies not only from the source which gives them existence (convention or the natural law), but also from the availability of means accorded them for accomplishing their end. A *perfect* society is self-sufficing, containing within itself all the resources needed for attaining its end. It is customary to name two perfect societies: the Church and the state. The Church is not a natural but a supernatural society, founded on divine positive law revealed to man. Whether particular states are perfect societies, as traditionally held, has now become questionable because of the growing interdependence of the international community. An *imperfect* society is not self-sufficing, but depends on other organizations at least for protection and tolerance, if not for promotion and encouragement. Such are all merely conventional societies. The family is in the unique position of a natural but imperfect society. Note that the words *perfect* and *imperfect* here mean that the society in concept is complete and independent or incomplete and dependent; they do not indicate how well or ill a particular society functions.

AUTHORITY ESSENTIAL TO SOCIETY

Authority is the right of a society to direct and control the members so that they cooperate toward the attainment of the end of that society. It should be evident that no society can function without authority, but this proposition is denied by the *anarchists*. They argue that social life and the absence of all restraint are compatible, that authority is necessary now only because of the imperfect condition of society. They say that society has evolved from despotic to monarchic, from monarchic to aristocratic, from aristocratic to democratic, and that the next step should be from democratic to anarchic. There is a gradual lessening of authority as man rises to a higher degree of development. Communists, despite their differences with the anarchists, have the same idea of the fully developed communist society when "the state will have withered away." The difference is rather about the means of accomplishing this end than about the character of the goal itself.

Anarchism takes an absurdly optimistic view of human nature. We must take human nature as it is, untinted with any rosy colors supplied by our imagination. A realistic appraisal shows that no society could endure without authority. Authority is needed:

1. *To remedy ignorance.* Only the more general principles of the natural law are evident to all; the remote conclusions are not easily grasped and must be enforced by one having the moral power or authority to do so for the common good and public order.

2. *To enforce justice.* Men are eager to claim benefits but prone to shirk duties; someone must see to it that both of these are distributed fairly, that the greedy are restrained and the slothful are stimulated. Besides direction, enforcement with the right to use penalties is necessary.

3. *To provide leadership.* Though all may agree on the end of human society, there may be many disputes on the means to be used in attaining the end; some one must be empowered to choose the means and to insist on the cooperative use of the means chosen. Cooperation is impossible without direction and control.

Authority is therefore essential to every society, since without it the society cannot exist or fulfill its function. The first two points mentioned stress the *substitutional* function of authority, by which it remedies human deficiencies either of intellect or of will. This kind of authority tends to diminish and become unnecessary the more it fulfills its function; thus paternal authority disappears when the child reaches adulthood and corrective authority ceases when the delinquent has been reformed. A chief difficulty of the anarchists is that they consider this function of authority alone. The third point mentioned brings out the *essential* function of authority, which would exist even in a society of perfect human beings. Because there could be several sets of equally effective means to the end, yet only one set can be used cooperatively, someone would have to choose between them and prescribe the one to use.

SOURCE OF AUTHORITY

In a *conventional* society authority comes from the members contracting to organize themselves, who vest the authority in a head or leader of their choosing, either a single person or some type of governing board. With no authority there would be no society; but, since the authority is wholly conferred by the members, they can withdraw it, limit it, or extend it as they please. The right of direction and control is hypothetical, for it affects a person only so long as he is a member; the extreme penalty for disobedience is expulsion from the society. Any member is free to repudiate the authority by resigning from the organization. Hence, if the family and the state were only conventional societies, they could have no more authority than the contracting parties in marriage or the founding fathers of the state possessed as individual persons, and association with these societies would be terminable at pleasure.

In a *natural* society the situation is very different. Men enter into natural societies by the prompting of nature and remain members by command of the natural law. Fulfillment of their duty as members of a natural society is enjoined on them by the natural law and cannot be extinguished by expulsion or resignation from the organization. A natural society has a scope of authority, an extent of direction and control, which the members as individuals never had or can have. Hence authority in a natural society cannot come from the individuals composing the society, but must come from the Author of that law, the natural law, from which natural societies derive their existence.

But is it not said that *all* authority, of any kind whatever, comes from God? To avoid confusion we must distinguish three possibilities:

1. *Conventional societies.* Here God is indeed the *ultimate* source of authority, but only in the sense in which He is the source of everything. He created the men who form the society, and gave them their faculties of intellect and will by which they can exercise direction and control of the society they establish. But the authority can be traced to God only *indirectly* and *remotely.*

2. *Natural societies.* Here God is the source of authority *directly* and *immediately,* inasmuch as He established the natural law which requires that men organize themselves, and through which He confers authority on the natural society so founded. God gives the authority directly to the society itself and not (as in conventional societies) to the founders to confer on the society at their discretion.

3. *Theocratic societies.* God by supernatural revelation founds a particular society among men, specifying its structure and determining its leaders, as in the case of the Jewish theocracy and the Christian Church. Here God is the source of authority not only directly and immediately, but *proximately* and *personally.*

The third case is outside our consideration and is mentioned only to show what we do not mean. When we say that in a natural society authority comes directly and immediately from God, the terms *directly* and *immediately* are to be taken in the second sense listed above, not in the third sense.

That a natural society receives its authority as described is evident from the definition. No society can exist without the means necessary for attaining its end and authority is such a means. The authority cannot come from men. For that would make it a conventional society. It must therefore come from God, either by revelation, and that is a theocratic society, or by the natural law, and that by definition is a natural society. The only medium could be the law, which as the eternal law is identified with God, and as the natural law is identified with man.

God confers the authority on a natural society at the first moment of its existence. Delay would leave the society in existence for some time without something essential to it.

Note that our discussion here is about the origin of authority in the *society as such,* and does not concern itself with how the authority comes to be vested in this or that particular leader within the society. This latter question we shall postpone to our treatment of the state, where the chief controversy lies.

SUMMARY

The *traditional* view is that man is naturally social and is led to form society by a dictate of the natural law operating through his rational and free nature. The *moral positivists* counter that man is not naturally social, that all society results from convention. The *evolutionists* hold that man's social nature is but a development of the gregarious instincts of his brute ancestors.

That man is naturally social is evident from the following properties of human nature:

(1) Man abhors solitude and craves companionship.
(2) Man cannot supply even his basic needs alone.
(3) Language fits man for communication and cooperation.
(4) Culture and progress are impossible outside society.

To guarantee this cooperation, men must bind themselves to it, and when they do, they create society. This obligation is on mankind generally, not on each individual.

Society is *defined* as an enduring union of a number of persons morally bound under authority to cooperate for a common good. The four causes of society are *material,* the members; *formal,* the moral bond; *efficient,* the founder; and *final,* the end or common good. Society is not a physical thing distinct from the members but a moral being consisting of a system of real relations coordinating the members' activities among themselves and to a common end.

The *common good* consists negatively in *order,* a maintenance of peace and affording of opportunity, and positively in *communion,* an increase of powers by their mutual supplementation. Institutions are means established for the storing and distribution of the common good. Social justice is the equal or proportionate sharing by the members in the common good.

Besides society-at-large, there are particular societies existing as unorganized *communities* or organized *associations.* Societies are *natural* or *conventional,* according as they are requirements of the natural law or have no other basis than the free agreement of men. Societies are *perfect* or *imperfect,* according as they are self-sufficing or rely on other organizations for help and protection. There are two natural societies, the family and the state, and two perfect societies, the Church and the state.

Anarchists think that society can get along without authority. This opinion is absurdly optimistic, for:

(1) What is socially good for man is not known by all.

(2) Benefits and duties must be distributed fairly.

(3) Some one must choose the correct means to the end.

Authority, the right of direction and control, is given to a natural society directly by God, since it is a means necessary to attain the end of such a society, and God cannot will the end without willing the means necessary to it. To confer it through the *natural law* is the only way appropriate to a natural society as opposed to a conventional and a theocratic society.

READINGS

The ancients did not treat of society apart from its specific forms, such as the family and the state.

* * *

1. The four following authors are of particular value:
   a. Messner, *Social Ethics,* a monumental work treating the whole subject fully; bk. I, pt. II, is pertinent here.
   b. Rommen, *The State in Catholic Thought,* ch. 1, on social being; ch. 13, on the common good.
   c. Simon, *The Nature and Functions of Authority.* This excellent lecture is expanded and developed in his later work: *The Philosophy of Democratic Government,* ch. 1.
   d. Sheed, *Society and Sanity,* is highly recommended.
2. The following have some helpful material:
   a. Le Buffe and Hayes, *The American Philosophy of Law,* pp. 311-322.
   b. Leibell, *Readings in Ethics,* pp. 743-763.
3. All books on sociology necessarily treat of society but more from the practical than from the philosophical standpoint. The following have interesting chapters on most of the forms of society and social disorders to be discussed later:
   a. Sorokin, *The Crisis of Our Age.*
   b. Lippmann, *The Good Society.*
   c. Casserley, *The Bent World.*

CHAPTER 24

THE FAMILY

DOMESTIC SOCIETY

If any group of human beings has the right to be called a society, that group is the family. In ancient times the family included all close blood relatives and not merely those who lived together; the word was also used to mean a whole household, including servants and other nonrelated persons, so long as they lived under one roof or on the same plantation. We take the more restricted meaning of the word: the family is a society consisting of husband or father, wife or mother, and their children.

The family or domestic society consists of two components or sub-societies: a horizontal component, the union of husband and wife, called *conjugal* society; and a vertical component, the union of parents and children, called *parental* society. These are not really two distinct societies, but two aspects or directions within the family. Accidentally a family may have one component only, but this is not the normal case.

The *material* cause of the family, as of all societies, consists of the members or persons constituting it: a man, a woman, and the children born from them. The *formal* cause is the moral bond between them, consisting of a definite group of rights and duties, guaranteed by contract in conjugal society and imposed by the nature of things in parental society. The *final* cause of the family is the good of all parties concerned, but especially of the child which is the natural product of relations between the sexes. The *efficient* cause of the family is the contract of marriage, or more properly the contracting parties, for by marriage the family is brought into existence and maintained.

MARRIAGE

Marriage may be considered as the act of getting married (wedding) or as the state of being married (wedlock). The first is the marriage contract, by which a man and a woman give and receive rights over each other's body for the performance of the generative act. As a state, marriage is a society or lasting union of a man and a woman resulting from such a contract. These define marriage not at its best, but in its bare essentials. We shall consider the state of marriage first, for people get married in order to live in the married state; hence the nature and conditions of the contract are determined from the state that the contract aims to produce.

The state of marriage implies four chief conditions:

1. There must be a union of *opposite sexes*. Since marriage has to do with the reproduction of the human race, this requirement is obvious. Thus marriage differs from all forms of perversion or unnatural sexual behavior. Whether marriage is always between only one man and only one woman will be discussed later.

2. Marriage is a *permanent* union. It must last at least as long as is necessary for the fulfillment of its primary purpose, the begetting and rearing of children. Hence it must endure at least until the last child is capable of living an independent life. Thus marriage differs from promiscuity. Whether marriage involves lifelong permanence will be considered later.

3. It is an *exclusive* union. The partners agree to share relations only with each other, so that extramarital acts are a violation of justice. Thus adultery is a crime against marriage.

4. Its permanence and exclusiveness are guaranteed by *contract*. Mere living together without being bound to do so does not constitute marriage, even though the partners actually remain together for life, because they do not form a society. This contract makes the difference between marriage and concubinage.

PROBLEM

The above is only a description of what marriage means as an actually existing institution. But ever since the beginning of ethics and the Greeks' first probing into human customs, the question was raised whether marriage is a natural institution necessary for the human race or only the prevailing convention we have grown to accept as a matter of course. If the former, marriage is the only possible arrangement between the sexes in conformity with the moral law; if the latter, marriage may still be the most desirable arrangement but not the only possible one even from the ethical standpoint. If marriage is a natural institution, the family is a natural society; otherwise it is not. The importance of the question is obvious:

(1) Is marriage merely a human convention? or
(2) Is marriage a natural institution?

Evolutionists as a group, and all modern materialists must be evolutionists, hold that man gradually developed from primitive promiscuity through various forms of polygamy to the monogamous marriage, the stage corresponding to his present development; future evolution will probably lead on to some more advanced arrangement; hence, though man is naturally social in a broad sense, marriage is a purely human institution that may be abandoned for something better. Those moral positivists who hold that man is not naturally social should logically deny that the family is a natural society, but they seem to be thinking rather of the state than of the family in this connection; at any rate Rousseau* says that the family is the only natural society. Those who hold that marriage is merely conventional may, motivated perhaps by personal reasons, advocate the abolition of the convention in favor of freer relations between the sexes, or they may think that on utilitarian grounds it is an excellent convention by all means to be maintained.

On the other hand, the thesis that marriage is a natural institution, besides expressing the prevailing and traditional belief, is the only one that can square with the natural law. A system of ethics based on the natural law has but to establish the connection between marriage and the natural law, in order to show that marriage is no mere convention but a natural institution.

MARRIAGE A NATURAL INSTITUTION

Aristotle's sagacious words deserve quoting because they contain the germ of our argument as well as a penetrating insight into human nature:

> Between man and wife friendship seems to exist by nature; for man is naturally inclined to form couples—even more than to form cities, inasmuch as the household is earlier and more necessary than the city, and reproduction is more common to man with the animals.† With the other animals the union extends only to this point, but human beings live together not only for the sake of reproduction but also for the various purposes of life; from the start the functions are divided, and those of man and woman are different; so they help each other by throwing their peculiar gifts into the common stock. It is for these reasons that both utility and pleasure seem to be found in this kind of friendship. But this friendship may be based also on virtue, if the parties are good; for each has its own virtue and they will delight in the fact. And children seem to be a bond of union (which is the reason why childless people part more easily); for children are a common good to both and what is common holds them together.‡

The Thomistic proof is built on this passage but casts the idea into a more formal type of argument:

Social Contract, bk. I, ch. 2.

†"Reproduction is more common to man with the animals" than forming cities is common to man with the animals. Reproduction is common to man and *all* animals, but political or quasi-political organization is common to man and *some* animals only, such as bees and ants.

‡Aristotle, *Nicomachean Ethics*, bk. VIII, ch. 12, 1162a 16-28.

That is said to be natural to which nature inclines, although it comes to pass through the intervention of the free will; thus acts of virtue and the virtues themselves are called natural; and in this way matrimony is natural, because natural reason inclines thereto in two ways. First, in relation to the principal end of matrimony, namely the good of the offspring. For nature intends not only the begetting of offspring, but also its education and development until it reach the perfect state of man as man, and that is the state of virtue. Hence, according to the Philosopher* we derive three things from our parents, namely existence, nourishment, and education. Now a child cannot be brought up and instructed unless it have certain and definite parents, and this would not be the case unless there were a tie between the man and a definite woman, and it is in this way that matrimony consists. Secondly, in relation to the secondary end of matrimony, which is the mutual services which married persons render one another in household matters. For just as natural reason dictates that men should live together, since one is not self-sufficient in all things concerning life, for which reason man is described as being naturally inclined to political society, so too among those works that are necessary for human life some are becoming to men, others to women. Wherefore nature inculcated that society of man and woman which consists in matrimony.†

The argument may be restated in the following fashion, carrying it along by steps and bringing out each point expressly:

1. Nature intends the continuance of the human race, because nature has given human beings the faculty and instinct for reproduction. Nature intends that this occur by a union of man and woman, because human beings are made to reproduce in the sexual manner. Hence in nature's plan the first and fundamental purpose of the sexual relation is the child. People may marry for a variety of motives, for love, for companionship, for money, for position. The idea of begetting children may be very secondary, perhaps only tolerated rather than desired, in the minds of many marrying couples; it need not be psychologically uppermost in their minds. But there is no doubt that it is primary in nature's design. Men eat mostly for the pleasure of it and rarely think of its necessity for sustaining life, yet they recognize on reflection that the latter is the primary purpose of eating. The same is true regarding the sexual relation; it may be done for pleasure, but its primary purpose is to sustain the race. In race preservation, nature has not trusted to logic by which man might reason to his duty in this regard, but has implanted an instinct so strong that most human beings follow it. Thus the whole economy of nature in establishing the sexes leads to the child.

2. The duty of caring for the child naturally devolves on the parents. The parents are the cause of the child's existence and therefore are

---

Ibid., ch. 11, 1161a 17.
†St. Thomas, *Summa Theologica,* III, Supplement, q. 41, a. 1. St. Thomas died before he could complete the *Summa Theologica.* The Supplement was added by his followers from others of his writings.

charged with caring for its welfare. There is nothing so helpless as the human infant. Some animals can fend for themselves shortly after birth, and none require a long period of care. Natural instinct prompts the parent animals, when both are necessary, to remain together until the offspring are sufficiently reared to care for themselves. In no case does this last until the next mating season, and therefore promiscuous mating does no harm to the offspring of animals and allows well for the fulfill-ment of nature's primary purpose. The same cannot be said of human beings. The human child cannot live at all without intense care for several years, and on the whole needs from fifteen to twenty years of rearing before it is really able to live a fully independent human life. The ones equipped by nature with the means for rearing the child and normally impelled to it by natural instinct and love are the parents. Other agencies are poor makeshifts in this regard. Therefore the parents are designated by nature as the child's proper guardians.

3. The duty of rearing the child belongs to both parents, and not to one alone. That this duty belongs to the mother is clear from the fact that she must bear the child and nurse it; otherwise it cannot survive even the first few days of life. But the father is equally the cause of the child's existence, and therefore is equally charged by nature with the child's welfare. Together they gave the child life and together they must care for it, not in lives apart and independent, but in that joint life which makes up the society of the family. Ordinarily neither mother nor child can procure the means of subsistence, and who else in nature's plan has this duty except the father, the one responsible for the condition of mother and child? The possibility that the mother may have wealth of her own is accidental and outside of nature's provision. The help of the father is necessary, not only in the first years of the child's life, but throughout the whole period of the child's rearing. In fact, it is rather toward the latter part of the training period that the father's influence is most neces-sary, when he must fit his children, especially the boys, to take their place in human life. Nature has given father and mother different capaci-ties that are psychologically as well as physically complementary, and the influence of the father's sternness as well as of the mother's sweetness is necessary for the adequate training of the child.

From these three points it follows that nature demands a permanent and exclusive union between the sexes, and one guaranteed by contract, in other words, that marriage is a natural institution. A momentary union for the sake of procreation alone is a betrayal and gross violation of nature's provisions for the human child. It also follows that any use of the sexual faculty outside marriage is contrary to nature and to the natural law, for it either fails to provide for the child or else is some form of un-natural perversion.

Remarks on the argument

1. *The argument shows why parents should remain together, but why must they bind themselves to this by contract?* Parental society requires

no contract, since the infant cannot make a contract and when it arrives at the use of reason finds itself already a member of parental society by disposition of nature itself. The same is not true of conjugal society, which is entered into freely by adults. Each must be assured of the other partner's faithfulness before assuming the heavy burdens that marriage entails. Public order as well as the virtue of the two partners requires that it be publicly known who is married to whom. Therefore a formal contract is necessary.

2. *If the argument for marriage as a natural institution is drawn wholly from the parents' obligation to the child, what about childless marriages?* The plan of nature must be judged from the normal instance, not from what is accidental. There is no marriage contract and no consequent married state unless the partners transfer to one another rights, and assume toward one another duties, which in the normal course of nature should issue in the existence of children. The begetting and rearing of children remains the primary end of marriage, even if through default of nature no child arrives. Nature sets the end, but does not guarantee that it will be attained in every case. Childless couples form a family in its conjugal relation, even though the parental relation never becomes actualized. They have the same rights and duties toward one another as any married couple, but their duties as parents are in abeyance so long as they have no child.

3. *Nature sometimes allows the child to be deprived of father or mother or both; how then is the help of both required by nature?* Here again the plan of nature must be judged from the normal instance. A man can get through life on one leg or without any, but this is not nature's design for the human frame. Loss of a parent, and much more of both, is recognized as a great misfortune in the child's life. An institution can supply material needs perhaps better than some parents, but it cannot give the child the love it craves and all that goes to make a home. Adoption into another family is the best remedy, but this supposes that there should be families, the very thing we have been proving.

4. *If marriage is a natural institution, is it not contrary to nature not to marry?* Marriage is a duty for the race but not for the individual, since its primary end is the racial and not the individual good. The individual's good can be obtained only by the individual's effort; thus no man can live by getting others to eat for him. But the good of the race can be obtained if a sufficient number tend toward it. Marriage would be a duty for each individual only if the human race would be in danger of dying out, but man's strong sexual propensities leave no fear in this regard. But, though marriage is not necessary for all, it is necessary for those who intend to have sexual experience.

PRIMARY AND SECONDARY ENDS OF MARRIAGE

As we have seen, the *primary* end of marriage is the good of the race to be achieved through the good of the children born of this particular union. It is not only the begetting but also the rearing of children. Rearing or education is taken here in the broadest sense for full physical, mental, and moral development, by which the children are fitted to face life, to pursue their last end, and to work with their fellows for the common good. This is the task married couples take on themselves, which they alone can most properly accomplish, and for which they bind themselves into a permanent contractual society rather than a temporary indiscriminate union. This is why marriage is marriage.

The *secondary* ends reinforce the primary end. They can be summed up in the mutual love and help which should exist between husband and wife. More specifically:

1. Sexual desire finds its only legitimate outlet in marriage. It is an utter mistake to see anything wrong in sex itself, which is a merely natural power and good in itself, but any use of it outside marriage is immoral. One who does not marry is bound to continence, a form of life for the few rather than the many.

2. Human love is something on a far higher plane than animal desire, something more lasting and spiritual, for it is directed to the other as a person with qualities of mind, heart, and soul. Whereas sex seeks selfish pleasure, love is the most unselfish thing in the world and seeks the good of the beloved. No marriage can be perfect without it.

3. Companionship results from the fact that the two sexes are ideally suited to each other, since the qualities of man and woman are naturally supplementary, each supplying what the other lacks. This mutual need appears in a practical as well as in a romantic way, and many unemotional marriages are successful on this prosaic level. Companionship remains long after the fires of passion are burnt out.

4. Self-perpetuation, the desire to leave behind an image of oneself, though scarcely present before childbirth, becomes prominent afterward and is a powerful motive in keeping the family together. It furnishes a new sense of identity between man and wife when each sees that the image of oneself is also the image of the other.

Some may be repelled by the treatment of marriage given so far, thinking that it concentrates on the biological and utilitarian aspects, and overlooks the most important thing in marriage, which is the love of husband and wife. Poets, dramatists, and novelists have said enough about love, and in media which alone can come close to expressing it. Love is too personal and exclusive a thing for the abstract and generalized discourse that scientific or philosophical writing is limited to. Our omission of the praise of human love is thus no oversight, but a tribute to all the artists who have done it so well.

But can we not say that love between husband and wife is at least as important as the begetting and rearing of children, and that therefore both of these are primary ends of marriage? There is no objection to putting it in this way, so long as we see these as two conjoined primary ends or two parts of the one primary end, and not as two alternative ends in the sense that we may choose either one while excluding the other.

Marriage does not cease if the partners cease to love each other, just as it does not cease when they are too old to have children. Even from the beginning there can be a valid marriage contract without genuine love, just as there can be a valid marriage contract between sterile persons.

When we ask about the essence of marriage, we ask about that without which marriage would not be marriage. This is the transference of the right to the generative act. It should not be mere biological satisfaction, but the culmination of all the human love husband and wife have for each other. And, since it is naturally fruitful, it should result in the creation of new life, in that permanent mingling of the qualities of the two wedded lovers in a new person who mirrors both. Love cannot be commanded, but it is morally wrong for married partners deliberately to exclude it and to indulge in hatred or indifference toward each other. Children, likewise, cannot always be summoned into being, but it is morally wrong deliberately to exclude them while performing the act that naturally should produce them. Hence our next topic.

BIRTH CONTROL

Any use of sex outside marriage is immoral, but there can also be immoral uses of sex within marriage. Unnatural acts performed by husband and wife are wrong from the very fact that they are unnatural. The only controversy on this point regards the now widespread practice of birth control. Is this also an unnatural act?

Birth control is the popular but inexact term used for *birth prevention* or *contraception:* the use of artificial means (mechanical, physical, or chemical) to prevent conception that might result from the marriage act. As taken here, it does not mean a control over births by abstinence or continence, or the limitation of intercourse to periods when conception is less likely to occur.

The practice of artificial contraception is propagandized as a method of counteracting overpopulation in countries that cannot support so many people, as a means of relieving economic distress in families already too large, and as a eugenic measure against the breeding of subnormal strains, but it seems to be practiced chiefly by the higher social brackets of civilized countries. However, our viewpoint is not economic or sociological, but ethical.

Hedonists, utilitarians, relativists, and those moral positivists who base all morality on convention have little or no opposition to this practice, since they see in man no obligation rationally to conform his conduct to his nature. But in a natural law philosophy there can be no defense for artificial contraception. The argument has already been given in our proof that marriage is a natural institution whose primary end is the begetting and rearing of children. This is the purpose for which nature has equipped man with the faculty of reproduction. Its use outside marriage is immoral, and even in marriage it is immoral deliberately to frustrate the marriage act of its natural issue. To frustrate a natural faculty of its primary purpose is to go against nature, to act in a manner directly contrary to the norm of morality, and to do something intrinsically wrong.

Artificial birth control is wrong for the reason that it is an unnatural vice of the same sort as solitary vice and homosexuality. These sins are attempts to secure sexual satisfaction while at the same time evading the responsibilities which nature attaches to this pleasure. The sexual power exists for the sake of the race and its continuance. The strong desire animals, including the human animal, feel for sex gratification is nature's means of alluring them to breed. To seek the satisfaction while at the same time defrauding nature is what is meant by perversion. Man alone is able willfully to pervert his own nature, but is bound not to do so by the natural moral law.

Since marriage is a natural institution, and artificial birth control is a violation of the primary end of marriage, artificial birth control is against the natural law. Hence it cannot be justified by eugenic, economic, sociological, political, humanitarian, or any other reasons. The remedy is to alleviate the economic and social situation, not to counsel sex perversion.

Are then married people obliged to have as many children as possible? No, provided they use no immoral means to prevent them. With mutual consent, husband and wife are always allowed to refrain. Marriage transfers rights, and it is a violation of the marriage contract to refuse these rights to the spouse who seriously demands them, but there is no obligation to demand them. Marital continence is not easy, but it is not as impossible as some seem to think.

What of the so-called "rhythm" method? It differs from artificial contraception in that no immoral means are used. Relations are limited to the comparatively sterile periods that nature itself provides. Since there is no obligation to demand marriage rights at all, there is no obligation to demand them at one time rather than another. Hence in the "rhythm" method the particular act done here and now is not performed unnaturally nor is there any obstacle placed to its natural issue. It is known that the act will be unfruitful, but nature itself has made it so. However, an act may be wrong not only because of the means used but also because of the end intended. Partners who limit relations to sterile periods exclusively would do so only because they intend to avoid having children. To enter marriage with the fixed intention of avoiding having any children under any circumstances is immoral, as robbing that marriage of its primary purpose. But accidental circumstances can arise which make the having of children undesirable at least for a time. Such reasons are practically reducible to four heads:

(1) *Medical,* the health of one of the partners
(2) *Eugenic,* a serious hereditary defect
(3) *Economic,* inability to support a larger family
(4) *Social,* such conditions as war or overpopulation

Two other requirements must be met: both partners must agree to abstain during the fertile period, and both must be able to do so without proximate danger of sin.

Since the means is not wrong in itself, and so long as the intention is not mere selfishness but the avoidance of a serious difficulty, the "rhythm" method is a morally justifiable solution. It is not at all the ideal of family relations, but a legitimate way of adjusting to difficult circumstances.

PROPERTIES OF MARRIAGE

Our whole discussion up to this point has had to do with marriage in its bare essentials. We have considered only those things without which the primary end of marriage cannot be attained at all. But nature also demands that marriage have certain properties that are necessary to attain the secondary ends, and to attain the primary end in its fullness and perfection. We said before that marriage must be between man and woman, but we did not say how many. We also said that marriage must be lasting, but we did not say how long. These questions are answered by the two main properties of marriage:

(1) Unity, as opposed to polygamy
(2) Indissolubility, as opposed to divorce

Polygamy

Unity of marriage means the marriage of only one man with only one woman at the same time. Such a marriage is called *monogamy;* marriage to two at the same time is *bigamy;* marriage to more than one at the same time without specifying the number is *polygamy*. Polygamy is said of either sex; it is:

(1) Polygyny, when one husband has more than one wife
(2) Polyandry, when one wife has more than one husband

Polygyny does not wholly frustrate the primary end of marriage. It places no hindrance to the birth of children, and allows at least the essentials of the child's rearing. Each mother can devote herself to the rearing of her own children while supported by the father. Unless the number of wives is extremely large, the father also should be able to assist somewhat in the training of the children.

But polygyny cannot realize the primary end of marriage perfectly, and can hardly fulfill the secondary ends at all. The father cannot give the same attention to the training of the children of several wives that he could give to those of one wife. The mutual love and help that should exist between husband and wife are weakened by being single in one direction and divided in the other. There can be no equality between husband and wife when she is only one among several, and there is little wonder that in polygamous countries the position of woman is not far above that of a slave. Jealousy among the wives is to be expected when each vies for the husband's favor and each is ambitious for her own children. Almost superhuman ingenuity is required of the husband to be perfectly fair to the wives and the children, and this kind of society seems possible only when the woman's condition is so degraded that her will does not count. Though such evils may occur in a monogamous family, they occur there only accidentally, through the fault of the parties concerned and not through the nature of the institution; but in a polygynous family these evils can be avoided only accidentally.

Polyandry is opposed both to the primary and to the secondary ends of marriage, and is therefore intrinsically wrong. In a sense polyandry is even worse than promiscuity, for the parties bind themselves to everything that makes promiscuity hideous. The only alleviating factor is that the several husbands would all be pledged to the support of one wife and all the children she would have. Thus wife and children would be assured of material support, but this is not the main element in marriage.

The excuse of polygyny, quicker propagation of the race, is absent in polyandry, for a woman cannot bear more children to many husbands than to one. The rearing of the children as nature intends becomes impossible, because the father cannot be determined with certainty and is thus unable to perform the function he has in natural law. The child also, unable to know his father, cannot call on him for help and guidance. The children would naturally quarrel over which husband is the father of which child. All the fathers might try to fulfill these functions to all the children or divide them arbitrarily, but this cannot be a truly parental relation. Thus, though practiced no doubt by individuals and by a few tribes here and there, it has never been the recognized form of marriage in any developed society.

Divorce

The second property of marriage is indissolubility, which means that the marriage cannot be dissolved, that it must last until the death of one of the partners. Married persons may break up their home in either of two ways:

(1) By separation from bed and board
(2) By attempted dissolution of the marriage bond

A *separation,* sometimes called *imperfect* divorce, means that the two parties cease to live together and to discharge marital functions, but remain married; the marriage bond remains intact so that neither party is free to contract a new marriage. It is easy to see that such a separation is sometimes necessary, but it should be undertaken only for the gravest of reasons, such as the danger of physical harm, and under proper authority, lest personal whim play too great a part as a motive. We are not speaking here of such separations, since they are not intended to dissolve marriage.

The term *divorce* is usually understood to mean *perfect* divorce, which is an attempt to dissolve the marriage bond itself so that the parties are free to contract new marriages with other persons. This alone is our question here. Divorce, like the marriage contract which it tries to dissolve, is regulated by ecclesiastical and civil law. We are obliged to consider the matter from the standpoint of the natural law alone, a limitation that necessarily makes our treatment incomplete.

The primary end of marriage requires that the marriage endure until the family is fully reared. The primary end of marriage, as we saw, is not only the begetting but also the rearing of children. Therefore by the natural law marriage must last until this end is accomplished, until the child is fully reared and able to live an independent life of its own. To rear one child normally takes from fifteen to twenty years. But if the parents must live together for that time, other children are ordinarily to be expected. Hence marriage must last for at least fifteen years after the birth of the youngest child. The woman is capable of bearing children up to the age of forty-five or so. Normally, therefore, marriage must last until husband and wife are sixty years old. This much at least the primary end of marriage demands.

The secondary ends of marriage require that the marriage last until the death of one of the partners. When married people have reached this age, hardly any reason could justify a separation. Life together could not have been too intolerable. Most separations occur in the early years of marriage, in the difficult period of mutual adjustment, when the romantic mist has blown away to reveal each to the other in the hard light of reality. It would be absurd to think that this has not already happened to an elderly couple who have shared all the joys and sorrows of life together for so long. The man is the natural support of the woman and must stand by her in her old age; the woman who has given to her husband her whole period of youth, beauty, and fertility deserves love and protection to the last. Likewise the woman who has taken her husband's support and protection in the years of his strength cannot leave him to loneliness at the end. Children, also, are the natural heirs and have a claim on the family property, which ought to be kept intact until by the parents' death it passes to them. And what kind of rearing would parents give to their children if they ruined it all by the bad example of breaking up their own home in their old age?

The chief reason against divorce is the havoc it works in the life of the child. Parents who divorce one another are considering themselves only, and ignoring the child whose good is the primary end of marriage. The child is the one who pays for the parents' selfishness. There is no substitute for the home. Parents who break up the home deprive the child of the environment in which by the intention of nature it should grow up. Cases happen in which the child profits by being removed from a bad home, but nature considers what is normal, not what is accidental. In fact, how can a home be bad except through the moral fault of at least one of the parents?

From this examination of the primary and secondary ends of marriage it follows that divorce is opposed to the natural law. In the early years of marriage husband and wife are forbidden to break the contract and seek new partners by the common duty they have toward the children nature normally supplies. In the latter years of marriage no justifying reason can be found for breaking the bond that has actually lasted so long.

Must we say that divorce is intrinsically wrong, so that no case of it can be permitted for any reason? Not absolutely, but conditionally. Divorce, being so contrary to the fundamental purposes of marriage and so serious a social evil, is intrinsically wrong if done at the mere discretion of the parties concerned. It is not intrinsically wrong if authorized by God, who in His providence can avert the naturally expected evil consequences. Can we prove by human reasoning on purely philosophical grounds either that God does or that He does not communicate this authority by the natural law to civil society? There seems to be no positive evidence to show that He does. On the other hand, conclusive evidence to show that He does not had best be sought from theological sources. A similar judgment applies to polygyny also.

Questions on the argument

The following difficulties are implicitly answered in the argument, but, because of the importance of the matter, should be given definite formulation:

1. *If marriage is a free contract, why can it not be freely terminated at the pleasure of the contracting parties?* Marriage is a free contract in the sense that one may either marry or not, but the conditions of marriage are laid down by nature and nature's Author, not by the contracting parties. Even in other matters the terms of a contract can be set down by law, either natural or positive; thus, one is free to enlist in the army, but having done so must serve out the term of enlistment. The term for marriage, set by the natural law, is until the death of one of the partners.

2. *Why be obliged to spend the rest of one's life with a companion one has ceased to love? Why cannot an unfortunate mistake be rectified?* Such questions only go to show what an important step marriage is. Those who enter it hastily with no sense of its serious obligations must pay the price of their folly. A contract for life is precisely that, and a person is obliged to live up to his word. Accidentally, divorce may be better for this or that individual, but it is ruinous to mankind generally. Laws are made for the common good, and individuals are bound to co-operate for the common good even at personal disadvantage.

3. *Would not such difficulties be obviated by trial marriages or companionate marriages?* These are not marriages at all, but legalized concubinage with an option for future promiscuity. They cannot properly fulfill the primary end of marriage, as the arguments we have already given sufficiently show.

4. *If separation without remarriage is allowable for serious reasons, why should not divorce with remarriage be allowable for the same reasons, since in both cases the family is broken up?* The difference here is in the intention of the separating partners. The first case does not involve the plan of subsequent marital infidelity, whereas the second case almost always does. The first case is a misfortune of the kind that occurs when one partner goes insane or is sent to prison; the second case is an immoral desire to form a new union with a more desirable person by violating the contract made with the first.

5. *Why could not divorce be restricted to extreme cases such as adultery?* In this matter the slightest entering wedge soon throws the door wide open. In those states where this is the only permitted cause for divorce, adultery is deliberately committed or simulated to obtain a divorce. Elsewhere the barriers have been gradually let down until the most trifling excuses are accepted. This so-called wedge argument has its value and is confirmed by history, but the only satisfactory answer to this question must be sought from theological sources.

6. *Why should not divorce be allowed in sterile marriages, since in them the primary end of marriage cannot be attained?* Here again we must note that nature plans for the normal, not for the exceptional, case. It is true that in sterile marriages the primary end cannot be attained, but this is the fault of nature, not of the parties concerned. The secondary ends of marriage remain, and they are sufficient for entering the married state so long as the primary end is not deliberately hindered. Nature seems to indicate that for the propagation of the race not all marriages need be fertile. Most couples when marrying do not know whether they are sterile or not, and cannot be sure for many years; yet from the outset, like any other married people, they must be assured of their partner's faithfulness. Even known sterility is not a bar to marriage, for a sterile person can fulfill the contract, which transfers a right to the generative act itself but not to actual fertility, the latter being nature's gift and not within the contracting party's power. The wedge argument applies here also; some would induce sterility to obtain a divorce, and lesser causes would be gradually admitted.

7. *Cannot the new husband or wife of a divorced person help in raising the children?* In some cases they can do so quite well, but in many cases they are bitterly resented by the children. Step-fathers and step-mothers are a byword, not because there are no successful ones, but because in general they are unable to take the dead parent's place. The case is vastly complicated when the real parent is still alive.

8. *People who have no intention of marrying again sometimes get a civil divorce; is this wrong?* The civil law makes no distinction between a *separation* and a *divorce*, declaring that the marriage contract is considered dissolved before the law, and leaving it to the individual conscience to decide whether it is really dissolved or not. People who intend only a separation may sometimes be obliged to secure a civil divorce to protect themselves from the other party, to obtain support and custody of the children, or to effect a civilly valid distribution of property. Divorce in these cases touches only the civil effects of marriage, but it should have ecclesiastical as well as civil authorization.

THE MARRIAGE CONTRACT

The married state of individuals begins by a contract entered into by the mutual free consent of the man and the woman. People are not born married and may remain unmarried throughout their lives. Nature does not select the partners for marriage. There must be something that determines *whether* one shall marry and *whom* one shall marry. Since nature does not determine it, the partners themselves do, and they do it by the marriage contract.

The marriage contract is a contract in the full sense of the word, and must fulfill all the conditions requisite for a contract in general, as well as some peculiar to itself. It is a bilateral onerous contract, by which the parties transfer to each other strict rights and thereby incur toward each other strict duties, which they henceforth owe to each other in justice. The essential right transferred is the right to the use of the other person's body for the performance of the generative act. Love, cohabitation, support, sharing of goods, and the like are consequent rights. The transference of the essential right is permanent and exclusive; failure to make it so invalidates the contract.

By its very nature as a contract marriage requires mutual free consent, and the absence of error and fear. Freedom of consent is particularly important in marriage, because marriage supposes love and love cannot be extorted, besides the fact that marriage imposes heavy burdens which no one is obliged to assume, much less to assume in company with a particular person.

An impediment to marriage is some inability in the contracting party that makes the marriage contract either invalid or illicit. The first kind render the contract null and void from the beginning so that the parties never were actually married. The second kind simply make it wrong for a person to marry under such conditions, but if he does so the marriage contract holds. The chief invalidating impediments in natural law are impotence, too close kinship, and being already married. The Church, because of its control over marriage in the supernatural order, and the state, for the sake of the common good, can establish additional impediments of either grade.

The ban of kinship may need a few remarks. The crime of incest has always been regarded even by pagans with particular horrror. Any marriage between parent and child is absolutely outlawed by nature as utterly opposed to the parental relation already existing. Marriage between brother and sister is not absolutely contrary to the natural law, but is under even more stringent conditions than polygyny and divorce; only God could allow it, and He would do so only if otherwise the race could not propagate. The reason for banning marriage between brother and sister is the fact that they grow up in the same home and develop during their immaturity a kind of love free from all passion; anything else would mean the utter ruin of the family and make the home an unlivable place.

CONCLUSION

There is nothing in human life more capable of abuse and mismanagement than sex. What is governed so easily and naturally in animals by means of their instinct must be regulated in man by his free will guided by his reason. Success or failure in life depends to a very great extent on the individual's ability to control this strongest of all passions. Marriage is the institution demanded by nature for securing this control. Any number of otherwise successful people have wrecked their lives by failing to succeed in their relations with the opposite sex. The selecting of the right partner in life and the preservation of fidelity to the marriage vow are not matters of accident but of wise human conduct. Marriage also requires traits of character that are not accidentally achieved, but must be sedulously developed. Success in the married state is possible only by the practice of the cardinal virtues, prudence, justice, fortitude, and temperance, in a high degree. Marriage therefore calls for a virtuous life and entails heavy responsibilities, but it also brings with it one of the best of earthly rewards, the founding and maintenance of a happy home.

SUMMARY

The family, the most primitive society, consists of two subsocieties: *conjugal,* the husband-wife relation, and *parental,* the parent-child relation. Marriage, which creates and maintains the family, means both the contract and the resulting state. The married state supposes a man and a woman united by contract in a permanent and exclusive union whose primary purpose is the begetting and rearing of children.

Is marriage merely a human convention or a natural institution? That it is the only arrangement between the sexes permitted by the natural law is proved thus:

(1) Nature's design in establishing sex is the propagation of the race, and is primarily directed to the child.
(2) The duty of caring for the child they beget falls on the parents, and this takes fifteen to twenty years.
(3) The rearing of the child belongs to both parents jointly; the father owes not only support but active help.

Therefore nature demands a permanent and exclusive union guaranteed by contract; that is, the natural law demands marriage.

While the *primary end* of marriage is the begetting and rearing of children, there are also *secondary ends:* to satisfy man's craving for sexual pleasure, human love, companionship, and self-perpetuation.

Birth control, in the sense of artificial contraception, is an unnatural use of sex within marriage, a frustration of a natural faculty, and therefore immoral. Eugenic, economic, social, political, and other reasons cannot justify it ethically. The "rhythm" method, since it is not unnatural, is allowable under certain conditions.

Marriage has two main properties: unity and indissolubility.

Polygamy, opposed to unity, has two forms. *Polygyny,* one husband with several wives, makes the primary end of marriage difficult as to the rearing of the children, and the secondary ends practically unattainable. *Polyandry,* one wife with several husbands, renders all the ends of marriage impossible. Both are against the natural law, especially the latter.

Divorce, opposed to indissolubility, means not a mere separation but an attempted dissolution of the marriage bond, so as to leave the partners free to remarry. The primary end of marriage requires the partners to remain together until the last child is reared; since they are then sixty years old, no justifying reason can be found for breaking the marriage. Accidentally divorce may not be harmful in individual cases, but it would be ruinous to mankind generally. Nature legislates for the common good and all must keep nature's laws.

The marriage *contract* is a bilateral onerous contract, by which each transfers to the other the right to the generative act. It must fulfill all the requisites for contracts in general regarding the contracting parties, the matter, and the mutual consent. Any fault in the essentials of the contract renders it invalid. The Church and the state may establish additional impediments rendering the contract either invalid or illicit.

READINGS

1. This is as good a place as any to suggest a reading of Aristotle's whole treatise on Friendship in the *Nicomachean Ethics,* books VIII and IX, though there are only passing remarks on marriage. Read his refutation of Plato's community of women in the *Politics,* bk. II, ch. 1-4, 1260b 28 to 1262b 35.
2. The treatise on marriage in the *Summa Theologica,* part III Supplement, qq. 41-68, is written from the standpoint of a theologian but discusses the philosophical aspect especially in qq. 41, 44-48, 51, 54, 65, 67. These are not found in the *Basic Writings.* Read Farrell's comments in his *Companion to the Summa,* vol. IV, ch. VIII.
3. The two Papal Encyclicals, Leo XIII's *Arcanum* (Christian Marriage) and Pius XI's *Casti Connubii* (Christian Marriage) should certainly be read. Handren, *No Longer Two,* is a commentary on *Casti Connubii.*
4. Cronin, *Science of Ethics,* vol. II, ch. XIII, XIV.
5. Rickaby, *Moral Philosophy,* pp. 263-277.
6. Leibell, *Readings in Ethics,* pp. 763-788, 820-848.
7. Messner, *Social Ethics,* bk. II, pt. I.
8. Haas, *Man and Society,* ch. VI, VII.
9. Le Buffe and Hayes, *The American Philosophy of Law,* pp. 272-287.
10. Sheed, *Society and Sanity,* ch. 8-10.
11. The following have a good philosophical background:
    a. Wayne, *Morals and Marriage,* an excellent little book for those contemplating marriage.
    b. Schmiedeler, *Marriage and the Family.*

c. Von Hildebrand's two short books, *Marriage* and *In Defense of Purity,* are well worth reading.

d. Leclercq, *Marriage and the Family.*

e. Joyce, *Christian Marriage.*

f. Healy, *Marriage Guidance.*

g. Clemens, *Marriage and the Family.*

h. Gerrard, *Marriage and Parenthood.*

i. Mihanovich, Schnepp, Thomas, *Marriage and the Family.*

j. Thibon, *What God Has Joined Together.*

k. Hope, *Life Together.*

l. Morrison, *God Is Its Founder.*

m. Magner, *The Art of Happy Marriage.*

n. Foerster, *Marriage and the Sex Problem.*

o. De Guchteneere's *Judgment on Birth Control;* Moore, *Birth Control;* D'Arcy, *Christian Morals,* pp. 124-139. There is a large pamphlet literature on this topic.

p. Thomas, *Marriage and Rhythm.*

CHAPTER 25

THE STATE

PROBLEM

W e said that there are two natural societies, domestic society (or the family) and political society (or the state). It was necessary to study the family first as the more primitive and fundamental institution. Now we go on to consider the more elaborate type of natural society known as the state. This part of ethics is sometimes called political philosophy, as midway between political science on the one hand and pure ethical theory on the other.

In this chapter we shall deal with the state itself, its origin, properties, purpose, and structure. In the following chapter we shall treat of the functioning of the state, or government. Only then can we give a definition summing up the nature of the state. The matter for the present chapter can be arranged under the following heads:

(1) Is the state a natural outgrowth of the family?
(2) How far does the state depend on contract?
(3) How far is the state sovereign?
(4) Is the state for man or man for the state?
(5) How is the state built up out of its elements?

Our first problem deals with the origin of the state itself as a political entity, the transition of a people from a nonorganized to a politically organized condition. On this point there are two main opinions:

(1) The state is a natural society because it arose as a natural outgrowth of the family.
(2) The state is a merely conventional society because it arose from a social contract freely entered into.

NATURAL ORIGIN THEORY

The Greeks took it for granted that the state is a natural society, although they do not call it that, perhaps because they have no word for *society* in general but use the word *polis,* city, to stand for both state and society.

Plato

Plato derives the state from man's economic needs, which of course are natural needs. He says:

A state, I said, arises, as I conceive, out of the needs of mankind; no one is self-sufficing, but all of us have many wants. Can any other origin of a State be imagined?

There can be no other.

Then, as we have many wants, and many persons are needed to supply them, one takes a helper for one purpose and another for another; and when these partners and helpers are gathered together in one habitation the body of inhabitants is termed a State.

True, he said.

And they exchange with one another, and one gives, and another receives, under the idea that the exchange will be for their good.

Very true.

Then, I said, let us begin and create in idea a State; and yet the true creator is necessity, who is the mother of our invention.*

Aristotle

Aristotle derives the state from the family, but not without due consideration for man's economic needs. Plato could hardly have stressed the family when he was going to abolish it among the rulers and guardians. But Aristotle is strong for the family. Here are his words:

He who thus considers things in their first growth and origin, whether a state or anything else, will obtain the clearest view of them. . . .

Out of these two relationships between man and woman, master and slave, the first thing to arise is the family. . . . The family is an association established by nature for the supply of men's everyday wants. . . . But when several families are united, and the association aims at something more than the supply of daily needs, the first society to be formed is the village. And the most natural form of the village appears to be that of a colony from the family, composed of children and grandchildren. . . .

When several villages are united in a single complete community, large enough to be nearly or quite self-sufficing, the state comes into existence, originating in the bare needs of life, and continuing in existence for the sake of a good life. And therefore, if the earlier forms of society are natural, so is the state, for it is the end of them, and the nature of a thing is its end. For what each thing is when fully developed, we call its nature, whether we are speaking of a man, a horse, or a family. Besides, the final cause and end of a thing is the best, and to be self-sufficing is the end and the best.

---

*Plato, *Republic,* bk. II, §369.

Hence it is evident that the state is a creature of nature, and that man is by nature a political animal. . . . And it is characteristic of man that he alone has any sense of good and evil, of just and unjust, and the like, and the association of living beings who have this sense makes a family and a state.

Further, the state is by nature clearly prior to the family and to the individual, since the whole is of necessity prior to the part. . . . The proof that the state is a creation of nature and prior to the individual is that the individual, when isolated, is not self-sufficient; and therefore he is like a part in relation to the whole. But he who is unable to live in society, or who has no need because he is sufficient for himself, must be either a beast or a god; he is no part of the state. A social instinct is implanted in all men by nature, and yet he who first founded the state was the greatest of benefactors. For man, when perfected, is the best of animals, but, when separated from law and justice, he is the worst of all.*

Restatement of Aristotle's argument

The foregoing passage from Aristotle was quoted at such length because of its fundamental importance. Before restating his argument, we have three preliminary remarks to make:

First, we have to speculate on the origin of the state by observing the forms of primitive society in existence today and by examining the traditions handed down among people now civilized. Of particular value are the Greeks, whose literature developed so early as to reflect both tribal and political life.

Second, we are interested in the passage of mankind from nonpolitical to political existence, the formation of the state as such, not of this or that particular state. The states in existence today have arisen by colonization, conquest, revolution, or similar causes, in which we see only the patterning of new states on the ready-made framework of old ones, not the original formation of political society.

Third, the first formation of the state must have been gradual. As a rule men do not consciously aim at things of which they have had no experience. As various needs arose and better solutions to them were devised, men were unconsciously framing the self-sufficient state. It was spontaneous, but also guided by reason as a product of many converging acts of human thought. The first states were not vast empires, but rather slight though real improvements on tribal organization.

With these remarks in mind, we can express Aristotle's theory under the following points:

1. *The most elementary form of society is the family.* The family is here taken in the broader sense to mean all blood relatives living together and any servants or others adopted into the household. It can provide for its own welfare in mere daily wants, but it cannot provide for a broader human life. The arts and appliances of civilization could

---

*Aristotle, *Politics,* bk. I, ch. 2, 1252a 24 to 1253a 39.

never be developed within one family; for these there is needed the cooperation of many minds and many hands through accumulated generations.

2. *As the family grows, the end it can attain also grows.* The children reach maturity and found new families, usually near by. In several generations a group of families all interrelated live close to one another. Division of labor comes in; people begin to specialize in different kinds of work and to exchange their products.

3. *The interrelated group has become a clan or tribe.* A clan is a smaller group with a tradition of descent from a common ancestor. A tribe is a larger group and may be an amalgamation of several clans; at least the blood relationship is not so clear. Some tribes never get beyond the tribal condition, either because of nomadic habits, or because they are wholly occupied in war, or because they show no ingenuity in developing the earth's resources. To form a state a peaceful industrious settlement is necessary: a central village where the people trade.

4. *The village community can supply more of its wants than a single family, but it is not yet self-sufficing.* Military organization against enemies from without, economic organization against famine and want, legal organization for settling internal disputes, are still wanting. These things are handled rather arbitrarily by the tribal chief with his council of elders. This chief may be the patriarch or founder of the whole family, or his eldest son, or one of his descendants appointed by him, or one elected by the tribe to be their leader, or one who simply assumes leadership and keeps it by his ability.

5. *From the village community or an aggregate of such villages the state is formed.* One village composed of people all descended from the same common ancestor may expand to such a size in such a favorable location, that it is now able to take care of all its needs and has become self-sufficing. More probably several such villages would aggregate together, organize for common defense, mutual trade, and a common legal system. As soon as these things have been determined upon and an authority has been established to enforce them, the state has come into existence.

We might summarize as follows: The family is demanded by the natural law. But the state is a natural outgrowth of the family, and becomes necessary for human living when a number of families realize the need of cooperation for their common good. Therefore in these circumstances the state is demanded by the natural law, and is therefore a natural society.

SOCIAL CONTRACT THEORY

The theory opposed to the natural origin of the state is the contractual theory. It is the only theory consistent with moral, legal, and juridical positivism, so we must expect the names familiar to us from those movements to recur.

Hobbes

To what we said previously about Thomas Hobbes' description of the state of nature we may add his description of the formation of political society:

> The only way to erect such a common power, as may be able to defend them from the invasion of foreigners and the injuries of one another, and thereby to secure them in such sort as that, by their own industry, and by the fruits of the earth, they may nourish themselves and live contentedly; is, to confer all their power and strength upon one man, or upon one assembly of men, that may reduce all their wills, by plurality of voices, unto one will: which is as much as to say, to appoint one man, or assembly of men, to bear their person; and everyone to own and acknowledge himself to be the author of whatsoever he, that so beareth their person, shall act or cause to be acted in those things which concern the common peace and safety; and therein to submit their wills, everyone to his will, and their judgments to his judgment. This is more than consent, or concord; it is a real unity of them all, in one and the same person, made by covenant of every man with every man, in such manner as if every man should say to every man, *"I authorize and give up my right of governing myself to this man, or to this assembly of men, on this condition, that thou give up thy right to him, and authorize all his actions in like manner."* This done, the multitude so united in one person, is called a *commonwealth,* in Latin *civitas.* This is the generation of that great *Leviathan,* or rather, to speak more reverently, of that *mortal god,* to whom we owe under the *immortal God,* our peace and defense.*

Since Hobbes' view cannot be gathered from one paragraph, however long, we append the following summary. Man by nature is not social but antisocial. In the state of nature, before the founding of the commonwealth, "man was a wolf to man," there was a "war of all against all," there was no right and wrong, no justice and injustice, for there was no law. Force and fraud governed men's actions. This condition was intolerable, and one powerful impulse, self-preservation, drove men to seek a remedy for constant warfare. The remedy was the *social contract,* by which men agreed to hand over all their liberties to some one man or body of men, provided every other man did likewise. Thus they created authority, to which all are now subject and which directs the destinies of all. The power of the ruler is the aggregate of the powers of the individuals. The social contract, once effected, is irrevocable. The sovereignty of the ruler is absolute within the terms of the contract, and rebellion can never be lawful; only if he can no longer protect his subjects does obligation to him cease. We have no rights except those granted back to us by the sovereign of the all-powerful state.

Rousseau

Jean Jacques Rousseau is as strong a proponent of the contractual theory as Hobbes, though the two differ in their interpretation of the social contract. Rousseau says:

---

*Hobbes, *Leviathan,* ch. XVII.

To find a form of association which may defend and protect with the whole force of the community the person and property of every associate, and by means of which, coalescing with all, each may nevertheless obey only himself, and remain as free as before. Such is the fundamental problem of which the social contract furnishes the solution. . .

In short, each giving himself to all, gives himself to nobody; and as there is not one associate over whom we do not acquire the same rights which we concede to him over ourselves, we gain the equivalent of all that we lose, and more power to preserve what we have.

If, then, we set aside what is not of the essence of the social contract, we shall find that it is reducible to the following terms: "Each of us puts in common his person and his whole power under the supreme direction of the general will; and in return we receive every member as an indivisible part of the whole."

Forthwith, instead of the individual personalities of all the contracting parties, this act of association produces a moral and collective body, which is composed of as many members as the assembly has voices, and which receives from this same act its unity, its common self, its life, and its will. This public person, which is thus formed by the union of all the individual members, formerly took the name of *City,* and now takes that of *Republic* or *Body Politic,* which is called by its members *State* when it is passive, *sovereign* when it is active, *power* when it is compared to similar bodies.*

The following supplies the background for the passages quoted. Man is not naturally antisocial, but only extrasocial. In the state of nature man lived a carefree life in the forests, sufficient for himself, bound by no obligations, subordinate to no one. Man is naturally good, and there was no war of all against all. But the establishment of private property, due to man's natural inventiveness, brought with it frauds, disputes, and conflict. Then the state had to be established as a necessary evil to keep the peace. The state was set up by the *social contract,* by which each man handed over all his power of self-rule to a sort of universal person, the *general will,* provided all the rest did the same. Thus the individual will became part of the general will, the individual person part of this general personality, the right of the state the accumulation of all individual rights. In obeying the general will a man really obeys himself as part of the general will, because in the social contract itself he has willed that the general will shall be his will, and shall prevail over any particular decision he makes. The general will is always sovereign, and, even if it appoints representatives, cannot transfer sovereignty to them. Especially in this last point Rousseau parts company with Hobbes.

Locke

A combination of the natural and contractual origin of the state is found in John Locke. He believes that man is naturally social, that there is a natural law conferring natural rights, but he thinks that political

*Rousseau, *Social Contract,* bk. I, ch. 6.

society could only begin by the social contract, which, however, men are impelled to make by the demands of their nature. He says:

> Men being, as has been said, by nature all free, equal, and independent, no one can be put out of this estate and subjected to the political power of another without his own consent. The only way whereby any one divests himself of his natural liberty, and puts on the bonds of civil society, is by agreeing with other men to join and unite into a community for their comfortable, safe, and peaceable living one amongst another. . . .
>
> And thus that which begins and actually constitutes any political society is nothing but the consent of any number of freemen capable of a majority to unite and incorporate into such a society. And this is that, and that only, which did or could give beginning to any lawful government in the world.*

Locke's opinion is good insofar as it makes society natural to man. There seems to be no warranted objection to placing an implicit contract as the actual instrument by which many particular states were founded. His critics point to his making such a contract a universal requirement for the origin of all states, to his basing every state on majority rule, to his requiring implicit renewal of the contract by each citizen on reaching adulthood, and to his making the chief function of the state the protection of property. But these are details. Our main contention here has not been to disprove a contract, but to insist that the state is a natural society and not an arbitrary creation of merely human devising. If there was a contract, men were impelled to make it by the requirements of human nature and the dictate of the natural moral law.

Criticism of the social contract

The following criticisms are directed against the theories of Hobbes and Rousseau, who deny that the state is a natural society:

1. Man is naturally social, not antisocial or extrasocial. He is neither utterly depraved nor thoroughly upright in nature, but inclined both to good and evil. There is no evidence that man ever lived in this state of nature, and it is probably not intended to be historical, but it does not give a correct view of human nature.

2. There never was a state of nonmorality without rights, duties, justice, or law. There was always the natural law, and from it rights and duties immediately flow. The first child would set up a whole system of rights and duties. There never was an utter absence of private property, for anything occupied becomes such, and this immediately involves justice and injustice.

3. The function of the family in preparing for the state cannot be overlooked. Human beings had to live at least temporarily in some society to be able to survive as a race. A mere animal life, whether predatory or carefree, is impossible for man, for no man can supply his needs unaided. Family life naturally develops into the clan or tribe, and from there to the state.

---

*Locke, *Second Treatise of Civil Government*, ch. VIII, §95, 99.

4. There are certain rights of the individual and of the family that it is immoral to transfer to another, for they belong to the dignity of the human person and to the very nature of the family. A social contract which requires the transference of all rights is contrary to the natural law.

5. A social contract that is not a requirement of human nature as such but a mere convention could not bind posterity. The unborn were not parties to the contract and might refuse to enter into it. No one would become a citizen of the state by birth, and anyone could resign from the state at will.

6. The social contract cannot have greater authority than the contracting parties give it. There are rights of the state which no individual can possess, because they concern the common good. In the contract theory there is no way in which the state can legitimately obtain them.

So much about the origin of the state as seen ethically rather than historically. The state is not only a natural society, as is also the family, but a self-sufficing or perfect society, which the family is not. We must examine the latter concept further.

SELF-SUFFICIENCY AND SOVEREIGNTY

The state is said to be a *perfect* society. Obviously we do not mean that the state is incapable of improvement, for nothing human is such, and the state is notorious for its defections from the ideal. The term *perfect society* means one that is self-sufficing, independent, autonomous, sovereign. As a society, whether it function well or ill, it is not tributary to or dependent on another society for the attainment of its end. It is because the family is not self-sufficing, is unable to protect itself and to provide its members with all they need for the good life, that the state is necessary. If the state itself were not self-sufficing, it would require a higher society on which it could depend. Such a series could not be infinite, and by the name *state* we mean precisely that society which is self-sufficing and independent.

Self-sufficiency here does not mean *autarky* or economic isolation. The state need not grow all its own food or produce all its own manufactures if it can obtain them by trade from other countries. It need not have an army that can stand off any other army in the world if it can secure its own protection by treaties and alliances. It must be independent in the sense that it acknowledges no dictation from other nations in its internal affairs and negotiates with them as an equal in external affairs. Such a state is self-governing, a law to itself, autonomous. Considered as a quality in the will of a people and their rulers, this autonomy is called *sovereignty,* the independent power of self-rule by which a state controls its citizens and its territory in such a way that there is no higher appeal in the political order. Sovereignty in the state corresponds somewhat to personality in the individual man.

Such qualities cannot be absolute or unlimited. As there are restrictions on the freedom and independence of the individual person, so also are there on the state. Its right to do what it pleases is limited by the natural law, by the natural rights of mankind, by the existence of other states with equal sovereignty. All nations form the world community to which they belong, like it or not, by the fact that they all exist on this same earth and cannot avoid each other. A League of Nations or United Nations does not form a superstate or destroy the sovereignty of individual states. Nor would a tighter federation of states destroy sovereignty, though it might limit it still further. A union of all mankind into a single world state would so absorb the sovereignty of individual states as practically to reduce them to mere provinces. We cannot debate this question here. Suffice it to note that it would not mean the end of political society but the substitution of one political state for many. And this one state would have to be self-sufficing, independent, autonomous, and sovereign.

THE STATE AND THE PERSON

The fact that the state is sovereign and in a sense supreme brings up the question of its relation to its members. How reconcile the autonomy of the individual person with the supremacy of the state? In the quotation from Aristotle given earlier, a statement is made that should not have escaped the reader's challenge:

> The state is by nature clearly prior to the family and to the individual, since the whole is of necessity prior to the part.*

This looks like the rankest totalitarianism, until we remember another quotation cited in the chapter on the family:

> Man is naturally inclined to form couples—even more so than to form cities, inasmuch as the household is earlier and more necessary than the city.†

Priority in *time* means *Which came earlier?* Priority in *nature* means *Which is for the sake of which?* The individual and the family are prior to the state in time, as the word "earlier" and the whole argument for the origin of the state indicate, but the phrase "more necessary" does not refer to time and seems to mean priority by nature.

Has Aristotle contradicted himself? We leave this question for historians of philosophy to answer. There is no doubt that among the Greeks ethical life was inconceivable apart from civic life, and all citizens took a more active part in civic affairs than is customary in modern life. But, whatever Aristotle himself may have thought, we are interested in the problem he raises:

(1) Is the state for man?

(2) Is man for the state?

If we must choose one or other of these without being permitted any

---

*Aristotle, *Politics,* bk. I, ch. 2, 1253a 19.

†Aristotle, *Nicomachean Ethics,* bk. VIII, ch. 12, 1162a 17. (For the context of these two passages, see pp. 318 and 300, respectively.)

qualification, we shall unhesitatingly choose the first: The state is for man, not man for the state. If Aristotle thinks otherwise, he is mistaken. We can excuse him on the grounds that no Greek developed the theory of the human person, which is one of Christianity's historic contributions to philosophy, and thus he failed to see that the dignity of the human person prevents man from being subordinated as a means to an end.

But an unqualified answer is too superficial. Individuals and families are often obliged to subordinate their private good to the common good, as is evident from the very idea of the state. Nor is it sufficient answer to say that the common good redounds to the benefit of all the individuals making up the community. An individual is sometimes obliged to sacrifice his life for the state, as in war, and gets no personal good out of it at all. If the state is for him, why must he die for it? There is, then, a qualified sense in which the individual is subordinate to the state. We must still say that the state is for man, but not for any single member of the state to the detriment of all.

A solution that gets at the metaphysical roots of this problem is developed by Jacques Maritain.* He argues from two apparently opposed passages in St. Thomas: "Every individual person is compared to the whole community, as part to whole"† and: "Man is not ordained to the body politic according to all that he is and has."‡ The whole man is a part of the state, but he is not a part of the state by reason of all that is in him. When a man runs, the whole man runs, but by reason of his muscles and not by reason of his knowledge of astronomy. So the whole man is an individual person, a member of the family, and a citizen of the state; but there is something different in him that sets him up in each of these relations.

The human being is a person, but not the highest type of person. Man is the highest creature and the only person in this material universe, but compared to the realm of angelic spirits man is at the bottom of the scale among created persons. As a person he is for himself under God and cannot be subordinated to a greater whole, but because his self-sufficiency is so limited he must band with his fellows to supply his needs.

Because he is a *person,* man transcends all temporal societies, for he has an eternal destiny and his immortal soul will outlast all the empires of this world. There is nothing above the human soul but God, and herein lies its high dignity. In this sense human society exists for each person and is subordinate to him. The state must not compromise man's natural rights because they are given by a higher law than the state's. The state itself is but one of the means granted to man by the natural law to help him in achieving his last end, and he casts it aside as an outworn

---

*Maritain, *Scholasticism and Politics,* ch. III; *Rights of Man and the Natural Law,* ch. I; *The Person and the Common Good.*
†St. Thomas, *Summa Theologica,* II-II, q. 64, a. 2.
‡I-II, q. 21, a. 4, 3rd obj.

instrument when he passes out of earthly society into the kingdom of heaven.

But because man is such a *lowly type* of person, subject indeed to no being but God above himself, but utterly dependent on his equals for every kind of service and abounding in needs and wants, both physical and intellectual, that only his fellow men can supply, man during his earthly life becomes a part of a larger whole whose common temporal good is greater than the individual temporal good of each member taken separately. In this sense the common welfare takes precedence over private comfort and security. Since the state exists to protect the life, liberty, and property of all, the individual may be called on to play his part in the common defense even at the expense of his own life, liberty, and property.

The theory continues with an exploration of the concepts of personality and individuality as verified in the one same individual person. The whole man is a person, and the whole man is an individual; personality and individuality are only mentally distinguished aspects. According to the Aristotelian theory that quantified matter is the principle of individuation, man is an individual by reason of his body. But man is a person by reason of his soul, since a person is an intellectual being, and man is intellectual by reason of his form or soul. So by reason of his individuality founded on his temporal needs man is a member of the political community and subordinate to it, but by reason of his personality based on his eternal destiny man transcends the political community and subordinates it to himself. These metaphysical speculations are not strictly necessary to answer the problem proposed.

STRUCTURE OF THE STATE

The building blocks of the state are the members, the individual human beings of whom the state is composed. How is the state built up out of these materials? Is it composed directly of individuals with no structures or subgroups in between, or is it made up of families which in turn are made up of individuals? Should we include other groupings larger than the family but smaller than the state? Are such groups essential to the state or only incidentally found in some states? There are three main views:

1. The *atomistic* concept of the state holds that the state is made up directly and proximately of individuals. Each citizen is like an atom in a homogeneous mass. He counts for one and no more than one, not representing others under him. No intermediate groups such as the family, the business firm, or the labor union are recognized as structural units in the state. They exist, of course, and the state must deal with them extensively, but they are not regarded as part of the state's essential make-up. In the state each individual is expected to act for his self-interest alone, banding with others only for mutual self-interest in a contractual relation. The atomistic view is characteristic of laissez faire individualism.

2. The *biological* concept of the state gives the state not merely a moral union but a physical entity over and above the members that compose it. It overdoes the analogy between a society and a living organism. Just as the organs and members of the living body have no life of their own but live with the life of the whole, so also the individual person and the family are thought to be as completely submerged in the state as a cell or organ in the living body. There are various interpretations of this view, but the most extreme as well as the most logical is the *totalitarian* concept, in which the individual counts for nothing. There is just a global mass of social humanity in which the individual has not even the independence of an atom.

3. The *organizational* concept of the state stands between these extremes. The state is seen as a complex structure of individuals and families, so that the family is an essential ingredient in the state's composition. Some individuals live singly outside families, and members of families have some relations to the state independently of their family status, but the very existence of the state depends on a healthy flourishing of family life among its people. Within modern states there are also a number of voluntary associations with semipolitical functions, carrying on work for the common good that the state would otherwise have to do by itself. These voluntary associations are not essential to the state in the same way as the family but are sort of properties pertaining to a well-developed state. This structure of individuals, families, voluntary associations, and the state forms a hierarchical arrangement. Some writers call this the *organic* theory and contrast it with the biological theory, which they call *organismic*. But the similarity of names is confusing, especially since other writers call organic any theory opposed to the atomistic. Care must be taken to stress that the state is not a physical organism but a moral organization, in which individuals and families retain their identity, rights, functions, and relative autonomy.

Of these three views the organizational one alone corresponds to the theory of man and society adopted here. It insists on the *principle of subsidiarity:* that no higher organization should take over work that a lower organization can do satisfactorily. The higher does not exist to absorb or extinguish the lower but to supplement and extend it. Otherwise the rights given by nature to the individual and to the family, and man's freedom to organize for lesser pursuits within the state, are rendered meaningless. On the other hand, the state should provide a favorable environment in which individuals, families, and voluntary associations can fulfill their functions properly. It has the right and duty to intervene when they fail to function as they ought or cannot harmonize their activities for the common good.

SUMMARY

The state is a *natural* society and not merely a conventional society, because the family naturally broadens out into the tribe with a central village and becomes a state when it achieves self-sufficiency under a common authority. Any group arriving at this condition is bound by the natural law to organize itself into political society.

Opposed to this is the *contractual theory* of Hobbes and Rousseau, according to which the state is an artificial product of human agreement. The *social contract* supposes a nonsocial and nonmoral state of nature, overlooks the natural expansion of the family, requires the transfer of inalienable rights, cannot logically bind posterity, and does not account for all the rights the state claims.

The state is a *perfect* society in the sense of being self-sufficing, independent, autonomous, and sovereign. It has all it needs to fulfill its end and depends on no higher society. But its sovereignty is not absolute, for it is limited by the natural law and the equal rights of other states.

The state is for man, not man for the state. But this cannot be said without qualification. The whole man is part of the state, but not by reason of all that is in him. Because he is a *person,* man transcends all temporal societies and is subordinate only to God. Because he is a *lowly type* of person, poor in self-sufficiency, the individual man is dependent on his fellows for his temporal welfare and must sacrifice his personal good for the common good. The state itself, however, is not for itself as a state, but for all its people.

The *structure* of the state is the arrangement of its components. The *atomistic* view has the state built up proximately of individuals, like atoms in a homogeneous mass. The *biological* view submerges the individual in the whole, like a cell in the living body. The *organizational* view sees the state as a hierarchical structure of individuals, families, and voluntary associations, which retain their identity, rights, and functions while directed to the common good by the state, according to the *principle of subsidiarity.*

READINGS

1. The great classics of political philosophy include such works as Plato's *Republic,* Aristotle's *Politics,* Cicero's *De Re Publica* and *De Legibus,* St. Thomas' *De Regimine Principum,* Machiavelli's *The Prince* and *Discourses,* Bodin's *De la République,* Bellarmine's *De Laicis,* Suarez' *De Legibus,* Hobbes' *Leviathan,* Locke's *Two Treatises on Government,* Rousseau's *Social Contract,* the *Federalist* papers, Mill's *Representative Government.* From this formidable array the student should find something to interest him.

2. On the matter of this chapter read Plato, *Republic,* bk. II, §§369-374, and *Laws,* bk. III, §§676-682.

3. Aristotle's *Politics,* bk. I, ch. 1 and 2.

4. Locke, *Second Treatise on Government,* ch. 1-4, 7-10.

5. Maritain, *Man and the State.* This short book sums up the results of his excellent work in political philosophy. Two earlier booklets of his are of particular value: *The Person and the Common Good* and *Rights of Man and the Natural Law.*

6. Simon, *Philosophy of Democratic Government,* is a unique and very rewarding work; chap. 1 is pertinent here.

7. Rommen, *The State in Catholic Thought,* ch. 4, 9-12, 17-18.

8. Messner, *Social Ethics,* bk. III, pts. I and II.

9. Cronin, *Science of Ethics,* vol. II, pp. 461-477, 491-499, 544-556.
10. Leibell, *Readings in Ethics,* pp. 743-763, 895-925.
11. Haas, *Man and Society,* ch. 15.
12. Cahill, *Framework of a Christian State,* ch. 23.
13. Le Buffe and Hayes, *The American Philosophy of Law,* ch. 14.
14. Rickaby, *Moral Philosophy,* pp. 297-319.
15. Catlin, *Story of Political Philosophers,* ch. 3, 5-9, 14.

CHAPTER 26

GOVERNMENT

PROBLEMS

A state is said to rule or govern. Government primarily means the actual exercise of the state's function, its direction of its citizens to their common good. To accomplish this purpose, a state can be organized in various ways. The particular organization used in a certain state is called its constitution. It determines the number of officers, how they are chosen, their coordination and subordination, their powers and duties, and the apportionment of authority among them. Government often means the constitution, especially when we speak of the form of government. Men tend to concretize abstractions and refer to the body of legislative and administrative officers, the group of persons officially exercising government, as *the government* of that particular state. So government means the act of governing, the constitution, and the persons holding political power.

There can be no society without authority. It is evident that, if authority exists anywhere in a state, it must exist in the government. How do they get it? How should they use it? We shall discuss the following topics:

(1) How is the recipient of authority designated?
(2) Is there any best form of government?
(3) How much should the state interfere in private life?
(4) What is the definition of the state?

RECIPIENT OF AUTHORITY

That authority is essential to every society, and that in a natural society authority comes directly and immediately from God, has already been discussed in the chapter on society in general. Then we were dealing with the origin of authority in society as such. Our present question is:

How is the person or group who is to bear and exercise this authority designated?

In a conventional society the same convention or agreement which establishes the society determines the mode of selecting its officials. In the natural society of the family the qualities of aggressiveness and leadership normally preponderant in the husband designate him as head of the family. How authority in *political* society begins to reside in one person or group of persons is a controverted matter. Among those who hold that civil authority comes from God, and all do who accept the state as a natural society, three main explanations have been devised:

(1) The divine right of kings
(2) The theory of popular consent
(3) The patriarchal theory

Divine right of kings

Though the theory of the divine right of kings is obsolete today, some remarks on it are necessary to make sure what we do not mean, and to bring the other views into sharper focus. It is well to note that the theory was most uncommon in the middle ages and arose to prominence only when feudalism had broken up and given place to the autocratic monarchies of the early modern period. Its chief proponent was King James I of England. Sir Robert Filmer's *Patriarcha,* a pamphlet defending the theory, called forth Locke's *Two Treatises of Government* in refutation.

The theory of the divine right of kings held that the actual rulers have their authority by an immediate personal grant from God. God not only gives authority to the state, but even selects the rulers, either by positive intervention as in the case of King Saul in the Jewish theocracy, or by tacit approval of the ruler selected by appointment, election, hereditary succession, or some other traditionally recognized manner. Most is made of the title of hereditary succession, as approved among the patriarchs and Jewish kings of the Old Testament, so that the hereditary monarchs of the European states are directly picked out by God for their positions. The kings, of course, were not loath to have their thrones bolstered by this theory, which would make it immoral to unseat them no matter how badly they governed.

Theory of popular consent

The endeavor of kings to bend philosophy to their service provoked an immediate reaction. The formerly prevailing view, that of popular consent, also called the *translation* or *transmission* theory, implicit and undeveloped in medieval writers, needed more express formulation. The challenge was met by St. Robert Bellarmine in his *De Laicis* (On the Laity) and by Francis Suarez in his *De Legibus* (On Laws) and *Defensio Fidei Catholicae* (Defense of the Catholic Faith), as well as by Locke and others later on.

Bellarmine and Suarez, whose opinions are substantially the same on this point, hold that the state is a natural society, that men are not free to form the state or not as they please, but are obliged to do so by their natural needs and inclinations, that all authority comes from God and is no mere product of human convention. But, though the people themselves do not give authority to the state, they are the ones who select the ruler who is to bear that authority. God immediately confers authority on the whole people civilly united; the people then determine the form of government and transfer the authority to an individual or a group, but the government thus set up exists by the consent of the governed.

The fact that families are descended from a common ancestor, that they live near one another, that they have common needs and interests, that they have organized themselves into a tribe with a central village, these are all dispository causes making the formation of a state naturally imperative. But the formation of an actual concrete state with a definite ruler and a definite type of organization requires the consent of the people, which is the proximate efficient cause of this particular state. The consent of the people may be either express or tacit, either direct or indirect, but in all cases it is the original title a ruler has for his authority. Though neither Bellarmine nor Suarez uses the exact words of Jefferson's phrase, "Governments derive their just powers from the consent of the governed," it aptly summarizes their opinion.

A few quotations from Bellarmine will clarify his thought:

> Political power considered in general, not descending in particular to Monarchy, Aristocracy, or Democracy, comes directly from God alone; for this follows of necessity from the nature of man, since that nature comes from Him Who made it; besides, this power derives from the natural law, since it does not depend upon the consent of men; for, willing or unwilling, they must be ruled over by someone, unless they wish the human race to perish, which is against a primary instinct of nature. . . .
>
> This power resides, as in its subject, immediately in the whole state, for this power is by Divine law, but Divine law gives this power to no particular man, therefore Divine law gives this power to the collected body. Furthermore, in the absence of positive law, there is no good reason why, in a multitude of equals, one rather than another should dominate. Therefore, power belongs to the collected body. . . .
>
> By the same natural law, this power is delegated by the multitude to one or several, for the State cannot of itself exercise this power; therefore, it is held to delegate it to some individual, or to several, and this authority of rulers considered thus in general is both by natural and by Divine law, nor could the entire human race assembled together decree the opposite, that is, that there should be neither rulers nor leaders. . . .
>
> Individual forms of government in specific instances derive from the law of nations, not from the natural law, for, as is evident, it depends on the consent of the people to decide whether kings, or consuls, or other magistrates are to be established in authority over them; and, if there

be legitimate cause, the people can change a kingdom into an aristocracy, or an aristocracy into a democracy, and vice versa.*

The difference between this theory and the contractualism of Hobbes and Rousseau should be apparent at a glance:

Hobbes-Rousseau	*Bellarmine-Suarez*
Man is not naturally social and forms the state only out of expediency.	Man is naturally social and is obliged by the natural law to form the state.
The state is an artificial institution and a pure invention of man.	The state is a natural society based on man's natural needs and instincts.
The social contract establishes political society itself as an institution.	The contract only determines the form of government and the ruler.
Authority is but an aggregate of individual human wills.	Authority comes from God to the people who transfer it to the ruler.
The ruler somehow gets rights the people have no power to give him.	The state gets its superior powers from God through the natural law.
The contracting parties bind posterity but with no valid authority to do so.	The natural law binds posterity to honor the state's just commitments.

Patriarchal theory

Some antiliberals of the nineteenth century, alarmed by the excesses of the French Revolution and the ensuing anticlerical governments, tried to avoid the pitfalls of the divine right of kings without admitting the rather thinly veiled democratic basis in the theory of Bellarmine and Suarez. Foreshadowed in the work of Joseph de Maistre† and Donoso Cortés,‡ the *patriarchal* or *designation* theory was proposed by Karl von Haller§ and defended, among others, by Aloysius Taparelli.‖ It was little noticed in England or America but very influential on the European continent.

It holds that, when civil society is first formed, some man or group of men may be so outstanding in fitness and leadership as to receive an immediate grant of authority through the natural law independently of the consent of the people. Some natural fact indicates this person or group. He may be the patriarch himself or the eldest son of the eldest branch of the family, or the tribal chieftain, or a victorious military leader, or a man who by gifts of intellect and will has done most to weld the people into a body politic.

The main point of this theory is that such a man receives his grant of authority immediately from God, independently of the consent of the

---

*Bellarmine, *De Laicis,* bk. III, ch. 6. See also Suarez, *De Legibus,* bk. III, ch. II, §§3, 4.
†De Maistre, *Du Pape* (On the Pope).
‡Donoso Cortés, *Ensayo sobre el Catolicismo, el Liberalismo y el Socialismo* (Essay on Catholicism, Liberalism, and Socialism).
§Haller, *Restauration der Staatswissenschaften* (Restoration of Political Sciences).
‖Taparelli, *Saggio Teoretico di Diritto Naturale* (Theoretical Essay on Natural Right).

people, for they are obliged by the natural law not to refuse his leadership. Even when no such man appears and the people choose their leader, he receives his authority so directly from God that it does not pass through the people.

Judgment on these opinions

The theory of the *divine right of kings* is easily disposed of. Except in the Jewish theocracy, no act of divine intervention designating the form of government and the person of the ruler has occurred in history. Hence ordinary civil rulers do not rule by divine appointment.

The *patriarchal theory* argues against the popular consent theory as follows:

1. The patriarch or chieftain already had some sort of authority in the tribe before it passed into statehood, and it is natural that he should keep it.

2. Authority is essentially an attribute of a ruler, whether an individual or a group, and cannot dwell in the community as such. The whole people are too unwieldy to exercise authority.

3. Popular consent, though one of the titles, is not the only title to political power. It cannot be proved historically that all original rulers were elected by the people.

The *popular consent theory* answers these arguments thus:

1. The patriarch or chieftain probably would become the ruler of a newly formed state. But not without the people's consent, at least tacit, if the state is to be formed as the natural law requires. There is no need of express consent in the form of a vote.

2. Formal authority ready for immediate use resides in the ruler, but basic authority resides in the whole community. Because they are too unwieldy a body, the people transfer the exercise of authority to an individual or group charged with the task of governing.

3. There are many titles to political power, but they are all derivative except the one basic title of popular consent. No other title is valid by itself but becomes so only when confirmed by at least tacit consent of the people. Rule against the people's will, maintained only by force, is the perversion of government.

There are additional arguments. During an interregnum there is no person in the state holding supreme authority; if authority vanishes, the state itself vanishes; the patriarchal theory cannot solve this difficulty, but the popular consent theory simply has the authority revert to the people. Also, natural law must provide some remedy for tyranny; tyrants can be removed only by revolution; no one can authorize a revolution except the people themselves, and to do so some form of authority must already dwell in them. By its very nature all government must be *for* the people, since its purpose is the common good; the popular consent theory says that it should also be *of* the people, arising from their consent and with their authorization; whether it should be *by* the people, so that they do the governing themselves, depends on the adoption of a democratic form. The popular consent theory does not require this last element but finds it congenial.

FORMS OF GOVERNMENT

This subject, which looms large in political science, can be passed over briefly by the moralist. From the earliest times political writers have tried to classify the forms of government. Plato* has a fivefold division based on a gradual falling-off from the ideal (aristocracy, timocracy, oligarchy, democracy, tyranny). Aristotle† has a sixfold division based on a double principle, the number of rulers and the goodness of their rule; he lists three good forms (monarchy, aristocracy, polity) and three perversions (tyranny, oligarchy, democracy). These ancient divisions have yielded in the popular mind to the threefold classification into monarchy, which may be absolute or limited; aristocracy, which may be of birth or wealth; and democracy, which may be pure or representative. These forms may be combined in so many ways that no two governments are exactly alike.

There is nothing ethically wrong with any of these forms or their combinations. Moralists think that the way a government functions is more important than the way it is constituted. Government is a means to the end of the state, the common good, the temporal welfare of the people. Any government which actually fulfills this end to the satisfaction of human expectation is good; any which does not, but governs for the benefit of the few at the expense of the many, is not good.

Recently there have been efforts to prove that representative democracy is the best form of government. A distinction must be made between the relatively best, the best for this people in these circumstances with these traditions and in this stage of its historical development, and the absolutely best, the best for an enlightened and mature people in almost ideal conditions. In the first case one type of government will be best for one people, another for another; which to adopt or maintain is a matter of political prudence. In the second case one can make out a good argument for democracy, since, other things being equal, it is more fitting for a free people not only to be ruled but also to share in the act of ruling. In actual fact, however, other things hardly ever are equal, and for democracy to work a people must have had a long apprenticeship in self-government.

In structure, all forms of government are ethically acceptable. In function, only those forms can be approved which actually succeed in realizing the end of the state. It is wrong to force on a people a type of government they do not want. Tyranny, the misuse of government, is per-

---

*Plato, *Republic*, bk. VIII.

†Aristotle, *Politics*, bk. III, ch. 7, 1279a 22 to 1279b 10. For the ancients democracy meant mob rule; hence it is listed among the perversions.

haps the worst moral crime that can be committed. Leaders of the state, and to some extent the people, have a serious moral obligation in justice to do what they can toward correcting the defects in their government.

GOVERNMENT CONTROL

Having seen how authority comes to reside in the governing body of a state, and the chief forms it takes, we must now ask how far the government should go in the exercise of its authority, in controlling the lives of its citizens. Including untenable extremes, we can list five possible views, grading them from the least to the most interference. Government should:

(1) Be abolished as unnecessary
(2) Be mostly negative and limited to mere policing
(3) Positively assist private initiative for the common good
(4) Assume direction and control of all public affairs
(5) Absorb the whole of human life

We shall discuss these opinions, beginning with the extremes and working toward the center. We have already said enough in the last chapter about the first opinion, *anarchism,* and the fifth opinion, *totalitarianism.* Both are clearly contrary to the natural law, since the first denies the rights of society and the other the rights of the person.

The second opinion is *individualism.* Last century it was called *liberalism,* but this term has become too equivocal a designation today. It is a theory of economics as well as politics. It was advocated by the Physiocrats in France,* who coined the phrase "laissez faire," and by the Economic Liberals in England,† where it was carried to an extreme in the Manchester School.‡ It is resentful of all government interference in business and wants no more government interference elsewhere that is strictly necessary. The activity of the state should be limited to keeping public order, protecting property, punishing criminals, and defense against foreign attack. Because its functions would be mainly negative, it is sometimes called the *watchman state.* It is also known as the *minimizing* theory, since it can be summed up in the statement: "The best government is the least government."

The fourth opinion, so far as it falls short of totalitarianism, is called *statism* and *paternalism.* Its corresponding economic theory is socialism, but it can exist without socialism, as in the mercantilist monarchies before the French Revolution. If not socalistic, it allows private property but leaves little scope for private enterprise in its use. It imposes the minutest regulations on all business and makes the undertaking of nearly all public works a state monopoly. Though free from theoretical convictions that the individual and the family are mere cogs in the state machine, in

---

*François Quesnay, Anne Robert Turgot.
†Adam Smith, David Ricardo.
‡Richard Cobden, John Bright.

practice it interferes unduly in the personal and family lives of its people and infringes on their natural rights. As the name *paternalism* indicates, it looks on its subjects as incapable children rather than responsible citizens. Lack of initiative and enterprise characterize people long subject to such a rule.

The third opinion seems to gravitate to the center and to maintain the proper balance between the claims of the individual and the state. It does not want any more government interference than is necessary, but is willing to admit it when necessary. It leaves the way open for private initiative, but is ready to come to its assistance when private initiative fails. It not only protects but positively promotes all enterprises undertaken for the common good. It carefully respects the rights of the individual and of the family, does not try to usurp their duties, and helps them rather by offering opportunities than by regimenting their behavior. On the other hand, it does not hesitate to correct abuses, by legislation if necessary, when it becomes apparent that private influences cannot cope with them. No government has ever put this theory into practice perfectly, but it represents the ideal of many governments, including our own. No term unequivocally designates this ideal and we shall simply call it the *middle way*. It can still be the middle way even if it has leanings to one side or the other, as in the conservative and liberal elements of our own country.

Individualism may work successfully for a while, especially in a land of unlimited opportunity, such as in the early days of our own country, but sooner or later proves inadequate to cope with the social stresses and strains of an advanced society. Paternalism may be necessary in colonial administration and among backward peoples not yet fit for self-rule, but even here should assume the role of a temporary educator rather than that of a permanent dictator. Whatever be the form of government or type of constitution in a state, the middle way represents the only way in which a government can exercise its powers consistently with the dignity of a mature and free people.

DEFINITION OF THE STATE

We can summarize our study of the state in a definition containing all the elements we have investigated:

The state is a perfect or self-sufficing natural society, consisting of many individuals and families, united under a common authority, for the attainment of the temporal welfare of the community.

1. It is a society, because it consists of many persons united together by a moral bond, which obliges them to use common means for a common end.

2. It is a natural society, for it is demanded by the natural law as the logical completion and extension of the other natural society, the family.

3. It is perfect or self-sufficing, for it is not subject or tributary to

any other natural society, and contains within itself all the means for attaining its end.

4. It consists proximately of families and remotely of individuals, for the family stands midway between the individual and the state. There are thus three natural units in human organization: the individual, the family, and the state. There should be room also for voluntary associations.

5. It has a common ruler possessing authority, for someone must oblige the members to use the means to attain the end. The ruler may be an individual, a group, or the whole people.

6. Its purpose is to promote man's temporal welfare, not that it should have no interest in man's last end, but that its function is only to provide the proper earthly conditions in which man may be free to work out his ultimate destiny.

7. It seeks the common good, the welfare of the community, taken both collectively and distributively. The state seeks the good of individuals and families by protecting them and offering them opportunities rather than by usurping their functions.

SUMMARY

Government means the act of governing, the constitution of the state, or the persons holding political power. Government supposes authority. How designate the *bearer of authority* in the state?

1. The *divine right of kings* theory, holding that the ruler is directly appointed by God, is deservedly obsolete.

2. The *popular* consent theory of Bellarmine and Suarez holds that God directly gives authority to the whole people civilly united, who then transfer its exercise to an individual or group according to the form of government they approve; the implied contract does not establish political society as such, but only the form of government and the ruler; all government exists by the consent, at least tacit, of the governed.

3. The *patriarchal* theory holds that a man or group can be so outstanding in qualities of leadership as to receive a grant of authority directly from God without the people's consent; authority dwells only in the ruler, not even basically in the people.

Of the last two theories, each of which has its probability, the popular consent theory seems preferable. It alone can explain an interregnum and a justified revolution. Any government in which there is not at least tacit consent of the people must be a tryranny and cannot be approved by the natural law.

The functioning of government is more important than its structure. Monarchy, aristocracy, and democracy are all ethically acceptable in principle. Some think that democracy is absolutely best, but in practice we must consider the relatively best: which form is best *for a people* depends on their traditions and circumstances.

How far should government interfere with private life? Theories run from *anarchism,* no interference at all, to *totalitarianism,* total absorption of everything into the state. *Individualism* and *paternalism* are more moderate but still exaggerate the function either of the individual or of the state. The ideal is the middle position, one of giving positive assistance to private initiative, correcting its abuses while scrupulously respecting its rights.

The state is *defined* as a perfect and self-sufficing natural society, consisting of many individuals and families, united under a common authority, for the attainment of the temporal welfare of the community.

READINGS

1. For the classics of political philosophy, see the readings for the previous chapter.
2. On the philosophy of government in general:
   a. D'Entrèves, *Aquinas, Selected Political Writings,* contains a translation of *De Regimine Principum* and of other political passages in St. Thomas' works; see D'Entrèves' excellent introduction on St. Thomas' political philosophy.
   b. Maritain, *Freedom in the Modern World,* pt. I and III; *True Humanism,* ch. 4-7; *Scholasticism and Politics,* ch. 1, 3-4 (in addition to the works mentioned in the last chapter).
   c. Sheed, *Society and Sanity,* ch. 11-16.
   d. There are two pertinent Encyclicals of Pope Leo XIII: *Immortale Dei* (Christian Constitution of States) and *Libertas Humana* (Human Liberty).
3. On the recipient of authority:
   a. James I's writings are found in McIlwain, *The Political Works of James I.*
   b. Bellarmine's *De Laicis* is translated by K. Murphy, *De Laicis, or the Treatise on Civil Government.*
   c. Suarez' *De Legibus* is translated in part in J. B. Scott, *Classics of International Law: Suarez;* read bk. III, ch. 2-4.
   d. Locke's *Two Treatises of Government* usually contains a reprint of Filmer's *Patriarcha,* of which Locke's *First Treatise* is a refutation. Locke's *Second Treatise* is the important one, giving Locke's positive view.
   e. Leibell, *Readings in Ethics,* pp. 895-899, pp. 913-971.
   f. Simon, *Philosophy of Democratic Government,* ch. 3.
   g. Rommen, *The State in Catholic Thought,* ch. 19-20.
   h. Catlin, *Story of Political Philosophers,* pp. 259-281.
   i. Figgis, *The Divine Right of Kings,* is the standard work on this subject.
   j. Cronin, *Science of Ethics,* vol. II, ch. 15-16, argues against Bellarmine and Suarez in favor of the patriarchal theory.
4. On forms of government:
   a. Plato's classification of constitutions is found in his *Republic,* bk. VIII and IX.
   b. Aristotle's classification is in his *Politics,* bk. III, ch. 6-9, 15-17, and throughout bk. IV.
   c. Cicero, *De Re Publica,* bk. I, ch. 22-47.
   d. Rommen, *The State in Catholic Thought,* ch. 21.
   e. Cronin, *Science of Ethics,* vol. II, ch. 17.
   f. Adler and Farrell, *The Theory of Democracy,* a series of articles in the *Thomist,* vol. III, IV, VI, VII (1941-1944), purporting to prove that democracy is the best form of government.
5. On state control and interference:
   a. Simon, *Philosophy of Democratic Government,* ch. 2, 4-5.
   b. Rommen, *The State in Catholic Thought,* ch. 13-14.
   c. Messner, *Social Ethics,* bk. III, pt. III.
   d. Haas, *Man and Society,* ch. 16-17.
   e. Catlin, *Story of Political Philosophers,* ch. 13, 20-22.
   f. Lippman, *The Public Philosophy,* argues that the natural law philosophy is the public philosophy inherent in the American form of government.

CHAPTER 27

CIVIL LAW

PROBLEMS

The state has at its command one major means for accomplishing its end: civil laws. All states pass laws, execute the laws passed, and bring offenders to justice. Thus the three powers, legislative, executive, and judicial, whether exercised by the same or different officials, are mentally distinguishable and all are necessary to every form of government. The apportionment and functioning of these powers is matter for political science. We shall limit ourselves to some questions involving the moral issue:

(1) Must natural law be supplemented by positive law?
(2) Is there a law between natural and positive law?
(3) Are we morally obliged to keep the civil law?
(4) Are there such things as purely penal laws?
(5) Why has the state the right to punish?
(6) Why has the state the right to tax?
(7) May the state limit freedom of speech and conscience?
(8) What can be done about unjust laws and tyranny?

NEED FOR POSITIVE LAW

If man is already governed by the natural law, it may seem that positive laws are superfluous. However, we have seen that the natural law is clear to all only in its most general precepts, that it is unequally known because knowledge of it must be gradually developed, and that in any case it lacks statement in an expressed formula. This formulation human legislators supply by framing positive laws based on natural law.

Human positive laws may assume two forms. *Declarative* positive laws simply declare in so many words what the natural law prescribes or draw conclusions deducible from the natural law. Such would be laws forbidding murder, theft, perjury, and the like. These differ from the natural law only in the mode of promulgation. *Determinative* positive laws determine or fix ways of acting in accordance with the natural law but not deducible from it. Such would be traffic laws, ways of collecting taxes, times and methods of electing magistrates, the conditions for contracts, and the like. No law which contradicts the natural law can be a true law, but it need not merely reecho the natural law.

The natural law needs to be supplemented by positive law, both declarative and determinative, for these main reasons:

1. *The dictates of right reason may be obscured in some persons.* In every community there are some with defective or perverted moral education. Against such individuals society must be protected by a code of laws drawn up by the more responsible members of society, expressly stating what right reason demands in accordance with the natural law and enforcing it.

2. *The natural law does not prescribe earthly penalties.* The sanction of the natural law often fails to have effect in earthly affairs because no one sees it applied, some are influenced only by what they experience, and some disbelieve in a hereafter. But these people cannot be allowed to destroy society. Hence society has the duty to compile a code of criminal law, specifying definite punishments for definite crimes and applying them justly.

3. *The natural law often allows a choice of means to the end.* In merely individual action each one may pursue his own method. But often the end must be achieved by concerted social action. Where teamwork is necessary, individual preferences must be sacrificed. Hence some social authority must decide among all these legitimate means and possible methods just which one is to be used in a given case.

4. *Complex social life continually changes.* To these changed conditions human society must be harmoniously adjusted, and new applications of the natural law must be made to fit the new situation. Thus the industrial revolution brought up problems undreamed of before, and, though the principles of justice remain the same, they must now be applied to this new form of social organization. To prevent untold confusion, positive laws must be passed providing a social and cooperative solution of these problems.

THE LAW OF NATIONS

The type of human law that most approaches the natural law is the law of nations or *jus gentium.*

The great lawgivers of antiquity were the Romans, whose legal system is the basis of nearly all modern law in the European tradition. The Romans developed their law in the early days of their Republic, but when they began to expand and incorporate other nations into their empire, they left a good deal of autonomy to their subject nations, allowing them to run most of their internal affairs according to their own laws. Difficulties arose when cases were to be decided between a Roman citizen and an individual of a subject nation or between individuals of different subject nations. They solved the problem by extracting the common elements from the laws and customs of all their subject peoples. This highest common factor they developed into the *jus gentium* or *law of nations*. It was gradual growth, but at the height of the Roman Empire it had become an impressive body of customary law. The new nations which resulted from the breakup of the Roman Empire continued to use this law of nations with which they were familiar, and on it built the structure of their own laws.

The other source of European law is the customs of the Germanic tribes, but on the Continent these were grafted onto Roman law. The only comparable rival to the Roman law of nations is the English *common law,* which is the basis of English and American law. The common law consists of unwritten precedents and decisions of the common courts handed down through the centuries, as distinguished from statute law, or acts of Parliament. The English common law is independent of the Roman law of nations, but has been greatly influenced by it.

The law of nations is not the same as the natural law. The law of nations is positive law, even though unwritten, for it is a sifting out of the common elements in the actual laws of various peoples. But, since it is founded on nothing else than universal human nature, it is in great part an embodiment of the natural law. The first clear distinction between the natural law and the law of nations is found in St. Isidore of Seville.

> Natural law is common to all peoples in that it is had by an instinct of nature, not by any human agreement, as the marriage of man and woman, the begetting and rearing of children, the common possession of all, the one freedom of all, the acquisition of those things that are taken in the air or sea or on land; likewise the restoring of property entrusted or lent, the repelling of violence by force. For this or whatever is like this could never constitute an injustice but must be considered in accord with natural equity.*
>
> The law of nations is the occupation of territory, the building and fortification of cities and castles, wars, captivities, enslavements, the recovery or rights of postliminy, treaties of peace and others, the scruple which protects ambassadors from violence, and prohibitions of marriage between persons of different nationality. This is therefore called the law of nations because nearly all nations have made such things their custom.†

The law of nations in the sense of the *jus gentium* is not the same as international law. International law aims to regulate the mutual relations of states as states. The *jus gentium* was a general law within all nations,

---

*Etymologia, bk. V, ch. 4.
†*Ibid.,* ch. 6 (translation of both passages taken from Le Buffe and Hayes, *Jurisprudence,* pp. 64-65).

not between nations, and dealt with activities of individuals without considering their nationality; it was supranational rather than international. The term *law of nations* is used by most modern writers to mean international law, thus causing much unfortunate ambiguity.

From this brief survey it can be seen that the *jus gentium* holds somewhat of a middle place between the natural law and the civil law. The *jus gentium* comes under the heading of positive law, but because of its fundamental and almost universal character it agrees closely with the natural law.

OBLIGATION OF CIVIL LAW

Besides the law of nations, there are the civil laws of particular states. God made man a social being, and in doing so He sanctioned the formation of the state as the necessary means of regulating man's social life and gave it the authority for this purpose. Hence in the natural order the state is the institution entrusted with the task of framing civil laws as the positive laws needed to supplement the natural law. But there cannot be a law unless there is an obligation to observe it. The argument may be put as follows:

Whatever is indispensable to man's life in society is prescribed by the natural law. For the natural law requires man to conform his conduct to the norm of morality, which includes man's social relations to his fellow man. But obedience to the civil law is indispensable to man's life in society. For society must be guided by law and the natural law must be supplemented by positive law. Therefore obedience to the civil law is prescribed by the natural law.

Man's obligation to obey the civil law brings up several points regarding the extent and seriousness of this obligation.

1. *Is the individual obliged or only the group?* One might argue that the state will not be destroyed by occasional disobedience of individual citizens, and therefore only the citizenry taken collectively and not the individual is morally obliged to obey the civil law. We see that the state continues despite individual acts of disobedience, but general disobedience would overthrow the state and make it futile. No one citizen has a better right to disobey than another; it is a case of all or none. To allow all to disobey would be to allow general disobedience. Therefore no one is allowed to disobey. We must not overlook the fact that the citizens as citizens are united into one body demanding cooperative action; each must contribute to the common good and he does so by keeping the laws.

2. *Must the lawmaker intend to bind in conscience?* Some argue that many modern lawmakers no longer believe in genuine moral obligation, and hence cannot intend civil laws to be morally binding. A formal and explicit intention of making the law binding in conscience is not necessary. Whatever be the theoretical beliefs of these lawmakers, they often have the practical intention of giving to their laws full authority, of making them bind as thoroughly as laws can bind. This is an implicit intention, and is sufficient to constitute a real law. Even when the legislator's authority does not demand their observance, the common good may.

3. *Is popular acceptance necessary for civil laws?* Not unless the nature of the state or of the law requires it. In a pure democracy, and in laws requiring a popular referendum, the people themselves are the lawmakers and the law becomes valid only by their consent. But ordinarily legislative authority is handed over to one person or a group, who have authority while in office to pass laws without the express consent of the people. Such laws should be changed by petitioning the lawmakers or electing new ones, not by disobedience. The refusal of the people to accept a law or general disobedience to it does not of itself nullify a law. At most it may arouse suspicion of some radical defect in the law, that it may be unreasonable or unjust or against the common good, and therefore not really a law; investigation can then verify or dissipate such a suspicion. Sometimes a legislator does not expressly repeal a law but tacitly lets it become a dead letter; this may be equivalent to repeal by the legislator and, if so, the law ceases to bind. But a true law cannot be got rid of except by repeal, express or tacit, by the authoritative legislator, and until he does so it continues to bind morally.

4. *How are laws to be interpreted?* Interpretation of a law is its genuine explanation according to the mind of the lawgiver. Laws may be interpreted by the lawgiver himself, or by lawyers and jurists of standing, or by custom which has the tacit approval of the lawgiver. Custom has been called the best interpreter of law. The custom must not be reprobated by the lawgiver, but must receive at least his tolerance and silent approval. It is this attitude of the lawgiver toward the custom that gives it authority as an interpreter of law, and prevents it from being an illegitimate assumption of authority by those subject to the law. With the tacit approval of the lawgiver, custom may not only interpret but also establish or abolish laws. A too rigid interpretation of the letter of the law may go contrary to its spirit and do more harm than good. Hence most governments admit the principle of *equity,* a tempering of the rigor of the law in the interest of reasonableness and natural justice.

PURELY PENAL LAWS

There are certain civil laws that many good people feel no qualm in violating. They know their conduct is illegal but they do not consider it immoral. A man who breaks traffic laws when there is no danger, or gets something through the customs office without paying duty, or operates a business without a license, does not feel that he has committed sin. A penal law is any law provided with a penalty, and a *purely penal law* is one which imposes no obligation in conscience but has a penalty attached for violation.

Purely penal laws pose a problem. They are commonly regarded by the people as genuine laws, yet a law which would impose no obligation whatever does not seem to have what the idea of a law demands. We seem to be faced with the dilemma that either these so-called laws are not really laws or that they do bind in conscience. In either case we go against the widespread opinion of well-meaning and conscientious persons.

Many writers of the intellectualist or Thomistic tradition will not admit the concept of purely penal law. They argue that a law is a work of reason and meant for the common good; if, therefore, a lawmaker intends a law at all, he must intend its full observance. Some say that all civil laws unless manifestly unjust bind in conscience, and their violation is a moral fault measured by the seriousness of the matter. Others require that a true law be really *necessary* for the common good, and admit that certain so-called laws are but rules and regulations for civil decorum and public good order, whose violation does not imply a breach of morals unless accompanied by contempt for authority. This group, then, either will not hear of purely penal laws at all, or, if they use the term, mean so-called laws that are not really laws.

Those of the voluntarist tradition, Scotistic or Suarezian, generally accept purely penal laws. Since for them law is essentially an act of the lawmaker's free will, he may choose not to invoke his power of binding in conscience. A common explanation of this theory is that a purely penal law imposes a disjunctive obligation: either obey the law literally or be willing to pay the penalty if caught breaking it. Thus the law is really a law because it does impose moral obligation, though a disjunctive one. The legislator, it is said, can intend to make the obligation disjunctive, with an option for fulfilling it in one way or the other, even though he indicates his preference for literal observance. By assessing heavy penalties out of all proportion to the crime, the legislator seems to show that he is not averse to allowing the act if one will pay the price. Some laws, especially those designed to raise revenue, may attain their end in this way, for the fines collected for breaking the law may exceed what the law would have brought in had it been kept by all. The fact that modern states rely so heavily on police machinery to enforce such laws, rather than on an appeal to duty, is considered an indication of the lawmaker's mind.

In summary, there are three possible views on the moral obligation of the civil law: all bind in conscience, or none do, or some do and some do not. The first view, though it has its defenders, is too severe and contrary to common opinion and practice. The second view is too lax and plainly false, for some civil laws are evidently necessary for the common good. The third view seems the only reasonable solution, but it brings up the problem of distinguishing which laws bind in conscience and which do not. Those which do not can be called purely penal laws with a disjunctive obligation, according to the voluntarist theory; or it can be said that they are mere directives and not really laws, according to the intellectualist theory. In either case civil laws which are thought not to bind in conscience can be recognized if their main purpose is raising revenue, if the penalty is much too severe for the offense, if police methods are exclusively resorted to, or if they involve mere technicalities of procedure.

PUNISHMENT

Laws are useless without enforcement, and enforcement supposes the right to punish. Punishment is applied by the executive power of the state, but the judgment that punishment is deserved is rendered by the judicial power. Punitive justice involves distributive and legal justice (sometimes also commutative) in the function of restoring the balance of equality upset by crime.

The following discussion has no reference to the punishment of animals, children, maniacs, or others who cannot be guilty of moral evil. This is not punishment in the strict sense, but a figurative extension of the term. There is a resemblance in the means used, but the purpose is quite different: not to repay for crime committed, but only to train or restrain irresponsible beings.

Punishment in the strict sense has three functions, one looking to the past and two to the future. As looking to the past, punishment is *retributive*, because it pays back the criminal for his crime, gives him his just deserts, reestablishes the equal balance of justice which has been outraged, and reasserts the authority of the lawgiver which the criminal has flouted. As looking to the future, punishment may take two forms. If directed to the improvement of the offender and his rehabilitation as a member of society, it is *corrective* or *medicinal*. If directed to forestalling similar crimes by others, showing by example what happens to offenders, it is *deterrent* or *preventive*.

An ideal punishment should fulfill all three functions, and thus serve all parties concerned. It should be:

(1) Retributive, vindicating the rights of the offended
(2) Corrective, rehabilitating the offender
(3) Deterrent, forewarning the community at large

This ideal, of course, is not always attainable. Perfect retribution implies restitution and a life taken cannot be restored. Capital punishment cannot correct the offender and some criminals are incorrigible. Punishments will not deter if the criminal thinks he can escape them, and not all are caught.

In most acts of wrongdoing punishable by society three things are usually involved:

(1) An injury against the individual
(2) A crime against the state
(3) A sin against God

For the *injury* done to the individual the offender is obliged to make restitution or compensation for the loss inflicted. This is only part of what is demanded by justice, for it merely restores things the way they were before the offense. It involves no payment for the crime as a crime, and therefore is not punishment. The offender simply did not get away with it this time and may try again later. The individual offended, as an individual, is not entitled to more than compensation, and this is one reason why vengeance is not a private affair. But the offense is a *crime* against the state as well as an injury to the individual. Hence, besides receiving compensation, the offended party can turn the criminal over to the state for punishment. The state has the right to exact retribution for the breach of public order and the assault on the majesty of the law, as well as the duty of trying to reform its wayward citizen and deter others from like crimes. The *sin,* however, still remains. Neither the individual offended nor the state can do anything about this. God can either forgive it or punish it as He wills; in fact, unlike human judges, His infinite wisdom, should He so will, enables Him to do both.

Basis of punishment

There is no difficulty about the corrective and deterrent aspects of punishment. Everyone sees that without them human society is impossible. But much has been written on retributive punishment in modern times, and some have thrown it out as a relic of benighted barbarism. They argue that it is mere revenge and is therefore immoral in itself, that it is but adding one evil to another and not the overcoming of evil by good. This is not really a new idea, but is found in Plato:

> No one punishes the evil-doer under the notion, or for the reason, that he has done wrong; only the unreasonable fury of the beast acts in that manner. But he who desires to inflict rational punishment does not retaliate for a past wrong which cannot be undone; he has regard to the future, and is desirous that the man who is punished, and he who sees him punished, may be deterred from doing wrong again. He punishes for the sake of prevention.*

Plato, as logic requires, connects his theory of punishment with his view that no one does wrong voluntarily. He also expresses the very modern notion that crime is a disease and should be treated as such. Many modern writers adopt Plato's theory on other grounds; they are determinists in psychology and utilitarians in ethics; no one can be guilty of crime if there is no free will, and there is nothing useful to the public welfare about merely retributive punishment.

It is well to pay tribute to the humanity of these well-meaning people, but we must not so emphasize mercy as to destroy justice. They are right in condemning revenge, but revenge and retributive punishment are not the same. Revenge aims at the emotional pleasure one gets from hurting an enemy, retributive punishment at securing justice simply. This is one reason why justice is best administered by a neutral party. Retribution

---

*Protagoras, §324. See also *Laws,* bk. **XI,** §934; *Gorgias,* §525.

is not merely adding one evil to another, unless one were to hold that justice itself is not a good. Some criminals probably are mentally diseased, but this is surely not true of all; if normal persons are morally responsible for the good they do, the same is true of their evil deeds. Many of the punishments used in former times were cruel, but that is an abuse and no argument against punishment itself.

The reason we cannot abolish the retributive function of punishment, and limit ourselves to the corrective and deterrent functions, is that all punishment to be justified must be based on retribution. Retribution may not be uppermost in mind but it must be present; otherwise the infliction of any punishment is morally wrong.

1. Punishment may not be inflicted unless a crime has been committed. If punishment were merely corrective and deterrent, we could inflict pain on any person to improve him or deter others from wrongdoing, whether he were guilty or not. But in these cases we can only threaten punishment, not inflict it. Guilt calls for retribution, and this is what gives us the right to inflict punishment so that it is not the use of an evil means to a good end. We may then also make the punishment corrective and deterrent as additional functions.

2. Punishment should be proportioned to the crime. But if the corrective and deterrent functions of punishment were the only ones, punishment should be proportioned to these. Not the guilt of the offender, but what is necessary to correct him or to protect society should measure the penalty. If the criminal could be frightened from ever doing this again, or be made such an example of as to deter many others from attempting it, we should be justified in punishing him far beyond his deserts. But this is absurd. All admit that for good reasons punishment may be mitigated, but never increased beyond what the guilt of the offender demands, no matter how much good it may do. Why? Because it is not deserved, just retribution does not call for it. Hence retribution is essential to punishment.

To sum up: It is immoral to punish unless the accused is guilty, no matter how much good the infliction of pain may do him or society. It is moral to punish the guilty even if there is no hope of correcting him or deterring others from crime. Therefore neither correction nor deterrence, but retribution is the basis on which punishment is justified. However, the corrective and deterrent functions of punishment are very important, and human rulers should devise their punishments with these uppermost in mind, leaving full retribution to God, but they cannot overlook retribution entirely for this alone makes punishment allowable.

Capital punishment

From the beginning of recorded history the state has used capital punishment rather freely, often excessively. If the death penalty is out of all proportion to the crime, the state does wrong in using it. We are speaking of it here only as applied to very serious crimes, such as murder and treason, which all who approve of capital punishment acknowledge as its proper sphere.

The state exists to maintain justice, and one of its chief purposes is the prevention and punishment of crime. In receiving its authority from God through the natural law, the state also receives from Him the right to use the necessary means for attainment of its end. The death penalty is used as such a means. It fulfills the retributive function of punishment by reestablishing as far as possible the balance of outraged justice and is thought to be the only effectual deterrent against the most serious crimes, especially those committed by criminals already under life sentence.

By its very nature capital punishment cannot be corrective. But correction, desirable though it be in a punishment, is not absolutely necessary; in the most serious crimes the claims of retribution and deterrence are so imperative that the corrective aspect must be sacrificed, if necessary. If capital punishment often fails as a deterrent, the fault may lie rather in the way it is administered than in the nature of the punishment itself. The law's long delays can empty the lesson of all its meaning. To be an effective deterrent, punishment should be swift, summary, and sure. Certainly, enough time must be allowed to gather evidence and to give the accused a fair trial, but in their effort to protect the criminal our judges, lawyers, and juries can lose the proper sense of civic responsibility.

Though the state has the right of capital punishment, it need not exercise the right if it can protect itself from criminals in another way. In former ages life imprisonment for all major criminals was impossible because the jails did not exist. If the state can prove that it can effectively handle crime without the death penalty, it may be argued that it not only need not but should not use it.

TAXATION

The state has from the natural law the right to the means necessary to accomplish its end. One of these means is revenue, and the ordinary way of raising revenue is by taxes. The state has therefore the right to tax its citizens. But this right is not unlimited. Legislators have a strict moral obligation not to impose too heavy a tax burden on the people, and those in charge of public funds are morally accountable for their use.

There is also a moral obligation to distribute the tax load as justly as possible. The only practical method is to make the taxes proportionate to the citizen's ability to pay, since there are many who not only cannot give anything but actually need help from the state. How the taxes ought to be arranged so as to fulfill the end of distributive justice is a matter for political and financial experts, and is beyond the scope of ethics as such.

If the state has the right to impose taxes, the citizen has the duty to pay taxes. One who is not too poor to pay some taxes yet pays none whatever is plainly failing in an important duty concerning the common good. But there are so many indirect taxes today that no one could avoid paying some taxes. Whether a man could fulfill his whole tax obligation in this way would depend on the amount and kind of his wealth.

Is one morally obliged to pay all the taxes imposed? If the tax is clearly unjust, there can be no moral obligation. The judgment that taxes are unjust must not be made hastily; people are always complaining about taxes even when there is no doubt of their necessity. On the other hand, the complete lack of conscience shown by too many public officials in spending the people's money makes the conviction all but inevitable that the state has not the right to all the revenue it asks. We must therefore distinguish between the duty of paying taxes in general, a real moral obligation, and the duty of paying this or that particular tax, a duty that is often not at all clear.

Are particular tax laws, then, purely penal laws? Those who reject the term entirely must give a negative answer. But those who admit purely penal laws in some sense, whether they mean only so-called laws that are mere directives or whether they mean real laws with a disjunctive obligation, consider it a solidly probable opinion that some particular tax laws are purely penal. Taxes have become too numerous and complicated for the ordinary citizen to handle, are accompanied by disproportionate penalties, and are often deducted at the source so that the citizen is not even trusted to do his duty; the state shows that it simply wants its money and makes no appeal to the public conscience. These are the usual indications of a purely penal law. It is therefore difficult to see a moral fault in a man who in general meets his tax obligations and supports the state, but occasionally evades a tax here and there, provided that in doing so he does not resort to such practices as lying or bribery. Conduct of this kind is certainly not recommended and a truly upright man would despise such pettifoggery.

PROTECTION OF CITIZENS' FREEDOMS

One of the ironies of history is the need for a Bill of Rights. The state, which exists to safeguard its citizens in the free exercise of their natural rights, has been a notorious violator of them. The history of the last few centuries portrays the victory of the people in their long struggle to get back from the state fundamental rights the state had usurped and liberties it had suppressed. Hardly had the victory been achieved when totalitarianism arose as the most ruthless destroyer of freedom yet to appear. We can discuss only three of these rights, perhaps the last to be won and the first to be lost in a people's fight to be free.

Free speech

The fact that speech is a natural ability means that man has a right to use it. Speech is not merely repeating what one has been told to say, but is the manifestation of one's own thoughts. Therefore a man has from the natural law the right to say what he thinks. But no right is wholly unlimited. A man can have no moral right to say things that are untrue or injurious to another person or harmful to the public welfare.

The state has the right to limit freedom of speech and of the press (which is only an extension of the right of speech) insofar as is necessary for the welfare of the community. Libel, obscenity, and the active fomenting of rebellion are rightly suppressed. The state has the duty to protect its citizens from these evils and their disastrous consequences.

It is one thing to admit that the state has the *right* to limit freedom of speech, and quite a different thing to ask how far the state should go in the *prudent exercise* of its right. History has shown that an overactive censorship is an unwise political policy, and that it is better to tolerate some abuses for the sake of liberty than to correct all abuses by suppressing liberty. A government afraid of criticism confesses its own weakness, and a government which stifles all criticism is tyrannical. Constructive criticism and free expression of opinion are the best way in which the government itself can find out how it stands with its people, what their needs are, and what reforms should be instituted for the common good. Certainly no government has the right to censor its citizens' mail (outside of wartime) or to spy on what things are said within the family. To do so is a direct invasion of the rights of the individual and the family.

A practically unrestricted right of free speech supposes an enlightened and responsible citizenry. If the government is not to restrict them, they must restrict themselves. A paradox occurs when a citizen abuses the right of free speech to advocate the overthrow of the government which guarantees free speech and the substitution of one that would abolish it. This behavior can be taken indulgently only as long as such persons are an uninfluential minority. Any government allowing it on a large scale is committing political suicide.

Freedom of conscience

Freedom of conscience is a natural and inalienable right. The only way in which a man can accept religious teaching is by being intellectually convinced of its truth. If he is convinced of its truth, he is morally bound to accept it; if he is convinced of its falsity, he is morally bound to reject it; if he is doubtful, he has the right to reserve judgment until further investigation convinces him one way or another. The state has no means at its command but the use or threat of physical coercion, which might produce a hypocritical conformity but cannot beget conviction. The state has therefore the obligation to respect the consciences of its citizens.

Religious persecution must be condemned as immoral and contrary to the natural law. Religious tolerance came late in history, though it was advocated in theory long before it could be put into practice. What retarded its advent was the failure to distinguish between the belief and the believer, between error and the erring. Any religion which considers itself as the only true religion must condemn contradictory religions as false. This attitude is not confined to religion, but includes any body of knowledge one is firmly convinced of. But intolerance toward the belief does not justify intolerance toward the believer. As a person he has to find truth for himself; he has the right to make the search and to accept the results he sincerely arrives at. It is said that error has no rights. In a sense this is so, for only persons have rights and error is not a person. In this sense neither has truth any rights. But the *person's* right must be respected. To grant it implies no approval of the beliefs he holds. There is nothing to prevent people of different faiths from living harmoniously side by side and agreeing to differ in religious belief, each respecting the other's political right to follow his conscience. In reading the history of religious conflicts it is well to mark the distinction between the official teachings of a religious body and the behavior of some of its overzealous but misguided members.

Church and state are independent but related societies. The Church is supreme in purely religious matters, the state in purely temporal matters. The Church must not interfere in matters of a merely civic character, nor the state in the teaching and practice of religion. But there will always be some relation between Church and the state, because the same persons who are members of one society are also members of the other. The two societies should harmoniously cooperate where their interests touch, and arrive at a working agreement. The Church can be a great help to the state by developing moral, virtuous, and law-abiding citizens. The state can help the Church by fostering religion and granting it free scope for its activity.

The *separation of Church and state* is a difficult problem because of the ambiguity in the word *separation*. How far does it go? If a religion holds that it is the only true Church, its theoretical ideal can be nothing less than that all men should be members of it. If the ideal were realized, Church and state would coincide in membership, but differ in purpose and function, and be at least *distinct,* if not separate. Even here provision would be necessary for the freedom of possible dissenters and minority groups to follow their own conscience openly and peaceably. In a pluralistic society such as ours, where the people profess many different religions and are split up into any number of sects, a practical separation of Church and state seems to be the only workable arrangement. As the facts of history show, it has succeeded admirably.

It is well to note that the term *separation of Church and state* is used in different senses in different parts of the world. For European and Latin-American anticlericals it often is only a euphemism for subordination of Church to state and suppression of religious freedom. This is the same thing as persecution. There has always been a movement in this direction in our own country, and the white-sheeted ghost of bigotry now and then comes back to haunt us.

Freedom from race prejudice

This important political and social question can be passed over with a word in a philosophical treatise, because no philosopher of note has ever attempted to defend racial discrimination. All human beings have the rights that go with human nature. To differentiate men by their color, race, caste, or class, and not on their dignity and value as human persons, is to succumb to one of the grossest of irrational prejudices. To deprive others of equal rights because of racial or other accidental characteristics is to commit serious injustice. There is a moral obligation on all, where such discrimination prevails, to cooperate in working for its removal. How to do it, especially where the prejudices are long ingrained, may tax the virtue of prudence to the limit, but the duty is there and must not be indefinitely postponed.

REBELLION AND REVOLUTION

Rebellion is open, organized, and armed resistance to constituted authority. Revolt, insurrection, sedition are more localized forms of the same thing. There will always be malcontents and disaffected groups even in the best of human societies. For the common good a government must try to keep them contented, which it can best do by scrupulous regard for minority rights, but no authority can allow itself to be openly defied. Since the state has the right to exist, it also has the right to put down rebellion by all efficient and legitimate means.

What if rebellion is provoked by abuse of power on the part of the ruler? Abuse of power does not by itself take away the right to power. A father unjustly punishing his son does not lose his paternal right, nor does a man putting his money to unjust use lose the ownership of it. Small abuses of power are occurring constantly and serious ones occasionally in every state, because rulers are only human and fallible. Such causes cannot justify rebellion, though they call for protest and redress.

What may a private citizen do when he is unjustly oppressed? Unjust laws are not laws at all and can impose no moral obligation. Injustice in a law must not lightly be presumed but clearly established.

1. Passive resistance or nonobedience is required if the citizen is ordered to do something intrinsically wrong, for no human law can cancel the already existing obligation of the natural law. A so-called law which is unjust but does not order the doing of something intrinsically wrong may be resisted or obeyed, as the subject thinks expedient. It is wrong to do injustice but not to suffer injustice. To prevent greater evils, one may have an incidental obligation to obey. But one must never do an act that is intrinsically wrong, no matter what the penalty.

2. Active resistance without physical force, by petitions, speeches, protests, books, pamphlets, editorials and propaganda of all sorts, is always morally allowed against unjust laws and tyrannical rulers. But it is characteristic of tyrants to deny any opportunity for such peaceful methods.

3. Active resistance with physical force is allowed against a tyrant

attempting to inflict grave personal injury, for the ruler in this case becomes an unjust aggressor. Such resistance may be extremely inexpedient, but it is not against the natural law. The rules of a blameless self-defense must be observed. If some citizens are unjustly attacked by a tyrannical ruler, others may come to their assistance against him.

Despite occasional injustice, it is wrong to stir up and wage civil war against a *rightful* ruler, that is, one who retains his right to rule. The right referred to here is not so much legal right as moral right. He may observe all legal and technical formalities and yet be a tyrant. Moral right means that he has not acted in such a way as to forfeit the office that still belongs to him in justice. If he is the rightful ruler, no one may rightfully depose him.

How can a ruler lose his right to rule? There are two ways. First, abuse of power may destroy the title on which the right is held. If the ruler took office bound by certain conditions and breaks his side of the contract, the people are not bound to theirs; in feudal times subjects were released from their oath of allegiance, and modern republics have the machinery of impeachment. Second, no matter how absolute a ruler may be, he always loses his moral right to rule by certain, continued, and excessive tyranny. In this case rebellion against him becomes a justified revolution.

Revolution is a fundamental change in political organization, or in a government or constitution; the overthrow or renunciation of one government or ruler, and the substitution of another, by the governed. Rebellion cannot be justified unless it is the means for accomplishing a legitimate revolution. In a revolution a new kind of government may be established, or the same type may be retained with new personnel. The theory behind a justified revolution is that the ruler lost his right to rule by his tyrannical behavior, and that sovereignty reverts to the people in whom it always dwells basically anyway (according to the theory of Bellarmine and Suarez). Consequently, it is not directed against a rightful ruler, since he has lost his right, nor is it by private authority, but by the public authority of the whole people civilly united.

The following conditions for a justified revolution are set down not as absolute requirements, for historical contingencies are too diverse, but as useful norms:

1. The government has become habitually tyrannical, works for its own selfish aims to the harm of the people, with no prospect of a change for the better within a reasonable time.

2. All legal and peaceful means have been exhausted to recall the ruler to a sense of duty.

3. There is reasonable probability that resistance will be successful, or at least that it will secure a betterment proportionate to the effort and suffering involved in civil war.

4. The judgment that the government is tyrannical should be truly representative of the people as a whole. It should not be a movement of a single faction or party, of one geographical district, of one social class or economic interest.

Nothing said here is intended to weaken the authority of legitimately established and functioning governments, whose laws the citizen is morally bound to obey. But the natural law, which condemns tyranny as one of the worst crimes because it works injustice on so many, cannot oblige men meekly to submit to being ground down in the dust with no hope of relief. The power of a ruler is too sacred a trust to be used irresponsibly yet kept indefinitely.

SUMMARY

Positive law, both *declarative* and *determinative,* is needed to supplement the natural law because:

(1) The ignorant need instruction and control by the wise
(2) Earthly penalties are required for the safety of society
(3) Concerted action demands teamwork and leadership
(4) Society must meet changed conditions harmoniously

The *jus gentium* or Roman *law of nations,* the source of most modern legal codes, was both a highest common factor among the positive laws of ancient civilized peoples and an approach to natural equity. The English *common law* is analogous to it in the latter function. They are both positive law embodying much of the natural law.

The natural law obliges men to maintain the state and obey the civil law, because the state is demanded by man's social nature and it accomplishes its end by the civil law. Laws are binding on each individual citizen, whatever be the theoretical beliefs of the lawmaker. General disobedience does not nullify a law, and contrary customs require at least tacit approval of the authorities.

Are there *purely penal laws,* laws which do not oblige in conscience but have a penalty attached for violation? Some say that they are real laws imposing a disjunctive obligation, either to keep the law or to pay the penalty if caught. Others think that they are not real laws but merely directives for public order. Others discard the concept entirely.

Punishment has three functions: retributive, corrective, and deterrent. It reestablishes the balance of outranged justice, rehabilitates the criminal, and prevents others from similar crimes. If we abolish the retributive function, we make all punishment unjust. It is immoral to punish unless the accused is guilty, no matter how much good the punishment may do him or society. It is moral to punish the guilty even if there is no hope of correcting him or deterring others from crime. Therefore neither correction nor deterrence but retribution is the basis of justified punishment.

The state has the right of *capital punishment,* which it exercises by the authority God gives it to attain its end. If it can curb criminals in another way, it need not use this right.

The state has the right to *tax,* since it needs revenue, but not to overtax. It must distribute the tax load fairly. The citizens must pay taxes, but *some* tax laws seem to be either purely penal laws or mere directives.

The state must acknowledge the citizen's right of *free speech,* and not limit it more than the common good demands. It is better to allow more than less freedom of speech, but some restriction is necessary.

The state must respect *freedom of conscience.* Religious persecution is morally wrong. We must distinguish the belief and the believer, condemning false beliefs while respecting the right of persons to profess what they sincerely believe. Separation of Church and state is often the best working arrangement.

The state is obliged in social justice to guarantee to its citizens freedom from the effects of *racial prejudice* and any other disabilities resulting from merely accidental differences of birth, race, color, caste, or class.

The state's right to *suppress rebellion* is implied in its right to existence. Occasional injustice does not destroy the state's right to rule. A citizen may resist tyrannical acts by civil disobedience and protest, by physical force only in self-defense against personal injury.

Citizens have the *right of revolution* only when the ruler has lost his right to rule. The conditions are habitual tyranny, no hope of improvement, the last resort, fair chance of success, and the backing of the people as a whole.

READINGS

1. Plato's passages on punishment (*Protagoras,* §324, *Gorgias,* §525, *Laws,* bk. XI, §934) occur in passing while treating of other matters, but it would be useful to read the surrounding context.
2. Aristotle's *Nicomachean Ethics,* bk. V, on justice, contains much pertinent matter. His treatment of revolutions in the *Politics,* bk. V, deals with the fact rather than the ethics of revolutions.
3. On human law read St. Thomas, *Summa Theologica,* I-II, qq. 95-97; q. 100, a. 2. Also II-II, q. 42, on sedition; q. 57, a. 3, on *jus gentium;* q. 64, aa. 2-3, and q. 69, a. 4, on capital punishment; q. 108, on vengeance, which St. Thomas considers a virtue (retributive justice).
4. Vitoria, *De Jure Gentium et Naturali* (On the Law of Nations and the Natural Law), translated in J. B. Scott, *The Spanish Orign of International Law: Francisco de Vitoria and his Law of Nations,* appendix E.
5. Suarez, *De Legibus* (On Laws), bk. II, ch. 16-20; bk. III, ch. 1; bk. IV, ch. 9; besides, the whole of book VII is on custom, treated at great length. Translated in J. B. Scott, *Classics of International Law: Suarez.*
6. Rommen, *The Natural Law,* ch. 14, and *The State in Catholic Thought,* ch. 15-16.
7. D'Entrèves, *Natural Law,* the whole book, but especially ch. 1.
8. Maritain, *Rights of Man and Natural Law.*
9. Simon, *Philosophy of Democratic Government,* ch. 2, 4-5.
10. Messner, *Social Ethics,* bk. I, pt. III; bk. III, pt. III.
11. Le Buffe and Hayes, *The American Philosophy of Law,* ch. 8, 10, 12.
12. Leibell, *Readings in Ethics,* pp. 326-341, 502-504, 987-1002, 1016-1032.
13. Douglas, *Ethics in Government,* and Graham, *Morality in American Politics,* are two books dealing with the practical aspects of ethics in political life.

14. Davitt, *Nature of Law,* is entirely concerned with the concept and history of purely penal law, contrasting the intellectualist and voluntarist approach to law.
15. Murray, *We Hold These Truths,* is an excellent discussion of the ethics of America's pluralistic society.
16. Famous works in defense of liberty; in accordance with their principles one can reserve the liberty of disagreeing with some of the things they say:
    a. Milton's *Areopagitica.*
    b. Locke's *Letter Concerning Toleration.*
    c. John Stuart Mill's essay *On Liberty.*

CHAPTER 28

EDUCATION

PROBLEM

That both the family and the state have an interest in education is admitted by all. Not only the propagation but also the education of children was put down as the primary end of marriage, and parents surely have the right to supervise their own children. The state also has the right to an educated citizenry, on which modern states so fully rely, and to secure which they so extensively engage in educational work. Our question is: *Who has the primary right, the parents or the state?*

Educators may dispute about the definition of education. We take it to mean any process of training the physical, mental, and moral powers of a human being to render him fit for the duties of life. Our question deals only with education during the formative period of a child's life and with education for the common duties of a human life. It does not deal with adult education, which is subsequent to the formative period, nor with vocational training, which is a requirement only for those pursuing that vocation. We are discussing the kind of education a child has a right to have and someone the duty to provide, a situation that sets up a special relation between teacher and pupil. Anyone who knows something has the right to teach it if he can get people to listen to him, but he cannot impose his teaching with authority. We are dealing here with education which the teacher has authority to impart and which the pupil has the duty to submit to respectfully, though his intellectual acceptance of what he is taught depends on his being convinced of its truth.

This main problem branches out into several others. We shall treat them as follows:

(1) The primary right of the parents
(2) The secondary rights of Church and state
(3) The founding and conducting of schools
(4) Academic freedom in the teachers

PARENTS' PRIMARY RIGHT

The right to educate their children belongs to the parents by the natural law, and is therefore a natural right. By the natural law parents have the *duty* to educate their children, for this belongs to the primary end of marriage, which is a natural institution required by the natural law. But one cannot have a duty without the right to fulfill that duty. Therefore by the natural law parents have the *right* to educate their children.

Since the parents are responsible for the child's existence, they are also responsible for all the child will need to live a decent and useful human life. They do not fulfill their duty simply by feeding, clothing, and sheltering the child; they must also see to it that the child, when grown, can take his place as a useful member of society, since society is natural to man. Therefore they must teach him the means of acquiring an independent livelihood, the means of communication with his fellow man, and the social virtues needed for life in common with others. More important still, the child is dependent on his parents for the formation of those good moral habits which the child will need for his own personal morality and for attaining his last end. The parents can do this and they can do it best. Hence they are picked out by nature for this work.

How much education is the child entitled to? At least the minimum essentials described above. Whether the child can expect more education than this depends on the child's ability, the circumstances of the family, the educational facilities available, and the prevalent level of culture. Parents should try to do the best they can for their children, but are not obliged to make extraordinary sacrifices. In this country one can hardly get along without knowing how to read and write, but this is not the case everywhere. The amount of education therefore depends on a combination of individual, family, and community requirements.

RIGHTS OF STATE AND CHURCH

The state has no right to interfere in what strictly belongs to the family. Education cannot belong to both family and state independently and on the same plane, for there would be a conflict of rights and duties. The family is prior to the state and had the obligation of educating the children before there was any state. The state is founded to supplement the family, not to destroy it, and hence cannot take away from the family its already existing right.

However, both Church and state have secondary rights in education, which by no means contravene the parents' primary right. Both Church and state have a right to all the means necessary for the fulfillment of their ends, and education comes within the scope of these means. The Church must have something to say about the education of her members, and the state of its citizens.

The Church has the right and the duty to oblige parents who are her members to give their children the proper religious education. But the Church has authority only over her members and uses no temporal sanc-

tions to obtain her ends. Since the members belong to the Church voluntarily, only a peculiar twist of logic could make them refuse to cooperate
with the Church's educational program.

The state has the right and the duty to compel parents to fulfill their
duty in educating their children. This is called a secondary right and
duty, because it is valid only when the parents themselves fail in their
duty. The state can compel parents to feed their children if they neglect
to do so, but has no right to interfere when the parents discharge their
obligation satisfactorily. The same is true in the matter of education. The
state's right is not so much to *do* the work of education as to see that it is
done. In this function it is only protecting the child.

SCHOOLS

Our discussion has been about education and not about schools, for
schooling is only a means, and not always an absolutely necessary one,
toward education. Parents had the duty of educating their children long
before there were any schools, and the duty would remain were all schools
abolished. Even today, if the parents have the ability and the leisure to
give adequate instruction to their children at home, they have no moral
obligation to send them to school at all. But few parents are qualified for
this task today, and the home-educated child is handicapped by lacking
the socializing influence of contact with those of his own age.

Ordinarily parents hand over the work of formal instruction and
mental training to schools. But not entirely; the parents themselves must
do the work of preschool education or hire someone to do it for them.
This is the most important part of education and is best done by the parents themselves. Even when the child goes to school, the parents must
continue their training out of school hours and must constantly watch the
child's progress at school. The mere handing over of the child to others
to educate does not absolve the parents of their responsibility. Parents
must inform themselves on the character of the schools to which they send
their children, and remove them if the influence threatens to prove harmful. In this respect the parents' right to educate their own children is
inalienable.

What are the rights of the Church regarding schools? The Church has
the right to teach her own members their religion and for this purpose
may open schools of religious instruction. Secular education does not directly belong to the Church's sphere of work, but, if it is either not being
given at all or is being given in a way hostile to religious faith, there is no
reason why the Church should not add a secular curriculum to the religious studies, and thus develop her schools (while preserving the denomi-
national aspect) into ordinary private schools. The Church got into the
work of secular education by historical accident, opening schools in the
early middle ages when there were no schools and no one else fit to start
any. The Church has adjusted to the modern educational scene differently
in different countries as circumstances seemed to warrant, either fitting

her religious program into the state school system or continuing to conduct her own independent schools. At least, the Church's schools are legitimate private schools, and she has the right to continue those in existence and to establish others, if this seems expedient for safeguarding the faith of her members.

What are the rights of the state regarding schools? The state has the right to open and conduct schools when private initiative is insufficient for this work. The state must look after the common welfare and promote all works that are socially necessary. If private schools are too few and small, they must be supplemented by state schools, and where there are no private schools, the state must furnish all the facilities. But, if this work is already being done adequately by private schools, the state has no right to put them out of business by unfair tax-supported competition.

The state has not the right to monopolize education. Education is a legitimate form of private enterprise, subject indeed to a certain amount of government regulation, but there is nothing in its nature that makes it a public or state monopoly. The reason is that the primary right to educate their children belongs to the parents. In undertaking the work of education the state is simply supplying the parents with facilities to fulfill their duty. If the parents have other facilities at their command, they have no obligation to use those the state provides.

The state's right in education is entirely secondary and supplementary. The state may not make attendance at state schools compulsory, either by law or by undue favoritism. It may not force parents to send their children to one definite school, public or private, rather than another, though it may refuse to accept children from other tax-supported districts. It may not close private schools already operating, unless they have proved to be public menaces or frauds, nor may it refuse to allow the opening of new private schools. Even in its own public schools the state is acting under the authority delegated to it by the parents, who have the primary right; the state is only their agent and trustee. Therefore, the state must conduct these schools with a regard for the parents' wishes, and not force on the children a type of education the parents disapprove. This does not put on them the impossible task of listening to every parents' whim, but they must give the general type of education the parents as a group demand. This is not true of private schools where they are optional, but would be true of them if they carried the whole educational burden, for then they would be in a position like that of a privately owned public utility, which is obliged to put the common good before private interests.

The state has the right to regulate education within certain limits. As a measure of public protection, it may set reasonable standards to which schools, both public and private, must conform. It may set standards of qualification for teachers. It may prevent the teaching of injurious and subversive doctrines, just as it can forbid the sale of tainted food. It may prescribe courses in citizenship and see that a patriotic spirit prevails in the schools; but it has no right to dominate the whole curriculum. The proper integration of courses in a school and the methods of teaching to be adopted are the business of educators, not of politicians.

Has not the state, especially a democratic state, a particular interest in the education of its future citizens, so that this right transcends that of parents? The state has a right to a sufficiently educated citizenry, especially a democratic state that depends on an intelligent vote; hence, if the parents do not fulfill their duty, the state may force them to do so, not only for the child's sake but also for the state's sake. But this right is always secondary. The state has the right to see that parents educate their children into competent citizens but no direct right to take over this duty itself. Otherwise the state is encroaching on an essential right of the family, crowding the family out of its rights, and thus verging on totalitarianism.

ACADEMIC FREEDOM

Academic freedom is the name given to a teacher's privilege of teaching the doctrines and opinions he holds, without undue censorship by the state or even by the school that employs him. It is understood that academic freedom is expected chiefly at the university level, but it is extended somewhat to secondary and primary education.

The reasons for some degree of academic freedom are obvious. Advancement in science and culture is possible only where investigators are free to pursue truth wherever it leads. The teacher is supposed to be an expert in his field, and it is illogical to put him under the dictation of those who know less about the subject than he. He cannot be morally obliged to play the hypocrite and teach what he thinks false. He earns his living by teaching and should not be in constant fear of dismissal because his superiors adopt a change of view or policy, so that he would have to teach one year the contradictory of what he had taught the previous year. This last remark shows the connection between academic freedom and tenure.

But it cannot be maintained that academic freedom is absolute. First of all, it is subject to the same limitations as the right of free speech, and may not be defamatory, obscene, subversive, or otherwise malicious, since no one can acquire a right to immoral conduct. But academic freedom is subject to further restrictions because of the teacher's fourfold relation:

(1) To his pupils
(2) To their parents
(3) To the school employing him
(4) To the community

Teacher's relation to pupils

Even the university professor is dealing with immature minds, unable to compete with him on the same level, as yet untrained to give an exact appraisal of all he says or to argue with him from a rich background of experience. Speaking to these impressionable minds with the authority of his position, he must consider not only his own convictions and theories, but what effect these will have on the minds of the young. He is supposed to be forming and developing youth, not merely using them as a sounding board for any sort of idea he may get. If he feels that loyalty to his own convictions requires him to preach doctrines commonly regarded as revolutionary and subversive, let him cross swords with his equals and not with babes; he has no business teaching. It is one thing to present the students with an intellectual challenge, another to make it a policy to unsettle all the ideals and convictions the students have received at home, and then leave them in this state of vacuity and disorientation. Such abusers of academic freedom are among the greatest enemies of youth.

Teacher's relation to parents

The teacher is the agent and trustee of the parents. He has no independent authority over the child, must work in harmony with the parents, supplement the training of the home, and in general give the type of education the parents contract for. On the other hand, parents send their children to him because he is supposed to be an expert in his field, and he cannot adjust his teaching or the school's curriculum to meet every ignorant or meddlesome parent's demand. Here arises a conflict of rights and duties, in which the application of the ordinary principles may become quite difficult. The best solution seems to be the establishment of many schools with a wide variety of curricula and policies, among which parents may choose, so that parents can get the kind of education they want for their children and the teachers can teach what they believe.

Teacher's relation to the school

The teacher has definite responsibilities to his employers and must fulfill the contract he makes with them. Before accepting the position he must inform himself on the ideals and policies of the school, for he has no right to take the position if he disagrees with them or intends to be disloyal to them. Academic freedom cannot be stretched to the point of allowing him publicly to oppose the policy of the school where he teaches; if he feels that he must, because of some change in his own views, he should seek other employment. The right of tenure may be invoked against arbitrary dismissal, but there can be no ethical ground for making it a reason why a school must tolerate treason in its own house. The school has a moral obligation to pupils and parents, and must be able to get rid of undesirable teachers as well as uncooperative pupils.

On the whole, we can consider the teacher in a threefold capacity: as a private individual expressing his personal opinions, as a scholar presenting the fruit of his research to the learned world, and precisely as a teacher in contact with his students. So far we have been discussing him in the last function. As a private individual, he may act as any other private person, so long as he makes clear that he is speaking for himself alone. As a scholar, he is somewhat in between; he is speaking to his equals and is open to their criticism on the same level, but he is under obligation to his school from which he derives his academic standing and on which his views may reflect; he cannot exempt himself entirely from their approval. This relation to his school puts some limitation on his academic freedom.

Let it be understood, however, that academic freedom certainly has its place, and a policy of overactive censorship, especially on the part of the state, would be most unwise. Any restriction of teaching should be done by the schools, which are capable of handling such matters, rather than by the state, which is capable of supplying the facilities for education but not of deciding what ought or ought not to be taught.

Teacher's relation to the community

How far should the teacher be free to use his position to promote social progress? Should education be the creature of the existing social order, perpetuating the *status quo*, or the creator of a new social order, an active instrument for social reconstruction? Should the teacher fit his students to take their place in society as now organized or should he inspire them with the goal of building a better social order that will be the work of the younger generation? This battle between traditional and progressive education, involving as it does the whole relation of education to politics, is too extensive for full treatment here, but a few remarks are called for.

Since human society is never in a perfect condition, to strive for social betterment is not only a laudable aim but a moral obligation. The question regarding the teacher is twofold:

(1) What sort of change is to be made in society?
(2) Is the teacher the one to promote such change?

The building of a social order can be understood to mean either the carrying on of the present work to higher perfection on the same foundations or the altering of the present structure so drastically as to eventuate in a new one on different foundations. Education is one of the means that society relies on for its own further development, and all would agree that here at least it operates within its legitimate sphere. Whether it should be used for the purpose of remaking society, of creating what amounts to social revolution, depends on many factors, not the least of them being the kind of new social structure to be built. Revolution can be justifiable, but not every revolution is justified. The first thing, then, that educational reconstructionists are obliged to do is to specify clearly and formulate exactly the social program they have in mind, so that they can submit it to the judgment of their fellow citizens. This is often the very thing that educational reconstructionists refuse to do, committed as they are to the doctrine that there are no ultimate goals and that progress is for the sake of progress we know not where.

Whether social reconstruction be justified or not, the question remains whether the *teacher* is the one to promote it. The form of government and the structure of society are political matters, to be decided by the ruling authority in the state; in a democracy this is the citizens, not the children in school nor their teachers precisely as teachers. If the latter judge that the citizens of today are so hopelessly conservative that the educators must take into their own hands the development of a new type of citizen for the future, they have ceased to be mere educators and have taken on themselves the role of legislators and governors. Who has given them such authority? They have the right, not as teachers but as citizens, to try to convince their fellow citizens of the worth of the changes they advocate, but they have not the right, as teachers, to introduce these changes surreptitiously by taking advantage of their pupils' innocence and disregarding the wishes of parents who may not want this kind of training for their children. It seems strange that they who make so much of the democratic method should constitute themselves into an autocratic elite, charged with the development of society and responsible to no one. To demand such a right under the guise of academic freedom is but a bid for political power.

SUMMARY

By *education* we mean any process of training the physical, mental, and moral powers of a human being to render him fit for the duties of life. We deal with general and formative education only.

By the natural law the *parents have the primary right* to educate their children, for education belongs to the primary end of marriage, and where there is a duty there is a right to exercise that duty. The amount of education depends on the child's capacity, the family's resources, and the cultural level of the community.

Church and state have *secondary or supplementary rights* in education, each within its proper sphere. They are not to interfere when parents do the work adequately, but they have the right to see that it is done.

Schools are the ordinary means of education, but do not take the whole burden from the parents. The *Church* has the right to establish religious schools and to add to religious teaching a secular curriculum. The *state* should respect the rights of private schools, supply facilities when private initiative is inadequate, give the general type of education the parents approve, set minimum standards and make inspections if necessary, prohibit subversive teachings and promote patriotism. The state must *not* monopolize education or dominate the whole curriculum.

Academic freedom, the teacher's privilege to teach what he believes without undue censorship, is a necessary part of the educator's life. But it has its limits. The teacher has special obligations to his *pupils,* because of their youth and inexperience, to the *parents,* whose agent and trustee he is, to the *school,* whose ideals and policies he is not allowed to subvert, and to the *community* of which he is a responsible and respected member. As a private individual he may say what he wishes, as a scholar he has some obligation to the school employing him, but precisely as a teacher he must form the minds of the young by continuing the child's home training according to the program of his school.

READINGS

1. Education is constantly referred to throughout Plato's works. His theory is described especially in the *Republic,* bk. II, §376, to bk. IV, §425; bk. VII, §521 to 541; the Laws, bk. VII.

2. Aristotle's views on education are found in his *Politics,* bk. VII, ch. 13, to the end of bk. VIII. Unfortunately, he does not get beyond elementary education. Both Plato and Aristotle are typically Greek in their stress on the educative value of music.

3. Both St. Augustine and St. Thomas have tracts entitled *De Magistro* (On the Teacher). Both are translated into English, the former in the *Ancient Christian Writers* series and the latter in M. E. Mayer, *The Philosophy of Teaching of St. Thomas Aquinas.* The content of these treatises is but remotely connected with the matter of this chapter.

4. Read Pius XI's Encyclical, *Divini Illius Magistri* (The Christian Education of Youth).

5. The following deal with the rights of family, Church, and state in education:
   a. Rommen, *The State in Catholic Thought,* ch. 15.
   b. Ward, *Christian Ethics,* ch. 14.
   c. Leibell, *Readings in Ethics,* pp. 848-891.
   d. Cronin, *Science of Ethics,* vol. II, pp. 486-491; reprinted in Leibell.
   e. Cahill, *Framework of a Christian State,* ch. 20.
   f. Redden and Ryan, *Catholic Philosophy of Education,* is a standard text in the educational field.

6. Kirk's *Academic Freedom* is one of the best on this knotty subject. MacIver's *Academic Freedom in Our Time* is a thorough modern study. Anything written on this topic should be read with cautious discrimination.

7. Dewey's *Democracy and Education* is one of the great classics of progressivism. Brameld, *Towards a Reconstructed Philosophy of Education,* and other works present the views of the more advanced reconstructionists.

8. Brubacher, *Eclectic Philosophy of Education,* is a book of readings from authors holding widely diverse positions.

CHAPTER 29

PROPERTY

PROBLEM

Man cannot live his life on earth without using the material goods with which the earth abounds. In doing so he makes them *his own*, his *property*. The more recent challenges to the right of property we shall leave to a later chapter. Here we limit ourselves to an investigation of the institution of private property as it has been accepted throughout most of the world's history and try to find what moral basis it has. We can distribute the matter under the following headings:

(1) What is ownership?
(2) Why may we use material goods for sustenance?
(3) What is theft and why is it wrong?
(4) What are the chief economic systems?
(5) How is the system of private property justified?

OWNERSHIP

The words *mine* and *thine* represent notions too elementary to be made simpler. The expression *one's own* universalizes the idea and makes it applicable to any person. A thing is said to be *one's own* when it is reserved to a certain person and all others are excluded from it. The one who holds a thing as *his own* is said to *own* it, to be its *owner*, to have the right of *ownership* over it. Things owned are said to *belong* to the owner and are called his *belongings*. So much any child knows. The English language feels more scientific when it dresses ideas in Latin derivatives; so *one's own* is *proper* (in its old meaning as contrasted with *common*), an *owner* is a *proprietor*, *ownership* is *proprietorship* and *belongings* are *property*.

Ownership may be defined as the *right of exclusive control and disposal over a thing at will*. It is:

1. *A right*. Thus we distinguish between ownership and the mere hold-

367

ing of a thing in one's possession. A thief has possession of stolen goods, but he does not own them because he cannot acquire a right to them.

2. *Exclusive.* This means keeping others from the use of the thing owned. A thing over which everybody has equal rights is not owned at all. Several or many persons may own a thing together, either in joint ownership or as a corporation, but anyone outside the group is excluded from the property.

3. *Control and disposal.* This means doing anything possible with it: keeping, changing, giving away, selling, using, consuming, destroying. Of itself ownership is unlimited, though limitation may come from another source: from rights of a higher order, from love of the neighbor, or from the civil law.

4. *Over a thing.* The matter of the right cannot be further detailed except to say that whatever can be controlled or disposed of can be owned. We think of it first as a material object, but it can be actions, services, good will, or credit.

5. *At will.* The owner acts for himself, in his own name, and need consult no one else as far as mere ownership is concerned. An agent or trustee may be given the right to control a thing or dispose of it, but only on behalf of the owner and in his name.

Property may be defined as *that which is owned* or that over which one has the exclusive right of control and disposal at will. Not everything is or can become property. The air, the sunlight, the ocean cannot be owned and can never be property; they must remain *common.* Wild beasts, fish in the sea, land in an unexplored wilderness are not actually owned but can be; they are potentially property but actually nobody's; they are *common* now but need not remain so.

There are various *kinds* of ownership, a few of which we can define briefly. Since a group can be an owner, and there is no limit to the size of this group, the whole community as such can own property: the federal government, the state, the county, the city. This is *public* as opposed to *private* ownership. In all ownership we must consider the substance of the thing owned as distinct from its use and fruits. *Perfect* ownership supposes right of control over all three; *imperfect* ownership over any one or two of these, but not over all three together. Lending, borrowing, renting, leasing, and the like render ownership imperfect. Only the one who retains control over the substance is properly called the *owner,* but it is obvious that the other has partial property rights in the matter, and hence some sort of limited ownership. Ownership over the substance is called *direct* ownership; over the use or fruits or both, *indirect.*

PROPERTY AS SUSTENANCE

The right of ownership or the right to property in its simplest and most primitive form enables man to take and use for his sustenance, comfort, and development the goods that nature's bounty provides. That man has a right to act in this way is evident from his natural right to life. The material goods of this world are naturally fitted to become man's property. In nature the lower beings are for the sake of the higher, for nature has so constructed them. Living things cannot maintain their lives except by the use and consumption of lower beings, both living and inanimate. Since man is the highest being on earth, all other things are for him. Nature does not portion out her goods to definite individuals. If no other man has already taken them, they are there for anyone to take. One who does so *appropriates* them, or makes them into his property.

Man has a natural capacity for ownership. He has intellect and will, by which he can indicate his intention of keeping material goods for his own use and of excluding others from them. His intellect and will naturally equip him to become a self-provider, with ingenuity to control nature and make it supply his wants. Animals cannot do this, but can only take what they find, as their instinct prompts them. Man, however, because of the control he can exert over nature, is naturally fitted for ownership.

The argument may be put as follows: The natural law gives a man a right to life, and also to the kind of life befitting a human being: a decent life with opportunity for physical, mental, and moral self-development. But the use of material goods is absolutely necessary for the maintenance of life and for proper self-development. Therefore the natural law gives every man the right to use the material goods of this world.

THEFT

The violation of the right of property is called *theft* or *stealing*. Hence the proof that man has a right to property is proof that theft is wrong. Theft can be defined as the *unjust taking of another's property,* and the taking is unjust when it goes against the owner's reasonable will. If nature were uniformly bountiful and no effort were needed to take and develop her products, there would be little motive for stealing. Its peculiar malice consists in the fact that one seizes the products another has gathered, labored on, and stored for his own use. No one reasonably wills to do for another, without compensation, what the other can equally well do for himself. Thus the thief virtually reduces another person to the status of a servant and, by disturbing the fundamental equality of mankind, commits an act of injustice. Even an owner who has not worked to acquire the goods that the thief steals owns them by some other legitimate title which does not cease without his consent. The wrong of theft is rectified first by restitution, the restoring of the stolen goods or their equivalent, and then by punishment, for theft is a crime upsetting the social order as well as an injury to the owner.

What happens when the right to life and the right to property come into apparent conflict? The general principle solving such conflicts is that the stronger right prevails. Obviously, property is for life, not life for property. Life is identified with the man himself; property is but a means to support life and minister to its needs. Life is indivisible, property divisible. A dead man has no use for property, but a live man who has lost his property can acquire new property and in the meantime be sustained by a share of another's excess property. Now the natural law cannot be contradictory, cannot give every man a right to life and to the means necessary for supporting life while at the same time giving some men such rights over property as to nullify other men's right to life. Therefore man's right to use material goods for the maintenance of his life prevails, as the stronger right, over any acquired right to property.

The argument as given refers to extreme need, but is valid, with due proportion, for serious but less drastic emergencies. If I am attacked and have no weapon of my own, I may use another's weapon even against his will in order to defend myself, unless he has equal need of it. If I am pursued by bandits, I may commandeer another's car or horse or any other means of escape. If the only way I can get out of a place in which my life is endangered lies through another's property, I need not worry about trespassing. In all such cases I must ask permission if time and circumstances permit, but, if this is impossible or the permission is refused, I may do these things anyway. I have no obligation to die or suffer very serious loss because some people are selfish. Of course, I must restore goods so taken as soon as the emergency is over. The owner is entitled to reimbursement for loss or damage done, to be paid eventually by the party at fault, if any. Civil law will have to decide disputes on indemnification.

If a man is starving, he should first try to obtain food by every legitimate means. He must seek honest work and if he finds it he must take it, even if it be of a menial character. He must contact public agencies of relief and not be too proud to accept their help. But if his every effort has met with rebuff and he sees that it is practically impossible for him to respect other people's property and at the same time to keep alive, the natural law then gives him the right to seize what he needs even though it is the property of another. This is not theft or stealing. Others have the duty to come to his relief, and if they do not their lesser right to their property yields to his greater right to his life.

We may sum up the points made so far. Man has a right to use the goods of this world. He has a right not only to the goods absolutely necessary for subsistence, but also to goods needed for a decent human life befitting his rational nature. Theft, or the unjust seizure of rightfully owned property, is morally wrong. But the right to property must yield to the right to life. It is not theft to seize goods needed for life or safety, even if they are someone else's property, unless he is in equal need. Rather, there is an obligation to share goods with those in extreme need, since supplying human needs is the primary function of property.

ECONOMIC SYSTEMS

We come now to a more intricate question, that of the *economic system* that ought to prevail in society. Here we no longer deal with the basic form of property stemming out of primitive human needs but with that more advanced form of property called *wealth*. Should nature's resources be left unowned for each to take what he needs, or be divided up among private owners, or be publicly owned and operated by the state? We can distinguish three primary economic systems:

1. Each one takes from nature's supply the goods that he needs for his use at present or in the near future, without hoarding up goods for the far future. Land, especially, is left common as the hunting ground of the tribe. Property does not extend much beyond personal movable implements. This is the system of *primitive collectivism* as found among savages and barbarians.

2. Nearly all the resources of nature and goods of the community are divided up among particular owners. The land is marked off and distributed, with trespassing forbidden or restricted. Only that is left common which everybody judges worthless. What individuals do not own, the state owns, but the bulk of the property is in private hands. This is the system of *private property* as found among civilized and semicivilized peoples.

3. The community or the state owns nearly everything, especially all the means of production, the farms and factories. The produce is distributed to the people in return for their work. Private property is allowed for use and consumption only. Here again hardly anything is left common as found in nature, though it may be called common in the sense of community-owned. This is the system of *socialism* and *communism*.

No enlightened person advocates a return to the first system. The second system has prevailed historically in almost all civilized countries up to the present century. The third system has now been substituted for the second in some countries and bids for world dominance. The issue can be stated in two questions:

(1) Is the system of private property ethically justified and, if so, on what principles?

(2) Should the system of private property be continued or be supplanted by socialism or communism?

These questions cannot be answered without a detailed examination of each system. Because of its almost universal acceptance and historical priority, the system of private property deserves to be studied first. Hence we save the second question for a later chapter and concentrate here on the first question.

PRIVATE PROPERTY AS AN ECONOMIC SYSTEM

What ethical justification has been offered for the institution of private property? There are two opinions, not opposed to each other, but differing in the extent to which they are willing to go:

(1) The system of private property rests on the *jus gentium*. It is in agreement with the natural law but not necessarily demanded by it. It is *a* morally acceptable system.

(2) The system of private property rests on the *natural law*. It is not

only in agreement with the natural law but demanded by it. It is the *only* morally acceptable system.

The *jus gentium* basis for private property

St. Thomas proves the system of private property from the law of nations or *jus gentium*. It may be well first to see his very cautious and enlightened treatment of this subject:

> Two things are competent to man in respect of exterior things. One is the power to procure and dispense them, and in this regard it is lawful for man to possess property. Moreover this is necessary to human life for three reasons. First because every man is more careful to procure what is for himself alone than that which is common to many or to all: since each one would shirk the labor and leave to another that which concerns the community, as happens where there is a great number of servants. Secondly, because human affairs are conducted in more orderly fashion if each man is charged with taking care of some particular thing himself, whereas there would be confusion if everyone had to look after any one thing indeterminately. Thirdly, because a more peaceful state is ensured to man if each one is contented with his own. Hence it is to be observed that quarrels arise more frequently where there is no division of the things possessed.
>
> The second thing that is competent to man with regard to external things is their use. In this respect man ought to possess external things, not as his own, but as common, so that, to wit, he is ready to communicate them to others in their need. . . .
>
> Community of goods is ascribed to the natural law, not that the natural law dictates that all things should be possessed in common, and that nothing should be possessed as one's own: but because the division of possessions is not according to the natural law, but rather arose from human agreement which belongs to positive law, as stated above (q. 57, aa. 2, 3). Hence the ownership of possessions is not contrary to the natural law, but an addition thereto devised by human reason.*

Several things are to be noted in this remarkable passage:

1. The first is that St. Thomas defends the institution of private property, and by the usual arguments, suggested by Aristotle's† criticism of Plato's communistic ideas.

2. The second is St. Thomas' approval of Aristotle's theory that property should be privately owned but its use should be common. This arrangement was especially applicable to the ancient and medieval system of large landed estates, privately held but with definitely understood public obligations. The modern counterpart is the social function of private capital invested in industries and corporations serving public needs and supplying livelihood to thousands of employees.

3. The third point is that St. Thomas bases the institution of private

---

Summa Theologica, II-II, q. 66, a. 2.
†*Politics,* bk. II, ch. 1-6, especially ch. 5, 1263a-1264b.

property on the law of nations, the *jus gentium,* which he discusses in question 57 to which he refers.

This third point is our present question. By his words St. Thomas seems to be making private property something allowed but not required by the natural law, something coming from human agreement sanctioned by positive law and permitted by the natural law, with an option for another arrangement equally in accord with the natural law. But this interpretation conflicts with St. Thomas' use of the terms *natural law* and *jus gentium.* The *jus gentium* is positive law in the sense that it has actually been derived from the positive laws of various peoples, but it is natural law in the sense that it embodies the necessary conclusions derived by human reason from the general principles of the natural law; thus it is positive law in origin but natural law in content. In deriving such conclusions human reason can fail to transcend the limitations of the age, and thus may include in *jus gentium* something no longer approved, as slavery, or omit something that now seems required, as free speech; but it represents the earnest effort of the human race to apply the natural law to social life, and on the whole is a clear enough mirror of the natural law itself.

Thus St. Thomas is by no means asserting that the institution of private property rests only on the *jus gentium* and does not pertain to the natural law. But he is so reserved in his treatment as to leave room for future speculation. He maintains that the institution of private property is a morally justified system, but he neither affirms nor denies that it is the only morally justified system.

The natural law basis for private property

The rise of socialism and communism renders this problem far more acute. Many think that we can go beyond St. Thomas' arguments and prove that the system of private property is the only method of managing the world's wealth consistent with the natural law, that private ownership is demanded by the requirements and aspirations of human nature, that socialism and communism cannot substitute for private ownership in these functions, and that private ownership is therefore a natural right. The positive part of the argument, leaving socialism and communism for a later chapter, pertains to our present matter. Being of the cumulative type, it is rather cumbersome in statement. We may reduce it to the following steps:

1. The argument begins with the fact we have already seen, that man *needs the goods of the earth* for his support, that nature has fitted these goods to become property by leaving them common, that man by his intellect and will is equipped by nature to be a self-provider and to tame the earth to minister to his needs, and that man is therefore a natural owner. On this indisputable basis the argument goes on to justify permanent ownership beyond one's immediate needs.

2. In the working up of nature's gifts, man impresses the *stamp of his*

personality on his products. Natural objects are changed by man's labor and bear the impress of his thought and energy. These objects which man has shaped after the design of his own mind should naturally belong to him; who else can have an equal right to them? Nature in leaving things common supplies only potential wealth, which becomes actual wealth only when man has developed it. To develop it man must possess it, for otherwise he cannot work on it; after development man can keep and use it, because it was for this purpose that he worked on it.

3. Nature does not provide continuously but *only in season*. A man must put away enough goods to last him through the winter; to do so he must own these goods and exclude others from them, thus acquiring the right to store and own this produce at least for a year. But there is no reason why ownership should stop then. A man pioneering in a new country clears the ground and sows the seed; that field is his at least until harvest. There is no reason why he should have to hand this field to others and clear a new field for next year's crop; so the field remains his permanently. Here he builds his house and settles with his family; there is no reason why he should have to vacate it or share it with others, for he was there first and has a right to privacy.

4. Man has the right and duty to *provide for his family*. He must rear his children and give them a start in life. He should then amass more goods than are necessary for his family's immediate use. He appropriates more land than he can now use with a view to the future needs of his growing children. At any time he may die or be disabled, and should leave his family well secured against the time when he can no longer work. If he has the right to provide for them, they have the right to receive these goods in the form of inheritance.

5. Inability to be expert in everything brought about a *division of labor*. Men specialize in certain kinds of work and exchange their products. Livelihood on this basis implies a right to store the products, to keep enough on hand to trade for present and future necessities. But storage is impossible without ownership. Besides, a storage of excess goods is the only way in which a man can provide for himself in sickness and old age, when he can no longer work. There is no reason why a man should have to be dependent on others during these times, for he fulfills his duty to society better and lightens its burden if he can take care of his own keep.

6. The *profit motive,* rooted in human nature, is the strongest motive in getting men to work. Men take pride in the work they have accomplished. If they cannot enjoy the fruits of their toil, they lose interest and turn to something else they think more profitable. They take care of the things they own, whereas it is notorious how common possessions are neglected and squandered. "What is everybody's business is nobody's business." Men also want to be independent, to choose their place of residence and their kind of work. They will not undertake projects for the taming of nature unless they can share in owning the results. Thus human progress and the advancement of civilization depend on private ownership.

7. The state is founded on *a solid middle class,* as Aristotle observed,* on families of fairly prosperous citizens who own a moderate amount of property. Their property is sufficient to give them the pride of ownership, yet not so abundant as to let them live in idleness. They have some resources for new undertakings and also the incentive to put their wealth to work. They are the equalizing influence between tyranny and anarchy, thus opposing the extreme tendencies of the rulers and the mob. Their continued prosperity depends on the maintenance of peace and order, without which business cannot function, and they exert pressure on the rulers to see that it is kept.

The above argument should be sufficient answer to the theory of the moral and legal positivists, that private property has no basis in natural law, that it is the mere result of a free compact entered into by men or of a grant by the state, and therefore entirely conventional. The system of private property is certainly in agreement with the natural law and approved by it. It is the system men naturally take to in the absence of any other, because it corresponds so well with the needs of human nature. Its historical development supplies ample confirmation. Since private property was the universal custom of civilized peoples applying the natural law to their social life, it was properly included within the *jus gentium.*

Does the argument also prove that the system of private property is so demanded by the natural law that there can be no substitute for it? Not without an examination of possible substitutes. But we had to present the positive side of the total argument and to detail rather precisely what functions any suggested alternative must fulfill. For it would have to fulfill these functions not only as well but better in order to justify the social upheaval necessary to introduce a new system.

SUMMARY

Ownership is the right of exclusive control and disposal over a thing at will. What is owned is *property.* Ownership is *public* if the property belongs to the community as such; otherwise it is *private.* Ownership is *perfect* if the owner controls the substance, use, and fruits, all three; otherwise it is *imperfect.* Ownership over the substance is *direct;* over the other two, *indirect.*

The natural law gives to every man the right to use the material goods of this world. Nature leaves things common; man is naturally a self-provider with ingenuity to make nature supply his wants.

Theft, as the unjust seizure of rightfully owned property, is wrong. But life comes before property. Nature cannot allow men to acquire such a right to property as to extinguish the right to life that nature has already given to all at birth. In grave need a man can commandeer another's property without the guilt of theft.

Politics, bk. IV, ch. 11, 1295b 25; ch. 12, 1296b 35.

There are three main *economic systems:* primitive collectivism, private property, and socialism or communism.

St. Thomas bases the system of private property on the *jus gentium.* Modern writers bring out more clearly how it is a demand of the *natural law,* for man should own the products on which he has put the stamp of his personality, nature is seasonal and a man must provide for the future of himself and family, division of labor requires storage of products for future trade, the profit motive is the most effective in getting men to work industriously, and the state functions best with a solid middle class of the moderately prosperous.

READINGS

1. Plato describes the origin of property together with the origin of the state in the *Republic,* bk. II, §369-374.
2. Read Aristotle's *Politics,* bk. II, ch. 1-6, 1260b 28 to 1266a 30.
3. St. Thomas' *Summa Theologica,* II-II, q. 66, is based on Aristotle and both are primary sources for the matter found here. It is not in the *Basic Writings.* Farrell's *Companion to the Summa,* vol. III, ch. VIII, pp. 205-210, contains his comments on the passage.
4. Locke, *Second Treatise on Government,* ch. V. Locke is a firm and even excessive defender of private property.
5. Leo XIII's *Rerum Novarum* (Condition of the Workingman), Pius XI's *Quadragesimo Anno* (Reconstruction of the Social Order), and John XXIII's *Mater et Magistra* (Christianity and Social Progress) can be found in many editions, some with excellent commentaries. They treat of many matters not pertinent to this chapter, but what they have to say on private property is much to the point.
6. Cronin, *The Science of Ethics,* vol. II, ch. IV, XII.
7. Messner, *Social Ethics,* bk. IV, pt. II.
8. Rickaby, *Moral Philosophy,* pp. 278-296.
9. Leibell, *Readings in Ethics,* pp. 583-598.
10. LeBuffe and Hayes, *The American Philosophy of Law,* pp. 248-260.
11. Ryan, *Distributive Justice,* ch. IV, XVIII.
12. Cahill, *Framework of the Christian State,* pp. 299-311.
13. Cronin, *Catholic Social Principles,* ch. XII.
14. Haas, *Man and Society,* ch. 9-10.

*   *   *

Many of these writers branch off into criticisms of socialism and communism, and also into criticisms of our present economic order with suggested remedies. These are beside the point of the present chapter.

CHAPTER 30

PROPERTY CONTRACTS

PROBLEM

The foregoing chapter was theoretical, asking whether there should be such a right as ownership and such a thing as property, and, if so, on what moral grounds the present system of private property rests. Taking that system as an existing fact, we now ask how one comes to acquire particular pieces of property and how certain business practices dealing with exchanges of property square with the moral law. We ask:

(1) What are the main titles to property?
(2) What are the obligations of buyers and sellers?
(3) Is there such a thing as a just price?
(4) Is monopoly necessarily evil?
(5) What are the duties of partners and stockholders?
(6) Why is interest taking allowable today?
(7) Are gambling and speculation wrong?

PROPERTY TITLES

How does this man come to own this or that piece of property? A man by the fact that he is a man has the right of ownership in general, yet he may never exercise this right, may never actually own anything. Something must make this man get this piece of property, that man that piece, a function fulfilled by the title. A *title* to property is an historical fact that changes the abstract right of ownership in general into the concrete right of ownership over this particular piece of property. There are seven chief titles to property:

1. *Occupancy* is the original way of changing into property the objects that nature leaves common. It is defined as the taking of a thing that

belongs to no one with manifest intent of holding it as one's own. It does not require dwelling or inhabiting, as the word *occupy* might suggest. There are three requirements: the thing taken must not actually be owned by anyone though capable of being owned, it must be effectively possessed with intent to hold it, and this intent must be made known to others by some suitable sign. The sign depends on custom: putting up a notice, fencing a field, staking a claim, recording the deed, keeping the thing on one's own person or in one's house. Some labor may be involved in securing possession, but the object itself is not the product of one's toil.

2. *Labor* cannot be the original title of ownership because the raw materials must first be owned before one has the right to work on them. But labor, transforming raw materials into useful objects, creates new values which belong to the worker as products of his energy. Mental no less than physical labor is a natural title to its fruits. When the material belongs to one owner and the labor to another, the ownership of the finished product has already been determined by a contract of hire; the owner of the material keeps the product and the worker is paid for his labor. Some think that labor is the only title to property, but can do so only by taking so broad a definition of labor as to include the act of occupancy, as John Locke* seems to do, or, like Karl Marx,† by restricting property to consumable goods distributed by the community to individuals in return for their labor.

3. *Gift* is a gratuitous transfer of ownership to another, and is implied in the owner's right of disposing of his property at will. In gift *alienation,* the ceasing of the first owner's right, and *acceptance,* the beginning of the new owner's right, occur simultaneously and with a view to one another.

4. *Trade* is any form of exchange, running all the way from *barter,* through *buying and selling,* up to and including the intricate enterprises of world *commerce.* In fact trade, whether money is used or not, is but mutual gift, but it is better to class it as a separate title because of the different attitude we have toward gifts and purchases. Trade is the logical consequence of the division of labor and necessary for the good of mankind, resting on the mutual help demanded by man's social nature, for each does help the other though personal gain be the motive.

5. *Inheritance* indicates that property on the death of the owner does not become common, to be occupied by the first comer, but passes to designated persons. If there is no will, the property goes to the natural heirs, the wife or husband and the children. Property is for the good not only of the individual but of the family, and after death should continue to fulfill the function of supporting them. Civil law determines inheritance; it should be based on natural justice and protect the natural heirs. By natural law the goods of a man dying intestate without relatives or dependents would become common, but the state usually settles the matter

---

*Locke, *Second Treatise on Government,* ch. V.
†Marx, *Capital,* vol. I, pt. I, ch. I, section 1.

by taking possession itself. *Bequest,* the disposing of property by a will, is a valid title, for a gift can be made to take effect at any time including the moment of death. In bequeathing his goods the owner is in duty bound to provide for his natural heirs, but beyond this he may make any disposal of his property he would be allowed to make when alive.

6. *Accession* is the title by which one gains ownership of the increment accruing to one's property. New trees in timberland, new births in a herd, new soil washed down on one's fields are examples of natural accession. The addition belongs to the owner of the property added to. Artificial accession, the inseparable mixing of two people's property without a previous agreement, such as painting a picture on another's canvas or building a house on another's land, can be settled by agreement or by the civil law. The property should go to the one who contributed the greater value, with compensation to the other.

7. *Prescription,* also called *adverse possession,* is the extinction of a previous owner's title and its transference to the present possessor through lapse of time. It concerns not only property itself but such easements as passing across others' land and fishing or mining in certain areas. For occupancy the goods must have no actual owner; for prescription the goods must, unknown to the present holder, be actually owned by someone else. Prescription is a civil title with a basis in natural law. To be valid it must fulfill these conditions: the matter must not be protected against prescription by civil law; the possessor must have intended ownership, been in constant peaceful possession, and in good faith; the time determined by the civil law must have elapsed. Without prescription much modern ownership would be uncertain. Most property is obtained from former owners, who must transmit it with a clear title. Memories fail, witnesses die, documents perish. New claimants could constantly arise, basing their pretensions on forgotten transactions centuries old. Present owners would be in jeopardy of having to prove and re-prove their right against all comers. The only remedy is the extinction of all titles and claims that go back beyond the time set by law. In all this the civil law is using the authority given to it by the natural law; it is an exercise of eminent domain.

Several of the seven titles to property (gift, trade, inheritance, and labor except labor for oneself) can be reduced to the general heading of *contract.* Not all contracts are about property and not all property is acquired by contract, but all deliberate transfer of property from one owner to another implies offer and acceptance resulting in a mutual agreement, and hence a contract. The contracts we deal with here involve the title of *trade.*

BUYING AND SELLING

The contract of *buying* and *selling,* or *purchase* and *sale,* is a contract whereby two persons agree to exchange a commodity for a certain price. It differs from *barter* by using money as the medium of exchange. The two are essentially the same sort of contract, but the idea of price brings up some special problems. The expression of consent to each other seals the contract by natural law, but the civil law may add certain formalities necessary for validity, as in the transfer of real estate, where it is important for the common good that the state know who owns the property.

The *seller* must own the object he sells, manifest its hidden defects, and deliver the actual article bought. Articles belonging to another, whether stolen or held by mistake, cannot be validly sold and anyone who possesses them must return them to the real owner as soon as his ownership becomes evident; a seller in bad faith must stand the loss, both refunding the price and seeing that the true owner gets his property, but no one need be disturbed about purchases made in good faith on the open market. The seller must manifest hidden substantial defects even without inquiry, for these touch the essence of the contract, but he need not manifest hidden accidental defects except on inquiry, when he must tell the truth; in any case he must lower the price proportionately.

The *buyer* must accept on delivery the goods contracted for and pay in full within a reasonable time, either specified in the contract or dictated by custom. Precious objects should not be bought for a song from children or simpletons, and the law protects them by making consent of their guardians necessary. The buyer need not inform the seller of the use he will make of the property or the profit he expects from it. But, to have a meeting of minds, both should know the *nature* of the goods even if they differ about their value.

Both buyer and seller, though neither need assist the other to make a good bargain since each is out for his own advantage, must see to it that the contract is valid according to the norms set down for contracts in general. They are also bound to see that justice is done, and therefore must agree on a just price.

THE JUST PRICE

In some economic circles the *just price* is regarded as a medieval notion inapplicable to the competitive methods of modern business. Since economics is not ethics, economists are privileged to ignore the idea of justice as being outside their field and to pursue their study in an ethical vacuum. In theory the two sciences must be kept distinct, but in practice no man can divide his life in that way. One does not cease to be a man by becoming a businessman. A business transaction has both a commercial and a moral aspect: commercial insofar as it involves a *price,* and moral insofar as it involves what is *just.* As it can be good or poor business, so it can be moral or immoral conduct, and these two spheres do not always coincide. To be viewed adequately as a piece of human endeavor the act must be seen from both standpoints.

It solves nothing to say that the just price is that which gives the seller a fair profit after deducting his own expenses. This is only a rule of thumb, supposing an already existing price structure, prices for materials, machines, labor, upkeep, and prices for the commodities needed for a man's support and purchased with his profit. We want to know how this price structure itself arises and what can make it just.

Our discussion will begin with *staple* commodities bought and sold in the market by people *in business,* not with rare articles or occasional private transactions outside the haunts of commerce. The former alone can give us a standard of value according to which prices can be scaled; the latter must also conform to the just price, but here it can be arrived at only by analogy and derivation from the former source.

The *price* of a thing is its value in terms of money. *Value* is the capacity of goods to satisfy human wants, and *money* is the accepted medium of exchange. The *just price,* then, is the true money value of the commodity, a price that can purchase other commodities having equal capacity for satisfying human wants as the commodity sold. The whole concept of commutative justice is based on the idea of equality, and trade itself with all its modern complexities is only a development of the same idea: that a man gets the equal of what he gives. The purpose of trade is social, to allow men to supply themselves with the commodities they need in exchange for those they have in surplus. Nor is this concept of equality contradictory to the idea of profit, for a man is entitled to the fruit of his superior industry and ingenuity, and he may make as good a bargain as is possible without violating justice. But there are limits set by justice, and human commerce is not allowed to have the antisocial purpose of battening on the calamities and misfortunes of others.

The problem is: How can the equal capacity of commodities for satisfying human wants be calculated? Two extreme views can be thought of:

(1) Each commodity has an exactly fixed money value.
(2) Any price the buyer is willing to pay is just.

The first extreme is impossible. There is no way of determining what any individual man will want, for human needs and desires differ too widely from person to person, vary too much from time to time in the same person, and depend on too many purely psychological factors such as taste and fashion. One will pay a king's ransom for an article that another would not take as a gift. Hence it is foolish to look for a just price as an absolutely fixed sum. It could only be a range within which prices fluctuate and the whole range varies with the times.

The second extreme is immoral. A starving man would be willing to pay all he possesses for a bit of food, for he cannot eat his money, but no one would be allowed to take such an advantage of his plight. Were prices determined by what an individual is willing to pay, we should have the absurd situation that, as a man's needs increase, the purchasing power of his money decreases, until in desperate straits it is practically worthless. The example given here is an extreme case, it is true, but it only goes to show how false the principle is. It would thwart the whole idea of money as a medium of exchange, of trade as a function of society, and of commutative justice as a moral virtue.

The just price, then, must be determined not by the usefulness of the commodity to this or that individual, but to men generally. The price must represent the judgment of the buying public on the value of the article, eliminating the subjective conditions peculiar to the individual. This judgment is expressed in the open market, where buyers and sellers freely compete with one another and thus establish a true equation between the capacities of different commodities for satisfying human wants. The competitive price is the *natural* price that will drive out all other prices, and this is also the just price where there is pure competition.

There is not much pure competition remaining. Wants are artificially created by our huge advertising programs and prices are monopolistically determined. But even an artificially induced want is a want and competes with other wants. Monopolistic prices can be judged outrageous or exorbitant, and the thing so priced will not sell, thus showing that the just price concept still obtains. Because there are conspiracies to boost or lower prices artificially, the government may step in and regulate prices; a price thus set by law is the *legal* price, and it is the just price if properly calculated to offset the distortion artificially induced. The government may also set legal prices to protect certain occupations, such as agriculture, which are essential to the public welfare.

The just price is elastic, a range between a *highest just price* and a *lowest just price*. Outside these limits justice is violated, but between them any price is just. The reason for this elasticity is that the wants of the buying and selling public continually alter and take some time to make themselves felt, so that the market lags a bit behind these changes. To sell above the highest just price is to take an antisocial advantage of the buyer's needs and to make a profit out of human misery; to buy below the lowest just price is to take the opposite advantage of the seller's need to get rid of his goods in exchange for what he needs more. To act thus is to be guilty of injustice, and one who does so is morally bound to make restitution even without a legal decision.

Possibility of loss or of long deferred payment may excuse from the market price, and so there is nothing wrong with the practice of a periodic "bargain sale" at reduced rates for the purpose of clearing out old stock or attracting new customers. The seller may raise the price if the article has personal or sentimental value for himself, because he deserves compensation for this loss; but not if it has such value for the buyer only, because the seller does not possess this extra value and loses nothing on account of it.

The prices of rare articles, such as curios, museum pieces, collector's items, objects of art and luxury, are determined by the narrow community that deals in such things. There is still a just price, but it is much more elastic. If the object is unique, the community may be narrowed down to one buyer and seller, and almost any price agreed on is just.

Auction is a sale in which the highest bidder becomes the purchaser. The highest bid determines the just price. Since no one is bound to buy in this manner, auctions work no injustice if the conventions are followed and free bidding is not interfered with.

MONOPOLY

Monopoly is exclusive control over a market. Monopolies may be private or public, natural or legal. *Private* monopoly is exercised by individuals or corporations, as the railroads in this country. *Public* monopoly is exercised by the state, as the postal service. *Natural* monopolies owe their existence to the nature of the marketable commodity: that it occurs only in certain places, or is worked by a secret process. *Legal* monopolies owe their existence directly or indirectly to legal enactment or concession, as in patents, copyrights, and franchises.

Monopoly is *just* when it uses its control for the common welfare. Thus copyright and patent rights secure to men the fruits of their ingenuity and industry, large outlays of capital for railroads and toll bridges need protection, the state may establish a monopoly over a luxury as a source of revenue. The putting of so much economic power into the hands of one or a few is not wrong in itself, any more than the putting of political power into the hands of one or a few, but it is very dangerous. The whole question is how that power is used, for or against the common good. Once a monopoly over important commodities and services has been secured, it ceases to have a purely private interest and becomes a matter of public and social interest. It can be administered fairly, but the temptations to abuse are enormous.

Monopoly is *unjust* when it uses its control against the common welfare. It is not unjust to undersell competitors, even though this act puts others out of business and tends to create a monopoly, provided one does not sell under the lowest just price. This is how competitive business works, though there are other obligations besides those of mere justice. The classic abuse of monopoly is to cut prices below the lowest just price for the purpose of driving out competitors and cornering the market, and then, when the monopolist has gained control and put everybody at his mercy, to raise the price above the highest just price. In such a process the monopolist has as his ultimate aim the charging of unjust prices and the using of economic dictatorship for his personal profit contrary to the common good.

PARTNERSHIP

Partnership is a contract by which several persons put together their money or labor or skill into a business and share the profit and loss proportionately. We limit ourselves to a few remarks on its ethical aspects.

In the *firm* or company each partner is bound by a personal obligation, and, in case of default, must make good out of his personal belongings for the total liability of the firm unless it is a "limited" firm. A *corporation* is a juridical person having corporate rights and duties, each member being bound in proportion to the amount of capital he has subscribed. Besides limiting the members' liability, the juridical person is endowed with a sort of immortality continuing in existence indefinitely though all the members have changed.

The ethical disadvantage of the corporation is the diminished sense of responsibility on the part of the stockholders who leave the whole management of the corporation to the directors. Many never reflect that their money may be put to the perpetration of the grossest injustices by unscrupulous directors. Securely shielded behind the impersonal front of the corporation, they may feel that they have sloughed off all personal responsibility onto the directors' shoulders. But it is impossible to get rid of moral responsibility in this way and the principles concerning *cooperation in evil* apply. As a rule people who have invested their money in reputable enterprises need not be disturbed, but if anything occurs to raise serious doubts they must investigate.

There is nothing wrong in principle with the more complex forms of business association such as trusts, cartels, syndicates, and holding companies, but they are open to serious abuse and require strict regulation.

INTEREST

Loan of money generally carries with it a contract of interest. Formerly all interest was called *usury,* from the Latin *usura,* the price for the use of a thing; but now usury means only excessive interest. It is well to note this in reading Aristotle's and St. Thomas' condemnation of *usury;* they do not mean excessive interest only, but any interest. Since they were only reflecting the common view of their day, we ask: Why was interest-taking formerly thought wrong and now is the accepted thing? According to Aristotle:

> The most hated sort [of wealth-getting], and with the greatest reason, is usury, which makes a gain out of money itself, and not from the natural object of it. For money was intended to be used in exchange, but not to increase at interest. And this term interest, which means the birth of money from money, is applied to the breeding of money because the offspring resembles the parent. Wherefore of all modes of getting wealth this is the most unnatural.*

St. Thomas accepts Aristotle's theory and works out the argument in greater detail. He says:

> To take usury for money lent is unjust in itself, because this is to sell what does not exist, and this evidently leads to inequality which is contrary to justice.
>
> In order to make this evident, we must observe that there are certain things the use of which consists in their consumption: thus we consume wine when we use it for drink, and we consume wheat when we use it for

*Aristotle, *Politics,* bk. I, ch. 10, 1258b 2-8.

food. . . . He commits injustice who lends wine or wheat, and asks for double payment, viz., one, the return of the thing in equal measure, the other, the price of the use, which is called usury. . . .

Now money, acording to the philosopher, was invented chiefly for the purpose of exchange: and consequently the proper and principal use of money is its consumption or alienation whereby it is sunk in exchange. Hence it is by its very nature unlawful to take payment for the use of money lent, which payment is known as usury: and just as a man is bound to restore other ill-gotten goods, so is he bound to restore the money which he has taken in usury.*

These views are no longer held, not because of any change in the moral principles of justice involved, but because of a change in the function of money. Interest was condemned as an attempt to get gain by no labor, expense, or risk from something which does not fructify (money) and hence can afford no just title for the gain.

In former ages Aristotle's statement that money is merely a medium of exchange was literally true. It could not be easily turned into capital. There were only handicrafts, no large factories. The only capital worth the name was land, and land, since it was owned by the nobility and was the title to their rank, was not generally on the market for sale. All that a man could do with his surplus money was to keep it locked in a chest or spend it on furnishings and luxuries.

The change in the function of money was brought about by the introduction of the capitalistic system, appearing first in the mercantile and later in the industrial form. When feudalism was breaking up and the new class of wealthy burghers was coming into prominence, the latter formed *joint stock companies* to finance projects greater than the wealth of any single man, the profit to be distributed in proportion to the amount contributed. Since the development of these enterprises and more so after the industrial revolution, money can always find profitable investments and can be readily turned into capital. By such investments money brings profit, breeds more money, and so does fructify.

Nowadays the person who lends money to another deprives himself of the opportunity of investing his money in profitable enterprises and is deserving of compensation for this loss. This is the modern function of interest. Now that anyone can readily invest his money and turn it into capital, there is no reason why he should ever lend money to another unless he can receive profit in the form of interest. To charge an excessive rate is unjust, and this has now become the crime of usury.

That this modern idea of interest does not rest on a change of moral principles, but only on a new interpretation of money, is confirmed by the fact that even the ancients admitted the right to compensation for the expenses of the transaction, the loss of the opportunity to seize good bargains, and the risk of not recovering the principal. In ancient times these were not always present or were negligible; now the reverse is true.

---

*St. Thomas, *Summa Theologica,* II-II, q. 78, a. 1.

The above refers to private loans only, in which the just rate of interest would be calculated to offset the loss of potential gain incurred in each case. But how explain the uniform rates of interest prevailing in the money markets? And how is a man justified in taking interest on money loaned to the capitalistic enterprises themselves, in supporting those very institutions that make interest-taking on private loans almost an economic necessity? An investor in stocks is entitled to dividends which are his share in the profits, but why is the holder of bonds, who owns no share in the company, entitled to interest on his money?

The answer must be based on the function of credit in the modern financial world. The granting of credit is the placing of economic power at somebody's disposal. This is an economic service, and as such is worth its price like any other service. He who makes his property available for another's use charges rent for it. He who makes his money or credit avaliable for another's use can likewise charge for this use in the form of interest. Interest in this sense has changed radically from interest on private loans. It ceases to be the old contract of interest and becomes much like one of hire or lease. It is rendering a service to the enterprise and thereby to the whole community, whose economic prosperity consists in the total complex of these enterprises. It sets up a market in money as in any other commodity, and the just price is determined in the same way as the price for any other service. The natural rate of interest is what people in general are willing to pay on the open market, and the legal rate is fixed by law.

CONTRACTS OF CHANCE

Contracts of chance have to do with some uncertain event whose outcome is due to luck or skill or a combination of the two. The chief forms are betting, gaming, and lottery, to which we must add insurance and market speculations. *Gambling* in the narrow sense is the same as gaming, but is often used to cover the first three or even all forms of venture. None of these is wrong in itself. However, contracts of chance, besides conforming to the requirements of contracts in general, must observe some special conditions of their own if they are to be conducted on a moral plane:

1. One must wager only what belongs to oneself and is not needed for satisfying other obligations, such as paying creditors or supporting one's family.

2. The matter of the contract must be something lawful in itself and understood in the same sense by all parties. Equality is not necessary but inequalities should be made known. Odds and handicaps should be offered by the favored side, but may be waived by the other side.

3. The outcome should be objectively uncertain and not a sure thing, if it is to be truly a contract of chance. Each may feel subjectively certain that he will win, but must not have so manipulated the matter beforehand as to cut down the other's chance. If one insists on betting against another's protestation of certainty, he is making a gift, not placing a bet.

4. There must be no cheating, either by fixing the outcome beforehand, or by an illegitimate style of play. What constitutes cheating depends on the conventions accepted in that kind of bet or game. Winnings through cheating are fraudulently acquired and must be refunded.

5. The loser must pay. This is evident from the whole supposition of the contract. One would have no right to take the winnings unless he is prepared to stand the losses, since this is the obligation he imposes on the other party and the obligation is mutual.

What if gambling is outlawed? If a civil law forbids gambling, it is either a purely penal law, leaving the contract valid and the obligation standing, or it is a law that binds morally, voiding the contract from the start so that the principles on evil contracts apply. In the former case one does no moral wrong in gambling but must pay. In the latter case one probably need not pay but commits a wrong in the act of gambling.

Gambling, though not in itself morally wrong, is so open to serious abuse that it should be strictly regulated. Some people get gambling in their blood and cannot stop until they have brought about their own and their family's ruin. For them gambling becomes a vice leading to many others. Just as some must practice total abstinence regarding drink, others must stay completely away from all forms of gambling, not because it is objectively wrong, but because of the subjective danger of excess in certain persons. Besides, professional gambling is conducted in such an atmosphere of general moral laxity as to provide many temptations beyond those of gambling itself.

Insurance has a purpose different from that of other contracts of chance, for it is not to make money quickly but to guard against loss. Gambling creates a risk where none existed before; insurance covers a risk that was already present. Insurance fills a definite need in modern society. Its contract, whose written form is called a policy, must follow the laws of contracts in general. Any fraudulent concealment or failure to live up to the terms of the contract is an act of injustice demanding restitution. Deliberately to cause damage in order to collect insurance money is the obvious crime here, removing the element of chance essential to the contract. Insurance companies must have the funds to pay indemnities for losses occurring at the normal rate, but not to cover all at once. Insurance has become so common and assumed such social significance that the civil law has the right and duty to regulate it strictly.

Operations on the stock exchange and similar markets are in the first instance but buying and selling, though on a grand scale. The size of the transaction does not change its nature or the moral principles on which it rests. It becomes a contract of chance when it assumes the form of *speculation,* which consists in betting on future changes of price and is thus a kind of gambling. In itself this is not morally wrong, and it follows the laws of betting. Those who engage in speculation, however, must consider not only themselves and their competitors, those willing to play the game, but also the producers of commodities and the vast horde of small investors whose interests are bound up with their own. Unscrupulous speculation on the market and its resulting artificial manipulation of prices can work serious harm to thousands of people and can wreck the economy of nations. To ruin others for one's own profit cannot be condoned by any law of justice or charity, and those who cause these evils bear a staggering load of moral responsibility.

SUMMARY

A *title* to property is an historical fact that changes the abstract right of ownership in general into the concrete right to this particular piece of property. There are seven titles:

(1) *Occupancy:* appropriating what belongs to no one
(2) *Labor:* adding new values to raw materials
(3) *Gift:* gratuitous transfer of ownership to another
(4) *Trade:* any kind of exchange including purchase
(5) *Inheritance:* gift to take effect at one's death
(6) *Accession:* increment accruing to one's property
(7) *Prescription:* possession in good faith over a long time

The title of property is transferred by *contract*. The *seller* must own the object he sells, manifest its hidden defects, and deliver the article bought; the *buyer* must accept the goods on delivery and pay within a reasonable time.

The *just price* is one that can purchase other commodities having equal capacity for satisfying human wants. It is neither an absolutely fixed money value nor any sum the buyer is willing to pay, but represents the judgment of the buying public in general, found by free competition on the open market. This is the *natural* price; if fixed by law, it is the *legal* price. The just price is elastic, a range between a *highest* and a *lowest* just price. To buy or sell outside these limits is unjust and demands restitution. Rare articles, bargain sales, and auctions are exceptions.

Monopoly, exclusive control over a market, is just when used for the common welfare, unjust when exploited for selfish ends.

Partnership is good in itself though monopolistic forms need regulation. In a *firm* each partner has total liability. In a *corporation* liability is limited by the proportion of shares held. Stockholders cannot slough off onto the directors responsibility for immoral use of their capital.

Interest was formerly condemned as an attempt to get gain from what does not fructify. Capitalism, with unlimited opportunities for investment, changed the function of money so that it can fructify. Interest compensates the lender for the gain he might otherwise have made and for the service he renders. Now only excessive interest, *usury*, is wrong.

Contracts of chance deal with an uncertain event. Gambling, though not wrong in itself under proper conditions, is a great moral danger to certain people. Cheating demands restitution and gambling debts must be paid. Insurance is a legitimate social necessity. Market speculation, a complex form of betting, is capable of wreaking great harm unless kept within responsible control.

READINGS

1. Aristotle is the founder of economics as well as of so many other sciences. Read the *Politics,* bk. I, ch. 8-11, 1256a-1259b.
2. Read St. Thomas on cheating and on usury, *Summa Theologica,* II-II, qq. 77 and 78. Not found in the *Basic Writings.*
3. Cronin, *The Science of Ethics,* vol. II, pp. 313-334.
4. Rickaby, *Moral Philosophy,* pp. 253-263.
5. Messner, *Social Ethics,* bk. IV, pt. I.
6. Leibell, *Readings in Ethics,* pp. 513-528, 565-580.
7. Farrell, *Companion to the Summa,* vol. III, ch. IX, pp. 234-244.
8. Ryan, *Distributive Justice,* ch. VII, X, XI, XVI.

CHAPTER 31

WORK AND WAGES

PROBLEM

The private property system under which we live has assumed the form in which most men get the property they need by working for it. By the wage contract a man hires out his labor to another for a definite sum of money known as a wage or salary. We single out the wage contract for special treatment because it brings up the whole question of industrial relations, the problem of capital and labor. We must discuss the following topics:

(1) Whether the wage system is just
(2) How the minimum just wage is determined
(3) Whether a man has a right to work
(4) Whether labor unions are justified
(5) Why and when workmen have a right to strike
(6) Whether lockouts and boycotts are justified

THE WAGE SYSTEM

A man who finds his business getting too large to be run by himself alone must either curtail its volume or engage the help of others. In the latter event, he may choose to take others into partnership and share with them the control of the business, or he may wish to keep the control in his own hands and merely hire others to do part of the work. Partnership usually supposes an investment of capital in the business, and is rewarded by a share in the profits. Employment does not suppose an investment in the business, and is rewarded by the definite monetary return contracted for. The wage system seems to be as old as history and is accepted everywhere. Though perhaps not the only possible arrangement between employer and employee, it is in itself a valid and just contract.

Under the wage system the workman gets a fixed wage but has no share in the profits and losses, whereas the owner gets the profits and also sustains the losses. Thus the workman has income security, which he needs most because of his lack of capital; the owner takes the risks and losses, which his reserve capital enables him to absorb, and he also has the profits as his compensation for the risks and losses. It is a fair bargain. Neither side can have it both ways. The *owner* may not take all the profits and then put off the losses on the laborer when profits fail. The paying of a fixed wage and a just wage is his first obligation, taking precedence over all others, even over payment for raw materials purchased. The *workman* is assured of a steady income from his labor, which is all he has to sell and on which he depends for his immediate support. Having been justly recompensed for his labor and having put nothing else into the business, he does not deserve a share in the profits just as he is not liable for the losses.

A fixed wage means that it is fixed over a certain period specified by contract, not that it is wholly static. The workman has no right to share in the immediate profits resulting from temporary fluctuations, but he has a right to share in the increasing wealth and prosperity of the community of which he forms a part, whether this community be the industry, the nation, or the whole world. Though the workman who is already being paid a just wage has no right to demand more merely because his company happens at the moment to be making a temporary increase in profit, which a prudent owner will hold as a cushion against possible reverses, any really lasting increase in efficiency of productivity should be reflected in a higher wage scale.

The foregoing is an extremely simple view of the matter, but it is necessary to get down to fundamentals or the problem cannot be seen at all. Our highly organized industrial society brings in a number of other factors, but the basic ones we have mentioned still remain. Many suggest a combination of the wage and partnership systems: that the worker be paid a fixed wage sufficient for his own and his family's support, and that over and above this he be given some shares in the business; that this be not in the form of an occasional bonus, but part of the employment contract. We have some discussion of such schemes in the chapter on social order. Note here that they do not eliminate the wage contract, which remains the basic source of the worker's income.

MINIMUM JUST WAGE

The minimum just wage means the least amount any regular workman ought to be paid for his work. By *regular workman* we mean here an adult competent full-time employee who makes his living by giving his whole working day to his employer. We do not mean children, the physically or mentally handicapped, or those engaged part-time or temporarily. These also must be paid justly but they cannot furnish a standard; their pay will be a fair proportion of the regular workman's wage.

The *minimum* just wage is not the minimum for a particular kind of work but for *any* work; it will apply only to the unskilled worker, since skilled work will be worth so much more. We shall make no attempt to calculate the actual minimum wage in dollars and cents, for this will vary with the times, but only to find the *principle* which ought to govern any such calculation. How can it be determined?

1. Not by the length of time spent in work, for any naive supposition that time itself has a definitely fixed and constant value is proved untrue by the fact that no man today could live on the wage given fifty years ago; the value of labor-time has fluctuated with the value of money, and time itself can form no standard.

2. Not by the value of the products of labor, for how much of this value is contributed by labor is hard to determine; besides, labor costs are included in the sale price of the product, thus supposing that the price of labor has already been set by some other standard.

3. Not by the usefulness of a certain laborer to his employer, for this is rewarded by wages above the minimum but cannot set a standard for the minimum itself; the minimum wage has no reference to the quality of the work, but means the least wage any regular workman should be paid if he is employed at all.

4. Not by the law of supply and demand, because labor is no ordinary commodity on a par with the rest, since it involves the dignity of the human person; in a way it is a commodity with fluctuations of value like any other, but differs in that there is a point below which it cannot go without degrading the human person to a subhuman condition. This is where human labor passes outside the field of economics and becomes a moral issue.

5. The only way in which the minimum just wage can be determined is from the function of human labor itself. *Why do men work?* Why are they willing to put in a day's labor for a sum of money? The answer is obvious: a man works to make a living, to support himself and his dependents. This is why a man will spend his life working for himself, as an independent farmer or artisan or shopkeeper. If a man instead of working for himself sells his labor to another, he does it for the same reason. Even the employer cannot stay in business unless it supports him, and, whatever other interests his work may afford him, this is the fundamental one. The same is true of the employee. If a man cannot make a living by his work, there is no reason why he should work. The minimum just wage, therefore, is a wage capable of supplying the essentials of a human life.

What are these essentials? More than bare subsistence, for a man is not a beast of burden and to treat him as such is to dishonor his human nature. More than would satisfy the simple wants of a savage, for a man has a right to share in the civilization of which he forms a part and in the general progress of humanity. His earnings must be graded to the standard of living common in the region where he dwells, though he has no right to demand luxuries and superfluities. Hence we mean the essentials of a human life precisely as *human,* a decent life befitting the rational kind of being man is by nature.

Is the minimum just wage a *personal* wage or a *family* wage, that is, must it be only enough for the worker alone or also enable him to support his dependents? It must be a family wage. The just price of labor, as of anything else, is determined in the open market by the common estimate of men, and the ordinary reason given by men for judging that a wage is too low is: "A man cannot support a family on such a wage." Besides, in the normal arrangement of nature the husband is the support of the family, and to fulfill this function he is not only urged by strong natural promptings but also bound by a strict obligation of the natural law. Therefore a wage sufficient only for the worker's personal support is not really sufficient even for this, for, since he is bound to share it with his family, not enough of it would be left even to support him personally. So the obligation of the natural law is clear: an employer who monopolizes all the earning-power of the father of a family is obliged by the natural law to pay him a wage that will enable him to fulfill his duties to his family under the same natural law. This is an obligation in commutative justice, because commutative justice is the virtue that regulates contractual exchanges.

Should this family wage be *relative* or *absolute,* that is, should it be scaled to the size of the particular workman's family or be adjusted to the average family? At first sight the above argument would seem to prove that it should be relative, for the workman must support the actual family he has, not some mathematical medium that may not be verified in his case. But a relative wage would lead to untold confusion and conflict. The employer would be faced with an almost hopeless task of clerical work, would be unable to estimate his labor cost for the coming year, and would have too strong a temptation to employ men of smaller families. There would be dissatisfaction among the employees paid differently for the same work, and those with the largest families, who most need work, would have the most difficulty finding and keeping it. Therefore the wage should be adjusted to the average family. Some sort of public subsidy might be necessary for very large families, but this is not strictly the employer's business; it devolves on society as a whole or on the state.

Have only married men a right to a family wage? No, this wage must be paid to all. The reason is that unmarried men have a right to marry, to save money for future marriage, and only a family wage will enable them to do so. This is one of the main reasons urging young men to work industriously. Even an elderly single man has the right to marry, though he may never exercise it, and he should not be penalized for not doing what he does not have to do. Besides, distinction in wages on this score would lead to trouble, for grasping employers would find pretexts to dismiss men when they marry, and hire unmarried men in their places.

The conclusion is that the minimum just wage must be sufficient to support a man and his family in reasonable and frugal comfort. What does such a wage entail? A right to:

(1) A home which is decent, private, and sanitary
(2) Sufficient and wholesome food
(3) Enough time off for sleep and relaxation
(4) Some inexpensive forms of recreation
(5) A small surplus for emergency and insurance

A word of caution may be useful here. While stressing the obligation of the employer, we must not forget the other side of the picture. Our American standard of living is so high that we have come to confuse necessities with luxuries, and our habits of spending are eliminating all regard for thrift, a quality needed for survival in most parts of the world. If a man wants luxuries, he should earn them by developing himself into a skilled worker who will receive a wage far above the minimum.

The changed condition of the modern family adds its problems. Formerly the husband walked to work and had to live nearby; now he needs a car. Formerly the wife contributed more to the family's sustenance by her personal services; she churned the butter, baked the bread, spun the wool, and made the clothes besides cooking the meals and sweeping the house. Now there are prepared foods, manufactured clothes, washing machines, vacuum cleaners, automatic kitchens, and countless other appliances. These cost money to buy and operate, and unless the wife is gainfully employed, must be paid for out of the husband's earnings. How many of these things are minimum requirements for a decent human life in our society so that any employer must pay enough to provide them?

EMPLOYMENT

Has a man a right to work, that is, to a steady job? The argument may be put very simply: If a man has a right to live, and can live only by work, then he has a right to work. The logic of the argument is perfect, but the second part of the hypothesis, that a man can live only by work, is normally and generally, but not universally and necessarily, true. The very rich are only an apparent exception because their capital works for them, but even outside this class there are always many who live by their wits and have no steady income. Some men turn green at the very mention of work, yet manage to stay alive. But work is the normal way of getting a living, and it can be taken as a general rule that a man has a right to work. Certainly the economic structure of modern society must be geared to it.

But if the jobs simply do not exist, how can workmen rightly demand them? In time of general calamity, such as widespread financial depression, workmen will suffer as well as everyone else. Employers are obliged to tide over short periods of depression and not to lay men off too quickly, for to take the losses as well as the profits is part of their risk, but it is absurd to think that they can run private businesses indefinitely at a loss.

Their own creditors, to whom they have obligations in justice, would close down on them; by trying to employ too many men they would soon be able to employ none. In such conditions the only one that can come to the workman's assistance is society itself and, as a last resort, the state. How to do it best is a matter of practical expediency and human ingenuity, but the duty itself is moral and binds in justice.

Under modern economic conditions society must see to it that there are enough jobs to go around for all who need them. Does this mean a planned economy? The phrase "planned economy" is often used to mean that the state should take over the work of private business, prescribing how much is to be produced and how many jobs are to be provided. Nothing of the kind is advocated here. But no enterprise can succeed without some planning. The state need not do the planning, but someone must; if private business cannot or will not, the state must either do it or see that it is done. Harmonious cooperation between them is the ideal.

The following groups are sore spots in the employment problem:

1. The first group is *temporarily unemployed* because of some financial crisis or industrial disturbance. The real cure is to remedy the financial or industrial situation, and to take measures to prevent a recurrence. Until we find a way of reducing these troubles, a partial remedy can be found in employment bureaus, in a combination of periodic occupations, in social insurance, in temporary subsidy to private companies, in the undertaking of public works.

2. The *unemployable* are a perennial problem. Since competitive business cannot afford to employ them, their care must be the duty of society in general. Institutions must be established for those who cannot be cared for privately. Those who are physically or mentally handicapped but not institutional cases may be given part-time employment, with the rest of their support made up by the state or by private foundations. The quarrelsome and the drunkard are the worst problems, but society cannot let them starve.

3. *Vagrants* deliberately put themselves outside the pale of human society, and thus cut themselves off from any real right to social assistance. Since these persons are often a menace to society, strict vagrancy laws should be enforced. Compulsory labor is probably unwise, except as a last resort, and even then it is doubtful whether it would do any good. On the other hand, there seems to be no ethical reason why a man may not adopt a wandering life, if he has no dependents and is willing to do temporary work for his daily needs.

LABOR UNIONS

The individual workman is at a distinct disadvantage in bargaining with his employer for a suitable wage. The workman is without capital or power or influence, is usually of lower educational attainments, is trained for only one kind of work, cannot travel but must take present opportunities, and needs a job immediately in order to live. The employer needs workmen but not any particular man, and thus can employ the man who will work for the lowest wage. The workman would have to take any terms the employer wanted to give him unless he could band with his fellow workers for the purpose of *collective bargaining*. A large group of workmen banded together can bargain with the employer on equal terms, since he is as dependent on them as they are on him.

That the labor union is ethically justified is hardly any longer in dispute. The labor union is the *only means* the workman has of obtaining the fair wages and fair treatment to which he as a person has a strict right. Unless the relation of capital and labor is to be regimented by the state, the individual worker is at the mercy of the employer. It is also a *legitimate means*. There is nothing contrary to justice or to the natural law in an association of workers or in collective bargaining. What it is lawful to do separately, it is lawful to do together. If employers and producers can organize themselves into associations, so can the workers. If employers can agree among themselves on what wages they will pay, so can the workers on what wages they will take.

Like everything else, labor unions are open to abuse. They have made exorbitant demands, called unjustified strikes, ruined fair-dealing employers, operated in restraint of trade, become hotbeds of radicalism, and been betrayed by unscrupulous leaders. The remedy is not to destroy the unions, but to correct the abuses. Capital also has been seriously abused by unjust management, as history from the beginning of the industrial revolution to today amply testifies, yet the remedy lay not necessarily in the abolition of capitalism, supposing it a legitimate system, but in the correction of its abuses. When management failed to correct its own abuses, legislation became necessary; if labor will not be clear-sighted enough to put its own house in order, it must submit to the same remedy. But in neither case does abuse destroy the use.

There is nothing wrong in principle with the *closed shop* or *union shop,* but in practice both are open to abuse. No one should be forced to join a union, it is true; but, if the situation is such that the union cannot achieve its end unless all the workers are organized or if some are taking the benefits gained by union activity while evading the burdens of membership, it seems right that those who will not join should be denied jobs. No one has a right to this particular job, and he who wants it should take the conditions attached to it. But if a large part of the workers do not want unionization, it would be unjust to force it on them. The so-called "right-to-work laws," outlawing the closed shop and union shop, seem justified only if the abuses cannot be handled by less drastic measures, a controverted issue dependent on local conditions.

Likewise the *closed union* is not wrong in principle. Unions have a right to limit membership and form a closed union, if otherwise their trade will be glutted with new men seeking to displace tried and reliable members who have given the union its prestige. But if limited membership is used, as sometimes happens, to create unduly high wages through artificial scarcity of workers, an unjust monopoly of labor is created against the public good.

STRIKES

The strike is the chief weapon in the hands of labor for enforcing its demands. Since the purpose of organized labor is to equalize the bargaining power between employer and employee, the only way to counteract refusal to pay fairly is by a concerted refusal to work.

A strike may be defined as an organized cessation of work by a number of workers to obtain their employer's assent to certain demands. In the strict sense a strike is of employees only, not of students or prisoners or other unpaid groups. A strike is a walk-out of a large enough number to cripple the business. It is an organized movement; even a large simultaneous quitting without organization is not a strike, unless the lack of organization is only pretended. The purpose of a strike is not to seek employment elsewhere, but to regain the old jobs on better terms; therefore a mass movement from one employer to another who pays better is not a strike against the first.

Are strikes morally justifiable? To answer this question we must first distinguish three main kinds of strike:

 (1) The *direct* strike, by workers actually laboring under the same industrial grievance
 (2) The *sympathetic* strike, by those who have no grievance of their own but act in support of others who have
 (3) The *general* strike, by all the workers of the community to support some political demand

The direct strike

The basic and original form of strike is the direct strike. Any workman has the right to quit his job provided he has fulfilled his contract, just as any employer who has fulfilled his contract need not rehire him. But an *organized* cessation of work, especially in a large and essential industry, ceases to be a private affair and assumes a social significance. It brings about serious evils to:

 (1) The employer, through loss of profits
 (2) The worker, through loss of wages needed for support
 (3) The consumer, through lack of goods and services
 (4) The public, through general economic dislocation

Application of the double-effect principle

Because it brings about these foreseen evils, which affect not only the persons concerned in the strike but the community at large, a direct strike involves among other principles that of double effect. It is quite possible and often happens that the four conditions are satisfied:

1. The direct strike is not wrong in itself. It contains four elements, none of which is essentially wrong. *Cessation of work* is not wrong in itself; otherwise, one could never quit work. Any other obligation to continue working would not oblige under serious hardship. *Organization* is not essentially wrong; if each may quit work separately, all may do it together, and for a common purpose, supposing that this purpose is good. *Just demands,* presented and refused, are the cause of the strike; no strike can be lawful unless these demands are just, but they can be and often are, such as insufficient pay or intolerable working conditions; the contract may have run its term, or been violated by the employers, or become null through an unforeseen change in the economic situation. *Circumstances* connected with a strike are not such that they must always and necessarily render it evil; violence and bloodshed have occurred in strikes, but there is nothing in the very idea of a strike that requires them.

2. The good effect is not obtained by means of the bad effect in any way that is morally wrong or violates anyone's rights. That the good effect is not obtained through the evils to the worker, to the consumer, or to the public is evident; it is possible, however, to use the exasperation of the public as an additional means of putting pressure on the employer. But is not the good effect obtained through the evil to the employer? The strike is so designed as to hit the employer where it hurts, in his pocketbook; this financial loss is the strikers' means of moving the employer to yield at last to their demands. True, but the fact that a strike works in this way does not make it morally wrong. Financial loss is a physical evil that one can have a right to inflict; a judge does so when he imposes a fine as punishment. The strikers do no injustice to their unjust employer when they stop work for the purpose of stopping his profits and thereby forcing him to stop his injustice toward them. To end the evil of loss to himself all the employer need do is to behave justly toward his men. Hence the principle of the *conflict of rights* comes in here to validate the double-effect principle.

3. The strikers must not intend the evil in itself, but only the just wages and proper working conditions to which they have a right. The strike must not be aimed at fomenting hatred and class war, but only at getting back the old jobs on better terms. Personal hatred on the part of individuals, though morally wrong for those indulging it, does not of itself invalidate an otherwise just cause, but it must not be the motive of the strike as such.

4. There must be sufficient proportion between the good and the evil effect. The more painful and widespread the evil, the greater must be the cause required to balance it. A strike among the military is unthinkable, among policemen and firemen almost never justifiable. A strike in a nationwide industry that would paralyze the country needs an overwhelmingly strong cause. This requirement does not put all the burden on the workingman, but emphasizes the duty of employers to anticipate trouble and to see that a really just cause for striking never arises. The proportion depends on many factors that must be separately determined for each concrete case.

Conditions of a justified strike

The fourth point can be developed more in detail by the following principles:

1. *There must be a just cause.* Too little pay, too long hours, brutal treatment, unsafe or unsanitary working conditions are certainly genuine grievances, whereas personal feuds, petty rivalries, and the ambitions of individual leaders are not. The workers may strike for the minimum just wage, and skilled workers for the wage prevalent for the kind of work they do. When negotiating a new contract, they may refuse to work for the minimum just wage, even though it is a just wage, and may demand more. No law obliges men to take the least they have a right to, and the very idea of bargaining supposes the hope of getting more. But the proportion is upset if the workers strike for the very last cent of the highest just wage, though they may ask it, or if the owners stage a lockout because the workers refuse to accept the bare minimum. To stick adamantly to either extreme, unless some important principle is at stake, is really a refusal to bargain, and neither side has the right to be stubborn at the expense of the public. This rule seems to be seriously violated in many cases.

2. *There should be proper authorization.* The decision to strike should come from the men themselves by a free and unintimidated vote. Organized workers must have their strike backed by their union. If the employer can bargain with his workers only through the union, the workers must also use the same channel. Hence "wildcat" strikes are outlawed, unless the circumstances are so unusual that the unions have ceased really to represent the workers and are repudiated by them. It would be out of proportion to authorize a strike that had no hope of even partial success.

3. *The strike must be the last resort.* Every other less painful means must have been exhausted. There is no need of trying plainly futile measures, but each side is morally bound to explore all avenues that offer any reasonable hope. This requirement is all the more important in strike threats that would paralyze the community, in which case the state as protector of the common good may be obliged to intervene. Arbitration, mediation, cooling-off periods, and fact-finding boards may be disagreeable to either side, but they must be used if they have a reasonable chance of success. If the means to avoid an evil are present, one who refuses to use them cannot consider the evil merely incidental to a good end, but deliberately wills the evil.

4. *Only rightful means may be used.* These are two: work stoppage, and persuasion of other workers to keep the work stopped until the demands are met. Strikers have no right to injure the employer in his person or property. There is no excuse for sabotage and little justification for the sit-down strike. Peaceful picketing is a lawful means of persuasion, but strikers are not entitled to use physical violence against those who try to cross the picket line, whether they be customers, nonstriking co-workers, or new workers genuinely seeking employment. Employers may hire peaceful workers to take the place of the strikers, but not professional strike-

breakers who, it is foreseen, will inevitably provoke violence. In a justified strike the strikers have a right to be returned to their jobs, for it was merely in defense of their rights that they struck in the first place. Whoever begins the use of violence in a strike does wrong; once it has begun, each one has the right of self-defense. But violence is not a legitimate means either of winning or breaking a strike as such.

The sympathetic strike

There is great difference of opinion regarding the sympathetic strike. Some see red at the very mention of it, while others think it but a natural extension of the direct strike. The moderate view distinguishes two possible cases.

1. The first case involves several groups of workmen belonging to different unions but hired by the same employer. One group strikes for an undoubtedly just demand but are too few to enforce it, and so they appeal to the other groups in the same plant or in different plants of the same company. This kind of sympathetic strike seems justified, provided all the other conditions for a just strike are fulfilled, because it is directed against the same unjust employer. It is not bringing harm to an innocent employer who does his duty by his workmen.

Such a strike may even be directed against several employers when they bind themselves into an employers' or producers' association to adopt a common policy toward their employees and this policy is unjust, or when one employer comes to the aid of another for the purpose of breaking a justified strike. Concerted effort on the part of management must be met by concerted effort on the part of labor. A real grievance is spread among all strikers, who direct their efforts against actually unjust employers.

2. The second case involves groups of workmen hired by different and unassociated employers. One group strike because of a grievance and to support them the other group go out on strike against their own wholly blameless employer. The idea seems to be that solidarity among the forces of labor must be achieved at all costs. This second type of sympathetic strike seems unlawful for several reasons:

It is a violation of the wage contract. These workers have no grievance against their own employer, yet refuse to do for him what they contracted to do. It is therefore a breach of commutative justice, for the wage contract is a bilateral onerous contract binding both sides equally.

The evil caused is out of proportion to the original demands. If such a sympathetic strike spreads far enough, the public at large rather than the unjust employer of the original strikers would be the chief ones to suffer from it.

There is no logical place where such a sympathetic strike should stop. All businesses are more or less connected. All use public utilities and, if these go out in sympathy, the whole city or country comes to a standstill. The logical conclusion of this type of sympathetic strike should be the general strike.

The general strike

The general strike is the favorite device of anarchists and revolutionaries, having for its ultimate purpose the overthrowing of capitalism and the putting of the means of production in the hands of the workers. We are not obliged to defend the capitalistic system and may advocate some other economic structure, but we may not try to bring about the change by such methods. The general strike aims not to remedy an evil, but to inflict injury; not to bring pressure on unjust persons to make them fulfill the demands of justice, but to destroy their property and overthrow the order of society. This is a grave moral crime. The general strike is a political rather than an economic weapon, and has the characteristics of rebellion or revolution. As a mere strike, it is out of all proportion. As a method of revolution, its morality depends on the justifiability of the revolution, toward which it could be a legitimate means. We are talking here of a serious strike. In some countries a general strike of a few hours or even of a whole day is used for political demonstration. This does not seem wrong if the people are willing to tolerate this sort of inconvenience and no permanent harm is done.

LOCKOUTS AND BOYCOTTS

The *lockout* is the inverse of the strike. The employer, unwilling to grant the demands of his striking employees, shuts down the whole plant, thus putting out of work even those who are not striking. This is the employer's weapon against the strike. As the workers are not obliged to submit to unjust treatment, neither is the employer. He cannot keep his plant running when key workers have quit and production is stalled, nor can he continue to pay wages without income. If the strike is justified, the lockout is not; but if the strike is unjustified, a lockout can be permissible so long as it conforms to the same conditions and restrictions that apply to the strike. But the *sympathetic lockout,* the closing down of all the factories of the region to break a strike in one of them, causes a disproportionate amount of suffering. The employer has wealth and credit to tide him over, but the workers have not.

A *boycott* is a concerted refusal to patronize a certain business establishment and a persuading of others to join in this refusal. A boycott is justifiable for the same reasons and on the same conditions as a strike. No one is obliged to trade in one place rather than another and may refuse to trade with unjust persons; there is no reason why he may not persuade others to do likewise, so long as he limits his efforts to persuasion and does not resort to violence. The *secondary boycott* is directed against other firms that do business with the boycotted firm; if they do not join in the boycott, they will be boycotted themselves. The secondary boycott is much like the sympathetic strike and follows the same principles. These other firms are not unjust and should not be made to suffer for something they cannot help. Often they cannot obtain materials or services elsewhere to keep themselves going, or they have contracts with the boycotted firm that they are bound in justice to fulfill. But if they cooperate with or connive at injustice, economic pressure can legitimately be brought against them.

CONCLUSION

The establishment and maintenance of good industrial relations is one of the most important problems of our age. Ethics is not called upon to solve it, but merely to point out some moral issues involved. It is not difficult to see in the abstract what ought to be done; the hard part is to get men to do what they know they ought. The ethical concept running through this whole discussion is that of justice. Justice itself never changes, but it must be applied to the new economic facts of the present day.

When our sense of social justice is outraged by the industrial unrest of today, we must not forget the enormous advances that social justice actually has made in the last hundred years. Capital, which formerly wielded its power with imperious recklessness, has been gradually though grudgingly brought to a better sense of public welfare; it still has a long enough way to go in eliminating greed and selfishness. Labor, once so powerless, has by dogged persistence won for itself a position of impregnable strength; it is time for it to assume a larger share of social responsibility.

Union leaders have a delicate and difficult task. They must be upright and just men, true leaders of their unions and jealous of their rights, but also men with a broad social vision embracing the welfare of the whole nation and not merely of the economic class they represent. The rank and file of labor have the obligation to attend meetings and vote, so as to make sure that the union will not fall prey to irresponsible leadership or adopt unjust policies. If a strike is to be called, workers have the duty to inform themselves on the justice of the strike, either by a direct study of the situation or, if they are incapable of this, by assuring themselves of the character and uprightness of their leaders.

Because it sets the pattern of industry, management's responsibility is inescapable. Despite its reforms hitherto, perhaps more of the vast wealth and energy devoted to expanding plants, developing new products, advertising and salesmanship, opening up new markets, paying dividends, and attracting the investment of capital could be diverted to that extremely important but often forgotten cog in their whole machinery: the contented employee. Further consideration of this matter is found in the chapter on social order.

SUMMARY

By the *wage contract* a man hires out his labor to another for a definite sum of money. Thus the workman has income security, which his lack of capital demands, while the employer takes the profits and losses, against which his capital acts as a cushion.

The *minimum just wage* is the least amount any regular unskilled workman should be paid. It is not determined like other commodities, because the dignity of the human person places a point below which it must not fall. It is determined by the reason why a man works: to earn a livelihood. It must be a *family wage,* one sufficient to supply the essentials of a decent human life for an average size family, whether the worker is married or not.

In our economy a man has a *right to work,* and society the duty to provide jobs. If no one else will, the state must. Means must be taken to cure unemployment, care for the unemployable, and regulate vagrancy.

Labor unions are morally justified as the only practical means of obtaining fair wages and fair treatment for the worker. By banding together for *collective bargaining,* workmen can overcome their disadvantage and make the employer as dependent on them as they are on him.

The *strike,* an organized cessation of work to obtain certain demands, is labor's chief weapon. The *direct* strike can be justified by the two principles of double effect and conflict of rights; the strikers have the right to demand justice by inflicting on the employer a loss of profits he seeks to gain unjustly. There is sufficient proportion if the strike is for a just grievance, is backed by a recognized union, is the last resort, and limits itself to peacefully persuasive means. The *sympathetic* strike is justified if directed against unjust employers only; otherwise it is an injustice against innocent people. The *general* strike is a political weapon, and immoral except as the means of a justified revolution. Lockouts and boycotts can be justified on the same principles as the strike.

Great strides have been made toward *social justice,* but both management and labor need a still higher sense of social responsibility.

READINGS

1. Pope Leo XIII's *Rerum Novarum* (Condition of the Workingman), Pius XI's *Quadragesimo Anno* (Reconstruction of the Social Order), and John XXIII's *Mater et Magistra* (Christianity and Social Progress) are among the most important documents on industrial relations. Their treatment of the subject is not primarily philosophical, but the ethical background is clearly brought out. The following commentaries on them are particularly useful:
   a. Nell-Breuning, *Reorganization of Social Economy.*
   b. Husslein, *The Christian Social Manifesto.*
   c. Hughes, *The Pope's New Order.*
   d. Miller, *Forty Years After: Pius XI on the Social Order.*
   e. Naughton, *Pius XII on World Problems,* pp. 102-132, shows how the tradition carries on after Pius XI.
2. Two leaders in writing on the moral aspect of industrial problems were John A. Ryan and Joseph Husslein, whose books, though old, are still useful. Especially well known and often reprinted is Ryan's *Distributive Justice.*
3. Leibell, *Readings in Ethics,* pp. 615-739, contains a number of useful readings, some from periodicals and pamphlets no longer obtainable.
4. Cronin, *The Science of Ethics,* vol. II, pp. 334-371.
5. Messner, *Social Ethics,* bk. II, pt. II.
6. Haas, *Man and Society,* ch. II, VIII, XI.
7. Callahan, *Catholic Attitude Toward a Familial Minimum Wage.*
8. Smith, *Spotlight on Labor Unions.*
9. McLean, *Morality of the Strike.*
10. Cronin, *Catholic Social Principles,* ch. IX, X, XI, contains an excellent classified and annotated bibliography.

11. Tannenbaum, *A Philosophy of Labor,* is an interesting and provocative little book, whether one accepts its conclusions or not.
12. Toner, *The Closed Shop.*
13. Johnston, *Business Ethics,* ch. 7, 10-11.

CHAPTER 32

COMMUNISM AND SOCIALISM

PROBLEM

The desire for a more equitable distribution of the world's goods is very ancient. The system of private property goes back further than our earliest historical records. So too do the abuses of private property, enormous wealth and dire poverty. As soon as any region became so settled that there was no longer any free land, all economic advancement had to be accomplished by the wealth already in one's possession. Because some men are more clever in trading than others, wealth tends to concentrate in the hands of a few. Classes of society based on wealth are established and the inequality is perpetuated. Thinkers began to speculate on the inequality of wealth, its causes and remedies.

Communism and socialism are proposed as remedies for this evil. Though in their present form these are modern theories, products of the industrial revolution, some of the basic ideas behind communism and socialism have an ancient lineage.

HISTORY OF UTOPIAN SCHEMES

The Institutions of Lycurgus* at Sparta embodied many features of communism: equal distribution of land, abolition of luxury, use of iron money valueless outside the state, common meals and dormitories, a rigid system of state education, prohibition of travel, and exclusion of strangers.

Plato's *Republic*† proposes a drastic communism, but quite unlike any

---

*Life of Lycurgus in Plutarch's *Lives.*
†See books III, IV, and V, especially the end of book III.

modern form. His motive was political, not economic. The state will be good only when ruled by the best men, the most qualified statesmen, the philosopher kings. To develop such persons a system of state education must be set up. All, men and women alike, will be given equal opportunity. From them the state will select its rulers by rigid examinations in which only the truly able will succeed. Thus the state will secure competent rulers. To eliminate fraud and graft, to secure public-spirited rulers who will administer the state for the common good and not for their private benefit, communism must be established for the guardians, the two upper classes of rulers and soldiers, but not for the third class of producers. The guardians would be allowed no property and the state would supply their needs. Lest they have any temptation to amass wealth or gain privileges for their wives and children, wives and children should be held in common as wards of the state. A strict system of eugenics will ensure the purity of the race and the development of the best talent.

St. Thomas More's *Utopia* is a satire on contemporary conditions, but contains communistic notions. In Utopia money is abolished and gold is held in dishonor, all persons must work, six hours a day are given to labor and the rest to learned leisure, property is held in common, there are common meals and apartments but the family is preserved, tolerance is accorded to all religions and opinions, and government is by an absolute monarch elected by the people.

The nineteenth century saw the rise of a number of socialist and communist movements. Claude de Saint-Simon advocated abolition of inheritance, socialization of the means of production, distribution based on merit, and a state ruled by economists and industrialists. Charles Fourier would organize the world into phalansteries or self-contained communal units consisting of land, shops, and dwellings, where each would contribute his labor and receive his share of the produce. Brook Farm in Massachusetts was the best known of his thirty-four establishments. Robert Owen, after successfully setting up a model textile factory, turned to the running of communal villages and cooperative communities. His foundation at New Harmony, Indiana, ended in discord. Pierre Proudhon insisted that property is theft, labor is the only measure of value, and man's ethical progress will make property and government unnecessary. He partly inspired the Paris Commune of 1871.

With the coming of Karl Marx the utopian era of socialism and communism ended. Marx made of socialism and communism a scientific theory and a practical movement. His *Communist Manifesto,* a brief call to the workmen of the world to unite, and his great work *Capital,* the bible of modern socialism and communism, are works of a far different spirit than anything which had preceded them.

Karl Marx, born in 1818 of Jewish parents at Trier in the Rhineland, attended the Universities of Bonn and Berlin, where he absorbed the then popular philosophy of Hegel, and took his doctorate at Jena with a thesis on the materialistic philosophy of Epicurus. As editor of a radical newspaper, he came in contact with the working classes and was deeply affected by their plight. He went to Paris, then the center of socialistic movements, where he was influenced by, though he disagreed with, Proudhon. On reading the materialistic works of Ludwig Feuerbach, he conceived his own distinctive philosophy, an application of Hegel's method to Feuerbach's content. In 1848 he published the *Communist Manifesto* with Friedrich Engels, his constant collaborator. Expelled successively from Paris and Brussels, he moved to London, where he spent the rest of his life in poverty, supported by Engels. He helped in the organization of the First International. He kept working on his great book, *Capital,* until his death in 1883.

EXPLANATION OF MARXISM

In our discussion of Marxism we shall first give a rapid bird's-eye view of the main points of the whole system, and then take up each point for evaluation and criticism. We can arrange the points as follows:

(1) In *philosophy:* dialectical materialism, the dialectical process applied to a materialistic content
(2) In *history:* economic interpretation of history, theory of class struggle
(3) In *economics:* labor theory of value, surplus-value, exploitation of the worker, concentration of wealth
(4) In *sociology:* progressive pauperization, industrial reserve army, cyclical financial crises
(5) In *politics:* inevitability of the revolution, dictatorship of the proletariat, the classless society

Philosophy: dialectical materialism

Marx's unique philosophy was a union of the dialectical method of Hegel with the historical materialism of Feuerbach. Marx thought that Hegel had the correct method of development but made the wrong thing evolve, thought instead of matter; Feuerbach, on the other hand, made reality consist of the right thing, matter, but left its development to chance, which explains nothing. Marx insists that his is not a vulgar mechanistic materialism.

The *Hegelian dialectic,* to give but the barest outline of it, is the process of development that pervades everything. For Hegel there is only one reality, which he calls the Idea. In a sense it is God because there is nothing else, but in another sense it is not God because it has not yet thought itself out and arrived at self-consciousness. The process of thinking itself out is the *dialectic.* Thinking consists in contrasting each thought with its opposite, whereupon there arises a higher thought which is the union of the two. Thus the thought of *being* leads to the thought of its opposite, which is *nothing;* the union is *becoming* or the passage from nothing to being. In every case the first stage which is simply given or posited is called the *thesis,* the negation of the thesis is the *antithesis,* and the union of the thesis and antithesis or the negation of the negation is the *synthesis.* What underlies this process is that reality itself is basically contradictory; thought first takes up one side of the contradiction (thesis), and then the other (antithesis), and finally succeeds in fusing the two (synthesis). Any thought contains only part of the truth; there is some truth also in the opposite, and only when both are reconciled in a higher union does the whole truth appear. The process continues because each synthesis now becomes a thesis for further development.

In thinking itself out, thought arrives at the main antithesis to itself, which is inert matter. At this point the Idea objectifies itself in matter, turns into its opposite, contradicts its unity and totality, fractions itself into this manifold world of experience, and spreads itself out to become Nature. This, for Hegel, is the creation of the world. World evolution continues along dialectical lines. The first inkling of synthesis is life, in which thought reappears in matter, organizing plants purposively, manifesting conscious instinct in animals, and arriving at self-consciousness in man, the spearhead of the process. In man the dialectic continues through human history, in which man has passed to higher and higher forms of social organization, culminating at present in the political state. Thus thought and matter, spirit and nature, are united in man. The final synthesis will be a combination of the thesis (the Idea thinking itself out) with the antithesis (the Idea spread out into Nature) into the synthesis (Nature gathered back into the Idea in full self-consciousness as Absolute Spirit). The whole process is the life of God, whose evolution is the universe, of which human history forms a leading part.

Marx kept the dialectic but substituted matter in place of thought. The Hegelian dialectic is an *idealism;* matter is but a transient appearance of the Idea in the stage of antithesis. Marx does not admit the existence of anything but matter. He nowhere defines exactly what he means by matter, but he certainly refers to the sensed world of bodies. He makes the dialectic a dialectical *materialism* instead of an idealism by having *matter* the evolving reality. He puts into matter itself the principle of its own evolution, which proceeds according to the three Hegelian stages and forms itself into our present universe. Marx is particularly interested in that part of the dialectic which refers to human history, which he says is conditioned by man's primitive material economic needs.

History: economic determinism

What Marx calls the *materialistic conception of history* is usually known as the *economic interpretation of history* or *economic determinism.* He thinks that the main motive explaining the whole of human behavior and therefore of history is economic. The way we produce goods and exchange products determines our life. Society gradually evolved from primitive collectivism, through savagery and barbarism, to civilization. At first men lived by hunting and fishing, then by domestication of animals and a nomad life, then by agriculture on settled farms, then by handicraft industry in the towns, and finally by power machinery and the factory system in huge industrial centers. The degree of civilization depends on the economic system. Religious, ethical, philosophical, artistic, social, and political ideas have their value in shaping history, but they are ultimately conditioned by economic motives. Any society will develop that type of religious belief, moral customs, philosophical outlook, artistic expression, social strata, and form of government which corresponds with the prevailing economy in that society's particular degree of cultural development.*

From this follows the theory of *class struggle*. Marx says: "The history of all hitherto existing society is the history of class struggle."† Classes arise out of the economic life of society: those who have and those who have not. In ancient times there were the masters and slaves, those who had and those who did not have freedom; in medieval times there were lords and serfs, those who owned and those who did not own the land; in modern times there are employers and employees, those who own the means of production and those who have nothing to sell but their labor. In history the lower class has always emancipated itself. This age can be no exception. The proletariat will rise against its oppressors, but this time it will destroy all class rule, and thus emancipate all society from the evil of class struggle. Marx thinks that not only is the *thesis* of primitive collectivism long past, but the *antithesis* of private property is now coming to an end, and the *synthesis* of communism is in sight.

Economics: surplus-value

Marx adopts from the liberal economists, Adam Smith, David Ricardo, and others, the *labor theory of value*, that labor is the sole source of economic value. The unit of wealth is a commodity, which, as Aristotle‡ had pointed out centuries before, has a twofold value: *use-value*, its capacity to satisfy a human want, depending on its physical and chemical properties, such as bread used for food; and *exchange-value*, the ratio according to which different use-values may be bartered for one another depending on the object's social desirability, such as bread to be sold in the market. Marx goes on to argue that exchange-value is wholly independent of use-value:

> As use-values, commodities are, above all, of different qualities but as exchange-values they are merely different quantities, and consequently do not contain an atom of use-value. If then we leave out of consideration the use-value of commodities, they have only one common property left, that of being products of labor. . . .
>
> A use-value, or useful article, therefore, has value only because human

---

*Marx, *A Contribution to the Critique of Political Economy* (1859), preface.
†Beginning of the *Communist Manifesto*.
‡Aristotle, *Politics,* bk. I, ch. 9, 1257a 7.

labor in the abstract has been embodied or materialized in it. How, then, is the magnitude of this value to be measured? Plainly, by the quantity of the value-creating substance, the labor, contained in the article. The quantity of labor, however, is measured by its duration, and labor-time in its turn finds its standard in weeks, days, and hours.*

Hence the value of an object consists solely in the amount of abstract homogeneous human labor socially necessary for its production. Since this cannot be accurately calculated, the actual price of a commodity fluctuates about its true value.

Marx's chief innovation is the concept of *surplus-value*. The modern workman, not owning machines and unable to compete by handicraft with those who do own them, must sell his labor-power to the capitalist, for labor-power is all he has. This labor-power has use-value and exchange-value like any other commodity. The use-value of labor-power is the improvement of the raw materials into the finished product. The exchange-value of labor-power is wages, what the workman gets in exchange for his work. The capitalist pays only the price of the exchange-value of the labor (wages), yet he takes the whole of the use-value of that labor (the finished product). The exchange-value of labor is a daily wage sufficient to buy the amount of goods necessary to sustain a man for a day, but in a day's work the workman produces goods of much higher value than that, so that the use-value of his labor far exceeds its exchange-value. This excess goes wholly to the capitalist, and for it no recompense is made to the workman. The workman may be able in the first few hours to create value equal to his wages, yet he is obliged to work several hours more. The value he creates in this second part of the day is what Marx calls *surplus-value*.† It may be defined as the use-value of the workman's labor-power minus its exchange-value.

The ratio of surplus-value is the measure of *exploitation of the worker*. Since the value of the finished product sold by the employer is measured wholly by the labor put into it, and the employer pays the workman only for part of that labor, the employer is robbing the workman to the extent of the surplus-value. The surplus-value is put back by the employer into his business and used to facilitate production; it thus produces more surplus-value, and so becomes *capital*.

The lower the wages the greater the surplus-value. The total capital may be divided into two parts: constant and variable. Constant capital is used for raw materials, machines, buildings, upkeep, and is not productive of more capital, for these expenses cannot be diminished without ruining the business. Variable capital is that used for wages and this is what creates surplus-value; the more wages are lowered, the more surplus-value there is for the employer in the form of profit. Marx's solution to this

---

*Marx, *Capital,* bk. I, pt. I, ch. I, sec. 1.

†Marx, *Wage Labor and Capital;* see Engels' very lucid introduction to this pamphlet. In *Karl Marx's Selected Works,* vol. I, p. 242 ff.

problem is to eliminate the capitalist and have the workers own the factory or farm. Then the total value of his labor, its full use-value, goes back to the worker.

Sociology: progressive pauperization

If surplus-value leads to an *accumulation of capital* by the employer, the unbridled competition which is the life of trade in the capitalistic system leads to its *concentration in monopolies.* As in the mercantile age, when capital was invested in raw materials, nations scrambled for colonies, so in the industrial age, when capital is invested in machinery, there is a scramble for markets. Since the cheapest product gets the market, competition means lower and lower wages. But competition is self-destructive, for logically there is no place where the forcing out of competitors should stop until everything is in the hands of one. Competition inevitably breeds monopoly, which, now that the zest of competition is eliminated, acts as a shackle on production and tends to bring about industrial stagnation. Industry becomes concentrated more and more in a few gigantic trusts, and capital becomes concentrated more and more in the hands of a few.

The effect of the factory system on the working masses is their gradual degradation. With the concentration of capital in the hands of the few, the rich grow richer and the poor poorer. The large companies squeeze out or absorb the smaller. Small manufacturers yield their plants to the big monopolies, and the former owners, once independent capitalists, now become proletarians working for the larger company. The middle class of society is gradually eliminated and swells the ranks of the proletariat.

The proletariat concentrate more and more around the centers of production, leaving the country and gathering in the industrial cities where they form the bulk of the slum population. This concentration is good for the capitalists because it provides them with a vast reserve of cheap labor. When the demand for work exceeds the supply of available jobs, wages go down, surplus-value goes up, and there is more profit to the capitalist. The invention of labor-saving devices decreases the number of workers needed and turns them out of the factories to swell the *industrial reserve army,* Marx's name for the unemployed.

The occurrence of *cyclical financial crises* accentuates the process. Every ten years or so a financial crisis occurs, a major one every twenty years, and these are getting progressively worse. They are necessarily bound up with the capitalistic system. When wages are low, industry makes use of the cheap labor to increase production. Now the markets become flooded, demand slackens off, the factory shuts down, and the workers are thrown out on the streets. These oscillations are unavoidable in an economy of unregulated competition, and the greater the concentration of industry the greater they must become. The time must come when a crisis of such magnitude will occur as to eventuate in the utter collapse of the capitalistic system.

Along with the constantly diminishing number of the magnates of capital, who usurp and monopolise all advantages of this process of transformation, grows the mass of misery, oppression, slavery, degradation, exploitation; but with this too grows the revolt of the working-class, a class always increasing in numbers, and disciplined, united, organised by the very mechanism of the process of capitalist production itself. The monopoly of capital becomes a fetter upon the mode of production, which has sprung up and flourished along with, and under it. Centralisation of the means of production and socialisation of labour at last reach a point where they become imcompatible with their capitalist integument. This integument is burst asunder. The knell of capitalist private property sounds. The expropriators are expropriated.*

Politics: the revolution

The dialectic of history shows the *inevitability of the revolution*. People can stand only so much. When the situation of the proletariat becomes absolutely unbearable, they will revolt. The Communists must be ready to take charge of this revolt and guide it the right way. Since it is inevitable, we may as well promote it and have done with it. As Marx and Engels put it:

In short the Communists everywhere support every revolutionary movement against the existing social and political order of things.

In all these movements they bring to the front, as the leading question in each, the property question, no matter what its degree of development at the time.

Finally, they labor everywhere for the union and agreement of the democratic parties of all countries.

The Communists disdain to conceal their views and aims. They openly declare that their ends can be attained only by the forcible overthrow of all existing social conditions. Let the ruling classes tremble at a Communistic revolution. The proletarians have nothing to lose but their chains. They have a world to win.

Workingmen of all countries, unite!†

Though they join them for tactical purposes of infiltration, Marxists have little sympathy with trade-unionism or with attempts to alleviate the condition of the working class. These, they say, are but palliatives, which can cause but temporary relief. The people must be taught to see that the capitalistic system itself is hopelessly rotten, that it cannot be patched up, but must be entirely scrapped in favor of a new economy. Let capitalism collapse, as it must. Then the revolution will come, when the exploiters will be driven out, the expropriators will be expropriated, the workers of the world will seize the means of production and set up the socialist or communist state.

This change can hardly be made without a wrench. The bourgeoisie

---

*Marx, *Capital,* vol. I, ch. XXXII, toward the end.
†*Communist Manifesto,* at the end.

will fight back, and to cope with them a transitory period of the *dictatorship of the proletariat* will be necessary, during which the Communist Party will be the spearhead of the revolutionary movement. The dictatorship of the proletariat, perhaps lasting some generations, will be followed by the period of *state socialism,* but the state will gradually wither away and give place to the long-desired era of pure communism. The end result will be the *classless society,* which will put a finish to the class struggle because there will be only one class. The era of exploitation will be over because the means of production will belong collectively to all. Then the communist utopia will be realized, for all men will share justly in the goods of the earth and the produce of their labor. Society, having passed dialectically from the thesis of the savage tribe's primitive collectivism, through the antithesis of private property by which civilization was developed, will at last be gathered into the synthesis of a new collectivism in which the evils of property will have been eliminated and the benefits of civilization retained for further progress.

EVALUATION OF MARXISM

This summary, inadequate as it must be in the space allotted, sketches the general outline of Marxist teachings. We must now turn to a critical appraisal of the points raised.

Criticism of dialectical materialism

As a system of philosophy, and not merely as an intellectual front for a revolutionary movement, dialectical materialism is not regarded very highly by philosophers. Hegelianism by itself is admired even by its opponents as an imposing structure of idealistic speculation. Materialism is probably as old as the human race and has had its adherents in every age. But the combination of the two is basically incoherent. One who finds neither element acceptable and their union incompatible has three main reasons for rejecting dialectical materialism.

Hegel's dialectic goes counter to two self-evident principles that are the foundation of all metaphysics and of all sane thinking, the principle of noncontradiction and the principle of causality. To take contradiction itself as the inner essence of all reality is to make both reality and knowledge impossible, for that which is self-contradictory can neither be nor be thought. Nor does it help to make the contradictory stages successive rather than simultaneous, for then the Idea is made to evolve out of itself what is not contained in itself or derived from any other source. Hence neither the Idea itself, as conceived by Hegel, nor its evolutionary dialectical process is admissible.

Materialism, the theory that nothing exists but matter, is countered by the arguments for the existence of God as a spiritual Being and for the human soul as the spiritual principle in man; these are discussed in other branches of philosophy. Marx insists that his dialectical materialism is a dynamic, not a mechanistic, materialism; this claim is true enough, but it ruins the system as a materialism, for mechanistic materialism limiting itself to the known properties of bare matter is the only kind of materialism that can be consistent with itself.

The combination is incoherent, for it invests matter with the qualities of spirit and spirit with the properties of matter. The human mind is reduced to a mere function of matter, whereby any explanation of reflective intelligence in man is rendered impossible, while at the same time matter is made a self-moving principle of development and orderly progress, a function impossible without a guiding intelligence.

Criticism of economic determinism

No one would deny that economic factors have largely influenced history. Before everything man must live, must find food, clothing, and shelter. But man does not live on bread alone. Marxists assert that they do not make economic motives the *sole* factors of history, but then they equivalently deny their assertion by making ethical, religious, philosophical, artistic, social, and political ideas the result of economic conditions. If there are other factors but these are reducible to economics, then economics is the *sole basic* factor in history.

Economic determinism is a distorted view of history. True, ancient civilization rested on a slave economy, but that form of economy was common to the whole ancient world. There was nothing distinctive in their economics that developed the Greeks' intellectual genius and the Romans' power in conquest. Even the peculiar position of the Jews is explained more by their religion than by their economics. The origin and spread of Christianity were not due to methods of production and exchange; here the religious motive introduced an economic change, abolition of slavery, rather than the other way round. Mohammedanism is the product of militant religious fanaticism. The Renaissance and the Reformation contained strong economic factors, it is true, but humanistic and religious causes were even more fundamental. Alexander, Caesar, Charlemagne, Napoleon, and other conquerors changed the course of history, but not so much for economic motives as for the love of glory and the pride of conquest. But materialism cannot admit the power of pure mind as a shaper of history. Certainly in all these movements an economic aspect can be discerned, but to make the economic motive primary is to oversimplify the really complex character of these events. There were other events in which the economic motive was primary, such as the descent of the Goths on the Roman Empire, the voyages of discovery to India and the New World, most of man's efforts at migration and colonization. These are important events in history but by no means make up the whole of it.

The class struggle theory is a gross exaggeration. Ancient history is full of wars of conquest between nations and despots, but relatively few class struggles are recorded. The masses were oppressed, but usually bore their yoke with mute resignation. Slave uprisings were quickly and ruthlessly suppressed. The castes of India and the masses of China remained in subjection for 3,000 years; movements to liberate them have come rather from the outside than from their own class-conscious efforts. Only in the late middle ages in Europe with the rise of the bourgeoisie did class struggle come to the fore, and only in the industrial revolution did it become a major force in history. Marx is cunningly selective in picking his events.

Even if class struggles have always occurred, they do not explain all the main events of history. The civilization of Greece was developed by free citizens, not by an uprising of slaves. The empire of Rome was a conquest of Roman arms, not a revolt of downtrodden masses. Christianity spread by the appeal of a religious idea, and is the very antithesis of hatred and violence. The Renaissance was a movement of educated people, not a rising of the lower classes against their masters. The Reformation was imposed from above by the kings and princes of northern Europe, and succeeded only in those countries where it was supported by the ruler. The voyages of discovery, which all admit had an undoubted economic motive, were financed and promoted by the ruling classes; they were no spontaneous revolt of the downtrodden seeking an outlet against oppression. Only after its discovery was America used as a refuge by the oppressed, whose oppression was as much religious as economic. Even the industrial revolution itself, though resulting in class struggles, was not produced by a class struggle but by inventive genius in the creation of new machines, and this genius was not restricted by class lines. The point of these examples is not to deny that class struggles have existed, but to show that they do not explain the whole of history.

Criticism of surplus-value

The theory of surplus-value is rejected by all reputable economists. It is untrue that exchange-value is wholly independent of use-value, and that the so-called surplus-value is necessarily exploitation.

The exchange-value of a commodity is not determined by labor alone. People will not buy articles merely because somebody has labored on them, but because they are somehow useful to the buyer. Plentiful things may have no exchange-value but great use-value, such as air and water. Rare things may have great exchange-value but hardly any use-value, such as objects of art. Hence the common element in all commodities is not labor, but the ability of a thing to satisfy some human need, its desirability or goodness, for which reason we call these things *goods*. If a thing is already plentiful and everybody's need for it is satisfied, it will not command a price no matter how much labor was spent on it. If a thing can satisfy a need better, it will sell at a higher price even though less labor went into it. Hence labor is but one of the factors determining the price of a desirable object; utility and scarcity are equally important. Marx admits this when he says that the only labor that counts is socially useful labor, and that if a thing is useless so also is the labor contained in it; but this admission contradicts all that he had said, for then utility and not labor would be the standard of value.

The theory of surplus-value depends on the labor theory of value, and stands or falls with it. The contract between employer and employee is simply one of hire. Marx supposes that the exchange-value or hire-value of labor is determined as the minimum amount required to support a man and his family; a man cannot work for less and the employer will not pay more. But this statement merely expresses the norm for a minimum wage, and wages are not held down to the minimum. One man is more experienced, talented, skillful, and reliable than another. The first man will be hired sooner and get more pay because he has more utility to the employer. The second man may have a larger family and so need more support, but gets less because he is a less desirable worker; he is certainly entitled to a minimum *just* wage, but can earn more if he makes his work more useful to his employer. Hence the exchange-value of labor is not measured solely by the number of hours spent at it. Nor is it correct to say that the value of skilled labor can always be expressed in terms of so much more unskilled labor, for few useful products can be made with unskilled labor alone. The quality of the labor is as important as its quantity.

It is not true that the capitalist necessarily exploits the worker. That capitalists have done so in the past and that some still do so, by paying too low wages and taking too much profit, is readily granted. But exploitation is an abuse of the system and by no means essential to it. Marx says that the capitalist appropriates all the surplus-value, which belongs properly to the laborer, and thus exploits him. If the capitalist manages his own plant, he certainly works in a way requiring more effort, skill, and training than the common laborer; Marx acknowledges this fact and would grant him the equivalent of a wage proportionate to his work; he too must live and such a return would not be regarded as profit. What Marx objects to is the kind of profit that is put back into the business, so that capital produces more capital. But how otherwise could any sort of economic development be possible? Does the capitalist, whether he manages his own plant or not, deserve no reward for all the risk and responsibility he takes or for the ingenuity and leadership he shows by putting his wealth into this enterprise? It is precisely because he has decided to use his capital in this way that he has made jobs and a livelihood possible for his workers. The idea of capital cannot be got rid of. Even if the state takes over all the means of production, it will need some resources to begin new enterprises and must have built up these resources from previous enterprises. In this sense communism itself is but state capitalism.

Criticism of progressive pauperization

Marx's views on the accumulation of capital and the concentration of industry have a fair amount of plausibility. The formation of huge trusts

and monopolies with the squeezing out of small firms has certainly occurred. Legislation has been necessary to correct this abuse, and it has
not been wholly successful. But not all the evils that Marx expected from
this concentration have come to pass. Trusts and monopolies have become
vast stock companies, so that the capital, rather than being concentrated
in the hands of a few, is scattered among many. However, it is all too
true that the control of these huge companies rests in the hands of a
powerful few, and decentralization of this control seems desirable. But the
elimination of the middle class was a groundless fear. Those who gave
up their small businesses to work for larger companies are paid good
salaries and are not pauperized. Many workers today invest part of their
wages in capitalistic enterprises, and thus become both workmen and
small capitalists.

When Marx wrote, there was real fear of progressive pauperization,
but his preoccupation with economics in history made him a poor prophet.
He failed to consider political and humanitarian influences. The rich have
indeed grown richer, but the poor have not grown poorer. Wages and
living standards have continually improved. The workers have not sunk
into growing insecurity, misery, oppression, slavery, degradation, and exploitation, as Marx gloomily predicted. Not everywhere in the world has
the position of labor grown as strong as it has in this country, but that
labor has prospered especially in the world's most industrialized nation
gives the lie to Marx's whole theory. Most of the demands for bettering
the condition of labor have been put into effect by government legislation
and by collective bargaining between labor unions and employers. It is
true that the workers will stand only so much, but they will not stand as
much as Marx thought they might, and they took means into their own
hands to improve their condition. This improvement has occurred within
the framework of capitalistic economy. Here we are not trying to prove
that capitalism is the best economic system, but only to show that socialism and communism are not necessary to remedy the workingman's
plight.

The industrial reserve army in the Marxist sense is a myth. There
always has been unemployment, but it is not desired by the capitalists
nor do they make a profit on it. Good times are beneficial both to capitalist
and proletarian, hard times hit proletarian and capitalist alike. The unemployed worker loses his wages, the capitalist loses his market and his
profits. New inventions put men out of work temporarily, but often result in the opening up of new industries with increased opportunities for
employment. The invention of the automobile ruined the carriage and
harness trade, but today the automotive and allied industries provide
millions of jobs more than the corresponding occupations in the horse-
and-buggy days.

Business cycles and financial crises are still with us. How they can
be avoided or controlled is a prime economic problem, but there is no
proof that they will necessitate a collapse of the capitalistic system. Panics

caused by huge frauds and swindles in the stock market, such as have occurred in the past, should be preventable by a vigilant government exercising the moderate control over business we have all come to recognize as necessary. The periodic shut down of factories has been largely corrected, either because management voluntarily geared itself to a steady rather than a fitful output or because it was forced to do so by collective bargaining with the unions. Privately owned enterprises can be regulated by law as effectively as socialistically operated factories. How far governmental regulation of business should go is a highly disputed point, but surely the state need not own industries in order to regulate them.

Criticism of the revolution

The inevitable collapse of capitalism through its own inherent rottenness shows no sign of imminence. The capitalistic system survived the world crisis of the 1930's and proved its efficiency in the stress of the world's greatest war. Communism owes what strength it has to militant agitators, not to any spontaneous rebellion by the workers. Marx thought that communism would appear in highly industrialized countries such as Germany or England, but the first country to adopt the communistic system was Russia, one of the least fit because least industrialized. Communism was imposed on Russia by a small minority when the nation was leaderless and demoralized, and was maintained only by the most ruthless oppression and terrorism. The Russian Revolution was no inevitable rising of the proletariat, but was deliberately engineered by trained revolutionaries who forcefully imposed their will on the helpless masses.

The classless society, the goal of communism, is as far off as ever. Certainly it has shown not the slightest sign of appearing in the communist governments so far established. Marxists answer that the process is still in the stage of dictatorship of the proletariat. But there is no indication that this period will ever come to an end. It is not even a dictatorship of the whole proletariat, but of a few dominant men. Communism, once but the economico-philosophical dream of Karl Marx and a few enthusiastic propagandists, has become a flaming revolutionary organization in absolute control of the world's largest country with tentacles stretched out over the whole earth. Will men who have so entrenched themselves in absolute power ever freely consent to let it "wither away"?

SOCIALISM

The previous discussion has been a criticism of Marx, whose orthodox followers today, accepting the development of Marx's doctrine by Lenin, are known as *communists*. Those who adopt milder views of the same general tendency and limit them more to the economic sphere are called *socialists*. The terms *communist* and *socialist* have been variously used at different times in the history of the Marxist movement. Today the main point of distinction seems to be that the communists believe in achieving their ends by violent revolution, the socialists by peaceful evolution in cooperation with existing governments and by legal procedures. Many socialists have dropped almost all Marxian theory from their program.

Stripped of any doctrinaire significance, the word *socialism* may mean only the opposite pole to *individualism*. One emphasizes the rights of society and the common welfare, the other the rights of the individual and personal liberty. Since both have rights, the only acceptable position is somewhere in between. Unless one wants to be a rugged individualist, one must admit some degree of *socialization*. We already have public education and social security, we have experimented with public power plants and utilities, we are toying with socialized medicine and compulsory insurance, we see other nations with nationalized railroads and subsidized merchant marine, and we can conceive of nationalized banks and stock exchanges. There is nothing morally wrong with these things, and each nation may decide for itself how far it wishes to go along the road of government-operated social service to its people. Even the welfare state, which some look on as being one step short of socialism, should not be criticized on ethical grounds but on those of expediency. Though the cost is heavy in taxes, it leaves most property in private hands and plenty of scope for private enterprise.

The case is different with organized doctrinaire socialism, which has as its goal the fully socialized state, in which *all* the means of production are taken from private hands and turned over to the state. Even when purged of the Marxian atheistic and materialistic ideology, and limited to the economic and politico-economic sphere, this kind of full-blown socialism is objectionable on ethical grounds. Its economic and political aim is indistinguishable from that of communism, the only difference being the peaceful rather than the violent mode by which the system is introduced. How could the program be implemented so as to reach the laudable goal of economic security without the sacrifice of the individual's inherent human rights?

There are many practical problems to be solved: how far to abolish private property, how to socialize the means of production without willful injustice, how to determine what to produce, how to distribute jobs and products, how to make men work diligently, how to get disagreeable work done, how to control migration at home and abroad, how to manage education and the family.

Any single one of these difficulties could perhaps be successfully overcome, but all of them taken together present an insurmountable obstacle. Have not the Soviet Socialist Republics overcome them? To an extent, but how? Their practice shows that only by a complete submersion of individual human rights and the institution of an absolutely totalitarian regime could the full socialistic program be inaugurated and maintained. But to deprive the individual of his natural rights is immoral.

It follows that the advocates of full socialism and communism, even as merely economic and politico-economic systems, must find a way of implementing their program without destroying the rights of the individual before they can offer a morally acceptable alternative to the private enterprise system. And they must prove that their system is not only as good but better—better enough to justify the dislocation inseparable from so vast a reorganization.

CONCLUSION

Both socialism and communism go counter to too many things fundamental in human nature. Their view of human nature is too high, too optimistic, when they think that men will spontaneously cooperate in harmony without the profit motive, and that such an enormous bureaucracy could function without a vast amount of corruption. Their view of human nature is too low, too degraded, when they think that men will not rebel against a stultifying regimentation unless it is enforced by tyranny and terror, and that the whole purpose of human life is confined to the temporal, mundane, economic sphere.

The only solution can be a compromise between the two goods, individual liberty and economic security. Economic liberalism, rugged individualism, laissez faire, is one exaggeration; socialism and communism exaggerate the other side. Man must have both liberty and security, but each limits the other. Just where to draw the line in this delicate balance is the crux of the whole economic problem, but neither extreme accords with right reason and human nature, which is the standard of moral action.

SUMMARY

Communism and socialism are proposed remedies for the inequality of wealth. Many utopian schemes were put forth both in ancient and modern times, but none of these can compare with that of Karl Marx, who made communism a scientific theory and a practical movement. Marx's system includes the following points:

1. *Dialectical materialism.* Marx combined the dialectical method of Hegel with the materialism of Feuerbach. Nothing exists but matter, which contains within itself the principle of its own development from thesis through antithesis to synthesis; man is the spearhead of this necessary evolution. *Criticism:* Hegel's dialectic is an idealism that runs counter to the principles of noncontradiction and of causality; materialism cannot explain the intellectual life of man; the combination of the two philosophies is incoherent.

2. *Economic determinism.* The underlying motive in all human history is economic; as the economy, so the civilization. Economic life establishes classes, the *haves* and the *have-nots,* and all history is the history of class struggles; the lower class always succeeds in emancipating itself. *Criticism:* This is a gross exaggeration of the role of economics and of the class struggle in history; it achieves plausibility only by selecting a few movements and neglecting whole areas of history.

3. *Surplus-value.* Exchange-value is entirely separate from use-value;

the capitalist takes the whole use-value of a man's labor while paying only for the exchange-value; the workman creates more value than he is paid for, and this surplus-value goes to the employer, who exploits the workman to that extent. The employer puts this surplus-value back into his business and this constitutes capital. The lower the wages, the more capital to the capitalist. *Criticism:* Labor is not the only source of value; labor-value differs qualitatively as well as quantitatively; the capitalist deserves a return for his risk, foresight, and ingenuity, and needs capital to begin new enterprises.

4. *Progressive pauperization.* Competition breeds monopoly, the rich grow richer and the poor poorer; the middle class is eliminated and swells the ranks of the proletariat, which concentrate in industrial centers and form a vast supply of cheap labor, the industrial reserve army. Financial crises, inseparable from the capitalistic system, accentuate the degrading process. *Criticism:* Wealth and industry do tend to concentrate, but the poor have not grown poorer; legislation and labor unions have largely remedied the workman's plight. Capitalists do not want unemployment because it hurts their markets; financial crises are not wholly beyond control.

5. *The Revolution.* The collapse of capitalism is inevitable; the masses will revolt, seize the means of production, establish the dictatorship of the proletariat, which after a phase of state socialism will emerge as the classless society, the communist utopia. *Criticism:* Capitalism survived war and depression; communism was imposed on Russia by a few and is maintained by terrorism; the classless society shows no signs of appearing.

Socialism relies on evolution rather than revolution. Moderate socialization is not immoral and the people may choose how much of it they want, even as far as the welfare state. But full doctrinaire socialism, even if limited to the economic and political sphere, cannot be morally justified unless it can solve its practical difficulties without destroying man's inherent rights.

Man must have both individual liberty and economic security. As rugged individualism exaggerates liberty, so communism and socialism exaggerate security. Neither corresponds with right reason or human nature taken completely.

READINGS

1. Every educated person should be familiar with the ideal states mentioned in the earlier part of the chapter, especially Plato's *Republic* and *Laws,* Aristotle's *Politics,* More's *Utopia.*
2. Hegel's dialectic process is described in his *Logic.* There is a good account of it in Marcuse, *Reason and Revolution: Hegel and the Rise of Social Theory.*
3. Feuerbach's *Essence of Christianity.* Its influence on Marx is described in Engels' book, *Ludwig Feuerbach and the Outcome of Classical German Philosophy.*
4. Marx and Engels' *Communist Manifesto* is an historic document of utmost significance.
5. Marx's *Capital* is called the "Bible" of communism. It is chiefly economic but embodies the whole system.

6. The works of Marx, Engels, Lenin, and Stalin are too numerous to mention. Convenient source works are:
   a. *Selected Works of Marx and Engels.*
   b. Lenin, *Selected Works.*
   c. Stalin, *Leninism, Selected Writings.*
   d. Burns, *Handbook of Marxism.*
7. The following are general surveys of Marxism, with stress on the philosophical side; some are sympathetic, some critical, some merely expository:
   a. Mayo, *Democracy and Marxism,* contains an excellent annotated bibliography.
   b. McFadden, *Philosophy of Communism.*
   c. MacMurray, *Philosophy of Communism.*
   d. Somerville, *Soviet Philosophy.*
   e. Hook, *Toward the Understanding of Karl Marx.*
   f. Hunt, *Theory and Practice of Marxism;* also *Marxism Past and Present.*
   g. Cole, *Meaning of Marxism.*
8. On dialectical materialism:
   a. Hook, *From Hegel to Marx.*
   b. Guest, *Textbook of Dialectical Materialism.*
   c. Cornforth, *Dialectical Materialism, an Introductory Course.*
   d. Wetter, *Dialectical Materialism.*
9. On the economic interpretation of history:
   a. Kautsky, *Ethics and the Materialist Conception of History.*
   b. Croce, *Historical Materialism and the Economics of Karl Marx.*
   c. Bober, *Karl Marx's Interpretation of History.*
   d. Federn, *Materialistic Conception of History.*
10. On the theory of value and surplus-value:
    a. Böhm-Bawerk, *Karl Marx and the Close of His System,* the classic refutation.
    b. Joseph, *The Labor Theory of Value in Karl Marx.*
    c. Lindsay, *Karl Marx's Capital.*
11. On the revolution:
    a. Lenin, *State and Revolution* and *The Proletarian Revolution and the Renegade Kautsky.*
    b. Berdyaev, *The Origin of Russian Communism.*
    c. Possony, *A Century of Conflict: Communist Techniques of World Revolution.*
12. On socialism:
    a. Shaw, *Essays in Fabian Socialism.*
    b. Sweezy, *Socialism.*
    c. Schumpter, *Capitalism, Socialism, and Democracy.*
    d. Von Mises, *Socialism.*
    e. Selsam, *Socialism and Ethics.*
13. On the Marxist view of morals and religion:
    a. Sheed, *Communism and Man.*
    b. Mauriac and others, *Communism and Christians.*
    c. Cameron, *Scrutiny of Marxism.*
    d. Gurian (ed.), *The Soviet Union, Background, Ideology, and Reality.*
    e. Hyde, *The Answer to Communism;* also *I Believed.*
    f. Crossman (ed.), *The God That Failed.*
    g. D'Arcy, *Communism and Christianity.*

CHAPTER 33

SOCIAL ORDER

PROBLEM

Earning a living is not the highest activity of man in point of dignity, but it consumes most of the ordinary person's time and effort. The economic side of man's nature, unlike the domestic and political, is not taken care of by a corresponding natural society. There already is an economic aspect both to the family and to the state, the one extending up and the other down into the middle region between these two societies. Families are alike and states are alike in having their essential functions prescribed for them by the natural law, but nature does not assign any definite association man must enter into for his economic support. That man must organize in some way for this purpose is evident, but *how* to do it is left to human ingenuity. As in most things human, man's efforts over the centuries in building up a socioeconomic order have been only partially successful. Its remarkable complexity is balanced by haphazard performance, its astonishing fertility in production by its glaring injustice in distribution.

Communism and extreme socialism, as we have seen, offer no satisfactory remedy but a treatment far worse than the disease. Must we then give wholehearted approval to capitalism? No, neither in its present form nor in any form. The world existed for many centuries with private property, yet without that specific form of it called capitalism. We shall not enter into a dispute about the proper definition of modern capitalism but can take it loosely as the economic system characterized by four things: private ownership, free enterprise, the profit motive, and invested funds. The last element is important in distinguishing it from earlier forms of the private property system. Capitalism, as a contingent historical occurrence, is thus not the only alternative to communism and socialism.

423

The system itself is contingent and so is the present form it has assumed. There are many details, adjuncts, and conditions not essential to the system of capitalism itself. Its development is constantly continuing, and there seems to be no final pattern into which it must necessarily congeal. When, if ever, it shall have changed so much as no longer to deserve the name of capitalism is a semantic question we cannot settle here. But, though capitalism is not the only alternative to communism and socialism, we are hard put to it to find another system of private property that could be substituted for it in an advanced society.

What then is the answer? There are several alternatives:

(1) Shall we look to the past and suggest a return to some precapitalist form of private property or a return to rugged individualism within capitalism?

(2) Shall we stand pat and do the best we can with our present amalgam of partly individualistic and partly state-controlled capitalism?

(3) Shall we advocate retention of the basic essentials of the capitalistic system with firm measures to correct its accidental defects?

(4) Shall we look to the future and try to frame some wholly new and different economic system that is neither capitalism nor socialism nor communism?

In other words should our attitude be reactionary, conservative, progressive, or radical?

ATTITUDES TOWARD ECONOMIC LIFE

The two extreme attitudes are impractical. We cannot turn back the clock of history and get people to give up the comforts of modern living for the simple life. Nor was this life wholly desirable. One can romanticize the past by overlooking its disagreeable features, which for the mass of mankind were far worse than anything we have today. The slave economy of ancient times made civilization possible by developing a leisured class, but only by the most hateful form of social injustice. The medieval knight could pursue his noble adventures only by the support of a horde of peasants and serfs who were excluded by birth from his privileges. Laissez-faire individualism, with its disregard for the dignity of the human person, proved its insufficiency within recent memory; the modern worker would embrace communism rather than return to it.

On the other hand, no one has proposed a totally new economic system that can be taken with any seriousness. Most utopias describe forms of communism, which we have already rejected. The working out of an ideal economy poses a challenging task for human ingenuity, but the finished blueprint would have to be highly practical as well as intellectually satisfying. The slightest knowledge of history shows that human institutions develop gradually and that men will not adopt a system that has no strong link with the past. To be practical, any such scheme would have to compromise with existing facts and thus could be no radical break with historical continuity. Even Marxism, which is a radical break, tries to justify itself on the basis of a necessary dialectic of history.

It seems that but two attitudes remain for those who reject communism and extreme socialism. One is *conservative* and pessimistic. In itself conservatism is indifferent; it all depends on what one wants to conserve, whether it be good or bad. The conservatism that cherishes all that is valuable in the culture of the past is the very life of civilization. The conservatism that perpetuates the diseases of society is a force that makes for death. It is the latter form that we are criticizing here, the attitude of wanting to maintain the economic status quo unchanged despite its acknowledged defects. We have arrived, they say, at an uneasy balance of individualism and statism. To stop the state's constant encroachment on private rights, we must fight hard for the retention of as much individualism as we can hold on to. Every suggestion for reform is suspected and branded as creeping socialism. If the present situation is bad, any other can only be worse. The best we can hope for in the losing battle is a stalemate. How should such an attitude be judged? It is natural that those whose economic situation is satisfactory should be loath to give up their advantages or compromise their position. But selfishness cannot be approved. The desire to preserve modes of conduct that are unjust is morally wrong. We are allowed to tolerate evils when they cannot be remedied, but the refusal even to seek a remedy for existing evils is not an ethically defensible position.

The other attitude is *progressive* and optimistic, recognizing the deficiencies of our present economic system and social order but seeking to remedy them gradually and peacefully. Utopia is impossible, and therefore our optimism should be restrained; but, though a perfect economy can never be achieved among fallible human beings, a better one is possible. The present arrangement manifests certain obvious defects that are not beyond improvement by human ingenuity. There has been constant progress in social and economic relations in the past, and there is no reason why the trend cannot be continued toward improvement while diverted somewhat in direction. Fear of the drift toward statism has much justification, and therefore the trend should be away from state intervention toward voluntary self-regulation. Violent agitation will accomplish nothing, but gradual pressure and persuasion can bring about more valuable if less spectacular results.

What are the areas in which improvement seems both desirable and possible, and what are the corrective measures most often proposed? This field is very controversial, and our remarks should be taken as tentative and suggestive. We can arrange them under the following headings:

(1) For the exclusive use of competition, a spirit of cooperation and mutual help

(2) For strife between management and labor, the institution of industrial councils embracing both

(3) For too much state control and bureaucracy, the substitution of voluntary associations

(4) For concentration of economic control in the hands of too few, a wider distribution of control

(5) For the stultifying effects of mass production, a training in the proper use of leisure

COMPETITION AND COOPERATION

Up to now a distinguishing mark of the capitalistic system has been the principle of competition. At the close of the feudal period, aristocracy of birth gave way to aristocracy of wealth. Business ability is no greater guarantee of morality than noble birth was; it is perhaps less, for the noble had security and traditions that the newcomer bourgeois lacked. Ability is determined by success and success by competition, which crowns the winner and eliminates the loser, for whom it makes no provision. Many have succeeded in economic competition without descent into the unethical, but it takes an extra measure of ability to win from those who do not play the game clean. In pure competition there are no rules to the game, and the most ruthless has the best chance of winning. Sanctions from other sources affect the economic sphere only indirectly. Thus the principle of pure competition puts a premium on selfishness and injustice, as well as on intelligence and energy.

On the other hand, there is no way to eliminate all competition and maintain free enterprise. Only were the state to set prices, fix wages, assign markets, allot quotas, and practically run all business would it be possible to do away with competition. This would be socialism, not free enterprise. Competition keeps the economy flexible, dynamic, progressive, resourceful, and efficient. But we now recognize that competition cannot be left wholly unregulated. We did not need Marx's partly justified criticism of laissez-faire capitalism to show us where it was heading. We learned from our own experience the need of putting a brake on unlimited individualism to protect the common good. Despite the limits imposed, competition still remains the chief principle on which free enterprise rests.

There is no question of abolishing competition, but of supplementing it with another principle, that of voluntary cooperation. Enterprise can remain free private enterprise while devoted to a common end as well as to an individual end. Citizens do not lose their freedom while voluntarily cooperating, and neither should business associations. Much cooperation actually goes on: against price slashing, against depletion of natural resources, against useless duplication of services, against false advertising, against a mad scramble for markets. Initiative for this cooperation had to come from legislation, but companies now recognize the value of most of this legislation and accept its protection. Now that the lesson has been learned, there is no reason why more cooperation cannot be initiated voluntarily without pressure from the law.

The population of the world is increasing so rapidly that it cannot be supported without a careful husbanding of the earth's resources. The earth can sustain a far larger population, but not by any haphazard methods of production and distribution. We know the answer of communism: abolish private enterprise and establish a state-dominated economy. In a sparsely settled country like America we can afford to brush this answer aside, but we cannot overlook the appeal it has to the teeming populations of Asia and the new nations of Africa, struggling to rise above their substandard living conditions. The capitalist economy must meet this problem and can do so only by a union of free enterprise with voluntary cooperation, the whole organized to work efficiently. Unless it sets up the machinery soon enough, the capitalistic system may not survive.

CLASS ANTAGONISM AND SOLIDARITY

At present, capital and management are lined up on one side and labor with its unions on the other. Because of the unfortunate history of long-standing hostility, it is assumed that these two groups are necessarily opposed. Here is the class struggle portrayed by the Marxists, who think it essential to the capitalistic system. There is organization among employers, the tightly knit organization of the company itself, and the looser grouping of various companies into employers' associations. Workers are organized into unions and local unions into industrywide unions and nationwide federations. Between the two there is collective bargaining, each trying to get as much as possible for itself, often with little consideration for the long-term benefit of both or for the nation and society as a whole. Even when relations are amicable, the atmosphere is that of each side protecting and furthering its own interests against the other's encroachments.

There has been too much class conflict, but Marxists are wrong in thinking it essential to capitalism. Collective bargaining cannot be eliminated in a free economy, but such negotiations need not be conducted in an antagonistic spirit of class against class. Two sides can vie with each other where their interests differ, yet unite where their interests agree. In the realm of sports we have each team striving its utmost to win the game, though both belong to the same league which scheduled the game and made common arrangements for the public's enjoyment. Economic rivalry is far more serious, but the analogy holds. The point is the same as that already made in the preceding section: cooperation and competition are not mutually exclusive, but there can be cooperation for the sake of legitimate competition. Just as more cooperation is needed between companies competing for the market, so more cooperation is needed between management and labor engaged in the same field of production.

The proposal to unite both the management group and the labor group concerned in the same industry into a larger organization for the benefit of the whole industry seems eminently reasonable. There have been overtures toward labor-management cooperation, some of which have been quite successful, and this movement should be sedulously encouraged. But the effort has been partial and sporadic; it needs definite organization into recognized bodies with detailed structure and function. Call them industry councils, vocational groups, occupational associations, corporative organizations, or any other suitable name.

These new common interest organizations would be supplementary to existing groups, in no way extinguishing or absorbing them. They would not try to do the work of labor unions or employers' associations, each of which would have to exist and retain its functions. Rather, these vocational groups would be central bodies for fact finding, policy making, standard setting, problem solving, and appeal and mediation service. They would not do collective bargaining, price fixing, or other detailed work proper to management or labor. Their general function would be to set the climate for individual enterprise. They would have to exercise some control, or there would be no reason for their existence, but a control reached by voluntary agreement and not by legislative fiat. Such industry councils should be hierarchically arranged on the local, regional, and national levels within the industry; then there could be higher organizations of allied industries, all culminating in a highest board with the most general overseeing capacity. Each level should solve its own problems and have recourse to a higher level only when the interests of more than one group are involved or no agreement can be reached. These industry councils would vary from industry to industry and from country to country in accordance with varying industrial, economic, and political factors. They should have a flexible structure, derived from and suited to their functions, to deal with changing conditions. Nor need they be limited to industry in the narrow sense but could be extended to agriculture, the professions, the financial interests, and any field of common occupational endeavor.

Such a plan seems grandiose and visionary only when we forget the actually existing tendency in this direction. What is needed is organization of these scattered efforts. Man's organizing genius is surely capable of filling the gaping hole in the social structure. That these organizations be free and voluntary, they must grow out of industry itself and develop from existing institutions. They should not be imposed by the state, as the next section will show.

STATISM AND SUBSIDIARITY

Like it or not, business is now regulated to a great extent by the government. The economic order teeters precariously between the extremes of freedom and control. Conservatives stress the evils of statism and its bureaucracy and ask for a return to more individualism. Liberals note the failure of disorganized individualism and call for increased state intervention in economic life. Neither alternative is acceptable and neither is necessary.

Government intervention came when and as it did because there was no mechanism in the business world for self-regulation. So huge and important a thing as man's economic life cannot simply be let go undirected and uncontrolled. Individualism was mistaken in thinking that there are natural economic laws which, if left alone, will automatically bring about the best results for all concerned. Individualism failed not only because it put a premium on waste, greed, and selfishness, but chiefly because it could not deal with the human person, who demanded respect for his dignity and enough security to make his freedom worth having. In the absence of any other power to help him, the state gradually became conscious of its duty to protect its citizens' welfare, stepped into the vacuum, and is now burdened with many functions that do not properly belong to political society as such.

Voluntary organizations such as the industry councils spoken of previously would take much of this burden off government. In the dilemma between no control offered by individualism and state control offered by socialism, there is a possible third horn, self-control. Industry councils would provide self-government of the industry by the industry. With a proper degree of self-regulation by industry itself, state regulation could be proportionately reduced.

There is no question of eliminating all government influence from economic affairs. That would be neither desirable nor possible. The state is responsible for the welfare of its people and cannot be left out of any consideration of man's economic life. Without state backing, help, and support, neither industry councils nor any other voluntary association could have any effect. There are fundamental laws regarding economic matters that any modern state must enact and enforce. But not everything should be the business of government. By the *principle of subsidiarity* a higher organization should not take over work that can be handled adequately by a lower organization. Industry councils functioning properly would make excessive government intervention unnecessary.

Hence it would subvert the whole idea of these industry councils if they were imposed by the state or made organs of the state. They should be relatively autonomous, self-governing bodies, acting as buffer groups between the individual and the state. Their function should be mainly advisory and consultative, but to give them no power would leave them ineffectual. They should be quasi-public institutions with quasi-legal rights, recognized by management, labor, and government as having authoritative status. They should be backed up by the state's authority, but neither set up, staffed, nor run by the state.

One of the common complaints against the modern state is its overgrown bureaucracy. One of the objections to the socialistic state is the still more enormous bureaucratic structure necessary in a government that reserves all enterprises to itself. The turning over of some economic functions to voluntary associations should relieve the state of much of its parasitic overgrowth of boards, offices, committees, authorities, and bureaus, with a corresponding reduction in the general tax burden. This is not suggested as a panacea for bureaucracy but should afford some mitigation.

BIGNESS AND DECENTRALIZATION

Concentration of wealth in the hands of a few was one of Marx's main criticisms of capitalist economy. He was wrong because ownership in corporations is shared among a large number of stockholders, thus partly diffusing the wealth. But he was right because control of this wealth is concentrated in the hands of a few directors of giant corporations. The problem of concentration is not the same as that of bigness, it is true, but the situation is aggravated by a concurrence of both: the economy is dominated by a few huge corporations, in each of which the directorship is lodged in a few persons. This centralization of economic power is not wrong in itself and often makes for greater efficiency, but it has its attendant evils: the crowding out of small businesses with the extinction of pride of ownership and sense of achievement, the danger of monopoly which can be used for selfish as opposed to social purposes, the pressure on government that can be exerted when the whole nation's economic life is dependent on a few powerful men. Some see in bigness a chief threat to our socioeconomic order and advocate a program of decentralization.

One such movement is *distributism*. As its name indicates, it seeks a greater distribution of property, both in ownership and control, as the only remedy against the servile state, whether in the form of socialism, communism, or monopoly capitalism. The means suggested are return to the land from the cities, benefits to rural areas, the making of farm life more attractive, tax favoritism to small farmers and businesses, more stringent antitrust laws, prohibiting large mergers and combines, discriminatory taxation against chain stores, and other modes of encouraging the little man. At least for the beginning of the program they would rely on a strong exercise of state power.

The aim is laudable but the means are questionable. No distinction is made between good and bad forms of bigness. There are things that can be done only with a large outlay of capital and a consequently large corporation to administer it; small businesses cannot afford to set up expensive research laboratories and management training centers. What small business could not do would have to be done by the government. Some tax revision might be good, but discriminatory taxation is unfair. The reliance on state power is too dangerous even for the initial stage; communism and socialism have recourse to it, and the prospect is that the initial stage will never be over.

The *cooperative movement* is another suggested scheme for decentralization. Its purpose is chiefly to eliminate the middleman by bringing producer in direct contact with consumer, thus saving money for both. There are thus both producers' cooperatives and consumers' cooperatives, and the two can form one larger cooperative. There is no giant corporation with directors and hired personnel; policies are determined in meetings of the members, in which each person has but one vote no matter how large his share. Thus there is diffused ownership and democratic control. The profit motive is played down, to be supplanted by the ideal of community service. Some propose *cooperatism* as a new form of society different from both capitalism and socialism and as an answer to both individualism and statism.

The cooperative movement, which has met with some marked success, especially in agriculture and the marketing of agricultural products, is good and should be encouraged. But to extend it to all fields of economic endeavor is a different matter. A factory cannot be run on democratic principles; a cooperative factory would have to hire managers and foremen with an unquestioned right to give orders; conditions of work would not differ much from the present factory owned by capital investors. Governing boards of cooperatives would differ little from those of our present corporations. Though each individual would have a vote equal to that of any other and no one could own a controlling number of shares, it would be possible to form blocs, cliques, and factions, and thus for a small group to gain control, making the diffusion of power only nominal. Nor should the profit motive be despised; to get more profit for producers and consumers is the motive behind the cooperative movement. Cooperatives deserve encouragement, especially where they have proved successful, but they are not a universal remedy.

A more modest approach is that of *profit sharing*. It is proposed as a supplement to the wage contract, not as a substitute for it. The worker would get his pay determined by collective bargaining and over and above this some share in the profits or even in the ownership of the business. Such schemes have been used successfully but by and large meet with resistance both from business and from labor. The purpose is to allay industrial unrest, to increase the worker's loyalty by making him feel a part of the enterprise, to make sustained production his advantage. But workers are suspicious that it is but a means of speeding up production, of tying them to the job, of giving them a poor substitute for increased wages, of hamstringing their unions' efforts at collective bargaining. Profit sharing might work better when this attitude of suspicion fostered by class antagonism has been outgrown.

A still more controverted issue is that of *management sharing*. Most employers will not hear of it and labor has been rather indifferent to it. To give ordinary laborers a place on the board of directors would be unrealistic. But recent efforts toward labor-management cooperation may finally break down much existing prejudice. Intelligent workers often have good suggestions, if not about handling the company's finances, at least about efficient ways of running the factory. Contrariwise, management may get better results by explaining the reasons for their decisions instead of simply handing out flat orders. Companies have become acutely conscious of "human relations," and these efforts may work out into better labor-management teamwork, if not into actual management sharing. Since management and labor do have different functions, perhaps they had best be kept distinct, with emphasis put on increasing communication, cooperation, and integration between them.

Perhaps bigness is a feature of the modern world we must learn to live with. The negative approach of trust-busting legislation has met with indifferent success. More can be accomplished by the positive approach of making farm life more attractive, dispersing industries into outlying areas, giving the worker a chance to own at least his own home, and demonstrating that everybody's prosperity depends most on increased production. After all, the goal is not an equal distribution of wealth but a standard of living that affords all, even the relatively poorest, a decent life befitting human dignity.

TECHNOLOGY AND LEISURE

The mention of human dignity leads to a consideration of the evils of technology and mass production. It is said that the gain in productiveness, making available to nearly all a vast variety of comforts and luxuries formerly beyond the dreams of the most wealthy, is matched by the degradation of the worker, chained to the machine, condemned to a stultifying routine of actions in which he has not the slightest interest. The assembly line reduces the worker to a robot, stunts his personality, and starves his artistic spirit, leaving him with no pride of ownership, no joy in creativeness, no satisfaction except his pay.

But what can be done about it? No one, least of all the worker himself, will return to handicraft methods of manufacture. It takes too much effort to produce too little. Comparing the two economies, we see that in the handicraft system it was possible to work at what one liked with a sense of pride and creativeness, but one worked long hours for a pittance; while now one may work at a routine noncreative task, it is true, but for short hours with good wages, making possible a style of living unthinkable for such workers a generation ago. Whenever was work free from drudgery? If the tedium of the factory were so much worse than the tedium of the farm, how explain the ceaseless movement from farm to factory? A sense of ownership may help the farmer plow his field for twelve hours a day six days a week, but the sense of ownership over the money he earns makes the factory worker tighten screws for eight hours a day five days a week, with a prospect of an even shorter working week. The creativeness of the worker was always limited by his ability to sell his product; not what he wants but what the buyer will want must be his guide if he expects to make a living by his work.

Nevertheless, the problem is there. Many leading industries recognize it and take some steps to alleviate it by fitting workers into jobs for which they are best suited, rotating them from one job to another, determining optimum length of work and rest periods, providing psychological counseling and social service facilities. But there is no way of turning all work into play, so that the man on the job can do only what he finds personally interesting. Automation, which will take over more and more of the disagreeable features of mass production, far from being feared, should be welcomed as a blessing. There will be initial dislocations and adjustments, toward easing which both management and labor should cooperate, but the final effect will be to make work easier, shorter, safer, and pleasanter.

The problem now is what to do with leisure time, how to educate the worker so that he can make the best use of the many free hours technology enables him to enjoy. The worker will still be economically bound to his machine, but he will be bound to it for less and less of his time. If he has any creativeness in his makeup, he will at least have some opportunity to exercise it, if not on the job then in his off time, whereas formerly most workers had no opportunity at all.

It is as foolish to paint too rosy a picture of the technological age as it is to over-romanticize the preindustrial period. We have only been trying to show that something can be said on both sides. One thing is certain: socialism and communism would produce far greater regimentation and stultification of the worker than need be feared under private enterprise. If this vexation cannot be eliminated from the capitalist economy, neither can it be eliminated from any workable economy in our modern age.

CONCLUSION

The preceding investigation has been unsatisfactory because it involves too much prophecy. The moral philosopher is not called upon to solve the economic ills of mankind but merely to point out the moral obligation of society to seek a solution for those ills. By detailing a few of the suggested remedies, we have shown at least that not all men are standing by idle in smug complacency at the present or wringing their hands in futile fear of the future. Many things can be done, and those mentioned here may not be the only ones or the best.

The obligation bears on society, not on single companies or single unions, much less on single individuals, except that they must show a willingness to cooperate with others in working out a solution and in adopting solutions agreed upon. The larger the industry or union, the greater the obligation of the leaders to point the way and to take the first steps along it. The advance toward social justice is a serious moral obligation that stands squarely on the leaders of society who have the power and influence to do something about it. It will not happen automatically but requires the cooperative effort of all under the leadership of the most able.

SUMMARY

Capitalism is not the only possible economic alternative to communism and socialism, but some form of it is the only practical alternative in an advanced society in our times. Should it be kept as it now is because there is no better, or can it be revised to eliminate some of its worst defects?

The first position is immoral if the second is possible. Proponents of the second position suggest the following:

1. For the exclusive use of *competition,* substitute a spirit of *cooperation* and mutual help. Competition is necessary to free enterprise, but unlimited competition was so greedy and wasteful that it had to be limited by law. Only greater cooperation can care for the increased population of the future.

2. For *strife* between management and labor, substitute *industry councils* embracing both. These would be bodies representing the whole industry or field of occupational endeavor, hierarchically arranged on various levels, not absorbing existing institutions, but growing out of them; backed by the state's authority but not staffed or run by the state.

3. For too much *state control* and bureaucracy, substitute *self-control* by the industry itself on all levels of management and labor. Voluntary associations, such as industry councils, seem to be the best answer to excessive interference of government.

4. For *concentration* of economic control in the hands of too few, substitute a wider *distribution* of control. Distributism would prohibit mergers, break up combines, help small business, promote rural life, all by means of state benefits and taxation. The cooperative movement eliminates the middleman, putting control in the owners rather than in boards of directors. Profit sharing would take the workers into the business as small owners, and management sharing would give them some control in its operation. These schemes all have some advantages and some drawbacks.

5. For the stultifying effects of *mass production,* substitute training in the proper use of *leisure.* Since technology is here to stay and even to increase, it will be better to adapt ourselves to it than to try to stop it. Education is faced with the great task of teaching the worker how to use profitably his vastly increased leisure.

To remedy our economic ills and establish social justice is a serious moral obligation on society. No one can do it alone, but all are obliged to seek remedies and to cooperate in the use of those agreed on.

READINGS

1. Pope Pius XI's *Quadragesimo Anno* (Reconstruction of the Social Order) should certainly be read as the document that brought these ideas most forceably to the world's notice. It inspired among others the following commentaries:
   a. Nell-Breuning, *Reconstruction of Social Economy,* ch. 10 and 11.
   b. Husslein, *Christian Social Manifesto,* ch. 30.
   c. Bruehl, *The Pope's Plan for Social Reconstruction,* ch. 17-29, but all of it is pertinent.
   d. Miller, *Forty Years After: Pius XI and the Social Order,* §§78-87. Pope John XXIII's *Mater et Magistra* repeats and extends the same views.
2. Other works, though not commentaries on the Encyclical, discuss the issues raised or lay the background for them:
   a. Munier, *Some American Approximations to Pius XI's "Industries and Professions."*
   b. Cronin, *Catholic Social Principles,* ch. 1, 7, 8, 13, 16.

   c. Messner, *Social Ethics,* bk. I, pt. IV; bk. II, pt. II; bk. IV, pt. III.

   d. Osgniach, *Must it be Communism?* pt. III.

   e. Drummond, *Social Justice.*

   f. Haas, *Man and Society,* ch. 12-14.

   g. Ferree, *The Act of Social Justice.*

   h. Mulcahy, *The Economics of Heinrich Pesch,* ch. 7.

3. The case for distributism is argued by Belloc in *The Servile State* and *The Restoration of Property* and by Chesterton in *What's Wrong With the World.* See Hewes, *Decentralize for Liberty;* also Kelso and Adler, *The Capitalist Manifesto.*

4. On the cooperative movement see Warbasse, *Cooperative Democracy;* Casselman, *The Cooperative Movement;* Ross, *Cooperative Plenty.*

5. Thompson, *Profit Sharing,* and Hartman, *Profit Sharing Manual,* treat this question from the economic standpoint.

6. On the evils of technology see Marcel, *Man Against Mass Society,* and his shorter statement of the same theme, *The Decline of Wisdom;* also Jünger, *The Failure of Technology.*

7. A good summary of the matter of this chapter is found in Johnston, *Business Ethics,* ch. 8 and 9.

CHAPTER 34

INTERNATIONAL

RELATIONS

PROBLEM

International relations are complicated by the fact that individual sovereign states have no earthly superior to whom they can appeal and whose authority they respect. The state itself is a society of individuals and families, and one of its chief functions is to judge disputes between them, but when states themselves conflict they have nothing ultimately to appeal to but force, and that is war. There is no more inefficient way of settling disputes than war. To avoid its horrors, if possible, or at least to reduce them as far as can be, states have developed the instrument known as international law. We must say something on:

    (1) The history and definition of international law
    (2) Whether international law is really law
    (3) Whether states are bound by the natural law
    (4) What duties in justice states have to one another
    (5) What duties in amity states have to one another

HISTORY

The ancients seem to have looked on foreign nations as enemies and their property as booty. Homer pictures the Greeks as supporting themselves by forays on other villages about Troy, and the custom was to kill or enslave the conquered. But there was some unwritten code of honor among warriors, for they held sacred the person of heralds and had truces for burying the dead and exchanging prisoners. The Amphictyonic League was an attempt to bring harmony among the Greek city-states and to establish among them some common rules of action, but it met with little success.

The Romans, as we have seen, developed the *jus gentium,* which is not international law but what they found to be the common element in the internal laws of all their subjugated peoples. The *jus gentium,* because it was common to all peoples with whom the Romans came into contact, closely approached the natural law and became one of the sources from which international law was later to be drawn. But the Romans felt no need for international law in the modern sense. Their final solution to the differences between nations was to absorb them all into their own vast Empire. Rome took on herself the task of keeping order in the civilized world, and her great achievement was the *Pax Romana.*

When the world emerged from the wreck of the Roman Empire, there was one great international institution to which all Christian nations could turn for an adjudication of disputes, the Church. A common faith and a common code of morality did much to standardize the behavior of kings and princes into a common Christian pattern, and to outlaw certain practices as unworthy of a Christian anywhere. The ideals of chivalry and knighthood, with their high sense of honor, exerted an enormous humanizing influence. Definite rules and customs, founded on the natural law, the *jus gentium,* and even the Church's Canon Law to some extent, governed the relations between states. Diplomatic negotiations, as we understand them now, seem to have originated among the medieval Italian city-states. Though without any force to impose her decisions and relying solely on her moral position, the Church arbitrated countless quarrels and did much to mitigate the horrors of war and conquest. Even so, the feudal period was all too barbarous; but at least between Christian peoples there was nothing like the wholesale enslavement of ancient times or the almost total war of today.

The breakdown of united Christendom in the sixteenth century and the ensuing lack of any common court of appeal acceptable to all Christian nations led to the formation of the concept of *international law* in the modern sense. Though it was prepared for by the work of Francis de Vitoria and Francis Suarez, who tried to codify existing customs and apply them to the rising nationalism of their day, the founding of international law is commonly attributed to Hugo Grotius, author of *The Rights of War and Peace.* He saw that henceforth, in the absence of a higher tribunal, relations between nations must be governed both by the natural law, which as the law of reason is common to all men, and by voluntary agreement among states, based on their enlightened self-interest. His codification of existing customs, tested by these criteria, passed into the texture of modern international law.

INTERNATIONAL LAW

International law is not the result of any definite enactment, but of long custom and usage. Its rules can be found in recognized writers commenting on these customs, in treaties between civilized nations, in state papers and diplomatic correspondence, in decisions of international tribunals, in court decisions of particular countries regarding citizenship, alien property, admiralty cases, and similar matters.

International law comprises the rules determining the conduct of political states in their dealings with each other. The main difficulty is to decide just which political organizations are *states*. In practice, a *state* is one so recognized by the nations of the world generally, and admitted to their circle. The theory on which this practice seems to be based is that a *state* is here taken in the strictest sense to mean one having the fullest degree of independent sovereignty.

This concept of the state supposes enough development and organization to make the state self-sufficient and capable of self-rule; it also supposes the actual possession of self-rule, full jurisdiction over the whole people in all departments of life, internal and external. Primitive and uncivilized tribes, though they have their natural rights, are not states because they lack the first requirement; the individual States of the United States, under the theory of divided sovereignty, have handed over control of foreign affairs to the federal government and thus fail in the second requirement.

The position of *client states,* whether they be called provinces, colonies, tributaries, dependencies, protectorates, or mandates, is a knotty question. Some of them retain a technical sovereignty and basic jurisdiction over all affairs, yet in practice have handed over to another state some of their affairs and especially their foreign relations. Those which are technically sovereign come under international law in theory, but foreign nations disregard this theoretical position in practice, since they cannot treat with them directly but only through the state that manages their foreign relations. Their position is somewhat like that of a minor, who has inherent personal rights equal to those of anyone else but is under his guardian's tutelage for the transaction of business. Some, especially colonies, gradually grow to a condition of full independence, but others show little tendency of ever doing so.

Natural and positive international law

Since law is defined as an ordinance of reason for the common good promulgated by him who has care of the community, it may be argued that international law is not truly law because there is no one who has care of the community of nations, no common authoritative ruler over all states. In fact, the requirement that the states be fully sovereign makes it impossible for any real law to exist between states.

To answer this difficulty it is necessary to distinguish between natural and positive international law. Some parts of international law arise out of the very nature of the state and are merely reaffirmations of the natural law or simple deductions from the natural law, such as the right of a nation to defend itself when unjustly attacked, or its duty to fulfill just contracts freely made. This is *natural* international law. Other parts of international law are the result of express or tacit agreements made between nations and not directly deducible from the natural law, such as the diplomatic immunity accorded ambassadors, or the internment of warships by neutrals in war time. This is *positive* international law.

Ethics is concerned with natural international law only, and this is truly law in the strict sense. Natural law is based on nature and ultimately on the Author of nature. It is imposed by God, who has supreme authority over all states and all possible human institutions. But positive international law depends only on compact and agreement, and relies for its enforcement only on the good faith of the contracting parties. There is nothing in the nature of things that demands the making of such contracts, and they are freely entered into for mutual benefit like contracts between private persons. Hence they are not laws in the strict sense.

But we cannot conclude that they have no binding force. Contracts between individuals, though not themselves laws, impose obligation from that precept of the natural law which says: *Just contracts must be kept.* The same is true of international agreements. Though they are entered into voluntarily and are not guaranteed by any higher authority on earth than the contracting parties, once made they bind nations and their rulers in conscience. Hence, the distinction between natural and positive international law, necessary for studying and formulating this law, is of less importance when there is the mere practical question of keeping its obligations. In both cases the obligation comes from the natural law ultimately, but in different ways: in one case, immediately; in the other, through the intermediacy of a voluntary contract. In the first case the obligation cannot be avoided; in the second, it can be avoided by refusing to be a party to the contract.

States bound by natural law

The solution just given is based on the supposition that states are bound by morality and the natural law. It is a deplorable fact that many states have behaved as if they were not bound by any consideration of morality, but this observation does not mean that they approved this kind of action in theory. Nations most ruthless in violating the rights of others often shout loudest when their own rights are attacked, thus offering lip service, when it suits them, to the idea of international morality. But some philosophers and jurists insist even in theory that international law is outside the scope of morality.

Moral positivists, holding that all morality comes from the state, must logically accept this conclusion. But one need not be a moral positivist to do so. One may attempt a compromise, admitting individual morality but denying international morality, on the grounds that the individual has a destiny beyond this world whereas the state is merely a temporal affair, that morality deals with eternal ideals of conduct whereas states are concerned with worldly needs and material wants, that an individual can afford to be idealistic but a state must be hardheadedly realistic.

Any such concept is entirely opposed to all we said previously about morality, the natural law, and the state. That states are bound by the natural law hardly needs any separate proof, but the following remarks will serve as a review:

1. The state is a natural institution, based on the natural law, from which it derives its whole title to existence. It cannot be exempt from the law which created it, maintains it, gives it all its rights and every shred of authority it possesses.

2. The state is composed of human beings and is carried on by their activity. No human being can be exempt from the natural moral law, which governs every possible form of human conduct. It is absurd to think that a man can get rid of obligations merely by associating with others, or that anything is allowable as long as men do it together.

3. International law cannot be based entirely on agreement, for what would oblige the states to keep their agreements except some previous agreement? An infinite series of agreements is impossible. We showed previously that the source of all obligation is the natural moral law, and this argument holds for states as well as for individuals.

4. That rights and duties exist between persons is as true of moral persons (societies) as of physical persons (individual men). The state is a moral person, and as a natural society has a sort of natural incorporation. Business firms have obligations in justice from the natural law; so likewise has the state.

5. The individual citizens of one state have natural rights and duties toward the citizens of other states. Justice does not end at the boundaries of states. Conflict of these rights and duties often cannot be settled except through the intermediacy of the states concerned, and these will be governed by international law based on the natural law.

INTERNATIONAL JUSTICE

Men as men are juridically equal because they all have the same human nature, the same origin and goal. On this foundation the virtue of justice rests. They can be subordinated to one another only because of some other reason, when they are organized to achieve some lesser end, as children are subordinated to parents, pupils to teachers, employees to employers, citizens to ruler. The family, the school, the business, the state are organized each for a definite earthly function as well as for helping men to their last end. Within these societies there is subordination, but between societies of the same kind there is juridical equality. Each is a moral person and must be treated as an equal by its equals, not merely as a means for another's convenience.

Thus each state exercising full sovereignty is the juridical equal of every other state. They all have the same end, to promote the temporal welfare of their peoples, and derive their authority from nature and nature's God, not from any other state. No such state is subordinate to any other and may not be treated as subordinate. The rights of a sovereign state are not scaled to its political size or strength, any more than the individual's rights are dependent on his physical size or strength. Whether or not states should curtail their sovereignty by becoming members of a world organization is a topic to be treated later, but even then the various states would be equal among themselves and not subordinate to one another, though they would come under the whole organization.

We must now discuss from the standpoint of morals some of the rights and duties states have in justice:

(1) Independence
(2) Entirety
(3) Property
(4) Colonization
(5) Free action

Independence

No state has the right wantonly to destroy the independent existence of another state. Independence is to a state what life is to an individual. As an individual has the right of self-defense against an unjust aggressor, so has a state. An individual may kill in self-defense under the proper conditions; so also a state may deprive another of independence if its own independent existence is so seriously threatened as to leave no other remedy, but this is the only reason. These questions will be treated under war.

A state may be destroyed not only by attack from without, but also by the fomentation of sedition and the stirring up of civil war. No state has the right to do this against its neighbor; a state has the right not only to bare existence, but also to a peaceful and orderly existence.

We should note one difference between the life of an individual and of a state. An individual may not take his own life, since he is a physical person, whose life is indivisible and incommunicable. A society, being a moral or juridical person, does not have these attributes. Societies can merge or divide, and even revive after extinction. A state can agree to unite with another or others in the formation of a larger state, as the thirteen American states formed the United States. What was formerly one state may split up into several, as in the dissolution of the Austro-Hungarian Empire after the first World War.

Entirety

Each sovereign state has a right to the whole of its territory and of its population. No state need submit to mutilation by its neighbors. Diseases of the kind that attack states are not cured by surgery; the principle, *the part for the sake of the whole,* which justifies individual mutilation cannot be applied to states, since the state exists for the benefit of the members. A state's right to expand is limited by its neighbor's right to all its land

and all its people. We are not speaking here of border regions to which there are conflicting claims, but of the seizure of neighboring territory which certainly belongs to another state.

The *nationalist ideal,* that the state and the nation, the political unit and the ethnic unit, should be coterminous, would be a legitimate ambition if it could be accomplished without trampling on the rights of other states equally sovereign, but this ideal is rarely attainable. There is nothing in the natural law which demands that all people of the same racial stock, language, and culture should be assimilated into the same political unit. Other things being equal, a homogeneous totality of population has certain advantages, but other things are hardly ever equal. The Swiss, for example, do not want to be divided among the neighboring states to which they have linguistic and cultural affinities. On the other hand, there is no reason why a number of small principalities should not voluntarily unite along nationalist lines, if they find it expedient and can do so without violating any rights.

Nor is it necessary, as the theory of *autarky* or economic self-sufficiency supposes, that the political unit be an economic unit. The self-sufficiency required for sovereignty does not mean that the country must produce all it consumes, but only that it can support itself adequately, either by produce or by trade or by any other means. A state need not be both agricultural and industrial, but can engage in a sort of economic symbiosis with another state. Remedy for surplus population is found in emigration and colonization, not in seizing the neighbor's territory.

Property

The state, being a moral or juridical person, can own property. The state's titles to property are about the same as those of individual ownership; the main difference is that the state has the additional title of legitimate conquest, but lacks the title of inheritance as a natural heir, though it can accept bequests.

Property can come under the jurisdiction of the state in three ways. There is exclusively state-owned property, such as warships, forts, highways, public buildings. Then there is the private property of its citizens both at home and abroad, for which the state has a responsibility, since to protect its people's property is one of the reasons for the state's existence. Lastly, the very territory of the state, though most of it is divided up among private owners, comes under the state's administration as far as foreign relations are concerned. Seizure of any of this territory by a foreign power is international theft, and culpable damage to it calls for indemnification.

Colonization

The state can take possession of territory not belonging to another state and own it by title of occupancy. Mere discovery does not suffice, but annexation and settlement are necessary. By occupancy a private citizen can turn part of a newly discovered land into his personal property, but such an action does not automatically bring it under the political jurisdiction of his state. The state must formally annex the territory and give notice of this act to the nations of the world; it must also establish a settlement sufficient to exercise political control.

The idea of colonization suggests several possibilities: land may be wholly unoccupied, or overrun by nomads, or very sparsely settled by politically unorganized primitive tribes, or adequately occupied by a people capable of statehood though not yet politically organized, or recognized as the territory of an existing state. The first and last of these suppositions offer no difficulty: unoccupied land is there for the first comer, and an existing state may not be deprived of its territory. A word on each of the other three possibilities:

1. Land that is merely overrun by nomadic hordes may be politically appropriated by any state willing to colonize it. Nomads have no real possession of the soil, and cannot reserve for their exclusive use a whole wilderness that they but occasionally visit and do nothing to develop. A state incorporating such land must give the nomads the opportunity to settle down or in some other way provide for their livelihood.

2. Land that is very sparsely settled by primitive tribes, whose members are too few or too uncivilized to form a political state of their own, is open to colonization. These tribes effectively occupy only their own villages and the immediate environs; over their vast hunting grounds they have no more definite control than nomads over the desert steppes. The world's teeming population cannot be kept out of these regions forever. Any state may send in a colony, being careful meanwhile to respect the natives' genuine rights. The land is incorporated into the state's political territory and put under its government, but the natives retain the personal ownership of their private property and must not be driven from their villages. The natives become citizens or at least wards of the state, which is now bound not only to respect but to defend their rights. These people are not deprived of political independence, for they have never had any political society. Great injustices have occurred in this type of colonization, not the least of them in our own country, but they are not essential to colonization as such.

3. Land that is adequately occupied by a people capable of statehood but not yet politically organized, or by a people with incipient political organization but not received into the community of nations, is not open for colonization. The territory is already occupied and cannot be seized again without violating the rights of the present possessors. These people have all the prerequisites for the formation of a state of their own, and are on the verge of doing so. They cannot rightfully be deprived of their independence. Instead of trying to annex it, more advanced nations should recognize this emergent state and assist it in its transition to full political stature. Greed and selfishness have often dictated the opposite policy, but we are talking here of morals.

Free action

A state has the right to develop itself in any way it sees fit that does not conflict with the strict right of another state. It may adopt the form of government it wishes, change its constitution to suit itself, enter into commercial relations with others, trade with whom it likes, impose what tariffs it thinks just, make treaties and carry on other negotiations. Some of these may be incidentally detrimental to other nations, but are not unjust unless they violate others' rights. States may not prevent the development of other states on the mere plea that they are threatened with rivalry, any more than individuals are allowed forcibly to extinguish legitimate competitors. Free competition is not aggression and does not justify counter-aggression.

Nations should have free access to the raw materials that nature provides, and should be able to obtain them by trade. These goods are intended by nature for all mankind, and no nation is allowed to monopolize them in such a way that the rest of the world must suffer. Here the laws of monopoly apply; a country has a right to a legitimate profit on its natural monopolies, but should not raise the price beyond the reach of other nations in genuine need of these products.

TREATIES

A treaty is a contract between sovereign states as states. It differs from a contract between a state and a private individual or corporation, and also from a contract between states not acting in a strictly political capacity, as when one government purchases food or munitions from another. To be binding a treaty must be an act of the sovereign authority in the state, which must ratify the result of previous diplomatic negotiations. The conditions for a valid treaty are the same as those for any valid contract. Treaties, because they are contracts, bind in commutative justice and derive their binding force from the natural law.

Do unjust treaties bind? If the terms of the treaty are clearly and certainly unjust, there can be no contract, for no one can be bound in justice to do or suffer injustice. A state forcing such a treaty on another is morally bound to withdraw it and repair any damage caused. The injustice of a treaty is not to be lightly presumed, but proved with objectively certain reasons. Any nation can trump up reasons for repudiating perfectly valid treaties when they prove burdensome, and by the use of propaganda can put a sanctimonious veneer on its conduct; this form of international dishonesty may soon destroy all faith between nations. The unilateral denunciation of a treaty as unjust before its fulfillment or expiration is very much to be suspected.

Do treaties made under duress bind? Ordinarily a contract made under duress is rendered null and void by positive law. But there is no positive law above states to regulate their actions or to set down conditions for the validity of their contracts. Hence treaties cannot become invalid for this reason. Moreover, the reason why positive law invalidates contracts made under duress is to protect the common good and discourage violence, but the invalidation of *treaties* made under duress would have the opposite effect. The typical treaty made under duress is the peace treaty at the end of a war. If an unjust aggressor is victorious, the treaty he imposes is unjust and therefore invalid. We are speaking here only of just treaties; at the end of a war even they are imposed under duress. The defeated nation is driven by force of arms to accept unfavorable conditions, but it was for the very purpose of imposing such conditions that the war was fought. If such treaties were invalid, wars could never end. It is surely wrong for a nation to accept a treaty to secure cessation of hostilities, and then to repudiate the treaty in order to get out of paying just reparations. The only case when just treaties made under duress do not bind is when the signer of the treaty is subjected to *personal* threats or violence, for then the presumption is that he is acting solely from motives of personal safety and is not truly the representative of his government.

When do treaties cease to bind? A treaty becomes extinct in the same way as any other contract:

(1) When its object is completely fulfilled
(2) By mutual consent of the parties
(3) When one of the parties ceases to exist
(4) When it becomes impossible of fulfillment
(5) When an essential condition no longer holds good
(6) If it conflicts with a higher or more universal law

If a treaty is valid at the time when it is made, there are as a rule only two reasons which can justify its repudiation:

(1) Failure of the other party to fulfill an essential part of his obligation
(2) Extinction of the state resulting from fulfillment of the treaty, unless that were part of the treaty itself

But the mere fact that a treaty becomes more burdensome to a state than was expected does not at all absolve a state from its obligation. This was the risk it took in making the treaty, and such risks are involved in all contracts, private as well as international.

INTERNATIONAL AMITY

The term *amity* means friendly relations, especially between states. Call it benevolence, helpfulness, humanity, cooperation, friendliness, good will, or any other name you prefer.

The duties of amity or friendship between states are about the same as the duties of love or charity between individuals. One state should come to the aid of another in distress, provided it can do so without serious hardship to itself, in the same way as an individual should help another in trouble. But there is one main difference between the state and the individual. An individual is allowed, though not obliged, to risk certain death in order to protect another; a state would not be allowed to do this, because its first obligation is to its own people whose rights it is not allowed to sacrifice. An individual is for himself, but a state is for its people.

Nationalism

Patriotism or love of country is a virtue akin to piety or love of parents, and must be developed by every citizen. It can go so far as to demand the supreme sacrifice of life itself, as in a just war. True *patriotism,* however, must be distinguished from its caricature, *nationalism,* just as proper self-love differs from selfishness. To love self we need not hate others.

The state, even though self-sufficient and sovereign, is not superior to the common humanity that binds all men into the great family of mankind. Political differences do not take away human likenesses, and the general welfare of the whole human race takes precedence over the welfare of any particular group. Each single state is organized for mutual helpfulness among its members, and this same principle that prevails within each state must also prevail between states. States exist for the sake of promoting a full human life, and the full development of man's social nature is not limited by any artificial political boundaries. Hence an exaggerated *nationalism,* which shows itself in hatred of all foreigners, is to some extent inhuman and therefore immoral, as contradicting man's essentially social nature. It is also poor service to one's own nation to seek its interests so exclusively as to make it a bad member among the family of nations. Selfishness can exist on a national as well as on an individual scale.

Intervention

The *principle of nonintervention,* defended especially by nineteenth century liberalism, is that no state may interfere in the internal affairs of another state for any reason, except where its own interests are involved. To do so is considered an infringement of sovereignty.

This opinion takes too narrow a view of sovereignty and violates the amity or helpfulness spoken of above. It is true that no state may meddle with another except for the most serious of reasons, but such reasons can and do sometimes exist. A state can come to the aid of a weaker state unjustly attacked by a stronger, can help a state put down unjustified insurrection, can establish order in a state hopelessly harassed by continual anarchy, can help a people throw off the yoke of unbearable tyranny, can enforce some policy absolutely necessary for the peace of the world. When one country appeals to another for assistance in such matters, there is no reason why the appeal must be rejected because of the fictitious principle of nonintervention. We may as well say that we have no right to interfere in a man's family when he is killing his wife or torturing his children. On the other hand, it would be wrong to try to run their family for them or to interfere when there is no call for it. Hence the principle of nonintervention is invalid as a sweeping generalization, but it has its validity within limits.

CONCLUSION

It is impossible for us to go deeper into the problem of international relations. Positive international law is quite outside our scope, except insofar as it may conflict with the natural law. The complexity of international relations in the modern world raises many difficult questions, answers to which have not yet been thoroughly worked out. Students of ethics, law, and politics have here a promisingly fertile field for their efforts. But they must remember that it is one thing to devise a solution in theory, and quite another to get the nations of the world to adopt it.

The point that remains of prime importance to the moralist is that the political state is as thoroughly subject to the natural moral law as the individual person. The acts of states are all the more important because they affect the lives of millions of people, and in our days even of the whole world. The rulers of states bear a responsibility proportionate to their power, and in a democracy this responsibility is partially shared by the people. In the course of history the world has paid a terrible price for international immorality, for injustice on a grand and global scale. Immoral conduct is inhuman conduct, and unless nations come to a better sense of justice and honor in their dealings we must be prepared to see more of man's inhumanity to man.

SUMMARY

International law, a gradual growth of custom and usage, comprises the rules determining the conduct of political states in their dealings with one another. A *state* here means one with full independent sovereignty, not client states whose foreign affairs are managed by others.

Since sovereign states have no superior, *is international law really law? Natural* international law, embodying precepts or conclusions from the natural law, is law in the strict sense. *Positive* international law, comprising free contracts between states, is not law in the strict sense, though the contracts bind like any others.

States are bound by the natural moral law, for they derive their rights and authority from the natural law, are composed of men subject in all their conduct to the natural law, rely on the natural law to give binding force to their contracts, are juridical persons with rights and duties based on the natural law, must see that natural justice is done between their own citizens and foreigners.

States have rights and duties to one another in *justice.* Every state has a right to:

1. *Independence.* This is a state's life; a state may defend itself against unjust attack and against undue interference by other states in its affairs.

2. *Entirety.* All its territory and population belong to it and must be

free from encroachment by other states seeking to satisfy nationalistic or economic ambitions.

3. *Property.* The state, like any society, can own and administer property; it must also protect its citizens' property and maintain its territory, even the part of it that is privately owned.

4. *Colonization.* The state may annex and settle unclaimed and politically unorganized regions, with proper respect for the rights of nomads and aborigines.

5. *Free action.* Each state may develop itself in its own way, with access to the earth's raw materials, which other states may not withhold from it by unjust monopoly.

Treaties, contracts between sovereign states as states, bind in justice like any other contract. Unjust treaties cannot bind, but the injustice must be certain. Treaties made under duress, such as peace treaties, bind unless the negotiator signs under threat of personal violence. A valid treaty may be repudiated only if the other party fails to fulfill it or if it would mean the extinction of the state.

States also have duties in *amity* or friendship to one another, but their duty to their own people comes first. Exaggerated *nationalism* is immoral, against man's duty to his fellow man of whatever nation. *Intervention* in another nation's internal affairs is wrong unless there are sufficient reasons to justify it.

READINGS

1. Vitoria faced the new moral problem of the Spanish conquest of the Americas. The translation of the text of his *De Indis* (On the Indians) and *De Jure Belli* (On the Right of War) is given in Scott's *Francisco de Vitoria and His Law of Nations,* together with Scott's comments.

2. Suarez' ideas on international law are gathered from his great work *De Legibus* (On Laws); the translation of bk. II, ch. XVII to XX, in Scott's *Classics of International Law: Suarez,* vol. II, gives a sample of his thinking that prepared the way for modern international law. See also Scott's *Catholic Conception of International Law,* treating of Vitoria, Suarez, and others.

3. Grotius' *Rights of War and Peace* is a classic well worth reading, but requiring some critical discrimination.

4. The position of modern Scholastic philosophers may be gathered from:
   a. Cronin, *The Science of Ethics,* vol. II, ch. XIX, pp. 633-662.
   b. Leibell, *Readings in Ethics,* pp. 1010-1032, 1059-1062.
   c. Eppstein, *The Catholic Tradition of the Law of Nations,* a classic on the subject, with numerous quotations and documents. See also his *Code of International Ethics.*
   d. Rommen, *The State in Catholic Thought,* ch. XXVIII.
   e. Messner, *Social Ethics,* bk. II, pt. IV.
   f. Haas, *Man and Society,* ch. 18.

CHAPTER 35

WAR

PROBLEM

War is the ultimate in human social failure. Unlike natural disasters, war is a wholly man-made affair, the result of man's greed, envy, hate, ambition, and passion, something utterly useless and unnecessary. No war taken as a whole can ever be justified, for it must start from some original injustice. Granted that the original injustice has been done, must it simply be suffered by the aggrieved nation or is there a right to resistance and redress? The behavior of mankind throughout history evidences a choice of the second alternative, but the mere fact that nations have acted in this way does not make it moral. Can any moral justification be made out, not for war itself as a whole, but for a nation fighting for its rights in a war not of its own making?

We shall first give the traditional teaching on war and then discuss the more terrible forms of modern warfare. We cannot judge whether or not the old views still prevail until we know what they are. We ask the following questions:

(1) What is man's normal condition, peace or war?
(2) How do we define war?
(3) What is the theory of the just war?
(4) How are the conditions of a just war to be applied?
(5) Is there an alternative to war?
(6) What can be said of modern nuclear warfare?
(7) Is there any possible excuse for total war?
(8) What is the outlook for the future?

449

MAN'S NORMAL CONDITION

We must face the fact that in the history of mankind wars have been almost continual. Thomas Hobbes wrote:

> Hereby it is manifest that during the time men live without a common power to keep them all in awe, they are in that condition which is called war; and such a war as is of every man against every man. For war consisteth not in battle only, or the act of fighting, but in a tract of time wherein the will to contend by battle is sufficiently known, and therefore the notion of time is to be considered in the nature of war, as it is in the nature of weather. For as the nature of foul weather lieth not in a shower or two of rain, but in an inclination thereto of many days together; so the nature of war consisteth not in actual fighting, but in the known disposition thereto, during all the time there is no assurance to the contrary. All other time is peace.*

If Hobbes could write thus in the seventeenth century, what would he say of our modern nations in which the whole population is permanently organized on a military basis? No nation today could delay preparations for war until it is attacked. It must have a huge store of armaments, a highly trained personnel, and complete plans of strategy ready to cover every possible emergency. Each nation must live in constant fear of its neighbors, while the armament race, war of nerves, cold war, economic blockade, espionage, propaganda, and ideological warfare fill the interval between open hostilities. By Hobbes' definition there has been no peace within the memory of any man now alive.

Despite the grain of truth in Hobbes' statement, we cannot accept his view that war is the normal and natural condition of man, that war is the positive reality and peace is only its negation. Which is the normal condition is not to be judged by the amount of time a nation spends in peace or war, but by an analysis of the nature of each. The normal does not mean the most frequent, but the standard by which things are measured. There are probably but few perfectly healthy persons in the world, yet disease cannot be regarded as the normal thing. International society is a chronic invalid indeed, but it is a fallacy to make its disease the very substance of its life.

St. Augustine's oft-quoted words containing his two famous definitions of peace as "well-ordered concord" and "tranquility of order" deserve to be read and pondered:

> Whoever gives even moderate attention to human affairs and to our common nature, will recognize that if there is no man who does not wish to be joyful, neither is there any one who does not wish to have peace. For even they who make war desire nothing but victory—desire, that is to say, to attain peace with glory. For what else is victory than the conquest of those who resist us? and when this is done there is peace. It is therefore with the desire for peace that wars are waged, even by those who

---

*Hobbes, *Leviathan,* ch. XIII.

take pleasure in exercising their warlike nature in command and battle. And hence it is obvious that peace is the end sought for by war. For every man seeks peace by waging war, but no man seeks war by making peace. For even they who intentionally interrupt the peace in which they are living have no hatred of peace, but only wish it changed into a peace that suits them better. They do not, therefore, wish to have no peace, but only one more to their mind. . . .*

The peace of the body then consists in the duly proportioned arrangement of the parts. The peace of the irrational soul is the harmonious repose of the appetites, and that of the rational soul the harmony of knowledge and action. The peace of body and soul is the well-ordered and harmonious life and health of the living creature. Peace between man and God is the well-ordered obedience of faith to eternal law. Domestic peace is the well-ordered concord between those of the family who rule and those who obey. Civil peace is a similar concord among the citizens. The peace of the celestial city is the perfectly ordered and harmonious enjoyment of God, and of one another in God. The peace of all things is the tranquility of order. Order is the distribution which allots things equal and unequal, each to its own place. . . . As, then, there may be life without pain, while there cannot be pain without some kind of life, so there may be peace without war, but there cannot be war without some kind of peace, because war supposes the existence of some natures to wage it, and these natures cannot exist without peace of one kind or another.†

The common philosophical tradition is that peace is the positive reality because it is the good, while war is the evil that consists in the privation of this good. The state exists for the sake of preserving and promoting peace, both within itself and with other states; war is the result of some state's failure as a political and social entity. A state does not exist for the sake of waging war and of using peace only as a breathing space to prepare for more war; rather, it is supposed to go to war only for the sake of achieving a just and honorable peace. No cynical observations on how nations really do act can destroy the moral obligation placed on every nation, and on every citizen of every nation, to work for peace.

DEFINITION OF WAR

Perhaps the most famous definition of war is that of Karl von Clausewitz: "War is an act of violence intended to compel our opponent to fulfill our will."‡ The merit of this definition is the utterly stark way in which it lays bare the essence of war: the end is to impose our will on another, and the means is violence. This definition very properly leaves out any consideration of right or justice as not belonging to war as such.

War in the strict sense in which we take it here is between one whole state, sovereign and independent, and another whole state, sovereign and independent; it is not between a state and some individuals, nor between

---

*St. Augustine, *City of God*, bk. XIX, ch. 12.
†*Ibid.*, ch. 13.
‡Clausewitz, *On War*, vol. I, beginning.

a government and its people. Sedition, insurrection, rebellion, revolution are often called civil war, but are not war in the strict sense. People in a condition of revolution are virtually in a condition of war, and it becomes formal war if the insurgents succeed in establishing a working *de facto* government in the territory they control. War is *armed* hostility; commercial rivalry and diplomatic tilts are not strictly war, nor is the so-called "cold war." War is *active* hostility; mere preparation for future aggression or defense is not war, but there must be actual fighting, though it may be intermittent.

War may be *defensive* or *aggressive*. There seems to be a fairly common opinion that the nation which declares war or makes the first attack is waging aggressive war, while the nation against which war is declared or which is attacked first is waging defensive war. But this view is too superficial and formalistic. Hear Suarez on the subject:

> It remains for us to explain what constitutes an aggressive war, and what, on the other hand, constitutes a defensive war; for sometimes that which is merely an act of defence may present the appearance of an aggressive act. . . . We have to consider whether the injustice is, practically speaking, simply about to take place; or whether it has already done so, and redress is sought through war. In this second case, the war is aggressive. In the former case, war has the character of self-defence, provided that it is waged with a moderation which is blameless.*

Hence a nation is fighting a defensive war if its sole purpose is to protect itself against actual or imminent aggression, even if its defense assumes the appearance of attack. Just as a man need not wait until he has been shot at before defending himself, so a nation need not wait until it is actually invaded before using means of defense. Moral certitude of the enemy's intention seems sufficient. The formality of declaring war has been discarded by some states, and modern nations must be prepared to meet a sneak attack. The advantage of striking the first blow is so great in modern warfare that no nation, not even one merely defending itself, can afford to give this edge to the enemy. This seems to be what some modern writers call *preemptive* as opposed to *preventive* war.

Since the word *aggression* is now taken almost always in a bad sense, it is more consonant with modern usage to divide war into *offensive* and *defensive*, according to the nation responsible for provoking (not necessarily beginning) hostilities, and into *just* and *unjust*, according to the nation having moral right on its side. Aggression can then be reserved for unjust offensive war. The mention of *just* and *unjust* leads to our next topic.

THEORY OF THE JUST WAR

The ancient writers did not discuss the morality of war. Plato and Aristotle saw it as a possibility even an ideal state would have to provide

---

*Suarez, *The Three Theological Virtues: On Charity*, disputation XIII (On War), section 1, no. 6.

for. The early Christians deplored the existence of war, and anyone should, but never condemned it as sinful in itself. The first noted writer to treat expressly of the morality of war was St. Augustine. While extolling the excellence of peace, he is realistic enough to recognize that war is not always avoidable. He suggests some conditions for a just war that St. Thomas later formalized. We give here a more modern version of the theory of the just war, first outlining the reasons why war was thought to be justifiable at all, and then the conditions under which a just war would have to be fought.

As an individual is allowed to use force in self-defense and also for the recovery of what is rightly his when recourse to higher authority is impossible, so may the state, and for the same reasons. War in itself is a physical evil; it becomes a moral evil only when there is injustice on the part of the one using the force. A nation against which injustice is being committed justly defends itself, according to the principle of the unjust aggressor. It may likewise seek the recovery of goods it has been unjustly deprived of, since there is no higher authority to which it can appeal. Though no war can be just on both sides (except subjectively, through mistaken judgment) and a war can be unjust on both sides (each nation violating the other's rights), it is possible for a war to be just on one side and unjust on the other.

The argument for the possibility of a just war can be stated thus: The state, since it is a natural society, has from the natural law the right to use the means necessary for its preservation and proper functioning. But conditions may be such that the only means by which a state can preserve itself in being, and can protect or recover its lawful rights, is by war. Therefore under such conditions the state has from the natural law the right to wage war.

A state which would not wage war, under any circumstances however serious, would condemn itself to extinction. If the natural law demanded this, God, the Author of the natural law, would both will and not will political society. He would will that it achieve its end, and at the same time deny to it the means necessary for attaining that end. If a state cannot protect the lives, liberty, and property of its citizens, it is failing in its chief function. If it cannot do this except through force, it must have the right to use force.

CONDITIONS OF A JUST WAR

Since even a just war is one of the worst physical evils that can occur in this world, it can be morally allowed only in accordance with certain conditions and reservations. St. Thomas reduces to systematic form the views of St. Augustine and specifies the conditions:

> In order for a war to be just, three things are necessary. First, the authority of the sovereign by whose command the war is to be waged. For it is not the business of a private individual to declare war, because he can seek for redress of his rights from the tribunal of his superior.

Moreover, it is not the business of a private individual to summon together the people, which has to be done in war time. And as the care of the common weal is committed to those who are in authority, it is their business to watch over the common weal of the city, kingdom or province subject to them. And just as it is lawful for them to have recourse to the sword in defending that common weal against internal disturbances, when they punish evil-doers, . . . so too it is their business to have recourse to the sword of war in defending the common weal against external enemies. . . . And for this reason Augustine says:* The natural order conducive to peace among mortals demands that the power to declare and counsel war should be in the hands of those who hold supreme authority.

Secondly, a just cause is required, namely that those who are attacked should be attacked because they deserve it on account of some fault. Wherefore Augustine says:† A just war is wont to be described as one that avenges wrongs, when a nation or state has to be punished, for refusing to make amends for the wrongs inflicted by its subjects, or to restore what it has seized unjustly.

Thirdly, it is necessary that the belligerents should have a rightful intention, so that they intend the advancement of the good, or the avoidance of evil. Hence Augustine says:‡ True religion looks upon as peaceful those wars that are waged not for motives of aggrandizement or cruelty, but with the object of securing peace, of punishing evil-doers, and of uplifting the good. For it may happen that the war is declared by the ligitimate authority, and for a just cause, and yet be rendered unlawful through a wicked intention. Hence Augustine says:§ The passion for inflicting harm, the cruel thirst for vengeance, an unpacific and relentless spirit, the fever of revolt, the lust for power, and suchlike things, all these are rightly condemned in war.‖

In the remaining articles of question 40, St. Thomas takes up the questions of ecclesiastics engaging in warfare, of laying ambushes, and of fighting on holy days. Except the second, these are obsolete medieval matters; they are mentioned here only to show that St. Thomas recognized that a war could be just in its cause yet become immoral because of the way it is fought. Hence, for a war to be morally allowable, the right use of means must be considered as well as the three conditions for a just war:

(1) Lawful authority
(2) Just cause
(3) Right intention

St. Thomas' opinions, stated so simply and generally, needed further development. Among his many commentators Vitoria, Suarez, and Bellarmine are outstanding in interpreting these conditions and applying them

---

Contra Faustum Manichaeum, bk. XXII, ch. 75.
†*Quaestiones in Heptateuchum*, bk. VI, q. 10, on Josue viii.
‡Not found in Augustine but in the *Decretum Gratiani* (Decree of Gratian, a medieval compilation of Canon Law), pt. II, causa 23, q. 1, canon 6.
§*Contra Faustum Manichaeum*, bk. XXII, ch. 74.
‖St. Thomas, *Summa Theologica*, II-II, q. 40, a. 1.

to the new nationalistic warfare of their day. Since these are the principles on which all pre-nuclear warfare was based, we must see them in greater detail.

Lawful authority

War is an act of the political state as such. Hence only the person or body designated in the constitution of the state as having the authority to declare war can do so legitimately. Killing is wrong only when unjust, but it is always unjust when done by private authority outside the case of blameless self-defense. The soldier gets his right to kill by being legally and publicly designated as an agent of his country in the prosecution of a just war. This formality, however, is not necessary in a purely defensive war, and the authority is rightly presumed. If the country is actually being overrun by the enemy, there is no need to wait for formal induction into the armed services.

Guerrilla warfare in the sense of raids unauthorized by any lawful government cannot be justified. But guerrilla tactics may be employed in a war declared by legitimate authority, especially in regions occupied by the enemy. Even the fact that a government has surrendered to an unjust invader does not mean that all underground resistance movements must cease for lack of proper authorization, for they began legitimately and may continue with hope of foreign assistance. When the government abdicated, sovereignty reverted to the people, who now tacitly acknowledge the leaders of the resistance as their temporary leaders. But after all possibility of success has been lost and the people have withdrawn their backing, guerrilla fighters would become outlaws.

Just cause

In every case it must be the violation, attempted or accomplished, of the nation's strict right. Such might be the carrying off of part of its population, the seizing of its territory or resources or property, or such a serious blow to the nation's honor as to weaken its authority and jeopardize its control. Territorial aggrandizement, glory and renown, envy of a neighbor's possessions, apprehension of a growing rival, personal spites and jealousies between monarchs, these and the like are invalid reasons. The just cause implies several subordinate conditions:

1. There must be a *sufficient proportion* between the good to be accomplished and the accompanying evil. War is so horrible an evil that only the most serious reasons can make it permissible. Nations must tolerate minor evils until changed times make their peaceful redress feasible. On the other hand, a nation need not be victimized by the Hitlerian technique of a series of small injuries and unjust demands, no one of which is worth fighting over, but adding up to a gradual loss of independence. Resistance is allowable as soon as the aggressive intent becomes morally certain.

2. War must be *the last resort*. Before a nation takes to war it must

have exhausted every peaceful means consistent with its dignity: negotiation, mediation, arbitration, diplomatic pressure, economic sanctions, ultimatums, and every other means known to enlightened statesmanship. Otherwise there is no proof that war is unavoidable and hence no sufficient proportion.

3. There must also be *fair hope of success*. This hope need not amount to moral certitude, for the fortunes of war involve too many unpredictable elements and moral certitude could occur only when the strongest nations are fighting the weakest. There is a fair hope when it is proportionate to the evils expected. To fight when there is not even possibility of victory is to impose evils on the nation to no purpose. However, a small nation may offer a token resistance to invasion as a protest against injustice and as a sign that it does not voluntarily submit to conquest.

4. The nation's cause must not only be just, but *known to be just*. This can be presumed in a purely defensive war, where there is no history of previous aggression on either side. But international relations have become so complex and affairs of state are kept so secret, that the ordinary citizen today is not always able to judge the justice of a war. Even the most bellicose nations refuse to admit that they are aggressors and put out reams of propaganda to deceive their own citizens as well as the rest of the world. After the war has been fought and all the documents are open to inspection, historians cannot always agree on war guilt.

This quandary can be handled in a practical way only by the rules for forming one's conscience. When the objective truth cannot be known, yet immediate action is imperative, there is no other recourse but to use reflex principles and arrive at a prudentially certain subjective judgment of conscience. Not only private citizens, but even statesmen themselves may be obliged to rely on their consciences when objective truth cannot be determined. Thus, though no war can be objectively just on both sides, the people and their leaders on both sides may be in a state of invincible ignorance, subjectively convinced of the justice of their cause, and acting with the right intention of saving their country. Bellarmine puts this clearly, as far as soldiers are concerned:

> The cause of war should be neither trivial nor doubtful, but weighty and certain, lest perchance the war bring about more harm than the hoped-for good; hence if there is any doubt a distinction must be made between the ruler and the soldiers, for the ruler himself sins, without doubt; for war is an act of retributive justice, but it is unjust to punish any one for a cause not yet proved; but the soldiers do not sin unless it is plainly evident that the war is unlawful, for subjects ought to obey their superior, nor should they criticize his commands, but they should rather suppose that their ruler has a good reason, unless they clearly know the contrary; just as when the offense of some particular individual is doubtful, the judge who condemns him sins, but not the executioner who carries out the sentence of death imposed on the condemned; for the executioner is not bound to criticize the sentence of the judge.*

*Bellarmine, *De Laicis*, ch. XV.

Bellarmine hastens to add that he is speaking of the regular army (to which he would add conscripts and draftees, if he had heard of them), but not of volunteers and mercenaries. Since these latter are not obliged to fight but offer themselves for it, they must make certain that the cause is just. One drafted by his country to fight in what seems to him to be a certainly unjust war must declare himself a conscientious objector; if this plea is not granted, he must make his cooperation in the war as remote as possible.

Right intention

A state may have objectively good grounds for war, or be subjectively convinced that it has, yet fight it for other reasons. It may use a just cause as an excuse to seek wrong ends, and thus spoil a good act by a bad intention. This intention may exist only in the minds of the rulers, while the people do no wrong in fighting because they have no such evil motives. Or an individual soldier fighting for his country in a just war kills for a motive of hatred and cruelty; his country's cause is good, but his own personal conduct is bad.

Note that a wrong intention will make the war subjectively immoral, but not necessarily unjust. It is not morally allowed to continue an unjust war and reparation must be made for the damage done; but in the prosecution of a just war an evil intention, if present at the beginning, can be corrected and the war continued for a worthy purpose.

Is a *punitive war*, a war undertaken to punish a guilty nation, ever justifiable? This is not understood to mean a war to force an unjust aggressor to give up his ill-gotten gains, which is mere restitution, but to go further and punish him for his crime. And even if the war was not undertaken for the purpose of punishment as its chief aim, still the question of punishing those responsible for unjust aggression and barbarous conduct arises at the end of the war. The older writers, St. Augustine, St. Thomas, Vitoria, Bellarmine, and Suarez, for example, think that a punitive war can be justified, as some of the quotations we have given indicate. Suarez is explicit:

> Just as within a state some lawful power to punish crime is necessary to the preservation of domestic peace; so in the world as a whole, there must exist, in order that the various states may dwell in concord, some power for the punishment of injuries inflicted by one state upon another; and this power is not to be found in any superior, for we assume that these states have no commonly acknowledged superior; therefore, the power in question must reside in the sovereign prince of the injured state, to whom, by reason of that injury, the opposing prince is made subject; and consequently, war of the kind in question has been instituted in place of a tribunal administering just punishment.*

This opinion is opposed by those who argue that punishment is an act of jurisdiction and must be inflicted by a superior on his inferior; since no state has jurisdiction over another, punishment of a guilty nation cannot

---

*Suarez, *The Three Theological Virtues: On Charity*, disp. XIII, sec. IV, no. 5.

be justified. This view seems too legalistic, as if there could be no law but positive law. Where there is a superior with jurisdiction, he and not the interested party is the one to pass sentence and administer punishment, but the mere fact that there happens to be no superior distinct from the parties concerned should not make the attainment of justice impossible. Where there is no positive law, we fall back on the natural law.

It may also be objected that punitive war has little application, that war guilt is too difficult to determine, that punishments devised in anger or by interested parties are seldom just, that punishment in such cases should be left to God or there will be no end to vengeance among nations. On the other hand, though there may seldom be occasion for a purely punitive war, the punitive motive can be added to other reasons for waging a just war. The determination of war guilt is sometimes impossible, but at other times quite clear. The victorious state can avoid harshness and passion by allowing a sufficient lapse of time and consulting the advice of neutrals. Right order and the future peace of the world demand that gangster nations be not permitted to do mass-murder with impunity and that they be taught that lesson here and now. All this, however, does not mean that punishment is mandatory. The remitting of punishment is an act of mercy and is in most instances to be strongly counseled, in some cases even demanded by enlightened prudence, but the *right* of punishment remains even if it is not exercised.

The same reasoning applies to the trial of *war criminals,* even though the whole war was not fought as a punitive war. It seems absurd to string a man on the gallows for a single peacetime murder, while letting those who have engaged in a set program of mass murder go scot-free, simply because nations have failed to enact a law providing for their punishment. It is hard to see how anyone who admits the existence of the natural law can call the punishment of war criminals unjust. Whether it is expedient or not is quite a different question. It does set a dangerous precedent, which future unjust aggressors who happen to be victorious can use with deadly ferocity against their blameless victims. Prudence and justice are both virtues, but their fruits are not always attainable in equal measure.

RIGHT USE OF MEANS

It is morally wrong to seek a good end through evil means. Hence a war might be justified in every other respect, yet become morally wrong because of the way in which it is fought. War is an ugly thing no matter how we look on it or for what noble purposes we may undertake it. The essential means is force, and the use of force is a brutal matter admitting of no finely drawn distinctions and delicate niceties. The soldier in the heat of battle can hardly be expected to fight with a gun in one hand and a textbook of ethics in the other. Much must be excused on the grounds of invincible ignorance, the clouding of reason by passion and fear, and the general background of war hysteria and propaganda. But none of this excuses us, as students of ethics, from a peacetime discussion of objective right and wrong in the fighting of a war.

The right use of means involves a number of details. We limit ourselves here to some more important points of conventional warfare.

1. How is *killing* in war justified? The purpose of a military campaign as a whole is to put the enemy's war machine out of commission so that he can no longer fight effectively. If this end could be attained without killing or hurting a single enemy soldier, there could be no excuse for bloodshed. But so far no method of stopping the enemy without killing has been devised or is likely in the foreseeable future.

Must killing in war be merely *indirect?* It would be ridiculous to try to apply the double-effect principle to the killing of enemy combatants. War cannot be waged realistically without *direct* killing. It may be justified on two titles.

The first title is that of *national defense.* In war an effective agent of an unjust government is an *unjust aggressor,* and his life is forfeit so long as he continues in that condition, that is, until he is disarmed. He need not be personally guilty of his nation's unjust war, nor need he be at the moment engaged in battle. It suffices that he is an active member of an armed force seeking to inflict or maintain injustice. His opposing number, the soldier of the just government fighting a just war, is commissioned by his country's public authority to eliminate the constant menace to its safety and its rights. The soldier acts not as a private individual, but as agent of his state and with its authority. War is not between person and person but between state and state, not a matter of individual but of national defense. The attack on the nation continues as long as the war lasts, not merely as long as this particular soldier is in danger.

The second title is that of *retributive justice,* empowering the injured state to execute mass murderers caught, as they are in battle, red-handed in the act. To use this title one must acknowledge the punitive element in a just war. Unlike the principle of self-defense, which is valid against material as well as formal aggressors, retributive justice is not applicable against enemy soldiers who are in good faith; however, it has its use where the commission of atrocities and barbarities gives proof enough of bad faith. Contrariwise, the principle of self-defense cannot be applied to captives, whereas the principle of retributive justice can.

2. The natural law is silent on the treatment of *prisoners,* except to urge the conflicting claims of justice and mercy, to counsel moderation in victory as in all things, and to remind civilized peoples of the excellence of humanity over brutality. Retributive justice warrants the execution of murderers even when disarmed, and those who willingly fight for a cause they know to be unjust fall under this heading. But today, when so many soldiers are conscripted, such evil intent is difficult to prove apart from overt acts of atrocity or treachery. The treatment of prisoners now customary among civilized peoples comes rather from international agreement than from the natural law. But no civilized nation today could be morally justified in refusing to subscribe to such agreements when the other nations of the world do so. States which are parties to such agreements are bound by the natural law to keep them unless they have been substantially broken by the enemy. Hence by international law and custom an implicit contract to spare prisoners' lives is involved in the acceptance of their surrender, and to kill them thereafter is an act of murderous treachery.

The same holds true regarding a refusal to take prisoners. The natural law does not oblige those fighting a just war to take prisoners. But once an international agreement has been made and as long as it holds, the natural law requires that the contract be kept, especially since the enemy soldiers, relying on the agreement, laid down their arms when they could have continued to fight in desperation. However, no nation in making such an agreement is presumed to intend thereby the exposure of its own forces to destruction, and, if it foresees that this will result, is justified in refusing to accept a surrender. Also, any army must protect itself against those who only pretend to surrender so as to kill at closer range; those who abuse the flag of truce or the sign of surrender forfeit any right they might have to quarter.

3. *Spies* are accorded different treatment. If caught, they must pay the penalty. They are effective agents and therefore combatants of the enemy who, in the hypothesis we are making here, is waging an unjust war; hence by the natural law they can be executed for their capital crime, and by international agreement they have not been exempted from this punishment. Spying is a strategem of war and not wrong in itself, though many of the methods commonly used are exceedingly questionable. If not wrong in itself, it can be used in a just war. But no means can be lawful in the prosecution of an unjust war, since the war itself is unlawful.

4. The distinction between *combatants* and *noncombatants* has been regarded as one of the triumphs of international law and a testimony to the advance of civilization from barbarism. The older writers, such as Vitoria, Bellarmine, and Suarez, refer rather to the *guilty* and the *innocent*. The term *guilty* here means objectively guilty, the effective agent of a nation waging unjust war, for no one in battle could examine each enemy soldier's conscience to determine his subjective guilt. Hence the terms *guilty* and *innocent* have up to now been taken to be practically the same as enemy *combatants* and *noncombatants,* supposing them on the unjust side. These older writers allow almost anything in war except the direct killing of the innocent. Suarez says:

> After war has been begun, and during the whole period thereof up to the attainment of victory, it is just to visit upon the enemy all losses which may seem necessary either for obtaining satisfaction or for securing victory, provided that these losses do not involve intrinsic injury to innocent persons, which would be in itself an evil. . . . The reason in support of this conclusion is as follows: if the end is permissible, the necessary means to that end are also permissible; and hence it follows that in the

whole course or duration of the war hardly anything done against the enemy involves injustice, except the slaying of the innocent. For all other damages are usually held to be necessary for attaining the end to which the war is directed.*

Lest Suarez be accused of arguing that a good end justifies evil means, reflect that the word *necessary* must be stressed. An end cannot be permissible if a means *necessary* to it be forbidden. If we already know that the end *is* permissible, so also must be the means *necessary* to it. Only thus could any argument for forceful defense, even personal self-defense, be valid. Suarez goes on to say that the killing of the innocent may be an incidental by-product in the legitimate prosecution of the war, according to the principle of double effect.

Who are combatants and who are noncombatants? An accurate determination could be made only by international agreement, but the natural law seems to approve the following general rule: Combatants are all those who belong to the armed forces of belligerent nations, and all who are actively and proximately cooperating in the military effort. Since cooperation shades imperceptibly from proximate to remote, the second part of this rule may be difficult to apply. Those who perform auxiliary military services, such as workers on arms, munitions, transport, communications, and the like, despite their technically civilian status, are actually combatants; their work is directly military in nature and can have no other purpose. The same is not true of farmers who grow food that will eventually be used by the armed forces, those who take civilian jobs to free men for military service, those who merely contribute money or lend moral support toward the war effort; their cooperation has been thought too remote to make them combatants. There are many borderline cases, but the general distinction seems clear enough as a norm for drawing up positive international agreements.

5. *Siege* is an old but not outmoded form of warfare consisting in bottling up the enemy within his stronghold, cutting off his supplies, and thus forcing him to capitulate. *Blockade* is an application of the same principle to a whole country, and usually implies control of the sea. Neither of these involves a direct killing of civilians, though indirectly it can produce the untold horrors of starvation. Siege and blockade are legitimate forms of warfare, and can be directed not merely against a military encampment but against a whole city or country as such. If the cause of the besieged is unjust, they bring these evils on themselves by continuing in their injustice and can stop them at any time, as they are obliged to do, by coming to terms. If their cause is just, they are allowed to hold out so long as there is hope of accomplishing a good proportionate to the evil suffered.

Submarines have enemy warships as their chief prey, but are also used to enforce or break a blockade. In this latter function they are legitimately

---

*Suarez, *The Three Theological Virtues: On Charity,* disp. XIII, sec. VII, no. 6.

used against the enemy's merchant marine. The main controversy concerns the use of submarines against neutral ships, against enemy passenger ships with no contraband aboard, and against enemy or neutral ships carrying both passengers and contraband of war. The natural law certainly forbids any attack on a neutral ship that is not supplying or aiding the enemy, and also the *direct* destruction of even enemy civilian lives, but further details must be regulated by international agreement.

6. *Reprisals* are acts of retaliation by inflicting evils equivalent to those suffered. The only case in which reprisals can be justified occurs when a means of war has been excluded only by treaty or international agreement and not by the natural law; if one side breaks the agreement, the other party cannot be held to it. But the fact that one side breaks the natural law and does something intrinsically wrong gives no permission to the other side to do so. The killing of *hostages* as an act of reprisal cannot be justified, unless the hostages come under the head of the "guilty" in the older writers' sense and deserve execution anyway. The practice of stopping sabotage in occupied countries by putting to death a certain number of innocent persons for each occurrence cannot be condoned on any moral principle.

7. As far as the natural law is concerned, the nation fighting a just war may commandeer all the *enemy property*, public or private, it needs to prosecute the war; and, if we add here the punitive aspect of war, it can confiscate all public property and even permanently annex the territory of the guilty nation. But this matter is regulated by custom and international agreement, and the signatories to such pacts are obliged to keep them. The customary rules are that property of military value may be seized or destroyed, but property of no military value must be respected; private property may be commandeered but at the end of the war must be returned to the owner or compensation made for its consumption; the invading power will exercise temporary administration over the public property of the occupied state until its final disposal is determined at the peace treaty.

8. The rights of *neutrals* in wartime must be respected. A nation has a strict right not to be drawn into a war against its will, and no considerations of *military necessity* can justify the violation of a neutral country's right, provided it remain genuinely neutral. So far the natural law. What sort of behavior is consistent with neutrality? The natural law is too vague to be a guide on this point, and recourse must be made to positive international agreements. Only by setting down definite overt acts can it be determined that a nation's sympathy with one side rather than another has stepped over the bounds of neutrality and become actual cooperation with a belligerent.

A nation has the right to come to the help of another fighting a just war, and, if it has pledged itself by treaty to do so, must fulfill its contract. But no state is morally allowed to make an alliance which would oblige it to fight in behalf of a nation provoking an unjust war, and any such contract would be invalid.

PACIFISM AND MILITARISM

So much on the traditional theory of the just war. It was an endeavor to find a middle ground between the extremes of pacifism and militarism. There are those who think that violence and bloodshed are so wrong that to use them even for defense is to use an evil means for a good end. There are others who look on war as a necessary element in a nation's growth and the natural means by which it plays its role in history.

Militarism was tacitly assumed in practice by most of the world's empires, but it had almost no philosophical defenders until the nineteenth century, when Fichte identified morality with struggle, Hegel made war a necessary stage in the passage from peace to victory, and Nietzsche extolled master morality as the ethics of the will-to-power. Hitler's Nazism was doubtless inspired by these views. Marxian communism, inheriting Hegel's dialectic without his idealism, carries out militaristic imperialism in our time, defining as "peace" anything, however violent, that furthers the communist aims, and branding as "warmongers" all who refuse to submit to their tyranny.

Pacifism is not a simple movement and exists on several levels. *Absolute* pacifists condemn all war. A man is not allowed to raise his hand against his neighbor even for personal defense; neither may a nation go to war to preserve its freedom. This attitude is usually adopted on religious grounds without attempt at philosophical justification. The pacifism of Gandhi* in India, rather than passing judgment on the wars of the past, was a practical movement for the elimination of war in the future. War will be impossible if people refuse to fight. Violence must be met by nonviolence, by the active nonviolent resistance of noncooperation. It is as wrong to run away as it is to fight. There must be no hatred toward the enemy and no show of cowardice, but simply a peaceful refusal to obey. If enough people can be persuaded to act thus, the enemy can achieve only a hollow victory and force ceases to be a factor in history. Gandhi's critics think his views noble but impractical. How does one persuade the vast bulk of humanity, especially those in communist countries, to refuse to fight?

Relative pacifists are less extreme. They recognize that in principle there can be such a thing as a just war, but deny that there can be a just *modern* war. Modern war, they say, has grown into such a horrible thing that it differs from older war not merely in degree but in kind. It is such that it essentially violates the principles of a just war. In particular they argue thus:

1. *The right use of means.* Modern weapons are immoral in themselves. They cannot be directed at military targets only. Their sphere of destruction is so widespread that they must by their very nature cause

---

*Gandhi, *Non-Violence in Peace and War.*

more damage to civilian life and property than to military personnel and installations. They cannot be used in such a way that civilian damage is merely a regrettable by-product. The wiping out of whole cities involves the destruction of the guilty and the innocent indiscriminately. This is but mass murder on a grand scale.

2. *Reasonable hope of success.* It is impossible to win a war nowadays. Both sides lose. The losses sustained even by the technically victorious side would nullify any benefit received. No injured rights could be so precious as to justify the wiping out of a nation's population and the rendering of a large part of its territory uninhabitable for years to come. Modern war is mass suicide as well as mass murder.

3. *The proportion of good to evil.* Modern war spreads to the whole world. Even if a single nation could achieve all its war aims, the good would be cancelled by the evils inflicted on all humanity through the poisoning of the atmosphere, producing diseases and mutations that would be passed on to future generations. Some go so far as to say that it would be better to accept communist slavery and try to oppose it from within by nonviolent methods, hoping to infiltrate into it and eventually control it, than to engage in mass suicide by fighting it. "Better red than dead" is the slogan of this group.

4. *Legitimate authority.* No one on earth has the authority to order a nation into modern war. The complications of modern diplomacy and efficiency of modern propaganda make it practically impossible for the ordinary citizen to determine the justice of his country's cause. How otherwise explain the millions who fought for Hitler? No longer can we blindly trust our leaders when the weight of evidence points to their probably being more wrong than right.

These and similar arguments cannot be taken lightly. Some writers call for a complete reworking of the whole question from the ground up, placing the ethics of war on a new footing. Others cannot see where any new footing could be found, but ask for a reinterpretation of the traditional principles to make them applicable to modern war. Still others see modern war as differing only in degree from wars of the past and capable of being judged by the old principles unmodified.

LIMITED NUCLEAR WAR

It is customary today to distinguish between *conventional* warfare, which includes all the wars fought hitherto, and *nuclear* warfare, which threatens to be the war of the future. The dropping of atomic bombs on Hiroshima and Nagasaki is regarded as the transition from one to the other. We need pass no moral judgment on this particular incident to discuss the principles of war in general. Past immoral use, if such it was, does not preclude a weapon's future legitimate use.

Conventional warfare is naturally limited by the limited destructiveness of the weapons. With the advance of science the limit is rapidly receding, so that nuclear warfare introduces a new element. The limitation must now be imposed by man since it no longer comes from the nature of the weapons. Since the only absolutely unlimited war would be one which wipes out humanity, only a war of lesser scope could claim to be moral. What are the proper limits and will man restrict himself to them in the use of his new-found power?

Bombing in itself is not intrinsically wrong. A bomb is simply a larger military weapon and, like any other, may be used against military targets; the killing of civilians, if any occurs, is incidental. Indiscriminate bombing of a city or area, with no attempt to distinguish military from nonmilitary objectives, has been rightly considered in conventional war as mass murder. The phrase *military necessity* used to justify acts of this kind is entirely meaningless, since it can be twisted to cover any act however immoral. Nor is it excused by the desire to destroy the enemy's morale and terrorize him into submission, for terror can also be produced by the grossest and most bestial atrocities without in any way making these acts moral. So conventional bombing can be moral or immoral, depending on how it is used.

Since a nuclear bomb is merely a bigger and more destructive bomb, its use is governed by the same principles. A military target may be extensive enough to warrant the use of a nuclear bomb without disproportionate civilian damage; for example, a fleet at sea or an isolated munitions plant. The enemy cannot claim sanctuary by putting such a plant in a civilian sector and has the responsibility of evacuating the civilian population from the danger spot. If it is allowed to destroy a military target with a hundred ordinary bombs, why not with one nuclear bomb? Nor can it be said that the atom bomb may have legitimate use, but not the hydrogen bomb. Though one works by fission and the other by fusion, it is not the method but the extent and control of the destructiveness that has moral significance. These two types of bomb overlap, the largest fission bomb being considerably more destructive and emitting more fallout that the smallest fusion bomb.

Nuclear bombs pose the problem of radioactive contamination that is absent in conventional bombs. The point of strike and its environs are not only destroyed but rendered uninhabitable for some time. The radioactive cloud is blown to civilian sectors and even to neutral countries. However, the amount reduces so rapidly as to come well within the limits of human tolerance, except near the center of the blast. Since there is natural radioactivity in the earth's crust and in cosmic rays, a nuclear explosion does not produce something entirely new but increases what is already there. Can a slightly added susceptibility to bone cancer and the possibility of mutational defects in the germ plasm be considered a by-product of the war that can be permitted to occur in the civilian population by the principle of double effect? It seems that it can. In any war the civilians suffer greatly anyway, and in a world war even neutral nations are seriously affected, at least economically, with repercussions on the rest of their life. To impose this on others is not out of proportion to a nation's right to its freedom. The hazard, however, must be reduced as far as possible and the endeavor to develop cleaner bombs is a moral requirement that is being increasingly recognized.

Guided missiles, whether intercontinental or of shorter range, cannot be considered wrong in themselves. What is important is the charge they carry and how accurately they are directed. If a nuclear bomb is justified, so also is this means of delivering it. It must be launched at military objectives only, and its accuracy must be such that civilian casualties caused by it are only incidental.

As bombs are legitimate weapons if used properly, so also are chemical and bacteriological warfare. The difficulty in these two types of warfare is one of control. Any means of waging war that is by its very nature uncontrollable cannot be condoned on any moral principle.

It was thought necessary to make these remarks here lest anyone argue from the very nature of the weapons used. Nuclear weapons are not of their very nature immoral. They can be controlled, they can be directed against military installations and personnel, they can be used in accordance with the principle of double effect, which allows direct attack against the guilty but permits only incidental harm to the innocent.

Despite what has been said, the terrible and extensive nature of the weapons used in a nuclear war even of a limited character imposes some restrictions not present in former wars. Some* think that we must make the following additions to the theory of the just war. They can be formulated in two propositions:

1. *Any war of aggression, even a just offensive war, is morally forbidden.* This statement goes counter to the traditional teaching on the just war, according to which war was a legitimate means of recovering violated rights. One reason is that the character of modern war requires much more serious reasons to justify it. Any nation that initiates war, even for the best of causes, needs overwhelmingly strong reasons to compensate for the damage done and for the danger of drawing the rest of the world into the conflict. In these days it is hard to conceive of any past grievance that could compensate for breaking an existing peace. Another reason is the existence of international tribunals and the United Nations. To bypass them at this critical juncture of their struggling existence by direct appeal to the sword would postpone indefinitely man's only hope of a peaceful world.

2. *A defensive war to preserve a nation's rights and freedom by the use of effective means is morally admissible.* There is no peace without justice, law, and order. Free field cannot be given to brutal violence and lack of conscience. A nation's defense is not restricted to conventional weapons, but to be adequate must match the weapons of the attackers.

---

*This material is taken from John Courtney Murray, "Remarks on the Moral Problem of War," *Theological Studies*, March, 1959, reprinted in *We Hold These Truths*, ch. 11, and in *Morality and Modern Warfare*, ch. 5.

Nuclear warfare of a limited character may be used morally under the following conditions:

— First, the war must be imposed on the nation by the enemy's obvious and grave injustice. Defensive war is not defined in terms of declaring war or crossing borders or dropping the first bombs, but the war must be thrust on the nation by an enemy's unjust act that can be met and stopped.

— Second, nuclear weapons, if used, must be indispensable for defense. The enemy must either already have resorted to nuclear weapons or there must be moral certitude that he will do so.

— Third, the proportion of good to evil, including the prospect of success, must be maintained. This proportion is not to be estimated only in terms of deaths and physical damage, but takes in such values as a nation's liberty and independence, which have always been a valid cause for war.

— Fourth, a new principle of limitation is introduced. Limitation, formerly inherent in the limited power of the weapons used, must now be voluntarily imposed. This principle of limitation bans a war of extermination and the unloosing of an evil that wholly escapes man's control.

TOTAL OR ALL-OUT WAR

It may be said that all the above discussion is unrealistic, for the next war is not going to be a limited war. Are we courageous enough to face the condition of total war, and to accept the alternatives of death if we try to fight it or of slavery if we refuse? Is the second really an out? When a nation that refuses to fight for itself has been reduced to slavery, it may then be forced to fight *for* its masters in their further conquests rather than *against* them. Do our moral principles oblige us to choose between being either "red or dead," or can we find a moral way of being neither?

We must first settle what is meant by *total* or *all-out* war.

— 1. In the extreme sense, it may mean a war that shatters the earth itself or so pollutes the atmosphere as to destroy all human life. Obviously, there could be no good end to be accomplished by such a war, since nobody would be left to enjoy it.

— 2. It may mean a war of extermination and obliteration against a whole people, systematically wiping out every one of them with all their cities and goods. If such extermination could be done at one blow, nobody would be left in that country to engage in defensive war, which we said is the only possibly justifiable modern war.

— 3. It may mean a war waged for the purpose of imposing absolute defeat on the enemy by the use of any and every means available, with no consideration of morality or immorality. Evidently, such a war is immoral by definition.

— 4. Total war may mean the concept of a whole nation in arms, a war in which the nation has mobilized all its personnel and all its resources for the war effort. More specifically, it involves the use of thermonuclear weapons that will take a huge toll of lives among the enemy.

It is only in this last sense that the morality of total war can be a subject of discussion. A total war of aggression is immoral for reasons given above. But is a total war of defense in the fourth sense explained above necessarily immoral? What of a nation that has total war thrust upon it, that is unjustly attacked by an enemy using the technique of total war. How can it defend itself? War is the repelling of force by force. If a nation has the right to defend itself, it has the right to use what force it needs to attain this end. If the enemy makes no distinction between combatants and noncombatants, military and civilians, how can the attacked nation adequately defend itself while respecting such a distinction in the enemy? All the defending nation's population is exposed to attack while most of the attacking nation's population is immune, and behind this immunity even the military can find some shelter.

We have here a very difficult question. On the one hand we may not use evil means to accomplish an end however good, and on the other we cannot admit that evil is inevitably destined to triumph because we are forbidden the only means that could oppose it. It is the moralist's duty to find a way between these two immoral extremes.

Some find it by insisting that total war is essentially immoral in any sense, even the one we are now discussing, but that it can be successfully opposed by limited war. Nuclear defense may be used against nuclear attack, but must be restricted to the smaller and cleaner bombs that can be pinpointed against the military. The disadvantage to the defenders will have to be made up in some other way, by more adequate preparation, by greater cleverness of strategy, by better use of resources, by building up an indefectible morale. Some* say that, if the conditions of a limited war do not prevail, it is our business to create such conditions and impose them on any potential enemy. The task is enormous, but the stakes are high enough to call forth the ultimate in human ingenuity. If we are morally obliged to defend ourselves against slavery and tyranny, yet may do so only by moral means, and if in the circumstances the only *moral* means is *limited* nuclear warfare, then we are obliged to develop a type of defense that can be successful even though limited.

This is a far cry from pacifism indeed, and is about as far as most reputable moralists are willing to go at present, if they go even that far. Yet not all are satisfied that this position is realistic enough. Limited nuclear defense may do for the present danger and the next conflict, if there is one, but is it a universal principle for all time? We pose the following questions and suggestions for what they are worth, not as maintaining them but as inviting discussion.

---

*Murray, *Op. cit.*

SPECULATIONS

How absolute is the distinction between *combatant* and *noncombatant?* Does it come from natural law or rest on convention? If the latter, is the convention so good that the natural law must condemn a nation that abandons it for any reason however grave, or is it a convention that should be maintained as long as possible but abandoned if conditions occur in which it would be moral to drop it?

How do we prove a *natural law* distinction here? War is of nation against nation. What is there in the natural law which demands that a nation must commit its defense to a specified portion of its population designated as combatants, and must regard its attackers as having made a similar distinction among themselves, so that the defenders can repel only the combatants among the attackers and must spare the remaining part of the population, even when the enemy refuses to recognize any such distinction but exploits his immunity to the full?

Is the distinction of combatant and noncombatant the same as the distinction of *guilty* and *innocent?* This never meant subjectively guilty or innocent. If it did, in these days of conscription when most of the military are subjectively innocent, nobody but the enemy's leaders could be killed. The distinction of *objectively* guilty and innocent was significant in conventional warfare when only armed men were dangerous. But who is the armed man in a nuclear war? Only those who push the buttons releasing the missiles or the whole nation? It is difficult to define a middle position. Perhaps the only objectively innocent ones left are children and invalids. If there is any warning of impending war, they should be evacuated from critical areas. Preparations to do so, despite the hugeness of the task, should be set up by every government.

Is not a whole industrial city these days a legitimate target of attack? It is the center for railroads, highways, shipping, all communication, manufacturing, fuel storage, food processing, and for the distribution of all the materials on which a modern mechanized army relies completely. The successful prosecution of the war demands that this center of the enemy's fighting potential be put out of commission. Cannot the city itself be regarded as the object of direct attack and the killing of any civilians present as an indirect consequence, according to the principle of double effect? The bombing of cities seems to be the modern equivalent of the siege, in which civilians normally outnumbered the military.

Is *massive retaliation* essentially immoral? Some say that it is not so long as it is not used. It is true that its main purpose is deterrence, but the nation must decide on what to do if it fails to deter. It can hardly tell the enemy that it will not retaliate, and its citizens must go on the assumption that it will. Reliance on massive retaliation alone would be a stupid policy. A modern nation must prepare for every eventuality. If the enemy engages only in a limited attack and the defender has nothing but massive nuclear weapons for defense, it will be tempted to use them in a situation that could not justify them. The defense must be matched to the attack or it is not defense.

Can the *actual use of massive retaliation* be morally justified? If each nation is threatening the other with extermination, we have a sort of mutual suicide or mutual murder pact that would be as immoral among nations as it is among individuals. But even if it is known that the enemy has such power, it cannot be known that he will use it to the full. A preemptive exterminatory strike against the enemy can therefore never be justified. If the enemy's first strike, actually delivered or certainly forthcoming, is less than exterminatory (the only realistic assumption, since no nation is presumed to seek self-destruction), a second strike must be expected. It can be deterred only by retaliation for the first. How otherwise can the survivors of the first be protected from the second?

Is it really *impossible to win* a nuclear war? Must we say that no country could recover from the blotting out of all its major metropolitan areas, and that the survivors would envy the dead? It depends on the extent of the destruction. Estimates have been made that, provided adequate preparations were made, a leading nation could lose a third of its population and all its major cities, yet build back to its former prosperity in about a generation. Meanwhile life would be on a lower order, but not more intolerable than that of our ancestors or of underprivileged peoples today. Is this too great a price to pay for freedom?

Is it immoral to *conduct nuclear tests* and *stockpile nuclear weapons* in peacetime? Certainly every effort at disarmament must be made. But no nation can be expected to disarm while its potential enemies remain armed. So long as some are unwilling to submit to a system of international inspection and control, mutual disarmament is an empty illusion. The only interim solution is to match arms for arms in the hope that neither side would dare to use them first, knowing the price of retaliation. This is the perpetuation of an irrational condition, but those who thrust it on the world by their refusal to cooperate must bear the responsibility. Unilateral disarmament would be a government's abdication of its moral duty to protect its people.

These and further questions must be asked and answered to each one's satisfaction, if he is to live morally in the modern world. Our remarks make no pretense at a definitive answer, but point out the magnitude and urgency of the problem.

CONCLUSION

War is one of the most regrettable things that have come to deface our fair world, a useless, wasteful, man-made evil. But we must live with the breed of men we find in this world, and if they make war on us we must defend ourselves. Otherwise the good must live as slaves of the wicked, who will then be free for every kind of violence and tyranny. In such a world there could be no peace. War is therefore an evil, but sometimes an unavoidable one. In a just war it is the duty of every citizen to support his country at the expense of fortune, liberty, and even of life itself if necessary, and his country has the right to call on him for such support. How to steer his country through the tangles of international complications without recourse to war's horrors is the virtue of the statesman.

SUMMARY

Despite its frequency, war is the disease of man's political life, peace its normal condition. Wars should be fought to secure peace, peace should not be but a preparation for more war. Peace is the positive good, war the evil that is its privation.

War is a condition of active armed hostility between two or more sovereign states. *Defensive* war is *just* when fought to repel an unjust aggressor, even when the defense takes the appearance of attack. *Offensive* war is *just* when fought to vindicate seriously violated rights; otherwise it is *unjust* aggression.

War is *not intrinsically wrong*. It may be the only means a state has to protect or recover its lawful rights or even to preserve itself in being; the natural law must give it the right to the means necessary to this end.

There are *three conditions for a just war:*

1. *Lawful authority.* War is an act of the state as such and must be properly authorized. This authorization gives the soldier his right to kill and use force. So long as there is hope, guerrilla fighting and underground resistance movements are lawful, even when the government that authorized them has fallen.

2. *Just cause.* This can be only the attempted or accomplished violation of a nation's strict rights. There must be *sufficient proportion* between the good intended and the evil permitted. War must be the *last resort* after the breakdown of all feasible forms of negotiation. There must be *fair hope of success* or there can be no proportion. The cause must be *known to be just;* if it is doubtful, subordinates can form their consciences and trust to the wisdom of their leaders.

3. *Right intention.* Objective grounds for war may exist, yet the nation may fight it for the wrong motives. *Punitive war* is accepted by the older writers; on this basis the punishment of war criminals can be defended.

Right use of means. A war otherwise justifiable can become wrong by the way it is fought. The killing of combatants, even direct killing, is allowed on the principles of national defense and of retributive justice. The treatment of prisoners, spies, noncombatants, and hostages; the use of siege, blockade, submarine warfare, and poison gas; the handling of enemy property and respect for the rights of neutrals; these and similar matters are but vaguely indicated by the natural law and are determined by custom and international agreement. Such contracts must be kept unless they are substantially broken by the other side. But no nation may do something intrinsically wrong because the other side does so.

Absolute *pacifism* condemns all war. Relative pacifism condemns modern war on the grounds that it necessarily violates the conditions of a just war.

Others consider that even *nuclear warfare* can be limited and can thus be made to conform to the accepted principles. They would add two new qualifications: that any war of aggression, even a just offensive war, is morally forbidden; and that the limitation of warfare, formerly automatic because of the small weapons used, must now be voluntarily imposed. Otherwise the proportion of good to evil is not kept.

Total war may mean the extermination of the human race, or of a whole people, or the use of any means however immoral, or the mobilization of a nation's whole manpower and resources for the prosecution of the war. In the first three senses it is utterly immoral. Many reject it also in the fourth sense, while others think that a nation attacked in this fashion may have recourse to it as the only adequate defense. The argument of the latter group is that a nation's right to existence and freedom implies the right to defense by means adequate to that end, and that the means are not intrinsically wrong.

There must be some way of facing these momentous issues that is both realistic and moral.

READINGS

1. Read something from the older writers who formed the theory of the just war, remembering that they had no notion of modern war:
   a. St. Augustine, *The City of God,* bk. XIX, ch. 5-17.
   b. St. Thomas, *Summa Theologica,* II-II, qq. 40, 41, 42; this is unfortunately not printed in the *Basic Writings.*
   c. Vitoria, *De Bello* (On War), found in Scott, *Francisco de Vitoria and His Law of Nations,* appendix F. Scott's commentary is found in the body of the book, ch. VIII and IX.
   d. St. Robert Bellarmine, *De Laicis or the Treatise on Civil Government,* ch. XIV and especially XV.
   e. Suarez, *The Three Theological Virtues: On Charity,* disputation XIII (On War). This is found in English in Scott's *Classics of International Law, Suarez,* vol. II, pp. 797-865. Scott, *The Catholic Conception of International Law,* ch. XII, comments on Suarez.
   f. Grotius, *The Rights of War and Peace,* especially books I and III.
2. The following modern works on war in general will be useful:
   a. Leibell, *Readings in Ethics,* pp. 1032-1059.
   b. Ryan, *Modern War and Basic Ethics.*
   c. Vann, *Morality and War.*
   d. Gigon, *The Ethics of Peace and War.*
   e. Eppstein, *The Catholic Tradition of the Law of Nations,* also *Code of International Ethics.*
   f. Rommen, *The State in Catholic Thought,* ch. XXIX.
   g. Gandhi, M. K., *Non-Violence in Peace and War.*
   h. Stratmann, *War and Christianity Today,* defends the pacifist position.
   i. D'Arcy, *Christian Morals,* pp. 140-157, criticism of pacifism.
3. On nuclear war:
   a. Kahn, *On Thermonuclear War,* though not treating of ethics, sets the stage by its analysis of what to expect in future wars.

b. Hodgson, *Nuclear Physics in Peace and War,* is a very clear summary. Chapter 7 is on the morality of nuclear war.

c. Thompson, *Morals and Missiles,* and Stein, *Nuclear Weapons, a Catholic Response,* present the pacifist case.

d. Nagle, *Morality and Modern Warfare,* is a good symposium.

e. Bennett, *Christians and the State,* ch. 12.

f. Ramsey, *War and the Christian Conscience.*

g. Batchelder, *The Irreversible Decision.*

h. Murray, John Courtney, *We Hold These Truths,* ch. 11.

i. Murray, Thomas E., *Nuclear Policy for War and Peace,* argues for limited war.

*   *   *

The most up-to-date matter on this topic is found in periodical literature.

O ur study of ethics should not end on the note of war. We have said that peace is the normal and natural relation that should exist between states, that war is the privation of this good and therefore an evil: a physical evil even for the nation that fights a just war, and a moral evil as well as a physical evil for the nation fighting an unjust war. We also noted that one of the reasons why wars have been unavoidable is that there is no higher authority to which states can appeal for the settlement of their disputes, at least no authority that nations will respect because it can enforce its decisions. The question that immediately comes to mind is: Why do not nations establish such an authority?

HISTORY

The idea of a world-wide society embracing all nations is not new but has been prevalent throughout the ages. As imaginative writers have put forth innumerable utopias portraying what they thought the ideal structure of a single state, so there have been many idealistic schemes of world union. The difference is that, although the ideal state has never existed, there do exist real states which function despite their defects; world union, on the other hand, has never yet even come near real accomplishment. However, there have been some more or less promising endeavors in that direction, roughly paralleling the development of international law.

In ancient times the Roman Empire took on itself the task of governing the then known world. Without consciously facing the problem, it solved it by the method of *one dominant nation,* and the solution was remarkably successful so long as the Empire preserved its vigor. Three main defects are apparent in this solution: the Empire itself had to be built up by war and conquest before it could maintain world peace; it never did include the whole world and its overextension contributed much to its downfall; and the solution was satisfactory to the dominant Romans but galling and irksome to their subjugated peoples. Communism looks to this sort of solution today; free peoples will have none of it.

Medieval society naturally turned to the Church as a model of international organization. Why could not nations produce in the political sphere what the Church had successfully accomplished in the religious sphere? Feudalism, with its hierarchical arrangement of overlord and vassal, its limitation and subordination of powers, supplied the means for effecting this organization and logically tended toward a union of the whole world. Dante in his *De Monarchia* envisions the Pope and the Emperor side by side, one supreme in the spiritual and the other in temporal matters, with all other rulers owing them fealty. This arrangement never got far beyond the stage of an ideal, and as a political venture the Holy Roman Empire was among the less successful, but the ideal colored the whole of medieval political thinking. This concept is past all hope of revival.

When the decline of feudalism and the breakup of united Christendom made the medieval ideal impossible, Renaissance writers like Grotius turned to international law as the means for keeping the peace. Nations might retain full sovereignty yet cooperate by voluntary agreement. The Congress of Vienna assembled after the French Revolution and the Napoleonic Wars, the Geneva Convention and the Court of Arbitration at The Hague, the League of Nations after the first World War and the United Nations of today are various attempts to mitigate or outlaw war and to maintain the peace of the world. They have had a moderate success in mediating small disputes, but none at all in preventing the two world wars that have wracked our century. If we succeed in avoiding a third world war, the credit for doing so will hardly go to the United Nations as at present constituted.

The difficulty seems to be that, so long as each nation is unwilling to part with any of its sovereignty, there is no way of making any international organization authoritative and effective. World wars are not caused by small countries, which can easily be kept in line by threat of intervention, but by the great powers. If each sovereign great power can veto any decision it does not like, the only decisions that are of value are unanimous ones, and if there is unanimity there is no dispute to settle. Hence a world organization along these lines seems to be either inadequate or superfluous, except as the expression of a hope that it will some day develop into an effective instrument.

PROBLEM

Can we say that, because efforts toward a really working international organization in the past have been unsuccessful, they must necessarily be so throughout all the future? Surely this would be an unwarranted conclusion. Here a distinction must be made between the absolute perfectionists and those who are willing to limit themselves to human possibilities. The ideal of the absolute perfectionist can never be realized, for all human works are imperfect and Utopia in this world can never be more than a dream. This limitation affects single states as well as international organizations. We cannot hope that all threat of war will forever be abolished from the earth, any more than we can hope to see our own government functioning without the slightest snarl or hitch. But approximations to the ideal are possible, and man is able by his own efforts aided by social cooperation to improve his condition. That is how he advanced this far, and who is to tell him he must stop? There is a mid-point between a foolish optimism and a paralyzing pessimism.

This problem is the concern of the moral philosopher and of the practical statesman. It can be phrased in two questions:

(1) Is mankind today morally obliged to work toward the establishment of an effective world organization?

(2) How can a world organization be set up that will have authority and will be effective of world peace?

The first question alone concerns the moral philosopher; the second is for the practical statesman and outside our province. When we examined the theory of the state we did not try to draw up a constitution for any country, and when we studied industrial relations we merely suggested a few of the practical means of bringing management and labor into accord; so now we merely point out to men politically organized their international obligations and leave to their ingenuity the construction of the instruments.

One may immediately object that there can be no obligation to do the impossible, and so until the second question is answered the first cannot be. This objection would be valid if we could prove that no effectual world organization is possible, neither now nor at any future time. But how can this be proved? If a man has an obligation to fulfill but the means he is now using are futile, he is not thereby freed from the duty of seeking better means. We are not yet certain that better means can never be devised. If the refusal of even one great power to cooperate with the rest of the world makes useless all present effort toward international organization, we have no certainty that this situation must be perpetual. Does not that nation brand itself as guilty of immoral conduct, thus confirming the existence of the moral obligation?

Hence the first question can be answered independently of the second. If a thing can be proved impossible, there is no sense trying to accomplish it. But if it cannot be proved possible except by actually doing it, we cannot wait for proof of possibility before starting to work at it. An international organization cannot be proved impossible and positive proof of its possibility can come only from success in the effort.

NECESSITY OF INTERNATIONAL ORGANIZATION

Our argument here is but a logical extension of the proof we used to show that man is morally obliged to organize himself into political society. We said that the state is the natural outgrowth of the family; that, when a number of families in a region find it impossible to defend themselves or to supply their needs singly, they are obliged by the natural law to cooperate for their common good; that, when a simple tribal organization becomes inadequate, they are further obliged to form themselves into the society called the state, and to set up governmental machinery with authority to carry on political functions. The formerly autonomous family was obliged to surrender part of its independence to create the sovereignty of the newly fashioned state.

Because of the diffusion of the human race across geographical barriers and the lack of contact between isolated sections, a number of political states sprang up in different parts of the world. It was formerly quite possible for each state to be wholly or nearly self-sufficient. It could defend itself against aggression from without and maintain law and order within, besides supplying its people with their comparatively simple needs. There were wars, all too fierce and frequent, but they were mostly localized. As yet there was no call for an international organization; travel was too difficult and much of the world's surface was undiscovered.

Today advancing civilization and scientific discovery have broken through all geographical barriers and brought every part of the world into closest contact with every other part. No longer can any nation live in isolation, no matter how hard it tries. National economy is geared to world economy, national peace is dependent on world peace. Over night any nation can find its livelihood throttled or its territory the battleground of a world war through no action of its own. The self-sufficiency of the individual state has all but disappeared. Small states, though still technically sovereign, are caught up in the orbits of a few great powers, and these are at loggerheads, threatening to embroil the whole world in their clash. There is plainly a need of something larger than the state itself to curb international lawlessness.

As human society outgrew the family, and, without destroying the family, required the formation of a larger organization, the state, so today human society is outgrowing the state and, without destroying it, is beginning to demand the formation of a still more extensive organization, a world society. Where the natural law is insufficient, it must be supplemented by positive law. Within each state the civil law can do efficiently enough its work of keeping order and making human life livable. But between states we find fear, suspicion, insecurity, deceit, disorder, and lawlessness, and the only court of appeal is force. Man is morally obliged to do his best to eliminate such evils from his international life. As now conducted man's international life does not square with the norm of morality, for it is not rational.

LIMITATION OF SOVEREIGNTY

To be authoritative, the world society, whatever form it may take at the dictation of political prudence, must have legislative, executive, and judicial power. To provide it with these powers, individual states will have to consent to some limitation of their sovereignty. Any suggestion of this sort raises an agonized protest from outraged nationalism and a vigorous waving of the flag. But this is beside the point. Limitation of sovereignty is not in any way contrary to true patriotism, but only to that vicious sort of nationalism which is akin to racial and religious prejudice or is committed to a program of militaristic imperialism. Exaggerated nationalism has never been a virtue but a vice, the very vice from which most of our international chaos springs.

Limitation of sovereignty is but a recognition of the ethical fact that no human right can be absolutely unlimited. What right have we to make national sovereignty into such a fetish that we must wreck the world in order to preserve it? Sovereignty is but a means to an end, the common good; when it swells to such a size that it blocks the path to the end, it must be trimmed down to its proper proportions. As the rights of the individual are limited by the rights of other individuals, as the rights of the family are limited by the rights of other families, so the rights of the state are limited by the rights of other states and of mankind in general.

Some say that the very concept of sovereignty requires that it be unlimited, that the notion of limited sovereignty is a contradiction in terms. There is good historical background for this interpretation, since the idea of sovereignty was developed to fit the claims of the newly emerged absolutist and autocratic monarchies of the sixteenth century. Jean Bodin,* originator of this concept, defines sovereignty as "the absolute and perpetual power of the commonwealth," and says that it "is not limited either in power, charge, or time," that the sovereign prince is "divided from the people," "is the image of God," and "need give account only to God." Democratic and other nonabsolutist states use the word *sovereignty* even in such a phrase as *sovereignty of the people,* but for them it can mean no more than independence, autonomy, nonsubjection to another state. But there still remains about it some aura of its former meaning, some connotation of irresponsibility. If sovereignty must mean absolute and unlimited power, it can belong to God alone, and never was or could be a real attribute of any state or prince. We have long ago repudiated any such fantastic claims of states and princes, and if the word *sovereignty* still has this meaning for us we had better drop it.

Each state has the right to autonomy and independence, full control over its domestic affairs, to *internal* sovereignty (if we wish to use that word). But there is no reason why it must continue to insist on absolute *external* sovereignty, why it should not accept the guidance and submit

---

*Bodin, *De la république,* bk. I, ch. 8. See Maritain, *Man and the State,* ch. II.

to the authority of a world organization in the control of such of its international affairs as have world-wide repercussions and can lead to a world-wide disaster, engulfing that very state itself. Small states today, though clinging to the fiction of unlimited sovereignty, are practically obliged to accept the guidance of the great powers in their international behavior. The great powers are the ones that need curbing, and, if this is not to be done by the system of the *one dominant nation*, it must be done by some organization superior to them all. Limitation of sovereignty is merely the acknowledgment of an existing fact, anyway. It would not destroy a nation's dignity, but only its lawless irresponsibility. An individual does not lose his dignity by becoming a citizen, nor should a state by becoming a member of an efficiently organized family of nations.

CONCLUSION

The world has already split into two camps lined up behind the two leading nations espousing two contradictory ideologies. The struggle that has already begun, whether it be carried through by cold war or hot war, by pressure of position or force of arms, must eventually result in the emergence of one dominant power. Should the forces of Communism be victorious, we know what to expect as the solution of the international riddle. If we come out successful, what solution will we have to offer? A variation of the one dominant nation scheme by keeping ourselves in the dominant position? Except for the difference of ideology and a more benevolent administration, this would be basically the solution our enemies want for themselves, and a betrayal of all that we as a nation stand for. Would we prefer a return to the *status quo* of international bumbling, with a world war breaking out every generation? Civilization is a hardy thing, but there must be limits to what it can take; how long we ourselves could survive in such a morass of unreason is questionable. Or will we have the vision and courage to rise to the next step logically indicated in the social organization of humanity?

This is undoubtedly the main moral problem before the world today. We may never see it solved in our lifetime, and some centuries may pass before it can be made a reality, but we cannot shirk the responsibility of seeking some solution and trying to lay the first stones in the edifice. The answer suggested above has been dismissed as visionary, even branded as traitorous by reliers on a vanished isolation. Those who think so are invited either to devise a solution of their own or to justify the present world disorder by what ethical reasons they can find.

Meanwhile the world rolls on. Whatever be the social conditions in which his lot is cast, the individual must live his life in such a way as to fulfill his moral duty and arrive at his last end. He who looks for Utopia here is the impractical visionary, not he who guides himself through the crumbling institutions of time to the lasting possession of the Highest Good.

SUMMARY

Attempts to organize the nations of the world in the interest of international harmony have all been futile. This does not prove that the nations never can be organized, but only that we have not yet found successful means to this end. It is not for ethics to find these means, but to point out our obligation to search for them.

That an *internatinal organization is necessary* is but a logical continuation of the argument that the state is necessary. The individual is insufficient and forms the family, the family is insufficient and forms the tribe, the tribe becomes insufficient and organizes itself into the political state. Today, because of the surmounting of geographical barriers, the state is no longer self-sufficient and must band with the other states of the world for their mutual safety and benefit.

To be *authoritative and effective* a world society needs legislative, executive, and judicial power, so that states will have to consent to some *limitation of sovereignty*. Sovereignty cannot be absolute anyway, but is limited by the natural law. A transfer of political sovereignty in matters that concern the peace of the world would not compromise a nation's dignity or independent equality with all other nations; it would only curb the lawless irresponsibility with which the great powers have pursued their selfish ambitions.

The present international chaos is immoral. If the above solution be too distasteful, right reason demands that some better one be sought.

READINGS

1. Read Kant's famous little essay, *Perpetual Peace*. It does not agree with all the ideas expressed here, but it has been influential in peace movements.
2. Two Popes, Benedict XV in the first World War and Pius XII in the second, have expressed themselves on world organization. John XXIII in his Encyclical, *Pacem in terris*, sums up and reinforces their statements. Though speaking as religious leaders, their views are based on the dictates of reason rather than of revelation. Their ideas can be found in:
   a. *Principles for Peace*, edited by the National Catholic Welfare Council.
   b. Gonella, *A World to Reconstruct*.
   c. Wright, *National Patriotism in Papal Teaching*, pt. III.
3. Mortimer Adler's *How to Think about War and Peace*, whether one agrees with all his conclusions or not, cannot be overlooked by anyone who wants to think clearly on this subject. In the same vein are:
   a. Hutchins' Aquinas Lecture, *St. Thomas and the World State*.
   b. Maritain, *Man and the State*, ch. I, II, VII.
4. The following books are useful:
   a. MacLean, *Dynamic World Order*, ch. XIX, XX.
   b. Sturzo, *Nationalism and Internationalism*, ch. 8, 9.
   c. Rommen, *The State in Catholic Thought*, ch. XXXI, XXXII.
   d. Haas, *Man and Society*, ch. 19.
   e. Dawson, *Judgment of the Nations*, ch. 6.
   f. Ebenstein, *Modern Political Thought*, reprints some provocative articles from prominent writers on the passage from nationalism to world order.

BIBLIOGRAPHY

Works of the classical philosophers who developed the ethical tradition followed in this text:

Plato, *The Dialogues of Plato,* translated by B. Jowett, 5 vols., Oxford University Press, 1892.
> Convenient reprint, omitting analyses and notes, in 2 vols., New York, Random House, 1937. Other translations and editions.

Aristotle, *Nicomachean Ethics, Politics.* In *The Works of Aristotle Translated into English,* edited by W. D. Ross, 12 vols., Oxford, Clarendon Press, 1921-1952.
> Convenient edition by Richard McKeon, *The Basic Works of Aristotle,* New York, Random House, 1941. Other translations and editions.

Cicero, *Tusculan Disputations, De Finibus, De Officiis, De Re Publica, De Legibus, Academica, Paradoxa Stoicorum.*
> Latin text and English translation in several volumes of the Loeb Classical Library, Cambridge, Mass., Harvard University Press.
> Other translations and editions.
> Cicero's philosophy is eclectic with a preference for Stoicism, but he helped to develop the natural law tradition.

St. Augustine, *De Civitate Dei* (The City of God), *De Libero Arbitrio* (On Free Will), *Contra Faustum Manichaeum* (Against Faustus the Manichean), *Quaestiones in Heptateuchum* (Questions on the Heptateuch), *De Mendacio* (On Lying), *Contra Mendacium* (Against Lying), *De Magistro* (On the Teacher).
> *The City of God,* translated by Marcus Dods, Edinburgh, T. & T. Clark, 1878. Older translation by John Healey, Everyman's Library, New York, Dutton, 1945.
> *De Libero Arbitrio* and *De Magistro* in Ancient Christian Writers series, Westminster, Md., Newman, 1950, 1955.
> *De Mendacio* and *Contra Mendacium* in *St. Augustine, Treatises on Various Subjects,* New York, Fathers of the Church, Inc., 1952.
> *Works of Aurelius Augustine,* 15 vols., Edinburgh, T. & T. Clark, 1876.

Boethius, *The Consolation of Philosophy,* translated by H. F. Stewart and E. K. Rand, Loeb Classical Library, Cambridge, Mass., Harvard University Press, 1936. Contains also *De Duabus Naturis.*

Abelard, Peter, *Ethics,* translated by J. R. McCallum, Oxford, Blackwell, 1935.
> Partial translation in Rand's *Classical Moralists.*
> Abelard calls attention to the function of conscience, but his teaching is incomplete and obscure.

481

St. Thomas Aquinas, *Summa Theologica, Summa Contra Gentiles, In X Libros Ethicorum, De Veritate, De Magistro, De Regimine Principum.*
  Summa Theologica, 22 vols. and *Summa Contra Gentiles,* 5 vols., translated by the English Dominican Fathers, New York, Benziger, 1911-1929.
  Three-volume edition of the *Summa Theologica,* New York, Benziger, 1947.
  Pegis, Anton, *Basic Writings of St. Thomas Aquinas,* 2 vols., New York, Random House, 1945.
  Pegis, Anton, *Introduction to St. Thomas Aquinas,* New York, Modern Library, 1948.
  Truth, English translation of *De Veritate,* 3 vols., Chicago, Regnery, 1953.
  On the Governance of Rulers, translation of *De Regimine Principum* by Gerald B. Phelan, New York, Sheed & Ward, 1938. Another edition entitled *On Kingship,* Toronto, Pontifical Institute of Mediaeval Studies, 1949. Another translation in d'Entrèves, *Aquinas, Selected Political Writings,* Oxford, Blackwell, 1954.
  Mayer, Mary Ellen, *The Philosophy of Teaching of St. Thomas Aquinas,* containing a translation of *De Magistro,* Milwaukee, Bruce, 1929.
  Conway, Pierre, *St. Thomas Aquinas on Aristotle's Love and Friendship,* translation of books VIII and IX of St. Thomas' *Commentary on Aristotle's Ethics,* Providence, R. I., Providence College Press, 1951.
Scotus, John Duns, *Commentaria Oxoniensia,* Quaracchi, 1912-1914.
  No English translation available.
Ockham, William of, *Super Quattuor Libros Sententiarum,* Lyons, 1495.
  No English translation available.
  Ockham belonged in general to the Scholastic tradition, but contributed more to its breakdown than to its development.
Cajetan, Thomas de Vio, *Commentaria* (Commentaries on the *Summa Theologica* of St. Thomas). Not in English; Latin text in the Leonine Edition of St. Thomas' works.
Vitoria, Francisco de, *De Indis* (On the Indians), *De Jure Belli* (On the Right of War), translated in J. B. Scott, *The Spanish Origin of International Law: Francisco de Vitoria and His Law of Nations,* Oxford, Clarendon Press, 1934.
Bellarmine, St. Robert, *De Laicis* (On the Laity). The part on civil government (part III) is found in *De Laicis, or the Treatise on Civil Government,* translated by K. Murphy, New York, Fordham University Press, 1928.
Suarez, Francisco, *De Legibus ac de Deo Legislatore* (On Laws and on God the Lawgiver), *Defensio Fidei Catholicae* (Defense of the Catholic Faith), *De Virtutibus Theologicis* (On the Theological Virtues, especially the third part, *De Caritate,* on charity).
  Translation of the important sections in J. B. Scott, *The Classics of International Law: Selections from Three Works of Francisco Suarez,* Oxford, Clarendon Press, 1944.
De Lugo, John, *De Justitia et Jure* (On Justice and Right), Venice, N. Pezzana, 1751.
  No English translation available.

Classical philosophers and moralists, ancient and modern, of various schools of thought. The list is roughly chronological and not at all exhaustive, containing only those referred to in the text. Some of them are to be read only with critical discrimination.

The *Bhagavadgita,* translated by Sir Edwin Arnold, Philadelphia, McKay, 1934.
  Another translation by Franklin Edgerton, Cambridge, Mass., Harvard University Press, 1944.

The *Dhammapada* and other Buddhist writings in Max Müller (editor), *The Sacred Books of the East,* vol. XII, New York, Scribner, 1901.

Lucretius, *On the Nature of Things,* translated by Cyril Bailey, Oxford, Clarendon Press, 1910.

Epictetus, *Discourses,* translated by T. W. Higginson, 2 vols., Boston, Little, Brown, 1891.

Marcus Aurelius, *Meditations,* translated by G. Long, New York, Burt, n.d.

Diogenes Laertius, *Lives and Opinions of Eminent Philosophers,* 2 vols., Loeb Classical Library, Cambridge, Mass., Harvard University Press, 1925.

Bodin, Jean, *De la république.* An old translation, *The Six Bookes of a Commonweale Written by J. Bodin,* done into English by Richard Knolles, London, G. Bishop, 1606. An abridged translation by M. J. Tooley, New York, Macmillan, 1955.

James I, *The Political Works of James I,* edited by Charles McIlwain, Cambridge, Mass., Harvard University Press, 1918.

Descartes, René, *Meditations, Objections and Replies.* In *Descartes Selections,* edited by Ralph M. Eaton, New York, Scribner, 1927.

Hobbes, Thomas, *Leviathan,* Oxford, Clarendon Press, 1909.

Spinoza, Baruch, *Ethics,* in *Philosophy of Spinoza,* translated by R. H. M. Elwes, New York, Tudor, n.d.
Theologico-Political Treatise and *Political Treatise,* in *Chief Works of Spinoza,* translated by R. H. M. Elwes, New York, Dover Publications, 1951.

Grotius, Hugo, *The Rights of War and Peace,* New York, Universal Classics Library, M. Walter Dunne, publisher, 1901.

Pufendorf, Samuel, *The Elements of Universal Jurisprudence,* English translation of *Elementa Jurisprudentiae Universalis,* Oxford, Clarendon Press, 1931.
De Jure Naturae et Gentium, translated by C. H. and W. A. Oldfather, New York, Oxford University Press, 1934.

Locke, John, *Two Treatises of Government,* New York, Hafner, 1947 (containing Sir Robert Filmer's *Patriarcha*).
Treatise of Civil Government and a Letter Concerning Toleration, New York, Appleton-Century, 1937.

Mandeville, Bernard de, *An Inquiry into the Origin of Moral Virtue,* in *The Fable of the Bees, etc.,* London, 1723.
Selections in Rand's *Classical Moralists,* Boston, Houghton Mifflin, 1909.

Shaftesbury, Anthony, Earl of, *Characteristics of Men, Manners, Opinions, and Times,* London, 1711. Selections in Rand.

Hutcheson, Francis, *An Inquiry into the Original of Our Ideas of Beauty and Virtue,* London, 1725. Selections in Rand.

Butler, Joseph, *Fifteen Sermons upon Human Nature,* London, 1726. Selections in Rand.

Hume, David, *Treatise of Human Nature,* edited by L. A. Selby-Bigge, Oxford, Clarendon Press, 1888.

Smith, Adam, *The Theory of Moral Sentiments,* in H. W. Schneider, *Smith's Moral and Political Philosophy,* New York, Hafner, 1948.

Reid, Thomas, *Essays on the Active Powers of Man,* Edinburgh, 1788. Selections in Rand.

Wilson, James, *Works,* 2 vols., Chicago, Callaghan, 1896. Also in R. G. Adams, *Selected Political Essays of James Wilson,* New York, Knopf, 1930.

Rousseau, Jean Jacques, *The Social Contract,* New York, Hafner, 1947. Also in *Famous Utopias,* New York, Tudor Publishing Co., n.d.

Kant, Immanuel, *Foundations of the Metaphysics of Morals, Critique of Practical Reason, Perpetual Peace, The Metaphysic of Morals, Religion Within the Limits of Reason Alone.* The first three in L. W. Beck, *Kant: Critique of Practical Reason,* Chicago, University of Chicago Press, 1949. The first two in T. K.

Abbott, *Kant's Theory of Ethics,* London, Longmans, Green, 1883. The first alone in H. J. Paton, *The Moral Law,* London, Hutchinson House, 1948.

Philosophy of Law (first part of Kant's *Metaphysic of Morals*), translated by W. Hastie, Edinburgh, T. & T. Clark, 1887.

Religion Within the Limits of Reason Alone, translated by Greene and Hudson, Chicago, Open Court, 1934.

Fichte, Johann Gottlieb, *The Science of Ethics as Based on the Science of Knowledge,* London, Kegan Paul, Trench, Trübner, 1897.

Hegel, Georg W. F., *Logic, Philosophy of Right.* The *Logic* in *The Logic of Hegel,* translated by William Wallace, Oxford University Press, 1892.

Philosophy of Right, translated by T. M. Knox, Oxford, Clarendon Press, 1949.

Schopenhauer, Arthur, *The World as Will and Idea,* translated by Haldane and Kemp, 3 vols., London, Trübner, 1883-1886.

Comte, Auguste, *The Positive Philosophy of Auguste Comte,* translated and condensed by Harriet Martineau, 2 vols., London, Trübner, n.d.

Bentham, Jeremy, *An Introduction to the Principles of Morals and Legislation,* London, W. Pickering, 1823.

Mill, John Stuart, *Utilitarianism,* Everyman's Library, New York, Dutton, 1931.

On Liberty; Representative Government, edited by R. B. McCallum, Oxford, Blackwell, 1946.

Spencer, Herbert, *The Principles of Ethics,* 2 vols., New York, Appleton, 1896.

The first part also published separately as *The Data of Ethics.*

Sidgwick, Henry, *The Methods of Ethics,* London, Macmillan, 1901.

Outlines of the History of Ethics for English Readers, London, Macmillan, 1886.

Kierkegaard, Søren, *Fear and Trembling* and *Sickness unto Death,* Princeton, Princeton University Press, 1941.

Nietzsche, Friedrich, *The Genealogy of Morals,* translated by H. Samuel, Edinburgh, T. N. Foulis, 1913.

Paulsen, Friedrich, *System of Ethics,* translated by Frank Thilly, New York, Scribner, 1899.

Green, Thomas Hill, *Prolegomena to Ethics,* Oxford, Clarendon Press, 1883.

Bradley, Francis Herbert, *Ethical Studies,* London, H. S. King, 1876.

Marx and Engels, *Communist Manifesto,* New York, International Publishers, n.d.

There are several editions of *Selected Works of Marx and Engels,* New York, International Publishers.

Marx, Karl, *Capital,* 3 vols., Chicago, Kerr, 1907.

Contribution to the Critique of Political Economy, New York, International Publishers, 1904.

Engels, Friedrich, *Herr Eugen Dühring's Revolution in Science* (commonly referred to as *Anti-Dühring*), Chicago, Kerr, 1907.

Ludwig Feuerbach, New York, International Publishers, 1934.

Origin of the Family, Private Property, and the State, Chicago, Kerr, 1902.

Lenin, V. I., *Materialism and Empirio-Criticism,* New York, International Publishers, 1927.

Stalin, Joseph, *Leninism,* New York, International Publishers, 1942.

Dialectical and Historical Materialism, New York, International Publishers, 1940.

Holmes, Oliver Wendell, *Collected Legal Papers,* New York, Harcourt, Brace, 1920.

Dewey, John, *Human Nature and Conduct,* New York, Holt, 1922.

The Quest for Certainty, New York, Minton-Balch, 1929.

Theory of Valuation, Chicago, University of Chicago Press, 1939.

Russell, Bertrand, *Mysticism and Logic,* New York, Longmans, Green, 1918.

Moore, G. E., *Principia Ethica,* Cambridge, Cambridge University Press, 1903.

Ethics, New York, Oxford University Press, 1912.

Perry, Ralph Barton, *General Theory of Value,* Cambridge, Harvard University Press, 1926.

Realms of Value, Cambridge, Harvard University Press, 1954.

Ross, W. D., *The Right and the Good,* Oxford, Clarendon Press, 1930.

Ewing, A. C., *The Definition of Good,* New York, Macmillan, 1947.

Ewing, A. C., *Ethics,* London, English Universities Press, 1953.

Ayer, A. J., *Language, Truth and Logic,* London, Gollancz, 1950.

Stevenson, C. L., *Ethics and Language,* New Haven, Yale University Press, 1946.

Lepley, Ray, *Value, a Cooperative Inquiry,* New York, Columbia University Press, 1949.

> *The Language of Value,* New York, Columbia University Press, 1957.

Sartre, Jean Paul, *On Being and Nothingness,* New York, Philosophical Library, 1956.

> *Existentialism,* New York, Philosophical Library, 1947.

Camus, Albert, *The Myth of Sisyphus,* New York, Knopf, 1957.

Marcel, Gabriel, *The Philosophy of Existence,* London, Harvill Press, 1948.

The following compilations and books of selected readings give convenient access to the sources:

Albert, Denise, and Peterfreund, *Great Traditions in Ethics,* New York, American Book Co., 1953.

Anshen, Ruth Nanda, *Moral Principles of Action,* New York, Harper, 1952.

Brubacher, John S., *Eclectic Philosophy of Education, a Book of Readings,* Englewood Cliffs, N. J., Prentice-Hall, 1951.

Burns, Emile, *Handbook of Marxism,* New York, International Publishers, 1935.

Burtt, Edwin, *The English Philosophers from Bacon to Mill,* New York, Modern Library, 1939.

Clark and Smith, *Readings in Ethics,* New York, Crofts, 1935.

Cummins and Linscott, *The World's Great Thinkers,* 4 vols., New York, Random House, 1947.

Ebenstein, William, *Modern Political Thought,* New York, Rinehart, 1954.

Husslein, Joseph, *Social Wellsprings,* 2 vols., Milwaukee, Bruce, 1940 (Encyclicals of Popes Leo XIII and Pius XI).

Jarrett and McMurrin, *Contemporary Philosophy,* New York, Holt, 1954.

Johnson, Oliver, *Ethics, a Source Book,* New York, Dryden, 1958.

Leibell, J. F., *Readings in Ethics,* Chicago, Loyola University Press, 1926.

Lin Yutang, *The Wisdom of China and India,* New York, Random House, 1942.

McKeon, Richard, *Basic Works of Aristotle,* New York, Random House, 1941.

Maritain, Jacques, *The Social and Political Writings of Jacques Maritain* (selected writings), New York, Scribner, 1955.

Melden, A. I., *Ethical Theories, a Book of Readings,* 2nd ed., Englewood Cliffs, N. J., Prentice-Hall, 1955.

Oates, W. J., *Basic Writings of St. Augustine,* 2 vols., New York, Random House, 1948.

Oates, W. J., *The Stoic and Epicurean Philosophers,* New York, Random House, 1940.

Pegis, Anton, *Basic Writings of St. Thomas Aquinas,* 2 vols., New York, Random House, 1945. Selections from this in *Introduction to St. Thomas Aquinas,* New York, Modern Library, 1948.

Rand, Benjamin, *The Classical Moralists,* Boston, Houghton Mifflin, 1909.

Rickaby, Joseph, *Aquinas Ethicus,* 2 vols., London, Burns, Oates & Washbourne, 1892.

Rickaby, Joseph, *Of God and His Creatures,* St. Louis, Herder, 1905 (selected translations from St. Thomas' *Summa Contra Gentiles*).

Sellars and Hospers, *Readings in Ethical Theory,* New York, Appleton-Century-Crofts, 1952.

Famous Utopias, New York, Tudor Publishing Co., n.d. (More, Rousseau, Bacon, Campanella).

Modern books on ethics or on ethical problems, primarily philosophical in character or at least dealing with a broad application of moral principles, and written from the Aristotelian-Thomistic point of view:

Adler, Mortimer, *A Dialectic of Morals,* Notre Dame, Indiana, The Review of Politics, 1941.

Bourke, Vernon, *Ethics,* New York, Macmillan, 1951.

Bourke, Vernon, *St. Thomas and the Greek Moralists,* Aquinas Lecture, Milwaukee, Marquette University Press, 1947.

Brennan, Sister Rose Emmanuella, *The Intellectual Virtues According to the Philosophy of St. Thomas,* Washington, D. C., Catholic University Press, 1941. Reprinted: Pacific Books, Palo Alto, Calif.

Brosnahan, Timothy, *Prolegomena to Ethics,* New York, Fordham University Press, 1941.

Bruehl, Charles, *This Way Happiness,* Milwaukee, Bruce, 1941.

Buckley, Joseph, *Man's Last End,* St. Louis, Herder, 1950.

Collins, James, *The Existentialists,* Chicago, Regnery, 1952.

Connell, Francis, *Morals in Politics and Professions,* Westminster, Md., Newman Bookshop, 1946.

Cronin, Michael, *The Science of Ethics,* 2 vols., New York, Benziger, 1922.

D'Arcy, Martin, *Christian Morals,* London, Longmans, Green, 1937.

Davitt, Thomas, *The Nature of Law,* St. Louis, Herder, 1951.

DeFinance, Joseph, *Ethica Generalis,* Rome, Gregorian University, 1959.

D'Entrèves, A. P., *Natural Law,* London, Hutchinson House, 1951.

Deploige, Simon, *The Conflict Between Ethics and Sociology,* St. Louis, Herder, 1938.

Doolan, Aegidius, *Order and Law,* Westminster, Md., Newman, 1954.

Farrell, Walter, *Companion to the Summa,* 4 vols., New York, Sheed & Ward, 1938. Volumes II and III on ethical subjects.

Gilson, Étienne, *Moral Values and Moral Life,* translated by Leo Ward, St. Louis, Herder, 1931.

Gilson, Étienne, *The Christian Philosophy of St. Thomas Aquinas,* New York, Random House, 1956.

Gilson, Étienne, *The Spirit of Mediaeval Philosophy,* New York, Scribner, 1936.

Hawkins, D. J. B., *Man and Morals,* London and New York, Sheed and Ward, 1960.

Hettinger, Franz, *Natural Religion,* New York, Pustet, 1890.

Higgins, Thomas, *Man as Man,* Milwaukee, Bruce, 1958.

Hildebrand, Dietrich von, *Christian Ethics,* New York, McKay, 1953.

Hildebrand, Dietrich von, *Fundamental Moral Attitudes,* New York, Longmans, Green, 1950.

Hildebrand, Dietrich von, *True Morality and Its Counterfeits,* New York, McKay, 1955.

Jaffa, Harry V., *Thomism and Aristotelianism,* Chicago, University of Chicago Press, 1952.

Klubertanz, George, *Philosophy of Human Nature,* New York, Appleton-Century-Crofts, 1953.

Maritain, Jacques, *Essay on Christian Philosophy,* New York, Philosophical Library, 1955.

Maritain, Jacques, *Freedom in the Modern World,* New York, Scribner, 1936.

Maritain, Jacques, *Man and the State,* Chicago, University of Chicago Press, 1951.

Maritain, Jacques, *The Person and the Common Good,* New York, Scribner, 1947.

Maritain, Jacques, *The Range of Reason,* New York, Scribner, 1942.

Maritain, Jacques, *The Rights of Man and the Natural Law,* New York, Scribner, 1943.

Maritain, Jacques, *Scholasticism and Politics,* New York, Macmillan, 1940.

Maritain, Jacques, *Science and Wisdom,* New York, Scribner, 1940.

Maritain, Jacques, *True Humanism,* New York, Scribner, 1938.

McGillivray, G. J., *Moral Principles and Practice,* New York, Sheed & Ward, 1933.

Messner, Johannes, *Social Ethics,* St. Louis, Herder, 1949.

Messner, Johannes, *Ethics and Facts,* St. Louis, Herder, 1952.

O'Connor, William R., *The Eternal Quest,* New York, Longmans, Green, 1947.

O'Connor, William R., *The Natural Desire for God,* Aquinas Lecture, Milwaukee, Marquette University Press, 1948.

Pieper, Josef, *Justice,* New York, Pantheon Books, 1955.

Pieper, Josef, *Fortitude and Temperance,* New York, Pantheon Books, 1954.

Pieper, Josef, *Prudence,* New York, Pantheon Books, 1956.

Regan, Robert, *Professional Secrecy in the Light of Moral Principles,* Washington, D. C., Augustinian Press, 1943.

Reinhardt, Kurt, *The Existentialist Revolt,* Milwaukee, Bruce, 1952.

Rickaby, Joseph, *Moral Philosophy,* Stonyhurst Series, London, Longmans, Green, 1910.

Rommen, Heinrich, *The Natural Law,* St. Louis, Herder, 1948.

Sheed, Frank J., *Society and Sanity,* New York, Sheed & Ward, 1953.

Simon, Yves, *The Nature and Functions of Authority,* Aquinas Lecture, Milwaukee, Marquette University Press, 1940.

Simon, Yves, *Critique de la Connaissance Morale,* Paris, Desclée de Brouwer, 1934.

Sutherland, Halliday, *The Laws of Life,* New York, Sheed & Ward, 1936.

Vann, Gerald, *Morals and Man,* New York, Sheed & Ward, 1960.

Ward, Leo, *Christian Ethics,* St. Louis, Herder, 1952.

Ward, Leo, *Philosophy of Value,* New York, Macmillan, 1930.

Ward, Leo, *Values and Reality,* New York, Sheed & Ward, 1935.

Wild, John, *Introduction to Realistic Philosophy,* New York, Harper, 1948.

Wild, John, *Plato's Modern Enemies and the Theory of Natural Law,* Chicago, University of Chicago Press, 1953.

Books useful for the study of applied ethics, but primarily economic, sociological, political, historical, legal, medical, or theological. On what points these works are useful has been indicated in the reading lists appended to each chapter. It will be convenient to distribute this section into several subdivisions.

1. Legal Ethics: Rights, Law, Justice

Gerhart, Eugene C., *American Liberty and "Natural Law,"* Boston, Beacon Press, 1953.

Haines, Charles G., *Revival of Natural Law Concepts,* Cambridge, Mass., Harvard University Press, 1930.

Harding, Arthur L. (ed.), *Natural Law and Natural Rights,* Dallas, Southern Methodist Press, 1955.

Kelsen, Hans, *What is Justice?* Berkeley, University of California Press, 1957. (Collected essays.)

Le Buffe and Hayes, *The American Philosophy of Law,* New York, Jesuit Educational Association, 1953.

McKinnon, Harold, *The Higher Law,* Berkeley, Calif., Gillick, 1946; reprinted in the *American Bar Association Journal,* February, 1947.

Ritchie, David G., *Natural Rights,* London, Allen & Unwin, 1894; reprinted 1952.

St. John-Stevas, Norman, *Life, Death, and the Law,* Bloomington, Indiana University Press, 1961.

Strauss, Leo, *Natural Rights and History,* Chicago, University of Chicago Press, 1953.

Human Rights, a symposium edited by Unesco, London, Wingate, n.d.

2. Medical Ethics: Life, Health

Bouscaren, T. L., *The Ethics of Ectopic Operations,* Milwaukee, Bruce, 1944.

Cunningham, Bert, *Morality of Organic Transplantation,* Washington, Catholic University Press, 1944.

Ficarra, Bernard, *Newer Ethical Problems in Medicine and Surgery,* Westminster, Md., Newman, 1951.

Flood, Peter (ed.), *New Problems in Medical Ethics,* 2 vols., Westminster, Md., Newman, 1953.

Flood, Peter (ed.), *Medical Experimentation on Man,* Chicago, Regnery, 1955.

Flood, Peter (ed.), *The Ethics of Brain Surgery,* Chicago, Regnery, 1955.

Good and Kelly, *Marriage, Morals and Medical Ethics,* New York, Kenedy, 1951.

Healy, Edwin, *Medical Ethics,* Chicago, Loyola University Press, 1956.

Kelly, Gerald, *Medico-Moral Problems,* St. Louis, Catholic Hospital Association, 1958.

Kenny, John P., *Principles of Medical Ethics,* Westminster, Md., Newman, 1952.

Lehane, Joseph, *Morality of American Civil Legislation Concerning Eugenical Sterilization,* Washington, Catholic University Press, 1944.

McFadden, Charles, *Medical Ethics,* revised, Philadelphia, F. A. Davis, 1949.

O'Donnell, Thomas, *Morals in Medicine,* Westminster, Md., Newman Press, 1956.

Schmiedeler, Edgar, *Sterilization in the United States,* Washington, National Catholic Welfare Conference, 1943.

Sullivan, Joseph V., *The Morality of Mercy Killing,* Westminster, Md., Newman Press, 1950.

3. Sociological Ethics: Society, Community

Casserley, J. V. Langmead, *The Bent World,* New York, Oxford University Press, 1955.

Durkheim, Émile, *Suicide,* Glencoe, Ill., Free Press, 1951.

Haas, Francis, *Man and Society,* 2nd edition, New York, Appleton-Century-Crofts, 1952.

Jünger, Friedrich, *The Failure of Technology,* Chicago, Regnery, 1956.

Lippmann, Walter, *The Good Society,* Boston, Little, Brown, 1937.

Marcel, Gabriel, *The Decline of Wisdom,* New York, Philosophical Library, 1955.

Marcel, Gabriel, *Man Against Mass Society,* Chicago, Regnery, 1952.

McKenny, Charles, *Moral Problems in Social Work,* Milwaukee, Bruce, 1951.

Niebuhr, Reinhold, *Moral Man and Immoral Society,* New York, Scribner, 1949.

Osgniach, Augustine, *Must it be Communism?* New York, Wagner, 1950.

Sorokin, Pitirim, *The Crisis of Our Age,* New York, Dutton, 1941.

4. Domestic Ethics: Marriage and the Family

Clemens, Alphonse, *Marriage and the Family,* Englewood Cliffs, N. J., Prentice-Hall, 1957.

De Guchteneere, R., *Judgment on Birth Control,* New York, Macmillan, 1931.

Foerster, F. W., *Marriage and the Sex Problem,* New York, Stokes, 1912.

Gerrard, Thomas, *Marriage and Parenthood,* New York, Wagner, 1937.

Handren, Walter, *No Longer Two,* commentary on "Casti Connubii," Westminster, Md., Newman, 1955.

Healy, Edwin, *Marriage Guidance,* Chicago, Loyola University Press, 1949.

Hildebrand, Dietrich von, *In Defense of Purity,* New York, Sheed & Ward, 1938.

Hildebrand, Dietrich von, *Marriage,* New York, Longmans, Green, 1942.

Hope, Wingfield, *Life Together,* New York, Sheed & Ward, 1944.
Joyce, George, *Christian Marriage,* London, Sheed & Ward, 1948.
Leclercq, Jacques, *Marriage and the Family,* New York, Pustet, 1942.
Magner, James, *The Art of Happy Marriage,* Milwaukee, Bruce, 1947.
Mihanovich, Schnepp, Thomas, *Marriage and the Family,* Milwaukee, Bruce, 1952.
Moore, Edward, *The Case Against Birth Control,* New York, Appleton-Century, 1931.
Morrison, Robert, *God Is Its Founder,* Milwaukee, Bruce, 1946.
Schmiedeler, Edgar, *Marriage and the Family,* New York, McGraw-Hill, 1946.
Thibon, Gustave, *What God has Joined Together,* Chicago, Regnery, 1952.
Thomas, John L., *Marriage and Rhythm,* Westminster, Md., Newman Press, 1957.
Wayne, T. G., *Morals and Marriage,* New York, Longmans, Green, 1936.

5. Political Ethics: The State, Government

Adler and Farrell, *The Theory of Democracy,* in the *Thomist,* vols. III, IV, VI, VII (1941-1944).
Cahill, Edward, *The Framework of the Christian State,* Dublin, Gill, 1932.
Catlin, George, *The Story of Political Philosophers,* New York, McGraw-Hill, 1939.
Douglas, Paul H., *Ethics in Government,* Cambridge, Mass., Harvard University Press, 1952.
Figgis, John, *The Divine Right of Kings,* Cambridge University Press, 1914.
Graham, George A., *Morality in American Politics,* New York, Random House, 1952.
Lippmann, Walter, *The Public Philosophy,* Boston, Little, Brown, 1955.
Murray, John Courtney, *We Hold These Truths,* New York, Sheed & Ward, 1960.
Newman, Jeremiah, *Studies in Political Morality,* Dublin, Scepter, 1962.
Rommen, Heinrich, *The State in Catholic Thought,* St. Louis, Herder, 1945.
Simon, Yves, *Philosophy of Democratic Government,* Chicago, University of Chicago Press, 1951.

6. Educational Ethics: Education, Schools

Brameld, Theodore, *Towards a Reconstructed Philosophy of Education,* New York, Dryden, 1956.
Brubacher, John S., *Modern Philosophies of Education,* New York, McGraw-Hill, 1950.
Dewey, John, *Democracy and Education,* New York, Macmillan, 1916.
Kirk, Russell, *Academic Freedom,* Chicago, Regnery, 1955.
MacIver, Robert, *Academic Freedom in Our Time,* New York, Columbia University Press, 1955.
Redden and Ryan, *A Catholic Philosophy of Education,* Milwaukee, Bruce, 1942.

7. Economic Ethics: Property, Business

Belloc, Hilaire, *The Restoration of Property, New York,* Sheed & Ward, 1936.
Belloc, Hilaire, *The Servile State,* London, T. N. Foulis, 1912.
Bunting, J. Whitney, *Ethics for Modern Business Practice,* New York, Prentice-Hall, 1953.
Casselman, Paul, *The Cooperative Movement,* New York, Philosophical Library, 1952.
Chesterton, G. K., *What's Wrong With the World,* New York, Dodd Mead, 1910.
Flubacher, Joseph, *The Concept of Ethics in the History of Economics,* New York, Vantage Press, 1950.
Gill, Eric, *Money and Morals,* London, Faber & Faber, 1937.
Hartman, R. S. (ed.), *Profit Sharing Manual,* Columbus, Ohio, Council of Profit Sharing Industries, 1948.
Hewes, Thomas, *Decentralize for Liberty,* New York, Dutton, 1947.

Johnston, Herbert, *Business Ethics,* New York, Pitman, 1956.

Kelso and Adler, *The Capitalist Manifesto,* New York, Random House, 1958.

Merrill, Harwood, *Responsibilities of Business Leadership,* Cambridge, Mass., Harvard University Press, 1948.

Mulcahy, Richard, *Economics of Heinrich Pesch,* New York, Holt, 1952.

Ross, J. Elliot, *Cooperative Plenty,* St. Louis, Herder, 1941.

Thompson, K. M., *Profit Sharing,* New York, Harper, 1949.

Warbasse, J. P., *Cooperative Democracy,* New York, Harper, 1942.

8. Industrial Ethics: Management, Labor

Bruehl, Charles, *The Pope's Plan for Social Reconstruction,* New York, Devin-Adair, 1939.

Callahan, John D., *The Catholic Attitude Toward a Familial Minimum Wage,* Washington, D. C., Catholic University Press, 1936.

Cronin, John F., *Catholic Social Principles,* Milwaukee, Bruce, 1950.

Drummond, William, *Social Justice,* Milwaukee, Bruce, 1955.

Ferree, William, *The Act of Social Justice,* Washington, D. C., Catholic University Press, 1942.

Hughes, Philip, *The Pope's New Order,* New York, Macmillan, 1944.

Husslein, Joseph, *The Christian Social Manifesto,* Milwaukee, Bruce, 1936.

McLean, Donald, *Morality of the Strike,* New York, Kenedy, 1921.

Miller, Raymond, *Forty Years After: Pius XI on the Social Order,* St. Paul, Radio Replies Press, 1948.

Munier, J. D., *Some Approximations to Pius X's "Industries and Professions,"* Washington, Catholic University Press, 1943.

Naughton, James, *Pius XII on World Problems,* New York, American Press, 1943.

Nell-Breuning, Oswald von, *Reconstruction of Social Economy,* Milwaukee, Bruce, 1936.

Ryan, John A., *Distributive Justice,* New York, Macmillan, 1942.

Smith, William J., *Spotlight on Labor Unions,* New York, Duell, Sloan & Pearce, 1946.

Smith, William J., *Spotlight on Social Order,* Rochester, N. Y., Christopher Press, 1953.

Tannenbaum, Frank, *A Philosophy of Labor,* New York, Knopf, 1951.

Toner, Jerome, *The Closed Shop,* Washington, D. C., American Council on Public Affairs, 1944.

9. Marxian Ethics: Communism, Socialism

Berdyaev, Nicholas, *The Origin of Russian Communism,* London, Bles, 1937.

Bober, M. M., *Karl Marx's Interpretation of History,* Cambridge, Mass., Harvard University Press, 1948.

Böhm-Bawerk, Eugen von, *Karl Marx and the Close of His System,* New York, A. M. Kelley, 1949.

Cameron, J. M., *Scrutiny of Marxism,* New York, Macmillan, 1948.

Cole, G. D. H., *Meaning of Marxism,* London, Gollancz, 1948.

Cornforth, Maurice, *Dialectical Materialism, Introductory Course,* London, Lawrence & Wishart, 1952.

Croce, Benedetto, *Historical Materialism and the Economics of Marx,* New York, Macmillan, 1914.

Crossman, R. H. S. (ed.), *The God That Failed,* New York, Harper, 1949.

D'Arcy, Martin, *Communism and Christianity,* New York, Devin-Adair, 1957.

Federn, Karl, *Materialist Conception of History,* London, Macmillan, 1939.

Guest, David, *Textbook of Dialectical Materialism,* New York, International Publishers, 1939.

Gurian, Waldemar (ed.), *The Soviet Union, Background, Ideology, and Reality,* Notre Dame, University of Notre Dame Press, 1951.

Hook, Sidney, *Toward the Understanding of Karl Marx,* New York, John Day, 1933.

Hook, Sidney, *From Hegel to Marx, New York,* Humanities Press, 1950.

Hunt, R. N. Carew, *Marxism Past and Present,* New York, Macmillan, 1955.

Hunt, R. N. Carew, *Theory and Practice of Communism,* New York, Macmillan, 1951.

Hyde, Douglas, *The Answer to Communism,* London, Paternoster Publications, 1949.

Hyde, Douglas, *I Believed,* New York, Putnam, 1950.

Joseph, H., *The Labor Theory of Value in Karl Marx,* London, Oxford University Press, 1923.

Kautsky, Karl, *Ethics and the Materialist Conception of History,* Chicago, Kerr, 1907.

Lindsay, A., *Karl Marx's "Capital,"* London, Oxford University Press, 1925.

Macmurray, John, *Philosophy of Communism,* London, Faber & Faber, 1933.

Marcuse, Herbert, *Reason and Revolution: Hegel and the Rise of Social Theory,* New York, Humanities Press, 1954.

Mauriac and others (symposium), *Communism and Christians,* Westminster, Md., Newman Press, 1949.

Mayo, H. B., *Democracy and Marxism,* New York, Oxford University Press, 1955.

McFadden, Charles, *The Philosophy of Communism,* New York, Benziger, 1939.

Possony, Stefan, *A Century of Conflict: Communist Techniques of World Revolution,* Chicago, Regnery, 1953.

Schumpeter, Joseph, *Capitalism, Socialism, and Democracy,* New York, Harpers, 1950.

Selsam, Howard, *Socialism and Ethics,* London, Lawrence, 1949.

Shaw, George Bernard, and others, *Essays in Fabian Socialism,* London, Constable, 1932.

Sheed, Frank, *Communism and Man,* New York, Sheed & Ward, 1939.

Somerville, J., *Soviet Philosophy,* New York, Philosophical Library, 1946.

Sweezy, Paul, *Socialism,* New York, McGraw-Hill, 1949.

Von Mises, Ludwig, *Socialism,* New Haven, Yale University Press, 1951.

Wetter, G., *Dialectical Materialism,* New York, Praeger, 1958.

10. International Ethics: World Community, War, Peace

Adler, Mortimer, *How to Think About War and Peace,* New York, Simon & Schuster, 1944.

Batchelder, Robert, *The Irreversible Decision,* Boston, Houghton Mifflin, 1962.

Bennett, John, *Christians and the State,* New York, Scribner, 1958.

Dawson, Christopher, *Judgment of the Nations,* New York, Sheed & Ward, 1942.

Eppstein, John, *The Catholic Tradition and the Law of Nations,* Washington, D. C., Catholic Association for International Peace, 1935.

Eppstein, John, *Code of International Ethics,* Westminster, Md., Newman, 1953.

Gandhi, M. K., *Non-Violence in Peace and War,* 2 vols., Ahmedabad, Navaijan Publishing Company, 1942-1948.

Gigon, H., *The Ethics of Peace and War,* London, Burns, Oates & Washbourne, 1935.

Gonella, Guido, *A World to Reconstruct,* Milwaukee, Bruce, 1944.

Hodgson, Peter, *Nuclear Physics in Peace and War,* New York, Hawthorn Books, 1961.

Hunter, Edward, *Brainwashing,* New York, Farrar, Straus & Cudahy, 1956.

Hutchins, Robert M., *St. Thomas and the World State,* Aquinas Lecture, Milwaukee, Marquette University Press, 1949.

Kahn, Herman, *On Thermonuclear War,* Princeton, Princeton University Press, 1961.

MacLean, Donald, *Dynamic World Order,* Milwaukee, Bruce, 1945.

Murray, Thomas E., *Nuclear Policy for War and Peace,* Cleveland, World Publishing Company, 1960.

Nagle, William, *Morality and Modern Warfare,* Baltimore, Helicon Press, 1960.

Ramsey, Paul, *War and the Christian Conscience,* Durham, N. C., Duke University Press, 1961.

Ryan, John K., *Modern War and Basic Ethics,* Milwaukee, Bruce, 1940.

Scott, James B., *The Catholic Conception of International Law,* Washington, D. C., Georgetown University Press, 1934.

Stratmann, F., *War and Christianity Today,* Westminster, Md., 1956.

Stein, Walter, *Nuclear Weapons, a Catholic Response,* New York, Sheed & Ward, 1961.

Sturzo, Luigi, *Nationalism and Internationalism,* New York, Roy Publishers, 1946.

Thompson, Charles S. (ed.), *Morals and Missiles,* London, Clarke, 1959.

Vann, Gerald, *Morality and War,* London, Burns, Oates & Washbourne, 1939.

Wright, John J., *National Patriotism in Papal Teaching,* Westminster, Md., Newman Bookshop, 1943.

Principles for Peace, edited by the National Catholic Welfare Conference, Washington, D. C., 1943.

INDEX